PHILOSOPHIC CLASSICS

BACON to KANT

PRENTICE-HALL PHILOSOPHY SERIES

Arthur E. Murphy, Ph.D., Editor

Books by Walter Kaufmann

Author

NIETZSCHE: PHILOSOPHER, PSYCHOLOGIST, ANTICHRIST (1950)
CRITIQUE OF RELIGION AND PHILOSOPHY (1958)
FROM SHAKESPEARE TO EXISTENTIALISM (1959)
THE FAITH OF A HERETIC (1961)

Editor and translator

THE PORTABLE NIETZSCHE (1954)
EXISTENTIALISM FROM DOSTOEVSKY TO SARTRE (1956)
JUDAISM AND CHRISTIANITY: ESSAYS BY LEO BAECK (1958)
GOETHE'S FAUST (1961)
PHILOSOPHIC CLASSICS: THALES TO ST. THOMAS (1961)
PHILOSOPHIC CLASSICS: BACON TO KANT (1961)
RELIGION FROM TOLSTOY TO CAMUS (1961)

PHILOSOPHIC CLASSICS

BACON to KANT

BASIC TEXTS
SELECTED AND EDITED WITH PREFACES
BY

Walter Kaufmann

PRENTICE-HALL, INC.
ENGLEWOOD CLIFFS, N.J.

First printing ...... *May, 1961*
Second printing .. *January, 1962*
Third printing .. *March, 1964*

66233-C

This volume is dedicated to

CLARENCE IRVING LEWIS

*Edgar Pierce Professor of Philosophy
in Harvard University
emeritus*

PREFACE

I

There is no better introduction to philosophy, whether one reads for oneself or takes a course, than to read some of the great philosophers. But few books are more difficult than Aristotle's *Metaphysics* or Spinoza's *Ethics* or Kant's *Critique of Pure Reason*. And even works that are less puzzling are sometimes like snippets of a conversation that one overhears on entering a room: what is said is clear, only one can't be sure one has got the point because one does not know just what has gone before. A slight point may be crucial to refute some earlier suggestion, and a seemingly pointless remark may contain a barbed allusion. Too often nonphilosophers despair: It does not occur to them that whenever they choose to begin, they can still get in at the beginning of the conversation. They need only to commence with Thales and the other pre-Socratics. Nobody should fear that going back so far will expose him to a tedious excursion. On the contrary, in quick succession one encounters some of the most fascinating thinkers of all time and finds oneself regretting that so little of their writings has survived.

Soon one comes to Socrates and Plato and becomes involved in philosophical discussions that continue to this day. In the early dialogues of Plato, the most brilliant literary power is employed to introduce us to philosophy; but one gains ever so much more from one's reading if one knows the pre-Socratics.

The later dialogues are much more difficult, and so is much of Aristotle, but no serious student will be satisfied to remain completely innocent of all these classics, and most teachers will want to read at least some of this material with their students.

Altogether, it is not the point of either this book or its companion volume to avoid all difficulties. On the contrary, philosophy begins in perplexity, as both Plato and Aristotle noted; and those who spurn perplexity and want unquestioned answers have not begun to understand philosophy. One of the first things one discovers in the study of philosophy is that intelligent and even brilliant men are frequently in disagreement, and that some of the most interesting problems seem to have no ready-made solutions. It might be argued that anyone who has not found this out still needs an education.

It is an uncomfortable discovery, however, and many people try to dodge it. Instead of being challenged by one great philosopher after another to reconsider preconceived opinions and to become more careful, thoughtful, and conscientious, many a student would like to learn, once and for all, the "central doctrines" of the great philosophers: that way one has something definite that one can memorize, and one does not have to think, oneself.

Alas, the "central doctrines" of a great philosopher often turn out to be very problematic in the context of the whole work in which they are said to be presented; and matters become yet less reassuring as we move to compare the first edition of some classics with the second, or one book with another by the same philosopher. Often, there are passages in which the "central doctrine" seems to be presented; but the philosopher did not always oblige us by ceasing to think after formulating his position in this manner: typically, he continued to reflect on the same topic and on other problems that have some relation to it; and in the end his position turns out to be hotly disputed by scholars. The greatest Plato scholars still argue not only about Plato's meaning in specific sentences but also about "central doctrines"; and the situation is no better in the case of Aristotle. No one who loves philosophy is seriously dismayed by that: what Plato and Aristotle teach us is not a body of assured results but rather a way of thinking—the delights of thinking.

The most damning comment on a course I ever heard came from a student who, after a semester's freshman course which he had taken with one of my colleagues, said that now he knew all about modern philosophy—adding only, as he noted my surprise, "at least since Descartes."

Carving up great books to excerpt "essential doctrines" is one of the sins against the spirit of philosophy. If the reading of a whole Platonic dialogue leaves a man more doubtful and less sure of himself than the perusal of a brief epitome, that is all to the good, as Plato himself noted many times; for example, at the end of the *Theaetetus*. It is part of the point of philosophy to make men a little less sure about things. And Socrates, who converted Plato to philosophy, insisted that what distinguished him from other men was not that he knew all, or even most, answers but rather that he realized his ignorance.

Nobody can be introduced to philosophy without being exposed to wonder and perplexity, without being made aware of his ignorance, and without discovering that the great philosophers, far from settling all our doubts, present us with a host of puzzles. Not the least of these is often what precisely the philosopher's position was. Those who have never read a complete book by a philosopher are very often sure about his doctrines, while those who have studied the man thoroughly are usually much less sure—and those who do feel sure often disagree with each other.

No reader of this book or its companion volume should feel that he now knows all about Plato or Kant, Aristotle or Spinoza. He will find many complete and unabridged works, supplemented with selections, but these, far from being tailored to some one interpretation of the man, should give some impression of the range of his thought and of the problems that confront interpreters. The reader should not emerge with a spurious sense that he knows what in fact he does not know; rather he should come, if possible, to love philosophy. The *Apology* may communicate the philosophic spirit, and the *Symposium* and the *Phaedrus*, also uncut, might convince the reader that here are works of great beauty which may well require many a delightful reading before they yield up even most of their treasures. It is thus that one is won for philosophy, not by reading books that make everything easy and simple.

II

There is a good deal of continuity in these selections: those from the pre-Socratics turn out to be relevant for an understanding of Plato, Aristotle, Epicurus, and a lot of later writers, and the previously suggested metaphor of the conversation should be taken seriously. Hobbes' objections to Descartes have been included with Descartes' replies before Thomas Hobbes is introduced in his own right; but even where the dialogue is not quite so explicit it is well to ask oneself to what ideas of his predecessors a philosopher is probably responding.

Where translations had to be used, versions in the public domain that could be reprinted without permissions and fees were usually available, but a great deal of effort was devoted to attempts to obtain some of the fine translations done in recent years by the best scholars. Professionals will appreciate instantly what it means (to give but a very few examples) that Kirk and Raven's work on *The*

Presocratic Philosophers (1957) could be used along with Cornford's and Hackforth's excellent translations of some of Plato's more difficult dialogues; that Aquinas is offered in the translation edited by Pegis; that there is an entirely new, previously unpublished version by Willis Doney of material from Malebranche, not hitherto available in English; and that Philip Wiener's revised versions of his fine Leibniz translations are presented.

A single case may be discussed in just a little more detail. Old translations, in the public domain but not respected by the scholars in the field, of much material by and about the pre-Socratics are available. The versions reprinted in two of the most popular texts come from Arthur Fairbanks' *The First Philosophers of Greece* (1898), of which R. D. Hicks showed in *The Classical Review* (1899, pp. 450 ff.) that "a pupil who followed the translation . . . would be liable to serious misconceptions at almost every step"—a verdict seconded by Gregory Vlastos in *The Philosophical Review* (October 1959). The student who wants versions based on the latest scholarship can turn to Kathleen Freeman's *Ancilla to The Pre-Socratic Philosophers* (1947) and find their fragments but none of the often equally important paraphrases or reports about their doctrines—though much of their thought is known to us only indirectly in this manner. For additional material he can consult Freeman's *The Pre-Socratic Philosophers: A Companion to Diels, Fragmente der Vorsokratiker* (1946). Or he can turn to Kirk and Raven and find many of the testimonies and those fragments—often all too few—which the authors cite in the course of their scholarly discussions. But to give only two examples, those who consult Kirk and Raven will miss out on a good many of Heraclitus' most striking sayings and on almost all of the abundant sayings of Democritus on ethics. In Freeman's *Ancilla*, on the other hand, they will miss the atomistic world view of Democritus, which is known almost exclusively from testimonies. What is offered in the following pages, then, is—quite apart from some emendations of the translations presented—no mere reprint but, at least in places, material never previously presented in anything like the present form.

Zeno represents an especially dramatic case. Few, if any, pre-Socratic fragments have elicited as much interest and discussion as his famous paradoxes; but in recent years some of the foremost scholars have repudiated earlier translations of this material and proposed new readings. No English version hitherto in print is really up to date. The section on Zeno, therefore, was contributed by Gregory Vlastos and constitutes an important contribution to pre-Socratic scholarship.

III

Nothing has been offered of Chinese and Indian philosophy. The little that might have been put into these two volumes could not have done justice to India or China and would only have taken away valuable space from Western thinkers. To do justice to Oriental thought, another volume as large as one of the present volumes would be necessary. The same reasoning applies to Western philosophy since Kant. Not enough could have been included along with the men from Bacon to Kant to be satisfactory for students of nineteenth or twentieth-century philosophy. It therefore seemed best to devote as much space as possible to philosophers of the seventeenth and eighteenth centuries.

The treatment of medieval thought also requires comment. In line with the points just made, it could be argued that the Middle Ages should have been left out entirely; but for two reasons a few samples of medieval philosophy have been presented. Unlike Oriental philosophy—which stands entirely apart from the development recorded in these volumes—and unlike philosophy since Kant, which comes afterwards as the sequel, medieval philosophy must be conceded to have been either a link or an interruption, and probably both, in the story that is here presented. Our understanding of Bacon, Descartes, and Spinoza is enhanced by even a slight knowledge of Augustine, Anselm, and Aquinas. Moreover, interest in St. Thomas Aquinas is widespread, and his thought is as much discussed in the twentieth century as ever before. It is therefore customary in many colleges to bring in just a little of medieval philosophy at the end of a course on Greek philosophy, and this makes good sense. But any great expansion of this section, either by way of offering more of the writings of the three men represented here or by way of introducing others, such as Erigena, Scotus, Eckhart, and Occam, was not feasible for the same reasons that led to the exclusion of Oriental and recent philosophy: not enough could have been offered for the serious student or for a semester's course, and the value of the remaining part of the volume would have been impaired too seriously by the required cuts. Everything considered, it seemed best to concentrate chiefly on one medieval philosopher—and to select St. Thomas Aquinas for this purpose.

Those who use one of these volumes as the basis of a one-term course need hardly to be told that there is more material here than can easily fit into one semester. But the editor does not apologize for offering some choice or for giving teachers who offer the same course years after year an easy opportunity for varying their fare.

The last quotation from Xenophanes may serve as a motto for both volumes: "Not from the beginning have the gods revealed all things to mortals, but by long seeking, men find what is better."

W. K.

ACKNOWLEDGMENTS

In making my selections for these two volumes, I have had the invaluable advantage of discussions with, and advice from, many of my colleagues: Dennis O'Brien, George Pitcher, and Gregory Vlastos at Princeton University; Richard Cartwright and Irving Copi at the University of Michigan; and Willis Doney at Dartmouth College. Having taught a variety of courses in the history of philosophy, they gave me the benefit of their considerable experience, and I am glad to have this opportunity to express my gratitude.

Professor Vlastos has also contributed the section on Zeno—both the translations and the editorial matter—and Professor Doney has contributed that on Malebranche. For this, too, I am deeply indebted to them.

Everybody with whom I have dealt at Prentice-Hall has been most cooperative and helpful, and special thanks are due Mrs. Maurine Lewis.

Acknowledgments to other publishers who have kindly given permission to reprint material in this volume will be found on page xvii.

NOTE: In many instances, the page numbers of a standard edition have been retained—in the running heads at the top of the page in the selections from Aristotle; in brackets at the end of the line in the selections from Plato (in the first volume) and in this volume's selections from Hobbes and Kant. This should facilitate the checking of scholarly citations as well as comparison with the original or with other editions. Moreover, where omissions are indicated, this device shows, at a glance, approximately how much has been omitted.

Acknowledgment is gratefully made to the following:

Cambridge University Press, for selections from Volume II of *The Philosophical Works of Descartes* translated by Elizabeth S. Haldane and G. R. T. Ross, published in 1955.

Professor Philip Wiener, for selections from his translations in *Leibniz Selections*, published in 1951 by Charles Scribner's Sons. Revised 1960.

CONTENTS

PHILOSOPHIC CLASSICS

BACON to KANT

FRANCIS BACON 1561–1626

It is customary and reasonable to begin "modern philosophy" with either Bacon or Descartes. Descartes is generally conceded to be much the greater philosopher: that is why some begin with him and disregard Bacon. But Francis Bacon was a remarkable man and an exceptionally fine writer; and he struck a new note. More than any other man, he is the herald of modern philosophy—its trumpeter.

He was educated at Trinity College, Cambridge, where he gained the conviction that philosophy, as then taught, was sterile. Instead of conceiving an enduring hatred of philosophy, he decided that the time had come to revolutionize it by abandoning the methods of scholasticism and making a fresh beginning.

After leaving the university, he went to Paris in 1576, but returned to England three years later, after his father's sudden death. He took up the law, and in 1584 gained a seat in Parliament. Henceforth he was prominent in public affairs, and some of the things he did have been subjects of controversy ever since. His political career reached its climax after the death of Queen Elizabeth, under the reign of James I. He became Solicitor-General in 1607, and Attorney-General six years later. In 1617 he was made Lord Keeper, and the following year Lord Chancellor and Baron Verulam. In 1621, he was created Viscount St. Albans; but within a week he was accused of bribery, pleaded guilty, and was condemned to a heavy fine (£40,000) and imprisonment in the Tower of London "during the king's pleasure." He was also disqualified from ever holding another public office. The king remitted the fine, and his imprisonment lasted four days. A general pardon was issued, but the parliamentary cen-

1

sure remained. Bacon himself, an all-time master of the aphorism, wrote: "I was the justest judge that was in England these fifty years; but it was the justest censure in Parliament that was these two hundred years." He insisted that, though he had accepted gifts from litigants as was the practice of the time, and one might condemn this practice by invoking higher standards than were then observed, his judgment had never once been swayed by any bribe.

In his subsequent retirement, he devoted himself entirely to research and writing. Many of his best known works, however, had appeared earlier: his famous *Essays*, in 1597; *Advancement of Learning*, in 1605; and *Novum Organum*, in 1620. The first edition of the *Essays* contained only ten items, the second (1612), thirty-eight, and the third, published during Bacon's retirement, in 1625, fifty-eight. In his later years, Bacon also reworked the material in the *Advancement* into a larger Latin work, *De dignitate et augmentis scientiarum* (1623). In this later form, the work was to constitute the first part of the grandly conceived *Instauratio Magna*. Of Bacon's many other works, the best known is probably his utopia, the *New Atlantis*. Bacon has also been credited with Shakespeare's plays by men who found it inconceivable that Shakespeare himself, a mere actor, should have written them; but few scholars even take this suggestion seriously.

Most of Bacon's philosophic writings have a programmatic tone. They possess great elan and elegance, are imaginative, not least in the form of expression, and have a quality, rare in philosophy, of inspiration. One specific contribution which is worked out in detail is the method of induction which Bacon proposes to replace the Aristotelian and scholastic addiction to deduction. If we want to know the cause of some phenomenon, we must tirelessly collect data and construct a table, first, of instances in which the phenomenon is present; then another table of otherwise similar instances in which the phenomenon is absent; finally, a "table of degrees," collecting instances in which the same phenomenon—Bacon uses the example of heat—is present in varying degrees. In such a manner one might discover that motion causes—or is the "form" of—heat. Critics have discussed the precise meaning of Bacon's "forms"; they have taken him to task for not grasping the importance of "working hypotheses"; and they have pointed out that he never appreciated the importance of mathematics, and thus did not correctly foresee the advances of modern science. There is more to deduction than he realized. Moreover, Bacon did not appreciate the major figures of modern science who had even then appeared: Copernicus, Kepler, Galileo, Harvey, and Gilbert.

For all his limitations, he is emphatically worth reading. And it is no mean tribute to him that perhaps the greatest work of modern philosophy, Kant's *Critique of Pure Reason*, begins with a motto from Francis Bacon.

Our first selection comes from the Preface to *The Great Instauration*. Down to "termination of infinite error," this passage was used by Kant as a motto.

The second selection is another introductory passage of the same work. Here Bacon summarizes many of his intentions. The few omissions, signalled by the customary three dots, are all short, the longest comprising about one page.

The next selection is the conclusion of the Preface to *Novum Organum*. The aphorisms that follow are taken from the first book of "Aphorisms concerning the interpretation of nature and the kingdom of man," which comprises the first part of *Novum Organum*.

THE GREAT INSTAURATION (*Renewal* or *Restoration*)

· · ·

Of myself I say nothing; but in behalf of the business which is in hand I entreat men to believe that it is not an opinion to be held, but a work to be done; and to be well assured that I am laboring to lay the foundation, not of any sect or doctrine, but of human utility and power. Next, I ask them to deal fairly by their own interests, and laying aside all emulations and prejudices in favor of this or that opinion, to join in consultation for the common good; and being now freed and guarded by the securities and helps which I offer from the errors and impediments of the way, to come forward themselves and take part in that which remains to be done. Moreover, to be of good hope, nor to imagine that this *Instauration* of mine is a thing infinite and beyond the power of man, when it is in fact the true end and termination of infinite error; and seeing also that it is by no means forgetful of the conditions of mortality and humanity (for it does not suppose that the work can be altogether completed within one generation, but provides for its being taken up by another); and finally that it seeks for the sciences not arrogantly in the little cells of human wit, but with reverence in the greater world. But it is the empty things that are vast: things solid are most contracted and lie in little room. And now I have only one favor more to ask (else injustice to me may perhaps imperil the business itself)—that men will consider well how far, upon that which I must needs assert (if I am to be consistent with myself), they are entitled to judge and decide upon these doctrines of mine; inasmuch as all that premature human reasoning which anticipates inquiry, and is abstracted from the facts rashly and sooner than is fit, is by me rejected (so far as the inquisition of nature is concerned) as a thing uncertain, confused, and ill built up; and I cannot be fairly asked to abide by the decision of a tribunal which is itself on its trial.

.   .   .

Red ←   ... in the ordinary logic almost all the work is spent about the syllogism. Of induction the logicians seem hardly to have taken any serious thought, but they pass it by with a slight notice, and hasten on to the formulae of disputation. I on the contrary, reject demonstration by syllogism, as acting too confusedly, and letting nature slip out of its hands. For although no one can doubt that things which agree in a middle term agree with one another (which is a proposition of mathematical certainty), yet it leaves an opening for deception; which is this. The syllogism consists of propositions; propositions of words; and words are the tokens and signs of notions. Now if the very notions of the mind (which are as the soul of words and the basis of the whole structure) be improperly and overhastily abstracted from facts, vague, not sufficiently definite, faulty in short in many ways, the whole edifice tumbles. I therefore reject the syllogism; and that not only as regards principles (for to principles the logicians themselves do not apply it) but also as regards middle propositions; which, though obtainable no doubt by the syllogism, are, when so obtained, barren of works, remote from practice, and altogether unavailable for the active department of the sciences. Although therefore I leave to the syllogism and these famous and boasted modes of demonstration their jurisdiction over popular arts and such as are matter of opinion (in which department I leave all as it is), yet in dealing with the nature of things I use induction throughout, and that in the minor propositions as well as the major. For I consider induction to be that form of demonstration which upholds the sense, and closes with nature, and comes to the very brink of operation, if it does not actually deal with it.

Hence it follows that the order of demonstration is likewise inverted. For hitherto the proceeding has been to fly at once from the sense and particulars, up to the most general propositions, as certain fixed poles for the argument to turn upon, and from these to derive the rest by middle terms: a short way, no doubt, but precipitate; and one which will never lead to nature, though it offers an easy and ready way to disputation. Now my plan is to proceed regularly and gradually from one axiom to another, so that the most general are not reached till the last; but then when you do come to them you find them to be not empty notions, but well defined, and such as nature would really recognize as her first principles, and such as lie at the heart and marrow of things.

But the greatest change I introduce is in the form itself of induction and the judgment made thereby. For the induction of which the logicians speak, which proceeds by simple enumeration, is a puerile thing; concludes at hazard; is always liable to be upset by contradictory in-

stance; takes into account only what is known and ordinary; and leads
to no result.

Now what the sciences stand in need of is a form of induction which
shall analyze experience and take it to pieces, and by a due process of
exclusion and rejection lead to an inevitable conclusion. And if that ordinary mode of judgment practiced by the logicians was so laborious,
and found exercise for such great wits, how much more labor must we
be prepared to bestow upon this other, which is extracted not merely
out of the depths of the mind, but out of the very bowels of nature.

Nor is this all. For I also sink the foundations of the sciences deeper
and firmer; and I begin the inquiry nearer the source than men have
done heretofore; submitting to examination those things which the common logic takes on trust. For first, the logicians borrow the principles of
each science from the science itself; secondly, they hold in reverence the
first notions of the mind; and lastly, they receive as conclusive the immediate informations of the sense, when well disposed. Now upon the
first point, I hold that true logic ought to enter the several provinces of
science armed with a higher authority than belongs to the principles of
those sciences themselves, and ought to call those putative principles to
account until they are fully established. Then with regard to the first
notions of the intellect: there is not one of the impressions taken by the
intellect when left to go its own way, but I hold it for suspected, and no
way established, until it has submitted to a new trial and a fresh judgment has been thereupon pronounced. And lastly, the information of the
sense itself I sift and examine in many ways. For certain it is that the
senses deceive; but then at the same time they supply the means of discovering their own errors; only the errors are here, the means of discovery are to seek.

The sense fails in two ways. Sometimes it gives no information, sometimes it gives false information. For first, there are very many things
which escape the sense, even when best disposed and no way obstructed;
by reason either of the subtlety of the whole body, or the minuteness of
the parts, or distance of place, or slowness or else swiftness of motion, or
familiarity of the object, or other causes. And again when the sense does
apprehend a thing its apprehension is not much to be relied upon. For
the testimony and information of the sense has reference always to man,
not to the universe; and it is a great error to assert that the sense is the
measure of things.

To meet these difficulties, I have sought on all sides diligently and
faithfully to provide helps for the sense—substitutes to supply its failures, rectifications to correct its errors; and this I endeavor to accomplish not so much by instruments as by experiments. For the subtlety of
experiments is far greater than that of the sense itself, even when assisted by exquisite instruments; such experiments, I mean, as are skill-
fully and artificially devised for the express purpose of determining the
point in question. To the immediate and proper perception of the sense
therefore I do not give much weight; but I contrive that the office of the

sense shall be only to judge of the experiment, and that the experiment itself shall judge of the thing. And thus I conceive that I perform the office of a true priest of the sense (from which all knowledge in nature must be sought, unless men mean to go mad) and a not unskillful interpreter of its oracles; and that while others only profess to uphold and cultivate the sense, I do so in fact. Such then are the provisions I make for finding the genuine light of nature and kindling and bringing it to bear. And they would be sufficient of themselves, if the human intellect were even, and like a fair sheet of paper with no writing on it. But since the minds of men are strangely possessed and beset, so that there is no true and even surface left to reflect the genuine rays of things, it is necessary to seek a remedy for this also.

Now the idols, or phantoms, by which the mind is occupied are either adventitious or innate. The adventitious come into the mind from without; namely, either from the doctrines and sects of philosophers, or from perverse rules of demonstration. But the innate are inherent in the very nature of the intellect, which is far more prone to error than the sense is. For let men please themselves as they will in admiring and almost adoring the human mind, this is certain: that as an uneven mirror distorts the rays of objects according to its own figure and section, so the mind, when it receives impressions of objects through the sense, cannot be trusted to report them truly, but in forming its notions mixes up its own nature with the nature of things.

And as the first two kinds of idols are hard to eradicate, so idols of this last kind cannot be eradicated at all. All that can be done is to point them out, so that this insidious action of the mind may be marked and reproved (else as fast as old errors are destroyed new ones will spring up out of the ill complexion of the mind itself, and so we shall have but a change of errors, and not a clearance); and to lay it down once for all as a fixed and established maxim, that the intellect is not qualified to judge except by means of induction, and induction in its legitimate form. This doctrine then of the expurgation of the intellect to qualify it for dealing with truth, is comprised in three refutations: the refutation of the Philosophies, the refutation of the Demonstrations, and the refutation of the Natural Human Reason. The explanation of which things, and of the true relation between the nature of things and the nature of the mind, is as the strewing and decoration of the bridal chamber of the Mind and the Universe, the Divine Goodness assisting; out of which marriage let us hope (and be this the prayer of the bridal song) there may spring helps to man, and a line and race of inventions that may in some degree subdue and overcome the necessities and miseries of humanity. This is the second part of the work.

But I design not only to indicate and mark out the ways, but also to enter them. And therefore the third part of the work embraces the Phenomena of the Universe; that is to say, experience of every kind, and such a natural history as may serve for a foundation to build philosophy upon. For a good method of demonstration or form of interpreting nature may keep the mind from going astray or stumbling, but it is not any excellence of method that can supply it with the material of knowledge. Those however who aspire not to guess and divine, but to discover and know; who propose not to devise mimic and fabulous worlds of their own, but to examine and dissect the nature of this very world itself; must go to facts themselves for everything. Nor can the place of this labor and search and world-wide perambulation be supplied by any genius or meditation or argumentation; no, not if all men's wits could meet in one. This therefore we must have, or the business must be forever abandoned. But up to this day such has been the condition of men in this matter, that it is no wonder if nature will not give herself into their hands. . . .

Next, with regard to the mass and composition of it: I mean it to be a history not only of nature free and at large (when she is left to her own course and does her work her own way),—such as that of the heavenly bodies, meteors, earth and sea, minerals, plants, animals,—but much more of nature under constraint and vexed; that is to say, when by art and the hand of man she is forced out of her natural state, and squeezed and molded. Therefore I set down at length all experiments of the mechanical arts, of the operative part of the liberal arts, of the many crafts which have not yet grown into arts properly so called, so far as I have been able to examine them and as they conduce to the end in view. Nay (to say the plain truth) I do in fact (low and vulgar as men may think it) count more upon this part both for helps and safeguards than upon the other; seeing that the nature of things betrays itself more readily under the vexations of art than in its natural freedom. . . .

Further, in the selection of the relations and experiments I conceive I have been a more cautious purveyor than those who have hitherto dealt with natural history. For I admit nothing but on the faith of eyes, or at least of careful and severe examination; so that nothing is exaggerated for wonder's sake, but what I state is sound and without mixture of fables or vanity. All received or current falsehoods also (which by strange negligence have been allowed for many ages to prevail and become established) I proscribe and brand by name; that the sciences may be no more troubled with them. For it has been well observed that the fables and superstitions and follies which nurses instill into children do serious injury to their minds; and the same consideration makes me anxious, having the management of the childhood as it were of philosophy in its course of natural history, not to let it accustom itself in the beginning to any vanity. Moreover, whenever I come to a new experiment of any subtlety (though it be in my own opinion certain and approved), I nevertheless subjoin a clear account of the manner in which I made it; that men knowing exactly how each point was made out, may see whether there be any error connected with it, and may arouse themselves to devise proofs more trustworthy and exquisite, if such can be found; and finally, I interpose everywhere admonitions and scruples

and cautions, with a religious care to eject, repress, and as it were ex-
orcise every kind of phantasm. . . .

For besides that I hope my speculations may in virtue of my continual
conversancy with nature have a value beyond the pretensions of my wit;
they will serve in the meantime for wayside inns, in which the mind may
rest and refresh itself on its journey to more certain conclusions. Nevertheless I wish it to be understood in the meantime that they are conclusions by which (as not being discovered and proved by the true form
of interpretation) I do not at all mean to bind myself. Nor need anyone
be alarmed at such suspensions of judgment, in one who maintains not
simply that nothing can be known, but only that nothing can be known
except in a certain course and way; and yet establishes provisionally
certain degrees of assurance, for use and relief until the mind shall arrive
at a knowledge of causes in which it can rest. For even those schools of
philosophy which held the absolute impossibility of knowing anything,
were not inferior to those which took upon them to pronounce. But then
they did not provide helps for the sense and understanding, as I have
done, but simply took away all their authority: which is quite a different
thing—almost the reverse.

The sixth part of my work (to which the rest is subservient and min-
istrant) discloses and sets forth that philosophy which by the legitimate,
chaste, and severe course of inquiry which I have explained and provided is at length developed and established. The completion however
of this last part is a thing both above my strength and beyond my hopes.
I have made a beginning of the work—a beginning, as I hope, not unimportant:—the fortune of the human race will give the issue;—such an
issue, it may be, as in the present condition of things and men's minds
cannot easily be conceived or imagined. For the matter in hand is no
mere felicity of speculation, but the real business and fortunes of the
human race, and all power of operation. For man is but the servant and
interpreter of nature: what he does and what he knows is only what he
has observed of nature's order in fact or in thought; beyond this he
knows nothing and can do nothing. For the chain of causes cannot by
any force be loosed or broken, nor can nature be commanded except by
being obeyed. And so those twin objects, *human knowledge* and *human
power,* do really meet in one; and it is from ignorance of causes that
operation fails.

.   .   .

Moreover I have one request to make. I have on my own part made it
my care and study that the things which I shall propound should not only
be true, but should also be presented to men's minds, how strangely soever preoccupied and obstructed, in a manner not harsh or unpleasant. It
is but reasonable however (especially in so great a restoration of learning
and knowledge) that I should claim of men one favor in return; which is
this:—If anyone would form an opinion or judgment either out of his own

observation, or out of the crowd of authorities, or out of the forms of demonstration (which have now acquired a sanction like that of judicial laws), concerning these speculations of mine, let him not hope that he can do it in passage or by the by; but let him examine the thing thoroughly; let him make some little trial for himself of the way which I describe and lay out; let him familiarize his thoughts with that subtlety of nature to which experience bears witness; let him correct by seasonable patience and due delay the depraved and deep-rooted habits of his mind; and when all this is done and he has begun to be his own master, let him (if he will) use his own judgment.

.   .   .

APHORISMS

CONCERNING

THE INTERPRETATION OF NATURE

AND

THE KINGDOM OF MAN

APHORISM

.   .   .

XIV

The syllogism consists of propositions, propositions consist of words, words are symbols of notions. Therefore if the notions themselves (which is the root of the matter) are confused and overhastily abstracted from the facts, there can be no firmness in the superstructure. Our only hope therefore lies in a true induction.

XV

There is no soundness in our notions whether logical or physical. Substance, Quality, Action, Passion, Essence itself, are not sound notions: much less are Heavy, Light, Dense, Rare, Moist, Dry, Generation, Corruption, Attraction, Repulsion, Element, Matter, Form, and the like; but all are fantastical and ill defined.

.   .   .

XXXII

The honor of the ancient authors, and indeed of all, remains untouched; since the comparison I challenge is not of wits or faculties, but of ways and methods, and the part I take upon myself is not that of a judge, but of a guide.

.   .   .

XXXVIII

The idols and false notions which are now in possession of the human understanding, and have taken deep root therein, not only so beset men's minds that truth can hardly find entrance, but even after entrance obtained, they will again in the very instauration of the sciences meet and trouble us, unless men being forewarned of the danger fortify themselves as far as may be against their assaults.

XXXIX

There are four classes of idols which beset men's minds. To these for distinction's sake I have assigned names,—calling the first class *Idols of the Tribe;* the second, *Idols of the Cave;* the third, *Idols of the Marketplace;* the fourth, *Idols of the Theater.*

XL

The formation of ideas and axioms by true induction is no doubt the proper remedy to be applied for the keeping off and clearing away of idols. To point them out, however, is of great use, for the doctrine of idols is to the interpretation of nature what the doctrine of the refutation of sophisms is to common logic.

XLI

The Idols of the Tribe have their foundation in human nature itself, and in the tribe or race of men. For it is a false assertion that the sense of man is the measure of things. On the contrary, all perceptions, as well of the sense as of the mind, are according to the measure of the individual and not according to the measure of the universe. And the human understanding is like a false mirror, which, receiving rays irregularly, distorts and discolors the nature of things by mingling its own nature with it.

XLII

The Idols of the Cave are the idols of the individual man. For everyone (besides the errors common to human nature in general) has a cave or den of his own, which refracts and discolors the light of nature; owing either to his own proper and peculiar nature or to his education and conversation with others; or to the reading of books, and the authority of those whom he esteems and admires; or to the differences of impressions, accordingly as they take place in a mind preoccupied and predisposed or in a mind indifferent and settled; or the like. So that the spirit of man (according as it is meted out to different individuals) is in fact a thing variable and full of perturbation, and governed as it were by chance. Whence it was well observed by Heraclitus that men look for sciences in their own lesser worlds, and not in the greater or common world.

XLIII

There are also idols formed by the intercourse and association of men with each other, which I call Idols of the Market-place, on account of the commerce and consort of men there. For it is by discourse that men associate; and words are imposed according to the apprehension of the vulgar. And therefore the ill and unfit choice of words wonderfully obstructs the understanding. Nor do the definitions or explanations wherewith in some things learned men are wont to guard and defend themselves, by any means set the matter right. But words plainly force and overrule the understanding, and throw all into confusion, and lead men away into numberless empty controversies and idle fancies.

XLIV

Lastly, there are idols which have immigrated into men's minds from the various dogmas of philosophies, and also from wrong laws of demonstration. These I call Idols of the Theater; because in my judgment all the received systems are but so many stage-plays, representing worlds of their own creation after an unreal and scenic fashion. Nor is it only of the systems now in vogue, or only of the ancient sects and philosophies, that I speak: for many more plays of the same kind may yet be composed and in like artificial manner set forth; seeing that errors the most widely different have nevertheless causes for the most part alike. Neither again do I mean this only of entire systems, but also of many principles and axioms in science, which by tradition, credulity, and negligence have come to be received.

But of these several kinds of idols I must speak more largely and exactly, that the understanding may be duly cautioned.

XLV

The human understanding is of its own nature prone to suppose the existence of more order and regularity in the world than it finds. And though there be many things in nature which are singular and unmatched, yet it devises for them parallels and conjugates and relatives which do not exist. Hence the fiction that all celestial bodies move in perfect circles; spirals and dragons being (except in name) utterly rejected. Hence too the element of fire with its orb is brought in, to make up the square with the other three which the sense perceives. Hence also the ratio of density of the so-called elements is arbitrarily fixed at ten to one. And so on of other dreams. And these fancies affect not dogmas only, but simple notions also.

XLVI

The human understanding when it has once adopted an opinion (either as being the received opinion or as being agreeable to itself) draws all things else to support and agree with it. And though there be a greater number and weight of instances to be found on the other side, yet these it either neglects and despises, or else by some distinction sets aside and rejects; in order that by this great and pernicious predetermination the authority of its former conclusions may remain inviolate. And therefore it was a good answer that was made by one who when they showed him hanging in a temple a picture of those who had paid their vows as having escaped shipwreck, and would have him say whether he did not now acknowledge the power of the gods,—"Aye," asked he again, "but where are they painted that were drowned after their vows?" And such is the way of all superstition, whether in astrology, dreams, omens, divine judgments, or the like; wherein men, having a delight in such vanities, mark the events where they are fulfilled, but where they fail, though this happen much oftener, neglect and pass them by. But with far more subtlety does this mischief insinuate itself into philosophy and the sciences; in which the first conclusion colors and brings into conformity with itself all that come after, though far sounder and better. Besides, independently of that delight and vanity which I have described, it is the peculiar and perpetual error of the human intellect to be more moved and excited by affirmatives than by negatives; whereas it ought properly to hold itself indifferently disposed towards both alike. Indeed in the establishment of any true axiom, the negative instance is the more forcible of the two.

XLVII

The human understanding is moved by those things most which strike and enter the mind simultaneously and suddenly, and so fill the imagination; and then it feigns and supposes all other things to be somehow, though it cannot see how, similar to those few things by which it is surrounded. But for that going to and fro to remote and heterogeneous instances by which axioms are tried as in the fire, the intellect is altogether slow and unfit, unless it be forced thereto by severe laws and overruling authority.

XLVIII

The human understanding is unquiet; it cannot stop or rest, and still presses onward, but in vain. Therefore it is that we cannot conceive of any end or limit to the world; but always as of necessity it occurs to us that there is something beyond. Neither again can it be conceived how eternity has flowed down to the present day: for that distinction which is commonly received of infinity in time past and in time to come can by no means hold; for it would thence follow that one infinity is greater than another, and that infinity is wasting away and tending to become finite. The like subtlety arises touching the infinite divisibility of lines, from the same inability of thought to stop. But this inability interferes more mischievously in the discovery of causes: for although the most general principles in nature ought to be held merely positive, as they are discovered, and cannot with truth be referred to a cause; nevertheless the human understanding being unable to rest still seeks something prior in the order of nature. And then it is that in struggling towards that which is further off it falls back upon that which is more nigh at hand,—namely, on final causes; which have relation clearly to the nature of man rather than to the nature of the universe, and from this source have strangely defiled philosophy. But he is no less an unskilled and shallow philosopher who seeks causes of that which is most general, than he who in things subordinate and subaltern omits to do so.

XLIX

The human understanding is no dry light, but receives an infusion from the will and affections; whence proceed sciences which may be called "sciences as one would." For what a man had rather were true he more readily believes. Therefore he rejects difficult things from impatience of research; sober things, because they narrow hope; the deeper things of nature, from superstition; the light of experience, from arrogance and pride, lest his mind should seem to be occupied with things mean and transitory; things not commonly believed, out of deference to the opinion of the vulgar. Numberless in short are the ways, and sometimes imperceptible, in which the affections color and infect the understanding.

L

But by far the greatest hindrance and aberration of the human understanding proceeds from the dullness, incompetency, and deceptions of the senses; in that things which strike the sense outweigh things which do not immediately strike it, though they be more important. Hence it is that speculation commonly ceases where sight ceases, insomuch that of things invisible there is little or no observation. Hence all the working of the spirits inclosed in tangible bodies lies hid and unobserved of men. So also all the more subtle changes of form in the parts of coarser substances (which they commonly call alteration, though it is in truth local motion through exceedingly small spaces) is in like manner unobserved. And yet unless these two things just mentioned be searched out and brought to light, nothing great can be achieved in nature, as far as the production of works is concerned. So again the essential nature of our common air, and of all bodies less dense than air (which are very many), is almost unknown. For the sense by itself is a thing infirm and erring; neither can instruments for enlarging or sharpening the senses do much: but all the truer kind of interpretation of nature is effected by instances and experiments fit and apposite; wherein the sense decides touching the experiment only, and the experiment touching the point in nature and the thing itself.

LI

The human understanding is of its own nature prone to abstractions and gives a substance and reality to things which are fleeting. But to resolve nature into abstractions is less to our purpose than to dissect her into parts; as did the school of Democritus, which went further into nature than the rest. Matter rather than forms should be the object of our attention, its configurations and changes of configuration, and simple action, and law of action or motion; for forms are figments of the human mind, unless you will call those laws of action forms.

LII

Conclusion

Such then are the idols which I call *Idols of the Tribe;* and which take their rise either from the homogeneity of the substance of the human spirit, or from its preoccupation, or from its narrowness, or from its restless motion, or from an infusion of the affections, or from the incompetency of the senses, or from the mode of impression.

LIII

The *Idols of the Cave* take their rise in the peculiar constitution, mental or bodily, of each individual; and also in education, habit, and accident. Of this kind there is a great number and variety; but I will instance those the pointing out of which contains the most important caution, and which have most effect in disturbing the clearness of the understanding.

LIV

Men become attached to certain particular sciences and speculations, either because they fancy themselves the authors and inventors thereof, or because they have bestowed the greatest pains upon them and become most habituated to them. But men of this kind, if they betake themselves to philosophy and contemplations of a general character, distort and color them in obedience to their former fancies; a thing especially to be noticed in Aristotle, who made his natural philosophy a mere bondservant to his logic, thereby rendering it contentious and well nigh useless. The race of chemists again out of a few experiments of the furnace have built up a fantastic philosophy, framed with reference to a few things; and Gilbert also, after he had employed himself most laboriously in the study and observation of the lodestone, proceeded at once to construct an entire system in accordance with his favorite subject.

LV

There is one principal and as it were radical distinction between different minds, in respect of philosophy and the sciences; which is this: that some minds are stronger and apter to mark the differences of things, others to mark their resemblances. The steady and acute mind can fix its contemplations and dwell and fasten on the subtlest distinctions; the lofty and discursive mind recognizes and puts together the finest and most general resemblances. Both kinds however easily err in excess, by catching the one at gradations the other at shadows.

LVI

There are found some minds given to an extreme admiration of antiquity, others to an extreme love and appetite for novelty; but few so duly tempered that they can hold the mean, neither carping at what has been well laid down by the ancients, nor despising what is well introduced by the moderns. This however turns to the great injury of the sciences and philosophy: since these affectations of antiquity and novelty are the humors of partisans rather than judgments; and truth is to be sought for not in the felicity of any age, which is an unstable thing, but in the light of nature and experience, which is eternal. These factions therefore must be abjured, and care must be taken that the intellect be not hurried by them into assent.

LVII

Contemplations of nature and of bodies in their simple form break up and distract the understanding, while contemplations of nature and bodies in their composition and configuration overpower and dissolve the understanding: a distinction well seen in the school of Leucippus and Democritus as compared with the other philosophies. For that school is so busied with the particles that it hardly attends to the structure; while the others are so lost in admiration of the structure that they do not penetrate to the simplicity of nature. These kinds of contemplation should therefore be alternated and taken by turns; that so the understanding may be rendered at once penetrating and comprehensive, and the inconveniences above mentioned, with the idols which proceed from them, may be avoided.

LVIII

Let such then be our provision and contemplative prudence for keeping off and dislodging the Idols of the Cave, which grow for the most part either out of the predominance of a favorite subject, or out of an excessive tendency to compare or to distinguish, or out of partiality for particular ages, or out of the largeness or minuteness of the objects contemplated. And generally let every student of nature take this as a rule, —that whatever his mind seizes and dwells upon with peculiar satisfaction is to be held in suspicion, and that so much the more care is to be taken in dealing with such questions to keep the understanding even and clear.

LIX

But the *Idols of the Market-place* are the most troublesome of all: idols which have crept into the understanding through the alliances of words and names. For men believe that their reason governs words; but it is also true that words react on the understanding; and this it is that has rendered philosophy and the sciences sophistical and inactive. Now words, being commonly framed and applied according to the capacity of the vulgar, follow those lines of division which are most obvious to the vulgar understanding. And whenever an understanding of greater acuteness or a more diligent observation would alter those lines to suit the true divisions of nature, words stand in the way and resist the change. Whence it comes to pass that the high and formal discussions of learned men end oftentimes in disputes about words and names; with which (according to the use and wisdom of the mathematicians) it would be more prudent to begin, and so by means of definitions reduce them to order. Yet even definitions cannot cure this evil in dealing with natural and material things; since the definitions themselves consist of words, and those words beget others: so that it is necessary to recur to individual instances, and those in due series and order; as I shall say presently when I come to the method and scheme for the formation of notions and axioms.

LX

The idols imposed by words on the understanding are of two kinds. They are either names of things which do not exist (for as there are things left unnamed through lack of observation, so likewise are there names which result from fantastic suppositions and to which nothing in reality corresponds), or they are names of things which exist, but yet

confused and ill-defined, and hastily and irregularly derived from realities. Of the former kind are Fortune, the Prime Mover, Planetary Orbits, Elements of Fire, and like fictions which owe their origin to false
and idle theories. And this class of idols is more easily expelled, because
to get rid of them it is only necessary that all theories should be steadily
rejected and dismissed as obsolete.

But the other class, which springs out of a faulty and unskillful abstraction, is intricate and deeply rooted. Let us take for example such a
word as *humid*, and see how far the several things which the word is
used to signify agree with each other; and we shall find the word *humid*
to be nothing else than a mark loosely and confusedly applied to denote
a variety of actions which will not bear to be reduced to any constant
meaning. For it both signifies that which easily spreads itself round any
other body; and that which in itself is indeterminate and cannot solid-
ize; and that which readily yields in every direction; and that which
easily divides and scatters itself; and that which easily unites and collects itself; and that which readily flows and is put in motion; and that
which readily clings to another body and wets it; and that which is
easily reduced to a liquid, or being solid easily melts. Accordingly when
you come to apply the word,—if you take it in one sense, flame is humid;
if in another, air is not humid; if in another, fine dust is humid; if in
another, glass is humid. So that it is easy to see that the notion is taken
by abstraction only from water and common and ordinary liquids, without
any due verification.

There are however in words certain degrees of distortion and error.
One of the least faulty kinds is that of names of substances, especially of
lowest species and well-deduced (for the notion of *chalk* and of *mud* is
good, of *earth* bad); a more faulty kind is that of actions, as *to generate, to corrupt, to alter;* the most faulty is of qualities (except such as
are the immediate objects of the sense) as *heavy, light, rare, dense,* and
the like. Yet in all these cases some notions are of necessity a little better than others, in proportion to the greater variety of subjects that fall
within the range of the human sense.

LXI

But the *Idols of the Theater* are not innate, nor do they steal into
the understanding secretly, but are plainly impressed and received into
the mind from the play-books of philosophical systems and the perverted rules of demonstration. To attempt refutations in this case would
be merely inconsistent with what I have already said: for since we agree
neither upon principles nor upon demonstrations there is no place for
argument. And this is so far well, inasmuch as it leaves the honor of the
ancients untouched. For they are no wise disparaged—the question between them and me being only as to the way. For as the saying is, the
lame man who keeps the right road outstrips the runner who takes a

wrong one. Nay it is obvious that when a man runs the wrong way, the more active and swift he is the further he will go astray.

But the course I propose for the discovery of sciences is such as leaves but little to the acuteness and strength of wits, but places all wits and understandings nearly on a level. For as in the drawing of a straight line or a perfect circle, much depends on the steadiness and practice of the hand, if it be done by aim of hand only, but if with the aid of rule or compass, little or nothing; so is it exactly with my plan. But though particular confutations would be of no avail, yet touching the sects and general divisions of such systems I must say something; something also touching the external signs which show that they are unsound; and finally something touching the causes of such great infelicity and of such lasting and general agreement in error; that so the access to truth may be made less difficult, and the human understanding may the more willingly submit to its purgation and dismiss its idols.

LXII

Idols of the Theater, or of Systems, are many, and there can be and perhaps will be yet many more. For were it not that now for many ages men's minds have been busied with religion and theology; and were it not that civil governments, especially monarchies, have been averse to such novelties, even in matters speculative; so that men labor therein to the peril and harming of their fortunes,—not only unrewarded, but exposed also to contempt and envy: doubtless there would have arisen many other philosophical sects like to those which in great variety flourished once among the Greeks. For as on the phenomena of the heavens many hypotheses may be constructed, so likewise (and more also) many various dogmas may be set up and established on the phenomena of philosophy. And in the plays of this philosophical theater you may observe the same thing which is found in the theater of the poets, that stories invented for the stage are more compact and elegant, and more as one would wish them to be, than true stories out of history.

In general however there is taken for the material of philosophy either a great deal out of a few things, or a very little out of many things; so that on both sides philosophy is based on too narrow a foundation of experiment and natural history, and decides on the authority of too few cases. For the rational school of philosophers snatches from experience a variety of common instances, neither duly ascertained nor diligently examined and weighed, and leaves all the rest to meditation and agitation of wit.

There is also another class of philosophers, who having bestowed much diligent and careful labor on a few experiments, have thence made bold to educe and construct systems; wresting all other facts in a strange fashion to conformity therewith.

And there is yet a third class, consisting of those who out of faith and veneration mix their philosophy with theology and traditions; among whom the vanity of some has gone so far aside as to seek the origin of science among spirits and genii. So that this parent stock of errors— this false philosophy—is of three kinds; the *sophistical*, the *empirical*, and the *superstitious*.

LXIII

The most conspicuous example of the first class was Aristotle, who corrupted natural philosophy by his logic: fashioning the world out of categories; assigning to the human soul, the noblest of substances, a genus from words of the second intention; doing the business of density and rarity (which is to make bodies of greater or less dimensions, that is, occupy greater or less spaces), by the frigid distinction of act and power; asserting that single bodies have each a single and proper motion, and that if they participate in any other, then this results from an external cause; and imposing countless other arbitrary restrictions on the nature of things: being always more solicitous to provide an answer to the question and affirm something positive in words, than about the inner truth of things; a failing best shown when his philosophy is compared with other systems of note among the Greeks. For the *homœomera* of Anaxagoras; the atoms of Leucippus and Democritus; the Heaven and Earth of Parmenides; the Strife and Friendship of Empedocles; Heraclitus's doctrine how bodies are resolved into the indifferent nature of fire, and remolded into solids; have all of them some taste of the natural philosopher,—some savor of the nature of things, and experience, and bodies; whereas in the physics of Aristotle you hear hardly anything but the words of logic; which in his metaphysics also, under a more imposing name, and more forsooth as a realist than a nominalist, he has handled over again. Nor let any weight be given to the fact that in his books on animals, and his *Problems*, and other of his treatises, there is frequent dealing with experiments. For he had come to his conclusion before: he did not consult experience, as he should have done, in order to the framing of his decisions and axioms; but having first determined the question according to his will, he then resorts to experience, and bending her into conformity with his placets leads her about like a captive in a procession: so that even on this count he is more guilty than his modern followers, the schoolmen, who have abandoned experience altogether.

LXIV

But the empirical school of philosophy gives birth to dogmas more deformed and monstrous than the sophistical or rational school. For it has its foundations not in the light of common notions (which, though it be a faint and superficial light, is yet in a manner universal, and has reference to many things) but in the narrowness and darkness of a few experiments. To those therefore who are daily busied with these experiments, and have infected their imagination with them, such a philosophy seems probable and all but certain; to all men else incredible and vain. Of this there is a notable instance in the alchemists and their dogmas; though it is hardly to be found elsewhere in these times, except perhaps in the philosophy of Gilbert. Nevertheless with regard to philosophies of this kind there is one caution not to be omitted; for I foresee that if ever men are roused by my admonitions to betake themselves seriously to experiment and bid farewell to sophistical doctrines, then indeed through the premature hurry of the understanding to leap or fly to universals and principles of things, great danger may be apprehended from philosophies of this kind; against which evil we ought even now to prepare.

LXV

But the corruption of philosophy by superstition and an admixture of theology is far more widely spread, and does the greatest harm, whether to entire systems or to their parts. For the human understanding is obnoxious to the influence of the imagination no less than to the influence of common notions. For the contentious and sophistical kind of philosophy ensnares the understanding; but this kind, being fanciful and tumid and half poetical, misleads it more by flattery. For there is in man an ambition of the understanding, no less than of the will, especially in high and lofty spirits.

Of this kind we have among the Greeks a striking example of Pythagoras, though he united with it a coarser and more cumbrous superstition; another in Plato and his school, more dangerous and subtle. It shows itself likewise in parts of other philosophies, in the introduction of abstract forms and final causes and first causes, with the omission in most cases of causes intermediate, and the like. Upon this point the greatest caution should be used. For nothing is so mischievous as the apotheosis of error; and it is a very plague of the understanding for vanity to become the object of veneration. Yet in this vanity some of the moderns have with extreme levity indulged so far as to attempt to found a system of natural philosophy on the first chapters of Genesis, on the book of Job, and other parts of the sacred writings; seeking for the dead among the living: which also makes the inhibition and repression of it the more important, because from this unwholesome mixture of things human and divine there arises not only a fantastic philosophy but also an heretical religion. Very meet it is therefore that we be sober-minded, and give to faith that only which is faith's.

LXVI

So much then for the mischievous authorities of systems, which are founded either on common notions, or on a few experiments, or on superstition. It remains to speak of the faulty subject-matter of contem-

plations, especially in natural philosophy. Now the human understanding
is infected by the sight of what takes place in the mechanical arts, in
which the alteration of bodies proceeds chiefly by composition or separation, and so imagines that something similar goes on in the universal
nature of things. From this source has flowed the fiction of elements,
and of their concourse for the formation of natural bodies. Again, when
man contemplates nature working freely, he meets with different species
of things, of animals, of plants, of minerals; whence he readily passes
into the opinion that there are in nature certain primary forms which
nature intends to educe, and that the remaining variety proceeds from
hindrances and aberrations of nature in the fulfillment of her work, or
from the collision of different species and the transplanting of one into
another. To the first of these speculations we owe our primary qualities
of the elements; to the other our occult properties and specific virtues;
and both of them belong to those empty *compendia* of thought wherein
the mind rests, and whereby it is diverted from more solid pursuits. It
is to better purpose that the physicians bestow their labor on the secondary qualities of matter, and the operations of attraction, repulsion, attenu-
ation, conspissation, dilatation, astriction, dissipation, maturation, and
the like; and were it not that by those two compendia which I have
mentioned (elementary qualities, to wit, and specific virtues) they corrupted their correct observations in these other matters,—either reducing
them to first qualities and their subtle and incommensurable mixtures,
or not following them out with greater and more diligent observation
to third and fourth qualities, but breaking off the scrutiny prematurely,
—they had made much greater progress. Nor are powers of this kind
(I do not say the same, but similar) to be sought for only in the medicines of the human body, but also in the changes of all other bodies.

But it is a far greater evil that they make the quiescent principles,
wherefrom, and not the moving principles, *whereby*, things are produced, the object of their contemplation and inquiry. For the former
tend to discourse, the latter to works. Nor is there any value in those
vulgar distinctions of motion which are observed in the received system of natural philosophy, as generation, corruption, augmentation,
diminution, alteration, and local motion. What they mean no doubt is
this: If a body, in other respects not changed, be moved from its place,
this is *local motion;* if without change of place or essence, it be changed
in quality, this is *alteration;* if by reason of the change the mass and
quantity of the body do not remain the same, this is *augmentation* or
diminution; if they be changed to such a degree that they change their
very essence and substance and turn to something else, this is *generation* and *corruption.* But all this is merely popular, and does not at all
go deep into nature; for these are only measures and limits, not kinds of
motion. What they intimate is *how far,* not *by what means,* or *from what
source.* For they do not suggest anything with regard either to the desires of bodies or to the development of their parts: it is only when that
motion presents the thing grossly and palpably to the sense as different

from what it was, that they begin to mark the division. Even when they
wish to suggest something with regard to the causes of motion, and to
establish a division with reference to them, they introduce with the
greatest negligence a distinction between motion natural and violent; a
distinction which is itself drawn entirely from a vulgar notion, since all
violent motion is also in fact natural; the external efficient simply setting nature working otherwise than it was before. But if, leaving all this,
anyone shall observe (for instance) that there is in bodies a desire of
mutual contact, so as not to suffer the unity of nature to be quite separated or broken and a vacuum thus made; or if anyone say that there is
in bodies a desire of resuming their natural dimensions or tension, so
that if compressed within or extended beyond them, they immediately
strive to recover themselves, and fall back to their old volume and extent; or if anyone say that there is in bodies a desire of congregating
towards masses of kindred nature,—of dense bodies, for instance, towards
the globe of the earth, of thin, and rare bodies towards the compass
of the sky; all these and the like are truly physical kinds of motion;—
but those others are entirely logical and scholastic, as is abundantly manifest from this comparison.

Nor again is it a less evil, that in their philosophies and contemplations their labor is spent in investigating and handling the first principles
of things and the highest generalities of nature; whereas utility and the
means of working result entirely from things intermediate. Hence it is
that men cease not from abstracting nature till they come to potential
and uninformed matter, nor on the other hand from dissecting nature
till they reach the atom; things which, even if true, can do but little
for the welfare of mankind.

LXVII

A caution must also be given to the understanding against the intemperance which systems of philosophy manifest in giving or withholding
assent; because intemperance of this kind seems to establish idols and
in some sort to perpetuate them, leaving no way open to reach and dis-
lodge them.

This excess is of two kinds: the first being manifest in those who are
ready in deciding; and render sciences dogmatic and magisterial; the
other in those who deny that we can know anything, and so introduce a
wandering kind of inquiry that leads to nothing; of which kinds the
former subdues, the latter weakens the understanding. For the philosophy of Aristotle, after having by hostile confutations destroyed all the
rest (as the Ottomans serve their brothers), has laid down the law on
all points: which done, he proceeds himself to raise new questions of his
own suggestion, and dispose of them likewise; so that nothing may remain that is not certain and decided,—a practice which holds and is in
use among his successors.

The school of Plato, on the other hand, introduced *Acatalepsia*, at first in jest and irony, and in disdain of the older sophists, Protagoras, Hippias, and the rest, who were of nothing else so much ashamed as of seeming to doubt about anything. But the New Academy made a dogma of it, and held it as a tenet. And though theirs is a fairer seeming way than arbitrary decisions; since they say that they by no means destroy all investigation, like Pyrrho and his Refrainers, but allow of some things to be followed as probable, though of none to be maintained as true; yet still when the human mind has once despaired of finding truth, its interest in all things grows fainter; and the result is that men turn aside to pleasant disputations and discourses and roam as it were from object to object, rather than keep on a course of severe inquisition. But, as I said at the beginning and am ever urging, the human senses and understanding, weak as they are, are not to be deprived of their authority, but to be supplied with helps.

LXVIII

So much concerning the several classes of idols, and their equipage: all of which must be renounced and put away with a fixed and solemn determination, and the understanding thoroughly freed and cleansed; the entrance into the kingdom of man, founded on the sciences, being not much other than the entrance into the kingdom of heaven, whereinto none may enter except as a little child.

· · ·

LXXI

The sciences which we possess come for the most part from the Greeks. For what has been added by Roman, Arabic, or later writers is not much nor of much importance; and whatever it is, it is built on the foundation of Greek discoveries. Now the wisdom of the Greeks was professorial and much given to disputations; a kind of wisdom most adverse to the inquisition of truth. Thus that name of Sophists, which by those who would be thought philosophers was in contempt cast back upon and so transferred to the ancient rhetoricians, Gorgias, Protagoras, Hippias, Polus, does indeed suit the entire class, Plato, Aristotle, Zeno, Epicurus, Theophrastus, and their successors Chrysippus, Carnades, and the rest. There was this difference only, that the former class was wandering and mercenary, going about from town to town, putting up their wisdom to sale, and taking a price for it; while the latter was more pompous and dignified, as composed of men who had fixed abodes, and who opened schools and taught their philosophy without reward. Still both sorts, though in other respects unequal, were professorial; both turned the matter into disputations, and set up and battled for philosophical sects and heresies;

so that their doctrines were for the most part (as Dionysius not unaptly rallied Plato) "the talk of idle old men to ignorant youths." But the elder of the Greek philosophers, Empedocles, Anaxagoras, Leucippus, Democritus, Parmenides, Heraclitus, Xenophanes, Philolaus, and the rest (I omit Pythagoras as a mystic), did not, so far as we know, open schools; but more silently and severely and simply,—that is, with less affectation and parade,—betook themselves to the inquisition of truth. And therefore they were in my judgment more successful; only that their works were in the course of time obscured by those slighter persons who had more which suits and pleases the capacity and tastes of the vulgar: time, like a river, bringing down to us things which are light and puffed up, but letting weighty matters sink. Still even they were not altogether free from the failing of their nation; but leaned too much to the ambition and vanity of founding a sect and catching popular applause. But the inquisition of truth must be despaired of when it turns aside to trifles of this kind. Nor should we omit that judgment, or rather divination, which was given concerning the Greeks by the Egyptian priest,—that "they were always boys, without antiquity of knowledge or knowledge of antiquity." Assuredly they have that which is characteristic of boys; they are prompt to prattle, but cannot generate; for their wisdom abounds in words but is barren of works. And therefore the signs which are taken from the origin and birthplace of the received philosophy are not good.

.   .   .

LXXVII

And as for the general opinion that in the philosophy of Aristotle at any rate there is great agreement; since after its publication the systems of older philosophers died away, while in the times which followed nothing better was found; so that it seems to have been so well laid and established as to have drawn both ages in its train; I answer in the first place, that the common notion of the falling off of the old systems upon the publication of Aristotle's works is a false one; for long afterwards, down even to the times of Cicero and subsequent ages, the works of the old philosophers still remained. But in the times which followed, when on the inundation of barbarians into the Roman empire human learning had suffered shipwreck, then the systems of Aristotle and Plato, like planks of lighter and less solid material, floated on the waves of time, and were preserved. Upon the point of consent also men are deceived, if the matter be looked into more keenly. For true consent is that which consists in the coincidence of free judgments, after due examination. But far the greater number of those who have assented to the philosophy of Aristotle have addicted themselves thereto from prejudgment and upon the authority of others; so that it is a following and going along together, rather than consent. But even if it had been a real and widespread consent, still so little ought consent to be deemed a sure and solid confirmation, that it is in fact a strong presumption the other way.

. . .

XCV

Those who have handled sciences have been either men of experiment or men of dogmas. The men of experiment are like the ant; they only collect and use: the reasoners resemble spiders, who make cobwebs out of their own substance. But the bee takes a middle course, it gathers its material from the flowers of the garden and of the field, but transforms and digests it by a power of its own. Not unlike this is the true business of philosophy: for it neither relies solely or chiefly on the powers of the mind, nor does it take the matter which it gathers from natural history and mechanical experiments and lay it up in the memory whole, as it finds it; but lays it up in the understanding altered and digested. Therefore from a closer and purer league between these two faculties, the experimental and the rational, (such as has never yet been made) much may be hoped.

XCVI

We have as yet no natural philosophy that is pure; all is tainted and corrupted: in Aristotle's school by logic; in Plato's by natural theology; in the second school of Platonists, such as Proclus and others, by mathematics, which ought only to give definiteness to natural philosophy, not to generate or give it birth. From a natural philosophy pure and unmixed, better things are to be expected.

. . .

CXXIX

. . . it will not be amiss to distinguish the three kinds and as it were grades of ambition in mankind. The first is of those who desire to extend their own power in their native country; which kind is vulgar and degenerate. The second is of those who labor to extend the power of their country and its dominion among men. This certainly has more dignity, though not less covetousness. But if a man endeavor to establish and extend the power and dominion of the human race itself over the universe, his ambition (if ambition it can be called) is without doubt both a more wholesome thing and a more noble than the other two.

RENÉ
DESCARTES   1596–1650

Descartes is quite generally considered the greatest French philosopher. He does not stand at the fount of a long national tradition, like Francis Bacon, who was followed by Hobbes, Locke, Berkeley, Hume, Bentham, J. S. Mill, and Russell, to name some of the major figures of British philosophy. Those who wish to classify Descartes call him the first of the "Continental Rationalists," and say that he was followed by Spinoza and Leibniz, neither of whom was French. Such fascinating writers as Montaigne, Pascal, Voltaire, and Rousseau—Frenchmen of unquestioned genius —are major literary figures and not very close to Descartes. On the whole, French philosophy has tended to be more literary and less technical than British or German philosophy.

Descartes served as a soldier during parts of the Thirty Years War. While serving in Germany and Holland, he came to feel more and more, as Bacon had, too, that his education—at the Jesuit college of La Flèche—had been thoroughly unsatisfactory, and that a new beginning must be made. But when he was about to publish his first book, *Le Monde*, in 1634, he heard that Galileo's *Dialogo dei due massimi sistemi del mondo*, published in 1632, had incurred the wrath of the Inquisition, and that the author had been forced in 1633 to recant the Copernican theory that the earth revolves around the sun. Descartes decided to withhold his book.

His first major philosophic work, the celebrated *Discours de la méthode*, appeared in 1637. It is the first philosophic classic in French, and is almost as remarkable for its literary excellence as for its solid contents. Next, Descartes wrote his great *Meditationes de prima philosophia*, reverting, as Bacon had done, to Latin. This work

26

was submitted to a number of outstanding critics, including Thomas Hobbes, and published in 1641 together with six sets of "Objections" and Descartes' "Replies to the Objections." Even more than the *Discourse,* the *Meditations* constitute one of the all-time classics of philosophy.

Descartes' *Principia philosophiae,* generally considered much less important than the other two works and never yet translated into English in its entirety, followed in 1644; his *Les passions de l'ame,* in 1650. In 1649 he had gone to Sweden, on the invitation of Queen Christina, who had conceived a great interest in philosophy; and it was in Sweden that he succumbed to pneumonia in 1650.

Unlike Bacon, Descartes was keenly aware of the importance of mathematics. Indeed, he was a first-rate mathematician, and it was he that first devised analytic geometry.

His importance for philosophy may be gleaned from his *Meditations* which did more than merely "influence" Spinoza, Malebranche, and Leibniz: Descartes' philosophy is their starting point, and their avowed purpose is to deal with his problems and to improve upon his solutions.

What follows is the complete text of the *Meditations* and of the "Objections" of Thomas Hobbes, together with Descartes' "Reply" to Hobbes. The translation of the *Meditations* is that of John Veitch, while the version of the "Objections" and "Reply," not translated by Veitch, is that of Elizabeth S. Haldane and G. R. T. Ross. Use of the Haldane and Ross version of the *Meditations* would not have ensured uniformity; as Haldane and Ross say, "This divergence of versions is inevitable, because the translation of the *Meditations* has been founded upon both the Latin and French text . . . thus best representing Descartes' final thoughts on the subject. But Descartes' critics had before them only the original Latin text. . . . Besides the variations explained by the above cause there are others due to abridged quotation or paraphrase of the original passage both by Descartes and by his critics." The brackets in the text are in all cases the translators' and not the editor's: they signify an attempt to do justice not only to the original Latin but also to a French version that appeared a few months later.

MEDITATIONS

Preface to the reader

I have already slightly touched upon the questions respecting the existence of God and the nature of the human soul, in the *Discourse on the
Method of rightly conducting the Reason, and seeking truth in the Sciences,* published in French in the year 1637; not, however, with the design
of there treating of them fully, but only, as it were, in passing, that I
might learn from the judgments of my readers in what way I should
afterwards handle them: for these questions appeared to me to be of such
moment as to be worthy of being considered more than once, and the
path which I follow in discussing them is so little trodden, and so remote
from the ordinary route, that I thought it would not be expedient to
illustrate it at greater length in French, and in a discourse that might be
read by all, lest even the more feeble minds should believe that this path
might be entered upon by them.

But, as in the discourse on Method, I had requested all who might find
aught meriting censure in my writings, to do me the favour of pointing
it out to me, I may state that no objections worthy of remark have been
alleged against what I then said on these questions, except two, to which
I will here briefly reply, before undertaking their more detailed discussion.

The first objection is that though, while the human mind reflects on
itself, it does not perceive that it is any other than a thinking thing, it does
not follow that its nature or essence consists only in its being a thing
which thinks; so that the word *only* shall exclude all other things which
might also perhaps be said to pertain to the nature of the mind.

To this objection I reply, that it was not my intention in that place to
exclude these according to the order of truth in the matter (of which I did
not then treat), but only according to the order of thought (perception);
so that my meaning was, that I clearly apprehended nothing, so far as I
was conscious, as belonging to my essence, except that I was a thinking
thing, or a thing possessing in itself the faculty of thinking. But I will
show hereafter how, from the consciousness that nothing besides thinking
belongs to the essence of the mind, it follows that nothing else does in
truth belong to it.

The second objection is that it does not follow, from my possessing the
idea of a thing more perfect than I am, that the idea itself is more perfect
than myself, and much less that what is represented by the idea exists.

But I reply that in the term *idea* there is here something equivocal; for
it may be taken either materially for an act of the understanding, and in
this sense it cannot be said to be more perfect than I, or objectively, for
the thing represented by that act, which, although it be not supposed to
exist out of my understanding, may, nevertheless, be more perfect than

myself, by reason of its essence. But, in the sequel of this treatise I will show more amply how, from my possessing the idea of a thing more perfect than myself, it follows that this thing really exists.

Besides these two objections, I have seen, indeed, two treatises of sufficient length relating to the present matter. In these, however, my conclusions, much more than my premises, were impugned, and that by arguments borrowed from the common-places of the atheists. But, as arguments of this sort can make no impression on the minds of those who shall rightly understand my reasonings, and as the judgments of many are so irrational and weak that they are persuaded rather by the opinions on a subject that are first presented to them, however false and opposed to reason they may be, than by a true and solid, but subsequently received, refutation of them, I am unwilling here to reply to these strictures from a dread of being, in the first instance, obliged to state them.

I will only say, in general, that all which the atheists commonly allege in favour of the non-existence of God arises continually from one or other of these two things, namely, either the ascription of human affections to deity, or the undue attribution to our minds of so much vigour and wisdom that we may essay to determine and comprehend both what God can and ought to do; hence all that is alleged by them will occasion us no difficulty, provided only we keep in remembrance that our minds must be considered finite, while Deity is incomprehensible and infinite.

Now that I have once, in some measure, made proof of the opinions of men regarding my work, I again undertake to treat of God and the human soul, and at the same time to discuss the principles of the entire first philosophy, without, however, expecting any commendation from the crowd for my endeavours, or a wide circle of readers. On the contrary, I would advise none to read this work, unless such as are able and willing to meditate with me in earnest, to detach their minds from commerce with the senses, and likewise to deliver themselves from all prejudice; and individuals of this character are, I well know, remarkably rare. But with regard to those who, without caring to comprehend the order and connection of the reasonings, shall study only detached clauses for the purpose of small but noisy criticism, as is the custom with many, I may say that such persons will not profit greatly by the reading of this treatise; and although perhaps they may find opportunity for cavilling in several places, they will yet hardly start any pressing objections, or such as shall be deserving of reply.

But since, indeed, I do not promise to satisfy others on all these subjects at first sight, nor arrogate so much to myself as to believe that I have been able to foresee all that may be the source of difficulty to each one, I shall expound, first of all, in the *Meditations,* those considerations by which I feel persuaded that I have arrived at a certain and evident knowledge of truth, in order that I may ascertain whether the reasonings which have prevailed with myself will also be effectual in convincing others. I will then reply to the objections of some men, illustrious for their genius and learning, to whom these meditations were sent for criticism before they were committed to the press; for these objections are so numerous and varied that I venture to anticipate that nothing, at least nothing of any moment, will readily occur to any mind which has not been touched upon in them.

Hence it is that I earnestly entreat my readers not to come to any judgment on the questions raised in the meditations until they have taken care to read the whole of the objections, with the relative replies.

Synopsis

of the

Six Following Meditations

In the First Meditation I expound the grounds on which we may doubt in general of all things, and especially of material objects, so long, at least, as we have no other foundations for the sciences than those we have hitherto possessed. Now, although the utility of a doubt so general may not be manifest at first sight, it is nevertheless of the greatest, since it delivers us from all prejudice, and affords the easiest pathway by which the mind may withdraw itself from the senses; and, finally, makes it impossible for us to doubt wherever we afterwards discover truth.

In the Second, the mind which, in the exercise of the freedom peculiar to itself, supposes that no object is, of the existence of which it has even the slightest doubt, finds that, meanwhile, it must itself exist. And this point is likewise of the highest moment, for the mind is thus enabled easily to distinguish what pertains to itself, that is, to the intellectual nature, from what is to be referred to the body. But since some, perhaps, will expect, at this stage of our progress, a statement of the reasons which establish the doctrine of the immortality of the soul, I think it proper here to make such aware, that it was my aim to write nothing of which I could not give exact demonstration, and that I therefore felt myself obliged to adopt an order similar to that in use among the geometers, viz., to premise all upon which the proposition in question depends, before coming to any conclusion respecting it. Now, the first and chief pre-requisite for the knowledge of the immortality of the soul is our being able to form the clearest possible conception (*conceptus*—concept) of the soul itself, and such as shall be absolutely distinct from all our notions of body; and how this is to be accomplished is there shown. There is required, besides this, the assurance that all objects which we clearly and distinctly think are true (really exist) in that very mode in which we think them: and this could not be established previously to the Fourth Meditation. Further, it is necessary, for the same purpose, that we possess a distinct conception of corporeal nature, which is given partly in the Second and partly in the Fifth and Sixth Meditations. And, finally, on these grounds, we are necessitated to conclude, that all those objects which are clearly and distinctly conceived to be diverse substances, as mind and body, are substances really reciprocally distinct; and this inference is made in the Sixth Meditation. The absolute distinction of mind and body is, besides, confirmed in this Second Meditation, by showing that we cannot conceive body unless as divisible; while, on the other hand, mind cannot be conceived unless as indivisible. For we are not able to conceive the half of a mind, as we can of any body, however small, so that the natures of these two substances are to be held, not only as diverse, but even in some measure as contraries. I have not, however, pursued this discussion further in the present treatise, as well for the reason that these considerations are sufficient to show that the destruction of the mind does not follow from the corruption of the body, and thus to afford to men the hope of a future life, as also because the premises from which it is competent for us to infer the immortality of the soul, involve an explication of the whole principles of physics: in order to establish, in the first place, that generally all substances, that is, all things which can exist only in consequence of having been created by God, are in their own nature incorruptible, and can never cease to be, unless God himself, by refusing his concurrence to them, reduce them to nothing; and, in the second place, that body, taken generally, is a substance, and therefore can never perish, but that the human body, in as far as it differs from other bodies, is constituted only by a certain configuration of members, and by other accidents of this sort, while the human mind is not made up of accidents, but is a pure substance. For although all the accidents of the mind be changed—although, for example, it think certain things, will others, and perceive others, the mind itself does not vary with these changes; while, on the contrary, the human body is no longer the same if a change take place in the form of any of its parts: from which it follows that the body may, indeed, without difficulty perish, but that the mind is in its own nature immortal.

In the Third Meditation, I have unfolded at sufficient length, as appears to me, my chief argument for the existence of God. But yet, since I was there desirous to avoid the use of comparisons taken from material objects, that I might withdraw, as far as possible, the minds of my readers from the senses, numerous obscurities perhaps remain, which, however, will, I trust, be afterwards entirely removed in the replies to the objections: thus, among other things, it may be difficult to understand how the idea of a being absolutely perfect, which is found in our minds, possesses so much objective reality [*i.e.*, participates by representation in so many degrees of being and perfection] that it must be held to arise from a course absolutely perfect. This is illustrated in the replies by the comparison of a highly perfect machine, the idea of which exists in the mind of some workmen; for as the objective (*i.e.*, representative) perfection of this idea must have some cause, viz., either the science of the workman, or of some other person from whom he has received the idea, in the same way the idea of God, which is found in us, demands God himself for its cause.

In the Fourth, it is shown that all which we clearly and distinctly perceive (apprehend) is true; and, at the same time, is explained wherein consists the nature of error; points that require to be known as well for confirming the preceding truths, as for the better understanding of those that are to follow. But, meanwhile, it must be observed, that I do not at all there treat of Sin, that is, of error committed in the pursuit of good and evil, but of that sort alone which arises in the determination of the true and the false. Nor do I refer to matters of faith, or to the conduct of life, but only to what regards speculative truths, and such as are known by means of the natural light alone.

In the Fifth, besides the illustration of corporeal nature, taken generically, a new demonstration is given of the existence of God, not free, perhaps, any more than the former, from certain difficulties, but of these the solution will be found in the replies to the objections. I further show in what sense it is true that the certitude of geometrical demonstrations themselves is dependent on the knowledge of God.

Finally, in the Sixth, the act of the understanding (*intellectio*) is distinguished from that of the imagination (*imaginatio*); the marks of this distinction are described; the human mind is shown to be really distinct from the body, and, nevertheless, to be so closely conjoined therewith, as together to form, as it were, a unity. The whole of the errors which arise from the senses are brought under review, while the means of avoiding them are pointed out; and, finally, all the grounds are adduced from which the existence of material objects may be inferred; not, however, because I deemed them of great utility in establishing what they prove, viz., that there is in reality a world, that men are possessed of bodies, and the like, the truth of which no one of sound mind ever seriously doubted; but because, from a close consideration of them, it is perceived that they are neither so strong nor clear as the reasonings which conduct us to the knowledge of our mind and of God; so that the latter are, of all which come under human knowledge, the most certain and manifest—a conclusion which it was my single aim in these Meditations to establish; on which account I here omit mention of the various other questions which, in the course of the discussion, I had occasion likewise to consider.

Meditations on the First Philosophy

IN WHICH THE EXISTENCE OF GOD, AND THE REAL DISTINCTION OF MIND AND BODY, ARE DEMONSTRATED

Meditation I

OF THE THINGS OF WHICH WE MAY DOUBT

Several years have now elapsed since I first became aware that I had accepted, even from my youth, many false opinions for true, and that consequently what I afterwards based on such principles was highly doubtful; and from that time I was convinced of the necessity of undertaking once in my life to rid myself of all the opinions I had adopted, and of commencing anew the work of building from the foundation, if I desired to establish a firm and abiding superstructure in the sciences. But as this enterprise appeared to me to be one of great magnitude, I waited until I had attained an age so mature as to leave me no hope that at any stage of life more advanced I should be better able to execute my design. On this account, I have delayed so long that I should henceforth consider I was doing wrong were I still to consume in deliberation any of the time that now remains for action. To-day, then, since I have opportunely freed my mind from all cares [and am happily disturbed by no passions], and since I am in the secure possession of leisure in a peaceable retirement, I will at length apply myself earnestly and freely to the general overthrow of all my former opinions. But, to this end, it will not be necessary for me to show that the whole of these are false—a point, perhaps, which I shall never reach; but as even now my reason convinces me that I ought not the less carefully to withhold belief from what is not entirely certain and indubitable, than from what is manifestly false, it will be sufficient to justify the rejection of the whole if I shall find in each some ground for doubt. Nor for this purpose will it be necessary even to deal with each belief individually, which would be truly an endless labour; but, as the removal from below of the foundation necessarily involves the downfall of the whole edifice, I will at once approach the criticism of the principles on which all my former beliefs rested.

All that I have, up to this moment, accepted as possessed of the highest truth and certainty, I received either from or through the senses. I observed, however, that these sometimes misled us; and it is the part of prudence not to place absolute confidence in that by which we have even once been deceived.

But it may be said, perhaps, that, although the senses occasionally mislead us respecting minute objects, and such as are so far removed from us as to be beyond the reach of close observation, there are yet many other of their informations (presentations), of the truth of which it is manifestly impossible to doubt; as for example, that I am in this place, seated by the fire, clothed in a winter dressing-gown, that I hold in my hands this piece of paper, with other intimations of the same nature. But how could I deny that I possess these hands and this body, and withal escape being classed with persons in a state of insanity, whose brains are so disordered and clouded by dark bilious vapours as to cause them pertinaciously to assert that they are monarchs when they are in the greatest poverty; or clothed [in gold] and purple when destitute of any covering; or that their head is made of clay, their body of glass, or that they are gourds? I should certainly be not less insane than they, were I to regulate my procedure according to examples so extravagant.

Though this be true, I must nevertheless here consider that I am a man, and that, consequently, I am in the habit of sleeping, and representing to myself in dreams those same things, or even sometimes others less prob-able, which the insane think are presented to them in their waking mo-ments. How often have I dreamt that I was in these familiar circumstances —that I was dressed, and occupied this place by the fire, when I was lying undressed in bed? At the present moment, however, I certainly look upon this paper with eyes wide awake; the head which I now move is not asleep; I extend this hand consciously and with express purpose, and I perceive it; the occurrences in sleep are not so distinct as all this. But I cannot forget that, at other times, I have been deceived in sleep by similar illusions; and, attentively considering those cases, I perceive so clearly that there exist no certain marks by which the state of waking can ever be distinguished from sleep, that I feel greatly astonished; and in amaze-ment I almost persuade myself that I am now dreaming.

Let us suppose, then, that we are dreaming, and that all these partic-ulars—namely, the opening of the eyes, the motion of the head, the forth-putting of the hands—are merely illusions; and even that we really possess neither an entire body nor hands such as we see. Nevertheless, it must be admitted at least that the objects which appear to us in sleep are, as it were, painted representations which could not have been formed unless in the likeness of realities; and, therefore, that those general ob-jects, at all events—namely, eyes, a head, hands, and an entire body—are not simply imaginary, but really existent. For, in truth, painters them-selves, even when they study to represent sirens and satyrs by forms the most fantastic and extraordinary, cannot bestow upon them natures ab-solutely new, but can only make a certain medley of the members of different animals; or if they chance to imagine something so novel that nothing at all similar has ever been seen before, and such as is, therefore, purely fictitious and absolutely false, it is at least certain that the colours of which this is composed are real.

And on the same principle, although these general objects, viz. [a body], eyes, a head, hands, and the like, be imaginary, we are nevertheless absolutely necessitated to admit the reality at least of some other objects still more simple and universal than these, of which, just as of certain real colours, all those images of things, whether true and real, or false and fantastic, that are found in our consciousness (*cogitatio*), are formed.

To this class of objects seem to belong corporeal nature in general and its extension; the figure of extended things, their quantity or magnitude, and their number, as also the place in, and the time during, which they exist, and other things of the same sort. We will not, therefore, perhaps reason illegitimately if we conclude from this that physics, astronomy, medicine, and all the other sciences that have for their end the considera-tion of composite objects, are indeed of a doubtful character; but that arithmetic, geometry, and the other sciences of the same class, which regard merely the simplest and most general objects, and scarcely inquire whether or not these are really existent, contain somewhat that is certain and indubitable: for whether I am awake or dreaming, it remains true that two and three make five, and that a square has but four sides; nor does it seem possible that truths so apparent can ever fall under a suspicion of falsity [or incertitude].

Nevertheless, the belief that there is a God who is all-powerful, and who created me, such as I am, has for a long time, obtained steady possession of my mind. How, then, do I know that he has not arranged that there should be neither earth, nor sky, nor any extended thing, nor figure, nor magnitude, nor place, providing at the same time, however, for [the rise in me of the perceptions of all these objects, and] the persuasion that these do not exist otherwise than as I perceive them? And further, as I sometimes think that others are in error respecting matters of which they believe themselves to possess a perfect knowledge, how do I know that I am not also deceived each time I add together two and three, or number the sides of a square, or form some judgment still more simple, if more simple indeed can be imagined? But perhaps Deity has not been willing that I should be thus deceived, for He is said to be supremely good. If, however, it were repugnant to the goodness of Deity to have created me subject to constant deception, it would seem likewise to be contrary to his goodness to allow me to be occasionally deceived; and yet it is clear that this is permitted. Some, indeed, might perhaps be found who would be disposed rather to deny the existence of a being so powerful than to believe that there is nothing certain. But let us for the present refrain from opposing this opinion, and grant that all which is here said of a Deity is fabulous: nevertheless, in whatever way it be supposed that I reached the state in which I exist, whether by fate, or chance, or by an endless series of antecedents and consequents, or by any other means, it is clear (since to be deceived and to err is a certain defect) that the probability of my being so imperfect as to be the constant victim of deception, will be increased exactly in proportion as the power possessed by the cause, to which they assign my origin, is lessened. To these reasonings I have assuredly nothing to reply, but am constrained at last to avow that there is nothing at all that I formerly believed to be true of which it is impossible to doubt, and that not through thoughtlessness or levity, but from cogent and maturely considered reasons; so that henceforward, if I desire to discover anything certain, I ought not the less carefully to refrain from assenting to those same opinions than to what might be shown to be manifestly false.

But it is not sufficient to have made these observations; care must be taken likewise to keep them in remembrance. For those old and customary opinions perpetually recur—long and familiar usage giving them the right of occupying my mind, even almost against my will, and subduing my belief; nor will I lose the habit of deferring to them and confiding in them so long as I shall consider them to be what in truth they are, viz., opinions to some extent doubtful, as I have already shown, but still highly probable, and such as it is much more reasonable to believe than deny. It is for this reason I am persuaded that I shall not be doing wrong, if, taking an opposite judgment of deliberate design, I become my own deceiver, by supposing, for a time, that all those opinions are entirely false and imaginary, until at length, having thus balanced my old by my new prejudices, my judgment shall no longer be turned aside by perverted usage from the path that may conduct to the perception of truth. For I am assured that, meanwhile, there will arise neither peril nor error from this course, and that I cannot for the present yield too much to distrust, since the end I now seek is not action but knowledge.

I will suppose, then, not that Deity, who is sovereignly good and the fountain of truth, but that some malignant demon, who is at once exceedingly potent and deceitful, has employed all his artifice to deceive me; I will suppose that the sky, the air, the earth, colours, figures, sounds, and all external things, are nothing better than the illusions of dreams, by means of which this being has laid snares for my credulity; I will consider myself as without hands, eyes, flesh, blood, or any of the senses, and as falsely believing that I am possessed of these; I will continue resolutely fixed in this belief, and if indeed by this means it be not in my power to arrive at the knowledge of truth, I shall at least do what is in my power, viz. [suspend my judgment], and guard with settled purpose against giving my assent to what is false, and being imposed upon by this deceiver, whatever be his power and artifice.

But this undertaking is arduous, and a certain indolence insensibly leads me back to my ordinary course of life; and just as the captive, who, perchance, was enjoying in his dreams an imaginary liberty, when he begins to suspect that it is but a vision, dreads awakening, and conspires with the agreeable illusions that the deception may be prolonged; so I, of my own accord, fall back into the train of my former beliefs, and fear to arouse myself from my slumber, lest the time of laborious wakefulness that would succeed this quiet rest, in place of bringing any light of day, should prove inadequate to dispel the darkness that will arise from the difficulties that have now been raised.

Meditation II

OF THE NATURE OF THE HUMAN MIND; AND THAT IT IS MORE EASILY KNOWN THAN THE BODY

The Meditation of yesterday has filled my mind with so many doubts, that it is no longer in my power to forget them. Nor do I see, meanwhile, any principle on which they can be resolved; and, just as if I had fallen all of a sudden into very deep water, I am so greatly disconcerted as to be made unable either to plant my feet firmly on the bottom or sustain myself by swimming on the surface. I will, nevertheless, make an effort, and try anew the same path on which I had entered yesterday, that is, proceed by casting aside all that admits of the slightest doubt, not less than if I had discovered it to be absolutely false; and I will continue always in this track until I shall find something that is certain, or at least, if I can do nothing more, until I shall know with certainty that there is nothing certain. Archimedes, that he might transport the entire globe from the place it occupied to another, demanded only a point that was firm and immovable; so also, I shall be entitled to entertain the highest expectations, if I am fortunate enough to discover only one thing that is certain and indubitable.

I suppose, accordingly, that all the things which I see are false (fictitious); I believe that none of those objects which my fallacious memory represents ever existed; I suppose that I possess no senses; I believe that body, figure, extension, motion, and place are merely fictions of my mind. What is there, then, that can be esteemed true? Perhaps this only, that there is absolutely nothing certain.

But how do I know that there is not something different altogether from the objects I have now enumerated, of which it is impossible to entertain the slightest doubt? Is there not a God, or some being, by whatever name I may designate him, who causes these thoughts to arise in my mind? But why suppose such a being, for it may be I myself am capable of producing them? Am I, then, at least not something? But I before denied that I possessed senses or a body; I hesitate, however, for what follows from that? Am I so dependent on the body and the senses that without these I cannot exist? But I had the persuasion that there was absolutely nothing in the world, that there was no sky and no earth, neither minds nor bodies; was I not, therefore, at the same time, persuaded that I did not exist? Far from it; I assuredly existed, since I was persuaded. But there is I know not what being, who is possessed at once of the highest power and the deepest cunning, who is constantly employing all his ingenuity in deceiving me. Doubtless, then, I exist, since I am deceived; and, let him deceive me as he may, he can never bring it about that I am nothing, so long as I shall be conscious that I am something. So that it must, in fine, be maintained, all things being maturely and carefully considered, that this proposition (*pronunciatum*) I am, I exist, is necessarily true each time it is expressed by me, or conceived in my mind.

But I do not yet know with sufficient clearness what I am, though assured that I am; and hence, in the next place, I must take care, lest perchance I inconsiderately substitute some other object in room of what is properly myself, and thus wander from truth, even in that knowledge (cognition) which I hold to be of all others the most certain and evident. For this reason, I will now consider anew what I formerly believed myself to be, before I entered on the present train of thought; and of my previous opinion I will retrench all that can in the least be invalidated by the grounds of doubt I have adduced, in order that there may at length remain nothing but what is certain and indubitable. What then did I formerly think I was? Undoubtedly I judged that I was a man. But what is a man? Shall I say a rational animal? Assuredly not; for it would be necessary forthwith to inquire into what is meant by animal, and what by rational, and thus, from a single question, I should insensibly glide into others, and these more difficult than the first; nor do I now possess enough of leisure to warrant me in wasting my time amid subtleties of this sort. I prefer here to attend to the thoughts that sprung up of themselves in my mind, and were inspired by my own nature alone, when I applied myself to the consideration of what I was. In the first place, then, I thought that I possessed a countenance, hands, arms, and all the fabric of members that appears in a corpse, and which I called by the name of body. It further occurred to me that I was nourished, that I walked, perceived, and thought, and all those actions I referred to the soul; but what the soul itself was I either did not stay to consider, or, if I did, I imagined that it was something extremely rare and subtile, like wind, or flame, or ether, spread through my grosser parts. As regarded the body, I did not even doubt of its nature, but thought I distinctly knew it, and if I had wished to describe it according to the notions I then entertained, I should have explained myself in this manner: By body I understand all that can be terminated by a certain figure; that can be comprised in a certain place, and so fill a certain space as therefrom to exclude every other body; that can be perceived either by touch, sight, hearing, taste, or smell; that can be moved in different ways, not indeed of itself, but by something foreign to it by which it is touched [and from which it receives the impression]; for the power of self-motion, as likewise that of perceiving and thinking, I held as by no means pertaining to the nature of body; on the contrary, I was somewhat astonished to find such faculties existing in some bodies.

But [as to myself, what can I now say that I am], since I suppose there exists an extremely powerful, and, if I may so speak, malignant being, whose whole endeavours are directed towards deceiving me? Can I affirm that I possess any one of all those attributes of which I have lately spoken as belonging to the nature of body? After attentively considering them in my own mind, I find none of them that can properly be said to belong to myself. To recount them were idle and tedious. Let us pass, then, to the attributes of the soul. The first mentioned were the powers of nutrition and walking; but, if it be true that I have no body, it is true likewise that I am capable neither of walking nor of being nourished. Perception is another attribute of the soul; but perception too is impossible without the body: besides, I have frequently, during sleep, believed that I perceived objects which I afterwards observed I did not in reality perceive. Thinking is another attribute of the soul; and here I discover what properly belongs to myself. This alone is inseparable from me. I am—I exist: this is certain; but how often? As often as I think; for perhaps it would even happen, if I should wholly cease to think, that I should at the same time altogether cease to be. I now admit nothing that is not necessarily true: I am therefore, precisely speaking, only a thinking thing, that is, a mind (*mens sive animus*), understanding, or reason,—terms whose signification was before unknown to me. I am, however, a real thing, and really existent; but what thing? The answer was, a thinking thing. The question now arises, am I aught besides? I will stimulate my imagination with a view to discover whether I am not still something more than a thinking being. Now it is plain I am not the assemblage of members called the human body; I am not a thin and penetrating air diffused through all these members, or wind, or flame, or vapour, or breath, or any of all the things I can imagine; for I supposed that all these were not, and, without changing the supposition, I find that I still feel assured of my existence.

But it is true, perhaps, that those very things which I suppose to be non-existent, because they are unknown to me, are not in truth different from myself whom I know. This is a point I cannot determine, and do not now enter into any dispute regarding it. I can only judge of things that are known to me: I am conscious that I exist, and I who know that I exist inquire into what I am. It is, however, perfectly certain that the knowledge of my existence, thus precisely taken, is not dependent on things, the existence of which is as yet unknown to me: and consequently it is not dependent on any of the things I can feign in imagination. Moreover, the phrase itself, I frame an image (*effingo*), reminds me of my error; for I should in truth frame one if I were to imagine myself to be anything, since to imagine is nothing more than to contemplate the figure or image of a corporeal thing; but I already know that I exist, and that it is possible at the same time that all those images, and in general all that relates to the nature of body, are merely dreams [or chimeras]. From this I discover that it is not more reasonable to say, I will excite my imagination that I may know more distinctly what I am, than to express myself as follows: I am now awake, and perceive something real; but because my perception is not sufficiently clear, I will of express purpose go to sleep that my dreams may represent to me the object of my perception with more truth and clearness. And, therefore, I know that nothing of all that I can embrace in imagination belongs to the knowledge which I have of myself, and that there is need to recall with the utmost care the mind from this mode of thinking, that it may be able to know its own nature with perfect distinctness.

But what, then, am I? A thinking thing, it has been said. But what is a thinking thing? It is a thing that doubts, understands [conceives], affirms, denies, wills, refuses, that imagines also, and perceives. Assuredly it is not little, if all these properties belong to my nature. But why should they not belong to it? Am I not that very being who now doubts of almost everything; who, for all that, understands and conceives certain things, who affirms one alone as true, and denies the others; who desires to know more of them, and does not wish to be deceived; who imagines many things, sometimes even despite his will; and is likewise percipient of many, as if through the medium of the senses. Is there nothing of all this as true as that I am, even although I should be always dreaming, and although he who gave me being employed all his ingenuity to deceive me? Is there also any one of these attributes that can be properly distinguished from my thought, or that can be said to be separate from myself? For it is of itself so evident that it is I who doubt, I who understand, and I who desire, that it is here unnecessary to add anything by way of rendering it more clear. And I am as certainly the same being who imagines; for, although it may be (as I before supposed) that nothing I imagine is true, still the power of imagination does not cease really to exist in me and to form part of my thoughts. In fine, I am the same being who perceives, that is, who apprehends certain objects as by the organs of sense, since, in truth, I see light, hear a noise, and feel heat. But it will be said that these presentations are false, and that I am dreaming. Let it be so. At all events it is certain that I seem to see light, hear a noise, and feel heat; this cannot be false, and this is what in me is properly called perceiving (*sentire*), which is nothing else than thinking. From this I begin to know what I am with somewhat greater clearness and distinctness than heretofore.

But, nevertheless, it still seems to me, and I cannot help believing, that corporeal things, whose images are formed by thought [which fall under the senses], and are examined by the same, are known with much greater distinctness than that I know not what part of myself which is not imaginable; although, in truth, it may seem strange to say that I know and comprehend with greater distinctness things whose existence appears to me doubtful, that are unknown, and do not belong to me, than others of whose reality I am persuaded, that are known to me, and appertain to my proper nature; in a word, than myself. But I see clearly what is the state of the case. My mind is apt to wander, and will not yet submit to be restrained within the limits of truth. Let us therefore leave the mind to itself once more, and, according to it every kind of liberty [permit it to consider the objects that appear to it from without], in order that, having afterwards withdrawn it from these gently and opportunely [and fixed it on the consideration of its being and the properties it finds in itself], it may then be the more easily controlled.

Let us now accordingly consider the objects that are commonly thought to be [the most easily, and likewise] the most distinctly known, viz., the bodies we touch and see; not, indeed, bodies in general, for these general notions are usually somewhat more confused, but one body in particular. Take, for example, this piece of wax; it is quite fresh, having been but recently taken from the beehive; it has not yet lost the sweetness of the honey it contained; it still retains somewhat of the odour of the flowers from which it was gathered; its colour, figure, size, are apparent (to the sight); it is hard, cold, easily handled; and sounds when struck upon with the finger. In fine, all that contributes to make a body as distinctly known as possible, is found in the one before us. But, while I am speaking, let it be placed near the fire—what remained of the taste exhales, the smell evaporates, the colour changes, its figure is destroyed, its size increases, it becomes liquid, it grows hot, it can hardly be handled, and, although struck upon, it emits no sound. Does the same wax still remain after this change? It must be admitted that it does remain; no one doubts it, or judges otherwise. What, then, was it I knew with so much distinctness in the piece of wax? Assuredly, it could be nothing of all that I observed by means of the senses, since all the things that fell under taste, smell, sight, touch, and hearing are changed, and yet the same wax remains. It was perhaps what I now think, viz., that this wax was neither the sweetness of honey, the pleasant odour of flowers, the whiteness, the figure, nor the sound, but only a body that a little before appeared to me conspicuous under these forms, and which is now perceived under others. But, to speak precisely, what is it that I imagine when I think of it in this way? Let it be attentively considered, and, retrenching all that does not belong to the wax, let us see what remains. There certainly remains nothing, except something extended, flexible, and movable. But what is meant by flexible and movable? Is it not that I imagine that the piece of wax, being round, is capable of becoming square, or of passing from a square into a triangular figure? Assuredly such is not the case, because I conceive that it admits of an infinity of similar changes; and I am, moreover, unable to compass this infinity by imagination, and consequently this conception which I have of the wax is not the product of the faculty of imagination. But what now is this extension? Is it not also unknown? for it becomes greater when the wax is melted, greater when it is boiled, and greater still when the heat increases; and I should not conceive [clearly and] according to truth, the wax as it is, if I did not suppose that the piece we are considering admitted even of a wider variety of extension than I ever imagined. I must, therefore, admit that I cannot even comprehend by imagination what the piece of wax is, and that it is the mind alone (*mens,* Lat.; *entendement,* F.) which perceives it. I speak of one piece in particular; for, as to wax in general, this is still more evident. But what is the piece of wax that can be perceived only by the [understanding of] mind? It is certainly the same which I see, touch, imagine; and, in fine, it is the same which, from the beginning, I believed it to be. But (and this it is of moment to observe) the perception of it is neither an act of sight, of touch, nor of imagination, and never was either of these, though it might formerly seem so, but is simply an intuition (*inspectio*) of the mind, which may be imperfect and confused, as it formerly was, or very clear and distinct, as it is at present, according as the attention is more or less directed to the elements which it contains, and of which it is composed.

But, meanwhile, I feel greatly astonished when I observe [the weakness of my mind, and] its proneness to error. For although, without at all giving expression to what I think, I consider all this in my own mind, words yet occasionally impede my progress, and I am almost led into error by the terms of ordinary language. We say, for example, that we see the same wax when it is before us, and not that we judge it to be the same from its retaining the same colour and figure: whence I should forthwith be disposed to conclude that the wax is known by the act of sight, and not by the intuition of the mind alone, were it not for the analogous instance of human beings passing on in the street below, as observed from a window. In this case I do not fail to say that I see the men themselves, just as I say that I see the wax; and yet what do I see from the window beyond hats and cloaks that might cover artificial machines, whose motions might be determined by springs? But I judge that there are human beings from these appearances, and thus I comprehend, by the faculty of judgment alone which is in the mind, what I believed I saw with my eyes.

The man who makes it his aim to rise to knowledge superior to the common, ought to be ashamed to seek occasions of doubting from the vulgar forms of speech: instead, therefore, of doing this, I shall proceed with the matter in hand, and inquire whether I had a clearer and more perfect perception of the piece of wax when I first saw it, and when I thought I knew it by means of the external sense itself, or, at all events, by the common sense (*sensus communis*), as it is called, that is, by the imaginative faculty; or whether I rather apprehend it more clearly at present, after having examined with greater care, both what it is, and in what way it can be known. It would certainly be ridiculous to entertain any doubt on this point. For what, in that first perception, was there distinct? What did I perceive which any animal might not have perceived? But when I distinguish the wax from its exterior forms, and when, as if I had stripped it of its vestments, I consider it quite naked, it is certain, although some error may still be found in my judgment, that I cannot, nevertheless, thus apprehend it without possessing a human mind.

But, finally, what shall I say of the mind itself, that is, of myself? for as yet I do not admit that I am anything but mind. What, then! I who seem to possess so distinct an apprehension of the piece of wax,—do I not know myself, both with greater truth and certitude, and also much more distinctly and clearly? For if I judge that the wax exists because I see it, it assuredly follows, much more evidently, that I myself am or exist, for the same reason: for it is possible that what I see may not in truth be wax, and that I do not even possess eyes with which to see anything; but it cannot be that when I see, or, which comes to the same thing, when I think I see, I myself who think am nothing. So likewise, if I judge that the wax exists because I touch it, it will still also follow that I am; and if I determine that my imagination, or any other cause, whatever it be, persuades me of the existence of the wax, I will still draw the same conclusion. And what is here remarked of the piece of wax is applicable to all the other things that are external to me. And further, if the [notion or] perception of wax appeared to me more precise and distinct, after that not only sight and touch, but many other causes besides, rendered it manifest to my apprehension, with how much greater distinctness must I now know myself, since all the reasons that contribute to the knowledge of the nature of wax, or of any body whatever, manifest still better the nature of my mind? And there are besides so many other things in the mind itself that contribute to the illustration of its nature, that those dependent on the body, to which I have here referred, scarcely merit to be taken into account.

But, in conclusion, I find I have insensibly reverted to the point I desired; for, since it is now manifest to me that bodies themselves are not properly perceived by the senses nor by the faculty of imagination, but by the intellect alone; and since they are not perceived because they are seen and touched, but only because they are understood [or rightly comprehended by thought], I readily discover that there is nothing more easily or clearly apprehended than my own mind. But because it is difficult to rid one's self so promptly of an opinion to which one has been long accustomed, it will be desirable to tarry for some time at this stage, that, by long continued meditation, I may more deeply impress upon my memory this new knowledge.

Meditation III

OF GOD: THAT HE EXISTS

I will now close my eyes, I will stop my ears, I will turn away my senses from their objects, I will even efface from my consciousness all the images of corporeal things; or at least, because this can hardly be accomplished, I will consider them as empty and false; and thus, holding converse only with myself, and closely examining my nature, I will endeavour to obtain by degrees a more intimate and familiar knowledge of myself. I am a thinking (conscious) thing, that is, a being who doubts, affirms, denies, knows a few objects, and is ignorant of many,—[who loves, hates], wills, refuses,—who imagines likewise, and perceives; for, as I before remarked, although the things which I perceive or imagine are perhaps nothing at all apart from me [and in themselves], I am neverthe-less assured that those modes of consciousness which I call perceptions and imaginations, in as far only as they are modes of consciousness, exist in me. And in the little I have said I think I have summed up all that I really know, or at least all that up to this time I was aware I knew. Now, as I am endeavouring to extend my knowledge more widely, I will use circumspection, and consider with care whether I can still dis-cover in myself anything further which I have not yet hitherto observed. I am certain that I am a thinking thing; but do I not therefore likewise know what is required to render me certain of a truth? In this first knowl-edge, doubtless, there is nothing that gives me assurance of its truth except the clear and distinct perception of what I affirm, which would not indeed be sufficient to give me the assurance that what I say is true, if it could ever happen that anything I thus clearly and distinctly per-ceived should prove false; and accordingly it seems to me that I may now take as a general rule, that all that is very clearly and distinctly apprehended (conceived) is true.

Nevertheless I before received and admitted many things as wholly certain and manifest, which yet I afterwards found to be doubtful. What, then, were those? They were the earth, the sky, the stars, and all the other objects which I was in the habit of perceiving by the senses. But what was it that I clearly [and distinctly] perceived in them? Nothing more than that the ideas and the thoughts of those objects were presented to my mind. And even now I do not deny that these ideas are found in my mind. But there was yet another thing which I affirmed, and which, from having been accustomed to believe it, I thought I clearly perceived, although, in truth, I did not perceive it at all; I mean the existence of objects external to me, from which those ideas proceeded, and to which they had a perfect resemblance; and it was here I was mistaken, or if I judged correctly, this assuredly was not to be traced to any knowledge I possessed (the force of my perception, Lat.).

But when I considered any matter in arithmetic and geometry, that was very simple and easy, as, for example, that two and three added together make five, and things of this sort, did I not view them with at least sufficient clearness to warrant me in affirming their truth? Indeed, if I afterwards judged that we ought to doubt of these things, it was for no other reason than because it occurred to me that a God might perhaps have given me such a nature as that I should be deceived, even respecting the matters that appeared to me the most evidently true. But as often as this preconceived opinion of the sovereign power of a God presents itself to my mind, I am constrained to admit that it is easy for him, if he wishes it, to cause me to err, even in matters where I think I possess the highest evidence; and, on the other hand, as often as I direct my attention to things which I think I apprehend with great clearness I am so persuaded of their truth that I naturally break out into expressions such as these: Deceive me who may, no one will yet ever be able to bring it about that I am not, so long as I shall be conscious that I am, or at any future time cause it to be true that I have never been, it being now true that I am, or make two and three more or less than five, in supposing which, and other like absurdities, I discover a manifest contradiction.

And in truth, as I have no ground for believing that Deity is deceitful, and as, indeed, I have not even considered the reasons by which the existence of a Deity of any kind is established, the ground of doubt that rests only on this supposition is very slight, and, so to speak, metaphysical. But, that I may be able wholly to remove it, I must inquire whether there is a God, as soon as an opportunity of doing so shall present itself; and if I find that there is a God, I must examine likewise whether he can be a deceiver; for, without the knowledge of these two truths, I do not see that I can ever be certain of anything. And that I may be enabled to examine this without interrupting the order of meditation I have proposed to myself [which is, to pass by degrees from the notions that I shall find first in my mind to those I shall afterwards discover in it], it is necessary at this stage to divide all my thoughts into certain classes, and to consider in which of these classes truth and error are, strictly speaking, to be found.

Of my thoughts some are, as it were, images of things, and to these alone properly belongs the name *idea;* as when I think [represent to my mind] a man, a chimera, the sky, an angel, or God. Others, again, have certain other forms; as when I will, fear, affirm, or deny, I always, indeed, apprehend something as the object of my thought, but I also embrace in thought something more than the representation of the object; and of this class of thoughts some are called volitions or affections, and others judgments.

Now, with respect to ideas, if these are considered only in themselves, and are not referred to any object beyond them, they cannot, properly speaking, be false; for whether I imagine a goat or a chimera, it is not less true that I imagine the one than the other. Nor need we fear that falsity may exist in the will or affections; for, although I may desire objects that are wrong, and even that never existed, it is still true that I desire them. There thus only remain our judgments, in which we must take diligent heed that we be not deceived. But the chief and most ordinary error that arises in them consists in judging that the ideas which are in us are like or conformed to the things that are external to us; for assuredly, if we but considered the ideas themselves as certain modes of our thought (consciousness), without referring them to anything beyond, they would hardly afford any occasion of error.

But, among these ideas, some appear to me to be innate, others adventitious, and others to be made by myself (factitious); for, as I have the power of conceiving what is called a thing, or a truth, or a thought, it seems to me that I hold this power from no other source than my own nature; but if I now hear a noise, if I see the sun, or if I feel heat, I have all along judged that these sensations proceeded from certain objects existing out of myself; and, in fine, it appears to me that sirens, hippogryphs, and the like, are inventions of my own mind. But I may even perhaps come to be of opinion that all my ideas are of the class which I call adventitious, or that they are all innate, or that they are all factitious, for I have not yet clearly discovered their true origin; and what I have here principally to do is to consider, with reference to those that appear to come from certain objects without me, what grounds there are for thinking them like these objects.

The first of these grounds is that it seems to me I am so taught by nature; and the second that I am conscious that those ideas are not dependent on my will, and therefore not on myself, for they are frequently presented to me against my will,—as at present, whether I will or not, I feel heat; and I am thus persuaded that this sensation or idea (*sensum vel ideam*) of heat is produced in me by something different from myself, viz., by the heat of the fire by which I sit. And it is very reasonable to suppose that this object impresses me with its own likeness rather than any other thing.

But I must consider whether these reasons are sufficiently strong and convincing. When I speak of being taught by nature in this matter, I understand by the word nature only a certain spontaneous impetus that impels me to believe in a resemblance between ideas and their objects, and not a natural light that affords a knowledge of its truth. But these two things are widely different; for what the natural light shows to be true can be in no degree doubtful, as, for example, that I am because I doubt, and other truths of the like kind: inasmuch as I possess no other faculty whereby to distinguish truth from error, which can teach me the falsity of what the natural light declares to be true, and which is equally trustworthy; but with respect to [seemingly] natural impulses, I have observed, when the question related to the choice of right or wrong in action, that they frequently led me to take the worse part; nor do I see that I have any better ground for following them in what relates to truth and error. Then, with respect to the other reason, which is that because these ideas do not depend on my will, they must arise from objects existing without me, I do not find it more convincing than the former; for, just as those natural impulses, of which I have lately spoken, are found in me, notwithstanding that they are not always in harmony with my will, so likewise it may be that I possess some power not sufficiently known to myself capable of producing ideas without the aid of external objects, and, indeed, it has always hitherto appeared to me that they are formed during sleep, by some power of this nature, without the aid of aught external. And, in fine, although I should grant that they proceeded from those objects, it is not a necessary consequence that they must be like them. On the contrary, I have observed, in a number of instances, that there was a great difference between the object and its idea. Thus, for example, I find in my mind two wholly diverse ideas of the sun; the one, by which it appears to me extremely small, draws its origin from the senses, and should be placed in the class of adventitious ideas; the other, by which it seems to be many times larger than the whole earth, is taken up on astronomical grounds, that is, elicited from certain notions born with me, or is framed by myself in some other manner. These two ideas cannot certainly both resemble the same sun; and reason teaches me that the one which seems to have immediately emanated from it is the most unlike. And these things sufficiently prove that hitherto it has not been from a certain and deliberate judgment, but only from a sort of blind impulse, that I believed in the existence of certain things different from myself, which, by the organs of sense, or by whatever other means it might be, conveyed their ideas or images into my mind [and impressed it with their likenesses].

But there is still another way of inquiring whether, of the objects whose ideas are in my mind, there are any that exist out of me. If ideas are taken in so far only as they are certain modes of consciousness, I do not remark any difference or inequality among them, and all seem, in the same manner, to proceed from myself; but, considering them as images, of which one represents one thing and another a different, it is evident that a great diversity obtains among them. For, without doubt, those that represent substances are something more, and contain in themselves, so to speak, more objective reality [that is, participate by representation in higher degrees of being or perfection] than those that represent only modes of accidents; and again, the idea by which I conceive a God [sovereign], eternal, infinite [immutable], all-knowing, all-powerful, and the creator of all things that are out of himself,—this, I say, has certainly in it more objective reality than those ideas by which finite substances are represented.

Now, it is manifest by the natural light that there must at least be as much reality in the efficient and total cause as in its effect; for whence can the effect draw its reality if not from its cause? and how could the cause communicate to it this reality unless it possessed it in itself? And hence it follows, not only that what is cannot be produced by what is not, but likewise that the more perfect,—in other words, that which contains in itself more reality,—cannot be the effect of the less perfect: and this is not only evidently true of those effects, whose reality is actual or formal, but likewise of ideas, whose reality is only considered as objective. Thus, for example, the stone that is not yet in existence, not only cannot now commence to be, unless it be produced by that which possesses in itself, formally or eminently, all that enters into its composition [in other words, by that which contains in itself the same properties that are in the stone, or others superior to them]; and heat can only be produced in a subject that was before devoid of it, by a cause that is of an order [degree or kind] at least as perfect as heat; and so of the others. But further, even the idea of the heat, or of the stone, cannot exist in me unless it be put there by a cause that contains, at least, as much reality as I conceive existent in the heat or in the stone: for, although that cause may not transmit into my idea anything of its actual or formal reality, we ought not on this account to imagine that it is less real; but we ought to consider that [as every idea is a work of the mind], its nature is such as of itself to demand no other formal reality than that which it borrows from our consciousness, of which it is but a mode [that is, a manner or way of thinking]. But in order that an idea may contain this objective reality rather than that, it must doubtless derive it from some cause in which is found at least as much formal reality as the idea contains an objective; for, if we suppose that there is found in an idea anything which was not in its cause, it must of course *derive this from nothing*. But, however imperfect may be the mode of existence by which a thing is objectively [or by representation] in the understanding by its idea, we certainly cannot, for all that, allege that this mode of existence is nothing, nor, consequently, that the idea owes its origin to nothing. Nor must it be imagined that, since the reality which is considered in these ideas is only objective, the same reality need not be formally (actually) in the causes of these ideas, but only objectively; for, just as the mode of existing objectively belongs to ideas by their peculiar nature, so likewise the mode of existing formally appertains to the causes of these ideas (at least to the first and principal), by their peculiar nature. And although an idea may give rise to another idea, this regress cannot, nevertheless, be infinite; we must in the end reach a first idea, the cause of which is, as it were, the archetype in which all the reality [or perfection] that is found objectively [or by representation] in these ideas is contained formally [and in act]. I am thus clearly taught by the natural light that ideas exist in me as pictures or images, which may in truth readily fall short of the perfection of the objects from which they are taken, but can never contain anything greater or more perfect.

And in proportion to the time and care with which I examine all those matters, the conviction of their truth brightens and becomes distinct. But, to sum up, what conclusion shall I draw from it all? It is this;—if the objective reality [or perfection] of any one of my ideas be such as clearly to convince me, that this same reality exists in me neither formally nor eminently, and if, as follows from this, I myself cannot be the cause of it, it is a necessary consequence that I am not alone in the world, but that there is besides myself some other being who exists as the cause of that idea; while, on the contrary, if no such idea be found in my mind, I shall have no sufficient ground of assurance of the existence of any other being besides myself, for, after a most careful search, I have, up to this moment, been unable to discover any other ground.

But, among these my ideas, besides that which represents myself, respecting which there can be here no difficulty, there is one that represents a God; others that represent corporeal and inanimate things; others angels; others animals; and, finally, there are some that represent men like myself. But with respect to the ideas that represent other men, or animals, or angels, I can easily suppose that they were formed by the mingling and composition of the other ideas which I have of myself, of corporeal things, and of God, although there were, apart from myself, neither men, animals, nor angels. And with regard to the ideas of corporeal objects, I never discovered in them anything so great or excellent which I myself did not appear capable of originating; for, by considering these ideas closely and scrutinising them individually, in the same way that I yesterday examined the idea of wax, I find that there is but little in them that is clearly and distinctly perceived. As belonging to the class of things that are clearly apprehended, I recognise the following, viz., magnitude or extension in length, breadth, and depth; figure, which results from the termination of extension; situation, which bodies of diverse figures preserve with reference to each other; and motion or the change of situation; to which may be added substance, duration, and number. But with regard to light, colours, sounds, odours, tastes, heat, cold and the other tactile qualities, they are thought with so much obscurity and confusion, that I cannot determine even whether they are true or false; in other words, whether or not the ideas I have of these qualities are in truth the ideas of real objects. For although I before remarked that it is only in judgments that formal falsity, or falsity properly so called, can be met with, there may nevertheless be found in ideas a certain material falsity, which arises when they represent what is nothing as if it were something. Thus, for example, the ideas I have of cold and heat are so far from being clear and distinct, that I am unable from them to discover whether cold is only the privation of heat, or heat the privation of cold; or whether they are or are not real qualities: and since, ideas being as it were images, there can be none that does not seem to us to represent some object, the idea which represents cold as something real and positive will not improperly be called false, if it be correct to say that cold is nothing but a privation of heat; and so in other cases. To ideas of this kind, indeed, it is not necessary that I should assign any author besides myself: for if they are false, that is, represent objects that are unreal, the natural light teaches me that they proceed from nothing; in other words, that they are in me only because something is wanting to the perfection of my nature; but if these ideas are true, yet because they exhibit to me so little reality that I cannot even distinguish the object represented from non-being, I do not see why I should not be the author of them.

With reference to those ideas of corporeal things that are clear and distinct, there are some which, as appears to me, might have been taken from the idea I have of myself, as those of substance, duration, number, and the like. For when I think that a stone is a substance, or a thing capable of existing of itself, and that I am likewise a substance, although I conceive that I am a thinking and non-extended thing, and that the stone, on the contrary, is extended and unconscious, there being thus the greatest diversity between the two concepts,—yet these two ideas seem to have this in common that they both represent substances. In the same way, when I think of myself as now existing, and recollect besides that I existed some time ago, and when I am conscious of various thoughts whose number I know, I then acquire the ideas of duration and number, which I can afterwards transfer to as many objects as I please. With respect to the other qualities that go to make up the ideas of corporeal objects, viz., extension, figure, situation, and motion, it is true that they are not formally in me, since I am merely a thinking being; but because they are only certain modes of substance, and because I myself am a substance, it seems possible that they may be contained in me eminently.

There only remains, therefore, the idea of God, in which I must consider whether there is anything that cannot be supposed to originate with myself. By the name God, I understand a substance infinite [eternal, immutable], independent, all-knowing, all-powerful, and by which I myself, and every other thing that exists, if any such there be, were created. But these properties are so great and excellent, that the more attentively I consider them the less I feel persuaded that the idea I have of them owes its origin to myself alone. And thus it is absolutely necessary to conclude, from all that I have before said, that God exists: for though the idea of substance be in my mind owing to this, that I myself am a substance, I should not, however, have the idea of an infinite substance, seeing I am a finite being, unless it were given me by some substance in reality infinite.

And I must not imagine that I do not apprehend the infinite by a true idea, but only by the negation of the finite, in the same way that I comprehend repose and darkness by the negation of motion and light: since, on the contrary, I clearly perceive that there is more reality in the infinite substance than in the finite, and therefore that in some way I possess the perception (notion) of the infinite before that of the finite, that is, the perception of God before that of myself, for how could I know that I doubt, desire, or that something is wanting to me, and that I am not wholly perfect, if I possessed no idea of a being more perfect than myself, by comparison of which I knew the deficiencies of my nature?

And it cannot be said that this idea of God is perhaps materially false, and consequently that it may have arisen from nothing [in other words, that it may exist in me from my imperfection], as I before said of the ideas of heat and cold, and the like: for, on the contrary, as this idea is very clear and distinct, and contains in itself more objective reality than any other, there can be no one of itself more true, or less open to the suspicion of falsity.

The idea, I say, of a being supremely perfect, and infinite, is in the highest degree true; for although, perhaps, we may imagine that such a being does not exist, we cannot, nevertheless, suppose that his idea represents nothing real, as I have already said of the idea of cold. It is likewise clear and distinct in the highest degree, since whatever the mind clearly and distinctly conceives as real or true, and as implying any perfection, is contained entire in this idea. And this is true, nevertheless, although I do not comprehend the infinite, and although there may be in God an infinity of things that I cannot comprehend, nor perhaps even compass by thought in any way; for it is of the nature of the infinite that it should not be comprehended by the finite; and it is enough that I rightly understand this, and judge that all which I clearly perceive, and in which I know there is some perfection, and perhaps also an infinity of properties of which I am ignorant, are formally or eminently in God, in order that the idea I have of him may become the most true, clear, and distinct of all the ideas in my mind.

But perhaps I am something more than I suppose myself to be, and it may be that all those perfections which I attribute to God, in some way exist potentially in me, although they do not yet show themselves, and are not reduced to act. Indeed, I am already conscious that my knowledge is being increased [and perfected] by degrees; and I see nothing to prevent it from thus gradually increasing to infinity, nor any reason why, after such increase and perfection, I should not be able thereby to acquire all the other perfections of the Divine nature; nor, in fine, why the power I possess of acquiring those perfections, if it really now exist in me, should not be sufficient to produce the ideas of them. Yet, on looking more closely into the matter, I discover that this cannot be; for, in the first place, although it were true that my knowledge daily acquired new degrees of perfection, and although there were potentially in my nature much that was not as yet actually in it, still all these excellences make not the slightest approach to the idea I have of the Deity, in whom there is no perfection merely potentially [but all actually] existent; for it is even an unmistakable token of imperfection in my knowledge, that it is augmented by degrees. Further, although my knowledge increase more and more, nevertheless I am not, therefore, induced to think that it will ever be actually infinite, since it can never reach that point beyond which it shall be incapable of further increase. But I conceive God as actually infinite, so that nothing can be added to his perfection. And, in fine, I readily perceive that the objective being of an idea cannot be produced by a being that is merely potentially existent, which, properly speaking, is nothing, but only by a being existing formally or actually.

And, truly, I see nothing in all that I have now said which it is not easy for any one, who shall carefully consider it, to discern by the natural light; but when I allow my attention in some degree to relax, the vision of my mind being obscured, and, as it were, blinded by the images of sensible objects, I do not readily remember the reason why the idea of a being more perfect than myself, must of necessity have proceeded from a being in reality more perfect. On this account I am here desirous to inquire further, whether I, who possess this idea of God, could exist supposing there were no God. And I ask, from whom could I, in that case, derive my existence? Perhaps from myself, or from my parents, or from some other causes less perfect than God; for anything more perfect, or even equal to God, cannot be thought or imagined. But if I [were independent of every other existence, and] were myself the author of my being, I should doubt of nothing, I should desire nothing, and, in fine, no perfection would be awanting to me; for I should have bestowed upon myself every perfection of which I possess the idea, and I should thus be God. And it must not be imagined that what is now wanting to me is perhaps of more difficult acquisition than that of which I am already possessed; for, on the contrary, it is quite manifest that it was a matter of much higher difficulty that I, a thinking being, should arise from nothing, than it would be for me to acquire the knowledge of many things of which I am ignorant, and which are merely the accidents of a thinking substance; and certainly, if I possessed of myself the greater perfection of which I have now spoken [in other words, if I were the author of my own existence], I would not at least have denied to myself things that may be more easily obtained [as that infinite variety of knowledge of which I am at present destitute]. I could not, indeed, have denied to myself any property which I perceive is contained in the idea of God, because there is none of these that seems to me to be more difficult to make or acquire; and if there were any that should happen to be more difficult to acquire, they would certainly appear so to me (supposing that I myself were the source of the other things I possess), because I should discover in them a limit to my power. And though I were to suppose that I always was as I now am, I should not, on this ground, escape the force of these reasonings, since it would not follow, even on this supposition, that no author of my existence needed to be sought after. For the whole time of my life may be divided into an infinity of parts, each of which is in no way dependent on any other; and, accordingly, because I was in existence a short time ago, it does not follow that I must now exist, unless in this moment some cause create me anew, as it were,—that is, conserve me. In truth, it is perfectly clear and evident to all who will attentively consider the nature of duration that the conservation of a substance, in each moment of its duration, requires the same power and act that would be necessary to create it, supposing it were not yet in existence; so that it is manifestly a dictate of the natural light that conservation and creation differ merely in respect of our mode of thinking [and not in reality]. All that is here required, therefore, is that I interrogate myself to discover whether I possess any power by means of which I can bring it about that I, who now am, shall exist a moment afterwards: for, since I am merely a thinking thing (or since, at least, the precise question, in the meantime, is only of that part of myself), if such a power resided in me, I should, without doubt, be conscious of it; but I am conscious of no such power, and thereby I manifestly know that I am dependent upon some being different from myself.

But perhaps the being upon whom I am dependent is not God, and I have been produced either by my parents, or by some causes less perfect than Deity. This cannot be: for, as I before said, it is perfectly evident that there must at least be as much reality in the cause as in its effect; and accordingly, since I am a thinking thing, and possess in myself an idea of God, whatever in the end be the cause of my existence, it must of necessity be admitted that it is likewise a thinking being, and that it possesses in itself the idea and all the perfections I attribute to Deity. Then it may again be inquired whether this cause owes its origin and existence to itself, or to some other cause. For if it be self-existent, it follows, from what I have before laid down, that this cause is God; for, since it possesses the perfection of self-existence, it must likewise, without doubt, have the power of actually possessing every perfection of which it has the idea,—in other words, all the perfections I conceive to belong to God. But if it owe its existence to another cause than itself, we demand again, for a similar reason, whether this second cause exists of itself or through some other, until, from stage to stage, we at length arrive at an ultimate cause, which will be God. And it is quite manifest that in this matter there can be no infinite regress of causes, seeing that the question raised respects not so much the cause which once produced me, as that by which I am at this present moment conserved.

Nor can it be supposed that several causes concerned in my production, and that from one I received the idea of one of the perfections I attribute to Deity, and from another the idea of some other, and thus that all those perfections are indeed found somewhere in the universe, but do not all exist together in a single being who is God; for, on the contrary, the unity, the simplicity or inseparability of all the properties of Deity, is one of the chief perfections I conceive him to possess; and the idea of this unity of all the perfections of Deity could certainly not be put into my mind by any cause from which I did not likewise receive the ideas of all the other perfections; for no power could enable me to embrace them in an inseparable unity, without at the same time giving me the knowledge of what they were [and of their existence in a particular mode].

Finally, with regard to my parents [from whom it appears I sprung], although all that I believed respecting them be true, it does not, nevertheless, follow that I am conserved by them, or even that I was produced by them, in so far as I am a thinking being. All that, at the most, they contributed to my origin was the giving of certain dispositions (modifications) to the matter in which I have hitherto judged that I or my mind, which is what alone I now consider to be myself, is enclosed; and thus there can here be no difficulty with respect to them, and it is absolutely necessary to conclude from this alone that I am, and possess the idea of a being absolutely perfect, that is, of God, that his existence is most clearly demonstrated.

There remains only the inquiry as to the way in which I received this idea from God; for I have not drawn it from the senses, nor is it even presented to me unexpectedly, as is usual with the ideas of sensible objects, when these are presented or appear to be presented to the external organs of the senses; it is not even a pure production or fiction of my mind, for it is not in my power to take from or add to it; and consequently there but remains the alternative that it is innate, in the same way as is the idea of myself. And, in truth, it is not to be wondered at that God, at my creation, implanted this idea in me, that it might serve, as it were, for the mark of the workman impressed on his work; and it is not also necessary that the mark should be something different from the work itself; but considering only that God is my creator, it is highly probable that he in some way fashioned me after his own image and likeness, and that I perceive this likeness, in which is contained the idea of God, by the same faculty by which I apprehend myself,—in other words, when I make myself the object of reflection, I not only find that I am an incomplete [imperfect] and dependent being, and one who unceasingly aspires after something better and greater than he is; but, at the same time, I am assured likewise that he upon whom I am dependent possesses in himself all the goods after which I aspire [and the ideas of which I find in my mind], and that not merely indefinitely and potentially, but infinitely and actually, and that he is thus God. And the whole force of the argument of which I have here availed myself to establish the existence of God, consists in this, that I perceive I could not possibly be of such a nature as I am, and yet have in my mind the idea of a God, if God did not in reality exist,—this same God, I say, whose idea is in my mind—that is, a being who possesses all those lofty perfections, of which the mind may have some slight conception, without, however, being able fully to comprehend them,—and who is wholly superior to all defect [and has nothing that marks imperfection]: whence it is sufficiently manifest that he cannot be a deceiver, since it is a dictate of the natural light that all fraud and deception spring from some defect.

But before I examine this with more attention, and pass on to the consideration of other truths that may be evolved out of it, I think it proper to remain here for some time in the contemplation of God himself—that I may ponder at leisure his marvellous attributes—and behold, admire, and adore the beauty of this light so unspeakably great, as far, at least, as the strength of my mind, which is to some degree dazzled by the sight, will permit. For just as we learn by faith that the supreme felicity of another life consists in the contemplation of the Divine majesty alone, so even now we learn from experience that a like meditation, though incomparably less perfect, is the source of the highest satisfaction of which we are susceptible in this life.

Meditation IV

OF TRUTH AND ERROR

I have been habituated these bygone days to detach my mind from the senses, and I have accurately observed that there is exceedingly little which is known with certainty respecting corporeal objects,—that we know much more of the human mind, and still more of God himself. I am thus able now without difficulty to abstract my mind from the contemplation of [sensible or] imaginable objects, and apply it to those which, as disengaged from all matter, are purely intelligible. And certainly the idea I have of the human mind in so far as it is a thinking thing, and not extended in length, breadth, and depth, and participating in none of the properties of body, is incomparably more distinct than the idea of any corporeal object; and when I consider that I doubt, in other words, that I am an incomplete and dependent being, the idea of a complete and independent being, that is to say of God, occurs to my mind with so much clearness and distinctness,—and from the fact alone that this idea is found in me, or that I who possess it exist, the conclusions that God exists, and that my own existence, each moment of its continuance, is absolutely dependent upon him, are so manifest,—as to lead me to believe it impossible that the human mind can know anything with more clearness and certitude. And now I seem to discover a path that will conduct us from the contemplation of the true God, in whom are contained all the treasures of science and wisdom, to the knowledge of the other things in the universe.

For, in the first place, I discover that it is impossible for him ever to deceive me, for in all fraud and deceit there is a certain imperfection: and although it may seem that the ability to deceive is a mark of subtlety or power, yet the will testifies without doubt of malice and weakness; and such, accordingly, can be found in God. In the next place, I am conscious that I possess a certain faculty of judging [or discerning truth from error], which I doubtless received from God, along with whatever else is mine; and since it is impossible that he should will to deceive me, it is likewise certain that he has not given me a faculty that will ever lead me into error, provided I use it aright.

And there would remain no doubt on this head, did it not seem to follow from this, that I can never therefore be deceived; for if all I possess be from God, and if he planted in me no faculty that is deceitful, it seems to follow that I can never fall into error. Accordingly, it is true that when I think only of God (when I look upon myself as coming from God, Fr.), and turn wholly to him, I discover [in myself] no cause of error or falsity: but immediately thereafter, recurring to myself, experience assures me that I am nevertheless subject to innumerable errors. When I come to inquire into the cause of these, I observe that there is not only present to my consciousness a real and positive idea of God, or of a being supremely perfect, but also, so to speak, a certain negative idea of nothing,—in other words, of that which is at an infinite distance from every sort of perfection, and that I am, as it were, a mean between God and nothing, or placed in such a way between absolute existence and non-existence, that there is in truth nothing in me to lead me into error, in so far as an absolute being is my creator; but that, on the other hand, as I thus likewise participate in some degree of nothing or of non-being, in other words, as I am not myself the supreme Being, and as I am wanting in many perfections, it is not surprising I should fall into error. And I hence discern that error, as far as error is not something real, which depends for its existence on God, but is simply defect; and therefore that, in order to fall into it, it is not necessary God should have given me a faculty expressly for this end, but that my being deceived arises from the circumstance that the power which God has given me of dicserning truth from error is not infinite.

Nevertheless this is not yet quite satisfactory; for error is not a pure negation [in other words, it is not the simple deficiency or want of some knowledge which is not due], but the privation or want of some knowledge which it would seem I ought to possess. But, on considering the nature of God, it seems impossible that he should have planted in his creature any faculty not perfect in its kind, that is, wanting in some perfection due to it: for if it be true, that in proportion to the skill of the maker the perfection of his work is greater, what thing can have been produced by the supreme Creator of the universe that is not absolutely perfect in all its parts? And assuredly there is no doubt that God could have created me such as that I should never be deceived; it is certain, likewise, that he always wills what is best: is it better, then, that I should be capable of being deceived than that I should not?

Considering this more attentively, the first thing that occurs to me is the reflection that I must not be surprised if I am not always capable of comprehending the reasons why God acts as he does; nor must I doubt of his existence because I find, perhaps, that there are several other things, besides the present respecting which I understand neither why nor how they were created by him; for, knowing already that my nature is extremely weak and limited, and that the nature of God, on the other hand, is immense, incomprehensible, and infinite, I have no longer any difficulty in discerning that there is an infinity of things in his power whose causes transcend the grasp of my mind: and this consideration alone is sufficient to convince me, that the whole class of final causes is of no avail in physical [or natural] things; for it appears to me that I cannot, without exposing myself to the charge of temerity, seek to discover the [impenetrable] ends of Deity.

It further occurs to be that we must not consider only one creature apart from the others, if we wish to determine the perfection of the works of Deity, but generally all his creatures together; for the same object that might perhaps, with some show of reason, be deemed highly imperfect if it were alone in the world, may for all that be the most perfect possible, considered as forming part of the whole universe: and although, as it was my purpose to doubt of everything, I only as yet know with certainty my own existence and that of God, nevertheless, after having remarked the infinite power of Deity, I cannot deny that he may have produced many other objects, or at least that he is able to produce them, so that I may occupy a place in the relation of a part to the great whole of his creatures.

Whereupon, regarding myself more closely, and considering what my errors are (which alone testify to the existence of imperfection in me), I observe that these depend on the concurrence of two causes, viz., the faculty of cognition which I possess, and that of election or the power of free choice,—in other words, the understanding and the will. For by the understanding alone, I [neither affirm nor deny anything, but] merely apprehend (*percipio*) the ideas regarding which I may form a judgment; nor is any error, properly so called, found in it thus accurately taken. And although there are perhaps innumerable objects in the world of which I have no idea in my understanding, it cannot, on that account, be said that I am deprived of those ideas [as of something that is due to my nature], but simply that I do not possess them, because, in truth, there is no ground to prove that Deity ought to have endowed me with a larger faculty of cognition than he has actually bestowed upon me; and however skillful a workman I suppose him to be, I have no reason, on that account, to think that it was obligatory on him to give to each of his works all the perfections he is able to bestow upon some. Nor, moreover, can I complain that God has not given me freedom of choice, or a will sufficiently ample and perfect, since, in truth, I am conscious of will so ample and extended as to be superior to all limits. And what appears to me here to be highly remarkable is that, of all the other properties I possess, there is none so great and perfect as that I do not clearly discern it could be still greater and more perfect. For, to take an example, if I consider the faculty of understanding which I possess, I find that it is of very small extent, and greatly limited, and at the same time I form the idea of another faculty of the same nature, much more ample and even infinite; and seeing that I can frame the idea of it, I discover, from this circumstance alone, that it pertains to the nature of God. In the same way, if I examine the faculty of memory or imagination, or any other faculty I possess, I find none that is not small and circumscribed, and in God immense [and infinite]. It is the faculty of will only, or freedom of choice, which I experience to be so great that I am unable to conceive the idea of another that shall be more ample and extended; so that it is chiefly my will which leads me to discern that I bear a certain image and similitude of Deity. For although the faculty of will is incomparably greater in God than in myself, as well in respect of the knowledge and power that are conjoined with it, and that render it stronger and more efficacious, as in respect of the object, since in him it extends to a greater number of things, it does not, nevertheless, appear to me greater, considered in itself formally and precisely: for the power of will consists only in this, that we are able to do or not to do the same thing (that is, to affirm or deny, to pursue or shun it), or rather in this alone, that in affirming or denying, pursuing or shunning, what is proposed to us by the understanding, we so act that we are not conscious of being determined to a particular action by any external force. For, to the possession of freedom, it is not necessary that I be alike indifferent towards each of two contraries; but on the contrary, the more I am inclined towards the one, whether because I clearly know that in it there is the reason of truth and goodness, or because God thus internally disposes my thought, the more freely do I choose and embrace it; and assuredly divine grace and natural knowledge, very far from diminishing liberty, rather augment and fortify it. But the indifference of which I am conscious when I am not impelled to one side rather than to another for want of a reason, is the lowest grade of liberty, and manifests defect or negation of knowledge rather than perfection, of will; for if I always clearly knew what was true and good, I should never have any difficulty in determining what judgment I ought to come to, and what choice I ought to make, and I should thus be entirely free without ever being indifferent.

From all this I discover, however, that neither the power of willing, which I have received from God, is of itself the source of my errors, for it is exceedingly ample and perfect in its kind; nor even the power of understanding, for as I conceive no object unless by means of the faculty that God bestowed upon me, all that I conceive is doubtless rightly conceived by me, and it is impossible for me to be deceived in it.

Whence, then, spring my errors? They arise from this cause alone, that I do not restrain the will, which is of much wider range than the understanding, within the same limits, but extend it even to things I do not understand, and as the will is of itself indifferent to such, it readily falls into error and sin by choosing the false in room of the true, and evil instead of good.

For example, when I lately considered whether aught really existed in the world, and found that because I considered this question, it very manifestly followed that I myself existed, I could not but judge that what I so clearly conceived was true, not that I was forced to this judgment by any external cause, but simply because great clearness of the understanding was succeeded by strong inclination in the will; and I believed this the more freely and spontaneously in proportion as I was less indifferent with respect to it. But now I not only know that I exist, in so far as I am thinking being, but there is likewise presented to my mind a certain idea of corporeal nature; hence I am in doubt as to whether the thinking nature which is in me, or rather which I myself am, is different from that corporeal nature, or whether both are merely one and the same thing, and I here suppose that I am as yet ignorant of any reason that would determine me to adopt the one belief in preference to the other: whence it happens that it is a matter of perfect indifference to me which of the two suppositions I affirm or deny, or whether I form any judgment at all in the matter.

This indifference, moreover, extends not only to things of which the understanding has no knowledge at all, but in general also to all those which it does not discover with perfect clearness at the moment the will is deliberating upon them; for, however probable the conjectures may be that dispose me to form a judgment in a particular matter, the simple knowledge that these are merely conjectures, and not certain and indubitable reasons, is sufficient to lead me to form one that is directly the opposite. Of this I lately had abundant experience, when I laid aside as false all that I had before held for true, on the single ground that I could in some degree doubt of it. But if I abstain from judging of a thing when I do not conceive it with sufficient clearness and distinctness, it is plain that I act rightly, and am not deceived; but if I resolve to deny or affirm, I then do not make a right use of my free will; and if I affirm what is false, it is evident that I am deceived: moreover, even although I judge according to truth, I stumble upon it by chance, and do not therefore escape the imputation of a wrong use of my freedom; for it is a dictate of the natural light, that the knowledge of the understanding ought always to precede the determination of the will.

And it is this wrong use of freedom of the will in which is found the privation that constitutes the form of error. Privation, I say, is found in the act, in so far as it proceeds from myself, but it does not exist in the faculty which I received from God, nor even in the act, in so far as it depends on him; for I have assuredly no reason to complain that God has not given me a greater power of intelligence or more perfect natural light than he has actually bestowed, since it is of the nature of a finite understanding not to comprehend many things, and of the nature of a created understanding to be finite; on the contrary, I have every reason to render thanks to God, who owed me nothing, for having given me all the perfections I possess, and I should be far from thinking that he has unjustly deprived me of, or kept back, the other perfections which he has not bestowed upon me.

I have no reason, moreover, to complain because he has given me a will more ample than my understanding, since, as the will consists only of a single element, and that indivisible, it would appear that this faculty is of such a nature that nothing could be taken from it [without destroying it]; and certainly, the more extensive it is, the more cause I have to thank the goodness of him who bestowed it upon me.

And, finally, I ought not also to complain that God concurs with me in forming the acts of this will, or the judgments in which I am deceived, because those acts are wholly true and good, in so far as they depend on God; and the ability to form them is a higher degree of perfection in my nature than the want of it would be. With regard to privation, in which alone consists the formal reason of error and sin, this does not require the concurrence of Deity, because it is not a thing [or existence]; and if it be referred to God as to its cause, it ought not to be called privation, but negation [according to the signification of these words in the schools]. For in truth it is no imperfection in Deity that he has accorded to me the power of giving or withholding my assent from certain things of which he has not put a clear and distinct knowledge in my understanding; but it is doubtless an imperfection in me that I do not use my freedom aright, and readily give my judgment on matters which I only obscurely and confusedly conceive.

I perceive, nevertheless, that it was easy for Deity so to have constituted me as that I should never be deceived, although I still remained free and possessed of a limited knowledge, viz., by implanting in my understanding a clear and distinct knowledge of all the objects respecting which I should ever have to deliberate; or simply by so deeply engraving on my memory the resolution to judge of nothing without previously possessing a clear and distinct conception of it, that I should never forget it. And I easily understand that, in so far as I consider myself as a single whole, without reference to any other being in the universe, I should have been much more perfect than I now am, had Deity created me superior to error; but I cannot therefore deny that it is not somehow a greater perfection in the universe, that certain of its parts are not exempt from defect, as others are, than if they were all perfectly alike.

And I have no right to complain because God, who placed me in the world, was not willing that I should sustain that character which of all others is the chief and most perfect; I have even good reason to remain satisfied on the ground that, if he has not given me the perfection of being superior to error by the first means I have pointed out above, which depends on a clear and evident knowledge of all the matters regarding which I can deliberate, he has at least left in my power the other means, which is, firmly to retain the resolution never to judge where the truth is not clearly known to me: for, although I am conscious of the weakness of not being able to keep my mind continually fixed on the same thought, I can nevertheless, by attentive and oft-repeated meditation, impress it so strongly on my memory that I shall never fail to recollect it as often as I require it, and I can acquire in this way the habitude of not erring; and since it is in being superior to error that the highest and chief perfection of man consists, I deem that I have not gained little by this day's meditation, in having discovered the source of error and falsity.

And certainly this can be no other than what I have now explained: for as often as I so restrain my will within the limits of my knowledge, that it forms no judgment except regarding objects which are clearly and distinctly represented to it by the understanding, I can never be deceived; because every clear and distinct conception is doubtless something, and as such cannot owe its origin to nothing, but must of necessity have God for its author—God, I say, who, as supremely perfect, cannot, without a contradiction, be the cause of any error; and consequently it is

necessary to conclude that every such conception [or judgment] is true.
Nor have I merely learned to-day what I must avoid to escape error
but also what I must do to arrive at the knowledge of truth; for I will
assuredly reach truth if I only fix my attention sufficiently on all the
thing I conceive perfectly, and separate these from others which I conceive more confusedly and obscurely: to which for the future I shall give
diligent heed.

Meditation V

OF THE ESSENCE OF MATERIAL THINGS; AND, AGAIN, OF GOD;
THAT HE EXISTS

Several other questions remain for consideration respecting the attributes of God and my own nature or mind. I will, however, on some
other occasion perhaps resume the investigation of these. Meanwhile,
as I have discovered what must be done, and what avoided to arrive
at the knowledge of truth, what I have chiefly to do is to essay to emerge
from the state of doubt in which I have for some time been, and to discover whether anything can be known with certainty regarding material
objects. But before considering whether such objects as I conceive exist
without me, I must examine their ideas in so far as these are to be
found in my consciousness, and discover which of them are distinct
and which confused.

In the first place, I distinctly imagine that quantity which the philosophers commonly call continuous, or the extension in length, breadth,
and depth that is in this quantity, or rather in the object to which it is
attributed. Further, I can enumerate in it many diverse parts, and attribute to each of these all sorts of sizes, figures, situations, and local
motions; and, in fine, I can assign to each of these motions all degrees
of duration. And I not only distinctly know these things when I thus consider them in general; but besides, by a little attention, I discover innumerable particulars respecting figures, numbers, motion, and the like,
which are so evidently true, and so accordant with my nature, that when
I now discover them I do not so much appear to learn anything new,
as to call to remembrance what I before knew, or for the first time to
remark what was before in my mind, but to which I had not hitherto directed my attention. And what I here find of most importance is, that
I discover in my mind innumerable ideas of certain objects, which cannot
be esteemed pure negations, although perhaps they possess no reality
beyond my thought, and which are not framed by me though it may be
in my power to think, or not to think them, but possess true and immutable natures of their own. As, for example, when I imagine a triangle, although there is not perhaps and never was in any place in the
universe apart from my thought one such figure, it remains true never-

theless that this figure possesses a certain determinate nature, form, or essence, which is immutable and eternal, and not framed by me, nor in any degree dependent on my thought; as appears from the circumstance, that diverse properties of the triangle may be demonstrated, viz., that its three angles are equal to two right, that its greatest side is subtended by its greatest angle, and the like, which, whether I will or not, I now clearly discern to belong to it, although before I did not at all think of them, when, for the first time, I imagined a triangle, and which accordingly cannot be said to have been invented by me. Nor is it a valid objection to allege, that perhaps this idea of a triangle came into my mind by the medium of the senses, through my having seen bodies of a triangular figure; for I am able to form in thought an innumerable variety of figures with regard to which it cannot be supposed that they were ever objects of sense, and I can nevertheless demonstrate diverse properties of their nature no less than of the triangle, all of which are assuredly true since I clearly conceive them; and they are therefore something, and not mere negations; for it is highly evident that all that is true is something [truth being identical with existence]; and I have already fully shown the truth of the principle, that whatever is clearly and distinctly known is true. And although this had not been demonstrated, yet the nature of my mind is such as to compel me to assent to what I clearly conceive while I so conceive it; and I recollect that even when I still strongly adhered to the objects of sense, I reckoned among the number of the most certain truths those I clearly conceived relating to figures, numbers, and other matters and pertain to arithmetic and geometry, and in general to the pure mathematics.

But now if because I can draw from my thought the idea of an object, it follows that all I clearly and distinctly apprehend to pertain to this object, does in truth belong to it, may I not from this derive an argument for the existence of God? It is certain that I no less find the idea of a God in my consciousness, that is, the idea of a being supremely perfect, than that of any figure or number whatever: and I know with not less clearness and distinctness that an [actual and] eternal existence pertains to his nature than that all which is demonstrable of any figure or number really belongs to the nature of that figure or number; and, therefore, although all the conclusions of the preceding Meditations were false, the existence of God would pass with me for a truth at least as certain as I ever judged any truth of mathematics to be, although indeed such a doctrine may at first sight appear to contain more sophistry than truth. For, as I have been accustomed in every other matter to distinguish between existence and essence, I easily believe that the existence can be separated from the essence of God, and that thus God may be conceived as not actually existing. But, nevertheless, when I think of it more attentively, it appears that the existence can no more be separated from the essence of God than the idea of a mountain from that of a valley, or the equality of its three angles to two right angles, from the essence of a [rectilineal] triangle; so that it is not less impossible to conceive a God, that is, a being supremely perfect, to whom existence is awanting, or who is devoid of a certain perfection, than to conceive a mountain without a valley.

But though, in truth, I cannot conceive a God unless as existing, any more than I can a mountain without a valley, yet, just as it does not folow that there is any mountain in the world merely because I conceive a mountain with a valley, so likewise, though I conceive God as existing, it does not seem to follow on that account that God exists; for my thought imposes no necessity on things; and as I may imagine a winged horse, though there be none such, so I could perhaps attribute existence to God, though no God existed. But the cases are not analogous, and a fallacy lurks under the semblance of this objection: for because I cannot conceive a mountain without a valley, it does not follow that there is any mountain or valley in existence, but simply that the mountain or valley, whether they do or do not exist, are inseparable from each other; whereas, on the other hand, because I cannot conceive God unless as existing, it follows that existence is inseparable from him, and therefore that he really exists: not that this is brought about by my thought, or that it imposes any necessity on things, but, on the contrary, the necessity which lies in the thing itself, that is, the necessity of the existence of God, determines me to think in this way, for it is not in my power to conceive a God without existence, that is a being supremely perfect, and yet devoid of an absolute perfection, as I am free to imagine a horse with or without wings.

Nor must it be alleged here as an objection, that it is in truth necessary to admit that God exists, after having supposed him to possess all perfections, since existence is one of them, but that my original supposition was not necessary; just as it is not necessary to think that all quadilateral figures can be inscribed in the circle, since, if I supposed this, I should be constrained to admit that the rhombus, being a figure of four sides, can be therein inscribed, which, however, is manifestly false. This objection is, I say, incompetent; for although it may not be necessary that I shall at any time entertain the notion of Deity, yet each time I happen to think of a first and sovereign being, and to draw, so to speak, the idea of him from the store-house of the mind, I am necessitated to attribute to him all kinds of perfections, though I may not then enumerate them all, nor think of each of them in particular. And this necessity is sufficient, as soon as I discover that existence is a perfection, to cause me to infer the existence of this first and sovereign being; just as it is not necessary that I should ever imagine any triangle, but whenever I am desirous of considering a rectilineal figure composed of only three angles, it is absolutely necessary to attribute those properties to it from which it is correctly inferred that its three angles are not greater than two right angles, although perhaps I may not then advert to this relation in particular. But when I consider what figures are capable of being inscribed in the circle, it is by no means necessary to hold that all quadrilateral figures are of this number; on the contrary, I cannot even imagine such to be the case, so long as I shall be unwilling to accept in thought aught that I do not clearly and distinctly conceive: and consequently there is a vast difference between false suppositions, as is the one in question, and the true ideas that were born with me, the first and chief of which is the idea of God. For indeed I discern on many grounds that this idea is not factitious, depending simply on my thought, but that it is the representation of a true and immutable nature: in the first place, because I can conceive no other being, except God, to whose essence existence [necessarily] pertains; in the second, because it is impossible to conceive two or more gods of this kind; and it being supposed that one such God exists, I clearly see that he must have existed from all eternity, and will exist to all eternity; and finally, because I apprehend many other properties in God, none of which I can either diminish or change.

But, indeed, whatever mode of probation I in the end adopt, it always returns to this, that it is only the things I clearly and distinctly conceive which have the power of completely persuading me. And although, of the objects I conceive in this manner, some, indeed, are obvious to every one, while others are only discovered after close and careful investigation; nevertheless, after they are once discovered, the latter are not esteemed less certain than the former. Thus, for example, to take the case of a right-angled triangle, although it is not so manifest at first that the square of the base is equal to the squares of the other two sides, as that the base is opposite to the greatest angle; nevertheless, after it is once apprehended, we are as firmly persuaded of the truth of the former as of the latter. And, with respect to God, if I were not preoccupied by prejudices, and my thoughts beset on all sides by the continual presence of the images of sensible objects, I should know nothing sooner or more easily than the fact of his being. For is there any truth more clear than the existence of a Supreme Being, or of God, seeing it is to his essence alone that [necessary and eternal] existence pertains? And although the right conception of this truth has cost me much close thinking, nevertheless at present I feel not only as assured of it as of what I deem most certain, but I remark further that the certitude of all other truths is so absolutely dependent on it, that without this knowledge it is impossible ever to know anything perfectly.

For although I am of such a nature as to be unable, while I possess a very clear and distinct apprehension of a matter, to resist the conviction of its truth, yet because my constitution is also such as to incapacitate me from keeping my mind continually fixed on the same object, and as I frequently recollect a past judgment without at the same time being able to recall the grounds of it, it may happen meanwhile that other reasons are presented to me which would readily cause me to change my opinion, if I did not know that God existed; and thus I should possess no true and certain knowledge, but merely vague and vacillating opinions. Thus, for example, when I consider the nature of the [rectilineal] triangle, it most clearly appears to me, who have been instructed in the principles of geometry, that its three angles are equal to two right angles, and I find it impossible to believe otherwise, while I apply my mind to the demonstration; but as soon as I cease from attending to the process of proof, although I still remember that I had a clear comprehension of it, yet I may readily come to doubt of the truth demonstrated, if I do not know that there is a God: for I may persuade myself that I have been so constituted by nature as to be sometimes deceived, even in matters which I think I apprehend with the greatest evidence and certitude, especially when I recollect that I frequently considered many things to be true and certain which other reasons afterwards constrained me to reckon as wholly false.

But after I have discovered that God exists, seeing I also at the same time observed that all things depend on him, and that he is no deceiver, and thence inferred that all which I clearly and distinctly perceive is of necessity true: although I no longer attend to the grounds of a judgment, no opposite reason can be alleged sufficient to lead me to doubt of its truth, provided only I remember that I once possessed a clear and distinct comprehension of it. My knowledge of it thus becomes true and certain. And this same knowledge extends likewise to whatever I remember to have formerly demonstrated, as the truths of geometry and the like: for what can be alleged against them to lead me to doubt of them? Will it be that my nature is such that I may be frequently deceived? But I already know that I cannot be deceived in judgments of the grounds of which I possess a clear knowledge. Will it be that I formerly deemed things to be true and certain which I afterwards discovered to be false? But I had no clear and distinct knowledge of any of those things, and, being as yet ignorant of the rule by which I am assured of the truth of a judgment, I was led to give my assent to them on grounds which I afterwards discovered were less strong than at the time I imagined them to be. What further objection, then, is there? Will it be said that perhaps I am dreaming (an objection I lately myself raised), or that all the thoughts of which I am now conscious have no more truth than the reveries of my dreams? But although, in truth, I should be dreaming, the rule still holds that all which is clearly presented to my intellect is indisputably true.

And thus I very clearly see that the certitude and truth of all science depends on the knowledge alone of the true God, insomuch that, before I knew him, I could have no perfect knowledge of any other thing. And now that I know him, I possess the means of acquiring a perfect knowledge respecting innumerable matters, as well relative to God himself and other intellectual objects as to corporeal nature, in so far as it is the object of pure mathematics [which do not consider whether it exists or not].

Meditation VI

OF THE EXISTENCE OF MATERIAL THINGS, AND OF THE REAL DISTINCTION BETWEEN THE MIND AND BODY OF MAN

There now only remains the inquiry as to whether material things exist. With regard to this question, I at least know with certainty that such things may exist, in as far as they constitute the object of the pure mathematics, since, regarding them in this aspect, I can conceive them clearly and distinctly. For there can be no doubt that God possesses the power of producing all the objects I am able distinctly to conceive, and I never considered anything impossible to him, unless when I experienced a contradiction in the attempt to conceive it aright. Further, the faculty of imagination which I possess, and of which I am conscious that I make use when I apply myself to the consideration of material things, is sufficient to persuade me of their existence: for, when I attentively consider what imagination is, I find that is simply a certain application of the cognitive faculty (*facultas cognoscitiva*) to a body which is immediately present to it, and which therefore exists.

And to render this quite clear, I remark, in the first place, the difference that subsists between imagination and pure intellection [or conception]. For example, when I imagine a triangle I not only conceive (*intelligo*) that it is a figure comprehended by three lines, but at the same time also I look upon (*intueor*) these three lines as present by the power and internal application of my mind (*acie mentis*), and this is what I call imagining. But if I desire to think of a chiliogon, I indeed rightly conceive that it is a figure composed of a thousand sides, as easily as I conceive that a triangle is a figure composed of only three sides; but I cannot imagine the thousand sides of a chiliogon as I do the three sides of a triangle, nor, so to speak, view them as present [with the eyes of my mind]. And although, in accordance with the habit I have of always imagining something when I think of corporeal things, it may happen that, in conceiving a chiliogon, I confusedly represent some figure to myself, yet it is quite evident that this is not a chiliogon, since it in no wise differs from that which I would represent to myself, if I were to think of a myriogon, or any other figure of many sides; nor would this representation be of any use in discovering and unfolding the properties that constitute the difference between a chiliogon and other polygons. But if the question turns on a pentagon, it is quite true that I can conceive its figure, as well as that of a chiliogon, without the aid of imagination; but I can likewise imagine it by applying the attention of my mind to its five sides, and at the same time to the area which they contain. Thus I observe that a special effort of mind is necessary to the act of imagination, which is not required to conceiving or understanding (*ad intelligen-*

dum); and this special exertion of mind clearly shows the difference between imagination and pure intellection (*imaginatio et intellectio pura*). I remark, besides, that this power of imagination which I possess, in as far as it differs from the power of conceiving, is in no way necessary to my [nature or] essence, that is, to the essence of my mind; for although I did not possess it, I should still remain the same that I now am, from which it seems we may conclude that it depends on something different from the mind. And I easily understand that, if some body exists, with which my mind is so conjoined and united as to be able, as it were, to consider it when it chooses, it may thus imagine corporeal objects; so that this mode of thinking differs from pure intellection only in this respect, that the mind in conceiving turns in some way upon itself, and considers some one of the ideas it possesses within itself; but in imagining it turns towards the body, and contemplates in it some object conformed to the idea which it either of itself conceived or apprehended by sense. I easily understand, I say, that imagination may be thus formed, if it is true that there are bodies; and because I find no other obvious mode of explaining it, I thence, with probability, conjecture that they exist, but only with probability; and although I carefully examine all things, nevertheless I do not find that, from the distinct idea of corporeal nature I have in my imagination, I can necessarily infer the existence of any body.

But I am accustomed to imagine many other objects besides that corporeal nature which is the object of the pure mathematics, as, for example, colours, sounds, tastes, pain, and the like, although with less distinctness; and, inasmuch as I perceive these objects much better by the senses, through the medium of which and of memory, they seem to have reached the imagination, I believe that, in order the more advantageously to examine them, it is proper I should at the same time examine what sense-perception is, and inquire whether from those ideas that are apprehended by this mode of thinking (consciousness), I cannot obtain a certain proof of the existence of corporeal objects.

And, in the first place, I will recall to my mind the things I have hitherto held as true, because perceived by the senses, and the foundations upon which my belief in their truth rested; I will, in the second place, examine the reasons that afterwards constrained me to doubt of them; and, finally, I will consider what of them I ought now to believe.

Firstly, then, I perceived that I had a head, hands, feet, and other members composing that body which I considered as part, or perhaps even as the whole, of myself. I perceived further, that that body was placed among many others, by which it was capable of being affected in diverse ways, both beneficial and hurtful; and what was beneficial I remarked by a certain sensation of pleasure, and what was hurtful by a sensation of pain. And, besides this pleasure and pain, I was likewise conscious of hunger, thirst, and other appetites, as well as certain corporeal inclinations towards joy, sadness, anger, and similar passions.

And, out of myself, besides the extension, figure, and motions of bodies, I likewise perceived in them hardness, heat, and the other tactile qualities, and, in addition, light, colours, odours, tastes, and sounds, the variety of which gave me the means of distinguishing the sky, the earth, the sea, and generally all the other bodies, from one another. And certainly, considering the ideas of all these qualities, which were presented to my mind, and which alone I properly and immediately perceived, it was not without reason that I thought I perceived certain objects wholly different from my thought, namely, bodies from which those ideas proceeded; for I was conscious that the ideas were presented to me without my consent being required, so that I could not perceive any object, however desirous I might be, unless it were present to the organ of sense; and it was wholly out of my power not to perceive it when it was thus present. And because the ideas I perceived by the senses were much more lively and clear, and even, in their own way, more distinct than any of those I could of myself frame by meditation, or which I found impressed on my memory, it seemed that they could not have proceeded from myself, and must therefore have been caused in me by some other objects: and as of those objects I had no knowledge beyond what the ideas themselves gave me, nothing was so likely to occur to my mind as the supposition that the objects were similar to the ideas which they caused. And because I recollected also that I had formerly trusted to the senses, rather than to reason, and that the ideas which I myself formed were not so clear as those I perceived by sense, and that they were even for the most part composed of parts of the latter, I was readily persuaded that I had no idea in my intellect which had not formerly passed through the senses. Nor was I altogether wrong in likewise believing that that body which, by a special right, I called my own, pertained to me more properly and strictly than any of the others; for in truth, I could never be separated from it as from other bodies: I felt in it and on account of it all my appetites and affections, and in fine I was affected in its parts by pain and the titillation of pleasure, and not in the parts of the other bodies that were separated from it. But when I inquired into the reason why, from this I know not what sensation of pain, sadness of mind should follow, and why from the sensation of pleasure joy should should arise, or why this indescribable twitching of the stomach, which I call hunger, should put me in mind of taking food, and the parchedness of the throat of drink, and so in other cases, I was unable to give any explanation, unless that I was so taught by nature; for there is assuredly no affinity, a least none that I am able to comprehend, between this irritation of the stomach and the desire of food, and more than between the perception of an object that causes pain and the consciousness of sadness which springs from the perception. And in the same way it seemed to me that all the other judgments I had formed regarding the objects of sense, were dictates of nature; because I remarked that those judgments were formed in me, before I had leisure to weigh and consider the reasons that might constrain me to form them.

But, afterwards, a wide experience by degrees sapped the faith I had reposed in my senses; for I frequently observed that towers, which at a distance seemed round, appeared square when more closely viewed, and that colossal figures, raised on the summits of these towers, looked like small statues, when viewed from the bottom of them; and, in other instances without number, I also discovered error in judgments founded on the external senses; and not only in those founded on the external, but even in those that rested on the internal senses; for is there aught more internal than pain? and yet I have sometimes been informed by parties whose arm or leg had been amputated, that they still occasionally seemed to feel pain in that part of the body which they had lost,—a circumstance that led me to think that I could not be quite certain even that any one of my members was affected when I felt pain in it. And to these grounds of doubt I shortly afterwards also added two others of very wide generality: the first of them was that I believed I never perceived anything when awake which I could not occasionally think I also perceived when asleep, and as I do not believe that the ideas I seem to perceive in my sleep proceed from objects external to me, I did not any more observe any ground for believing this of such as I seem to perceive when awake; the second was that since I was as yet ignorant of the author of my being, or at least supposed myself to be so, I saw nothing to prevent my having been so constituted by nature as that I should be deceived even in matters that appeared to me to possess the greatest truth. And, with respect to the grounds on which I had before been persuaded of the existence of sensible objects, I had no great difficulty in finding suitable answers to them; for as nature seemed to incline me to many things from which reason made me averse, I thought that I ought not to confide much in its teachings. And although the perceptions of the senses were not dependent on my will, I did not think that I ought on that ground to conclude that they proceeded from things different from myself, since perhaps there might be found in me some faculty, though hitherto unknown to me, which produced them.

But now that I begin to know myself better, and to discover more clearly the author of my being, I do not, indeed, think that I ought rashly to admit all which the senses seem to teach, nor, on the other hand, is it my conviction that I ought to doubt in general of their teachings.

And, firstly, because I know that all which I clearly and distinctly conceive can be produced by God exactly as I conceive it, it is sufficient that I am able clearly and distinctly to conceive one thing apart from another, in order to be certain that the one is different from the other, seeing they may at least be made to exist separately, by the omnipotence of God; and it matters not by what power this separation is made, in order to be compelled to judge them different; and, therefore, merely because I know with certitude that I exist, and because, in the meantime, I do not observe that aught necessarily belongs to my nature or essence beyond my being a thinking thing, I rightly conclude that my essence consists only in my being a thinking thing [or a substance whose whole essence or nature is merely thinking]. And although I may, or rather, as I will shortly say, although I certainly do possess a body with which I am very closely conjoined; nevertheless, because, on the one hand, I have a clear and distinct idea of myself, in as far as I am only a thinking and unextended thing, and as, on the other hand, I possess a distinct idea of body, in as far as it is only an extended and unthinking thing, it is certain that I [that is, my mind, by which I am what I am] is entirely and truly distinct from my body, and may exist without it.

Moreover, I find in myself diverse faculties of thinking that have each their special mode: for example, I find I possess the faculties of imagining and perceiving, without which I can indeed clearly and distinctly conceive myself as entire, but I cannot reciprocally conceive them without conceiving myself, that is to say, without an intelligent substance in which they reside, for [in the notion we have of them, or to use the terms of the schools] in their formal concept, they comprise some sort of intellection; whence I perceive that they are distinct from myself as modes are from things. I remark likewise certain other faculties, as the power of changing place, of assuming diverse figures, and the like, that cannot be conceived and cannot therefore exist, any more than the preceding, apart from a substance in which they inhere. It is very evident, however, that these faculties, if they really exist, must belong to some corporeal or extended substance, since in their clear and distinct concept there is contained some sort of extension, but no intellection at all. Farther, I cannot doubt but that there is in me a certain passive faculty of perception, that is, of receiving and taking knowledge of the ideas of sensible things; but this would be useless to me, if there did not also exist in me, or in some other thing, another active faculty capable of forming and producing those ideas. But this active faculty cannot be in me [in as far as I am but a thinking thing], seeing that it does not presuppose thought, and also that those ideas are frequently produced in my mind without my contributing to it in any way, and even frequently contrary to my will. This faculty must therefore exist in some substance different from me, in which all the objective reality of the ideas that are produced by this faculty is contained formally or eminently, as I before remarked: and this substance is either a body, that is to say, a corporeal nature in which is contained formally [and in effect] all that is objectively [and by representation] in those ideas; or it is God himself, or some other creature, of a rank superior to body, in which the same is contained eminently. But as God is no deceiver, it is manifest that he does not of himself and immediately communicate those ideas to me, nor even by the intervention of any creature in which their objective reality is not formally, but only eminently, contained. For as he has given me no faculty whereby I can discover this to be the case, but, on the contrary, a very strong inclination to believe that those ideas arise from corporeal objects, I do not see how he could be vindicated from the charge of deceit, if in truth they proceeded from any other source, or were produced by other causes than corporeal things: and accordingly it must be concluded, that corporeal objects exist. Nevertheless they are not perhaps exactly such as we perceive by the senses, for their comprehension by the senses is, in many instances, very obscure and confused; but it is at least necessary to admit that all which I clearly and distinctly conceive as in them, that is, generally speaking, all that is comprehended in the object of speculative geometry, really exists external to me.

But with respect to other things which are either only particular, as, for example, that the sun is of such a size and figure, etc., or are conceived with less clearness and distinctness, as light, sound, pain, and the like, although they are highly dubious and uncertain, nevertheless on the ground alone that God is no deceiver, and that consequently he has permitted no falsity in my opinions which he has not likewise given me a faculty of correcting, I think I may with safety conclude that I possess in myself the means of arriving at the truth. And, in the first place, it cannot be doubted that in each of the dictates of nature there is some truth: for by nature, considered in general, I now understand nothing more than God himself, or the order and disposition established by God in created things; and by my nature in particular I understand the assemblage of all that God has given me.

But there is nothing which that nature teaches me more expressly [or more sensibly] than that I have a body which is ill affected when I feel pain, and stands in need of food and drink when I experience the sensations of hunger and thirst, etc. And therefore I ought not to doubt but that there is some truth in these informations.

Nature likewise teaches me by these sensations of pain, hunger, thirst, etc., that I am not only lodged in my body as a pilot in a vessel, but that I am besides so intimately conjoined, and as it were intermixed with it, that my mind and body compose a certain unity. For if this were not the case, I should not feel pain when my body is hurt, seeing I am merely a thinking thing, but should perceive the wound by the understanding alone, just as a pilot perceives by sight when any part of his vessel is damaged; and when my body has need of food or drink, I should have a clear knowledge of this, and not be made aware of it by the confused sensations of hunger and thirst: for, in truth, all these sensations of hunger, thirst, pain, etc., are nothing more than certain confused modes of thinking, arising from the union and apparent fusion of mind and body.

Besides this, nature teaches me that my own body is surrounded by many other bodies, some of which I have to seek after, and others to shun. And indeed, as I perceive different sorts of colours, sounds, odours, tastes, heat, hardness, etc., I safely conclude that there are in the bodies from which the diverse perceptions of the senses proceed, certain varieties corresponding to them, although, perhaps, not in reality like them; and since, among these diverse perceptions of the senses, some are agreeable, and others disagreeable, there can be no doubt that my body, or rather my entire self, in as far as I am composed of body and mind, may be variously affected, both beneficially and hurtfully, by surrounding bodies.

But there are many other beliefs which, though seemingly the teaching of nature, are not in reality so, but which obtained a place in my mind through a habit of judging inconsiderately of things. It may thus easily happen that such judgments shall contain error: thus, for example, the opinion I have that all space in which there is nothing to affect [or make an impression on] my senses is void; that in a hot body there is something in every respect similar to the idea of heat in my mind; that in a white or green body there is the same whiteness or greenness which I perceive; that in a bitter or sweet body there is the same taste, and so in other instances; that the stars, towers, and all distant bodies, are of the same size and figure as they appear to our eyes, etc. But that I may avoid everything like indistinctness of conception, I must accurately define what I properly understand by being taught by nature. For nature is here taken in a narrower sense than when it signifies the sum of all the things which God has given me; seeing that in that meaning the notion comprehends much that belongs only to the mind [to which I am not here to be understood as referring when I use the term nature]; as, for example, the notion I have of the truth, that what is done cannot be undone, and all the other truths I discern by the natural light [without the aid of the body]; and seeing that it comprehends likewise much besides that belongs only to body, and is not here any more contained under the name nature, as the quality of heaviness, and the like, of which I do not speak,—the term being reserved exclusively to designate the things which God has given to me as a being composed of mind and body. But nature, taking the term in the sense explained, teaches me to shun what causes in me the sensation of pain, and to pursue what affords me the sensation of pleasure, and other things of this sort; but I do not discover that it teaches me, in addition to this, from these diverse perceptions of the senses, to draw any conclusions respecting external objects without a previous [careful and mature] consideration of them by the mind: for it is, as appears to me, the office of the mind alone, and not of the composite whole of mind and body, to discern the truth in those matters. Thus, although the impression a star makes on my eye is not larger than that from the flame of a candle, I do not, nevertheless, experience any real or positive impulse determining me to believe that the star is not greater than the flame; the true account of the matter being merely that I have so judged from my youth without any rational ground. And, though on approaching the fire I feel heat, and even pain on approaching it too closely, I have, however, from this no ground for holding that something resembling the heat I feel is in the fire, any more than that there is something similar to the pain; all that I have ground for believing is, that there is something in it, whatever it may be, which excites in me those sensations of heat or pain. So also, although there are spaces in which I find nothing to excite and affect my senses, I must not therefore conclude that those spaces contain in them no body; for I see that in this, as in many other similar matters, I have been accustomed to pervert the order of nature, because these perceptions of the senses, although given me by nature merely to signify to my mind what things are beneficial and hurtful to the composite whole of which it is a part, and being sufficiently clear and distinct for that purpose, are nevertheless used by me as infallible rules by which to determine immediately the essence of the bodies that exist out of me, of which they can of course afford me only the most obscure and confused knowledge.

But I have already sufficiently considered how it happens that, notwithstanding the supreme goodness of God, there is falsity in my judgments. A difficulty, however, here presents itself, respecting the things which I am taught by nature must be pursued or avoided, and also respecting the internal sensations in which I seem to have occasionally detected error [and thus to be directly deceived by nature]: thus, for example, I may be so deceived by the agreeable taste of some viand with which poison has been mixed, as to be induced to take the poison. In this case, however, nature may be excused, for it simply leads me to desire the viand for its agreeable taste, and not the poison, which is unknown to it; and thus we can infer nothing from this circumstance beyond that our nature is not omniscient; at which there is assuredly no ground for surprise, since, man being of a finite nature, his knowledge must likewise be of limited perfection. But we also not unfrequently err in that to which we are directly impelled by nature, as is the case with invalids who desire drink or food that would be hurtful to them. It will here, perhaps, be alleged that the reason why such persons are deceived is that their nature is corrupted; but this leaves the difficulty untouched, for a sick man is not less really the creature of God than a man who is in full health; and therefore it is as repugnant to the goodness of God that the nature of the former should be deceitful as it is for that of the latter to be so. And, as a clock, composed of wheels and counter-weights, observes not the less accurately all the laws of nature when it is ill made, and points out the hours incorrectly, than when it satisfies the desire of the maker in every respect; so likewise if the body of man be considered as a kind of machine, so made up and composed of bones, nerves, muscles, veins, blood, and skin, that although there were in it no mind, it would still exhibit the same motions which it at present manifests involuntarily, and therefore without the aid of the mind [and simply by the dispositions of its organs], I easily discern that it would also be as natural for such a body, supposing it dropsical, for example, to experience the parchedness of the throat that is usually accompanied in the mind by the sensation of thirst, and to be disposed by this parchedness to move its nerves and its other parts in the way required for drinking, and thus increase its malady and do itself harm, as it is natural for it, when it is not indisposed to be stimulated to drink for its good by a similar cause; and although looking to the use for which a clock was destined by its maker, I may say that it is deflected from its proper nature when it incorrectly indicates the hours, and on the same principle, considering the machine of the human body as having been formed by God for the sake of the motions which it usually manifests, although I may likewise have ground for thinking that it does not follow the order of its nature when the throat is parched and drink does not tend to its preservation, nevertheless I yet plainly discern that this latter acceptation of the term nature is very different from the other; for this is nothing more than a certain denomination, depending entirely on my thought, and hence called extrinsic, by which I compare a sick man and an imperfectly constructed clock with the idea I have of a man in good health and a well-made clock; while by the other acceptation of nature is understood something which is truly found in things, and therefore possessed of some truth.

But certainly, although in respect of a dropsical body, it is only by way of exterior denomination that we say its nature is corrupted, when, without requiring drink, the throat is parched; yet, in respect of the composite whole, that is, of the mind in its union with the body, it is not a pure denomination, but really an error of nature, for it to feel thirst when drink would be hurtful to it: and, accordingly, it still remains to be considered why it is that the goodness of God does not prevent the nature of man thus taken from being fallacious.

To commence this examination accordingly, I here remark, in the first place, that there is a vast difference between mind and body, in respect that body, from its nature, is always divisible, and that mind is entirely indivisible. For in truth, when I consider the mind, that is, when I consider myself in so far only as I am a thinking thing, I can distinguish in myself no parts, but I very clearly discern that I am somewhat absolutely one and entire; and although the whole mind seems to be united to the whole body, yet, when a foot, an arm, or any other part is cut off, I am conscious that nothing has been taken from my mind; nor can the faculties of willing, perceiving, conceiving, etc., properly be called its parts, for it is the same mind that is exercised [all entire] in willing, in perceiving, and in conceiving, etc. But quite the opposite holds in corporeal or extended things; for I cannot imagine any one of them [how small soever it may be], which I cannot easily sunder in thought, and which, therefore, I do not know to be divisible. This would be sufficient to teach me that the mind or soul of man is entirely different from the body, if I had not already been apprised of it on other grounds.

I remark, in the next place, that the mind does not immediately receive the impression from all the parts of the body, but only from the brain, or perhaps even from one small part of it, viz., that in which the common sense (*sensus communis*) is said to be, which as often as it is affected in the same way, gives rise to the same perception in the mind, although meanwhile the other parts of the body may be diversely disposed, as is proved by innumerable experiments, which it is unnecessary here to enumerate.

I remark, besides, that the nature of body is such that none of its parts can be moved by another part a little removed from the other, which cannot likewise be moved in the same way by any one of the parts that lie between those two, although the most remote part does not act at all. As, for example, in the cord A, B, C, D [which is in tension], if its last part D be pulled, the first part A will not be moved in a different way than it would be were one of the intermediate parts B or C to be pulled, and the last part D meanwhile to remain fixed. And in the same way, when I feel pain in the foot, the science of physics teaches me that this sensation is experienced by means of the nerves dispersed over the foot, which, extending like cords from it to the brain, when they are contracted in the foot, contract at the same time the inmost parts of the brain in which they have their origin, and excite in these parts a certain motion appointed by nature to cause in the mind a sensation of pain, as if existing in the foot: but as these nerves must pass through the tibia, the leg, the loins, the back, and neck, in order to reach the brain, it may happen that although their extremities in the foot are not affected, but only certain of their parts that pass through the loins or neck, the same movements, nevertheless, are excited in the brain by this motion as would have been caused there by a hurt received in the foot, and hence the mind will necessarily feel pain in the foot, just as if it had been hurt; and the same is true of all the other perceptions of our senses.

I remark, finally, that as each of the movements that are made in the part of the brain by which the mind is immediately affected, impresses it with but a single sensation, the most likely supposition in the circumstances is, that this movement causes the mind to experience, among all the sensations which it is capable of impressing upon it, that one which is the best fitted, and generally the most useful for the preservation of the human body when it is in full health. But experience shows us that all the perceptions which nature has given us are of such a kind as I have mentioned; and accordingly, there is nothing found in them that does not manifest the power and goodness of God. Thus, for example, when the nerves of the foot are violently or more than usually shaken, the motion passing through the medulla of the spine to the innermost parts of the brain affords a sign to the mind on which it experiences a sensation, viz., of pain, as if it were in the foot, by which the mind is admonished and excited to do its utmost to remove the cause of it as dangerous and hurtful to the foot. It is true that God could have so constituted the nature of man as that the same motion in the brain would have informed the mind of something altogether different: the motion might, for example, have been the occasion on which the mind became conscious of itself, in so far as it is in the brain, or in so far as it is in some place intermediate between the foot and the brain, or, finally, the occasion on which it perceived some other object quite different, whatever that might be; but nothing of all this would have so well contributed to the preservation of the body as that which the mind actually feels. In the same way, when we stand in need of drink, there arises from this want a certain parchedness in the throat that moves its nerves, and by means of them the internal parts of the brain, and this movement affects the mind with the sensation of thirst, because there is nothing on that occasion which is more useful for us than to be made aware that we have need of drink for the preservation of our health; and so in other instances.

Whence it is quite manifest, that notwithstanding the sovereign goodness of God, the nature of man, in so far as it is composed of mind and body, cannot but be sometimes fallacious. For, if there is any cause which excites, not in the foot, but in some one of the parts of the nerves that stretch from the foot to the brain, or even in the brain itself, the same movement that is ordinarily created when the foot is ill affected, pain will be felt, as it were, in the foot, and the sense will thus be naturally deceived; for as the same movement in the brain can but impress the mind with the same sensation, and as this sensation is much more frequently excited by a cause which hurts the foot than by one acting in a different quarter, it is reasonable that it should lead the mind to feel pain in the foot rather than in any other part of the body. And if it sometimes happens that the parchedness of the throat does not arise, as is usual, from drink being necessary for the health of the body, but from quite the opposite cause, as is the case with the dropsical yet it is much better that it should be deceitful in that instance, than if, on the contrary, it were continually fallacious when the body is well-disposed; and the same holds true in other cases.

And certainly this consideration is of great service, not only in enabling me to recognise the errors to which my nature is liable, but likewise in rendering it more easy to avoid or correct them: for, knowing that all my senses more usually indicate to me what is true than what is false, in matters relating to the advantage of the body, and being able almost always to make use of more than a single sense in examining the same object, and besides this, being able to use my memory in connecting present with past knowledge, and my understanding which has already discovered all the causes of my errors, I ought no longer to fear that falsity may be met with in what is daily presented to me by the senses. And I ought to reject all the doubts of those bygone days as hyperbolical and ridiculous, especially the general uncertainty respecting sleep, which I could not distinguish from the waking state: for I now find a very marked difference between the two states, in respect that our memory can never connect our dreams with each other and with the course of life, in the way it is in the habit of doing with events that occur when we are awake. And, in truth, if some one, when I am awake, appeared to me all of a sudden and as suddenly disappeared, as do the images I see in sleep, so that I could not observe either whence he came or whither he went, I should not without reason esteem it either a spectre or phantom formed in my brain, rather than a real man. But when I perceive objects with regard to which I can distinctly determine both the place whence they come, and that in which they are, and the time at which they appear to me, and when, without interruption, I can connect the perception I have of them with the whole of the other parts of my life, I am perfectly sure that what I thus perceive occurs while I am awake and not during sleep. And I ought not in the least degree to doubt of the truth of those presentations, if, after having called together all my senses, my memory, and my understanding for the purpose of examining them, no deliverance is given by any one of these faculties which is repugnant to that of any other: for since God is no deceiver, it necessarily follows that I am not herein deceived. But because the necessities of action frequently oblige us to come to a determination before we have had leisure for so careful an examination, it must be confessed that the life of man is frequently obnoxious to error with respect to individual objects; and we must, in conclusion, acknowledge the weakness of our nature.

THE THIRD SET OF OBJECTIONS [BY HOBBES] WITH THE AUTHOR'S REPLY

FIRST OBJECTION

(In reference to Meditation I, *Concerning those matters that may be brought within the sphere of the doubtful.*)

It is sufficiently obvious from what is said in this Meditation, that we have no criterion for distinguishing dreaming from waking and from what the senses truly tell us; and that hence the images present to us when we are awake and using our senses are not accidents inhering in external objects, and fail to prove that such external objects do as a fact exist. And therefore, if we follow our senses without using any train of reasoning, we shall be justified in doubting whether or not anything exists. Hence we acknowledge the truth of this Meditation. But, since Plato and other ancient Philosophers have talked about this want of certitude in the matters of sense, and since the difficulty in distinguishing the waking state from dreams is a matter of common observation, I should have been glad if our author, so distinguished in the handling of modern speculations, had refrained from publishing those matters of ancient lore.

REPLY

The reasons for doubt here admitted as true by this Philosopher were propounded by me only as possessing verisimilitude, and my reason for employing them was not that I might retail them as new, but partly that I might prepare my readers' minds for the study of intellectual matters and for distinguishing them from matters corporeal, a purpose for which such arguments seem wholly necessary; in part also because I intended to reply to these very arguments in the subsequent Meditations; and partly in order to show the strength of the truths I afterwards propound, by the fact that such metaphysical doubts cannot shake them. Hence, while I have sought no praise from their rehearsal, I believe that it was impossible for me to omit them, as impossible as it would be for a medical writer to omit the description of a disease when trying to teach the method of curing it.

OBJECTION II

(In opposition to the Second Meditation, *Concerning the nature of the Human Mind.*)

I am a thing that thinks; *quite correct. From the fact that I think, or have an image, whether sleeping or waking, it is inferred that I am exercising thought; for* I think and I am exercising thought *mean the same thing. From the fact that I am exercising thought it follows that* I am, *since that which thinks is not nothing. But, where it is added,* this is the mind, the spirit, the understanding, the reason, *a doubt arises. For it does not seem to be good reasoning to say:* I am exercising thought, *hence* I am thought; *or* I am using my intellect, *hence* I am intellect. *For in the same way I might say,* I am walking; *hence* I am the walking. *It is hence an assumption on the part of M. Descartes that that which understands is the same as the exercise of understanding which is an act of that which understands, or, at least, that that which understands is the same as the understanding, which is a power possessed by that which thinks. Yet all Philosophers distinguish a subject from its faculties and activities, i.e. from its properties and essences; for the* entity *itself is one thing, its essence another. Hence it is possible for a thing that thinks to be the subject of the mind, reason, or understanding, and hence to be something corporeal; and the opposite of this has been assumed, not proved. Yet this inference is the basis of the conclusion that M. Descartes seems to wish to establish.*

In the same place he says, I know that I exist; *the question is, who am I—the being that I know? It is certain that the knowledge of this being thus accurately determined does not depend on those things which I do not yet know to exist.*

It is quite certain that the knowledge of this proposition, I exist, *depends upon that other one,* I think, *as he has himself correctly shown us. But whence comes our knowledge of this proposition,* I think? *Certainly from that fact alone, that we can conceive no activity whatsoever apart from its subject, e.g. we cannot think of leaping apart from that which leaps, of knowing apart from a knower, or of thinking without a thinker.*

And hence it seems to follow that that which thinks is something corporeal; for, as it appears, the subjects of all activities can be conceived only after a corporeal fashion, or as in material guise, as M. Descartes himself afterwards shows, when he illustrates by means of wax, this wax was understood to be always the same thing, i.e. the identical matter underlying the many successive changes, though its colour, consistency, figure and other activities were altered. Moreover it is not by another thought that I infer that I think; for though anyone may think that he has thought (to think so is precisely the same as remembering), yet we cannot think

*that we are thinking, nor similarly know that we know. For this would
entail the repetition of the question an infinite number of times; whence
do you know, that you know, that you know, that you know?*

*Hence, since the knowledge of this proposition, I exist, depends upon
the knowledge of that other, I think, and the knowledge of it upon the
fact that we cannot separate thought from a matter that thinks, the proper
inference seems to be that that which thinks is material rather than immaterial.*

REPLY

Where I have said, *this is the mind, the spirit, the intellect, or the
reason,* I understood by these names not merely faculties, but rather what
is endowed with the faculty of thinking; and this sense the two former
terms commonly, the latter frequently bear. But I used them in this sense
so expressly and in so many places that I cannot see what occasion there
was for any doubt about their meaning.

Further, there is here no parity between walking and thinking; for
walking is usually held to refer only to that action itself, while thinking
applies now to the action, now to the faculty of thinking, and again to
that in which the faculty exists.

Again I do not assert that that which understands and the activity of
understanding are the same thing, nor indeed do I mean that the thing
that understands and the understanding are the same, if the term understanding be taken to refer to the faculty of understanding; they are
identical only when the understanding means the thing itself that understands. I admit also quite gladly that, in order to designate that thing or
substance, which I wished to strip of everything that did not belong to it,
I employed the most highly abstract terms I could; just as, on the contrary this Philosopher uses terms that are as concrete as possible, e.g.
subject, matter, body, to signify that which thinks, fearing to let it be
sundered from the body.

But I have no fear of anyone thinking that his method of coupling diverse things together is better adapted to the discovery of the truth than
mine, that gives the greatest possible distinctness to every single thing.
But, dropping the verbal controversy, let us look to the facts in dispute.

A thing that thinks, he says, *may be something corporeal; and the opposite of this has been assumed; not proved.* But really I did not assume
the opposite, neither did I use it as a basis for my argument; I left it
wholly undetermined until Meditation VI, in which its proof is given.

Next he quite correctly says, that *we cannot conceive any activity apart
from its subject,* e.g. thought apart from that which thinks, since that
which thinks is not nothing. But, wholly without any reason, and in opposition to the ordinary use of language and good Logic, he adds, *hence
it seems to follow that that which thinks is something corporeal;* for *the
subjects of all activities are* indeed *understood as falling within the sphere
of substance* (or even, if you care, *as wearing the guise of matter,* viz.

metaphysical matter), but not on that account are they to be defined as bodies.

On the other hand both logicians and as a rule all men are wont to say that substances are of two kinds, spiritual and corporeal. And all that I proved, when I took wax as an example, was that its colour, hardness, and figure did not belong to the formal nature of the wax itself [i.e. that we can comprehend everything that exists necessarily in the wax, without thinking of these]. I did not there treat either of the formal nature of the mind, or even of the formal nature of body.

Again it is irrelevant to say, as this Philosopher here does, that one thought cannot be the subject of another thought. Who, except my antagonist himself, ever imagined that it could? But now, for a brief explanation of the matter,—it is certain that no thought can exist apart from a thing that thinks; no activity, no accident can be without a substance in which to exist. Moreover, since we do not apprehend the substance itself immediately through itself, but by means only of the fact that it is the subject of certain activities, it is highly rational, and a requirement forced on us by custom, to give diverse names to those substances that we recognize to be the subjects of clearly diverse activities or accidents, and afterwards to inquire whether those diverse names refer to one and the same or to diverse things. But there are *certain* activities, which we call *corporeal*, e.g. magnitude, figure, motion, and all those that cannot be thought of apart from extension in space; and the substance in which they exist is called *body*. It cannot be pretended that the substance that is the subject of figure is different from that which is the subject of spatial motion, etc., since all these activities agree in presupposing extension. Further, there are other activities, which we call *thinking* activities, e.g. understanding, willing, imagining, feeling, etc., which agree in falling under the description of thought, perception, or consciousness. The substance in which they reside we call a *thinking thing* or *the mind*, or any other name we care, provided only we do not confound it with corporeal substance, since thinking activities have no affinity with corporeal activities, and thought, which is the common nature in which the former agree, is totally different from extension, the common term for describing the latter.

But after we have formed two distinct concepts of those two substances, it is easy, from what has been said in the sixth Meditation, to determine whether they are one and the same or distinct.

OBJECTION III

What then is there distinct from my thought? What can be said to be separate from me myself?

Perchance some one will answer the question thus—I, the very self that thinks, am held to be distinct from my own thought; and, though it is not really separate from me, my thought is held to be diverse from me, just in the way (as has been said before) that leaping is distinguished from

*the leaper. But if M. Descartes shows that he who understands and the
understanding are identical we shall lapse back into the scholastic mode
of speaking. The understanding understands, the vision sees, will wills,
and by exact analogy, walking, or at least the faculty of walking will walk.
Now all this is obscure, incorrect, and quite unworthy of M. Descartes'
wonted clearness.*

REPLY

I do not deny that I, the thinker, am distinct from my own thought, in
the way in which a thing is distinct from its mode. But when I ask, *what
then is there distinct from my thought,* this is to be taken to refer to the
various modes of thought there recounted, not to my substance; and when
I add, *what can be said to be separate from me myself,* I mean only that
these modes of thinking exist entirely in me. I cannot see on what pretext
the imputation here of doubt and obscurity rests.

OBJECTION IV

Hence it is left for me to concede that I do not even understand by the
imagination what this wax is, but conceive it by the mind alone.

*There is a great difference between imagining, i.e. having some idea,
and conceiving with the mind, i.e. inferring, as the result of a train of
reasoning, that something is, or exists. But M. Descartes has not explained
to us the sense in which they differ. The ancient peripatetics also have
taught clearly enough that substance is not perceived by the senses, but is
known as a result of reasoning.*

*But what shall we now say, if reasoning chance to be nothing more than
the uniting and stringing together of names or designations by the word
is? It will be a consequence of this that reason gives us no conclusion
about the nature of things, but only about the terms that designate them,
whether, indeed, or not there is a convention (arbitrarily made about their
meanings) according to which we join these names together. If this be so,
as is possible, reasoning will depend on names, names on the imagination,
and imagination, perchance, as I think, on the motion of the corporeal
organs. Thus mind will be nothing but the motions in certain parts of an
organic body.*

REPLY

I have here explained the difference between imagination and a pure
mental concept, as when in my illustration I enumerated the features in
wax that were given by the imagination and those solely due to a conception of the mind. But elsewhere also I have explained how it is that one
and the same thing, e.g. a pentagon, is in one way an object of the understanding, in another way of the imagination [for example how in order to
imagine a pentagon a particular mental act is required which gives us this

figure (i.e. its five sides and the space they enclose) which we dispense with wholly in our conception]. Moreover, in reasoning we unite not names but the things signified by the names; and I marvel that the opposite can occur to anyone. For who doubts whether a Frenchman and a German are able to reason in exactly the same way about the same things, though they yet conceive the words in an entirely diverse way? And has not my opponent condemned himself in talking of conventions arbitrarily made about the meanings of words? For, if he admits that words signify anything, why will he not allow our reasonings to refer to this something that is signified, rather than to the words alone? But, really, it will be as correct to infer that earth is heaven or anything else that is desired, as to conclude that mind is motion [for there are no other two things in the world between which there is not as much agreement as there is between motion and spirit, which are of two entirely different natures].

OBJECTION V

In reference to the third Meditation—concerning God—some of these (thoughts of men) are, so to speak, images of things, and to these alone is the title 'idea' properly applied; examples are my thought of a man, or of a Chimera, of Heavens, of an Angel, or [even] of God.

When I think of a man, I recognize an idea, or image, with figure and colour as its constituents; and concerning this I can raise the question whether or not it is the likeness of a man. So it is also when I think of the heavens. When I think of the chimera, I recognize an idea or image, being able at the same time to doubt whether or not it is the likeness of an animal, which, though it does not exist, may yet exist or has at some other time existed.

But, when one thinks of an Angel, what is noticed in the mind is now the image of a flame, now that of a fair winged child, and this, I may be sure, has no likeness to an Angel, and hence is not the idea of an Angel. But believing that created beings exist that are the ministers of God, invisible and immaterial, we give the name of Angel to this object of belief, this supposed being, though the idea used in imagining an Angel is, nevertheless, constructed out of the ideas of visible things.

It is the same way with the most holy name of God; we have no image, no idea corresponding to it. Hence we are forbidden to worship God in the form of an image, lest we should think we could conceive Him who is inconceivable.

Hence it appears that we have no idea of God. But just as one born blind who has frequently been brought close to a fire and has felt himself growing warm, recognizes that there is something which made him warm, and, if he hears it called fire, concludes that fire exists, though he has no acquaintance with its shape or colour, and has no idea of fire nor image that he can discover in his mind; so a man, recognizing that there must be some cause of his images and ideas, and another previous cause of this cause and so on continuously, is finally carried on to a conclusion, or to the supposition of some eternal cause, which, never having begun to be, can have no cause prior to it: and hence he necessarily concludes that something eternal exists. But nevertheless he has no idea that he can assert to be that of this eternal being, and he merely gives a name to the object of his faith or reasoning and calls it God.

Since now it is from this position, viz. that there is an idea of God in our soul, that M. Descartes proceeds to prove the theorem that God (an all-powerful, all-wise Being, the creator of the world) exists, he should have explained this idea of God better, and he should have deduced from it not only God's existence, but also the creation of the world.

REPLY

Here the meaning assigned to the term idea is merely that of images depicted in the corporeal imagination; and, that being agreed on, it is easy for my critic to prove that there is no proper idea of Angel or of God. But I have, everywhere, from time to time, and principally in this place, shown that I take the term idea to stand for whatever the mind directly perceives; and so when I will or when I fear, since at the same time I perceive that I will and fear, that very volition and apprehension are ranked among my ideas. I employed this term because it was the term currently used by Philosophers for the forms of perception of the Divine mind, though we can discover no imagery in God; besides I had no other more suitable term. But I think I have sufficiently well explained what the idea of God is for those who care to follow my meaning; those who prefer to wrest my words from the sense I give them, I can never satisfy. The objection that here follows, relative to the creation of the world, is plainly irrelevant [for I proved that God exists, before asking whether there is a world created by him, and from the mere fact that God, i.e. a supremely perfect being exists, it follows that if there be a world it must have been created by him].

OBJECTION VI

But other (*thoughts*) possess other forms as well. For example, in willing, fearing, affirming, denying, though I always perceive something as the subject of my thought, yet in my thought I embrace something more than the similitude of that thing; and, of the thoughts of this kind, some are called volitions or affections, and others judgments.

When a man wills or fears, he has indeed an image of the thing he fears or of the action he wills; but no explanation is given of what is further embraced in the thought of him who wills or fears. If indeed fearing be thinking, I fail to see how it can be anything other than the thought of the thing feared. In what respect does the fear produced by the onrush of a lion differ from the idea of the lion as it rushes on us, together with its effect (produced by such an idea in the heart), which impels the fearful man towards that animal motion we call flight? Now this motion of flight

is not thought; whence we are left to infer that in fearing there is no think-
ing save that which consists in the representation of the thing feared. The
same account holds true of volition.

Further you do not have affirmation and negation without words and
names; consequently brute creatures cannot affirm or deny, not even in
thought, and hence are likewise unable to judge. Yet a man and a beast
may have similar thoughts. For, when we assert that a man runs, our
thought does not differ from that which a dog has when it sees its master
running. Hence neither affirmation nor negation add anything to the bare
thought, unless that increment be our thinking that the names of which
the affirmation consists are the names of the same thing in [the mind of]
him who affirms. But this does not mean that anything more is contained
in our thought than the representation of the thing, but merely that that
representation is there twice over.

REPLY

It is self-evident that seeing a lion and fearing it at the same time is
different from merely seeing it. So, too, it is one thing to see a man running, another thing to affirm to oneself that one sees it, an act that needs
no language. I can see nothing here that needs an answer.

OBJECTION VII

It remains for me to examine in what way I have received that idea from
God. I have neither derived it from the senses; nor has it ever come to me
contrary to my expectation, as the ideas of sensible things are wont to do,
when these very things present themselves to the external organs of sense
or seem to do so. Neither also has it been constructed as a fictitious idea
by me, for I can take nothing from it and am quite unable to add to it.
Hence the conclusion is left that it is innate in me, just as the idea of my
own self is innate in me.

If there is no idea of God (now it has not been proved that it exists),
as seems to be the case, the whole of this argument collapses. Further
(if it is my body that is being considered) the idea of my own self pro-
ceeds [principally] from sight; but (if it is a question of the soul) there
is no idea of the soul. We only infer by means of the reason that there is
something internal in the human body, which imparts to it its animal mo-
tion, and by means of which it feels and moves; and this, whatever it be,
we name the soul, without employing any idea.

REPLY

If there is an idea of God (as it is manifest there is), the whole of this
objection collapses. When it is said further that we have no idea of the
soul but that we arrive at it by an inference of reason, that is the same

as saying that there is no image of the soul depicted in the imagination, but that that which I have called its idea does, nevertheless, exist.

OBJECTION VIII

But the other idea of the sun is derived from astronomical reasonings, i.e. is elicited from certain notions that are innate in me.

It seems that at one and the same time the idea of the sun must be single whether it is beheld by the eyes, or is given by our intelligence as many times larger than it appears. For this latter thought is not an idea of the sun, but an inference by argument that the idea of the sun would be many times larger if we viewed the sun from a much nearer distance.

But at different times the ideas of the sun may differ, e.g. when one looks at it with the naked eye and through a telescope. But astronomical reasonings do not increase or decrease the idea of the sun; rather they show that the sensible idea is misleading.

REPLY

Here too what is said not to be an idea of the sun, but is, nevertheless, described, is exactly what I call an idea. [But as long as my critic refuses to come to terms with me about the meaning of words, none of his objections can be other than frivolous.]

OBJECTION IX

For without doubt those ideas, which reveal substance to me, are something greater, and, so to speak, contain within them more objective reality than those which represent only modes or accidents. And again, that by means of which I apprehend a supreme God who is eternal, infinite, omniscient, all-powerful, and the creator of all else there is besides, assuredly possesses more objective reality than those ideas that reveal to us finite substances.

I have frequently remarked above that there is no idea either of God or of the soul; I now add that there is no idea of substance. For substance (the substance that is a material, subject to accidents and changes) is perceived and demonstrated by the reason alone, without yet being conceived by us, or furnishing us with any idea. If that is true, how can it be maintained that the ideas which reveal substance to me are anything greater or possess more objective reality than those revealing accidents to us? Further I pray M. Descartes to investigate the meaning of more reality. Does reality admit of more and less? Or, if he thinks that one thing can be more a thing than another, let him see how he is to explain it to our intelligence with the clearness called for in demonstration, and such as he himself has at other times employed.

REPLY

I have frequently remarked that I give the name idea to that with which reason makes us acquainted just as I also do to anything else that is in any way perceived by us. I have likewise explained how reality admits of more and less: viz. in the way in which substance is greater than mode; and if there be real qualities or incomplete substances, they are things to a greater extent than modes are, but less than complete substances. Finally, if there be an infinite and independent substance, it is more a thing than a substance that is finite and dependent. Now all this is quite self-evident [and so needs no further explanation].

OBJECTION X

Hence there remains alone the idea of God, concerning which we must consider whether it is not something that is capable of proceeding from me myself. By the name God I understand a substance that is infinite [eternal, immutable], independent, all-knowing, all-powerful, and by which both I myself and everything else, if anything else does exist, have been created. Now all these characteristics are such that, the more diligently I attend to them, the less do they appear capable of proceeding from me alone; hence, from what has been already said, we must conclude that God necessarily exists.

When I consider the attributes of God, in order to gather thence the idea of God, and see whether there is anything contained in it that cannot proceed from ourselves, I find, unless I am mistaken, that what we assign in thought to the name of God neither proceeds from ourselves nor needs to come from any other source than external objects. For by the word God I mean a substance, *i.e. I understand that God exists (not by means of an idea but by reasoning). This substance is* infinite *(i.e. I can neither conceive nor imagine its boundaries or extreme parts, without imagining further parts beyond them): whence it follows that corresponding to the term* infinite *there arises an idea not of the Divine infinity, but of my own bounds or limitations. It is also* independent, *i.e. I have no conception of a cause from which God originates; whence it is evident that I have no idea corresponding to the term* independent, *save the memory of my own ideas with their commencement at divers times and their consequent dependence.*

Wherefore to say that God is independent, *is merely to say that God is to be reckoned among the number of those things, of the origin of which we have no image. Similarly to say that God is* infinite, *is identical with saying that He is among those objects of the limits of which we have no conception. Thus any idea of God is ruled out; for what sort of idea is that which has neither origin nor termination?*

Take the term all-knowing. *Here I ask: what idea does M. Descartes employ in apprehending the intellectual activity of God?*

All-powerful. *So too, what is the idea by which we apprehend power, which is relative to that which lies in the future, i.e. does not exist? I certainly understand what power is by means of an image, or memory of past events, inferring it in this wise—Thus did He, hence thus was He able to do; therefore as long as the same agent exists He will be able to act so again, i.e. He has the power of acting. Now these are all ideas that can arise from external objects.*

Creator of everything that exists. *Of creation some image can be constructed by me out of the objects I behold, e.g. the birth of a human being or its growth from something small as a point to the size and figure it now possesses. We have no other idea than this corresponding to the term creator. But in order to prove creation it is not enough to be able to imagine the creation of the world. Hence although it had been demonstrated that an* infinite, independent, all-powerful, etc. *being exists, nevertheless it does not follow that a creator exists. Unless anyone thinks that it is correct to infer, from the fact that there is a being which we believe to have created everything, that hence the world was at some time created by him.*

Further, when M. Descartes says that the idea of God and that of the soul are innate in us, I should like to know whether the minds of those who are in a profound and dreamless sleep yet think. If not, they have at that time no ideas. Whence no idea is innate, for what is innate is always present.

REPLY

Nothing that we attribute to God can come from external objects as a copy proceeds from its exemplar, because in God there is nothing similar to what is found in external things, i.e. in corporeal objects. But whatever is unlike them in our thought [of God], must come manifestly not from them, but from the cause of that diversity existing in our thought [of God].

Further I ask how my critic derives the intellectual comprehension of God from external things. But I can easily explain the idea which I have of it, by saying that by idea I mean whatever is the form of any perception. For does anyone who understands something not perceive that he does so? and hence does he not possess that form or idea of mental action? It is by extending this indefinitely that we form the idea of the intellectual activity of God; similarly also with God's other attributes.

But, since we have employed the idea of God existing in us for the purpose of proving His existence, and such mighty power is comprised in this idea, that we comprehend that it would be contradictory, if God exists, for anything besides Him to exist, unless it were created by Him; it clearly follows, from the fact that His existence has been demonstrated, that it has been also proved that the whole world, or whatever things other than God exist, have been created by Him.

Finally when I say that an idea is innate in us [or imprinted in our souls by nature], I do not mean that it is always present to us. This would make no idea innate. I mean merely that we possess the faculty of sum-moning up this idea.

OBJECTION XI

The whole force of the argument lies in this—that I know I could not exist, and possess the nature I have, that nature which puts me in posses-sion of the idea of God, unless God did really exist, the God, I repeat, the idea of whom is found in me.

Since, then, it has not been proved that we possess an idea of God, and the Christian religion obliges us to believe that God is inconceivable, which amounts, in my opinion, to saying that we have no idea of Him, it follows that no proof of His existence has been effected, much less of His work of creation.

REPLY

When it is said that we cannot conceive God, to conceive means to comprehend adequately. For the rest, I am tired of repeating how it is that we can have an idea of God. There is nothing in these objections that invalidates my demonstrations.

OBJECTION XII

(Directed against the fourth Meditation, *Concerning the true and the false.*)

And thus I am quite sure that error, in so far as it is error, is nothing real, but merely defect. Hence in order to go astray, it is not necessary for me to have a faculty specially assigned to me by God for this purpose.

It is true that ignorance is merely a defect, and that we stand in need of no special positive faculty in order to be ignorant; but about error the case is not so clear. For it appears that stones and inanimate things are unable to err solely because they have no faculty of reasoning, or im-agining. Hence it is a very direct inference that, in order to err, a faculty of reasoning, or at least of imagination is required; now both of these are positive faculties with which all beings that err, and only beings that err, have been endowed.

Further, M. Descartes says—I perceive that they (*viz. my mistakes*) depend upon the cooperation of two causes, viz. my faculty of cognition, and my faculty of choice, or the freedom of my will. *But this seems to be contradictory to what went before. And we must note here also that the freedom of the will has been assumed without proof, and in opposition to the opinion of the Calvinists.*

REPLY

Although in order to err the faculty of reasoning (or rather of judging, or affirming and denying) is required, because error is a lack of this power it does not hence follow that this defect is anything real, just as it does not follow that blindness is anything real, although stones are not said to be blind merely because they are incapable of vision. I marvel that in these objections I have as yet found nothing that is properly argued out. Further I made no assumption concerning freedom which is not a matter of universal experience; our natural light makes this most evident and I cannot make out why it is said to be contradictory to previous statements.

But though there are many who, looking to the Divine foreordination, cannot conceive how that is compatible with liberty on our part, nevertheless no one, when he considers himself alone, fails to experience the fact that to will and to be free are the same thing [or rather that there is no difference between what is voluntary and what is free]. But this is no place for examining other people's opinions about this matter.

OBJECTION XIII

For example, whilst I, during these days, sought to discuss whether anything at all existed, and noted that, from the very fact that I raised this question, it was an evident consequence that I myself existed, I could not indeed refrain from judging that what I understood so clearly was true; this was not owing to compulsion by some external force, but because the consequence of the great mental illumination was a strong inclination of the will, and I believed the above truth the more willingly and freely, the less indifferent I was towards it.

This term, great mental illumination, *is metaphorical, and consequently is not adapted to the purposes of argument. Moreover everyone who is free from doubt claims to possess a similar illumination, and in his will there is the same inclination to believe that of which he does not doubt, as in that of one who truly knows. Hence while this illumination may be the cause that makes a man obstinately defend or hold some opinion, it is not the cause of his knowing it to be true.*

Further, not only to know a thing to be true, but also to believe it or give assent to it, have nothing to do with the will. For, what is proved by valid argument or is recounted as credible, is believed by us whether we will or no. It is true that affirming and denying, maintaining or refuting propositions, are acts of will; but it does not follow on that account that internal assent depends upon the will.

Therefore the demonstration of the truth that follows is not adequate— and it is in this misuse of our free-will, that this privation consists that constitutes the form of error.

REPLY

It does not at all matter whether or not the term *great illumination* is proper to argument, so long as it is serviceable for explanation, as in fact it is. For no one can be unaware that by mental illumination is meant clearness of cognition, which perhaps is not possessed by everyone who thinks he possesses it. But this does not prevent it from being very different from a bigoted opinion, to the formation of which there goes no perceptual evidence.

Moreover when it is here said that when a thing is clearly perceived we give our assent whether we will or no, that is the same as saying that we desire what we clearly know to be good whether willing or unwilling; for the word *unwilling* finds no entrance in such circumstances, implying as it does that we will and do not will the same thing.

OBJECTION XIV

(To the fifth Meditation, *On the essence of material things.*)

As, for example, when I imagine a triangle, though perhaps such a figure does not exist at all outside my thought, or never has existed, it has nevertheless a determinate nature, or essence, or immutable and eternal form, which is not a fiction of my construction, and does not depend on my mind, as is evident from the fact that various properties of that triangle may be demonstrated.

If the triangle exists nowhere at all, I do not understand how it can have any nature; for that which exists nowhere does not exist. Hence it has no existence or nature. The triangle in the mind comes from the triangle we have seen, or from one imaginatively constructed out of triangles we have beheld. Now when we have once called the thing (from which we think that the idea of triangle originates) by the name triangle, although the triangle itself perishes, yet the name remains. In the same way if, in our thought, we have once conceived that the angles of a triangle are together all equal to two right angles, and have given this other name to the triangle—possessed of three angles equal to two right angles— although there were no angle at all in existence, yet the name would remain; and the truth of this proposition will be of eternal duration—a triangle is possessed of three angles equal to two right angles. But the nature of the triangle will not be of eternal duration, if it should chance that triangle perished.

In like manner the proposition, man is animal, will be eternally true, because the names it employs are eternal, but if the human race were to perish there would no longer be a human nature.

Whence it is evident that essence in so far as it is distinguished from existence is nothing else than a union of names by means of the verb is. And thus essence without existence is a fiction of our mind. And it appears

*that as the image of a man in the mind is to the man so is essence to exist-
ence; or that the essence of Socrates bears to his existence the relation
that this proposition,* Socrates is a man, *to this other,* Socrates is or exists.
Now the proposition, Socrates is a man, *means, when Socrates does not
exist, merely the connection of its terms; and* is, *or to be, has underlying
it the image of the unity of a thing designated by two names.*

REPLY

The distinction between essence and existence is known to all; and all
that is here said about eternal names in place of concepts or ideas of an
eternal truth, has been already satisfactorily refuted.

OBJECTION XV

(Directed against the sixth Meditation—*Concerning the existence of
material things.*)

For since God has evidently given me no faculty by which to know this
(*whether or not our ideas proceed from bodies*), but on the contrary has
given me a strong propensity towards the belief that they do proceed
from corporeal things, I fail to see how it could be made out that He is
not a deceiver, if our ideas proceeded from some other source than corporeal things. Consequently corporeal objects must exist.
*It is the common belief that no fault is committed by medical men who
deceive sick people for their health's sake, nor by parents who mislead
their children for their good; and that the evil in deception lies not in
the falsity of what is said, but in the bad intent of those who practise it.
M. Descartes must therefore look to this proposition,* God can in no case
deceive us, *taken universally, and see whether it is true; for if it is not
true, thus universally taken, the conclusion,* hence corporeal things exist,
does not follow.

REPLY

For the security of my conclusion we do not need to assume that we
can never be deceived (for I have gladly admitted that we are often
deceived), but that we are not deceived when that error of ours would
argue an intention to deceive on the part of God, an intention it is contradictory to impute to Him. Once more this is bad reasoning on my critic's
part.

FINAL OBJECTION

For now I perceive how great the difference is between the two (i.e.
between waking and dreaming) from the fact that our dreams are never
conjoined by our memory [with each other and] with the whole of the

rest of our life's action [as happens with the things which occur in waking moments].

I ask whether it is really the case that one, who dreams he doubts whether he dreams or no, is unable to dream that his dream is connected with the idea of a long series of past events. If he can, those things which to the dreamer appear to be the actions of his past life may be regarded as true just as though he had been awake. Besides, since, as M. Descartes himself asserts, all certitude and truth in knowledge depend alone upon our knowing the true God, either it will be impossible for an Atheist to infer from the memory of his previous life that he wakes, or it will be possible for a man to know that he is awake, apart from knowledge of the true God.

REPLY

One who dreams cannot effect a real connection between what he dreams and the ideas of past events, though he can dream that he does connect them. For who denies that in his sleep a man may be deceived? But yet when he has awakened he will easily detect his error.

But an Atheist is able to infer from the memory of his past life that he is awake; still he cannot know that this sign is sufficient to give him the certainty that he is not in error, unless he knows that it has been created by a God who does not deceive.

THOMAS HOBBES   1588-1679

*H*obbes was born prematurely: his mother was badly frightened when the Spanish Armada approached Great Britain. He later said of himself that he was a child of fear, alluding to the importance he assigned to fear in his philosophy.

He studied at Oxford and later came to know personally both Bacon and Descartes. He also visited Galileo in 1636.

Unlike Bacon and Descartes, he is often considered a one-book philosopher. Though in the course of his exceptionally long life he wrote prolifically, his enduring fame is tied to a work he published in his sixties: *Leviathan* (1651). In forceful English, the book propounds his highly unsentimental views on man and the state. Except for his "Objections" to Descartes, all of our selections from Hobbes come from this book. The text and the page numbers in brackets are those of the original edition.

Of his other writings, the following may at least be mentioned briefly. In 1628 he published a remarkable translation of Thucydides, whose hardheaded and brilliant realism appealed to him. No doubt, Hobbes was more congenial to the great Athenian than was Jowett, whose more faithful translation was made in the Victorian era; but in the case of Pericles' praise of democracy in his great funeral oration, which is reprinted in the companion volume, Jowett's version is incomparably better and was therefore selected after careful comparison. Hobbes' translation was partly intended to warn his compatriots against democracy (in the Peloponnesian War, democratic Athens was defeated by Sparta), and his heart did not catch fire, as Jowett's did, when he came to Pericles' speech.

Hobbes continued his studies of mathematics and natural science

92

in Paris and, unlike Bacon, recognized the great significance of Copernicus and Kepler, Galileo and Harvey. He proposed to approach the study of man and government in a scientific and materialistic manner. He made many trips to the continent, and fled to Paris in 1640, when the Long Parliament took over in London. It was in Paris that he published *De cive* in 1642, in Latin. An expanded version appeared in 1647 in Amsterdam; an English version in 1651; a French translation, two years earlier. *Leviathan or the matter, form and authority of government*, written in Paris, appeared in London in 1651; a Latin version in 1668.

In 1652, Cromwell permitted Hobbes to return to England. Although Hobbes had been a royalist, and his *Leviathan* was odious to both Catholics and Protestants, Hobbes' argument for the almost unlimited power of the sovereign was not restricted to kings. Rather, Hobbes had tried to show that only a strong sovereign—conceivably an assembly—could keep the peace and guarantee that security which men need and desire above all. He did not claim any divine sanction for the ruler but only the sanction of the common interest. When Cromwell was firmly established, he had no reason to consider Hobbes' doctrine seditious—any more than Charles II, whom Hobbes had tutored in Paris, did a few years later, when the monarchy was restored.

In 1656, Hobbes published *Quaestiones de libertate, necessitate et casu*. He also set to work on a trilogy, of which the earlier *De cive* was to form the final part: part one was *De corpore* (1655 in English), part two, *De homine* (1658 in English)—both in Latin in 1668. In his eighties, Hobbes wrote a history of the period of 1640-1660, which he called *Behemoth*. Held back at the king's request, the book was published in 1679 without the author's permission, and created a great stir. In 1675, Hobbes published a complete English translation of both the *Iliad* and the *Odyssey*. A little earlier, at 84, Hobbes published his autobiography, in Latin verse.

His last years were troubled by charges of heresy, though Hobbes was held in high esteem outside of England. His defense, *An Historical Narration concerning Heresy and the Punishment thereof*, was published posthumously in 1680, the year after he had died at the age of 91.

LEVIATHAN

Part I. Of man [3]

CHAP. I.   OF SENSE

Concerning the Thoughts of man, I will consider them first *Singly,* and afterwards in *Trayne,* or dependance upon one another. *Singly,* they are every one a *Representation* or *Apparence,* of some quality, or other Accident of a body without us; which is commonly called an *Object.* Which Object worketh on the Eyes, Eares, and other parts of mans body; and by diversity of working, produceth diversity of Apparences.

The Originall of them all, is that which we call SENSE; (For there is no conception in a mans mind, which hath not at first, totally, or by parts, been begotten upon the organs of *Sense.*) The rest are derived from that originall.

To know the naturall cause of Sense, is not very necessary to the business now in hand; and I have elsewhere written of the same at large. Nevertheless, to fill each part of my present method, I will briefly deliver the same in this place.

The cause of Sense, is the Externall Body, or Object, which presseth the organ proper to each Sense, either immediatly, as in the Tast and Touch; or mediately, as in Seeing, Hearing, and Smelling: which pressure, by the mediation of Nerves, and other strings, and membranes of the body, continued inwards to the Brain, and Heart, causeth there a resistance, or counter-pressure, or endeavour of the heart, to deliver it self: which endeavour because *Outward,* seemeth to be some matter without. And this *seeming,* or *fancy,* is that which men call *Sense;* and consisteth, as to the Eye, in a *Light,* or *Colour figured;* To the Eare, in a *Sound;* To the Nostrill, in an *Odour;* To the Tongue and Palat, in a *Savour;* And to the rest of the body, in *Heat, Cold, Hardnesse, Softnesse,* and such other qualities, as we discern by *Feeling.* All which qualities called *Sensible,* are in the object that causeth them, but so many several motions of the matter, by which it presseth our organs diversly. Neither in us that are pressed, are they any thing else, but divers motions; (for motion, produceth nothing but motion.) But their apparence to us is Fancy, the same waking, that dreaming. And as pressing, rubbing, or striking the Eye, makes us fancy a light; and pressing the Eare, produceth a dinne; so do the bodies also we see, or hear, produce the same by their strong, though unobserved action. For if those Colours, and Sounds, were in the Bodies, or Objects that cause them, they could [4] not bee severed from them, as by glasses, and in Ecchoes by reflection, wee see they are; where we know the thing we see, is in one place; the apparence, in another. And though at some certain distance, the reall, and very object seem invested with the fancy it begets in us; Yet still the object is one thing, the image or fancy is another. So that Sense in all cases, is nothing els but originall fancy, caused (as I have said) by the pressure, that is, by the motion, of externall things upon our Eyes, Eares, and other organs thereunto ordained.

But the Philosophy-schooles, through all the Universities of Christendome, grounded upon certain Texts of *Aristotle*, teach another doctrine; and say, For the cause of *Vision*, that the thing seen, sendeth forth on every side a *visible species* (in English) a *visible shew, apparition*, or *aspect*, or *a being seen;* the receiving whereof into the Eye, is *Seeing*. And for the cause of *Hearing*, that the thing heard, sendeth forth an *Audible species*, that is, an *Audible aspect*, or *Audible being seen;* which entring at the Eare, maketh *Hearing*. Nay for the cause of *Understanding* also, they say the thing Understood sendeth forth *intelligible species*, that is, an *intelligible being seen;* which comming into the Understanding, makes us Understand. I say not this, as disapproving the use of Universities: but because I am to speak hereafter of their office in a Commonwealth, I must let you see on all occasions by the way, what things would be amended in them; amongst which the frequency of insignificant Speech is one.

CHAP. II.   OF IMAGINATION

That when a thing lies still, unlesse somewhat els stirre it, it will lye still for ever, is a truth that no man doubts of. But that when a thing is in motion, it will eternally be in motion, unless somewhat els stay it, though the reason be the same, (namely, that nothing can change it selfe,) is not so easily assented to. For men measure, not onely other men, but all other things, by themselves: and because they find themselves subject after motion to pain, and lassitude, think every thing els growes weary of motion, and seeks repose of its own accord; little considering, whether it be not some other motion, wherein that desire of rest they find in themselves, consisteth. From hence it is, that the Schooles say, Heavy bodies fall downwards, out of an appetite to rest, and to conserve their nature in that place which is most proper for them; ascribing appetite and Knowledge of what is good for their conservation, (which is more than man has) to things inanimate, absurdly.

When a Body is once in motion, it moveth (unless something els hinder it) eternally; and whatsoever hindreth it, cannot in an instant, but in time, and by degrees quite extinguish it: And as wee see in the water, though the wind cease, the waves give not over rowling for a long time after; so also it happeneth in that motion, which is made in the   [5] internall parts of a man, then, when he Sees, Dreams, &c. For after the object is removed, or the eye shut, wee still retain an image of the thing seen, though more obscure than when we see it. And this is it, the Latines call *Imagination*, from the image made in seeing; and apply the same, though improperly, to all the other senses. But the Greeks call it *Fancy;* which signifies *apparence,* and is as proper to one sense, as to another. IMAGINATION therefore is nothing but *decaying sense;* and is found in men, and many other living Creatures, aswell sleeping, as waking.

The decay of Sense in men waking, is not the decay of the motion made in sense; but an obscuring of it, in such manner, as the light of the Sun obscureth the light of the Starres; which starrs do no less exercise their vertue by which they are visible, in the day, than in the night. But because amongst many stroaks, which our eyes, eares, and other organs receive from externall bodies, the predominant onely is sensible; therefore the light of the Sun being predominant, we are not affected with the action of the starrs. And any object being removed from our eyes, though the impression it made in us remain; yet other objects more present succeeding, and working on us, the Imagination of the past is obscured, and made weak; as the voyce of a man is in the noyse of the day. From whence it followeth, that the longer the time is, after the sight, or Sense of any object, the weaker is the Imagination. For the continuall change of mans body, destroyes in time the parts which in sense were moved: So that distance of time, and of place, hath one and the same effect in us. For as at a great distance of place, that which wee look at, appears dimme, and without distinction of the smaller parts; and as Voyces grow weak, and inarticulate: so also after great distance of time, our imagination of the Past is weak; and wee lose (for example) of Cities wee have seen, many particular Streets; and of Actions, many particular Circumstances. This *decaying sense,* when wee would express the thing it self, (I mean *fancy* it selfe,) wee call *Imagination,* as I said before: But when we would express the *decay,* and signifie that the Sense is fading, old, and past, it is called *Memory.* So that *Imagination* and *Memory,* are but one thing, which for divers considerations hath divers names.

Much memory, or memory of many things, is called *Experience.* Againe, Imagination being only of those things which have been formerly perceived by Sense, either all at once, or by parts at severall times; The former, (which is the imagining the whole object, as it was presented to the sense) is *simple Imagination;* as when one imagineth a man, or horse, which he hath seen before. The other is *Compounded;* as when from the sight of a man at one time, and of a horse at another, we conceive in our mind a Centaure.

.   .   .

CHAP. VI.   OF THE INTERIOUR BEGINNINGS OF VOLUNTARY   [23]
MOTIONS; COMMONLY CALLED THE PASSIONS. AND THE
SPEECHES BY WHICH THEY ARE EXPRESSED.

There be in Animals, two sorts of *Motions* peculiar to them: One called *Vitall;* begun in generation, and continued without interruption through their whole life; such as are the *course* of the *Bloud,* the *Pulse,* the *Breathing*, the *Concoction, Nutrition, Excretion*, &c; to which Motions there needs no help of Imagination: The other is *Animall motion*, otherwise called *Voluntary motion;* as to *go*, to *speak*, to *move* any of our limbes, in such manner as is first fancied in our minds. That Sense, is Motion in the organs and interiour parts of mans body, caused by the action of the things we See, Heare, &c; And that Fancy is but the Reliques of the same Motion, remaining after Sense, has been already sayd in the first and second Chapters. And because *going, speaking*, and the like Voluntary motions, depend alwayes upon a precedent thought of *whither, which way*, and *what;* it is evident, that the Imagination is the first internall beginning of all Voluntary Motion. And although unstudied men, doe not conceive any motion at all to be there, where the thing moved is invisible; or the space it is moved in, is (for the shortnesse of it) insensible; yet that doth not hinder, but that such Motions are. For let a space be never so little, that which is moved over a greater space, whereof that little one is part, must first be moved over that. These small beginnings of Motion, within the body of Man, before they appear in walking, speaking, striking, and other visible actions, are commonly called ENDEAVOUR.

This Endeavour, when it is toward something which causes it, is called APPETITE, or DESIRE; the later, being the generall name; and the other, often-times restrayned to signifie the Desire of Food, namely *Hunger* and *Thirst*. And when the Endeavour is fromward something, it is generally called AVERSION. These words *Appetite*, and *Aversion* we have from the *Latines;* and they both of them signifie the motions, one of approaching, the other of retiring. So also do the Greek words for the same, which are ὁρμή, and ἀφορμή. For Nature it selfe does often presse upon men those truths, which afterwards, when they look for somewhat beyond Nature, they stumble at. For the Schooles find in meere Appetite to go, or move, no actuall Motion at all: but because some Motion they must acknowledge, they call it Metaphoricall Motion; which is but an absurd speech: for though Words may be called metaphoricall; Bodies, and Motions cannot.

That which men Desire, they are also sayd to LOVE: and to HATE those things, for which they have Aversion. So that Desire, and [24] Love, are the same thing; save that by Desire, we alwayes signifie the Absence of the Object; by Love, most commonly the Presence of the same. So also by Aversion, we signifie the Absence; and by Hate, the Presence of the Object.

· · ·

For *Appetite* with an opinion of attaining, is called HOPE.
The same, without such opinion, DESPAIRE.
Aversion, with opinion of *Hurt* from the object, FEARE.
The same, with hope of avoyding that Hurt by resistence, COURAGE.
Sudden *Courage*, ANGER.
Constant *Hope*, CONFIDENCE of our selves.
Constant *Despayre*, DIFFIDENCE of our selves.

Anger for great hurt done to another, when we conceive the same to be done by Injury, INDIGNATION.   [26]

Desire of good to another, BENEVOLENCE, GOOD WILL, CHARITY. If to man generally, GOOD NATURE.

Desire of Riches, COVETOUSNESSE: a name used alwayes in signification of blame; because men contending for them, are displeased with one anothers attaining them; though the desire in it selfe, be to be blamed, or allowed, according to the means by which those Riches are sought.

Desire of Office, or precedence, AMBITION: a name used also in the worse sense, for the reason before mentioned.

Desire of things that conduce but a little to our ends; And fear of things that are but of little hindrance, PUSILLANIMITY. *weaknes, Cowardice*

Contempt of little helps, and hindrances, MAGNANIMITY.

Magnanimity, in danger of Death, or Wounds, VALOUR, FORTITUDE.

Magnanimity, in the use of Riches, LIBERALITY.

Pusillanimity, in the same WRETCHEDNESSE, MISERABLENESSE; or PARSIMONY; as it is liked, or disliked.

Love of Persons for society, KINDNESSE.

Love of Persons for Pleasing the sense onely, NATURALL LUST.

Love of the same, acquired from Rumination, that is, Imagination of Pleasure past, LUXURY.

Love of one singularly, with desire to be singularly beloved, THE PASSION OF LOVE. The same, with fear that the love is not mutuall, JEALOUSIE.

Desire, by doing hurt to another, to make him condemn some fact of his own, REVENGEFULNESSE.

.   .   .

CHAP. IX.   OF THE SEVERALL SUBJECTS OF KNOWLEDGE
[Contains a chart reproduced on the facing page.]

.   .   .

CHAP. XI.   OF THE DIFFERENCE OF MANNERS

By Manners, I mean not here, Decency of behaviour; as how one man should salute another, or how a man should wash his mouth, or pick his teeth before company, and such other points of the *Small Moralls;* But those qualities of man-kind, that concern their living together in Peace, and Unity. To which end we are to consider, that the Felicity of this life, consisteth not in the repose of a mind satisfied. For there is no such *Finis ultimus,* (utmost ayme,) nor *Summum Bonum,* (greatest Good,) as is spoken of in the Books of the old Morall Philosophers. Nor can a man any more live, whose Desires are at an end, than he, whose Senses and Imaginations are at a stand. Felicity is a continuall progresse of the desire, from one object to another; the attaining of the former, being still but the way to the later. The cause whereof is, That the object of mans desire, is not to enjoy once onely, and for one instant of time; but to assure for

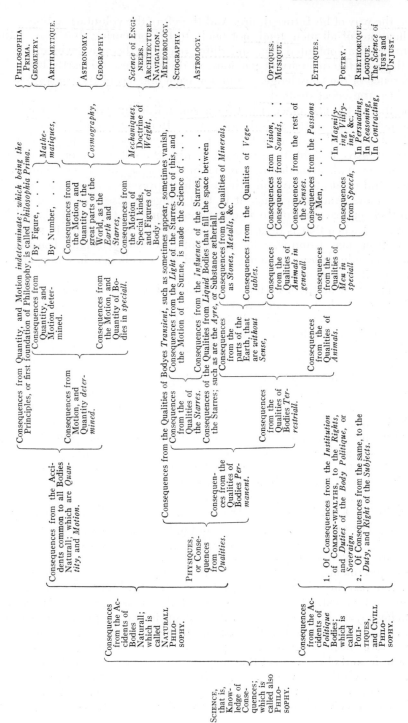

SCIENCE, that is, Knowledge of Consequences; which is called also PHILOSOPHY.

- Consequences from the Accidents of Bodies Naturall; which is called NATURALL PHILOSOPHY.
  - Consequences from the Accidents common to all Bodies Naturall; which are *Quantity*, and *Motion*.
    - Consequences from Quantity, and Motion *indeterminate; which being the Principles, or first foundation of Philosophy, is called Philosophia Prima*. → PHILOSOPHIA PRIMA.
    - Consequences from Motion, and Quantity *determined*.
      - Consequences from Quantity, and Motion determined. *Mathematiques,*
        - By Figure, . . . → GEOMETRY.
        - By Number, . . . → ARITHMETIQUE.
      - Consequences from the Motion, and Quantity of Bodies in *speciall*.
        - Consequences from the Motion, and Quantity of the great parts of the World, as the *Earth* and *Starres*, *Cosmography,*
          - ASTRONOMY.
          - GEOGRAPHY.
        - Consequences from the Motion of Special kinds, and Figures of Body, *Mechaniques, Doctrine of Weight,*
          - Science of ENGINEERS.
          - ARCHITECTURE.
          - NAVIGATION.
  - PHYSIQUES, or Consequences from *Qualities*.
    - Consequences from the Qualities of Bodyes *Transient*, such as sometimes appear, sometimes vanish, → METEOROLOGY.
    - Consequences from the Qualities of Bodies *Permanent*.
      - Consequences from the Qualities of the *Starres*.
        - Consequences from the *Light* of the Starres. Out of this, and the Motion of the Sunne, is made the Science of . . . → SCIOGRAPHY.
        - Consequences from the *Influence* of the Starres, . . . → ASTROLOGY.
      - Consequences of the Qualities from *Liquid* Bodies that fill the space between the Starres; such as are the *Ayre*, or Substance aetheriall.
      - Consequences from the Qualities of Bodies *Terrestriall*.
        - Consequences from the parts of the Earth, that are *without Sense*,
          - Consequences from the Qualities of *Minerals*, as *Stones, Metalls,* &c.
          - Consequences from the Qualities of *Vegetables*.
        - Consequences from the Qualities of *Animals*.
          - Consequences from the Qualities of *Animals in generall*
            - Consequences from *Vision*, . . → OPTIQUES.
            - Consequences from *Sounds*, . . → MUSIQUE.
            - Consequences from the rest of the *Senses*.
          - Consequences from the Qualities of *Men in speciall*
            - Consequences from the *Passions* of Men, . . . → ETHIQUES.
            - Consequences from *Speech*,
              - In *Magnifying, Vilifying*, &c. → POETRY.
              - In *Persuading*, → RHETHORIQUE.
              - In *Reasoning*, → LOGIQUE.
              - In *Contracting*, → The *Science* of Just and Unjust.
- Consequences from the Accidents of *Politique* Bodies; which is called POLITIQUES, and CIVILL PHILOSOPHY.
  1. Of Consequences from the *Institution* of COMMON-WEALTHS, to the *Rights*, and *Duties* of the *Body Politique*, or *Soveraign*.
  2. Of Consequences from the same, to the *Duty*, and *Right* of the *Subjects*.

ever, the way of his future desire. And therefore the voluntary actions, and inclinations of all men, tend, not onely to the procuring, but also to the assuring of a contented life; and differ onely in the way: which ariseth partly from the diversity of passions, in divers men; and partly from the difference of the knowledge, or opinion each one has of the causes, which produce the effect desired.

So that in the first place, I put for a generall inclination of all mankind, a perpetuall and restlesse desire of Power after power, that ceaseth onely in Death. And the cause of this, is not alwayes that a man hopes for a more intensive delight, than he has already attained to; or that he cannot be content with a moderate power: but because he cannot assure the power and means to live well, which he hath present, without the acquisition of more. And from hence it is, that Kings, whose power is greatest, turn their endeavours to the assuring it at home by Lawes, or abroad by Wars: and when that is done, there succeedeth a new desire; in some, of Fame from new Conquest; in others, of ease and sensuall pleasure; in others, of admiration, or being flattered for excellence in some art, or other ability of the mind.

Competition of Riches, Honour, Command, or other power, enclineth to Contention, Enmity, and War: Because the way of one Com-   [48] petitor, to the attaining of his desire, is to kill, subdue, supplant, or repell the other. Particularly, competition of praise, enclineth to a reverence of Antiquity. For men contend with the living, not with the dead; to these ascribing more than due, that they may obscure the glory of the other.

Desire of Ease, and sensuall Delight, disposeth men to obey a common Power: Because by such Desires, a man doth abandon the protection might be hoped for from his own Industry, and labour. Fear of Death, and Wounds, disposeth to the same; and for the same reason. On the contrary, needy men, and hardy, not contented with their present condition; as also, all men that are ambitious of Military command, are enclined to continue the causes of warre; and to stirre up trouble and sedition: for there is no honour Military but by warre; nor any such hope to mend an ill game, as by causing a new shuffle.

Desire of Knowledge, and Arts of Peace, enclineth men to obey a common Power: For such Desire, containeth a desire of leasure; and consequently protection from some other Power than their own.

Desire of Praise, disposeth to laudable actions, such as please them whose judgment they value; for of those men whom we contemn, we contemn also the Praises. Desire of Fame after death does the same. And though after death, there be no sense of the praise given us on Earth, as being joyes, that are either swallowed up in the unspeakable joyes of Heaven, or extinguished in the extreme torments of Hell: yet is not such Fame vain; because men have a present delight therein, from the foresight of it, and of the benefit that may redound thereby to their posterity: which though they now see not, yet they imagine; and any thing that is pleasure in the sense, the same also is pleasure in the imagination.

To have received from one, to whom we think our selves equall, greater benefits than there is hope to Requite, disposeth to counterfeit love; but really secret hatred; and puts a man into the estate of a desperate debtor, that in declining the sight of his creditor, tacitely wishes him there, where he might never see him more. For benefits oblige; and obligation is thraldome; and unrequitable obligation, perpetuall thraldome; which is to ones equall, hatefull. But to have received benefits from one, whom we acknowledge for superiour, enclines to love; because the obligation is no new depression: and cheerfull acceptation, (which men call *Gratitude*,) is such an honour done to the obliger, as is taken generally for retribution. Also to receive benefits, though from an equall, or inferiour, as long as there is hope of requitall, disposeth to love: for in the intention of the receiver, the obligation is of ayd, and service mutuall; from whence proceedeth an Emulation of who shall exceed in benefiting; the most noble and profitable contention possible; wherein the victor is pleased with his victory, and the other revenged by confessing it.

To have done more hurt to a man, then he can, or is willing to expiate, enclineth the doer to hate the sufferer. For he must expect re|venge, or forgivenesse; both which are hatefull.

Feare of oppression, disposeth a man to anticipate, or to seek   [49] ayd by society: for there is no other way by which a man can secure his life and liberty.

Men that distrust their own subtilty, are in tumult, and sedition, better disposed for victory, then they that suppose themselves wise, or crafty. For these love to consult, the other (fearing to be circumvented,) to strike first. And in sedition, men being alwayes in the procincts of battell, to hold together, and use all advantages of force, is a better stratagem, than any that can proceed from subtilty of Wit.

Vain-glorious men, such as without being conscious to themselves of great sufficiency, delight in supposing themselves gallant men, are enclined onely to ostentation; but not to attempt: because when danger or difficulty appears, they look for nothing but to have their insufficiency discovered.

Vain-glorious men, such as estimate their sufficiency by the flattery of other men, or the fortune of some precedent action, without assured ground of hope from the true knowledge of themselves, are enclined to rash engaging; and in the approach of danger, or difficulty, to retire if they can: because not seeing the way of safety, they will rather hazard their honour, which may be salved with an excuse; than their lives, for which no salve is sufficient.

Men that have a strong opinion of their own wisdome in matter of government, are disposed to Ambition. Because without publique Employment in counsell or magistracy, the honour of their wisdome is lost. And therefore Eloquent speakers are enclined to Ambition; for Eloquence seemeth wisdome, both to themselves and others.

Pusillanimity disposeth men to Irresolution, and consequently to lose the occasions, and fittest opportunities of action. For after men have been in deliberation till the time of action approach, if it be not then manifest what is best to be done, 'tis a signe, the difference of Motives, the one way and the other, are not great: Therefore not to resolve then, is to lose the occasion by weighing of trifles; which is Pusillanimity.

Frugality, (though in poor men a Vertue,) maketh a man unapt to atchieve such actions, as require the strength of many men at once: For it weakeneth their Endeavour, which is to be nourished and kept in vigor by Reward.

Eloquence, with flattery, disposeth men to confide in them that have it; because the former is seeming Wisdome, the later seeming Kindnesse. Adde to them Military reputation, and it disposeth men to adhære, and subject themselves to those men that have them. The two former, having given them caution against danger from him; the later gives them caution against danger from others.

Want of Science, that is, Ignorance of causes, disposeth, or rather constraineth a man to rely on the advise, and authority of others. For all men whom the truth concernes, if they rely not on their own, must rely on the opinion of some other, whom they think wiser than themselves, and see not why he should deceive them.

Ignorance of the signification of words; which is, want of [50] understanding, disposeth men to take on trust, not onely the truth they know not; but also the errors; and which is more, the non-sense of them they trust: For neither Error, nor non-sense, can without a perfect understanding of words, be detected.

From the same it proceedeth, that men give different names, to one and the same thing, from the difference of their own passions: As they that approve a private opinion, call it Opinion; but they that mislike it, Hæresie: and yet hæresie signifies no more than private opinion; but has onely a greater tincture of choler.

From the same also it proceedeth, that men cannot distinguish, without study and great understanding, between one action of many men, and many actions of one multitude; as for example, between the one action of all the Senators of *Rome* in killing *Catiline,* and the many actions of a number of Senators in killing *Cæsar*; and therefore are disposed to take for the action of the people, that which is a multitude of actions done by a multitude of men, led perhaps by the perswasion of one.

Ignorance of the causes, and originall constitution of Right, Equity, Law, and Justice, disposeth a man to make Custome and Example the rule of his actions; in such manner, as to think that Unjust which it hath been the custome to punish; and that Just, of the impunity and approbation whereof they can produce an Example, or (as the Lawyers which onely use this false measure of Justice barbarously call it) a Precedent; like little children, that have no other rule of good and evill manners, but the correction they receive from their Parents, and Masters; save that children are constant to their rule, whereas men are not so; because grown strong, and stubborn, they appeale from custome to reason, and from reason to custome, as it serves their turn; receding from custome when their interest requires it, and setting themselves against treason, as oft as reason is against them: Which is the cause, that the doctrine of Right and Wrong, is perpetually disputed, both by the Pen and the Sword: Whereas the doctrine of Lines, and Figures, is not so; because men care not, in that subject what be truth, as a thing that crosses no mans ambition, profit, or lust. For I doubt not, but if it had been a thing contrary to any mans right of dominion, or to the interest of men that have dominion, *That the three Angles of a Triangle, should be equall to two Angles of a Square;* that doctrine should have been, if not disputed, yet by the burning of all books of Geometry, suppressed, as farre as he whom it concerned was able.

Ignorance of remote causes, disposeth men to attribute all events, to the causes immediate, and Instrumentall: For these are all the causes they perceive. And hence it comes to passe, that in all places, men that are grieved with payments to the Publique, discharge their anger upon the Publicans, that is to say, Farmers, Collectors, and other Officers of the publique Revenue; and adhære to such as find fault with the publike Government; and thereby, when they have engaged themselves beyond hope of justification, fall also upon the Supreme Authority, for feare [51] of punishment, or shame of receiving pardon.

Ignorance of naturall causes disposeth a man to Credulity, so as to believe many times impossibilities: For such know nothing to the contrary, but that they may be true; being unable to detect the Impossibility. And Credulity, because men love to be hearkened unto in company, disposeth them to lying: so that Ignorance it selfe without Malice, is able to make a man both to believe lyes, and tell them; and sometimes also to invent them.

Anxiety for the future time, disposeth men to enquire into the causes of things: because the knowledge of them, maketh men the better able to order the present to their best advantage.

Curiosity, or love of the knowledge of causes, draws a man from consideration of the effect, to seek the cause; and again, the cause of that cause; till of necessity he must come to this thought at last, that there is some cause, whereof there is no former cause, but is eternall; which is it men call God. So that it is impossible to make any profound enquiry into naturall causes, without being enclined thereby to believe there is one God Eternall; though they cannot have any Idea of him in their mind, answerable to his nature. For as a man that is born blind, hearing men talk of warming themselves by the fire, and being brought to warm himself by the same, may easily conceive, and assure himselfe, there is somewhat there, which men call *Fire,* and is the cause of the heat he feeles; but cannot imagine what it is like; nor have an Idea of it in his mind, such as they have that see it: so also, by the visible things of this world, and their admirable order, a man may conceive there is a cause of them, which men call God; and yet not have an Idea, or Image of him in his mind.

And they that make little, or no enquiry into the naturall causes of things, yet from the feare that proceeds from the ignorance it selfe, of

what it is that hath the power to do them much good or harm, are enclined
to suppose, and feign unto themselves, severall kinds of Powers Invisible;
and to stand in awe of their own imaginations; and in time of distress to
invoke them; as also in the time of an expected good successe, to give
them thanks; making the creatures of their own fancy, their Gods. By
which means it hath come to passe, that from the innumerable variety of
Fancy, men have created in the world innumerable sorts of Gods. And
this Feare of things invisible, is the naturall Seed of that, which every one
in himself calleth Religion; and in them that worship, or feare that Power
otherwise than they do, Superstition.

And this seed of Religion, having been observed by many; some of those
that have observed it, have been enclined thereby to nourish, dresse, and
forme it into Lawes; and to adde to it of their own invention, any opinion
of the causes of future events, by which they thought they should best
be able to govern others, and make unto themselves the greatest use of
their Powers.

CHAP. XII.   OF RELIGION   [52]

Seeing there are no signes, nor fruit of *Religion*, but in Man onely;
there is no cause to doubt, but that the seed of *Religion*, is also onely in
Man; and consisteth in some peculiar quality, or at least in some eminent
degree thereof, not to be found in other Living creatures.

And first, it is peculiar to the nature of Man, to be inquisitive into the
Causes of the Events they see, some more, some lesse; but all men so
much, as to be curious in the search of the causes of their own good and
evill fortune.

Secondly, upon the sight of any thing that hath a Beginning, to think
also it had a cause, which determined the same to begin, then when it did,
rather than sooner or later.

Thirdly, whereas there is no other Felicity of Beasts, but the enjoying
of their quotidian Food, Ease, and Lusts; as having little, or no foresight
of the time to come, for want of observation, and memory of the order,
consequence, and dependance of the things they see; Man observeth how
one Event hath been produced by another; and remembreth in them
Antecedence and Consequence; And when he cannot assure himselfe of
the true causes of things, (for the causes of good and evill fortune for the
most part are invisible,) he supposes causes of them, either such as his
own fancy suggesteth; or trusteth to the Authority of other men, such as
he thinks to be his friends, and wiser than himselfe.

The two first, make Anxiety. For being assured that there be causes of
all things that have arrived hitherto, or shall arrive hereafter; it is impossible for a man, who continually endeavoureth to secure himselfe
against the evill he feares, and procure the good he desireth, not to be in
a perpetuall solicitude of the time to come; So that every man, especially
those that are over provident, are in an estate like to that of *Prometheus*.
For as *Prometheus*, (which interpreted, is, *The Prudent man*,) was bound

to the hill *Caucasus,* a place of large prospect, where, an Eagle feeding on his liver, devoured in the day, as much as was repayred in the night: So that man, which looks too far before him, in the care of future time, hath his heart all the day long, gnawed on by feare of death, poverty, or other calamity; and has no repose, nor pause of his anxiety, but in sleep.

This perpetuall feare, alwayes accompanying mankind in the ignorance of causes, as it were in the Dark, must needs have for object something. And therefore when there is nothing to be seen, there is nothing to accuse, either of their good, or evill fortune, but some *Power,* or Agent *Invisible*: In which sense perhaps it was, that some of the old Poets said, that the Gods were at first created by humane Feare: which spoken of the [53] Gods, (that is to say, of the many Gods of the Gentiles) is very true. But the acknowledging of one God Eternall, Infinite, and Omnipotent, may more easily be derived, from the desire men have to know the causes of naturall bodies, and their severall vertues, and operations; then from the feare of what was to befall them in time to come. For he that from any effect hee seeth come to passe, should reason to the next and immediate cause thereof, and from thence to the cause of that cause, and plonge himselfe profoundly in the pursuit of causes; shall at last come to this, that there must be (as even the Heathen Philosophers confessed) one First Mover; that is, a First, and an Eternall cause of all things; which is that which men mean by the name of God: and all this without thought of their fortune; the solicitude whereof, both enclines to fear, and hinders them from the search of the causes of other things; and thereby gives occasion of feigning of as many Gods, as there be men that feigne them.

And for the matter, or substance of the Invisible Agents, so fancyed; they could not by naturall cogitation, fall upon any other conceipt, but that it was the same with that of the Soule of man; and that the Soule of man, was of the same substance, with that which appeareth in a Dream, to one that sleepeth; or in a Looking-glasse, to one that is awake; which, men not knowing that such apparitions are nothing else but creatures of the Fancy, thing to be reall, and externall Substances; and therefore call them Ghosts; as the Latines called them *Imagines,* and *Urbræ;* and thought them Spirits, that is, thin aëreall bodies; and those Invisible Agents, which they feared, to bee like them; save that they appear, and vanish when they please. But the opinion that such Spirits were Incorporeall, or Immateriall, could never enter into the mind of any man by nature; because, though men may put together words of contradictory signification, as *Spirit,* and *Incorporeall;* yet they can never have the imagination of any thing answering to them: And therefore, men that by their own meditation, arrive to the acknowledgement of one Infinite, Omnipotent, and Eternall God, choose rather to confesse he is Incomprehensible, and above their understanding; than to define his Nature by *Spirit Incorporeall,* and then confesse their definition to be unintelligible: or if they give him such a title, it is not *Dogmatically,* with intention to make the Divine Nature understood; but *Piously,* to honour him with attributes, of significations, as remote as they can from the grossenesse of Bodies Visible.

Then, for the way by which they think these Invisible Agents wrought their effects; that is to say, what immediate causes they used, in bringing things to passe, men that know not what it is that we call *causing,* (that is, almost all men) have no other rule to guesse by, but by observing, and remembering what they have seen to precede the like effect at some other time, or times before, without seeing between the antecedent and subsequent Event, any dependance or connexion at all: And therefore from the like things past, they expect the like things to come; and hope for good or evill luck, superstitiously, from things that have no part at all in   [54] the causing of it: As the Athenians did for their war at *Lepanto,* demand another *Phormio;* The Pompeian faction for their warre in *Afrique,* another *Scipio;* and others have done in divers other occasions since. In like manner they attribute their fortune to a stander by, to a lucky or unlucky place, to words spoken, especially if the name of God be amongst them; as Charming, and Conjuring (the Leiturgy of Witches;) insomuch as to believe, they have power to turn a stone into bread, bread into a man, or any thing, into any thing.

Thirdly, for the worship which naturally men exhibite to Powers invisible, it can be no other, but such expressions of their reverence, as they would use towards men; Gifts, Petitions, Thanks, Submission of Body, Considerate Addresses, sober Behaviour, premeditated Words, Swearing (that is, assuring one another of their promises,) by invoking them. Beyond that reason suggesteth nothing; but leaves them either to rest there; or for further ceremonies, to rely on those they believe to be wiser than themselves.

Lastly, concerning how these Invisible Powers declare to men the things which shall hereafter come to passe, especially concerning their good or evill fortune in generall, or good or ill successe in any particular undertaking, men are naturally at a stand; save that using to conjecture of the time to come, by the time past, they are very apt, not onely to take casuall things, after one or two encounters, for Prognostiques of the like encounter ever after, but also to believe the like Prognostiques from other men, of whom they have once conceived a good opinion.

And in these foure things, Opinion of Ghosts, Ignorance of second causes, Devotion towards what men fear, and Taking of things Casuall for Prognostiques, consisteth the Naturall seed of *Religion;* which by reason of the different Fancies, Judgements, and Passions of severall men, hath grown up into ceremonies so different, that those which are used by one man, are for the most part ridiculous to another.

. . .

CHAP. XIII.   OF THE NATURALL CONDITION OF MANKIND, AS CONCERNING THEIR FELICITY, AND MISERY

Nature hath made men so equall, in the faculties of body, and mind; as that though there bee found one man sometimes manifestly stronger in body, or of quicker mind then another; yet when all is reckoned together, the difference between man, and man, is not so considerable, as that one man can thereupon claim to himselfe any benefit, to which another may not pretend, as well as he. For as to the strength of body, the weakest has strength enough to kill the strongest, either by secret machination, or by confederacy with others, that are in the same danger with himselfe.

And as to the faculties of the mind, (setting aside the arts grounded upon words, and especially that skill of proceeding upon generall, and infallible rules, called Science; which very few have, and but in few things; as being not a native faculty, born with us; nor attained, (as Prudence,) while we look after somewhat els,) I find yet a greater equality amongst men, than that of strength. For Prudence, is but Experience; which equall time, equally bestowes on all men, in those things [61] they equally apply themselves unto. That which may perhaps make such equality incredible, is but a vain conceipt of ones owne wisdome, which almost all men think they have in a greater degree, than the Vulgar; that is, than all men but themselves, and a few others, whom by Fame, or for concurring with themselves, they approve. For such is the nature of men, that howsoever they may acknowledge many others to be more witty, or more eloquent, or more learned; Yet they will hardly believe there be many so wise as themselves: For they see their own wit at hand, and other mens at a distance. But this proveth rather that men are in that point equall, than unequall. For there is not ordinarily a greater signe of the equall distribution of any thing, than that every man is contented with his share.

From this equality of ability, ariseth equality of hope in the attaining of our Ends. And therefore if any two men desire the same thing, which neverthelesse they cannot both enjoy, they become enemies; and in the way to their End, (which is principally their owne conservation, and sometimes their delectation only,) endeavour to destroy, or subdue one an other. And from hence it comes to passe, that where an Invader hath no more to feare, than an other mans single power; if one plant, sow, build, or possesse a convenient Seat, others may probably be expected to come prepared with forces united, to dispossesse, and deprive him, not only of the fruit of his labour, but also of his life, or liberty. And the Invader again is in the like danger of another.

And from this diffidence of one another, there is no way for an man to secure himselfe, so reasonable, as Anticipation; that is, by force, or wiles, to master the persons of all men he can, so long, till he see no other power great enough to endanger him: And this is no more than his own conservation requireth, and is generally allowed. Also because there be some, that taking pleasure in contemplating their own power in the acts of conquest, which they pursue farther than their security requires; if others, that otherwise would be glad to be at ease within modest bounds, should not by invasion increase their power, they would not be able, long time, by standing only on their defence, to subsist. And by con-

sequence, such augmentation of dominion over men, being necessary to
a mans conservation, it ought to be allowed him.

Againe, men have no pleasure, (but on the contrary a great deale of
griefe) in keeping company, where there is no power able to over-awe
them all. For every man looketh that his companion should value him,
at the same rate he sets upon himselfe: And upon all signes of contempt,
or undervaluing, naturally endeavours, as far as he dares (which amongst
them that have no common power to keep them in quiet, is far enough to
make them destroy each other,) to extort a greater value from his con-
temners, by dommage; and from others, by the example.

So that in the nature of man, we find three principall causes of quar-
rell. First, Competition; Secondly, Diffidence; Thirdly, Glory.

The first, maketh men invade for Gain; the second, for Safety; [62]
and the third, for Reputation. The first use Violence, to make themselves
Masters of other mens persons, wives, children, and cattell; the second,
to defend them; the third, for trifles, as a word, a smile, a different opinion, and any other signe of undervalue, either direct in their Persons, or
by reflexion in their Kindred, their Friends, their Nation, their Profession,
or their Name.

Hereby it is manifest, that during the time men live without a common
Power to keep them all in awe, they are in that condition which is called
Warre; and such a warre, as is of every man, against every man. For
Warre, consisteth not in Battell onely, or the act of fighting; but in a
tract of time, wherein the Will to contend by Battell is sufficiently known:
and therefore the notion of *Time*, is to be considered in the nature of
Warre; as it is in the nature of Weather. For as the nature of Foule
weather, lyeth not in a showre or two of rain; but in an inclination thereto
of many dayes together: So the nature of War, consisteth not in actuall
fighting; but in the known disposition thereto, during all the time there is
is no assurance to the contrary. All other time is Peace.

Whatsoever therefore is consequent to a time of Warre, where every
man is Enemy to every man; the same is consequent to the time, wherein
men live without other security, than what their own strength, and their
own invention shall furnish them withall. In such condition, there is no
place for Industry; because the fruit thereof is uncertain: and consequently no Culture of the Earth; no Navigation, nor use of the commodities that may be imported by Sea; no commodious Building; no
Instruments of moving, and removing such things as require much force;
no Knowledge of the face of the Earth; no account of Time; no Arts; no
Letters; no Society; and which is worst of all, continuall feare, and danger
of violent death; And the life of man, solitary, poore, nasty, brutish, and
short.

It may seem strange to some man, that has not well weighed these
things; that Nature should thus dissociate, and render men apt to invade, and destroy one another: and he may therefore, not trusting to
this Inference, made from the Passions, desire perhaps to have the same
confirmed by Experience. Let him therefore consider with himselfe,

Read

when taking a journey, he armes himselfe, and seeks to go well accompanied; when going to sleep, he locks his dores; when even in his house he locks his chests; and this when he knowes there bee Lawes, and publike Officers, armed, to revenge all injuries shall bee done him; what opinion he has of his fellow subjects, when he rides armed; of his fellow Citizens, when he locks his dores; and of his children, and servants, when he locks his chests. Does he not there as much accuse mankind by his actions, as I do by my words? But neither of us accuse mans nature in it. The Desires, and other Passions of man, are in themselves no Sin. No more are the Actions, that proceed from those Passions, till they know a Law that forbids them: which till Lawes be made they cannot know: nor can any Law be made, till they have agreed upon the Person that shall make it.

It may peradventure be thought, there was never such a time, [63] nor condition of warre as this; and I believe it was never generally so, over all the world: but there are many places, where they live so now. For the savage people in many places of *America*, except the government of small Families, the concord whereof dependeth on naturall lust, have no government at all; and live at this day in that brutish manner, as I said before. Howsoever, it may be perceived what manner of life there would be, where there were no common Power to feare; by the manner of life, which men that have formerly lived under a peacefull government, use to degenerate into, in a civill Warre.

But though there had never been any time, wherein particular men were in a condition of warre one against another; yet in all times, Kings, and Persons of Soveraigne authority, because of their Independency, are in continuall jealousies, and in the state and posture of Gladiators; having their weapons pointing, and their eyes fixed on one another; that is, their Forts, Garrisons, and Guns upon the Frontiers of their Kingdomes; and continuall Spyes upon their neighbours; which is a posture of War. But because they uphold thereby, the Industry of their Subjects; there does not follow from it, that misery, which accompanies the Liberty of particular men.

To this warre of every man against every man, this also is consequent; that nothing can be Unjust. The notions of Right and Wrong, Justice and Injustice have there no place. Where there is no common Power, there is no Law: where no Law, no Injustice. Force, and Fraud, are in warre the two Cardinall vertues. Justice, and Injustice are none of the Faculties neither of the Body, nor Mind. If they were, they might be in a man that were alone in the world, as well as his Senses, and Passions. They are Qualities, that relate to men in Society, not in Solitude. It is consequent also to the same condition, that there be no Propriety, no Dominion, no *Mine* and *Thine* distinct; but onely that to be every mans, that he can get; and for so long, as he can keep it. And thus much for the ill condition, which man by meer Nature is actually placed in; though with a possibility to come out of it, consisting partly in the Passions, partly in his Reason.

The Passions that encline men to Peace, are Feare of Death; Desire of such things as are necessary to commodious living; and a Hope by their Industry to obtain them. And Reason suggesteth convenient Articles of Peace, upon which men may be drawn to agreement. These Articles, are they, which otherwise are called the Lawes of Nature: whereof I shall speak more particularly, in the two following Chapters.

CHAP. XIV.   OF THE FIRST AND SECOND NATURALL LAWES,   [64]
AND OF CONTRACTS

THE RIGHT OF NATURE, which Writers commonly call *Jus Naturale*, is the Liberty each man hath, to use his own power, as he will himselfe, for the preservation of his own Nature; that is to say, of his own Life; and consequently, of doing any thing, which in his own Judgement, and Reason, hee shall conceive to be the aptest means thereunto.

By LIBERTY, is understood, according to the proper signification of the word, the absence of externall Impediments: which Impediments, may oft take away part of a mans power to do what hee would; but cannot hinder him from using the power left him, according as his judgement, and reason shall dictate to him.

A LAW OF NATURE, (*Lex Naturalis,*) is a Precept, or generall Rule, found out by Reason, by which a man is forbidden to do, that, which is destructive of his life, or taketh away the means of preserving the same; and to omit, that, by which he thinketh it may be best preserved. For though they that speak of this subject, use to confound *Jus,* and *Lex, Right* and *Law;* yet they ought to be distinguished; because Right, consisteth in liberty to do, or to forbeare; Whereas Law, determineth, and bindeth to one of them: so that Law, and Right, differ as much, as Obligation, and Liberty; which in one and the same matter are inconsistent.

And because the condition of Man, (as hath been declared in the precedent Chapter) is a condition of Warre of every one against every one; in which case every one is governed by his own Reason; and there is nothing he can make use of, that may not be a help unto him, in preserving his life against his enemies; It followeth, that in such a condition, every man has a Right to every thing; even to one anothers body. And therefore, as long as this naturall Right of every man to every thing endureth, there can be no security to any man, (how strong or wise soever he be,) of living out the time, which Nature ordinarily alloweth men to live. And consequently it is a precept, or generall rule of Reason, *That every man, ought to endeavour Peace, as farre as he has hope of obtaining it; and when he cannot obtain it, that he may seek, and use, all helps, and advantages of Warre.* The first branch of which Rule, containeth the first, and Fundamentall Law of Nature; which is, *to seek Peace, and follow it.* The Second, the summe of the Right of Nature; which is, *By all means we can, to defend our selves.*

From this Fundamentall Law of Nature, by which men are commanded to endeavour Peace, is derived this second law; *That a man be*

willing, when others are so too, as farre-forth, as for Peace, and de- [65]
fence of himselfe he shall think it necessary, to lay down this right to all
things; and be contented with so much liberty against other men, as he
would allow other men against himselfe. For as long as every man
holdeth this Right, of doing any thing he liketh; so long are all men in
the condition of Warre. But if other men will not lay down their Right,
as well as he; then there is no Reason for any one, to devest himselfe of
his: For that were to expose himselfe to Prey, (which no man is bound
to) rather than to dispose himselfe to Peace. This is that Law of the
Gospell; *Whatsoever you require that others should do to you, that do ye
o them.* And that Law of all men, *Quod tibi fieri non vis, alteri ne
feceris.*

To *lay downe* a mans *Right* to any thing, is to *devest* himselfe of the
Liberty, of hindring another of the benefit of his own Right to the same.
For he that renounceth, or passeth away his Right, giveth not to any
other man a Right which he had not before; because there is nothing to
which every man had not Right by Nature: but onely standeth out of
his way, that he may enjoy his own originall Right, without hindrance
from him; not without hindrance from another. So that the effect which
redoundeth to one man, by another mans defect of Right, is but so much
diminution of impediments to the use of his own Right originall.

Right is layd aside, either by simply Renouncing it; or by Transferring
it to another. By *Simply* RENOUNCING; when he cares not to whom the
benefit thereof redoundeth. By TRANSFERRING; when he intendeth the
benefit thereof to some certain person, or persons. And when a man hath
in either manner abandoned, or granted away his Right; then is he said
to be OBLIGED, or BOUND, not to hinder those, to whom such Right is
granted, or abandoned, from the benefit of it: and that he *Ought*, and
it is his DUTY, not to make voyd that voluntary act of his own: and that
such hindrance is INJUSTICE, and INJURY, as being *Sine Jure;* the Right
being before renounced, or transferred. So that *Injury*, or *Injustice*, in the
controversies of the world, is somewhat like to that, which in the disputations of Scholers is called *Absurdity.* For as it is there called an
Absurdity, to contradict what one maintained in the Beginning: so in
the world, it is called Injustice, and Injury, voluntarily to undo that,
which from the beginning he had voluntarily done. The way by which
a man either simply Renounceth, or Transferreth his Right, is a Declaration or Signification, by some voluntary and sufficient signe, or signes,
that he doth so Renounce, or Transferre; or hath so Renounced, or
Transferred the same, to him that accepteth it. And these Signes are
either Words onely, or Actions onely; or (as it happeneth most often)
both Words, and Actions. And the same are the BONDS, by which men
are bound, and obliged: Bonds, that have their strength, not from their
own Nature, (for nothing is more easily broken then a mans word,) but
from Feare of some evill consequence upon the rupture.

Whensoever a man Transferreth his Right, or Renounceth it; it is
either in consideration of some Right reciprocally transferred to himselfe;

or for some other good he hopeth for thereby. For it is a voluntary   [66]
act: and of the voluntary acts of every man, the object is some *Good to himselfe*. And therefore there be some Rights, which no man can be understood by any words, or other signes, to have abandoned, or transferred. As first a man cannot lay down the right of resisting them, that assault him by force, to take away his life; because he cannot be understood to ayme thereby, at any Good to himselfe. The same may be sayd of Wounds, and Chayns, and Imprisonment; both because there is no benefit consequent to such patience; as there is to the patience of suffering another to be wounded, or imprisoned: as also because a man cannot tell, when he seeth men proceed against him by violence, whether they intend his death or not. And lastly the motive, and end for which this renouncing, and transferring of Right is introduced, is nothing else but the security of a mans person, in his life, and in the means of so preserving life, as not to be weary of it. And therefore if a man by words, or other signes, seem to despoyle himselfe of the End, or which those signes were intended; he is not to be understood as if he meant it, or that it was his will; but that he was ignorant of how such words and actions were to be interpreted.

Te mutuall transferring of Right, is that which men call CONTRACT.

.   .   .

CHAP. XV.   OF OTHER LAWES OF NATURE

From the law of Nature, by which we are obliged to transferre to another, such Rights, as being retained, hinder the peace of Mankind, there followeth a Third; which is this, *That men performe their Covenants made*: without which, Covenants are in vain, and but Empty words; and the Right of all men to all things remaining, wee are still in the condition of Warre.

And in this law of Nature, consisteth the Fountain and Originall of JUSTICE. For where no Covenant hath preceded, there hath no Right been transferred, and every man has right to every thing; and consequently, no action can be Unjust. But when a Covenant is made, then to break it is *Unjust:* And the definition of INIUSTICE, is no other than *the not Performance of Covenant.* And whatsoever is not Unjust, is *Just.*

But because Covenants of mutuall trust, where there is a feare of not performance on either part, (as hath been said in the former Chapter,) are invalid; though the Originall of Justice be the making of Covenants; yet Injustice actually there can be none, till the cause of such feare be taken away; which while men are in the naturall condition of Warre, cannot be done. Therefore before the names of Just, and Unjust can have place, there must be some coërcive Power, to compell men equally to the performance of their Covenants, by the terrour of some punishment, greater than the benefit they expect by the breach of   [72] their Covenant; and to make good that Propriety, which by mutuall Contract men acquire, in recompence of the universall Right they abandon: and such power there is none before the erection of a Common-wealth. And this is also to be gathered out of the ordinary definition of Justice in the Schooles: For they say, that *Justice is the constant Will of giving to every man his own.* And therefore where there is no *Own*, that is, no Propriety, there is no Injustice; and where there is no coërcive Power erected, that is, where there is no Common-wealth, there is no Propriety; all men having Right to all things: Therefore where there is no Common-wealth, there nothing is Unjust. So that the nature of Justice, consisteth in keeping of valid Covenants: but the Validity of Covenants begins not but with the Constitution of a Civill Power, sufficient to com-pell men to keep them: And then it is also that Propriety begins.

The Foole hath sayd in his heart, there is no such thing as Justice; and sometimes also with his tongue; seriously alleaging, that every mans conservation, and contentment, being committed to his own care, there could be no reason, why every man might not do what he thought con-duced thereunto: and therefore also to make, or not make; keep, or not keep Covenants, was not against Reason, when it conduced to ones benefit. He does not therein deny, that there be Covenants; and that they are sometimes broken, sometimes kept; and that such breach of them may be called Injustice, and the observance of them Justice: but he questioneth, whether Injustice, taking away the feare of God, (for the same Foole hath said in his heart there is no God,) may not sometimes stand with that Reason, which dictateth to every man his own good; and particularly then, when it conduceth to such a benefit, as shall put a man in a condition, to neglect not onely the dispraise, and revilings, but also the power of other men. The Kingdome of God is gotten by violence: but what if it could be gotten by unjust violence? were it against Reason so to get it, when it is impossible to receive hurt by it? and if it be not against Reason, it is not against Justice: or else Justice is not to be approved for good. From such reasoning as this, Successfull wickednesse hath obtained the name of Vertue: and some that in all other things have disallowed the violation of Faith; yet have allowed it, when it is for the getting of a Kingdome. And the Heathen that believed, that *Saturn* was deposed by his son *Jupiter,* believed neverthelesse the same *Jupiter* to be the avenger of Injustice: Somewhat like to a piece of Law in *Cokes* Commentaries on *Litleton;* where he sayes, If the right Heire of the Crown be attainted of Treason; yet the Crown shall descend to him, and *eo instante* the Atteyn-der be voyd: From which instances a man will be very prone to inferre; that when the Heire apparent of a Kingdome, shall kill him that is in possession, though his father; you may call it Injustice, or by what other name you will; yet it can never be against Reason, seeing all the voluntary actions of men tend to the benefit of themselves; and those actions are most Reasonable, that conduce most to their ends. This specious [73] reasoning is neverthelesse false.

For the question is not of promises mutuall, where there is no security of performance on either side; as when there is no Civill Power erected over the parties promising; for such promises are no Covenants: But either where one of the parties has performed already; or where there is a Power to make him performe; there is the question whether it be against reason, that is, against the benefit of the other to performe, or not. And I say it is not against reason. For the manifestation whereof, we are to consider; First, that when a man doth a thing, which notwithstanding any thing can be foreseen, and reckoned on, tendeth to his own destruction, howsoever some accident which he could not expect, arriving may turne it to his benefit; yet such events do not make it reasonably or wisely done. Secondly, that in a condition of Warre, wherein every man to every man, for want of a common Power to keep them all in awe, is an Enemy, there is no man can hope by his own strength, or wit, to defend himselfe from destruction, without the help of Confederates; where every one expects the same defence by the Confederation, that any one else does: and therefore he which declares he thinks it reason to deceive those that help him, can in reason expect no other means of safety, than what can be had from his own single Power. He therefore that breaketh his Covenant, and consequently declareth that he thinks he may with reason do so, cannot be received into any Society, that unite themselves for Peace and Defence, but by the errour of them that receive him; nor when he is received, be retayned in it, without seeing the danger of their errour; which errours a man cannot reasonably reckon upon as the means of his security: and therefore if he be left, or cast out of Society, he perisheth; and if he live in Society, it is by the errours of other men, which he could not foresee, nor reckon upon; and consequently against the reason of his preservation; and so, as all men that contribute not to his destruction, forbear him only out of ignorance of what is good for themselves.

As for the Instance of gaining the secure and perpetual felicity of Heaven, by any way; it is frivolous: there being but one way imaginable; and that is not breaking, but keeping of Covenant.

And for the other Instance of attaining Soveraignty by Rebellion; it is manifest, that though the event follow, yet because it cannot reasonably be expected, but rather the contrary; and because by gaining it so, others are taught to gain the same in like manner, the attempt thereof is against reason. Justice therefore, that is to say, Keeping of Covenant, is a Rule of Reason, by which we are forbidden to do any thing destructive to our life; and consequently a Law of Nature.

There be some that proceed further; and will not have the Law of Nature, to be those Rules which conduce to the preservation of mans life on earth; but to the attaining of an eternall felicity after death; to which they think the breach of Covenant may conduce; and consequently be just and reasonable; (such are they that think it a work of merit to   [74] kill, or depose, or rebell against, the Soveraigne Power constituted over them by their own consent.) But because there is no naturall knowledge of mans estate after death; much lesse of the reward that is then to be given to breach of Faith; but onely a beliefe grounded upon other mens saying, that they know it supernaturally, or that they know those, that knew them, that knew others, that knew it supernaturally; Breach of Faith cannot be called a Precept of Reason, or Nature.

Others, that allow for a Law of Nature, the keeping of Faith, do neverthelesse make exception of certain persons; as Heretiques, and such as use not to performe their Covenant to others: And this also is against reason. For if any fault of a man, be sufficient to discharge our Covenant made; the same ought in reason to have been sufficient to have hindred the making of it.

The names of Just, and Injust, when they are attributed to Men, signifie one thing; and when they are attributed to Actions, another. When they are attributed to Men, they signifie Conformity, or Inconformity of Manners, to Reason. But when they are attributed to Actions, they signifie the Conformity or Inconformity to Reason, not of Manners, or manner of life, but of particular Actions. A Just man therefore, is he that taketh all the care he can, that his Actions may be all Just: and an Unjust man, is he that neglecteth it. And such men are more often in our Language stiled by the names of Righteous, and Unrighteous; then Just, and Unjust; though the meaning be the same. Therefore a Righteous man, does not lose that Title, by one, or a few unjust Actions, that proceed from sudden Passion, or mistake of Things, or Persons: nor does an Unrighteous man, lose his character, for such Actions, as he does, or forbeares to do, for feare: because his Will is not framed by the Justice, but by the apparent benefit of what he is to do. That which gives to humane Actions the relish of Justice, is a certain Noblenesse or Gallantnesse of courage, (rarely found,) by which a man scorns to be beholding for the contentment of his life, to fraud, or breach of promise. This Justice of the Manners, is that which is meant, where Justice is called a Vertue; and Injustice a Vice.

But the Justice of Actions denominates men, not Just, *Guiltlesse:* and the Injustice of the same, (which is also called Injury,) gives them but the name of *Guilty.*

Again, the Injustice of Manners, is the disposition, or aptitude to do Injurie; and is Injustice before it proceed to Act; and without supposing any individuall person injured. But the Injustice of an Action, (that is to say Injury,) supposeth an individuall person Injured; namely him, to whom the Covenant was made: And therefore many times the injury is received by one man, when the dammage redoundeth to another. As when the Master commandeth his servant to give mony to a stranger; if it be not done, the Injury is done to the Master, whom he had before Covenanted to obey; but the dammage redoundeth to the stranger, to whom he had no Obligation; and therefore could not Injure him. And so also in Common-wealths, private men may remit to one another [75] their debts; but not robberies or other violences, whereby they are endamaged; because the detaining of Debt, is an Injury to themselves; but Robbery and Violence, are Injuries to the Person of the Common-wealth.

Whatsoever is done to a man, conformable to his own Will signified to the doer, is no Injury to him. For if he that doeth it, hath not passed away his originall right to do what he please, by some Antecedent Covenant, there is no breach of Covenant; and therefore no Injury done him. And if he have; then his Will to have it done being signified, is a release of that Covenant: and so again there is no Injury done him.

Justice of Actions, is by Writers divided into *Commutative, and Distributive:* and the former they say consisteth in proportion Arithmeticall; the later in proportion Geometricall. Commutative therefore, they place in the equality of value of the things contracted for; And Distributive, in the distribution of equall benefit, to men of equall merit. As if it were Injustice to sell dearer than we buy; or to give more to a man than he merits. The value of all things contracted for, is measured by the Appetite of the Contractors: and therefore the just value, is that which they be contented to give. And Merit (besides that which is by Covenant, where the performance on one part, meriteth the performance of the other part, and falls under Justice Commutative, not Distributive,) is not due by Justice; but is rewarded of Grace onely. And therefore this distinction, in the sense wherein it useth to be expounded, is not right. To speak properly, Commutative Justice, is the Justice of a Contractor; that is, a Performance of Covenant, in Buying, and Selling; Hiring, and Letting to Hire; Lending, and Borrowing; Exchanging, Bartering, and other acts of Contract.

And Distributive Justice, the Justice of an Arbitrator; that is to say, the act of defining what is Just. Wherein, (being trusted by them that make him Arbitrator,) if he performe his Trust, he is said to distribute to every man his own: and this is indeed Just Distribution, and may be called (though improperly) Distributive Justice; but more properly Equity; which also is a Law of Nature, as shall be shewn in due place.

As Justice dependeth on Antecedent Covenant; so does Gratitude depend on Antecedent Grace; that is to say, Antecedent Free-gift: and is the fourth Law of Nature; which may be conceived in this Forme, *That a man which receiveth Benefit from another of meer Grace, Endeavour that he which giveth it, have no reasonable cause to repent him of his good will.* For no man giveth, but with intention of Good to himselfe; because Gift is Voluntary; and of all Voluntary Acts, the Object is to every man his own Good; of which if men see they shall be frustrated, there will be no beginning of benevolence, or trust; nor consequently of mutuall help; nor of reconciliation of one man to another; and therefore they are to remain still in the condition of *War;* which is contrary to the first and Fundamentall Law of Nature, which commandeth men to *Seek Peace.* The breach of this Law, is called *Ingratitude;* and hath the   [76] same relation to Grace, that Injustice hath to Obligation by Covenant.

A fifth Law of Nature, is Compleasance; that is to say, *That every man strive to accommodate himselfe to the rest.* For the understanding whereof, we may consider, that there is in mens aptnesse to Society, a diversity of Nature, rising from their diversity of Affections; not unlike to that we see in stones brought together for building of an Ædifice. For as that stone which by the asperity, and irregularity of Figure, takes more room from others, than it selfe fills; and for the hardnesse, cannot be easily made plain, and thereby hindereth the building, is by the builders cast away as unprofitable, and troublesome: so also, a man that by asperity of Nature, will strive to retain those things which to himselfe are superfluous, and to others necessary; and for the stubbornness of his Passions, cannot be corrected, is to be left, or cast out of Society, as combersome thereunto. For seeing every man, not onely by Right, but also by necessity of Nature, is supposed to endeavour all he can, to obtain that which is necessary for his conservation; He that shall oppose himselfe against it, for things superfluous, is guilty of the warre that thereupon is to follow; and therefore doth that, which is contrary to the fundamentall Law of Nature, which commandeth *to seek Peace*. The observers of this Law, may be called Sociable, (the Latines call them *Commodi;*) The contrary, *Stubborn, Insociable, Froward, Intractable.*

A sixth Law of Nature, is this, *That upon caution of the Future time, a man ought to pardon the offences past of them that repenting, desire it.* For Pardon, is nothing but granting of Peace; which though granted to them that persevere in their hostility, be not Peace, but Feare; yet not granted to them that give caution of the Future time, is signe of an aversion to Peace; and therefore contrary to the Law of Nature.

A seventh is, *That in Revenges,* (that is, retribution of Evil for Evil,) *Men look not at the greatnesse of the evill past, but the greatnesse of the good to follow.* Whereby we are forbidden to inflict punishment with any other designe, than for correction of the offender, or direction of others. For this Law is consequent to the next before it, that commandeth Pardon, upon security of the Future time. Besides, Revenge without respect to the Example, and profit to come, is a triumph, or glorying in the hurt of another, tending to no end; (for the End is alwayes somewhat to Come;) and glorying to no end, is vain-glory, and contrary to reason; and to hurt without reason, tendeth to the introduction of Warre; which is against the Law of Nature; and is commonly stiled by the name of *Cruelty.*

. . .

Part II. Of common-wealth [85]

CHAP. XVII.   OF THE CAUSES, GENERATION, AND DEFINITION OF A COMMON-WEALTH

The finall Cause, End, or Designe of men (who naturally love Liberty, and Dominion over others,) in the introduction of that restraint upon themselves, (in which wee see them live in Common-wealths,) is the foresight of their own preservation, and of a more contented life thereby; that is to say, of getting themselves out from that miserable condition of Warre, which is necessarily consequent (as hath been shewn) to the naturall Passions of men, when there is no visible Power to keep them in awe, and tye them by feare of punishment to the performance of their Covenants, and observation of those Lawes of Nature set down in the fourteenth and fifteenth Chapters.

For the Lawes of Nature (as *Justice, Equity, Modesty, Mercy,* and (in summe) *doing to others, as wee would be done to,*) of themselves, without the terrour of some Power, to cause them to be observed, are contrary to our naturall Passions, that carry us to Partiality, Pride, Revenge, and the like. And Covenants, without the Sword, are but Words, and of no strength to secure a man at all. Therefore notwithstanding the Lawes of Nature, (which every one hath then kept, when he has the will to keep them, when he can do it safely,) if there be no Power erected, or not great enough for our security; every man will, and may lawfully rely on his own strength and art, for caution against all other men. And in all places, where men have lived by small Families, to robbe and spoyle one another, has been a Trade, and so farre from being reputed against the Law of Nature, that the greater spoyles they gained, the greater was their honour; and men observed no other Lawes therein, but the Lawes of Honour; that is, to abstain from cruelty, leaving to men their lives, and instruments of husbandry. And as small Familyes did then; so now do Cities and Kingdomes which are but greater Families (for their own security) enlarge their Dominions, upon all pretences of danger, and fear of Invasion, or assistance that may be given to Invaders, endeavour as much as they can, to subdue, or weaken their neighbours, by open force, and secret arts, for want of other Caution, justly; and are remembred for it in after ages with honour.

Nor is it the joyning together of a small number of men, that gives them this security; because in small numbers, small additions on the one side or the other, make the advantage of strength so great, as is sufficient   [86] to carry the Victory; and therefore gives encouragement to an Invasion. The Multitude sufficient to confide in for our Security, is not determined by any certain number, but by comparison with the Enemy we feare; and is then sufficient, when the odds of the Enemy is not of so visible and conspicuous moment, to determine the event of warre, as to move him to attempt.

And be there never so great a Multitude; yet if their actions be directed according to their particular judgements, and particular appetites, they can expect thereby no defence, nor protection, neither against a Common enemy, nor against the injuries of one another. For being distracted in opinions concerning the best use and application of their strength, they do not help, but hinder one another; and reduce their strength by mutuall opposition to nothing: whereby they are easily, not onely subdued by a very few that agree together; but also when there is no common enemy, they make warre upon each other, for their particular interests. For if we could suppose a great Multitude of men to consent in the observation of Justice, and other Lawes of Nature, without a common Power to keep them all in awe; we might as well suppose all Man-kind to do the same; and then there neither would be, nor need to be any Civill Government, or Common-wealth at all; because there would be Peace without subjection.

Nor is it enough for the security, which men desire should last all the time of their life, that they be governed, and directed by one judgement, for a limited time; as in one Battell, or one Warre. For though they obtain a Victory by their unanimous endeavour against a forraign enemy; yet afterwards, when either they have no common enemy, or he that by one part is held for an enemy, is by another part held for a friend, they must needs by the difference of their interests dissolve, and fall again into a Warre amongst themselves.

It is true, that certain living creatures, as Bees, and Ants, live sociably one with another, (which are therefore by *Aristotle* numbred amongst Politicall creatures;) and yet have no other direction, than their particular judgements and appetites; nor speech, whereby one of them can signifie to another, what he thinks expedient for the common benefit: and therefore some man may perhaps desire to know, why Man-kind cannot do the same. To which I answer,

First, that men are continually in competition for Honour and Dignity, which these creatures are not; and consequently amongst men there ariseth on that ground, Envy and Hatred, and finally Warre; but amongst these not so.

Secondly, that amongst these creatures, the Common good differeth not from the Private; and being by nature enclined to their private, they procure thereby the common benefit. But man, whose Joy consisteth in comparing himselfe with other men, can relish nothing but what is eminent.

Thirdly, that these creatures, having not (as man) the use of reason, do not see, nor think they see any fault, in the administration of [87] their common businesse: whereas amongst men, there are very many, that thinke themselves wiser, and abler to govern the Publique, better than the rest; and these strive to reforme and innovate, one this way, another that way; and thereby bring it into Distraction and Civill warre.

Fourthly, that these creatures, though they have some use of voice, in making knowne to one another their desires, and other affections; yet they want that art of words, by which some men can represent to others, that which is Good, in the likenesse of Evill; and Evill, in the likenesse of Good; and augment, or diminish the apparent greatnesse of Good and Evill; discontenting men, and troubling their Peace at their pleasure.

Fiftly, irrational creatures cannot distinguish betweene *Injury,* and *Dammage;* and therefore as long as they be at ease, they are not offended with their fellowes: whereas Man is then most troublesome, when he is most at ease: for then it is that he loves to shew his Wisdome, and controule the Actions of them that governe the Common-wealth.

Lastly, the agreement of these creatures is Naturall; that of men, is by Covenant only, which is Artificiall: and therefore it is no wonder if there be somewhat else required (besides Covenant) to make their Agreement constant and lasting; which is a Common Power, to keep them in awe, and to direct their actions to the Common Benefit.

The only way to erect such a Common Power, as may be able to defend them from the invasion of Forraigners, and the injuries of one another, and thereby to secure them in such sort, as that by their owne industrie, and by the fruites of the Earth, they may nourish themselves and live contentedly; is, to conferre all their power and strength upon one Man, or upon one Assembly of men, that may reduce all their Wills, by plurality of voices, unto one Will: which is as much as to say, to appoint one Man, or Assembly of men, to beare their Person; and every one to owne, and acknowledge himselfe to be Author of whatsoever he that so beareth their Person, shall Act, or cause to be Acted, in those things which concerne the Common Peace and Safetie; and therein to submit their Wills, every one to his Will, and their Judgements, to his Judgment. This is more than Consent, or Concord; it is a reall Unitie of them all, in one and the same Person, made by Covenant of every man with every man, in such manner, as if every man should say to every man, *I Authorise and give up my Right of Governing my selfe, to this Man, or to this Assembly of men, on this condition, that thou give up thy Right to him, and Authorise all his Actions in like manner.* This done, the Multitude so united in one Person, is called a COMMON-WEALTH, in latine CIVITAS. This is the Generation of that great LEVIATHAN, or rather (to speake more reverently) of that *Mortall God,* to which wee owe under the *Immortall God,* our peace and defence. For by this Authoritie, given him by every particular man in the Common-Wealth, he hath the use of so much Power and   [88] Strength conferred on him, that by terror thereof, he is inabled to forme the wills of them all, to Peace at home, and mutuall ayd against their enemies abroad. And in him consisteth the Essence of the Commonwealth; which (to define it,) is *One Person, of whose Acts a great Multitude, by mutuall Covenants one with another, have made themselves every one the Author, to the end he may use the strength and means of them all, as he shall think expedient, for their Peace and Common Defence.*

And he that carryeth this Person, is called SOVERAIGNE, and said to have *Soveraigne Power;* and every one besides, his SUBJECT.

The attaining to this Soveraigne Power, is by two wayes. One, by Naturall force; as when a man maketh his children, to submit themselves, and their children to his government, as being able to destroy them if they refuse; or by Warre subdueth his enemies to his will, giving them their lives on that condition. The other, is when men agree amongst themselves, to submit to some Man, or Assembly of men, voluntarily on confidence to be protected by him against all others. This later, may be called a Politicall Common-wealth, or Common-wealth by *Institution;* and the former, a Common-wealth by *Acquisition.* And first, I shall speak of a Common-wealth by Institution.

· · ·

CHAP. XXI.   OF THE LIBERTY OF SUBJECTS

LIBERTY, or FREEDOME, signifieth (properly) the absence of Opposition; (by Opposition, I mean externall Impediments of motion;) and may be applyed no lesse to Irrationall, and Inanimate creatures, than to Rationall.

For whatsoever is so tyed, or environed, as it cannot move, but within a certain space, which space is determined by the opposition of some externall body, we say it hath not Liberty to go further. And so of all living creatures, whilest they are imprisoned, or restrained, with walls, or chayns; and of the water whilest it is kept in by banks, or vessels, that otherwise would spread it selfe into a larger space, we use to say, they are not at Liberty, to move in such manner, as without those externall impediments they would. But when the impediment of motion, is in the constitution of the thing it selfe, we use not to say, it wants the Liberty; but the Power to move; as when a stone lyeth still, or a man is fastned to his bed by sicknesse.

And according to this proper, and generally received meaning of [108] the word, A FREE-MAN, *is he, that in those things, which by his strength and wit he is able to do, is not hindred to doe what he has a will to.* But when the words *Free,* and *Liberty,* are applyed to any thing but *Bodies,* they are abused; for that which is not subject to Motion, is not subject to Impediment: And therefore, when 'tis said (for example) The way is Free, no Liberty of the way is signified, but of those that walk in it without stop. And when we say a Guift is Free, there is not meant any Liberty of the Guift, but of the Giver, that was not bound by any law, or Covenant to give it. So when we *speak Freely,* it is not the Liberty of voice, or pronunciation, but of the man, whom no law hath obliged to speak otherwise then he did. Lastly, from the use of the word *Free-will,* no Liberty can be inferred of the will, desire, or inclination, but the Liberty of the man; which consisteth in this, that he finds no stop, in doing what he has the will, desire, or inclination to doe.

Feare, and Liberty are consistent; as when a man throweth his goods into the Sea for *feare* the ship should sink, he doth it neverthelesse very willingly, and may refuse to doe it if he will: It is therefore the action, of one that was *free:* so a man sometimes pays his debt, only for *feare* of Imprisonment, which because no body hindred him from detaining, was the action of a man at *liberty.* And generally all actions which men doe in Common-wealths, for *feare* of the law, are actions, which the doers had *liberty* to omit.

Liberty, and Necessity are consistent: As in the water, that hath not only *liberty,* but a *necessity* of descending by the Channel; so likewise in the Actions which men voluntarily doe: which, because they proceed from their will, proceed from *liberty;* and yet, because every act of mans will, and every desire, and inclination proceedeth from some cause, and that from another cause, in a continuall chaine, (whose first link is in the hand of God the first of all causes,) they proceed from *necessity.* So that to him that could see the connexion of those causes, the *necessity* of all mens voluntary actions, would appeare manifest. And therefore God, that seeth, and disposeth all things, seeth also that the *liberty* of man in doing what he will, is accompanied with the *necessity* of doing that which God will, & no more, nor lesse. For though men may do many things, which God does not command, nor is therefore Author of them; yet they can have no passion, nor appetite to any thing, of which appetite Gods will is not the cause. And did not his will assure the *necessity* of mans will, and consequently of all that on mans will dependeth, the *liberty* of men would be a contradiction, and impediment to the omnipotence and *liberty* of God. And this shall suffice, (as to the matter in hand) of that naturall *liberty*, which only is properly called *liberty*.

But as men, for the atteyning of peace, and conservation of themselves thereby, have made an Artificiall Man, which we call a Common-wealth; so also have they made Artificiall Chains, called *Civill Lawes*, which they themselves, by mutuall covenants, have fastned at one end, to the   [109] lips of that Man, or Assembly, to whom they have given the Soveraigne Power; and at the other end to their own Ears. These Bonds in their own nature but weak, may neverthelesse be made to hold, by the danger, though not by the difficulty of breaking them.

In relation to these Bonds only it is, that I am to speak now, of the *Liberty* of *Subjects*. For seeing there is no Common-wealth in the world, wherein there be Rules enough set down, for the regulating of all the actions, and words of men, (as being a thing impossible:) it followeth necessarily, that in all kinds of actions, by the laws prætermitted, men have the Liberty, of doing what their own reasons shall suggest, for the most profitable to themselves. For if wee take Liberty in the proper sense, for corporall Liberty; that is to say, freedome from chains, and prison, it were very absurd for men to clamor as they doe, for the Liberty they so manifestly enjoy. Againe, if we take Liberty, for an exemption from Lawes, it is no lesse absurd, for men to demand as they doe, that Liberty, by which all other men may be masters of their lives. And yet as absurd as it is, this is it they demand; not knowing that the Lawes are of no power to protect them, without a Sword in the hands of a man, or men, to cause those laws to be put in execution. The Liberty of a Subject, lyeth therefore only in those things, which in regulating their actions, the Soveraign hath prætermitted: such as is the Liberty to buy, and sell, and otherwise contract with one another; to choose their own aboad, their own diet, their own trade of life, and institute their children as they themselves think fit; & the like.

Neverthelesse we are not to understand, that by such Liberty, the Soveraign Power of life, and death, is either abolished, or limited. For it has been already shewn, that nothing the Soveraign Representative can doe to a Subject, on what pretence soever, can properly be called Injustice, or Injury; because every Subject is Author of every act the Sovereign doth; so that he never wanteth Right to any thing, otherwise than as he himself is the Subject of God, and bound thereby to observe the laws of Nature. And therefore it may, and doth often happen in Common-wealths, that a Subject may be put to death, by the command of the Soveraign Power; and yet neither doe the other wrong: As when *Jeptha* caused his daughter to be sacrificed: In which, and the like cases, he that so dieth, had Liberty to doe the action, for which he is neverthelesse, without Injury put to death. And the same holdeth also in a Soveraign Prince, that putteth to death an Innocent Subject. For though the action be against the law of Nature, as being contrary to Equitie, (as was the killing of *Uriah,* by *David;*) yet it was not an Injurie to *Uriah;* but to *God.* Not to *Uriah,* because the right to doe what he pleased, was given him by *Uriah* himself: And yet to *God,* because *David* was *Gods* Subject; and prohibited all Iniquitie by the law of Nature. Which distinction, *David* himself, when he repented the fact, evidently confirmed, saying, *To thee only have I sinned.*

The Obligation of Subjects to the Soveraign, is understood to [114] last as long, and no longer, than the power lasteth, by which he is able to protect them. For the right men have by Nature to protect themselves, when none else can protect them, can by no Covenant be relinquished. The Soveraignty is the Soule of the Common-wealth; which once departed from the Body, the members doe no more receive their motion from it. The end of Obedience is Protection; which, wheresoever a man seeth it, either in his own, or in anothers sword, Nature applyeth his obedience to it, and his endeavour to maintaine it. And though Soveraignty, in the intention of them that make it, be immortall; yet is it in its own nature, not only subject to violent death, by forreign war; but also through the ignorance, and passions of men, it hath in it, from the very institution, many seeds of a naturall mortality, by Intestine Discord.

If a Subject be taken prisoner in war; or his person, or his means of life be within the Guards of the enemy, and hath his life and corporall Libertie given him, on condition to be Subject to the Victor, he hath Libertie to accept the condition; and having accepted it, is the subject of him that took him; because he had no other way to preserve himself. The case is the same, if he be deteined on the same termes, in a forreign country. But if a man be held in prison, or bonds, or is not trusted with the libertie of his bodie; he cannot be understood to be bound by Covenant to subjection; and therefore may, if he can, make his escape by any means whatsoever.

If a Monarch shall relinquish the Soveraignty, both for himself, and his heires; His Subjects returne to the absolute Libertie of Nature; because, though Nature may declare who are his Sons, and who are the nerest of his Kin; yet it dependeth on his own will, (as hath been said in the precedent chapter,) who shall be his Heyr. If therefore he will have no Heyre, there is no Soveraignty, nor Subjection. The case is the same, if he dye without known Kindred, and without declaration of his Heyre. For then there can no Heire be known, and consequently no Subjection be due.

If the Soveraign Banish his Subject; during the Banishment, he is not Subject. But he that is sent on a message, or hath leave to travell, is still Subject; but it is, by Contract between Soveraigns, not by vertue of the covenant of Subjection. For whosoever entreth into anothers dominion, is Subject to all the Laws thereof; unlesse he have a privilege by the amity of the Soveraigns, or by speciall licence.

If a Monarch subdued by war, render himself Subject to the Victor; his Subjects are delivered from their former obligation, and become obliged to the Victor. But if he be held prisoner, or have not the liberty of his own Body; he is not understood to have given away the Right of Soveraigntie; and therefore his Subjects are obliged to yield obedience to the Magistrates formerly placed, governing not in their own name, but in his. For, his Right remaining, the question is only of the Administration; that is to say, of the Magistrates and Officers; which, if   [115] he have not means to name, he is supposed to approve those, which he himself had formerly appointed.

BARUCH
SPINOZA   1632–1677

No other philosopher of the seventeenth and eighteenth centuries, if of any century, has been so widely and so greatly admired both by professional philosophers and by non-philosophers as Baruch Spinoza. He has often been called Christlike and saintly, but he was literally a heretic, and in the twentieth century he has frequently been linked with Freud.

He was born in Amsterdam, a Jew, whose parents had fled there from Portugal to escape persecution. Trained in the Jewish tradition under the guidance of a celebrated Talmudist, Saul Levi Morteira, he also studied with Manasseh ben Israel, who persuaded Cromwell to allow Jews to return to England. Fluent in Hebrew, Spanish, and Portuguese as well as Dutch, the eight-year-old Spinoza studied Latin, science, and the philosophy of Descartes with a Dutch physician, Franz van der Ende.

After his father's death, he became involved in a law suit over his inheritance with his half-sister. He won, but renounced it. Passions had been inflamed, he was accused of heresy, a zealot tried to kill him, but the synagogue of Amsterdam urged him to compromise by leaving van der Ende and making gestures of conformity. Spinoza refused and was formally excommunicated by the Jewish community of Amsterdam, in 1656, when he was 23. In the twentieth century, the new state of Israel revoked the ban.

Without the least wish to join any other religious community, Spinoza settled down in a suburb of Amsterdam, a few years later moved to Rhynsburg, then to Voorburg near the Hague, and finally to the Hague itself where he lived first in a widow's house and then, until his death, in a painter's. He lived very simply, supporting himself by grinding and polishing lenses. This was the craft he had learned in keeping with the Jewish tradition of the time which required scholars to learn some trade. The glass dust probably hastened his death by consumption. He died at 44, two years before Hobbes died at 91.

His first philosophic work was an exposition of Descartes' philosophy, *more geometrico,* in the manner of a geometric treatise (1663). Spinoza did not accept Descartes' system, though he admired it, and his approach was not meant to prove it right but to exhibit as clearly and concisely as possible its presuppositions and structure.

His second book, also in Latin, was the *Tractatus theologico-politicus* (1670). This treatise, revolutionary in many respects, argued at length that the Bible does not aim at truth, but only at pious and obedient behavior. Spinoza does not merely fail to cite Scripture to prove claims, as the scholastic philosophers had done and as even John Locke, born the same year as Spinoza, did very occasionally in his political works; Spinoza explicitly denies the authority of the Bible in matters of truth. He also catalogues contradictions in Scripture and argues that the Five Books of Moses could not have been written by Moses. Spinoza might be called the grandfather of modern Bible criticism, but his interest in these questions is inseparable from his moral and political concerns. In the twelfth century, Abraham Ibn Ezra, a great Jewish Bible scholar, had carefully listed some contradictions and hinted that some passages in the Pentateuch could hardly have been written by Moses, while Maimonides, his younger contemporary had argued that Scripture must always be interpreted as agreeing with reason. Spinoza rejected this idea no less than the idea that reason must be subordinated to Scripture. He proposes—writing soon after the Thirty Years War—that religion and truth should be separated altogether. That is the best safeguard against fanaticism. Pious conduct flourishes best in an atmosphere of free speech; and laws concerning speculative matters are quite useless, only promoting strife, and distracting attention from moral conduct.

This book attracted a great deal of attention, became the butt of many attacks, but also brought Spinoza a call to the chair of philosophy at the university of Heidelberg, in Germany. Although the invitation made a point of his academic freedom, Spinoza rejected it because he thought that such a position would inevitably impinge on his freedom to speak and write as he saw fit.

An early fragment *On the Improvement of the Intellect* and a late fragment, *Political Treatise,* written in Latin like his other works, were published posthumously in 1677, together with his main work, *Ethica, ordine geometrico demonstrata*—the celebrated *Ethics.* He also wrote a compendium of Hebrew grammar and some post-humously published letters which illuminate both his character and some difficult points in his philosophy.

All of the following selections are from the *Ethics*. The translation used is the classical one by R. H. M. Elwes.

THE ETHICS

Part I. Concerning God

DEFINITIONS

I

By that which is *self-caused*, I mean that of which the essence involves existence, or that of which the nature is only conceivable as existent.

II. A thing is called *finite after its kind*, when it can be limited by another thing of the same nature; for instance, a body is called finite because we always conceive another greater body. So, also, a thought is limited by another thought, but a body is not limited by thought, nor a thought by body.

III. By *substance*, I mean that which is in itself, and is conceived through itself: in other words, that of which a conception can be formed independently of any other conception.

IV. By *attribute*, I mean that which the intellect perceives as constituting the essence of substance.

V. By *mode*, I mean the modifications [1] of substance, or that which exists in, and is conceived through, something other than itself.

VI. By *God*, I mean a being absolutely infinite—that is, a substance consisting in infinite attributes, of which each expresses eternal and infinite essentiality.

Explanation.—I say absolutely infinite, not infinite after its kind: for, of a thing infinite only after its kind, infinite attributes may be denied; but that which is absolutely infinite, contains in its essence whatever expresses reality, and involves no negation.

VII. That thing is called free, which exists solely by the necessity of its own nature, and of which the action is determined by itself alone. On the other hand, that thing is necessary, or rather constrained, which is determined by something external to itself to a fixed and definite method of existence or action.

---

[1] "*Affectiones.*"

VIII. By *eternity*, I mean existence itself, in so far as it is conceived necessarily to follow solely from the definition of that which is eternal.

Explanation.—Existence of this kind is conceived as an eternal truth, like the essence of a thing, and, therefore, cannot be explained by means of continuance or time, though continuance may be conceived without a beginning or end.

AXIOMS

I. Everything which exists, exists either in itself or in something else.

II. That which cannot be conceived through anything else must be conceived through itself.

III. From a given definite cause an effect necessarily follows; and, on the other hand, if no definite cause be granted, it is impossible that an effect can follow.

IV. The knowledge of an effect depends on and involves the knowledge of a cause.

V. Things which have nothing in common cannot be understood, the one by means of the other; the conception of one does not involve the conception of the other.

VI. A true idea must correspond with its ideate or object.

VII. If a thing can be conceived as non-existing, its essence does not involve existence.

PROPOSITIONS

PROP. I. *Substance is by nature prior to its modifications.*

Proof.—This is clear from Deff. iii. and v.

PROP. II. *Two substances, whose attributes are different have nothing in common.*

Proof.—Also evident from Def. iii. For each must exist in itself, and be conceived through itself; in other words, the conception of one does not imply the conception of the other.

PROP. III. *Things which have nothing in common cannot be one the cause of the other.*

Proof.—If they have nothing in common, it follows that one cannot be apprehended by means of the other (Ax. v.), and, therefore, one cannot be the cause of the other (Ax. iv.).   *Q.E.D.*

PROP. IV. *Two or more distinct things are distinguished one from the other, either by the difference of the attributes of the substances, or by the difference of their modifications.*

Proof.—Everything which exists, exists either in itself or in something else (Ax. i.),—that is (by Deff. iii. and v.), nothing is granted in addition to the understanding, except substance and its modifications. Nothing is, therefore, given besides the understanding, by which several things may be distinguished one from the other, except the substances, or, in other words (see Ax. iv.), their attributes and modifications.   *Q.E.D.*

QED : "*Quod erat demonstrandum*"
" Which was to be demonstrated"

PROP. V.   *There cannot exist in the universe two or more substances having the same nature or attribute.*

Proof.—If several distinct substances be granted, they must be distinguished one from the other, either by the difference of their attributes, or by the difference of their modifications (Prop. iv.). If only by the difference of their attributes, it will be granted that there cannot be more than one with an identical attribute. If by the difference of their modifications—as substance is naturally prior to its modifications (Prop. i.),—it follows that setting the modifications aside, and considering substance in itself, that is truly, (Deff. iii. and vi.), there cannot be conceived one substance different from another,—that is (by Prop. iv.), there cannot be granted several substances, but one substance only.   *Q.E.D.*

PROP. VI.   *One substance cannot be produced by another substance.*

Proof.—It is impossible that there should be in the universe two substances with an identical attribute, *i.e.* which have anything common to them both (Prop. ii.), and, therefore (Prop. iii.), one cannot be the cause of another, neither can one be produced by the other.   *Q.E.D.*

Corollary.—Hence it follows that a substance cannot be produced by anything external to itself. For in the universe nothing is granted, save substances and their modifications (as appears from Ax. i. and Deff. iii. and v.). Now (by the last Prop.) substance cannot be produced by another substance, therefore it cannot be produced by anything external to itself.   *Q.E.D.*   This is shown still more readily by the absurdity of the contradictory. For, if substance be produced by an external cause, the knowledge of it would depend on the knowledge of its cause (Ax. iv.), and (by Def. iii.) it would itself not be substance.

PROP. VII.   *Existence belongs to the nature of substance.*

Proof.—Substance cannot be produced by anything external (Corollary, Prop. vi.), it must, therefore, be its own cause—that is, its essence necessarily involves existence, or existence belongs to its nature.

PROP. VIII.   *Every substance is necessarily infinite.*

Proof.—There can only be one substance with an identical attribute, and existence follows from its nature (Prop. vii.); its nature, therefore, involves existence, either as finite or infinite. It does not exist as finite, for (by Def. ii.) it would then be limited by something else of the same kind, which would also necessarily exist (Prop. vii.); and there would be two substances with an identical attribute, which is absurd (Prop. v.). It therefore exists as infinite.   *Q.E.D.*

Note I.—As finite existence involves a partial negation, and infinite existence is the absolute affirmation of the given nature, it follows (solely from Prop. vii.) that every substance is necessarily infinite.

Note II.—No doubt it will be difficult for those who think about things loosely, and have not been accustomed to know them by their primary causes, to comprehend the demonstration of Prop. vii.: for such persons make no distinction between the modifications of substances and the substances themselves, and are ignorant of the manner in which things are produced; hence they attribute to substances the beginning which they observe in natural objects. Those who are ignorant of true causes, make complete confusion—think that trees might talk just as well as men—that men might be formed from stones as well as from seed; and imagine that any form might be changed into any other. So, also, those who confuse the two natures, divine and human, readily attribute human passions to the deity, especially so long as they do not know how passions originate in the mind. But, if people would consider the nature of substance, they would have no doubt about the truth of Prop. vii. In fact, this proposition would be a universal axiom, and accounted a truism. For, by substance, would be understood that which is in itself, and is conceived through itself —that is, something of which the conception requires not the conception of anything else; whereas modifications exist in something external to themselves, and a conception of them is formed by means of a conception of the thing in which they exist. Therefore, we may have true ideas of non-existent modifications; for, although they may have no *actual* existence apart from the conceiving intellect, yet their essence is so involved in something external to themselves that they may through it be conceived. Whereas the only truth substances can have, external to the intellect, must consist in their existence, because they are conceived through themselves. Therefore, for a person to say that he has a clear and distinct —that is, a true—idea of a substance, but that he is not sure whether such substance exists, would be the same as if he said that he had a true idea, but was not sure whether or no it was false (a little consideration will make this plain); or if anyone affirmed that substance is created, it would be the same as saying that a false idea was true—in short, the height of absurdity. It must, then, necessarily be admitted that the existence of substance as its essence is an eternal truth. And we can hence conclude by another process of reasoning—that there is but one such substance. I think that this may profitably be done at once; and, in order to proceed regularly with the demonstration, we must premise:—

1. The true definition of a thing neither involves nor expresses anything beyond the nature of the thing defined. From this it follows that—

2. No definition implies or expresses a certain number of individuals, inasmuch as it expresses nothing beyond the nature of the thing defined. For instance, the definition of a triangle expresses nothing beyond the actual nature of a triangle: it does not imply any fixed number of triangles.

3. There is necessarily for each individual existent thing a cause why it should exist.

4. This cause of existence must either be contained in the nature and definition of the thing defined, or must be postulated apart from such definition.

It therefore follows that, if a given number of individual things exist in nature, there must be some cause for the existence of exactly that number, neither more nor less. For example, if twenty men exist in the universe (for simplicity's sake, I will suppose them existing simultaneously, and to have had no predecessors), and we want to account for the existence of these twenty men, it will not be enough to show the cause of human existence in general; we must also show why there are exactly twenty men, neither more nor less: for a cause must be assigned for the existence of each individual. Now this cause cannot be contained in the actual nature of man, for the true definition of man does not involve any consideration of the number twenty. Consequently, the cause for the existence of these twenty men, and, consequently, of each of them, must necessarily be sought externally to each individual. Hence we may lay down the absolute rule, that everything which may consist of several individuals must have an external cause. And, as it has been shown already that existence appertains to the nature of substance, existence must necessarily be included in its definition; and from its definition alone existence must be deducible. But from its definition (as we have shown, Notes ii., iii.), we cannot infer the existence of several substances; therefore it follows that there is only one substance of the same nature. *Q.E.D.*

PROP. IX. *The more reality or being a thing has the greater the number of its attributes* (Def. iv.).

PROP. X. *Each particular attribute of the one substance must be conceived through itself.*

Proof.—An attribute is that which the intellect perceives of substance, as constituting its essence (Def. iv.). and, therefore, must be conceived through itself (Def. iii.). *Q.E.D.*

Note.—It is thus evident that, though two attributes are, in fact, conceived as distinct—that is, one without the help of the other—yet we cannot, therefore, conclude that they constitute two entities, or two different substances. For it is the nature of substance that each of its attributes is conceived through itself, inasmuch as all the attributes it has have always existed simultaneously in it, and none could be produced by any other; but each expresses the reality or being of substance. It is, then, far from an absurdity to ascribe several attributes to one substance; for nothing in nature is more clear than that each and every entity must be conceived under some attribute, and that its reality or being is in proportion to the number of its attributes expressing necessity or eternity and infinity. Consequently it is abundantly clear, that an absolutely infinite being must necessarily be defined as consisting in infinite attributes, each of which expresses a certain eternal and infinite essence.

If anyone now ask, by what sign shall he be able to distinguish different substances, let him read the following propositions, which show that there is but one substance in the universe, and that it is absolutely infinite, wherefore such a sign would be sight for in vain.

PROP. XI. *God, or substance, consisting of infinite attributes, of which each expresses eternal and infinite essentiality, necessarily exists.*

Proof.—If this be denied, conceive, if possible, that God does not exist: then his essence does not involve existence. But this (by Prop. vii.) is absurd. Therefore God necessarily exists.

Another proof.—Of everything whatsoever a cause or reason must be assigned, either for its existence, or for its non-existence—*e.g.* if a triangle exist, a reason or cause must be granted for its existence; if, on the contrary, it does not exist, a cause must also be granted, which prevents it from existing, or annuls its existence. This reason or cause must either be contained in the nature of the thing in question, or be external to it. For instance, the reason for the non-existence of a square circle is indicated in its nature, namely, because it would involve a contradiction. On the other hand, the existence of substance follows also solely from its nature, inasmuch as its nature involves existence. (See Prop. vii.)

But the reason for the existence of a triangle or a circle does not follow from the nature of those figures, but from the order of universal nature in extension. From the latter it must follow, either that a triangle necessarily exists, or that it is impossible that it should exist. So much is self-evident. It follows therefrom that a thing necessarily exists, if no cause or reason be granted which prevents its existence.

If, then, no cause or reason can be given, which prevents the existence of God, or which destroys his existence, we must certainly conclude that he necessarily does exist. If such a reason or cause should be given, it must either be drawn from the very nature of God, or be external to him —that is, drawn from another substance of another nature. For if it were of the same nature, God, by that very fact, would be admitted to exist. But substance of another nature could have nothing in common with God (by Prop. ii.), and therefore would be unable either to cause or to destroy his existence.

As, then, a reason or cause which would annul the divine existence cannot be drawn from anything external to the divine nature, such cause must perforce, if God does not exist, be drawn from God's own nature, which would involve a contradiction. To make such an affirmation about a being absolutely infinite and supremely perfect, is absurd; therefore, neither in the nature of God, nor externally to his nature, can a cause or reason be assigned which would annul his existence. Therefore, God necessarily exists. *Q.E.D.*

 Another proof.—The potentiality of non-existence is a negation of power, and contrariwise the potentiality of existence is a power, as is obvious. If, then, that which necessarily exists is nothing but finite beings, such finite beings are more powerful than a being absolutely infinite, which is obviously absurd; therefore, either nothing exists, or else a being absolutely infinite necessarily exists also. Now we exist either in ourselves, or in something else which necessarily exists (see Axiom i. and Prop. vii.). Therefore a being absolutely infinite—in other words, God (Def. vi.)— necessarily exists. *Q.E.D.*

Note.—In this last proof, I have purposely shown God's existence *à posteriori*, so that the proof might be more easily followed, not because, from the same premises, God's existence does not follow *à priori*. For, as the potentiality of existence is a power, it follows that, in proportion as reality increases in the nature of a thing, so also will it increase its strength for existence. Therefore a being absolutely infinite, such as God, has from himself an absolutely infinite power of existence, and hence he does absolutely exist. Perhaps there will be many who will be unable to see the force of this proof, inasmuch as they are accustomed only to consider those things which flow from external causes. Of such things, they see that those which quickly come to pass—that is, quickly come into existence—quickly also disappear; whereas they regard as more difficult of accomplishment—that is, not so easily brought into existence—those things which they conceive as more complicated.

However, to do away with this misconception, I need not here show the measure of truth in the proverb, "What comes quickly, goes quickly," nor discuss whether, from the point of view of universal nature, all things are equally easy, or otherwise: I need only remark, that I am not here speaking of things, which come to pass through causes external to themselves, but only of substances which (by Prop. vi.) cannot be produced by any external cause. Things which are produced by external causes, whether they consist of many parts or few, owe whatsoever perfection or reality they possess solely to the efficacy of their external cause, and therefore their existence arises solely from the perfection of their external cause, not from their own. Contrariwise, whatsoever perfection is possessed by substance is due to no external cause; wherefore the existence of substance must arise solely from its own nature, which is nothing else but its essence. Thus, the perfection of a thing does not annul its existence, but, on the contrary, asserts it. Imperfection, on the other hand, does annul it; therefore we cannot be more certain of the existence of anything, than of the existence of a being absolutely infinite or perfect—that is, of God. For inasmuch as his essence excludes all imperfection, and involves absolute perfection, all cause for doubt concerning his existence is done away, and the utmost certainty on the question is given. This, I think, will be evident to every moderately attentive reader.

PROP. XII. *No attribute of substance can be conceived from which it would follow that substance can be divided.*

Proof.—The parts into which substance as thus conceived would be divided, either will retain the nature of substance, or they will not. If the former, then (by Prop. viii.) each part will necessarily be infinite, and (by Prop. vi.) self-caused, and (by Prop. v.) will perforce consist of a different attribute, so that, in that case, several substances could be formed out of one substance, which (by Prop. vi.) is absurd. Moreover, the parts (by Prop. ii.) would have nothing in common with their whole, and the whole (by Def. iv. and Prop. x.) could both exist and be conceived without its parts, which everyone will admit to be absurd. If we adopt the second alternative—namely, that the parts will not retain the nature of substance —then, if the whole substance were divided into equal parts, it would lose the nature of substance, and would cease to exist, which (by Prop. vii.) is absurd.

PROP. XIII. *Substance absolutely infinite is indivisible.*

Proof.—If it could be divided, the parts into which it was divided would either retain the nature of absolutely infinite substance, or they would not. If the former, we should have several substances of the same nature, which (by Prop. v.) is absurd. If the latter, then (by Prop. vii.) substance absolutely infinite could cease to exist, which (by Prop. xi.) is also absurd.

Corollary.—It follows, that no substance, and consequently no extended substance, in so far as it is substance, is divisible.

Note.—The indivisibility of substance may be more easily understood as follows. The nature of substance can only be conceived as infinite, and by a part of substance, nothing else can be understood than finite substance, which (by Prop. viii.) involves a manifest contradiction.

PROP. XIV. *Besides God no substance can be granted or conceived.*

Proof.—As God is a being absolutely infinite, of whom no attribute that expresses the essence of substance can be denied (by Def. vi.), and he necessarily exists (by Prop. xi.); if any substance besides God were granted, it would have to be explained by some attribute of God, and thus two substances with the same attribute would exist, which (by Prop. v.) is absurd; therefore, besides God no substance can be granted, or, consequently, be conceived. If it could be conceived, it would necessarily have to be conceived as existent; but this (by the first part of this proof) is absurd. Therefore, besides God no substance can be granted or conceived. *Q.E.D.*

Corollary I.—Clearly, therefore: 1. God is one, that is (by Def. vi.) only one substance can be granted in the universe, and that substance is absolutely infinite, as we have already indicated (in the note to Prop. x.).

Corollary II.—It follows: 2. That extension and thought are either attributes of God or (by Ax. i.) accidents (*affectiones*) of the attributes of God.

PROP. XV. *Whatsoever is, is in God, and without God nothing can be, or be conceived.*

Proof.—Besides God, no substance is granted or can be conceived (by Prop. xiv.), that is (by Def. iii.) nothing which is in itself and is conceived through itself. But modes (by Def. v.) can neither be, nor be conceived without substance; wherefore they can only be in the divine nature, and can only through it be conceived. But substances and modes form the sum total of existence (by Ax. i.), therefore, without God nothing can be, or be conceived. *Q.E.D.*

Note.—Some assert that God, like a man, consists of body and mind, and is susceptible of passions. How far such persons have strayed from the truth is sufficiently evident from what has been said. But these I pass over. For all who have in anywise reflected on the divine nature deny that God has a body. Of this they find excellent proof in the fact that we understand by body a definite quantity, so long, so broad, so deep, bounded by a certain shape, and it is the height of absurdity to predicate such a thing of God, a being absolutely infinite. But meanwhile by the other reasons with which they try to prove their point, they show that they think corporeal or extended substance wholly apart from the divine nature, and say it was created by God. Wherefrom the divine nature can have been created, they are wholly ignorant; thus they clearly show, that they do not know the meaning of their own words. I myself have proved sufficiently clearly, at any rate in my own judgment (Coroll. Prop. vi., and Note 2,

Prop. viii.), that no substance can be produced or created by anything other than itself. Further, I showed (in Prop. xiv.), that besides God no substance can be granted or conceived. Hence we drew the conclusion that extended substance is one of the infinite attributes of God. However, in order to explain more fully, I will refute the arguments of my adversaries, which all start from the following points:—

Extended substance, in so far as it is substance, consists, as they think, in parts, wherefore they deny that it can be infinite, or, consequently, that it can appertain to God. This they illustrate with many examples, of which I will take one or two. If extended substance, they say, is infinite, let it be conceived to be divided into two parts; each part will then be either finite or infinite. If the former, then infinite substance is composed of two finite parts, which is absurd. If the latter, then one infinite will be twice as large as another infinite, which is also absurd.

Further, if an infinite line be measured out in foot lengths, it will consist of an infinite number of such parts; it would equally consist of an infinite number of parts, if each part measured only an inch: therefore, one infinity would be twelve times as great as the other.

Lastly, if from a single point there be conceived to be drawn two diverging lines which at first are at a definite distance apart, but are produced to infinity, it is certain that the distance between the two lines will be continually increased, until at length it changes from definite to indefinable. As these absurdities follow, it is said, from considering quantity as infinite, the conclusion is drawn, that extended substance must necessarily be finite, and, consequently, cannot appertain to the nature of God.

The second argument is also drawn from God's supreme perfection. God, it is said, inasmuch as he is a supremely perfect being, cannot be passive; but extended substance, in so far as it is divisible, is passive. It follows, therefore, that extended substance does not appertain to the essence of God.

Such are the arguments I find on the subject in writers, who by them try to prove that extended substance is unworthy of the divine nature, and cannot possibly appertain thereto. However, I think an attentive reader will see that I have already answered their propositions; for all their arguments are founded on the hypothesis that extended substance is composed of parts, and such a hypothesis I have shown (Prop. xii., and Coroll. Prop. xiii.) to be absurd. Moreover, anyone who reflects will see that all these absurdities (if absurdities they be, which I am not now discussing), from which it is sought to extract the conclusion that extended substance is finite, do not at all follow from the notion of an infinite quantity, but merely from the notion that an infinite quantity is measurable, and composed of finite parts: therefore, the only fair conclusion to be drawn is that infinite quantity is not measurable, and cannot be composed of finite parts. This is exactly what we have already proved (in Prop. xii.). Wherefore the weapon which they aimed at us has in reality recoiled upon themselves. If, from this absurdity of theirs, they persist in drawing the conclusion that extended substance must be finite, they will in good sooth be acting like a man who asserts that circles have the properties of squares, and, finding himself thereby landed in absurdities, proceeds to deny that circles have any centre, from which all lines drawn to the circumference are equal. For, taking extended substance, which can only be conceived as infinite, one, and indivisible (Props. viii., v., xii.) they assert, in order to prove that it is finite, that it is composed of finite parts, and that it can be multiplied and divided.

So, also, others, after asserting that a line is composed of points, can produce many arguments to prove that a line cannot be infinitely divided. Assuredly it is not less absurd to assert that extended substance is made up of bodies or parts, than it would be to assert that a solid is made up of surfaces, a surface of lines, and a line of points. This must be admitted by all who know clear reason to be infallible, and most of all by those who deny the possibility of a vacuum. For if extended substance could be so divided that its parts were really separate, why should not one part admit of being destroyed, the others remaining joined together as before? And why should all be so fitted into one another as to leave no vacuum? Surely in the case of things, which are really distinct one from the other, one can exist without the other, and can remain in its original condition. As, then, there does not exist a vacuum in nature (of which anon), but all parts are bound to come together to prevent it, it follows from this also that the parts cannot be really distinguished, and that extended substance in so far as it is substance cannot be divided.

If anyone asks me the further question, Why are we naturally so prone to divide quantity? I answer, that quantity is conceived by us in two ways; in the abstract and superficially, as we imagine it; or as substance, as we conceive it solely by the intellect. If, then, we regard quantity as it is represented in our imagination, which we often and more easily do, we shall find that it is finite, divisible, and compounded of parts; but if we regard it as it is represented in our intellect, and conceive it as substance, which it is very difficult to do, we shall then, as I have sufficiently proved, find that it is infinite, one, and indivisible. This will be plain enough to all, who make a distinction between the intellect and the imagination, especially if it be remembered, that matter is everywhere the same, that its parts are not distinguishable, except in so far as we conceive matter as diversely modified, whence its parts are distinguished, not really, but modally. For instance, water, in so far as it is water, we conceive to be divided, and its parts to be separated one from the other; but not in so far as it is extended substance; from this point of view it is neither separated nor divisible. Further, water, in so far as it is water, is produced and corrupted; but, in so far as it is substance, it is neither produced nor corrupted.

I think I have now answered the second argument; it is, in fact, founded on the same assumption as the first—namely, that matter, in so far as it is substance, is divisible, and composed of parts. Even if it were so, I do not know why it should be considered unworthy of the divine nature, inasmuch as besides God (by Prop. xiv.) no substance can be granted, wherefrom it could receive its modifications. All things, I repeat, are in God, and all things which come to pass, come to pass solely through the laws of the infinite nature of God, and follow (as I will shortly show) from the necessity of his essence. Wherefore it can in nowise be said, that God is passive in respect to anything other than himself, or that extended substance is unworthy of the Divine nature, even if it be supposed divisible, so long as it is granted to be infinite and eternal. But enough of this for the present.

.   .   .

PROP. XXVIII.—*Every individual thing, or everything which is finite and has a conditioned existence, cannot exist or be conditioned to act, unless it be conditioned for existence and action by a cause other than itself, which also is finite, and has a conditioned existence; and likewise this cause cannot in its turn exist, or be conditioned to act, unless it be conditioned for existence and action by another cause, which also is finite, and has a conditioned existence, and so on to infinity.*

Proof.—Whatsoever is conditioned to exist and act, has been thus conditioned by God (by Prop. xxvi. and Prop. xxiv., Coroll.)

But that which is finite, and has a conditioned existence, cannot be produced by the absolute nature of any attribute of God; for whatsoever follows from the absolute nature of any attribute of God is infinite and eternal (by Prop. xxi.). It must, therefore, follow from some attribute of God, in so far as the said attribute is considered as in some way modified; for substance and modes make up the sum total of existence (by Ax. i. and Def. iii., v.), while modes are merely modifications of the attributes of God. But from God, or from any of his attributes, in so far as the latter is modified by a modification infinite and eternal, a conditioned thing cannot follow. Wherefore it must follow from, or be conditioned for, existence and action by God or one of his attributes, in so far as the latter are modified by some modification which is finite, and has a conditioned existence. This is our first point. Again, this cause or this modification (for the reason by which we established the first part of this proof) must in its turn be conditioned by another cause, which also is finite, and has a conditioned existence, and, again, this last by another (for the same reason); and so on (for the same reason) to infinity. *Q.E.D.*

Note.—As certain things must be produced immediately by God, namely those things which necessarily follow from his absolute nature, through the means of these primary attributes, which, nevertheless, can neither exist nor be conceived without God, it follows:—1. That God is absolutely the proximate cause of those things immediately produced by him. I say absolutely, not after his kind, as is usually stated. For the effects of God cannot either exist or be conceived without a cause (Prop. xv. and Prop. xxiv., Coroll.). 2. That God cannot properly be styled the remote cause of individual things, except for the sake of distinguishing these from what he immediately produces, or rather from what follows from his absolute nature. For, by a remote cause, we understand a cause which is in no way conjoined to the effect. But all things which are, are in God, and so depend on God, that without him they can neither be nor be conceived.

Prop. XXIX. *Nothing in the universe is contingent, but all things are conditioned to exist and operate in a particular manner by the necessity of the divine nature.*

Proof.—Whatsoever is, is in God (Prop. xv.). But God cannot be called a thing contingent. For (by Prop. xi.) he exists necessarily, and not contingently. Further, the modes of the divine nature follow therefrom necessarily, and not contingently (Prop. xvi.); and they thus follow, whether we consider the divine nature absolutely, or whether we consider it as in any way conditioned to act (Prop. xxvii.). Further, God is not only the cause of these modes, in so far as they simply exist (by Prop. xxiv., Coroll.), but also in so far as they are considered as conditioned for operating in a particular manner (Prop. xxvi.). If they be not conditioned by God (Prop. xxvi.), it is impossible, and not contingent, that they should condition themselves; contrariwise, if they be conditioned by God, it is impossible, and not contingent, that they should render themselves unconditioned. Wherefore all things are conditioned by the necessity of the divine nature, not only to exist, but also to exist and operate in a particular manner, and there is nothing that is contingent. *Q.E.D.*

Note.—Before going any further, I wish here to explain, what we should understand by nature viewed as active (*natura naturans*), and nature viewed as passive (*natura naturata*). I say to explain, or rather call attention to it, for I think that, from what has been said, it is sufficiently clear, that by nature viewed as active we should understand that which is in itself, and is conceived through itself, or those attributes of substance, which express eternal and infinite essence, in other words (Prop. xiv., Coroll. i., and Prop. xvii., Coroll. ii.) God, in so far as he is considered as a free cause.

By nature viewed as passive I understand all that which follows from the necessity of the nature of God, or of any of the attributes of God, that is, all the modes of the attributes of God, in so far as they are considered as things which are in God, and which without God cannot exist or be conceived.

.   .   .

Prop. XXXII. *Will cannot be called a free cause, but only a necessary cause.*

Proof.—Will is only a particular mode of thinking, like intellect; therefore (by Prop. xxviii.) no volition can exist, nor be conditioned to act, unless it be conditioned by some cause other than itself, which cause is conditioned by a third cause, and so on to infinity. But if will be supposed infinite, it must also be conditioned to exist and act by God, not by virtue of his being substance absolutely infinite, but by virtue of his possessing an attribute which expresses the infinite and eternal essence of thought (by Prop. xxiii.). Thus, however it be conceived, whether as finite or infinite, it requires a cause by which it should be conditioned to exist and act. Thus (Def. vii.) it cannot be called a free cause, but only a necessary or constrained cause. *Q.E.D.*

Coroll. I.—Hence it follows, first, that God does not act according to freedom of the will.

Coroll. II.—It follows, secondly, that will and intellect stand in the same relation to the nature of God as do motion, and rest, and absolutely all natural phenomena, which must be conditioned by God (Prop. xxix.) to exist and act in a particular manner. For will, like the rest, stands in need of a cause, by which it is conditioned to exist and act in a particular manner. And although, when will or intellect be granted, an infinite number of results may follow, yet God cannot on that account be said to act from freedom of the will, any more than the infinite number of results from motion and rest would justify us in saying that motion and rest act by free will. Wherefore will no more appertains to God than does anything else in nature, but stands in the same relation to him as motion, rest, and the like, which we have shown to follow from the necessity of the divine nature, and to be conditioned by it to exist and act in a particular manner.

.   .   .

APPENDIX.—In the foregoing I have explained the nature and properties of God. I have shown that he necessarily exists, that he is one: that he is, and acts solely by the necessity of his own nature; that he is the free cause of all things, and how he is so; that all things are in God, and so depend on him, that without him they could neither exist nor be conceived; lastly, that all things are predetermined by God, not through his free will or absolute fiat, but from the very nature of God or infinite power. I have further, where occasion offered, taken care to remove the prejudices, which might impede the comprehension of my demonstrations. Yet there still remain misconceptions not a few, which might and may prove very grave hindrances to the understanding of the concatenation of things, as I have explained it above. I have therefore thought it worth while to bring these misconceptions before the bar of reason.

All such opinions spring from the notion commonly entertained, that all things in nature act as men themselves act, namely, with an end in view. It is accepted as certain, that God himself directs all things to a definite goal (for it is said that God made all things for man, and man that he might worship him). I will, therefore, consider this opinion, asking first, why it obtains general credence, and why all men are naturally so prone to adopt it? secondly, I will point out its falsity; and, lastly, I will show how it has given rise to prejudices about good and bad, right and wrong, praise and blame, order and confusion, beauty and ugliness, and the like. However, this is not the place to deduce these misconceptions from the nature of the human mind: it will be sufficient here, if I assume as a starting point, what ought to be universally admitted, namely, that all men are born ignorant of the causes of things, that all have the desire to seek for what is useful to them, and that they are conscious of such desire. Herefrom it follows, first, that men think themselves free inasmuch as they are conscious of their volitions and desires, and never even dream, in their ignorance, of the causes which have disposed them so to wish and desire. Secondly, that men do all things for an end, namely, for that which is useful to them, and which they seek. Thus it comes to pass that they only look for a knowledge of the final causes of events, and when these are learned, they are content, as having no cause for further doubt. If they cannot learn such causes from external sources, they are compelled to turn to considering themselves, and reflecting what end would have induced them personally to bring about the given event, and thus they necessarily judge other natures by their own. Further, as they find in themselves and outside themselves many means which assist them not a little in their search for what is useful, for instance, eyes for seeing, teeth for chewing, herbs and animals for yielding food, the sun for giving light, the sea for breeding fish, &c., they come to look on the whole of nature as a means for obtaining such conveniences. Now as they are aware, that they found these conveniences and did not make them, they think they have cause for believing, that some other being has made them for their use. As they look upon things as means, they cannot believe them to be self-created; but, judging from the means which they are accustomed to prepare for themselves, they are bound to believe in some ruler or rulers of the universe endowed with human freedom, who have arranged and adapted everything for human use. They are bound to estimate the nature of such rulers (having no information on the subject) in accordance with their own nature, and therefore they assert that the gods ordained everything for the use of man, in order to bind man to themselves and obtain from him the highest honour. Hence also it follows, that everyone thought out for himself, according to his abilities, a different way of worshipping God, so that God might love him more than his fellows, and direct the whole course of nature for the satisfaction of his blind cupidity and insatiable avarice. Thus the prejudice developed into superstition, and took deep root in the human mind; and for this reason everyone strove most zealously to understand and explain the final causes of things; but in their endeavour to show that nature does nothing in vain, *i.e.*, nothing which is useless to man, they only seem to have demonstrated that nature, the gods, and men are all mad together. Consider, I pray you, the result: among the many helps of nature they were bound to find some hindrances, such as storms, earthquakes, diseases, &c.: so they declared that such things happen, because the gods are angry at some wrong done them by men, or at some fault committed in their worship. Experience day by day protested and showed by infinite examples, that good and evil fortunes fall to the lot of pious and impious alike; still they would not abandon their inveterate prejudice, for it was more easy for them to class such contradictions among other unknown things of whose use they were ignorant, and thus to retain their actual and innate condition of ignorance, than to destroy the whole fabric of their reasoning and start afresh. They therefore laid down as an axiom, that God's judgments far transcend human understanding. Such a doctrine might well have sufficed to conceal the truth from the human race for all eternity, if mathematics had not furnished another standard of verity in considering solely the essence and properties of figures without regard to their final causes. There are other reasons (which I need not mention here) besides mathematics, which might have caused men's minds to be directed to these general prejudices, and have led them to the knowledge of the truth.

I have now sufficiently explained my first point. There is no need to show at length, that nature has no particular goal in view, and that final causes are mere human figments. This, I think, is already evident enough, both from the causes and foundations on which I have shown such prejudice to be based, and also from Prop. xvi., and the Corollary of Prop. xxxii., and, in fact, all those propositions in which I have shown, that everything in nature proceeds from a sort of necessity, and with the utmost perfection. However, I will add a few remarks, in order to overthrow this doctrine of a final cause utterly. That which is really a cause it considers as an effect, and *vice versâ:* it makes that which is by nature first to be last, and that which is highest and most perfect to be most imperfect. Passing over the questions of cause and priority as self-evident, it is plain from Props. xxi., xxii., xxiii. that that effect is most perfect which is produced immediately by God; the effect which requires for its production several intermediate causes is, in that respect, more imperfect. But if those things which were made immediately by God were made to enable him to attain his end, then the things which come after, for the sake of which the first were made, are necessarily the most excellent of all.

Further, this doctrine does away with the perfection of God: for, if God acts for an object, he necessarily desires something which he lacks. Certainly, theologians and metaphysicians draw a distinction between the object of want and the object of assimilation; still they confess that God made all things for the sake of himself, not for the sake of creation. They are unable to point to anything prior to creation, except God himself, as an object for which God should act, and are therefore driven to admit (as they clearly must), that God lacked those things for whose attainment he created means, and further that he desired them.

We must not omit to notice that the followers of this doctrine, anxious to display their talent in assigning final causes, have imported a new method of argument in proof of their theory—namely, a reduction, not to the impossible, but to ignorance; thus showing that they have no other method of exhibiting their doctrine. For example, if a stone falls from a roof on to someone's head, and kills him, they will demonstrate by their new method, that the stone fell in order to kill the man; for, if it had not by God's will fallen with that object, how could so many circumstances (and there are often many concurrent circumstances) have all happened together by chance? Perhaps you will answer that the event is due to the facts that the wind was blowing, and the man was walking that way. "But why," they will insist, "was the wind blowing, and why was the man at that very time walking that way?" If you again answer, that the wind had then sprung up because the sea had begun to be agitated the day before, the weather being previously calm, and that the man had been invited by a friend, they will again insist: "But why was the sea agitated, and why was the man invited at that time?" So they will pursue their questions from cause to cause, till at last you take refuge in the will of God—in other words, the sanctuary of ignorance. So, again, when they survey the frame of the human body, they are amazed; and being ignorant of the causes of so great a work of art, conclude that it has been fashioned, not mechanically, but by divine and supernatural skill, and has been so put together that one part shall not hurt another.

Hence anyone who seeks for the true causes of miracles, and strives to understand natural phenomena as an intelligent being, and not to gaze at them like a fool, is set down and denounced as an impious heretic by those, whom the masses adore as the interpreters of nature and the gods. Such persons know that, with the removal of ignorance, the wonder which forms their only available means for proving and preserving their authority would vanish also. But I now quit this subject, and pass on to my third point.

After men persuaded themselves, that everything which is created is created for their sake, they were bound to consider as the chief quality in everything that which is most useful to themselves, and to account those things the best of all which have the most beneficial effect on mankind. Further, they were bound to form abstract notions for the explanation of the nature of things, such as *goodness, badness, order, confusion, warmth, cold, beauty, deformity*, and so on; and from the belief that they are free agents arose the further notions *praise* and *blame, sin* and *merit*.

I will speak of these latter hereafter, when I treat of human nature; the former I will briefly explain here.

Everything which conduces to health and the worship of God they have called *good*, everything which hinders these objects they have styled *bad*; and inasmuch as those who do not understand the nature of things do not verify phenomena in any way, but merely imagine them after a fashion, and mistake their imagination for understanding, such persons firmly believe that there is an *order* in things, being really ignorant both of things and their own nature. When phenomena are of such a kind, that the impression they make on our senses requires little effort of imagination, and can consequently be easily remembered, we say that they are *well-ordered*; if the contrary, that they are *ill-ordered* or *confused*. Further, as things which are easily imagined are more pleasing to us, men prefer order to confusion—as though there were any order in nature, except in relation to our imagination—and say that God has created all things in order; thus, without knowing it, attributing imagination to God, unless, indeed, they would have it that God foresaw human imagination, and arranged everything, so that it should be most easily imagined.

If this be their theory, they would not, perhaps, be daunted by the fact that we find an infinite number of phenomena, far surpassing our imagination, and very many others which confound its weakness. But enough has been said on this subject. The other abstract notions are nothing but modes of imagining, in which the imagination is differently affected, though they are considered by the ignorant as the chief attributes of things, inasmuch as they believe that everything was created for the sake of themselves; and, according as they are affected by it, style it good or bad, healthy or rotten and corrupt. For instance, if the motion which objects we see communicate to our nerves be conducive to health, the objects causing it are styled *beautiful;* if a contrary motion be excited, they are styled *ugly.*

Things which are perceived through our sense of smell are styled fragrant or fetid; if through our taste, sweet or bitter, full-flavoured or insipid; if through our touch, hard or soft, rough or smooth, &c.

Whatsoever affects our ears is said to give rise to noise, sound, or harmony. In this last case, there are men lunatic enough to believe, that even God himself takes pleasure in harmony; and philosophers are not lacking who have persuaded themselves, that the motion of the heavenly bodies gives rise to harmony—all of which instances sufficiently show that everyone judges of things according to the state of his brain, or rather mistakes for things the forms of his imagination. We need no longer wonder that there have arisen all the controversies we have witnessed, and finally scepticism: for, although human bodies in many respects agree, yet in very many others they differ; so that what seems good to one seems bad to another; what seems well ordered to one seems confused to another; what is pleasing to one displeases another, and so on. I need not further enumerate, because this is not the place to treat the subject at length, and also because the fact is sufficiently well known. It is commonly said: "So many men, so many minds; everyone is wise in his own way; brains differ as completely as palates." All of which proverbs show, that men judge of things according to their mental disposition, and rather imagine than understand: for, if they understood phenomena, they would, as mathematics attest, be convinced, if not attracted, by what I have urged.

We have now perceived, that all the explanations commonly given of nature are mere modes of imagining, and do not indicate the true nature of anything, but only the constitution of the imagination; and, although they have names, as though they were entities, existing externally to the imagination, I call them entities imaginary rather than real; and, therefore, all arguments against us drawn from such abstractions are easily rebutted.

Many argue in this way. If all things follow from a necessity of the absolutely perfect nature of God, why are there so many imperfections in nature? such, for instance, as things corrupt to the point of putridity, loathsome deformity, confusion, evil, sin, &c. But these reasoners are, as I have said, easily confuted, for the perfection of things is to be reckoned only from their own nature and power; things are not more or less perfect, according as they delight or offend human senses, or according as they are serviceable or repugnant to mankind. To those who ask why God did not so create all men, that they should be governed only by reason, I give no answer but this: because matter was not lacking to him for the creation of every degree of perfection from highest to lowest; or, more strictly, because the laws of his nature are so vast, as to suffice for the production of everything conceivable by an infinite intelligence, as I have shown in Prop. xvi.

Such are the misconceptions I have undertaken to note; if there are any more of the same sort, everyone may easily dissipate them for himself with the aid of a little reflection.

Part II. Of the nature and origin of the mind

.   .   .

PROP. XLIV. *It is not in the nature of reason to regard things as contingent, but as necessary.*

Proof.—It is in the nature of reason to perceive things truly (II. xli.), namely (I. Ax. vi.), as they are in themselves—that is (I. xxix.), not as contingent, but as necessary. *Q.E.D.*

Corollary I.—Hence it follows, that it is only through our imagination that we consider things, whether in respect to the future or the past, as contingent.

Note.—How this way of looking at things arises, I will briefly explain. We have shown above (II. xvii. and Coroll.) that the mind always regards things as present to itself, even though they be not in existence, until some causes arise which exclude their existence and presence. Further (II. xviii.), we showed that, if the human body has once been affected by two external bodies simultaneously, the mind, when it afterwards imagines one of the said external bodies, will straightway remember the other—that is, it will regard both as present to itself, unless there arise causes which exclude their existence and presence. Further, no one doubts that we imagine time, from the fact that we imagine bodies to be moved some more slowly than others, some more quickly, some at equal speed. Thus, let us suppose that a child yesterday saw Peter for the first time in the morning, Paul at noon, and Simon in the evening; then, that to-day he again sees Peter in the morning. It is evident, from II. Prop. xviii, that, as soon as he sees the morning light, he will imagine that the sun will traverse the same parts of the sky, as it did when he saw it on the preceding day; in other words, he will imagine a complete day, and, together with his imagination of the morning, he will imagine Peter; with noon, he will imagine Paul; and with evening, he will imagine Simon—that is, he will imagine the existence of Paul and Simon in relation to a future time; on the other hand, if he sees Simon in the evening, he will refer Peter and Paul to a past time, by imagining them simultaneously with the imagination of a past time. If it should at any time happen, that on some other evening the child should see James instead of Simon, he will, on the following morning, associate with his imagination of evening sometimes Simon, sometimes James, not both together: for the child is supposed to have seen, at evening, one or other of them, not both together. His imagination will therefore waver; and, with the imagination of future evenings, he will associate first one, then the other—that is, he will imagine them in the future, neither of them as certain, but both as contingent. This wavering of the imagination will be the same, if the imagination be concerned with things which we thus contemplate, standing in relation to time past or time present: consequently, we may imagine things as contingent, whether they be referred to time present, past, or future.

Corollary II.—It is in the nature of reason to perceive things under a certain form of eternity (*sub quâdam æternitatis specie*).

Proof.—It is in the nature of reason to regard things, not as contingent, but as necessary (II. xliv.). Reason perceives this necessity of things (II. xli.) truly—that is (I. Ax. vi.), as it is in itself. But (I. xvi.) this necessity of things is the very necessity of the eternal nature of God; therefore, it is in the nature of reason to regard things under this form of eternity. We may add that the bases of reason are the notions (II. xxxviii.), which answer to things common to all, and which (II. xxxvii.) do not answer to the essence of any particular thing: which must therefore be conceived without any relation to time, under a certain form of eternity.

.   .   .

PROP. XLVIII. *In the mind there is no absolute or free will; but the mind is determined to wish this or that by a cause, which has also been determined by another cause, and this last by another cause, and so on to infinity.*

Proof.—The mind is a fixed and definite mode of thought (II. xi.), therefore it cannot be the free cause of its actions (I. xvii. Coroll. ii.); in other words, it cannot have an absolute faculty of positive or negative volition; but (by I. xxviii.) it must be determined by a cause, which has also been determined by another cause, and this last by another, &c. *Q.E.D.*

Note.—In the same way it is proved, that there is in the mind no absolute faculty of understanding, desiring, loving, &c. Whence it follows, that these and similar faculties are either entirely fictitious, or are merely abstract or general terms, such as we are accustomed to put together from particular things. Thus the intellect and the will stand in the same relation to this or that idea, or this or that volition, as "lapidity" to this or that stone, or as "man" to Peter and Paul. The cause which leads men to consider themselves free has been set forth in the Appendix to Part I. But, before I proceed further, I would here remark that, by the will to affirm and decide, I mean the faculty, not the desire. I mean, I repeat, the faculty, whereby the mind affirms or denies what is true or false, not the desire, wherewith the mind wishes for or turns away from any given thing. After we have proved, that these faculties of ours are general notions, which cannot be distinguished from the particular instances on which they are based, we must inquire whether volitions themselves are anything besides the ideas of things. We must inquire, I say, whether there is in the mind any affirmation or negation beyond that, which the idea, in so far as it is an idea, involves. On which subject see the following proposition, and II. Def. iii., lest the idea of pictures should suggest itself. For by ideas I do not mean images such as are formed at the back of the eye, or in the midst of the brain, but the conceptions of thought.

PROP. XLIX. *There is in the mind no volition or affirmation and negation, save that which an idea, inasmuch as it is an idea, involves.*

Proof.—There is in the mind no absolute faculty of positive or negative volition, but only particular volitions, namely, this or that affirmation, and this or that negation. Now let us conceive a particular volition, namely, the mode of thinking whereby the mind affirms, that the three interior angles of a triangle are equal to two right angles. This affirmation involves the conception or idea of a triangle, that is, without the idea of a triangle it cannot be conceived. It is the same thing to say, that the concept A must involve the concept B, as it is to say, that A cannot be conceived without B. Further, this affirmation cannot be made (II. Ax. iii.) without the idea of a triangle. Therefore, this affirmation can neither be nor be conceived, without the idea of a triangle. Again, this idea of a triangle must involve this same affirmation, namely, that its three interior angles are equal to two right angles. Wherefore, and *vice versâ*, this idea of a triangle can neither be nor be conceived without this affirmation, therefore, this affirmation belongs to the essence of the idea of a triangle, and is nothing besides. What we have said of this volition (inasmuch as we have selected it at random) may be said of any other volition, namely, that it is nothing but an idea.   *Q.E.D.*

Corollary.—Will and understanding are one and the same.

Proof.—Will and understanding are nothing beyond the individual volitions and ideas (II. xlviii. and note). But a particular volition and a particular idea are one and the same (by the foregoing Prop.); therefore, will and understanding are one and the same.   *Q.E.D.*

Note.—We have thus removed the cause which is commonly assigned for error. For we have shown above, that falsity consists solely in the privation of knowledge involved in ideas which are fragmentary and confused. Wherefore, a false idea, inasmuch as it is false, does not involve certainty. When we say, then, that a man acquiesces in what is false, and that he has no doubts on the subject, we do not say that he is certain, but only that he does not doubt, or that he acquiesces in what is false, inasmuch as there are no reasons, which should cause his imagination to waver (see II. xliv. note). Thus, although the man be assumed to acquiesce in what is false, we shall never say that he is certain. For by certainty we mean something positive (II. xliii. and note), not merely the absence of doubt.

However, in order that the foregoing proposition may be fully explained, I will draw attention to a few additional points, and I will furthermore answer the objections which may be advanced against our doctrine. Lastly, in order to remove every scruple, I have thought it worth while to point out some of the advantages, which follow therefrom. I say "some," for they will be better appreciated from what we shall set forth in the fifth part.

I begin, then, with the first point, and warn my readers to make an accurate distinction between an idea, or conception of the mind, and the images of things which we imagine. It is further necessary that they should distinguish between idea and words, whereby we signify things. These three—namely, images, words, and ideas—are by many persons either entirely confused together, or not distinguished with sufficient accuracy or care, and hence people are generally in ignorance, how absolutely necessary is a knowledge of this doctrine of the will, both for philosophic purposes and for the wise ordering of life. Those who think that ideas consist in images which are formed in us by contact with external bodies, persuade themselves that the ideas of those things, whereof we can form no mental picture, are not ideas, but only figments, which we invent by the free decree of our will; they thus regard ideas as though they were inanimate pictures on a panel, and, filled with this misconception, do not see that an idea, inasmuch as it is an idea, involves an affirmation or negation. Again, those who confuse words with ideas, or with the affirmation which an idea involves, think that they can wish something contrary to what they feel, affirm, or deny. This misconception will easily be laid aside by one, who reflects on the nature of knowledge, and seeing that it in no wise involves the conception of extension, will therefore clearly understand, that an idea (being a mode of thinking) does not consist in the image of anything, nor in words. The essence of words and images is put together by bodily motions, which in no wise involve the conception of thought.

These few words on this subject will suffice: I will therefore pass on to consider the objections, which may be raised against our doctrine. Of these, the first is advanced by those, who think that the will has a wider scope than the understanding, and that therefore it is different therefrom. The reason for their holding the belief, that the will has wider scope than the understanding, is that they assert, that they have no need of an increase in their faculty of assent, that is of affirmation or negation, in order to assent to an infinity of things which we do not perceive, but that they have need of an increase in their faculty of understanding. The will is thus distinguished from the intellect, the latter being finite and the former infinite. Secondly, it may be objected that experience seems to teach us especially clearly, that we are able to suspend our judgment before assenting to things which we perceive; this is confirmed by the fact that no one is said to be deceived, in so far as he perceives anything, but only in so far as he assents or dissents.

For instance, he who feigns a winged horse, does not therefore admit that a winged horse exists; that is, he is not deceived, unless he admits in addition that a winged horse does exist. Nothing therefore seems to be taught more clearly by experience, than that the will or faculty of assent is free and different from the faculty of understanding. Thirdly, it may be objected that one affirmation does not apparently contain more reality than another; in other words, that we do not seem to need for affirming, that what is true is true, any greater power than for affirming, that what is false is true. We have, however, seen that one idea has more reality or perfection than another, for as objects are some more excellent than others, so also are the ideas of them some more excellent than others; this also seems to point to a difference between the understanding and the will. Fourthly, it may be objected, if man does not act from free will, what will happen if the incentives to action are equally balanced, as in the case of Buridan's ass? Will he perish of hunger and thirst? If I say that he would, I shall seem to have in my thoughts an ass or the statue of a man rather than an actual man. If I say that he would not, he would then determine his own action, and would consequently possess the faculty of going and doing whatever he liked. Other objections might also be raised, but, as I am not bound to put in evidence everything that anyone may dream, I will only set myself to the task of refuting those I have mentioned, and that as briefly as possible.

To the *first* objection I answer, that I admit that the will has a wider scope than the understanding, if by the understanding be meant only clear and distinct ideas; but I deny that the will has a wider scope than the perceptions, and the faculty of forming conceptions; nor do I see why the faculty of volition should be called infinite, any more than the faculty of feeling: for, as we are able by the same faculty of volition to affirm an infinite number of things (one after the other, for we cannot affirm an infinite number simultaneously), so also can we, by the same faculty of feeling, feel or perceive (in succession) an infinite number of bodies. If it be said that there is an infinite number of things which we cannot perceive, I answer, that we cannot attain to such things by any thinking, nor, consequently, by any faculty of volition. But, it may still be urged, if God wished to bring it about that we should perceive them, he would be obliged to endow us with a greater faculty of perception, but not a greater faculty of volition than we have already. This is the same as to say that, if God wished to bring it about that we should understand an infinite number of other entities, it would be necessary for him to give us a greater understanding, but not a more universal idea of entity than that which we have already, in order to grasp such infinite entities. We have shown that will is a universal entity or idea, whereby we explain all particular volitions—in other words, that which is common to all such volitions.

As, then, our opponents maintain that this idea, common or universal to all volitions, is a faculty, it is little to be wondered at that they assert, that such a faculty extends itself into the infinite, beyond the limits of the understanding: for what is universal is predicated alike of one, of many, and of an infinite number of individuals.

To the *second* objection I reply by denying, that we have a free power of suspending our judgment: for, when we say that anyone suspends his judgment, we merely mean that he sees, that he does not perceive the matter in question adequately. Suspension of judgment is, therefore, strictly speaking, a perception, and not free will. In order to illustrate the point, let us suppose a boy imagining a horse, and perceiving nothing else. Inasmuch as this imagination involves the existence of the horse (II. xvii. Coroll.), and the boy does not perceive anything which would exclude the existence of the horse, he will necessarily regard the horse as present: he will not be able to doubt of its existence, although he be not certain thereof. We have daily experience of such a state of things in dreams; and I do not suppose that there is anyone, who would maintain that, while he is dreaming, he has the free power of suspending his judgment concerning the things in his dream, and bringing it about that he should not dream those things, which he dreams that he sees; yet it happens, notwithstanding, that even in dreams we suspend our judgment, namely, when we dream that we are dreaming.

Further, I grant that no one can be deceived, so far as actual perception extends—that is, I grant that the mind's imaginations, regarded in themselves, do not involve error (II. xvii., note); but I deny, that a man does not, in the act of perception, make any affirmation. For what is the perception of a winged horse, save affirming that a horse has wings? If the mind could perceive nothing else but the winged horse, it would regard the same as present to itself: it would have no reasons for doubting its existence, nor any faculty of dissent, unless the imagination of a winged horse be joined to an idea which precludes the existence of the said horse, or unless the mind perceives that the idea which it possesses of a winged horse is inadequate, in which case it will either necessarily deny the existence of such a horse, or will necessarily be in doubt on the subject.

I think that I have anticipated my answer to the *third* objection, namely, that the will is something universal which is predicated of all ideas, and that it only signifies that which is common to all ideas, namely, an affirmation, whose adequate essence must, therefore, in so far as it is thus conceived in the abstract, be in every idea, and be, in this respect alone, the same in all, not in so far as it is considered as constituting the idea's essence: for, in this respect, particular affirmations differ one from the other, as much as do ideas. For instance, the affirmation which involves the idea of a circle, differs from that which involves the idea of a triangle, as much as the idea of a circle differs from the idea of a triangle.

Further, I absolutely deny, that we are in need of an equal power of thinking, to affirm that that which is true is true, and to affirm that that which is false is true. These two affirmations, if we regard the mind, are in the same relation to one another as being and not-being; for there is nothing positive in ideas, which constitutes the actual reality of falsehood (II. xxxv. note, and xlvii. note).

We must therefore conclude, that we are easily deceived, when we confuse universals with singulars, and the entities of reason and abstractions with realities. As for the *fourth* objection, I am quite ready to admit, that a man placed in the equilibrium described (namely, as perceiving nothing but hunger and thirst, a certain food and a certain drink, each equally distant from him) would die of hunger and thirst. If I am asked, whether such an one should not rather be considered an ass than a man; I answer, that I do not know, neither do I know how a man should be considered, who hangs himself, or how we should consider children, fools, madmen, &c.

It remains to point out the advantages of a knowledge of this doctrine as bearing on conduct, and this may be easily gathered from what has been said. The doctrine is good,

1. Inasmuch as it teaches us to act solely according to the decree of God, and to be partakers in the Divine nature, and so much the more, as we perform more perfect actions and more and more understand God. Such a doctrine not only completely tranquillizes our spirit, but also shows us where our highest happiness or blessedness is, namely, solely in the knowledge of God, whereby we are led to act only as love and piety shall bid us. We may thus clearly understand, how far astray from a true estimate of virtue are those who expect to be decorated by God with high rewards for their virtue, and their best actions, as for having endured the direst slavery; as if virtue and the service of God were not in itself happiness and perfect freedom.

2. Inasmuch as it teaches us, how we ought to conduct ourselves with respect to the gifts of fortune, or matters which are not in our own power, and do not follow from our nature. For it shows us, that we should await and endure fortune's smiles or frowns with an equal mind, seeing that all things follow from the eternal decree of God by the same necessity, as it follows from the essence of a triangle, that the three angles are equal to two right angles.

3. This doctrine raises social life, inasmuch as it teaches us to hate no man, neither to despise, to deride, to envy, or to be angry with any. Further, as it tells us that each should be content with his own, and helpful to his neighbour, not from any womanish pity, favour, or superstition, but solely by the guidance of reason, according as the time and occasion demand, as I will show in Part III.

4. Lastly, this doctrine confers no small advantage on the commonwealth; for it teaches how citizens should be governed and led, not so as to become slaves, but so that they may freely do whatsoever things are best.

I have thus fulfilled the promise made at the beginning of this note, and I thus bring the second part of my treatise to a close. I think I have therein explained the nature and properties of the human mind at sufficient length, and, considering the difficulty of the subject, with sufficient clearness. I have laid a foundation, whereon may be raised many excellent conclusions of the highest utility and most necessary to be known, as will, in what follows, be partly made plain.

Part III. On the origin and nature of the emotions

Most writers on the emotions and on human conduct seem to be treating rather of matters outside nature than of natural phenomena following nature's general laws. They appear to conceive man to be situated in nature as a kingdom within a kingdom: for they believe that he disturbs rather than follows nature's order, that he has absolute control over his actions, and that he is determined solely by himself. They attribute human infirmities and fickleness, not to the power of nature in general, but to some mysterious flaw in the nature of man, which accordingly they bemoan, deride, despise, or, as usually happens, abuse: he, who succeeds in hitting off the weakness of the human mind more eloquently or more acutely than his fellows, is looked upon as a seer. Still there has been no lack of very excellent men (to whose toil and industry I confess myself much indebted), who have written many noteworthy things concerning the right way of life, and have given much sage advice to mankind. But no one, so far as I know, has defined the nature and strength of the emotions, and the power of the mind against them for their restraint.

I do not forget, that the illustrious Descartes, though he believed, that the mind has absolute power over its actions, strove to explain human emotions by their primary causes, and, at the same time, to point out a way, by which the mind might attain to absolute dominion over them. However, in my opinion, he accomplishes nothing beyond a display of the acuteness of his own great intellect, as I will show in the proper place. For the present I wish to revert to those, who would rather abuse or deride human emotions than understand them. Such persons will, doubtless think it strange that I should attempt to treat of human vice and folly geometrically, and should wish to set forth with rigid reasoning those matters which they cry out against as repugnant to reason, frivolous, absurd, and dreadful. However, such is my plan. Nothing comes to pass in nature, which can be set down to a flaw therein; for nature is always the same, and everywhere one and the same in her efficacy and power of action; that is, nature's laws and ordinances, whereby all things come to pass and change from one form to another, are everywhere and always the same; so that there should be one and the same method of understanding the nature of all things whatsoever, namely, through nature's universal laws and rules. Thus the passions of hatred, anger, envy, and so on, considered in themselves, follow from this same necessity and efficacy of nature; they answer to certain definite causes, through which they are understood, and possess certain properties as worthy of being known as the properties of anything else, whereof the contemplation in itself affords us delight. I shall, therefore, treat of the nature and strength of the emotions according to the same method, as I employed heretofore in my investigations concerning God and the mind. I shall consider human actions and desires in exactly the same manner, as though I were concerned with lines, planes, and solids.

DEFINITIONS

I. By an *adequate* cause, I mean a cause through which its effect can be clearly and distinctly perceived. By an *inadequate* or partial cause, I mean a cause through which, by itself, its effect cannot be understood.

II. I say that we *act* when anything takes place, either within us or externally to us, whereof we are the adequate cause; that is (by the foregoing definition) when through our nature something takes place within us or externally to us, which can through our nature alone be clearly and distinctly understood. On the other hand, I say that we are passive as regards something when that something takes place within us, or follows from our nature externally, we being only the partial cause.

III. By *emotion* I mean the modifications of the body, whereby the active power of the said body is increased or diminished, aided or constrained, and also the ideas of such modifications.

N.B. If we can be the adequate cause of any of these modifications, I then call the emotion an activity, otherwise I call it a passion, or state wherein the mind is passive.

POSTULATES

I. The human body can be affected in many ways, whereby its power of activity is increased or diminished, and also in other ways which do not render its power of activity either greater or less.

N.B. This postulate or axiom rests on Postulate i. and Lemmas v. and vii., which see after II. xiii.

II. The human body can undergo many changes, and, nevertheless, retain the impressions or traces of objects (cf. II. Post. v.), and, consequently, the same images of things (see note II, xvii.).

PROPOSITIONS

PROP. I. *Our mind is in certain cases active, and in certain cases passive. In so far as it has adequate ideas it is necessarily active, and in so far as it has inadequate ideas, it is necessarily passive.*

Proof.—In every human mind there are some adequate ideas, and some ideas that are fragmentary and confused (II. xl. note). Those ideas which are adequate in the mind are adequate also in God, inasmuch as he constitutes the essence of the mind (II. xl. Coroll.), and those which are inadequate in the mind are likewise (by the same Coroll.) adequate in God, not inasmuch as he contains in himself the essence of the given mind alone, but as he, at the same time, contains the minds of other things. Again, from any given idea some effect must necessarily follow (I. 36); of this effect God is the adequate cause (III. Def. i.), not inasmuch as he is infinite, but inasmuch as he is conceived as affected by the given idea (II. ix.). But of that effect whereof God is the cause, inasmuch as he is affected by an idea which is adequate in a given mind, of that effect, I repeat, the mind in question is the adequate cause (II. xi. Coroll.). Therefore our mind, in so far as it has adequate ideas (III. Def. ii.), is in certain cases necessarily active; this was our first point. Again, whatsoever necessarily follows from the idea which is adequate in God, not by virtue of his possessing in himself the mind of one man only, but by virtue of his containing, together with the mind of that one man, the minds of other things also, of such an effect (II. xi. Coroll.) the mind of the given man is not an adequate, but only a partial cause; thus (III. Def. ii.) the mind, inasmuch as it has inadequate ideas, is in certain cases necessarily passive; this was our second point. Therefore our mind, &c. *Q.E.D.*

Corollary.—Hence it follows that the mind is more or less liable to be acted upon, in proportion as it possesses inadequate ideas, and, contrariwise, is more or less active in proportion as it possesses adequate ideas.

PROP. II. *Body cannot determine mind to think, neither can mind determine body to motion or rest or any state different from these, if such there be.*

Proof.—All modes of thinking have for their cause God, by virtue of his being a thinking thing, and not by virtue of his being displayed under any other attribute (II. vi.). That, therefore, which determines the mind to thought is a mode of thought, and not a mode of extension; that is (II. Def. i.), it is not body. This was our first point. Again, the motion and rest of a body must arise from another body, which has also been determined to a state of motion or rest by a third body, and absolutely everything which takes place in a body must spring from God, in so far as he is regarded as affected by some mode of extension, and not by some mode of thought (II. vi.); that is, it cannot spring from the mind, which is a mode of thought. This was our second point. Therefore body cannot determine mind, &c. *Q.E.D.*

Note.—This is made more clear by what was said in the note to II. vii., namely, that mind and body are one and the same thing, conceived first under the attribute of thought, secondly, under the attribute of extension. Thus it follows that the order or concatenation of things is identical, whether nature be conceived under the one attribute or the other; consequently the order of states of activity and passivity in our body is simultaneous in nature with the order of states of activity and passivity in the mind. The same conclusion is evident from the manner in which we proved II. xii.

Nevertheless, though such is the case, and though there be no further room for doubt, I can scarcely believe, until the fact is proved by experience, that men can be induced to consider the question calmly and fairly, so firmly are they convinced that it is merely at the bidding of the mind, that the body is set in motion or at rest, or performs a variety of actions depending solely on the mind's will or the exercise of thought. However, no one has hitherto laid down the limits to the powers of the body, that is, no one has as yet been taught by experience what the body can accomplish solely by the laws of nature, in so far as she is regarded as extension. No one hitherto has gained such an accurate knowledge of the bodily mechanism, that he can explain all its functions; nor need I call attention to the fact that many actions are observed in the lower animals, which far transcend human sagacity, and that somnambulists do many things in their sleep, which they would not venture to do when awake: these instances are enough to show, that the body can by the sole laws of its nature do many things which the mind wonders at.

Again, no one knows how or by what means the mind moves the body, nor how many various degrees of motion it can impart to the body, nor how quickly it can move it. Thus, when men say that this or that physical action has its origin in the mind, which latter has dominion over the body, they are using words without meaning, or are confessing in specious phraseology that they are ignorant of the cause of the said action, and do not wonder at it.

But, they will say, whether we know or do not know the means whereby the mind acts on the body, we have, at any rate, experience of the fact that unless the human mind is in a fit state to think, the body remains inert. Moreover, we have experience, that the mind alone can determine whether we speak or are silent, and a variety of similar states which, accordingly, we say depend on the mind's decree. But, as to the first point, I ask such objectors, whether experience does not also teach, that if the body be inactive the mind is simultaneously unfitted for thinking? For when the body is at rest in sleep, the mind simultaneously is in a state of torpor also, and has no power of thinking, such as it possesses when the body is awake. Again, I think everyone's experience will confirm the statement, that the mind is not at all times equally fit for thinking on a given subject, but according as the body is more or less fitted for being stimulated by the image of this or that object, so also is the mind more or less fitted for contemplating the said object.

But, it will be urged, it is impossible that solely from the laws of nature considered as extended substance, we should be able to deduce the causes of buildings, pictures, and things of that kind, which are produced only by human art; nor would the human body, unless it were determined and led by the mind, be capable of building a single temple. However, I have just pointed out that the objectors cannot fix the limits of the body's power, or say what can be concluded from a consideration of its sole nature, whereas they have experience of many things being accomplished solely by the laws of nature, which they would never have believed possible except under the direction of mind: such are the actions performed by somnambulists while asleep, and wondered at by their performers when awake. I would further call attention to the mechanism of the human body, which far surpasses in complexity all that has been put together by human art, not to repeat what I have already shown, namely, that from nature, under whatever attribute she be considered, infinite results follow. As for the second objection, I submit that the world would be much happier, if men were as fully able to keep silence as they are to speak. Experience abundantly shows that men can govern anything more easily than their tongues, and restrain anything more easily than their appetites; whence it comes about that many believe, that we are only free in respect to objects which we moderately desire, because our desire for such can easily be controlled by the thought of something else frequently remembered, but that we are by no means free in respect to what we seek with violent emotion, for our desire cannot then be allayed with the remembrance of anything else. However, unless such persons had proved by experience that we do many things which we afterwards repent of, and again that we often, when assailed by contrary emotions, see the better and follow the worse, there would be nothing to prevent their believing that we are free in all things. Thus an infant believes that of its own free will it desires milk, an angry child believes that it freely desires vengeance, a timid child believes that it freely desires to run away; further, a drunken man believes that he utters from the free decision of his mind words which, when he is sober, he would willingly have withheld: thus, too, a delirious man, a garrulous woman, a child, and others of like complexion, believe that they speak from the free decision of their mind, when they are in reality unable to restrain their impulse to talk. Experience teaches us no less clearly than reason, that men believe themselves to be free, simply because they are conscious of their actions, and unconscious of the causes whereby those actions are determined; and, further, it is plain that the dictates of the mind are but another name for the appetites, and therefore vary according to the varying state of the body. Everyone shapes his actions according to his emotion, those who are assailed by conflicting emotions know not what they wish; those who are not attacked by any emotion are readily swayed this way or that. All these considerations clearly show that a mental decision and a bodily appetite, or determined state, are simultaneous, or rather are one and the same thing, which we call decision, when it is regarded under and explained through the attribute of thought, and a conditioned state, when it is regarded under the attribute of extension, and deduced from the laws of motion and rest. This will appear yet more plainly in the sequel. For the present I wish to call attention to another point, namely, that we cannot act by the decision of the mind, unless we have a remembrance of having done so. For instance, we cannot say a word without remembering that we have done so. Again, it is not within the free power of the mind to remember or forget a thing at will. Therefore the freedom of the mind must in any case be limited to the power of uttering or not uttering something which it remembers. But when we dream that we speak, we believe that we speak from a free decision of the mind, yet we do not speak, or, if we do, it is by a spontaneous motion of the body. Again, we dream that we are concealing something, and we seem to act from the same decision of the mind as that, whereby we keep silence when awake concerning something we know. Lastly, we dream that from the free decision of our mind we do something, which we should not dare to do when awake.

Now I should like to know whether there be in the mind two sorts of decisions, one sort illusive, and the other sort free? If our folly does not carry us so far as this, we must necessarily admit, that the decision of the mind, which is believed to be free, is not distinguishable from the imagination or memory, and is nothing more than the affirmation, which an idea, by virtue of being an idea, necessarily involves (II. xlix.). Wherefore these decisions of the mind arise in the mind by the same necessity, as the ideas of things actually existing. Therefore those who believe, that they speak or keep silence or act in any way from the free decision of their mind, do but dream with their eyes open.

PROP. III. *The activities of the mind arise solely from adequate ideas; the passive states of the mind depend solely on inadequate ideas.*

Proof.—The first element, which constitutes the essence of the mind, is nothing else but the idea of the actually existent body (II. xi. and xiii.), which (II. xv.) is compounded of many other ideas, whereof some are adequate and some inadequate (II. xxix. Coroll., II. xxxviii. Coroll.). Whatsoever therefore follows from the nature of mind, and has mind for its proximate cause, through which it must be understood, must necessarily follow either from an adequate or from an inadequate idea. But in so far as the mind (III. i.) has inadequate ideas, it is necessarily passive: wherefore the activities of the mind follow solely from adequate ideas, and accordingly the mind is only passive in so far as it has inadequate ideas. Q.E.D.

Note.—Thus we see, that passive states are not attributed to the mind, except in so far as it contains something involving negation, or in so far as it is regarded as a part of nature, which cannot be clearly and distinctly perceived through itself without other parts: I could thus show, that passive states are attributed to individual things in the same way that they are attributed to the mind, and that they cannot otherwise be perceived, but my purpose is solely to treat of the human mind.

PROP. IV. *Nothing can be destroyed, except by a cause external to itself.*

Proof.—This proposition is self-evident, for the definition of anything affirms the essence of that thing, but does not negative it; in other words, it postulates the essence of the thing, but does not take it away. So long therefore as we regard only the thing itself, without taking into account external causes, we shall not be able to find in it anything which could destroy it. Q.E.D.

PROP. V. *Things are naturally contrary, that is, cannot exist in the same object, in so far as one is capable of destroying the other.*

Proof.—If they could agree together or co-exist in the same object, there would then be in the said object something which could destroy it; but this, by the foregoing proposition, is absurd, therefore things, &c. Q.E.D.

PROP. VI. *Everything, in so far as it is in itself, endeavours to persist in its own being.*

Proof.—Individual things are modes whereby the attributes of God are expressed in a given determinate manner (I. xxv. Coroll.); that is (I.

xxxiv.), they are things which express in a given determinate manner the power of God, whereby God is and acts; now no thing contains in itself anything whereby it can be destroyed, or which can take away its existence (III. iv.); but contrariwise it is opposed to all that could take away its existence (III. v.). Therefore, in so far as it can, and in so far as it is in itself, it endeavours to persist in its own being. *Q.E.D.*

PROP. VII. *The endeavour, wherewith everything endeavours to persist in its own being, is nothing else but the actual essence of the thing in question.*

Proof.—From the given essence of any thing certain consequences necessarily follow (I. xxxvi.), nor have things any power save such as necessarily follows from their nature as determined (I. xxix.); wherefore the power of any given thing, or the endeavour whereby, either alone or with other things, it acts, or endeavours to act, that is (III. vi.), the power or endeavour, wherewith it endeavours to persist in its own being, is nothing else but the given or actual essence of the thing in question. *Q.E.D.*

PROP. VIII. *The endeavour, whereby a thing endeavours to persist in its being, involves no finite time, but an indefinite time.*

Proof.—If it involved a limited time, which should determine the duration of the thing, it would then follow solely from that power whereby the thing exists, that the thing could not exist beyond the limits of that time, but that it must be destroyed; but this (III. iv.) is absurd. Wherefore the endeavour wherewith a thing exists involves no definite time; but, contrariwise, since (III. iv.) it will be the same power whereby it already exists always continue to exist, unless it be destroyed by some external cause, this endeavour involves an indefinite time.

PROP. IX. *The mind, both in so far as it has clear and distinct ideas, and also in so far as it has confused ideas, endeavours to persist in its being for an indefinite period, and of this endeavour it is conscious.*

Proof.—The essence of the mind is constituted by adequate and inadequate ideas (III. iii.), therefore (III. vii.), both in so far as it possesses the former, and in so far as it possesses the latter, it endeavours to persist in its own being, and that for an indefinite time (III. viii.). Now as the mind (II. xxiii.) is necessarily conscious of itself through the ideas of the modifications of the body, the mind is therefore (III. vii.) conscious of its own endeavour.

Note.—This endeavour, when referred solely to the mind, is called *will,* when referred to the mind and body in conjunction it is called *appetite;* it is, in fact, nothing else but man's essence, from the nature of which necessarily follow all those results which tend to its preservation; and which man has thus been determined to perform.

Further, between appetite and desire there is no difference, except that the term desire is generally applied to men, in so far as they are conscious of their appetite, and may accordingly be thus defined: *Desire is appetite with consciousness thereof.* It is thus plain from what has been said, that in no case do we strive for, wish for, long for, or desire anything, because we deem it to be good, but on the other hand we deem a thing to be good, because we strive for it, wish for it, long for it, or desire it.

PROP. X.   *An idea, which excludes the existence of our body, cannot be postulated in our mind, but is contrary thereto.*

Proof.—Whatsoever can destroy our body, cannot be postulated therein (III. v.). Therefore neither can the idea of such a thing occur in God, in so far as he has the idea of our body (II. ix. Coroll.); that is (II. xi. xiii.), the idea of that thing cannot be postulated as in our mind, but contrariwise, since (II. xi. xiii.) the first element, that constitutes the essence of the mind, is the idea of the human body as actually existing, it follows that the first and chief endeavour of our mind is the endeavour to affirm the existence of our body: thus, an idea, which negatives the existence of our body, is contrary to our mind, &c.   *Q.E.D.*

PROP. XI.   *Whatsoever increases or diminishes, helps or hinders the power of activity in our body, the idea thereof increases or diminishes, helps or hinders the power of thought in our mind.*

Proof.—This proposition is evident from II. vii. or from II. xiv.

Note.—Thus we see, that the mind can undergo many changes, and can pass sometimes to a state of greater perfection, sometimes to a state of lesser perfection. These passive states of transition explain to us the emotions of pleasure and pain. By *pleasure* therefore in the following propositions I shall signify *a passive state wherein the mind passes to a greater perfection.* By *pain* I shall signify *a passive state wherein the mind passes to a lesser perfection.* Further, the emotion of pleasure in reference to the body and mind together I shall call *stimulation* (*titillatio*) or *merriment* (*hilaritas*), the emotion of pain in the same relation I shall call *suffering* or *melancholy.* But we must bear in mind, that stimulation and suffering are attributed to man, when one part of his nature is more affected than the rest, merriment and melancholy, when all parts are alike affected. What I mean by desire I have explained in the note to Prop. ix. of this part; beyond these three I recognize no other primary emotion; I will show as I proceed, that all other emotions arise from these three. But, before I go further, I should like here to explain at greater length Prop. x. of this part, in order that we may clearly understand how one idea is contrary to another. In the note to II. xvii. we showed that the idea, which constitutes the essence of mind, involves the existence of body, so long as the body itself exists. Again, it follows from what we pointed out in the Coroll. to II. viii., that the present existence of our mind depends solely on the fact, that the mind involves the actual existence of the body. Lastly, we showed (II. xvii. xviii. and note) that the power of the mind, whereby it imagines and remembers things, also depends on the fact, that it involves the actual existence of the body. Whence it follows, that the present existence of the mind and its power of imagining are removed, as soon as the mind ceases to affirm the present existence of the body. Now the cause, why the mind ceases to affirm this existence of the body, cannot be the mind itself (III. iv.), nor again the fact that the body ceases to exist. For (by II. vi.) the cause, why the mind affirms the existence of the body, is not that the body began to exist; therefore, for the same reason, it does not cease to affirm the existence of the body, because the body ceases to exist; but (II. xvii.) this result follows from another idea, which excludes the present existence of our body and, consequently, of our mind, and which is therefore contrary to the idea constituting the essence of our mind.

.   .   .

PROP. XIV. *If the mind has once been affected by two emotions at the same time, it will, whenever it is afterwards affected by one of the two, be also affected by the other.*

Proof.—If the human body has once been affected by two bodies at once, whenever afterwards the mind conceives one of them, it will straightway remember the other also (II. xviii.). But the mind's conceptions indicate rather the emotions of our body than the nature of external bodies (II. xvi. Coroll. ii.); therefore, if the body, and consequently the mind (III. Def. iii.) has been once affected by two emotions at the same time, it will, whenever it is afterwards affected by one of the two, be also affected by the other.

PROP. XV. *Anything can, accidentally, be the cause of pleasure, pain, or desire.*

Proof.—Let it be granted that the mind is simultaneously affected by two emotions, of which one neither increases nor diminishes its power of activity, and the other does either increase or diminish the said power (III. Post. i.). From the foregoing proposition it is evident that, whenever the mind is afterwards affected by the former, through its true cause, which (by hypothesis) neither increases nor diminishes its power of action, it will be at the same time affected by the latter, which does increase or diminish its power of activity, that is (III. xi. note) it will be affected with pleasure or pain. Thus the former of the two emotions will, not through itself, but accidentally, be the cause of pleasure or pain. In the same way also it can be easily shown, that a thing may be accidentally the cause of desire.   *Q.E.D.*

Corollary.—Simply from the fact that we have regarded a thing with the emotion of pleasure or pain, though that thing be not the efficient cause of the emotion, we can either love or hate it.

Proof.—For from this fact alone it arises (III. xiv.), that the mind afterwards conceiving the said thing is affected with the emotion of pleasure or pain, that is (III. xi. note), according as the power of the mind and body may be increased or diminished, &c.; and consequently (III. xii.), according as the mind may desire or shrink from the conception of it (III. xiii. Coroll.), in other words (III. xiii. note), according as it may love or hate the same.   *Q.E.D.*

Note.—Hence we understand how it may happen, that we love or hate a thing without any cause for our emotion being known to us; merely, as the phrase is, from *sympathy* or *antipathy*. We should refer to the same category those objects, which affect us pleasurably or painfully, simply because they resemble other objects which affect us in the same way. This I will show in the next Prop. I am aware that certain authors, who were the first to introduce these terms "sympathy" and "antipathy," wished to signify thereby some occult qualities in things; nevertheless I think we may be permitted to use the same terms to indicate known or manifest qualities.

.   .   .

PROP. XXXVIII. *If a man has begun to hate an object of his love, so that love is thoroughly destroyed, he will, causes being equal, regard it with more hatred than if he had never loved it, and his hatred will be in proportion to the strength of his former love.*

.   .   .

PROP. XLIV. *Hatred which is completely vanquished by love passes into love: and love is thereupon greater than if hatred had not preceded it.*

Proof.—The proof proceeds in the same way as Prop. xxxviii. of this Part: for he who begins to love a thing, which he was wont to hate or regard with pain, from the very fact of loving feels pleasure. To this pleasure involved in love is added the pleasure arising from aid given to the endeavour to remove the pain involved in hatred (III. xxxvii.), accompanied by the idea of the former object of hatred as cause.

Note.—Though this be so, no one will endeavour to hate anything, or to be affected with pain, for the sake of enjoying this greater pleasure; that is, no one will desire that he should be injured, in the hope of recovering from the injury, nor long to be ill for the sake of getting well. For everyone will always endeavour to persist in his being, and to ward off pain as far as he can. If the contrary is conceivable, namely, that a man should desire to hate someone, in order that he might love him the more thereafter, he will always desire to hate him. For the strength of the love is in proportion to the strength of the hatred, wherefore the man would desire, that the hatred be continually increased more and more, and, for a similar reason, he would desire to become more and more ill, in order that he might take a greater pleasure in being restored to health: in such a case he would always endeavour to be ill, which (III. vi.) is absurd.

.   .   .

DEFINITIONS OF THE EMOTIONS

I. *Desire* is the actual essence of man, in so far as it is conceived, as determined to a particular activity by some given modification of itself.

Explanation.—We have said above, in the note to Prop. ix. of this part, that desire is appetite, with consciousness thereof; further, that appetite is the essence of man, in so far as it is determined to act in a way tending to promote its own peristence. But, in the same note,

I also remarked that, strictly speaking, I recognize no distinction between appetite and desire. For whether a man be conscious of his appetite or not, it remains one and the same appetite. Thus, in order to avoid the appearance of tautology, I have refrained from explaining desire by appetite; but I have taken care to define it in such a manner, as to comprehend, under one head, all those endeavours of human nature, which we distinguish by the terms appetite, will, desire, or impulse. I might, indeed, have said, that desire is the essence of man, in so far as it is conceived as determined to a particular activity; but from such a definition (cf. II. xxiii.) it would not follow that the mind can be conscious of its desire or appetite. Therefore, in order to imply the cause of such consciousness, it was necessary to add, *in so far as it is determined by some given modification, &c.* For, by a modification of man's essence, we understand every disposition of the said essence, whether such disposition be innate, or whether it be conceived solely under the attribute of thought, or solely under the attribute of extension, or whether, lastly, it be referred simultaneously to both these attributes. By the term desire, then, I here mean all man's endeavours, impulses, appetites, and volitions, which vary according to each man's disposition, and are, therefore, not seldom opposed one to another according as a man is drawn in different directions, and knows not where to turn.

II. *Pleasure* is the transition of a man from a less to a greater perfection.

III. *Pain* is the transition of a man from a greater to a less perfection.

Explanation.—I say transition: for pleasure is not perfection itself. For, if man were born with the perfection to which he passes, he would possess the same, without the emotion of pleasure. This appears more clearly from the consideration of the contrary emotion, pain. No one can deny, that pain consists in the transition to a less perfection, and not in the less perfection itself: for a man cannot be pained, in so far as he partakes of perfection of any degree. Neither can we say, that pain consists in the absence of a greater perfection. For absence is nothing, whereas the emotion of pain is an activity; wherefore this activity can only be the activity of transition from a greater to a less perfection—in other words, it is an activity whereby a man's power of action is lessened or constrained (cf. III. xi. note). I pass over the definitions of merriment, stimulation, melancholy, and grief, because these terms are generally used in reference to the body, and are merely kinds of pleasure or pain.

.   .   .

VI. *Love* is pleasure, accompanied by the idea of an external cause.

Explanation.—This definition explains sufficiently clearly the essence of love; the definition given by those authors who say that love is *the lover's wish to unite himself to the loved object* expresses a property, but not the essence of love; and, as such authors have not sufficiently discerned love's essence, they have been unable to acquire a true conception of its properties, accordingly their definition is on all hands admitted to be very obscure. It must, however, be noted, that when I say that it is a property of love, that the lover should wish to unite himself to the beloved object, I do not here mean by *wish* consent, or conclusion, or a free decision of the mind (for I have shown such, in II. xlviii., to be fictitious); neither do I mean a desire of being united to the loved object when it is absent, or of continuing in its presence when it is at hand; for love can be conceived without either of these desires; but by *wish* I mean the contentment, which is in the lover, on account of the presence of the beloved object, whereby the pleasure of the lover is strengthened, or at least maintained.

VII. *Hatred* is pain, accompanied by the idea of an external cause.

Explanation.—The observations are easily grasped after what has been said in the explanation of the preceding definition (cf. also III. xiii. note).

.　.　.

XXVII. *Repentance* is pain accompanied by the idea of some action, which we believe we have performed by the free decision of our mind.

Explanation.—The causes of these emotions we have set forth in III. li. note, and in III. liii. liv. lv. and note. Concerning the free decision of the mind see II. xxxv. note. This is perhaps the place to call attention to the fact, that it is nothing wonderful that all those actions, which are commonly called *wrong*, are followed by pain and all those, which are called *right*, are followed by pleasure. We can easily gather from what has been said, that this depends in great measure on education. Parents, by reprobating the former class of actions, and by frequently chiding their children because of them, and also by persuading to and praising the later class, have brought it about, that the former should be associated with pain and the latter with pleasure. This is confirmed by experience. For custom and religion are not the same among all men, but that which some consider sacred others consider profane, and what some consider honourable others consider disgraceful. According as each man has been educated, he feels repentance for a given action or glories therein.

.　.　.

Part IV. Of human bondage, or the strength of the emotions

PREFACE

Human infirmity in moderating and checking the emotions I name bondage: for, when a man is a prey to his emotions, he is not his own master, but lies at the mercy of fortune: so much so, that he is often compelled, while seeing that which is better for him, to follow that which is worse. Why this is so, and what is good or evil in the emotions, I propose to show in this part of my treatise. But, before I begin, it would

be well to make a few prefatory observations on perfection and imperfection, good and evil.

When a man has purposed to make a given thing, and has brought it
to perfection, his work will be pronounced perfect, not only by himself,
but by everyone who rightly knows, or thinks that he knows, the intention and aim of its author. For instance, suppose anyone sees a work
(which I assume to be not yet completed), and knows that the aim of
the author of that work is to build a house, he will call the work imperfect; he will, on the other hand, call it perfect, as soon as he sees
that it is carried through to the end, which its author had purposed
for it. But if a man sees a work, the like whereof he has never seen
before, and if he knows not the intention of the artificer, he plainly cannot know, whether that work be perfect or imperfect. Such seems to be
the primary meaning of these terms.

But, after men began to form general ideas, to think out types of
houses, buildings, towers, &c., and to prefer certain types to others, it
came about, that each man called perfect that which he saw agree with
the general idea he had formed of the thing in question, and called
imperfect that which he saw agree less with his own preconceived type,
even though it had evidently been completed in accordance with the
idea of its artificer. This seems to be the only reason for calling natural
phenomena, which, indeed, are not made with human hands, perfect
or imperfect: for men are wont to form general ideas of things natural,
no less than of things artificial, and such ideas they hold as types, believing that Nature (who they think does nothing without an object)
has them in view, and has set them as types before herself. Therefore,
when they behold something in Nature, which does not wholly conform
to the preconceived type which they have formed of the thing in question, they say that Nature has fallen short or has blundered, and has left
her work incomplete. Thus we see that men are wont to style natural
phenomena perfect or imperfect rather from their own prejudices, than
from true knowledge of what they pronounce upon.

Now we showed in the Appendix to Part I., that Nature does not
work with an end in view. For the eternal and infinite Being, which we
call God or Nature, acts by the same necessity as that whereby it exists.
For we have shown, that by the same necessity of its nature, whereby
it exists, it likewise works (I. xvi.). The reason or cause why God or
Nature exists, and the reason why he acts, are one and the same. Therefore, as he does not exist for the sake of an end, so neither does he act
for the sake of an end; of his existence and of his action there is neither
origin nor end. Wherefore, a cause which is called final is nothing else
but human desire, in so far as it is considered as the origin or cause of
anything. For example, when we say that to be inhabited is the final
cause of this or that house, we mean nothing more than that a man,
conceiving the conveniences of household life, had a desire to build a
house. Wherefore, the being inhabited, in so far as it is regarded as a
final cause, is nothing else but this particular desire, which is really

the efficient cause; it is regarded as the primary cause, because men are generally ignorant of the causes of their desires. They are, as I have often said already, conscious of their own actions and appetites, but ignorant of the causes whereby they are determined to any particular desire. Therefore, the common saying that Nature sometimes falls short, or blunders, and produces things which are imperfect, I set down among the glosses treated of in the Appendix to Part I. Perfection and imperfection, then, are in reality merely modes of thinking, or notions which we form from a comparison among one another of individuals of the same species; hence I said above (II. Def. vi.), that by reality and perfection I mean the same thing. For we are wont to refer all the individual things in nature to one genus, which is called the highest genus, namely, to the category of Being, whereto absolutely all individuals in nature belong. Thus, in so far as we refer the individuals in nature to this category, and comparing them one with another, find that some possess more of being or reality than others, we, to this extent, say that some are more perfect than others. Again, in so far as we attribute to them anything implying negation—as term, end, infirmity, etc.,—we, to this extent, call them imperfect, because they do not affect our mind so much as the things which we call perfect, not because they have any intrinsic deficiency, or because Nature has blundered. For nothing lies within the scope of a thing's nature, save that which follows from the necessity of the nature of its efficient cause, and whatsoever follows from the necessity of the nature of its efficient cause necessarily comes to pass.

As for the terms *good* and *bad*, they indicate no positive quality in things regarded in themselves, but are merely modes of thinking, or notions which we form from the comparison of things one with another. Thus one and the same thing can be at the same time good, bad, and indifferent. For instance, music is good for him that is melancholy, bad for him that mourns; for him that is deaf, it is neither good nor bad.

Nevertheless, though this be so, the terms should still be retained. For, inasmuch as we desire to form an idea of man as a type of human nature which we may hold in view, it will be useful for us to retain the terms in question, in the sense I have indicated.

In what follows, then, I shall mean by "good" that which we certainly know to be a means of approaching more nearly to the type of human nature, which we have set before ourselves; by "bad," that which we certainly know to be a hindrance to us in approaching the said type. Again, we shall say that men are more perfect, or more imperfect, in proportion as they approach more or less nearly to the said type. For it must be specially remarked that, when I say that a man passes from a lesser to a greater perfection, or *vice versâ*, I do not mean that he is changed from one essence or reality to another; for instance, a horse would be as completely destroyed by being changed into a man, as by being changed into an insect. What I mean is, that we conceive the thing's power of action, in so far as this is understood by its nature, to be increased or diminished. Lastly, by perfection in general I shall, as I have said, mean reality—in other words, each thing's essence, in so far as it exists, and operates in a particular manner, and without paying any regard to its duration. For no given thing can be said to be more perfect, because it has passed a longer time in existence. The duration of things cannot be determined by their essence, for the essence of things involves no fixed and definite period of existence; but everything, whether it be more perfect or less perfect, will always be able to persist in existence with the same force wherewith it began to exist; wherefore, in this respect, all things are equal.

. . .

PROP. XXIII. *Man, in so far as he is determined to a particular action because he has inadequate ideas, cannot be absolutely said to act in obedience to virtue; he can only be so described, in so far as he is determined for the action because he understands.*

Proof.—In so far as a man is determined to an action through having inadequate ideas, he is passive (III. i.), that is (III. Deff. i. and iii.), he does something, which cannot be perceived solely through his essence, that is (by IV. Def. viii.), which does not follow from his virtue. But, in so far as he is determined for an action because he understands, he is active; that is, he does something, which is perceived through his essence alone, or which adequately follows from his virtue. *Q.E.D.*

PROP. XXIV. *To act absolutely in obedience to virtue is in us the same thing as to act, to live, or to preserve one's being (these three terms are identical in meaning) in accordance with the dictates of reason on the basis of seeking what is useful to one's self.*

Proof.—To act absolutely in obedience to virtue is nothing else but to act according to the laws of one's own nature. But we only act, in so far as we understand (III. iii.): therefore to act in obedience to virtue is in us nothing else but to act, to live, or to preserve one's being in obedience to reason, and that on the basis of seeking what is useful for us (IV. xxii. Coroll.). *Q.E.D.*

. . .

PROP. XXXIV. *In so far as men are assailed by emotions which are passions, they can be contrary one to another.*

Proof.—A man, for instance Peter, can be the cause of Paul's feeling pain, because he (Peter) possesses something similar to that which Paul hates (III. xvi.), or because Peter has sole possession of a thing which Paul also loves (III. xxxii. and note), or for other causes (of which the chief are enumerated in III. lv. note); it may therefore happen that Paul should hate Peter (Def. of Emotions, vii.), consequently it may easily happen also, that Peter should hate Paul in return, and that each should endeavour to do the other an injury (III. xxxix.), that is (IV. xxx.), that they should be contrary one to another. But the emotion of pain is always a passion or passive state (III. lix.); hence men, in so far as they are assailed by emotions which are passions, can be contrary one to another. *Q.E.D.*

Note.—I said that Paul may hate Peter, because he conceives that Peter possesses something which he (Paul) also loves; from this it seems, at first sight, to follow, that these two men, through both loving the same thing, and, consequently, through agreement of their respective natures, stand in one another's way; if this were so, Props. xxx. and xxxi. of this Part would be untrue. But if we give the matter our unbiassed attention, we shall see that the discrepancy vanishes. For the two men are not in one another's way in virtue of the agreement of their natures, that is, through both loving the same thing, but in virtue of one differing from the other. For, in so far as each loves the same thing, the love of each is fostered thereby (III. xxxi.), that is (Def. of the Emotions, vi.) the pleasure of each is fostered thereby. Wherefore it as far from being the case, that they are at variance through both loving the same thing, and through the agreement in their natures. The cause for their opposition lies, as I have said, solely in the fact that they are assumed to differ. For we assume that Peter has the idea of the loved object as already in his possession, while Paul has the idea of the loved object as lost. Hence the one man will be affected with pleasure, the other will be affected with pain, and thus they will be at variance one with another. We can easily show in like manner, that all other causes of hatred depend solely on differences, and not on the agreement between men's natures.

Prop. XXXV. *In so far only as men live in obedience to reason, do they always necessarily agree in nature.*

Proof.—In so far as men are assailed by emotions that are passions, they can be different in nature (IV. xxxiii.), and at variance one with another. But men are only said to be active, in so far as they act in obedience to reason (III. iii.); therefore, whatsoever follows from human nature in so far as it is defined by reason must (III. Def. ii.) be understood solely through human nature as its proximate cause. But, since ever man by the laws of his nature desires that which he deems good, and endeavours to remove that which he deems bad (IV. xix.); and further, since that which we, in accordance with reason, deem good or bad, necessarily is good or bad (II. xli.); it follows that men, in so far as they live in obedience to reason, necessarily do only such things as are necessarily good for human nature, and consequently for each individual man (IV. xxxi. Coroll.); in other words, such things as are in harmony with each man's nature. Therefore, men in so far as they live in obedience to reason, necessarily live always in harmony one with another. *Q.E.D.*

Corollary I.—There is no individual thing in nature, which is more useful to man, than a man who lives in obedience to reason. For that thing is to man most useful, which is most in harmony with his nature (IV. xxxi. Coroll.); that is, obviously, man. But man acts absolutely according to the laws of his nature, when he lives in obedience to reason (III. Def. ii.), and to this extent only is always necessarily in harmony with the nature of another man (by the last Prop.); wherefore among individual things nothing is more useful to man, than a man who lives in obedience to reason. *Q.E.D.*

Corollary II.—As every man seeks most that which is useful to him, so are men most useful one to another. For the more a man seeks what is useful to him and endeavours to preserve himself, the more is he endowed with virtue (IV. xx.), or, what is the same thing (IV. Def. viii.), the more is he endowed with power to act according to the laws of his own nature, that is to live in obedience to reason. But men are most in natural harmony, when they live in obedience to reason (by the last Prop.); therefore (by the foregoing Coroll.) men will be most useful one to another, when each seeks most that which is useful to him. *Q.E.D.*

Note.—What we have just shown is attested by experience so conspicuously, that it is in the mouth of nearly everyone: "Man is to man a God." Yet it rarely happens that men live in obedience to reason, for things are so ordered among them, that they are generally envious and troublesome one to another. Nevertheless they are scarcely able to lead a solitary life, so that the definition of man as a social animal has met with general assent; in fact, men do derive from social life much more convenience than injury. Let satirists then laugh their fill at human affairs, let theologians rail, and let misanthropes praise to their utmost the life of untutored rusticity, let them heap contempt on men and praises on beasts; when all is said, they will find that men can provide for their wants much more easily by mutual help, and that only by uniting their forces can they escape from the dangers that on every side beset them: not to say how much more excellent and worthy of our knowledge it is, to study the actions of men than the actions of beasts. But I will treat of this more at length elsewhere.

PROP. XXXVI. *The highest good of those who follow virtue is common to all, and therefore all can equally rejoice therein.*

Proof.—To act virtuously is to act in obedience with reason (IV. xxiv.), and whatsoever we endeavour to do in obedience to reason is to understand (IV. xxvi.); therefore (IV. xxviii.) the highest good for those who follow after virtue is to know God; that is (II. xlvii. and note) a good which is common to all and can be possessed by all men equally, in so far as they are of the same nature. *Q.E.D.*

Note.—Someone may ask how it would be, if the highest good of those who follow after virtue were not common to all? Would it not then follow, as above (IV. xxxiv.), that men living in obedience to reason, that is (IV. xxxv.), men in so far as they agree in nature, would be at variance one with another? To such an inquiry I make answer, that it follows not accidentally but from the very nature of reason, that man's highest good is common to all, inasmuch as it is deduced from the very essence of man, in so far as defined by reason; and that a man could neither be, nor be conceived without the power of taking pleasure in this highest good. For it belongs to the essence of the human mind (II.

xlvii.), to have an adequate knowledge of the eternal and infinite essence of God.

· · ·

PROP. L. *Pity, in a man who lives under the guidance of reason, is in itself bad and useless.*

Proof.—Pity (Def. of the Emotions, xviii.) is a pain, and therefore (IV. xli.) is in itself bad. The good effect which follows, namely, our endeavour to free the object of our pity from misery, is an action which we desire to do solely at the dictation of reason (IV. xxxvii.); only at the dictation of reason are we able to perform any action, which we know for certain to be good (IV. xxvii.); thus, in a man who lives under the guidance of reason, pity in itself is useless and bad.   *Q.E.D.*

Note.—He who rightly realizes, that all things follow from the necessity of the divine nature, and come to pass in accordance with the eternal laws and rules of nature, will not find anything worthy of hatred, derision, or contempt, nor will he bestow pity on anything, but to the utmost extent of human virtue he will endeavour to do well, as the saying is, and to rejoice. We may add, that he, who is easily touched with compassion, and is moved by another's sorrow or tears, often does something which he afterwards regrets; partly because we can never be sure that an action caused by emotion is good, partly because we are easily deceived by false tears. I am in this place expressly speaking of a man living under the guidance of reason. He who is moved to help others neither by reason nor by compassion, is rightly styled inhuman, for (III. xxvii.) he seems unlike a man.

PROP. LI. *Approval is not repugnant to reason, but can agree therewith and arise therefrom.*

Proof.—Approval is love towards one who has done good to another (Def. of the Emotions, xix.); therefore it may be referred to the mind, in so far as the latter is active (III. lix.), that is (III. iii.), in so far as it understands; therefore, it is in agreement with reason, &c.   *Q.E.D.*

Another Proof.—He, who lives under the guidance of reason, desires for others the good which he seeks for himself (IV. xxxvii.); wherefore from seeing someone doing good to his fellow his own endeavour to do good is aided; in other words, he will feel pleasure (III. xi. note) accompanied by the idea of the benefactor. Therefore he approves of him. *Q.E.D.*

Note.—Indignation as we defined it (Def. of the Emotions, xx.) is necessarily evil (IV. xlv.); we may, however, remark that, when the sovereign power for the sake of preserving peace punishes a citizen who has injured another, it should not be said to be indignant with the criminal, for it is not incited by hatred to ruin him, it is led by a sense of of duty to punish him.

PROP. LII. *Self-approval may arise from reason, and that which arises from reason is the highest possible.*

Proof.—Self-approval is pleasure arising from a man's contemplation of himself and his own power of action (Def. of the Emotions, xxv.). But a man's true power of action or virtue is reason herself (III. iii.), as the said man clearly and distinctly contemplates her (II. xl. xliii.); therefore self-approval arises from reason. Again, when a man is contemplating himself, he only perceives clearly and distinctly or adequately, such things as follow from his power of action (III. Def. ii.), that is (III. iii.), from his power of understanding; therefore in such contemplation alone does the highest possible self-approval arise. *Q.E.D.*

Note.—Self-approval is in reality the highest object for which we can hope. For (as we showed in IV. xxv.) no one endeavours to preserve his being for the sake of any ulterior object, and, as this approval is more and more fostered and strengthened by praise (III. liii. Coroll.), and on the contrary (III. lv. Coroll.) is more and more disturbed by blame, fame becomes the most powerful of incitements to action, and life under disgrace is almost unendurable.

PROP. LIII. *Humility is not a virtue, or does not arise from reason.*

Proof.—Humility is pain arising from a man's contemplation of his own infirmities (Def. of the Emotions, xxvi). But, in so far as a man knows himself by true reason, he is assumed to understand his essence, that is, his power (III. vii). Wherefore, if a man in self-contemplation perceives any infirmity in himself, it is not by virtue of his understanding himself, but (III. lv.) by virtue of his power of activity being checked. But, if we assume that a man perceives his own infirmity by virtue of understanding something stronger than himself, by the knowledge of which he determines his own power of activity, this is the same as saying that we conceive that a man understands himself distinctly (IV. xxvi.), because his power of activity is aided. Wherefore humility, or the pain which arises from a man's contemplation of his own infirmity, does not arise from the contemplation or reason, and is not a virtue but a passion. *Q.E.D.*

PROP. LIV. *Repentance is not a virtue, or does not arise from reason; but he who repents of an action is doubly wretched or infirm.*

Proof.—The first part of this proposition is proved like the foregoing one. The second part is proved from the mere definition of the emotion in question. (Def. of the Emotions, xxvii.). For the man allows himself to be overcome, first, by evil desires; secondly, by pain.

Note.—As men seldom live under the guidance of reason, these two emotions, namely, Humility and Repentance, as also Hope and Fear, bring more good than harm; hence, as we must sin, we had better sin in that direction. For, if all men who are a prey to emotion were all equally proud, they would shrink from nothing, and would fear nothing; how then could they be joined and linked together in bonds of union? The crowd plays the tyrant, when it is not in fear; hence we need not wonder that the prophets, who consulted the good, not of a few, but of all, so strenuously commended Humility, Repentance, and Reverence. Indeed those who are prey to these emotions may be led much more easily than others to live under the guidance of reason, that is, to become free and to enjoy the life of the blessed.

. . .

PROP. LXVII. *A free man thinks of death least of all things; and his wisdom is a meditation not of death but of life.*

Proof.—A free man is one who lives under the guidance of reason, who is not led by fear (IV. lxiii.), but who directly desires that which is good (IV. lxiii. Coroll.), in other words (IV. xxiv.), who strives to act, to live, and to preserve his being on the basis of seeking his own true advantage; wherefore such an one thinks of nothing less than of death, but his wisdom is a meditation of life. *Q.E.D.*

PROP. LXVIII. *If men were born free, they would, so long as they remained free, form no conception of good and evil.*

Proof.—I call free him who is led solely by reason; he, therefore, who is born free, and who remains free, has only adequate ideas; therefore (IV. lxiv. Coroll.) he has no conception of evil, or consequently (good and evil being correlative) of good. *Q.E.D.*

Note.—It is evident, from IV. iv., that the hypothesis of this Proposition is false and inconceivable, except in so far as we look solely to the nature of man, or rather to God; not in so far as the latter is infinite, but only in so far as he is the cause of man's existence.

This, and other matters which we have already proved, seem to have been signified by Moses in the history of the first man. For in that narrative no other power of God is conceived, save that whereby he created man, that is the power wherewith he provided solely for man's advantage; it is stated that God forbade man, being free, to eat of the tree of the knowledge of good and evil, and that, as soon as man should have eaten of it, he would straightway fear death rather than desire to live. Further, it is written that when man had found a wife, who was in entire harmony with his nature, he knew that there could be nothing in nature which could be more useful to him; but that after he believed the beasts to be like himself, he straightway began to imitate their emotions (III. xxvii.), and to lose his freedom; this freedom was afterwards recovered by the patriarchs, led by the spirit of Christ; that is, by the idea of God, whereon alone it depends, that man may be free, and desire for others the good which he desires for himself, as we have shown above (IV. xxxvii.).

. . .

PROP. LXX. *The free man, who lives among the ignorant, strives, as far as he can, to avoid receiving favours from them.*

Proof.—Everyone judges what is good according to his disposition (III. xxxix. note); wherefore an ignorant man, who has conferred a benefit on another, puts his own estimate upon it, and, if it appears to be estimated less highly by the receiver, will feel pain (III. xlii.). But the free man only desires to join other men to him in friendship (IV. xxxvii.), not repaying their benefits with others reckoned as of like value, but guiding himself and others by the free decision of reason, and doing only such things as he knows to be of primary importance. Therefore the free man, lest he should become hateful to the ignorant, or follow their desires rather than reason, will endeavour, as far as he can, to avoid receiving their favours.

Note.—I say, *as far as he can.* For though men be ignorant, yet are they men, and in cases of necessity could afford us human aid, the most excellent of all things: therefore it is often necessary to accept favours from them, and consequently to repay such favours in kind; we must, therefore, exercise caution in declining favours, lest we should have the appearance of despising those who bestow them, or of being, from avaricious motives, unwilling to requite them, and so give ground for offence by the very fact of striving to avoid it. Thus, in declining favours, we must look to the requirements of utility and courtesy.

PROP. LXXI. *Only free men are thoroughly grateful one to another.*

Proof.—Only free men are thoroughly useful one to another, and associated among themselves by the closest necessity of friendship (IV. xxxv. and Coroll. i.), only such men endeavour, with mutual zeal of love, to confer benefits on each other (IV. xxxvii.), and, therefore, only they are thoroughly grateful one to another. *Q.E.D.*

Note.—The goodwill, which men who are led by blind desire have for one another, is generally a bargaining or enticement, rather than pure goodwill. Moreover, ingratitude is not an emotion. Yet it is base, inasmuch as it generally shows, that a man is affected by excessive hatred, anger, pride, avarice, &c. He who, by reason of his folly, knows not how to return benefits, is not ungrateful, much less he who is not gained over by the gifts of a courtesan to serve her lust, or by a thief to conceal his thefts, or by any similar persons. Contrariwise, such an one shows a constant mind, inasmuch as he cannot by any gifts be corrupted, to his own or the general hurt.

PROP. LXXII. *The free man never acts fraudulently, but always in good faith.*

Proof.—If it be asked: What should a man's conduct be in a case where he could be breaking faith free himself from the danger of present death? Would not his plan of self-preservation completely persuade him to deceive? this may be answered by pointing out that, if reason persuaded him to act thus, it would persuade all men to act in a similar manner, in which case reason would persuade men not to agree in good faith to unite their forces, or to have laws in common, that is, not to have any general laws, which is absurd.

PROP. LXXIII. *The man, who is guided by reason, is more free in a State, where he lives under a general system of law, than in solitude, where he is independent.*

Proof.—The man, who is guided by reason, does not obey through fear (IV. lxiii.): but, in so far as he endeavours to preserve his being according to the dictates of reason, that is (IV. lxvi. note), in so far as he endeavours to live in freedom, he desires to order his life according to the general good (IV. xxxvii.), and, consequently (as we showed in IV. xxxvii. note ii.), to live according to the laws of his country. Therefore the free man, in order to enjoy greater freedom, desires to possess the general rights of citizenship. *Q.E.D.*

Note.—These and similar observations, which we have made on man's true freedom, may be referred to strength, that is, to courage and nobility of character (III, lix. note). I do not think it worth while to prove separately all the properties of strength; much less need I show, that he that is strong hates no man, is angry with no man, envies no man, is indignant with no man, despises no man, and least of all things is proud. These propositions, and all that relate to the true way of life and religion, are easily proved from IV. xxxvii. and xlvi.; namely, that hatred should be overcome with love, and that every man should desire for others the good which he seeks for himself. We may also repeat what we drew attention to in the note to IV. l., and in other places; namely, that the strong man has ever first in his thoughts, that all things follow from the necessity of the divine nature; so that whatsoever he deems to be hurtful and evil, and whatsoever, accordingly, seems to him impious, horrible, unjust, and base, assumes that appearance owing to his own disordered, fragmentary, and confused view of the universe. Wherefore he strives before all things to conceive things as they really are, and to remove the hindrances to true knowledge, such as are hatred, anger, envy, derision, pride, and similar emotions, which I have mentioned above. Thus he endeavours, as we said before, as far as in him lies, to do good, and to go on his way rejoicing. How far human virtue is capable of attaining to such a condition, and what its powers may be, I will prove in the following Part.

APPENDIX

What I have said in this Part concerning the right way of life has not been arranged, so as to admit of being seen at one view, but has been set forth piece-meal, according as I thought each Proposition could most readily be deduced from what preceded it. I propose, therefore, to re-arrange my remarks and to bring them under leading heads.

I. All our endeavours or desires so follow from the necessity of our nature, that they can be understood either through it alone, as their proximate cause, or by virtue of our being a part of nature, which cannot be adequately conceived through itself without other individuals.

II. Desires, which follow from our nature in such a manner, that they can be understood through it alone, are those which are referred to the mind, in so far as the latter is conceived to consist of adequate ideas: the remaining desires are only referred to the mind, in so far as it conceives things inadequately, and their force and increase are generally defined not by the power of man, but by the power of things external to us: wherefore the former are rightly called actions, the latter passions, for the former always indicate our power, the latter, on the other hand, show our infirmity and fragmentary knowledge.

III. Our actions, that is, those desires which are defined by man's power or reason, are always good. The rest may be either good or bad.

IV. Thus in life it is before all things useful to perfect the understanding, or reason, as far as we can, and in this alone man's highest happiness or blessedness consists, indeed blessedness is nothing else but the contentment of spirit, which arises from the intuitive knowledge of God: now, to perfect the understanding is nothing else but to understand God, God's attributes, and the actions which follow from the necessity of his nature. Wherefore of a man, who is led by reason, the ultimate aim or highest desire, whereby he seeks to govern all his fellows, is that whereby he is brought to the adequate conception of himself and of all things within the scope of his intelligence.

V. Therefore, without intelligence there is not rational life: and things are only good, in so far as they aid man in his enjoyment of the intellectual life, which is defined by intelligence. Contrariwise, whatsoever things hinder man's perfecting of his reason, and capability to enjoy the rational life, are alone called evil.

VI. As all things whereof man is the efficient cause are necessarily good, no evil can befall man except through external causes; namely, by virtue of man being a part of universal nature, whose laws human nature is compelled to obey, and to conform to in almost infinite ways.

VII. It is impossible, that man should not be a part of nature, or that he should not follow her general order; but if he be thrown among individuals whose nature is in harmony with his own, his power of action will thereby be aided and fostered, whereas, if he be thrown among such as are but very little in harmony with his nature, he will hardly be able to accommodate himself to them without undergoing a great change himself.

VIII. Whatsoever in nature we deem to be evil, or to be capable of injuring our faculty for existing and enjoying the rational life, we may endeavour to remove in whatever way seems safest to us; on the other hand, whatsoever we deem to be good or useful for preserving our being, and enabling us to enjoy the rational life, we may appropriate to our use and employ as we think best. Everyone without exception may, by sovereign right of nature, do whatsoever he thinks will advance his own interest.

IX. Nothing can be in more harmony with the nature of any given thing than other individuals of the same species; therefore (cf. vii.) for man in the preservation of his being and the enjoyment of the rational life there is nothing more useful than his fellow-man who is led by reason. Further, as we know not anything among individual things which is more excellent than a man led by reason, no man can better display the power of his skill and disposition, than in so training men, that they come at last to live under the dominion of their own reason.

X. In so far as men are influenced by envy or any kind of hatred, one towards another, they are at variance, and are therefore to be feared in proportion, as they are more powerful than their fellows.

XI. Yet minds are not conquered by force, but by love and high-mindedness.

XII. It is before all things useful to men to associate their ways of life, to bind themselves together with such bonds as they think most fitted to gather them all into unity, and generally to do whatsoever serves to strengthen friendship.

XIII. But for this there is need of skill and watchfulness. For men are diverse (seeing that those who live under the guidance of reason are few), yet are they generally envious and more prone to revenge than to sympathy. No small force of character is therefore required to take every-one as he is, and to restrain one's self from imitating the emotions of others. But those who carp at mankind, and are more skilled in railing at vice than in instilling virtue, and who break rather than strengthen men's dispositions, are hurtful both to themselves and others. Thus many from too great impatience of spirit, or from misguided religious zeal, have pre-ferred to live among brutes rather than among men; as boys or youths, who cannot peaceably endure the chidings of their parents, will enlist as soldiers and choose the hardships of war and the despotic discipline in preference to the comforts of home and the admonitions of their father: suffering any burden to be put upon them, so long as they may spite their parents.

XIV. Therefore, although men are generally governed in everything by their own lusts, yet their association in common brings many more advan-tages than drawbacks. Wherefore it is better to bear patiently the wrongs they may do us, and to strive to promote whatsoever serves to bring about harmony and friendship.

XV. Those things, which beget harmony, are such as are attributable to justice, equity, and honourable living. For men brook ill not only what is unjust or iniquitous, but also what is reckoned disgraceful, or that a man should slight the received customs of their society. For winning love those qualities are especially necessary which have regard to religion and piety (cf. IV. xxxvii. notes, i. ii.; xlvi. note; and lxxiii. note).

XVI. Further, harmony is often the result of fear: but such harmony is insecure. Further, fear arises from infirmity of spirit, and moreover be-longs not to the exercise of reason: the same is true of compassion, though this latter seems to bear a certain resemblance to piety.

XVII. Men are also gained over by liberality, especially such as have not the means to buy what is necessary to sustain life. However, to give aid to every poor man is far beyond the power and the advantage of any private person. For the riches of any private person are wholly inadequate to meet such a call. Again, an individual man's resources of character are too limited for him to be able to make all men his friends. Hence providing for the poor is a duty, which falls on the State as a whole, and has regard only to the general advantage.

XVIII. In accepting favours, and in returning gratitude our duty must be wholly different (cf. IV. lxx. note; lxxi. note).

XIX. Again, meretricious love, that is, the lust of generation arising from bodily beauty, and generally every sort of love, which owns anything save freedom of soul as its cause, readily passes into hate; unless indeed, what is worse, it is a species of madness; and then it promotes discord rather than harmony (cf. III. xxxi. Coroll.).

XX. As concerning marriage, it is certain that this is in harmony with reason, if the desire for physical union be not engendered solely by bodily beauty, but also by the desire to beget children and to train them up wisely; and moreover, if the love of both, to wit, of the man and of the woman, is not caused by bodily beauty only, but also by freedom of soul.

XXI. Furthermore, flattery begets harmony; but only by means of the vile offence of slavishness or treachery. None are more readily taken with flattery than the proud, who wish to be first, but are not.

XXII. There is in abasement a spurious appearance of piety and religion. Although abasement is the opposite to pride, yet is he that abases himself most akin to the proud (IV. lvii. note).

XXIII. Shame also brings about harmony, but only in such matters as cannot be hid. Further, as shame is a species of pain, it does not concern the exercise of reason.

XXIV. The remaining emotions of pain towards men are directly opposed to justice, equity, honour, piety, and religion; and, although indignation seems to bear a certain resemblance to equity, yet is life but lawless, where every man may pass judgment on another's deeds, and vindicate his own or other men's rights.

XXV. Correctness of conduct (*modestia*), that is, the desire of pleasing men which is determined by reason, is attributable to piety (as we said in IV. xxxvii. note i.). But, if it spring from emotion, it is ambition, or the desire whereby men, under the false cloak of piety, generally stir up discords and seditions. For he who desires to aid his fellows either in word or in deed, so that they may together enjoy the highest good, he, I say, will before all things strive to win them over with love: not to draw them into admiration, so that a system may be called after his name, nor to give any cause for envy. Further, in his conversation he will shrink from talking of men's faults, and will be careful to speak but sparingly of human infirmity: but he will dwell at length on human virtue or power, and the way whereby it may be perfected. Thus will men be stirred not by fear, nor by aversion, but only by the emotion of joy, to endeavour, so far as in them lies, to live in obedience to reason.

XXVI. Besides men, we know of no particular thing in nature in whose mind we may rejoice, and whom we can associate with ourselves in friendship or any sort of fellowship; therefore, whatsoever there be in nature besides man, a regard for our advantage does not call on us to preserve, but to preserve or destroy according to its various capabilities, and to adapt to our use as best we may.

XXVII. The advantage which we derive from things external to us, besides the experience and knowledge which we acquire from observing them, and from recombining their elements in different forms, is principally the preservation of the body; from this point of view, those things are most useful which can so feed and nourish the body, that all its parts may rightly fulfil their functions. For, in proportion as the body is capable of being affected in a greater variety of ways, and of affecting external bodies in a great number of ways, so much the more is the mind capable of thinking (IV. xxxviii. xxxix.). But there seem to be very few things of this kind in nature; wherefore for the due nourishment of the body we must use many foods of diverse nature. For the human body is composed of very many parts of different nature, which stand in continual need of varied nourishment, so that the whole body may be equally capable of doing everything that can follow from its own nature, and consequently that the mind also may be equally capable of forming many perceptions.

XXVIII.   Now for providing these nourishments the strength of each individual would hardly suffice, if men did not lend one another mutual aid. But money has furnished us with a token for everything: hence it is with the notion of money, that the mind of the multitude is chiefly engrossed: nay, it can hardly conceive any kind of pleasure, which is not accompanied with the idea of money as cause.

XXIX.   This result is the fault only of those, who seek money, not from poverty or to supply their necessary wants, but because they have learned the arts of gain, wherewith they bring themselves to great splendour. Certainly they nourish their bodies, according to custom, but scantily, believing that they lose as much of their wealth as they spend on the preservation of their body. But they who know the true use of money, and who fix the measure of wealth solely with regard to their actual needs, live content with little.

XXX.   As, therefore, those things are good which assist the various parts of the body, and enable them to perform their functions; and as pleasure consists in an increase of, or aid to, man's power, in so far as he is composed of mind and body; it follows that all those things which bring pleasure are good. But seeing that things do not work with the object of giving us pleasure, and that their power of action is not tempered to suit our advantage, and, lastly, that pleasure is generally referred to one part of the body more than to the other parts; therefore most emotions of pleasure (unless reason and watchfulness be at hand), and consequently the desires arising therefrom, may become excessive. Moreover we may add that emotion leads us to pay most regard to what is agreeable in the present, nor can we estimate what is future with emotions equally vivid. (IV. xliv. note, and lx. note.)

XXXI.   Superstition, on the other hand, seems to account as good all that brings pain, and as bad all that brings pleasure. However, as we said above (IV. xlv. note), none but the envious take delight in my infirmity and trouble. For the greater the pleasure whereby we are affected, the greater is the perfection whereto we pass, and consequently the more do we partake of the divine nature: no pleasure can ever be evil, which is regulated by a true regard for our advantage. But contrariwise he, who is led by fear and does good only to avoid evil, is not guided by reason.

XXXII. But human power is extremely limited, and is infinitely surpassed by the power of external causes; we have not, therefore, an absolute power of shaping to our use those things which are without us. Nevertheless, we shall bear with an equal mind all that happens to us in contravention to the claims of our own advantage, so long as we are conscious, that we have done our duty, and that the power which we possess is not sufficient to enable us to protect ourselves completely; remembering that we are a part of universal nature, and that we follow her order. If we have a clear and distinct understanding of this, that part of our nature which is defined by intelligence, in other words the better part of ourselves, will assuredly acquiesce in what befalls us, and in such acquiescence will endeavour to persist. For, in so far as we are intelligent beings, we cannot desire anything save that which is necessary, nor yield absolute acquiescence to anything, save to that which is true: wherefore, in so far as we have a right understanding of these things, the endeavour of the better part of ourselves is in harmony with the order of nature as a whole.

Part V. On the power of the understanding, or of human freedom

. . .

PROP. II. *If we remove a disturbance of the spirit, or emotion, from the thought of an external cause, and unite it to other thoughts, then will the love or hatred towards that external cause, and also the vacillations of spirit which arise from these emotions, be destroyed.*

Proof.—That, which constitutes the reality of love or hatred, is pleasure or pain, accompanied by the idea of an external cause (Def. of the Emotions, vi. vii.); wherefore, when this cause is removed, the reality of love or hatred is removed with it; therefore these emotions and those which arise therefrom are destroyed. *Q.E.D.*

PROP. III. *An emotion, which is a passion, ceases to be a passion, as soon as we form a clear and distinct idea thereof.*

Proof.—An emotion, which is a passion, is a confused idea (by the general Def. of the Emotions). If, therefore, we form a clear and distinct idea of a given emotion, that idea will only be distinguished from the emotion, in so far as it is referred to the mind only, by reason (II. xxi. and note); therefore (III. iii.), the emotion will cease to be a passion. *Q.E.D.*

Corollary.—An emotion therefore becomes more under our control, and the mind is less passive in respect to it, in proportion as it is more known to us.

. . .

PROP. VI. *The mind has greater power over the emotions and is less subject thereto, in so far as it understands all things as necessary.*

Proof.—The mind understands all things to be necessary (I. xxix.) and to be determined to existence and operation by an infinite chain of causes; therefore (by the foregoing Proposition), it thus far brings it about, that it is less subject to the emotions arising therefrom, and (III. xlviii.) feels less emotion towards the things themselves. *Q.E.D.*

Note.—The more this knowledge, that things are necessary, is applied to particular things, which we conceive more distinctly and vividly, the greater is the power of the mind over the emotions, as experience also testifies. For we see, that the pain arising from the loss of any good is mitigated, as soon as the man who has lost it perceives, that it could not by any means have been preserved. So also we see that no one pities an infant, because it cannot speak, walk, or reason, or lastly, because it passes so many years, as it were, in unconsciousness. Whereas, if most people were born full-grown and only one here and there as an infant, everyone would pity the infants; because infancy would not then be looked on as a state natural and necessary, but as a fault or delinquency in Nature; and we may note several other instances of the same sort.

.   .   .

PROP. XV. *He who clearly and distinctly understands himself and his emotions loves God, and so much the more in proportion as he more understands himself and his emotions.*

Proof.—He who clearly and distinctly understands himself and his emotions feels pleasure (III, liii.), and this pleasure is (by the last Prop.) accompanied by the idea of God; therefore (Def. of the Emotions, vi.) such an one loves God, and (for the same reason) so much the more in proportion as he more understands himself and his emotions. *Q.E.D.*

PROP. XVI. *This love towards God must hold the chief place in the mind.*

Proof.—For this love is associated with all the modifications of the body (V. xiv.) and is fostered by them all (V. xv.); therefore (V. xi.), it must hold the chief place in the mind. *Q.E.D.*

PROP. XVII. *God is without passions, neither is he affected by any emotion of pleasure or pain.*

Proof.—All ideas, in so far as they are referred to God, are true (II. xxxii.), that is (II. Def. iv.) adequate; and therefore (by the general Def. of the Emotions) God is without passions. Again, God cannot pass either to a greater or to a lesser perfection (I. xx. Coroll. ii.); therefore (by Def. of the Emotions, ii. iii.) he is not affected by any emotion of pleasure or pain.

Corollary.—Strictly speaking, God does not love or hate anyone. For God (by the foregoing Prop.) is not affected by any emotion of pleasure or pain, consequently (Def. of the Emotions, vi. vii.) he does not love or hate anyone.

PROP. XVIII. *No one can hate God.*

Proof.—The idea of God which is in us is adequate and perfect (II. xlvi. xlvii.); wherefore, in so far as we contemplate God, we are active

(III. iii.); consequently (III. lix.) there can be no pain accompanied by the idea of God, in other words (Def. of the Emotions, vii.), no one can hate God. *Q.E.D.*

Corollary.—Love towards God cannot be turned into hate.

Note.—It may be objected that, as we understand God as the cause of all things, we by that very fact regard God as the cause of pain. But I make answer, that, in so far as we understand the causes of pain, it to that extent (V. iii.) ceases to be a passion, that is, it ceases to be pain (III. lix.); therefore, in so far as we understand God to be the cause of pain, we to that extent feel pleasure.

PROP. XIX. *He, who loves God, cannot endeavour that God should love him in return.*

Proof.—For, if a man should so endeavour, he would desire (V. xvii. Coroll.) that God, whom he loves, should not be God, and consequently he would desire to feel pain (III. xix.); which is absurd (III. xxviii.). Therefore, he who loves God, &c. *Q.E.D.*

PROP. XX. *This love towards God cannot be stained by the emotion of envy or jealousy: contrariwise, it is the more fostered, in proportion as we conceive a greater number of men to be joined to God by the same bond of love.*

Proof.—This love towards God is the highest good which we can seek for under the guidance of reason (IV. xxviii.), it is common to all men (IV. xxxvi.), and we desire that all should rejoice therein (IV. xxxvii.); therefore (Def. of the Emotions, xxiii.), it cannot be stained by the emotion of envy, nor by the emotion of jealousy (V. xviii. see definition of Jealousy, III. xxxv. note); but, contrariwise, it must needs be the more fostered, in proportion as we conceive a greater number of men to rejoice therein. *Q.E.D.*

Note.—We can in the same way show, that there is no emotion directly contrary to this love, whereby this love can be destroyed; therefore we may conclude, that this love towards God is the most constant of all the emotions, and that, in so far as it is referred to the body, it cannot be destroyed, unless the body be destroyed also. As to its nature, in so far as it is referred to the mind only, we shall presently inquire.

I have now gone through all the remedies against the emotions, or all that the mind, considered in itself alone, can do against them. Whence it appears that the mind's power over the emotions consists:—

I. In the actual knowledge of the emotions (V. iv. note).

II. In the fact that it separates the emotions from the thought of an external cause, which we conceive confusedly (V. ii. and iv. note).

III. In the fact, that, in respect to time, the emotions referred to things, which we distinctly understand, surpass those referred to what we conceive in a confused and fragmentary manner (V. vii.).

IV. In the number of causes whereby those modifications [2] are fostered,

---

[2] *Affectiones.* Camerer reads *affectus*—emotions.

which have regard to the common properties of things or to God (V. ix. xi.).

V. Lastly, in the order wherein the mind can arrange and associate, one with another, its own emotions (V. x. note and xii. xiii. xiv.).

But, in order that this power of the mind over the emotions may be better understood, it should be specially observed that the emotions are called by us strong, when we compare the emotion of one man with the emotion of another, and see that one man is more troubled than another by the same emotion; or when we are comparing the various emotions of the same man one with another, and find that he is more affected or stirred by one emotion than by another. For the strength of every emotion is defined by a comparison of our own power with the power of an external cause. Now the power of the mind is defined by knowledge only, and its infirmity or passion is defined by the privation of knowledge only: it therefore follows, that that mind is most passive, whose greatest part is made up of inadequate ideas, so that it may be characterized more readily by its passive states than by its activities: on the other hand, that mind is most active, whose greatest part is made up of adequate ideas, so that, although it may contain as many inadequate ideas as the former mind, it may yet be more easily characterized by ideas attributable to human virtue, than by ideas which tell of human infirmity. Again, it must be observed, that spiritual unhealthiness and misfortunes can generally be traced to excessive love for something which is subject to many variations, and which we can never become masters of. For no one is solicitous or anxious about anything, unless he loves it; neither do wrongs, suspicions, enmities, &c. arise, except in regard to things whereof no one can be really master.

We may thus readily conceive the power which clear and distinct knowledge, and especially that third kind of knowledge (II. xlvii. note), founded on the actual knowledge of God, possesses over the emotions: if it does not absolutely destroy them, in so far as they are passions (V. iii. and iv. note); at any rate, it causes them to occupy a very small part of the mind (V. xiv.). Further, it begets a love towards a thing immutable and eternal (V. xv.), whereof we may really enter into possession (II. xlv); neither can it be defiled with those faults which are inherent in ordinary love; but it may grow from strength to strength, and may engross the greater part of the mind, and deeply penetrate it.

And now I have finished with all that concerns this present life: for, as I said in the beginning of this note, I have briefly described all the remedies against the emotions. And this everyone may readily have seen for himself, if he has attended to what is advanced in the present note, and also to the definitions of the mind and its emotions, and, lastly, to Propositions i. and iii. of Part III. It is now, therefore, time to pass on to those matters, which appertain to the duration of the mind, without relation to the body.

PROP. XXXII. *Whatsoever we understand by the third kind of knowledge, we take delight in, and our delight is accompanied by the idea of God as cause.*

Proof.—From this kind of knowledge arises the highest possible mental acquiescence, that is (Def. of the Emotions, xxv.), pleasure, and this acquiescence is accompanied by the idea of the mind itself (V. xxvii.), and consequently (V. xxx.) the idea also of God as cause. *Q.E.D.*

Corollary.—From the third kind of knowledge necessarily arises the intellectual love of God. From this kind of knowledge arises pleasure accompanied by the idea of God as cause, that is (Def. of the Emotions, vi.), the love of God; not in so far as we imagine him as present (V. xxix.), but in so far as we understand him to be eternal; this is what I call the intellectual love of God.

PROP. XXXIII. *The intellectual love of God, which arises from the third kind of knowledge, is eternal.*

Proof.—The third kind of knowledge is eternal (V. xxxi. I. Ax. iii.); therefore (by the same Axiom) the love which arises therefrom is also necessarily eternal. *Q.E.D.*

Note.—Although this love towards God has (by the foregoing Prop.) no beginning, it yet possesses all the perfections of love, just as though it had arisen as we feigned in the Coroll. of the last Prop. Nor is there here any difference, except that the mind possesses as eternal those same perfections which we feigned to accrue to it, and they are accompanied by the idea of God as eternal cause. If pleasure consists in the transition to a greater perfection, assuredly blessedness must consist in the mind being endowed with perfection itself.

PROP. XXXIV. *The mind is, only while the body endures, subject to those emotions which are attributable to passions.*

Proof.—Imagination is the idea wherewith the mind contemplates a thing as present (II. xvii. note); yet this idea indicates rather the present disposition of the human body than the nature of the external thing (II. xvi. Coroll. ii.). Therefore emotion (see general Def. of Emotions) is imagination, in so far as it indicates the present disposition of the body; therefore (V. xxi.) the mind is, only while the body endures, subject to emotions which are attributable to passions. *Q.E.D.*

Corollary.—Hence it follows that no love save intellectual love is eternal.

Note.—If we look to men's general opinion, we shall see that they are indeed conscious of the eternity of their mind, but that they confuse eternity with duration, and ascribe it to the imagination or the memory which they believe to remain after death.

PROP. XXXV. *God loves himself with an infinite intellectual love.*

Proof.—God is absolutely infinite (I. Def. vi.), that is (II. Def. vi.), the nature of God rejoices in infinite perfection; and such rejoicing is (II. iii.) accompanied by the idea of himself, that is (I. xi. and Def. i.), the idea of his own cause: now this is what we have (in V. xxxii. Coroll.) described as intellectual love.

PROP. XXXVI. *The intellectual love of the mind towards God is that very love of God whereby God loves himself, not in so far as he is infinite, but in so far as he can be explained through the essence of the human mind regarded under the form of eternity; in other words, the intellectual love of the mind towards God is part of the infinite love wherewith God loves himself.*

Proof.—This love of the mind must be referred to the activities of the mind (V. xxxi. Coroll. and III. iii.); it is itself, indeed, an activity whereby the mind regards itself accompanied by the idea of God as cause (V. xxxii. and Coroll.); that is (I. xxv. Coroll. and II. xi. Coroll.), an activity whereby God, in so far as he can be explained through the human mind, regards himself accompanied by the idea of himself; therefore (by the last Prop.), this love of the mind is part of the infinite love wherewith God loves himself. *Q.E.D.*

Corollary.—Hence it follows that God, in so far as he loves himself, loves man, and, consequently, that the love of God towards men, and the intellectual love of the mind towards God are identical.

Note.—From what has been said we clearly understand, wherein our salvation, or blessedness, or freedom, consists: namely, in the constant and eternal love towards God, or in God's love towards men. This love or blessedness is, in the Bible, called Glory, and not undeservedly. For whether this love be referred to God or to the mind, it may rightly be called acquiescence of spirit, which (Def. of the Emotions, xxv. xxx.) is not really distinguished from glory. In so far as it is referred to God, it is (V. xxxv.) pleasure, if we may still use that term, accompanied by the idea of itself, and, in so far as it is referred to the mind, it is the same (V. xxvii.).

Again, since the essence of our mind consists solely in knowledge, whereof the beginning and the foundation is God (I. xv. and II. xlvii. note), it becomes clear to us, in what manner and way our mind, as to its essence and existence, follows from the divine nature and constantly depends on God. I have thought it worth while here to call attention to this, in order to show by this example how the knowledge of particular things, which I have called intuitive or of the third kind (II. xl. note ii.), is potent, and more powerful than the universal knowledge, which I have styled knowledge of the second kind. For, although in Part I. I showed in general terms, that all things (and consequently, also, the human mind) depend as to their essence and existence on God, yet that demonstration, though legitimate and placed beyond the chances of doubt, does not affect our own mind so much, as when the same conclusion is derived from the actual essence of some particular thing, which we say depends on God.

PROP. XXXVII. *There is nothing in nature, which is contrary to this intellectual love, or which can take it away.*

Proof.—This intellectual love follows necessarily from the nature of the mind, in so far as the latter is regarded through the nature of God as an eternal truth (V. xxxiii. and xxix.). If, therefore, there should be anything which would be contrary to this love, that thing would be contrary to that which is true; consequently, that, which should be able to take away this love, would cause that which is true to be false; an obvious absurdity. Therefore there is nothing in nature which, &c. *Q.E.D.*

Note.—The Axiom of Part IV. has reference to particular things, in so far as they are regarded in relation to a given time and place: of this, I think, no one can doubt.

Prop. XXXVIII. *In proportion as the mind understands more things by the second and third kind of knowledge, it is less subject to those emotions which are evil, and stands in less fear of death.*

Proof.—The mind's essence consists in knowledge (II. xi.); therefore, in proportion as the mind understands more things by the second and third kinds of knowledge, the greater will be the part of it that endures (V. xxix. and xxiii.), and, consequently (by the last Prop.), the greater will be the part that is not touched by the emotions, which are contrary to our nature, or in other words, evil (IV. xxx.). Thus, in proportion as the mind understands more things by the second and third kinds of knowledge, the greater will be the part of it, that remains unimpaired, and, consequently, less subject to emotions, &c. *Q.E.D.*

Note.—Hence we understand that point which I touched on in IV. xxxix. note, and which I promised to explain in this Part; namely, that death becomes less hurtful, in proportion as the mind's clear and distinct knowledge is greater, and, consequently, in proportion as the mind loves God more. Again, since from the third kind of knowledge arises the highest possible acquiescence (V. xxvii.), it follows that the human mind can attain to being of such a nature, that the part thereof which we have shown to perish with the body (V. xxi.) should be of little importance when compared with the part which endures. But I will soon treat of the subject at greater length.

Prop. XXXIX. *He, who possesses a body capable of the greatest number of activities, possess a mind whereof the greatest part is eternal.*

Proof.—He, who possesses a body capable of the greatest number of activities, is least agitated by those emotions which are evil (IV. xxxviii.)—that is (IV. xxx.), by those emotions which are contrary to our nature; therefore (V. x.), he possesses the power of arranging and associating the modifications of the body according to the intellectual order, and, consequently, of bringing it about, that all the modifications of the body should be referred to the idea of God; whence it will come to pass that (V. xv.) he will be affected with love towards God, which (V. xvi.) must occupy or constitute the chief part of the mind; therefore (V. xxxiii.), such a man will possess a mind whereof the chief part is eternal. *Q.E.D.*

Note.—Since human bodies are capable of the greatest number of activities, there is no doubt but that they may be of such a nature, that they may be referred to minds possessing a great knowledge of themselves and of God, and whereof the greatest or chief part is eternal, and, therefore, that they should scarcely fear death. But, in order that this may be understood more clearly, we must here call to mind, that we live in a state of perpetual variation, and, according as we are changed for the better or the worse, we are called happy or unhappy.

For he, who, from being an infant or a child, becomes a corpse, is called unhappy; whereas it is set down to happiness, if we have been able to live through the whole period of life with a sound mind in a sound body. And, in reality, he, who, as in the case of an infant or a child, has a body capable of very few activities, and depending, for the most part, on external causes, has a mind which, considered in itself alone, is scarcely conscious of itself, or of God, or of things; whereas, he, who has a body capable of very many activities, has a mind which, considered in itself alone, is highly conscious of itself, of God, and of things. In this life, therefore, we primarily endeavour to bring it about, that the body of a child, in so far as its nature allows and conduces thereto, may be changed into something else capable of very many activities, and referable to a mind which is highly conscious of itself, of God, and of things; and we desire so to change it, that what is referred to its imagination and memory may become insignificant, in comparison with its intellect, as I have already said in the note to the last Proposition.

PROP. XL. *In proportion as each thing possesses more of perfection, so is it more active, and less passive; and, vice versâ, in proportion as it is more active, so is it more perfect.*

Proof.—In proportion as each thing is more perfect, it possesses more of reality (II. Def. vi.), and, consequently (III. iii. and note), it is to that extent more active and less passive. This demonstration may be reversed, and thus prove that, in proportion as a thing is more active, so is it more perfect.   *Q.E.D.*

Corollary.—Hence it follows that the part of the mind which endures, be it great or small, is more perfect than the rest. For the eternal part of the mind (V. xxiii. xxix.) is the understanding, through which alone we are said to act (III. iii.); the part which we have shown to perish is the imagination (V. xxi.), through which only we are said to be passive (III. iii. and general Def. of the Emotions); therefore, the former, be it great or small, is more perfect than the latter.   *Q.E.D.*

Note.—Such are the doctrines which I had purposed to set forth concerning the mind, in so far as it is regarded without relation to the body; whence, as also from I. xxi. and other places, it is plain that our mind, in so far as it understands, is an eternal mode of thinking, which is determined by another eternal mode of thinking, and this other by a third, and so on to infinity; so that all taken together at once constitute the eternal and infinite intellect of God.

PROP. XLI. *Even if we did not know that our mind is eternal, we should still consider as of primary importance piety and religion, and generally all things which, in Part IV., we showed to be attributable to courage and high-mindedness.*

Proof.—The first and only foundation of virtue, or the rule of right living is (IV. xxii. Coroll. and xxiv.) seeking one's own true interest. Now, while we determined what reason prescribes as useful, we took no account of the mind's eternity, which has only become known to us in this Fifth Part. Although we were ignorant at that time that the mind is eternal, we nevertheless stated that the qualities attributable to courage and high-mindedness are of primary importance. Therefore, even if we were still ignorant of this doctrine, we should yet put the aforesaid precepts of reason in the first place. *Q.E.D.*

Note.—The general belief of the multitude seems to be different. Most people seem to believe that they are free, in so far as they may obey their lusts, and that they cede their rights, in so far as they are bound to live according to the commandments of the divine law. They therefore believe that piety, religion, and, generally, all things attributable to firmness of mind, are burdens, which, after death, they hope to lay aside, and to receive the reward for their bondage, that is, for their piety and religion; it is not only by this hope, but also, and chiefly, by the fear of being horribly punished after death, that they are induced to live according to the divine commandments, so far as their feeble and infirm spirit will carry them.

If men had not this hope and this fear, but believed that the mind perishes with the body, and that no hope of prolonged life remains for the wretches who are broken down with the burden of piety, they would return to their own inclinations, controlling everything in accordance with their lusts, and desiring to obey fortune rather than themselves. Such a course appears to me not less absurd than if a man, because he does not believe that he can by wholesome food sustain his body for ever, should wish to cram himself with poisons and deadly fare; or if, because he sees that the mind is not eternal or immortal, he should prefer to be out of his mind altogether, and to live without the use of reason; these ideas are so absurd as to be scarcely worth refuting.

PROP. XLII. *Blessedness is not the reward of virtue, but virtue itself; neither do we rejoice therein, because we control our lusts, but, contrariwise, because we rejoice therein, we are able to control our lusts.*

Proof.—Blessedness consists in love towards God (V. xxxvi. and note), which love springs from the third kind of knowledge (V. xxxii. Coroll.); therefore this love (III. iii. lix.) must be referred to the mind, in so far as the latter is active; therefore (IV. Def. viii.) it is virtue itself. This was our first point. Again, in proportion as the mind rejoices more in this divine love or blessedness, so does it the more understand (V. xxxii.); that is (V. iii. Coroll.), so much the more power has it over the emotions, and (V. xxxviii.) so much the less is it subject to those emotions which are evil; therefore, in proportion as the mind rejoices in this divine love or blessedness, so has it the power of controlling lusts. And, since human power in controlling the emotions consists solely in the understanding, it follows that no one rejoices in blessedness, because he has controlled his lusts, but, contrariwise, his power of controlling his lusts arises from this blessedness itself. *Q.E.D.*

Note.—I have thus completed all I wished to set forth touching the mind's power over the emotions and the mind's freedom. Whence it appears, how potent is the wise man, and how much he surpasses the ignorant man, who is driven only by his lusts. For the ignorant man is not only distracted in various ways by external causes without ever gaining the true acquiescence of his spirit, but moreover lives, as it were unwitting of himself, and of God, and of things, and as soon as he ceases to suffer, ceases also to be.

Whereas the wise man, in so far as he is regarded as such, is scarcely at all disturbed in spirit, but, being conscious of himself, and of God, and of things, by a certain eternal necessity, never ceases to be, but always possesses true acquiescence of his spirit.

If the way which I have pointed out as leading to this result seems exceedingly hard, it may nevertheless be discovered. Needs must it be hard, since it is so seldom found. How would it be possible, if salvation were ready to our hand, and could without great labour be found, that it should be by almost all men neglected? But all things excellent are as difficult as they are rare.

JOHN
LOCKE   1632–1704

Born in Wrington, Somerset, Locke is the only one of
the three great "British Empiricists" who was an Eng-
lishman. Berkeley was Irish, Hume a Scotsman. Locke attended
Christ Church, Oxford, where he got his B.A. in 1656, an M.A. in
1658, and in 1659, a position as Senior Student, which he lost on
political grounds in 1684.

He was active in politics, traveled a great deal, and lived for
several years in Paris and in Holland. After the "Glorious Revolution" of 1688, he not only returned to England, but became Comis-
sioner of Appeals and, later, Commissioner of Trade and Plantages.

His major work, *Essay Concerning Human Understanding*, appeared in 1690, after about 20 years' intermittent work on it. The
book, although overly-long and long-winded, is important, interesting, and has been extremely influential.

Of Locke's other writings, his *Two Treatises of Government* deserve special mention. They, too, appeared in 1690. The first attacked
the patriarchal absolutism of Sir Robert Filmer, a royalist of the
time; the second developed Locke's own ideas. Locke also wrote
several "Letters" concerning toleration. His political views greatly
influenced Jefferson and the whole structure of the American government.

In 1695, Locke published *The Reasonableness of Christianity as
Delivered in the Scriptures,* and later the same year, and again in
1697, *Vindications* of this work. There has been some controversy
as to whether he was a Unitarian.

All of the following selections come from his *Essay Concerning
Human Understanding*. The *Essay* went through several editions

while Locke was still living, and he added some passages—here printed in square brackets. A complete edition, with ample editorial material, was edited by Alexander Campbell Fraser in 1894. In 1695, John Wynne published *An Abridgement of Mr. Locke's Essay Concerning Human Understanding*, with the author's consent, and by 1737 there was a "Fifth Edition Corrected." In the twentieth century, abridged versions were edited by Mary Whiton Calkins and A. S. Pringle-Pattison, among others, and the latter also supplied many helpful footnotes; but neither of them marked all omissions. The following text is indebted to several previous editors, especially Pringle-Pattison.

OF HUMAN UNDERSTANDING

Book I

CHAPTER I. INTRODUCTION

1. *An enquiry into the understanding pleasant and useful.* Since it is the *understanding* that sets man above the rest of sensible beings, and gives him all the advantage and dominion which he has over them, it is certainly a subject, even for its nobleness, worth our labour to enquire into. The understanding, like the eye, whilst it makes us see and perceive all other things, takes no notice of itself; and it requires art and pains to set it at a distance, and make it its own object. But whatever be the difficulties that lie in the way of this enquiry; whatever it be that keeps us so much in the dark to ourselves; sure I am that all the light we can let in upon our own minds, all the acquaintance we can make with our own understandings, will not only be very pleasant, but bring us great advantage in directing our thoughts in the search of other things.

2. *Design*—This, therefore, being my purpose, to enquire into the original, certainty, and extent of human Knowledge, together with the grounds and degrees of Belief, Opinion, and Assent, I shall not at present meddle with the physical consideration of the mind, or trouble myself to examine wherein its essence consists, or by what motions of our spirits, or alterations of our bodies, we come to have any sensation by our organs, or any ideas in our understandings; and whether those ideas do, in their formation, any or all of them, depend on matter or no. These are speculations which, however curious and entertaining, I shall decline, as lying out of my way in the design I am now upon. It shall suffice to my present purpose, to consider the discerning faculties of a man as they are em-

ployed about the objects which they have to do with: and I shall imagine I have not wholly misemployed myself in the thoughts I shall have on this occasion, if, in this historical, plain method, I can give any account of the ways whereby our understandings come to attain those notions of things we have, and can set down any measures of the certainty of our knowledge, or the grounds of those persuasions which are to be found amongst men, so various, different, and wholly contradictory; and yet asserted somewhere or other with such assurance, and confidence, that he that shall take a view of the opinions of mankind, observe their opposition, and at the same time consider the fondness and devotion wherewith they are embraced, the resolution and eagerness wherewith they are maintained, may perhaps have reason to suspect that either there is no such thing as truth at all, or that mankind hath no sufficient means to attain a certain knowledge of it.

3. *Method.*—It is therefore worth while to search out the *bounds* between Opinion and Knowledge, and examine by what measures, in things whereof we have no certain knowledge, we ought to regulate our assent, and moderate our persuasions. In order whereunto, I shall pursue this following method:—

First, I shall enquire into the *original* of those *ideas*, notions, or whatever else you please to call them, which a man observes, and is conscious to himself he has in his mind; and the ways whereby the understanding comes to be furnished with them.

Secondly, I shall endeavour to show what *knowledge* the understanding hath by those *ideas*, and the certainty, evidence, and extent of it.

Thirdly, I shall make some enquiry into the nature and grounds of Faith or Opinion; whereby I mean that assent which we give to any proposition as true, of whose truth yet we have no certain knowledge: and here we shall have occasion to examine the reasons and degrees of *Assent*.

4. *Useful to know the extent of our comprehension.*—If by this enquiry into the nature of the understanding, I can discover the powers thereof, *how far* they reach, to what things they are in any degree proportionate, and where they fail us, I suppose it may be of use, to prevail with the busy mind of man to be more cautious in meddling with things exceeding its comprehension, to stop when it is at the utmost extent of its tether, and to sit down in a quiet ignorance of those things which, upon examination, are found to be beyond the reach of our capacities. We should not then perhaps be so forward, out of an affectation of an universal knowledge, to raise questions, and perplex ourselves and others with disputes about things to which our understandings are not suited, and of which we cannot frame in our minds any clear or distinct perceptions, or whereof (as it has, perhaps, too often happened) we have not any notions at all. If we can find out how far the understanding can extend its view, how far it has faculties to attain certainty, and in what cases it can only judge and guess, we may learn to content ourselves with what is attainable by us in this state.

.   .   .

8. *What 'idea' stands for.*—Thus much I thought necessary to say concerning the occasion of this enquiry into human understanding. But, before I proceed on to what I have thought on this subject, I must here, in the entrance, beg pardon of my reader for the frequent use of the word *idea* which he will find in the following treatise. It being that term which, I think, serves best to stand for whatsoever is the object of the understanding when a man thinks, I have used it to express whatever is meant by *phantasm, notion, species,* or whatever it is which the mind can be employed about in thinking; and I could not avoid frequently using it.

I presume it will be easily granted me, that there are such *ideas* in men's minds; every one is conscious of them in himself, and men's words and actions will satisfy him that they are in others.

Our first enquiry then shall be, how they come into the mind.

CHAPTER II. NO INNATE PRINCIPLES IN THE MIND

1. *The way shown how we come by any knowledge, sufficient to prove it not innate.*—It is an established opinion amongst some men, that there are in the understanding certain *innate principles;* some primary notions, κοιναὶ ἔννοιαι, characters, as it were stamped upon the mind of man, which the soul receives in its very first being, and brings into the world with it. It would be sufficient to convince unprejudiced readers of the falseness of this supposition, if I should only show (as I hope I shall in the following parts of this discourse) how men, barely by the use of their natural faculties, may attain to all the knowledge they have, without the help of any innate impressions; and may arrive at certainty, without any such original notions or principles. For I imagine any one will easily grant, that is would be impertinent to suppose the ideas of colours innate in a creature to whom God hath given sight, and a power to receive them by the eyes from external objects: and no less unreasonable would it be to attribute several truths to the impressions of nature and innate characters, when we may observe in ourselves faculties fit to attain as easy and certain knowledge of them as if they were originally imprinted on the mind.

But because a man is not permitted without censure to follow his own thoughts in the search of truth, when they lead him ever so little out of the common road, I shall set down the reasons that made me doubt of the truth of that opinion, as an excuse for my mistake, if I be in one; which I leave to be considered by those who, with me, dispose themselves to embrace truth wherever they find it.

2. *General assent the great argument.*—There is nothing more commonly taken for granted, than that there are certain principles, both *speculative* and *practical* (for they speak of both), universally agreed upon by all mankind; which therefore, they argue, must needs be the constant impressions which the souls of men receive in their first beings,

and which they bring into the world with them, as necessarily and really as they do any of their inherent faculties.

3. *Universal consent proves nothing innate.*—This argument, drawn from universal consent, has this misfortune in it, that if it were true in matter of fact, that there were certain truths wherein all mankind agreed, it would not prove them innate, if there can be any other way shown, how men may come to that universal agreement in the things they do consent in; which I presume may be done.

.   .   .

5. *Not on the mind naturally imprinted, because not known to children, idiots,* &c.—For, first, it is evident, that all children and idiots have not the least apprehension or thought of them: and the want of that is enough to destroy that universal assent, which must needs be the necessary concomitant of all innate truths: it seeming to me near a contradiction to say, that there are truths imprinted on the soul which it perceives or understands not; imprinting, if it signify anything, being nothing else but the making certain truths to be perceived. No proposition can be said to be in the mind which it never yet knew, which it was never yet conscious of. For if any one may, then, by the same reason, all propositions that are true, and the mind is capable ever of assenting to, may be said to be in the mind, and to be imprinted; since if any one can be said to be in the mind, which it never yet knew, it must be only because it is capable of knowing it; and so the mind is of all truths it ever shall know. Nay, thus truths may be imprinted on the mind which it never did, nor ever shall know: for a man may live long, and die at last in ignorance of many truths which his mind was capable of knowing, and that with certainty. So that if the capacity of knowing be the natural impression contended for, all the truths a man ever comes to know will, by this account, be every one of them innate: and this great point will amount to no more, but only to a very high improper way of speaking. But then, to what end such contest for certain innate maxims? If truths can be imprinted on the understanding without being perceived, I can see no difference there can be between any truths the mind is capable of knowing in respect of their original: they must all be innate, or all adventitious; in vain shall a man go about to distinguish them. He therefore that talks of innate notions in the understanding, cannot (if he intend thereby any distinct sort of truths) mean such truths to be in the understanding as it never perceived, and is yet wholly ignorant of. For if these words 'to be in the understanding' have any propriety, they signify to be understood. If therefore these two propositions: 'Whatsoever is, is,' and, 'It is impossible for the same thing to be, and not to be,' are by nature imprinted, children cannot be ignorant of them; infants, and all that have souls, must necessarily have them in their understandings, know the truth of them, and assent to it.

.   .   .

CHAPTER III. NO INNATE PRACTICAL PRINCIPLES

1. *No moral principles so clear and so generally received as the fore-mentioned speculative maxims.*—If those speculative maxims whereof we discoursed in the foregoing chapter have not an actual universal assent from all mankind, as we there proved, it is much more visible concerning *practical principles*, that they come short of an universal reception. . . .

2. *Faith and justice not owned as principles by all men.*—Whether there be any such moral principles wherein all men do agree, I appeal to any who have been but moderately conversant in the history of mankind, and looked abroad beyond the smoke of their own chimneys. Where is that practical truth that is universally received without doubt or question, as it must be if innate? Justice, and keeping of contracts, is that which most men seem to agree in. This is a principle which is thought to extend itself to the dens of thieves, and the confederacies of the greatest villains; and they who have gone farthest towards the putting off of humanity itself, keep faith and rules of justice one with another. I grant that outlaws themselves do this one amongst another; but it is without receiving these as the innate laws of nature. They practise them as rules of convenience within their own communities: but it is impossible to conceive that he embraces justice as a practical principle who acts fairly with his fellow-highwayman, and at the same plunders or kills the next honest man he meets with.

.   .   .

CHAPTER IV. CONSIDERATIONS ON INNATE PRINCIPLES

8. *Idea of God not innate.*—If any idea can be imagined innate, the *idea of God* may, of all others, for many reasons, be thought so; since it is hard to conceive how there should be innate moral principles without an innate idea of a Deity: without a notion of a law-maker, it is impossible to have a notion of a law, and an obligation to observe it. Besides the atheists taken notice of amongst the ancients, and left branded upon the records of history, hath not navigation discovered, in these latter ages, whole nations, at the Bay of Soldania, in Brazil, in Boranday, and the Caribbee Islands, &c., amongst whom there was to be found no notion of a God, no religion? . . . Perhaps, if we should with attention mind the lives and discourses of people not so far off, we should have too much reason to fear that many, in more civilized countries, have no very strong and clear impressions of a Deity upon their minds; and that the complaints of atheism made from the pulpit are not without reason. . . .

9. *The name of God not universal or obscure in meaning.*—But had all mankind everywhere a notion of a God (whereof yet history tells us the

contrary), it would not from thence follow that the idea of him was innate, ... especially if it be such an idea as is agreeable to the common light of reason, and naturally deducible from every part of our knowledge, as that of a God is. For the visible marks of extraordinary wisdom and power appear so plainly in all the work of the creation, that a rational creature who will but seriously reflect on them, cannot miss the discovery of a Deity; and the influence that the discovery of such a Being must necessarily have on the minds of all that have but once heard of it, is so great, and carries such a weight of thought and communication with it, that it seems stranger to me that a whole nation of men should be anywhere found so brutish as to want the notion of a God, than that they should be without any notion of numbers, or fire.

. . .

Book II

CHAPTER I.   OF IDEAS IN GENERAL AND THEIR ORIGINAL

1. *Idea is the object of thinking.*—Every man being conscious to himself that he thinks, and that which his mind is applied about whilst thinking being the ideas that are there, it is past doubt that men have in their minds several ideas, such as are those expresed by the words, 'whiteness, hardness, sweetness, thinking, motion, man, elephant, army, drunkenness', and others. It is in the first place then to be enquired, How he comes by them? I know it is a received doctrine, that men have native ideas and original characters stamped upon their minds in their very first being. This opinion I have at large examined already; and, I suppose, what I have said in the foregoing Book will be much more easily admitted, when I have shown whence the understanding may get all the ideas it has, and by what ways and degrees they may come into the mind; for which I shall appeal to every one's own observation and experience.

2. *All ideas come from sensation or reflection.*—Let us then suppose the mind to be, as we say, white paper, void of all characters, without any ideas; how comes it to be furnished? Whence comes it by that vast store, which the busy and boundless fancy of man has painted on it with an almost endless variety? Whence has it all the materials of reason and knowledge? To this I answer, in one word, from EXPERIENCE; in that all our knowledge is founded, and from that it ultimately derives itself. Our observation, employed either about external sensible objects, or about the internal operations of our minds, perceived and reflected on by ourselves, is that which supplies our understandings with all the materials of thinking. These two are the fountains of knowledge, from whence all the ideas we have or can naturally have, do spring.

3. *The objects of sensation one source of ideas.*—First, our senses,

conversant about particular sensible objects, do convey into the mind several distinct perceptions of things, according to those various ways wherein those objects do affect them; and thus we come by those *ideas* we have of yellow, white, heat, cold, soft, hard, bitter, sweet, and all those which we call sensible qualities; which when I say the senses convey into the mind, I mean, they from external objects convey into the mind what produces there those perceptions. This great source of most of the ideas we have, depending wholly upon our senses, and derived by them to the understanding, I call, SENSATION.

4. *The operations of our minds the other source of them.*—Secondly, the other fountain, from which experience furnisheth the understanding with ideas, is the perception of the operations of our mind within us, as it is employed about the ideas it has got; which operations, when the soul comes to reflect on and consider, do furnish the understanding with another set of ideas which could not be had from things without: and such are perception, thinking, doubting, believing, reasoning, knowing, willing, and all the different actings of our own minds; which we being conscious of, and observing in ourselves, do from these receive into our understanding as distinct ideas, as we do from bodies affecting our senses. This source of ideas every man has wholly in himself: and though it be not sense, as having nothing to do with external objects, yet it is very like it, and might properly enough be called internal sense. But as I call the other Sensation, so I call this REFLECTION, the ideas it affords being such only as the mind gets by reflecting on its own operations within itself. By Reflection, then, in the following part of this discourse, I would be understood to mean that notice which the mind takes of its own operations, and the manner of them, by reason whereof there come to be ideas of these operations in the understanding. These two, I say, viz., external material things as the objects of Sensation, and the operations of our own minds within as the objects of Reflection are, to me, the only originals from whence all our ideas take their beginnings. The term *operations* here, I use in a large sense, as comprehending not barely the actions of the mind about its ideas, but some sort of passions arising sometimes from them, such as is the satisfaction or uneasiness arising from any thought.

5. *All our ideas are of the one or the other of these.*—The understanding seems to me not to have the least glimmering of any ideas which it doth not receive from one of these two. *External objects* furnish the mind with the ideas of sensible qualities, which are all those different perceptions they produce in us; and *the mind* furnishes the understanding with ideas of its own operations. These, when we have taken a full survey of them, and their several modes, combinations, and relations, we shall find to contain all our whole stock of ideas; and that we have nothing in our minds which did not come in one of these two ways. Let any one examine his own thoughts, and thoroughly search into his understanding, and then let him tell me, whether all the original ideas he has there, are any other than of the objects of his senses, or

of the operations of his mind considered as objects of his reflection; and how great a mass of knowledge soever he imagines to be lodged there, he will, upon taking a strict view, see that he has not any idea in his mind but what one of these two have imprinted, though perhaps with infinite variety compounded and enlarged by the understanding, as we shall see hereafter.

6. *Observable in children.*—He that attentively considers the state of a child at his first coming into the world, will have little reason to think him stored with plenty of ideas that are to be the matter of his future knowledge. It is by degrees he comes to be furnished with them: and though the ideas of obvious and familiar qualities imprint themselves before the memory begins to keep a register of time and order, yet it is often so late before some unusual qualities come in the way, that there are few men that cannot recollect the beginning of their acquaintance with them: and if it were worth while, no doubt a child might be so ordered as to have but a very few even of the ordinary ideas till he were grown up to a man. But all that are born into the world being surrounded with bodies that perpetually and diversely affect them, variety of ideas, whether care be taken about it or no, are imprinted on the minds of children. Light and colours are busy and at hand everywhere when the eye is but open; sounds and some tangible qualities fail not to solicit their proper senses, and force an entrance to the mind; but yet I think it will be granted easily, that if a child were kept in a place where he never saw any other but black and white till he were a man, he would have no more ideas of scarlet or green, than he that from his childhood never tasted an oyster or a pine-apple has of those particular relishes.

7. *Men are differently furnished with these according to the different objects they converse with.*—Men then come to be furnished with fewer or more simple ideas from without, according as the objects they converse with afford greater or less variety; and from the operations of their minds within, according as they more or less reflect on them. For, though he that contemplates the operations of his mind cannot but have plain and clear ideas of them; yet, unless he turn his thoughts that way, and considers them *attentively*, he will no more have clear and distinct ideas of all the operations of his mind, and all that may be observed therein, than he will have all the particular ideas of any landscape, or of the parts and motions of a clock, who will not turn his eyes to it, and with attention heed all the parts of it. The picture or clock may be so placed, that they may come in his way every day; but yet he will have but a confused idea of all the parts they are made up of, till he applies himself with attention to consider them each in particular.

8. *Ideas of reflection later, because they need attention.*—And hence we see the reason why it is pretty late before most children get ideas of the operations of their own minds; and some have not any very clear or perfect ideas of the greatest part of them all their lives. Because, though they pass there continually, yet, like floating visions, they make not

deep impressions enough to leave in the mind clear, distinct, lasting ideas, till the understanding turns inwards upon itself, reflects on its own operations, and makes them the object of its own contemplation. Children, when they come first into it, are surrounded with a world of new things, which, by a constant solicitation of their senses, draw the mind constantly to them, forward to take notice of new, and apt to be delighted with the variety of changing objects. Thus the first years are usually employed and diverted in looking abroad. Men's business in them is to acquaint themselves with what is to be found without; and so, growing up in a constant attention to outward sensations, seldom make any considerable reflection on what passes within them till they come to be of riper years; and some scarce ever at all.

9. *The soul begins to have ideas when it begins to perceive.*—To ask, at what *time* a man has first any ideas, is to ask when he begins to perceive; having ideas, and perception, being the same thing. I know it is an opinion, that the soul always thinks; and that it has the actual perception of ideas in itself constantly, as long as it exists; and that actual thinking is as inseparable from the soul, as actual extension is from the body: which if true, to enquire after the beginning of a man's ideas is the same as to enquire after the beginning of his soul. For by this account, soul and its ideas, as body and its extension, will begin to exist both at the same time.

.   .   .

CHAPTER II.   OF SIMPLE IDEAS

1. *Uncompounded appearances.*—The better to understand the nature, manner, and extent of our knowledge, one thing is carefully to be observed concerning the ideas we have; and that is, that some of them are *simple*, and some *complex*.

Though the qualities that affect our senses are, in the things themselves, so united and blended that there is no separation, no distance between them; yet it is plain the ideas they produce in the mind enter by the senses simple and unmixed. For though the sight and touch often take in from the same object at the same time different ideas; as a man sees at once motion and colour, the hand feels softness and warmth in the same piece of wax; yet the simple ideas thus united in the same subject are as perfectly distinct as those that come in by different senses. The coldness and hardness which a man feels in a piece of ice being as distinct ideas in the mind as the smell and whiteness of a lily, or as the taste of sugar and smell of a rose: and there is nothing can be plainer to a man than the clear and distinct perception he has of those simple ideas; which, being each in itself uncompounded, contains in it nothing but one uniform appearance or conception in the mind, and is not distinguishable into different ideas.

2. *The mind can neither make nor destroy them.*—These simple ideas, the materials of all our knowledge, are suggested and furnished to the mind only by those two ways above mentioned, viz., sensation and reflection. When the understanding is once stored with these simple ideas, it has the power to repeat, compare, and unite them, even to an almost infinite variety, and so can make at pleasure new complex ideas. But it is not in the power of the most exalted wit or enlarged understanding, by any quickness or variety of thought, to invent or frame one new simple idea in the mind, not taken in by the ways before mentioned; nor can any force of the understanding destroy those that are there. The dominion of man in this little world of his own understanding, being much-what the same as it is in the great world of visible things, wherein his power, however managed by art and skill, reaches no farther than to compound and divide the materials that are made to his hand, but can do nothing towards the making the least particle of new matter, or destroying one atom of what is already in being. The same inability will every one find in himself, who shall go about to fashion in his understanding any simple idea not received in by his senses from external objects, or by reflection from the operations of his own mind about them. I would have any one try to fancy any taste which had never affected his palate, or frame the idea of a scent he had never smelt; and when he can do this, I will also conclude, that a blind man hath ideas of colours, and a deaf man true distinct notions of sounds.

3. This is the reason why, though we cannot believe it impossible to God to make a creature with other organs, and more ways to convey into the understanding the notice of corporeal things than those five, as they are usually counted, which he has given to man: yet I think it is *not possible* for any one to *imagine* any other qualities in bodies, howsoever constituted, whereby they can be taken notice of, besides sounds, tastes, smells, visible and tangible qualities. And had mankind been made with but four senses, the qualities then which are the object of the fifth sense, had been as far from our notice, imagination, and conception, as now any belonging to a sixth, seventh, or eighth sense, can possibly be: which, whether yet some other creatures, in some other parts of this vast and stupendous universe, may not have, will be a great presumption to deny. He that will not set himself proudly at the top of all things, but will consider the immensity of this fabric, and the great variety that is to be found in this little and inconsiderable part of it which he has to do with, may be apt to think, that in other mansions of it there may be other and different intelligible beings, of whose faculties he has as little knowledge or apprehension, as a worm shut up in one drawer of a cabinet hath of the senses or understanding of a man; such variety and excellency being suitable to the wisdom and power of the Maker. I have here followed the common opinion of man's having but five senses, though perhaps there may be justly counted more, but either supposition serves equally to my present purpose.

CHAPTER III. OF IDEAS OF ONE SENSE

1. *Division of simple ideas.*—The better to conceive the ideas we receive from sensation, it may not be amiss for us to consider them in reference to the different ways whereby they make their approaches to our minds, and make themselves perceivable by us.

First, then, There are some which come into our minds *by one sense* only.

Secondly. There are others that convey themselves into the mind *by more senses than one.*

Thirdly. Others that are had from *reflection* only.

Fourthly. There are some that make themselves way, and are suggested to the mind *by all the ways of sensation and reflection.*

We shall consider them apart under these several heads.

First, There are some ideas which have admittance only through one sense, which is peculiarly adapted to receive them. Thus light and colours, as white, red, yellow, blue, with their several degrees or shades and mixtures, as green, scarlet, purple, sea-green, and the rest come in only by the eyes; all kinds of noises, sounds, and tones, only by the ears; the several tastes and smells, by the nose and palate. And if these organs, or the nerves which are the conduits to convey them from without to their audience in the brain, the mind's presence-room (as I may so call it), are, any of them, so disordered as not to perform their functions, they have no postern to be admitted by, no other way to bring themselves into view, and be perceived by the understanding.

The most considerable of those belonging to the touch are heat, and cold, and solidity; all the rest, consisting almost wholly in the sensible configuration, as smooth and rough; or else, more or less firm adhesion of the parts, as hard and soft, tough and brittle, are obvious enough.

2. *Few simple ideas have names.*—I think it will be needless to enumerate all the particular simple ideas belonging to each sense. Nor indeed is it possible if we would, there being a great many more of them belonging to most of the senses than we have names for. The variety of smells, which are as many almost, if not more than species of bodies in the world, do most of them want names. Sweet and stinking commonly serve our turn for these ideas, which in effect is little more than to call them pleasing or displeasing; though the smell of a rose and violet, both sweet, are certainly very distinct ideas. Nor are the different tastes that by our palates we receive ideas of, much better provided with names. Sweet, bitter, sour, harsh, and salt, are almost all the epithets we have to denominate that numberless variety of relishes which are to be found distinct, not only in almost every sort of creatures, but in the different parts of the same plant, fruit, or animal. The same may be said of colours and sounds. I shall therefore, in the account of simple ideas I am here giving, content myself to set down only such as are most material to our present purpose, or are in themselves less apt to be taken notice of, though

they are very frequently the ingredients of our complex ideas; amongst which, I think, I may well account solidity, which therefore I shall treat of in the next chapter.

CHAPTER IV. OF SOLIDITY

1. *We receive this idea from touch.*—The idea of solidity we receive by our touch; and it arises from the resistance which we find in body to the entrance of any other body into the place it possesses, till it has left it. There is no idea which we receive more constantly from sensation than solidity. Whether we move or rest, in what posture soever we are, we always feel something under us that supports us, and hinders our farther sinking downwards; and the bodies which we daily handle make us perceive that whilst they remain between them, they do, by an insurmountable force, hinder the approach of the parts of our hands that press them. That which thus hinders the approach of two bodies, when they are moving one towards another, I call *solidity*. I will not dispute whether this acceptation of the word solid be nearer to its original signification than that which mathematicians use it in: it suffices that, I think, the common notion of solidity will allow, if not justify, this use of it; but if any one think it better to call it *impenetrability*, he has my consent. Only I have thought the term solidity the more proper to express this idea, not only because of its vulgar use in that sense, but also because it carries something more of positive in it than impenetrability, which is negative, and is, perhaps, more a consequence of solidity than solidity itself. This, of all other, seems the idea most intimately connected with and essential to body, so as nowhere else to be found or imagined, but only in matter; and though our senses take no notice of it, but in masses of matter, of a bulk sufficient to cause a sensation in us; yet the mind, having once got this idea from such grosser sensible bodies, traces it farther, and considers it, as well as figure, in the minutest particle of matter that can exist, and finds it inseparably inherent in body, wherever or however modified.

.   .   .

3. *Distinct from space.*—This resistance, whereby it keeps other bodies out of the space which it possesses, is so great, that no force, how great soever, can surmount it. All the bodies in the world, pressing a drop of water on all sides, will never be able to overcome the resistance which it will make, as soft as it is, to their approaching one another, till it be removed out of their way: whereby our idea of solidity is distinguished both from pure space, which is capable neither of resistance nor motion, and from the ordinary idea of hardness. For a man may conceive two bodies at a distance so as they may approach one another without touching or displacing any solid thing till their superficies come to meet; whereby, I think, we have the clear idea of space without solidity. For

(not to go so far as annihilation of any particular body) I ask, whether a man cannot have the idea of the motion of one single body alone, without any other succeeding immediately into its place? I think it is evident he can: the idea of motion in one body no more including the idea of motion in another, than the idea of a square figure in one body includes the idea of a square figure in another. I do not ask, whether bodies do so exist, that the motion of one body cannot really be without the motion of another? To determine this either way is to beg the question for or against a vacuum. But my question is, whether one cannot have the idea of one body moved, whilst others are at rest? And I think this no one will deny: if so, then the place it deserted gives us the idea of pure space without solidity, whereinto another body may enter without either resistance or protrusion of anything. When the sucker in a pump is drawn, the space it filled in the tube is certainly the same, whether any other body follows the motion of the sucker or no; nor does it imply a contradiction that upon the motion of one body, another that is only contiguous to it should not follow it. The necessity of such a motion is built only on the supposition, that the world is full, but not on the distinct ideas of space and solidity; which are as different as resistance and not-resistance, protrusion and not-protrusion. And that men have ideas of space without body, their very disputes a vacuum plainly demonstrate, as is showed in another place.

4. *From hardness.*—Solidity is hereby also differenced from hardness, in that solidity consists in repletion, and so an utter exclusion of other bodies out of the space it possesses; but hardness, in a firm cohesion of the parts of matter, making up masses of a sensible bulk, so that the whole does not easily change its figure. And, indeed, hard and soft are names that we give to things only in relation to the constitutions of our own bodies; that being generally called hard by us which will put us to pain sooner than change figure by the pressure of any part of our bodies; and that, on the contrary, soft which changes the situation of its parts upon an easy and unpainful touch.

But this difficulty of changing the situation of the sensible parts amongst themselves, or of the figure of the whole, gives no more solidity to the hardest body in the world than to the softest; nor is an adamant one jot more solid than water. For though the two flat sides of two pieces of marble will more easily approach each other, between which there is nothing but water or air, than if there be a diamond between them; yet it is not that the parts of the diamond are more solid than those of water, or resist more, but because the parts of water being more easily separable from each other, they will by a side-motion be more easily removed and give way to the approach of the two pieces of marble: but if they could be kept from making place by that side-motion, they would eternally hinder the approach of these two pieces of marble as much as the diamond. The softest body in the world will as invincibly resist the coming together of any two other boides, if it be not put out of the way, but remain between them, as the hardest that can be found or imagined. He that shall fill a yielding soft body well with air or water will quickly find its resistance: and he that thinks that nothing but bodies that are hard can keep his hands from approaching one another, may be pleased to make a trial with the air enclosed in a football. [The experiment I have been told was made at Florence, with a hollow globe of gold filled with water, and exactly closed, farther shows the solidity of so soft a body as water. For the golden globe thus filled being put into a press which was driven by the extreme force of screws, the water made itself way through the pores of that very close metal, and finding no room for a nearer approach of its particles within, got to the outside, where it rose like a dew, and so fell in drops before the sides of the globe could be made to yield to the violent compression of the engine that squeezed it.]

5. *On solidity depend impulse, resistance, and protrusion.*—By this idea of solidity is the extension of body distinguished from the extension of space. The extension of body being nothing but the cohesion or continuity of solid, separable, movable parts; and the extension of space, the continuity of unsolid, inseparable, and immovable parts. Upon the solidity of bodies also depend their mutual impulse, resistance, and protrusion. Of pure space then, and solidity, there are several (amongst which I confess myself one) who persuade themselves they have clear and distinct ideas; and that they can think on space without anything in it that resists or is protruded by body. This is the idea of pure space, which they think they have as clear as any idea they can have of the extension of body. . . .

6. *What it is.*—If any one asks me, *what this solidity is*, I send him to his senses to inform him: let him put a flint or a football between his hands, and then endeavour to join them, and he will know. If he thinks this is not a sufficient explanation of solidity, what it is, and wherein it consists, I promise to tell him what it is, and wherein it consists, when he tells me what thinking is, or wherein it consists; or explains to me what extension or motion is, which perhaps seems much easier. The simple ideas we have are such as experience teaches them us; but if, beyond that, we endeavour by words to make them clearer in the mind, we shall succeed no better than if we went about to clear up the darkness of a blind man's mind by talking, and to discourse into him the ideas of light and colours. The reason of this I shall show in another place.

CHAPTER V. OF SIMPLE IDEAS OF DIVERS SENSES

The ideas we get by more than one sense are of *space* or *extension*, *figure, rest* and *motion*: for these make perceivable impressions both on the eyes and touch; and we can receive and convey into our minds the ideas of the extension, figure, motion, and rest of bodies, both by seeing and feeling. But having occasion to speak more at large of these in another place, I here only enumerate them.

CHAPTER VI.　OF SIMPLE IDEAS OF REFLECTION

1. *Are the operations of the mind about its other ideas.*—The mind, receiving the ideas mentioned in the foregoing chapters from without, when it turns its view inward upon itself, and observes its own actions about those ideas it has, takes from thence other ideas, which are as capable to be the objects of its contemplation as any of those it received from foreign things.

2. *The idea of perception, and idea of willing, we have from reflection.* —The two great and principal actions of the mind, which are most frequently considered, and which are so frequent that every one that pleases may take notice of them in himself, are these two: *perception* or *thinking,* and *volition* or *willing.* The power of thinking is called the *Understanding,* and the power of volition is called the *Will;* and these two powers of abilities in the mind are denominated *faculties.* Of some of the modes of these simple ideas of reflection, such as are *remembrance, discerning, reasoning, judging, knowledge, faith,* &c., I shall have occasion to speak hereafter.

CHAPTER VII.　OF SIMPLE IDEAS OF BOTH SENSATION
AND REFLECTION

1. There be other simple ideas which convey themselves into the mind by all the ways of sensation and reflection; viz., *pleasure* or *delight,* and its opposite, *pain* or *uneasiness; power; existence; unity.*

2. *Pleasure and pain.* Delight or uneasiness, one or other of them, join themselves to almost all our ideas both of sensation and reflection; and there is scarce any affection of our senses from without, any retired thought of our mind within, which is not able to produce in us pleasure or pain. By pleasure and pain, I would be understood to signify whatsoever delights or molests us; whether it arises from the thoughts of our minds, or anything operating on our bodies. For whether we call it satisfaction, delight, pleasure, happiness, &c., on the one side, or uneasiness, trouble, pain, torment, anguish, misery, &c., on the other, they are still but different degrees of the same thing, and belong to the ideas of pleasure and pain, delight or uneasiness; which are the names I shall most commonly use for those two sorts of ideas.

3. The infinite wise Author of our being, to excite us to these actions of thinking and motion that we are capable of, has been pleased to join to several thoughts and several sensations a perception of delight. If this were wholly separated from all our outward sensations and inward thoughts, we should have no reason to prefer one thought or action to another, negligence to attention, or motion to rest. And so we should neither stir our bodies, nor employ our minds, but let our thoughts (if I may so call it) run adrift, without any direction or design; and suffer the ideas of our minds, like unregarded shadows, to make their appear-

ances there as it happened, without attending to them. In which state man, however furnished with the faculties of understanding and will, would be a very idle, unactive creature, and pass his time only in a lazy, lethargic dream. . . .

4. Pain has the same efficacy and use to set us on work that pleasure has, we being as ready to employ our faculties to avoid that, as to pursue this: only this is worth our consideration, that pain is often produced by the same objects and ideas that produce pleasure in us. . . . Thus heat, that is very agreeable to us in one degree, by a little greater increase of it proves no ordinary torment; and the most pleasant of all sensible objects, light itself, if there be too much of it, if increased beyond a due proportion to our eyes, causes a very painful sensation. Which is wisely and favourably so ordered by nature, that when any object does by the vehemency of its operation disorder the instruments of sensation, whose structures cannot but be very nice and delicate, we might by the pain be warned to withdraw before the organ be quite put out of order, and so be unfitted for its proper functions for the future.

. . .

7. *Existence and unity.*—Existence and unity are two other ideas that are suggested to the understanding by every object without, and every idea within. When ideas are in our minds, we consider them as being actually there, as well as we consider things to be actually without us: which is, that they exist, or have existence. And whatever we can consider as one thing, whether a real being or idea, suggests to the understanding the idea of unity.

8. *Power.*—Power also is another of those simple ideas which we receive from sensation and reflection. For, observing in ourselves that we do and can think, and that we can at pleasure move several parts of our bodies which were at rest, the effects also that natural bodies are able to produce in one another occurring every moment to our senses, we both these ways get the idea of power.

9. *Succession.*—Besides these there is another idea, which though suggested by our senses yet is more constantly offered us by what passes in our own minds; and that is the idea of succession. For if we look immediately into ourselves, and reflect on what is observable there, we shall find our ideas always, whilst we are awake or have any thought, passing in train, one going and another coming without intermission.

10. *Simple ideas the materials of all our knowledge.*—These, if they are not all, are at least (as I think) the most considerable of those simple ideas which the mind has, and out of which is made all its other knowledge: all of which it receives only by the two forementioned ways of sensation and reflection.

Nor let any one think these too narrow bounds for the capacious mind of man to expatiate in, which takes its flight farther than the stars, and cannot be confined by the limits of the world. I grant all this, but desire any one to assign any simple idea which is not received from one of those inlets before mentioned, or any complex idea not made out of those simple ones.

Nor will it be so strange to think these few simple ideas sufficient to employ the quickest thought or largest capacity, and to furnish the materials of all that various knowledge and more various fancies and opinions of all mankind, if we consider how many words may be made out of the various composition of twenty-four letters; or if, going one step farther, we will but reflect on the variety of combinations may be made with barely one of the above-mentioned ideas, viz., number, whose stock is inexhaustible and truly infinite: and what a large and immense field doth extension alone afford the mathematicians?

CHAPTER VIII. SOME FARTHER CONSIDERATIONS CONCERNING OUR SIMPLE IDEAS

1. *Positive ideas from privative causes.*—Concerning the simple ideas of sensation it is to be considered, that whatsoever is so constituted in nature as to be able by affecting our senses to cause any perception in the mind, doth thereby produce in the understanding a simple idea; which, whatever be the external cause of it, when it comes to be taken notice of by our discerning faculty, it is by the mind looked on and considered there to be a real positive idea in the understanding, as much as any other whatsoever; though perhaps the cause of it be but a privation in the subject.

2. Thus the ideas of heat and cold, light and darkness, white and black, motion and rest, are equally clear and positive ideas in the mind; though perhaps some of the causes which produce them are barely privations in those subjects from whence our senses derive those ideas. These the understanding, in its view of them, considers all as distinct positive ideas without taking notice of the causes that produce them: which is an enquiry not belonging to the idea as it is in the understanding, but to the nature of the things existing without us. These are two very different things, and carefully to be distinguished; it being one thing to perceive and know the idea of white or black, and quite another to examine what kind of particles they must be, and how ranged in the superficies, to make any object appear white or black.

3. A painter or dyer who never enquired into their causes, hath the ideas of white and black and other colours as clearly, perfectly, and distinctly in his understanding, and perhaps more distinctly than the philosopher who hath busied himself in considering their natures, and thinks he knows how far either of them is in its cause positive or privative; and the idea of black is no less positive in his mind than that of white, however the cause of that colour in the external object may be only a privation.

4. If it were the design of my present understaking to enquire into the natural causes and manner of perception, I should offer this as a reason why a privative cause might, in some cases at least, produce a positive idea, viz., that all sensation being produced in us only by different de-

grees and modes of motion in our animal spirits, variously agitated by external objects, the abatement of any former motion must as necessarily produce a new sensation as the variation or increase of it; and so introduce a new idea, which depends only on a different motion of the animal spirits in that organ.

5. But whether this be so or no I will not here determine, but appeal to every one's own experience, whether the shadow of a man, though it consists of nothing but the absence of light (and the more the absence of light is, the more discernible is the shadow), does not, when a man looks on it, cause as clear and positive an idea in his mind as a man himself, though covered over with clear sunshine. And the picture of a shadow is a positive thing. Indeed, we have negative names, which stand not directly for positive ideas, but for their absence, such as *insipid, silence, nihil,* &c., which words denote positive ideas, v.g., *taste, sound, being,* with a signification of their absence.

6. And thus one may truly be said to see darkness. . . . The privative causes I have here assigned of positive ideas are according to the common opinion; but in truth it will be hard to determine whether there be really any ideas from a privative cause, till it be determined whether rest be any more a privaton than motion.

7. *Ideas in the mind, qualities in bodies.*—To discover the nature of our ideas the better, and to discourse of them intelligibly, it will be convenient to distinguish them, as they are ideas or perceptions in our minds, and as they are modifications of matter in the bodies that cause such perceptions in us; that so we may not think (as perhaps usually is done) that they are exactly the images and resemblances of something inherent in the subject; most of those of sensation being in the mind no more the likeness of something existing without us than the names that stand for them are the likeness of our ideas, which yet upon hearing they are apt to excite in us.

8. Whatsoever the mind perceives in itself, or is the immediate object of perception, thought, or understanding, that I call *idea*; and the power to produce any idea in our mind, I call *quality* of the subject wherein that power is. Thus a snowball having the power to produce in us the ideas of white, cold, and round, the powers to produce those ideas in us as they are in the snowball, I call qualities; and as they are sensations or perceptions in our understandings, I call them ideas; which ideas, if I speak of them sometimes as in the things themselves, I would be understood to mean those qualities in the objects which produce them in us.

9. *Primary qualities of bodies.*—Qualities thus considered in bodies are, First, such as are utterly inseparable from the body, in what estate soever it be; such as, in all the alterations and changes it suffers, all the force can be used upon it, it constantly keeps; and such as sense constantly finds in every particle of matter which has bulk enough to be perceived, and the mind finds inseparable from every particle of matter, though less than to make itself singly be perceived by our senses: v.g.,

take a grain of wheat, divide it into two parts, each part has still solidity, extension, figure, and mobility; divide it again, and it retains still the same qualities: and so divide it on, till the parts become insensible; they must retain still each of them all those qualities. . . . [These I call *original* or *primary qualities* of body, which I think we may observe to produce simple ideas in us, viz., solidity, extension, figure, motion or rest, and number.

10. *Secondary qualities of bodies.*—Secondly, such qualities, which in truth are nothing in the objects themselves, but powers to produce various sensations in us by their primary qualities, i.e., by the bulk, figure, texture, and motion of their insensible parts, as colours, sounds, tastes, &c., these I call *secondary qualities*. To these might be added a third sort, which are allowed to be barely powers, though they are as much real qualities in the subject as those which I, to comply with the common way of speaking, call qualities, but, for distinction, secondary qualities. For the power in fire to produce a new colour or consistence in wax or clay by its primary qualities, is as much a quality in fire as the power it has to produce in *me* a new idea or sensation of warmth or burning, which I felt not before, by the same primary qualities, viz., the bulk, texture, and motion of its insensible parts.]

11. *How primary qualities produce their ideas.*—The next thing to be considered is, how bodies produce ideas in us; and that is manifestly by impulse, the only way which we can conceive bodies operate in.

12. If, then, external objects be not united to our minds when they produce ideas in it, and yet we perceive these original qualities in such of them as singly fall under our senses, it is evident that some motion must be thence continued by our nerves or animal spirits, by some parts of our bodies, to the brains or the seat of sensation, there to produce in our minds the particular ideas we have of them. And since the extension, figure, number, and motion of bodies of an observable bigness, may be perceived at a distance by the sight, it is evident some singly imperceptible bodies must come from them to the eyes, and thereby convey to the brain some motion which produces these ideas which we have of them in us.

13. *How secondary.*—After the same manner that the ideas of these original qualities are produced in us, we may conceive that the ideas of secondary qualities are also produced, viz., by the operation of insensible particles on our senses. . . . The different motions and figures, bulk and number of such particles, affecting the several organs of our senses, produce in us those different sensations which we have from the colours and smells of bodies; v.g., that a violet, by the impulse of such insensible particles of matter of peculiar figures and bulks, and in different degrees and modifications of their motions, causes the ideas of the blue colour and sweet scent of that flower to be produced in our minds. It being no more impossible to conceive that God should annex such ideas to such motions with which they have no similitude, than that he should annex the idea of pain to the motion of a piece of steel dividing our flesh, with which that idea hath no resemblance.

14. What I have said concerning colours and smells may be understood also of tastes and sounds, and other the like sensible qualities; which, whatever reality we by mistake attribute to them, are in truth nothing in the objects themselves, but powers to produce various sensations in us, and depend on those primary qualities, viz., bulk, figure, texture, and motion of parts, as I have said.

15. *Ideas of primary qualities are resemblances; of secondary, not.—* From whence I think it is easy to draw this observation, that the ideas of primary qualities of bodies are resemblances of them, and their patterns do really exist in the bodies themselves; but the ideas produced in us by these secondary qualities have no resemblance of them at all. There is nothing like our ideas existing in the bodies themselves. They are, in the bodies we denominate from them, only a power to produce those sensations in us: and what is sweet, blue, or warm in idea, is but the certain bulk, figure, and motion of the insensible parts in the bodies themselves, which we call so.

16. Flame is denominated hot and light; snow, white and cold; and manna, white and sweet, from the ideas they produce in us. Which qualities are commonly thought to be the same in those bodies that those ideas are in us, the one the perfect resemblance of the other, as they are in a mirror; and it would by most men be judged very extravagant, if one should say otherwise. And yet he that will consider that the same fire that at one distance produces in us the sensation of warmth, does at a nearer approach produce in us the far different sensation of pain, ought to bethink himself what reason he has to say, that his idea of warmth which was produced in him by the fire, is actually in the fire, and his idea of pain which the same fire produced in him the same way is not in the fire. Why is whiteness and coldness in snow, and pain not, when it produces the one and the other idea in us, and can do neither, but by the bulk, figure, number, and motion of its solid parts?

17. The particular bulk, number, figure, and motion of the parts of fire or snow are really in them, whether any one's senses perceive them or no; and therefore they may be called *real qualities*, because they really exist in those bodies. But light, heat, whiteness, or coldness, are no more really in them than sickness or pain is in manna. Take away the sensation of them; let not the eyes see light or colours, nor the ears hear sounds; let the palate not taste, nor the nose smell; and all colours, tastes, odours, and sounds, as they are such particular ideas, vanish and cease, and are reduced to their causes, i.e., bulk, figure, and motion of parts.

18. A piece of manna of a sensible bulk is able to produce in us the idea of a round or square figure; and, by being removed from one place to another, the idea of motion. This idea of motion represents it as it really is in the manna moving; a circle or square are the same, whether in idea or existence, in the mind or in the manna; and this, both motion and figure are really in the manna, whether we take notice of them or no: this everybody is ready to agree to. Besides, manna, by the bulk, figure, texture, and motion of its parts, has a power to produce the sensations

of sickness, and sometimes of acute pains or gripings, in us. That these
ideas of sickness and pain are not in the manna, but effects of its operations on us, and are nowhere when we feel them not: this also every one
readily agrees to. And yet men are hardly to be brought to think that
sweetness and whiteness are not really in manna, which are but the effects
of the operations of manna by the motion, size, and figure of its particles
on the eyes and palate: as the pain and sickness caused by manna are
confessedly nothing but the effects of its operations on the stomach ...
Why the pain and sickness, ideas that are the effects of manna, should be
thought to be nowhere when they are not felt; and yet the sweetness and
whiteness, effects of the same manna on other parts of the body, by ways
equally as unknown, should be thought to exist in the manna, when they
are not seen nor tasted, would need some reason to explain.

19. Let us consider the red and white colours in porphyry: hinder
light but from striking on it, and its colours vanish; it no longer produces
any such ideas in us. Upon the return of light, it produces these appearances on us again. Can any one think any real alterations are made in
the porphyry by the presence or absence of light, and that those ideas
of whiteness and redness are really in porphyry in the light, when it is
plain *it has no colour in the dark?* It has indeed such a configuration
of particles, both night and day, as are apt, by the rays of light rebound-
ing from some parts of that hard stone, to produce in us the idea of
redness, and from others the idea of whiteness: but whiteness or redness
are not in it at any time, but such a texture that hath the power to produce
such a sensation in us.

.   .   .

22. I have, in what just goes before, been engaged in physical enquiries
a little farther than perhaps I intended. But it being necessary to make
the nature of sensation a little understood, and to make the difference
between the *qualities* in bodies and the *ideas* produced by them in the
mind to be distinctly conceived, without which it were impossible to
discourse intelligibly of them, I hope I shall be pardoned this little excursion into natural philosophy, it being necessary in our present enquiry
to distinguish the *primary* and *real* qualities of bodies, which are always
in them (viz., solidity, extension, figure, number, and motion or rest, and
are sometimes perceived by us, viz., when the bodies they are in are
big enough singly to be discerned), from those *secondary* and *imputed*
qualities, which are but the powers of several combinations of those
primary ones, when they operate without being distinctly discerned:
whereby we also may come to know what ideas are, and what are not,
resemblances of something really existing in the bodies we denominate
from them.

23. *Three sorts of qualities in bodies.*—The qualities then that are in
bodies, rightly considered, are of three sorts:

First, the bulk, figure, number, situation, and motion or rest of their
solid parts. Those are in them, whether we perceive them or no; and

when they are of that size that we can discover them, we have by these an idea of the thing as it is in itself, as is plain in artificial things. These I call *primary qualities*.

Secondly, the power that is in any body, by reason of its insensible primary qualities, to operate after a peculiar manner on any of our senses, and thereby produce in *us* the different ideas of several colours, sounds, smells, tastes, &c. These are usually called *sensible qualities*.

Thirdly, the power that is in any body, by reason of the particular constitution of its primary qualities, to make such a change in the bulk, figure, texture, and motion of another body, as to make it operate on our senses differently from what it did before. Thus the sun has a power to make wax white, and fire, to make lead fluid. These are usually called *powers*.

The first of these, as has been said, I think may be properly called real, original, or primary qualities, because they are in the things themselves, whether they are perceived or no: and upon their different modifications it is that the secondary qualities depend.

The other two are only powers to act differently upon other things, which powers result from the different modifications of those primary qualities.

24. *The first are resemblances; the second thought resemblances, but are not; the third neither are, nor are thought so.*—But though these two latter sorts of qualities are powers barely, and nothing but powers, relating to several other bodies, and resulting from the different modifications of the original qualities, yet they are generally otherwise thought of . . . V.g., the idea of heat or light which we receive by our eyes or touch from the sun, are commonly thought real qualities existing in the sun, and something more than mere powers in it. But when we consider the sun in reference to wax, which it melts or blanches, we look upon the whiteness and softness produced in the wax, not as qualities in the sun, but effects produced by powers in it: whereas, if rightly considered, these qualities of light and warmth, which are perceptions in me when I am warmed or enlightened by the sun, are no otherwise in the sun than the changes made in the wax, when it is blanched or melted, are in the sun. They are all of them equally powers in the sun, depending on its primary qualities. . . .

25. The reason why the one are ordinarily taken for real qualities, and the other only for bare powers, seems to be because the ideas we have of distinct colours, sounds, &c., containing nothing at all in them of bulk, figure, or motion, we are not apt to think them the effects of these primary qualities which appear not to our senses to operate in their production, and with which they have not any apparent congruity, or conceivable connexion. Hence it is that we are so forward to imagine that those ideas are the resemblances of something really existing in the objects themselves. . . . But, in the other case, in the operations of bodies changing the qualities one of another, we plainly discover that the

quality produced hath commonly no resemblance with anything in the thing producing it; wherefore we look on it as a bare effect of power. . . .

. . .

CHAPTER XII. OF COMPLEX IDEAS

1. *Made by the mind out of simple ones.*—We have hitherto considered those ideas, in the reception whereof the mind is only passive, which are those simple ones received from sensation and reflection before mentioned, whereof the mind cannot make one to itself, nor have any idea which does not wholly consist of them. [But as the mind is wholly passive in the reception of all its simple ideas, so it exerts several acts of its own, whereby out of its simple ideas, as the materials and foundations of the rest, the other are framed. The acts of the mind wherein it exerts its power over its simple ideas are chiefly these three: (1) Combining several simple ideas into one compound one; and thus all complex ideas are made. (2) The second is bringing two ideas, whether simple or complex, together, and setting them by one another, so as to take a view of them at once, without uniting them into one; by which it gets all its ideas of relations. (3) The third is separating them from all other ideas that accompany them in their real existence; this is called abstraction: and thus all its general ideas are made. This shows man's power and its way of operation to be much-what the same in the material and intellectual world. For, the materials in both being such as he has no power over, either to make or destroy, all that man can do is either to unite them together, or to set them by one another, or wholly separate them. I shall here begin with the first of these in the consideration of complex ideas, and come to the other two in their due places.] As simple ideas are observed to exist in several combinations united together, so the mind has a power to consider several of them united together as one idea; and that not only as they are united in external objects, but as itself has joined them. Ideas thus made up of several simple ones put together I call *complex;* such as are beauty, gratitude, a man, an army, the universe; which, though complicated of various simple ideas or complex ideas made up of simple ones, yet are, when the mind pleases, considered each by itself as one entire thing, and signified by one name.

2. *Made voluntarily.*—In this faculty of repeating and joining together its ideas, the mind has great power in varying and multiplying the objects of its thoughts infinitely beyond what sensation or reflection furnished it with: but all this still confined to those simple ideas which it received from those two sources, and which are the ultimate materials of all its compositions. For simple ideas are all from things themselves; and of these the mind can have no more nor other than what are suggested to it. It can have no other ideas of sensible qualities than what come from without by the senses, nor any ideas of other kind of operations of a thinking substance than what it finds in itself: but when it has once

got these simple ideas, it is not confined barely to observation, and what offers itself from without; it can, by its own power, put together those ideas it has, and make new complex ones which it never received so united.

3. *Are either modes, substances, or relations.*—Complex ideas, however compounded and decompounded, though their number be infinite, and the variety endless wherewith they fill and entertain the thoughts of men, yet I think they may be all reduced under these three heads: 1. *Modes.* 2. *Substances.* 3. *Relations.*

4. *Modes.*—First, *Modes* I call such complex ideas which, however compounded, contain not in them the supposition of subsisting by themselves, but are considered as dependences on, or affections of substances; such as are the ideas signified by the words triangle, gratitude, murder, &c. And if in this I use the word mode in somewhat a different sense from its ordinary signification, I beg pardon; it being unavoidable in discourses differing from the ordinary received notions, either to make new words, or to use old words in somewhat a new signification: the latter whereof, in our present case, is perhaps the more tolerable of the two.

5. *Simple and mixed modes.*—Of these modes there are two sorts which deserve distinct consideration. First, there are some which are only variations or different combinations of the same simple idea, without the mixture of any other, as a dozen, or score; which are nothing but the ideas of so many distinct units added together: and these I call *simple modes,* as being contained within the bounds of one simple idea. Secondly, there are others compounded of simple ideas of several kinds, put together to make one complex one; v.g., beauty, consisting of a certain composition of colour and figure, causing delight in the beholder; theft, which, being the concealed change of the possession of anything, without the consent of the proprietor, contains, as is visible, a combination of several ideas of several kinds: and these I call *mixed modes.*

6. *Substances, single or collective.*—Secondly, the ideas of *substances* are such combinations of simple ideas as are taken to represent distinct particular things subsisting by themselves, in which the supposed or confused idea of substance, such as it is, is always the first and chief. Thus, if to substance be joined the simple idea of a certain dull whitish colour, with certain degrees of weight, hardness, ductility, and fusibility, we have the idea of lead; and a combination of the ideas of a certain sort of figure, with the powers of motion, thought, and reasoning, joined to substance, make the ordinary idea of a man. Now of substances also there are two sorts of ideas, one of single substances, as they exist separately, as of a man or a sheep; the other of several of those put together, as an army of men, or flock of sheep; which collective ideas of several substances thus put together, are as much each of them one single idea as that of a man or an unit.

7. *Relation.*—Thirdly, the last sort of complex ideas is that we call *relation,* which consists in the consideration and comparing one idea with another. Of these several kinds we shall treat in their order.

8. *The abstrusest ideas from the two sources.*—If we will trace the progress of our minds, and with attention observe how it repeats, adds together, and unites its simple ideas received from sensation or reflection, it will lead us farther than at first perhaps we should have imagined. And I believe we shall find, if we warily observe the originals of our notions, that even the most abstruse ideas, how remote soever they may seem from sense, or from any operation of our own minds, are yet only such as the understanding frames to itself, by repeating and joining together ideas that it had either from objects of sense, or from its own operations about them: so that those even large and abstract ideas are *derived from sensation or reflection,* being no other than what the mind, by the ordinary use of its own faculties, employed about ideas received from objects of sense, or from the operations it observes in itself about them, may and does attain unto. This I shall endeavour to show in the ideas we have of space, time, and infinity, and some few other, that seem the most remote from those originals.

．　　．　　．

CHAPTER XXI. OF POWER

1. *This idea how got.*—The mind being every day informed, by the senses, of the alteration of those simple ideas it observes in things without; and taking notice how one comes to an end and ceases to be, and another begins to exist which was not before; reflecting also, on what passes within itself, and observing a constant change of its ideas, sometimes by the impression of outward objects on the senses, and sometimes by the determination of its own choice; and concluding from what it has so constantly observed to have been, that the like changes will for the future be made in the same things by like agents, and by the like ways; considers in one thing the possibility of having any of its simple ideas changed, and in another the possibility of making that change; and so comes by that idea which we call *power.* Thus we say, fire has a power to melt gold, i.e., to destroy the consistency of its insensible parts, and consequently its hardness, and make it fluid; and gold has a power to be melted: that the sun has a power to blanch wax; and wax a power to be blanched by the sun, whereby the yellowness is destroyed, and whiteness made to exist in its room. In which and the like cases, the power we consider is in reference to the change of perceivable ideas. For we cannot observe any alteration to be made in, or operation upon, anything, but by the observable change of its sensible ideas: nor conceive any alteration to be made, but by conceiving a change of some of its ideas.

2. *Power active and passive.*—Power thus considered is twofold, viz., as able to make, or able to receive, any change: the one may be called *active,* and the other *passive,* power. Whether matter be not wholly destitute of active power, as its author, God, is truly above all passive power; and whether the intermediate state of created spirits be not that

alone which is capable of both active and passive power, may be worth consideration. I shall not now enter into that enquiry: my present business being not to search into the original of power, but how we come by the idea of it. But since active powers make so great a part of our complex ideas of natural substances (as we shall see hereafter), yet they being not, perhaps, so truly active powers as our hasty thoughts are apt to represent them, I judge it not amiss, by this intimation, to direct our minds to the consideration of God and spirits, for the clearest idea of active power.

3. *Power includes relation.*—I confess power includes in it some kind of *relation* (a relation to action or change), as indeed, which of our ideas, of what kind soever, when attentively considered, does not? For our ideas of extension, duration, and number, do they not all contain in them a secret relation of the parts? Figure and motion have something relative in them much more visibly: and sensible qualities, as colours and smells, &c., what are they but the powers of different bodies in relation to our perception? And if considered in the things themselves, do they not depend on the bulk, figure, texture, and motion of the parts? All which include some kind of relation in them. Our idea therefore of power, I think, may well have a place amongst other simple ideas, and be considered as one of them, being one of those that make a principal ingredient in our complex ideas of substances, as we shall hereafter have occasion to observe.

4. *The clearest idea of active power had from spirit.*—We are abundantly furnished with the idea of passive power, by almost all sorts of sensible things. In most of them we cannot avoid observing their sensible qualities, nay, their very substances, to be in a continual flux: and therefore with reason we look on them as liable still to the same change. Nor have we of active power (which is the more proper signification of the word power) fewer instances. Since whatever change is observed, the mind must collect a power somewhere, able to make that change, as well as a possibility in the thing itself to receive it. But yet, if we will consider it attentively, bodies by our senses do not afford us so clear and distinct an idea of active power as we have from reflection on the operations of our minds. For all power relating to action, and there being but two sorts of action whereof we have any idea, viz., thinking and motion, let us consider whence we have the clearest ideas of the powers which produce these actions. (1) Of thinking, body affords us no idea at all: it is only from reflection that we have that. (2) Neither have we from body any idea of the beginning of motion. A body at rest affords us no idea of any active power to move; and when it is set in motion itself, that motion is rather a passion than an action in it. For when the ball obeys the stroke of a billiard-stick, it is not any action of the ball, but bare passion: also when by impulse it sets another ball in motion that lay in its way, it only communicates the motion it had received from another, and loses in itself so much as the other received; which gives us but a very obscure idea of an active power of moving in body, whilst we observe it only to

transfer but not produce any motion. . . . The idea of the beginning of motion we have only from reflection on what passes in ourselves, where we find by experience, that, barely by willing it, barely by a thought of the mind, we can move the parts of our bodies which were before at rest. So that it seems to me, we have, from the observation of the operation of bodies by our senses, but a very imperfect, obscure idea of active power, since they afford us not any idea in themselves of the power to begin any action, either motion or thought. But if, from the impulse bodies are observed to make one upon another, any one thinks he has a clear idea of power, it serves as well to my purpose, sensation being one of those ways whereby the mind comes by its ideas: only I thought it worth while to consider here by the way, whether the mind doth not receive its idea of active power clearer from reflection on its own operations, than it doth from any external sensation.

.   .   .

CHAPTER XXIII.   OF OUR COMPLEX IDEAS OF SUBSTANCES

1. *Ideas of substances, how made.*—The mind being, as I have declared, furnished with a great number of the simple ideas conveyed in by the senses, as they are found in exterior things, or by reflection on its own operations, takes notice also, that a certain number of these simple ideas go constantly together; which being presumed to belong to one thing, and words being suited to common apprehensions, and made use of for quick dispatch, are called, so united in one subject, by one name; which, by inadvertency, we are apt afterward to talk of and consider as one simple idea, which indeed is a complication of many ideas together: because, as I have said, not imagining how these simple ideas can subsist by themselves, we accustom ourselves to suppose some *substratum* wherein they do subsist, and from which they do result, which therefore we call *substance*.

2. *Our idea of substance in general.*—So that if any one will examine himself concerning his notion of pure substance in general, he will find he has no other idea of it at all, but only a supposition of he knows not what support of such qualities which are capable of producing simple ideas in us; which qualities are commonly called accidents. If any one should be asked, what is the subject wherein colour or weight inheres, he would have nothing to say, but the solid extended parts: and if he were demanded, what is it that that solidity and extension inhere in, he would not be in a much better case than the Indian before mentioned, who saying that the world was supported by a great elephant, was asked, what the elephant rested on; to which his answer was, a great tortoise: but being again pressed to know what gave support to the broad-backed tortoise, replied, something, he knew not what. And thus here, as in all other cases where we use words without having clear and distinct ideas, we talk like children; who being questioned what such a thing is which

they know not, readily give this satisfactory answer, that it is *something;* which in truth signifies no more, when so used, either by children or men, but that they know not what; and that the thing they pretend to know, and talk of, is what they have no distinct idea of at all, and so are perfectly ignorant of it, and in the dark. The idea, then, we have, to which we give the general name substance, being nothing but the supposed, but unknown, support of those qualities we find existing, which we imagine cannot subsist *sine re substante,* without something to support them, we call that support *substantia;* which, according to the true import of the word, is, in plain English, standing under, or upholding.

3. *Of the sorts of substances.*—An obscure and relative idea of substance in general being thus made, we come to have the ideas of *particular sorts of substances,* by collecting such combinations of simple ideas as are, by experience and observation of men's senses, taken notice of to exist together, and are therefore supposed to flow from the particular internal constitution or unknown essence of that substance. Thus we come to have the ideas of a man, horse, gold, water, &c., of which substances, whether any one has any other clear idea, farther than of certain simple ideas coexisting together, I appeal to every one's own experience. It is the ordinary qualities observable in iron or a diamond, put together, that make the true complex idea of those substances, which a smith or a jeweller commonly knows better than a philosopher; who, whatever substantial forms he may talk of, has no other idea of those substances than what is framed by a collection of those simple ideas which are to be found in them. Only we must take notice, that our complex ideas of substances, besides all these simple ideas they are made up of, have always the confused idea of something to which they belong and in which they subsist. And therefore, when we speak of any sort of substance, we say it is a thing having such or such qualities; as body is a thing that is extended, figured, and capable of motion; a spirit, a thing capable of thinking; and so hardness, friability, and power to draw iron, we say, are qualities to be found in a loadstone. These and the like fashions of speaking intimate that the substance is supposed always something besides the extension, figure, solidity, motion, thinking, or other observable ideas, though we know not what it is.

4. *No clear idea of substance in general.*—Hence, when we talk or think of any particular sort of corporeal substances, as horse, stone, &c., though the idea we have of either of them be but the complication or collection of those several simple ideas of sensible qualities which we use to find united in the thing called horse or stone; yet because we cannot conceive how they should subsist alone, nor one in another, we suppose them existing in, and supported by, some common subject; which support we denote by the name substance, though it be certain we have no clear or distinct idea of that thing we suppose a support.

5. *As clear an idea of spirit as body.*—The same happens concerning the operations of the mind, viz., thinking, reasoning, fearing, &c., which we concluding not to subsist of themselves, nor apprehending how they

can belong to body, or be produced by it, we are apt to think these the
actions of some other substance, which we call spirit; whereby yet it is
evident, that having no other idea or notion of matter, but something
wherein those many sensible qualities which affect our senses do subsist;
by supposing a substance wherein thinking, knowing, doubting, and a
power of moving, &c. do subsist; we have as clear a notion of the substance of spirit as we have of body; the one being supposed to be (without knowing what it is) the *substratum* to those simple ideas we have
from without; and the other supposed (with a like ignorance of what it
is) to be the *substratum* to those operations which we experiment in
ourselves within. It is plain, then, that the idea of corporeal substance
in matter is as remote from our conceptions and apprehensions as that of
spiritual substance or spirit; and therefore, from our not having any notion
of the substance of spirit, we can no more conclude its non-existence
than we can, for the same reason, deny the existence of body: it being
as rational to affirm there is no body, because we have no clear and
distinct idea of the substance of matter, as to say there is no spirit, because
we have no clear and distinct idea of the substance of a spirit.

6. *Of the sorts of substances.*—Whatever therefore be the secret and
abstract nature of substance in general, all the ideas we have of particular
distinct sorts of substances are nothing but several combinations of simple
ideas coexisting in such, though unknown, cause of their union, as makes
the whole subsist of itself. It is by such combinations of simple ideas,
and nothing else, that we represent particular sorts of substances to ourselves. Such are the ideas we have of their several species in our minds;
and such only do we, by their specific names, signify to others, v.g., man,
horse, sun, water, iron; upon hearing which words, every one who understands the language frames in his mind a combination of those several
simple ideas which he has usually observed or fancied to exist together
under that denomination; all which he supposes to rest in, and be, as it
were, adherent to, that unknown common subject, which inheres not in
anything else. Though in the meantime it be manifest, and every one
upon enquiry into his own thoughts will find, that he has no other idea
of any substance but what he has barely of those sensible qualities,
which he supposes to inhere, with a supposition of such a substratum,
as gives, as it were, a support to those qualities or simple ideas, which
he has observed to exist united together. Thus the idea of the sun, what
is it but an aggregate of those several simple ideas, bright, hot, roundish,
having a constant regular motion, at a certain distance from us, and
perhaps some other? As he who thinks and discourses of the sun, has
been more or less accurate in observing those sensible qualities, ideas,
or properties, which are in that thing which he calls the sun.

7. *Powers a great part of our complex ideas of substances.*—For he
has the perfectest idea of any of the particular sorts of substances who
has gathered and put together most of those simple ideas which do exist
in it, among which are to be reckoned its active powers and passive
capacities; which, though not simple ideas, yet in this respect, for brevity's

sake, may conveniently enough be reckoned amongst them; . . . We immediately by our senses perceive in fire its heat and colour; which are, if rightly considered, nothing but powers in it to produce those ideas in us: we also by our senses perceive the colour and brittleness of charcoal, whereby we come by the knowledge of another power in fire, which it has to change the colour and consistency of wood. By the former, fire immediately, by the latter it mediately, discovers to us these several powers, which therefore we look upon to be a part of the qualities of fire, and so make them a part of the complex idea of it. For all those powers that we take cognizance of, terminating only in the alteration of some sensible qualities in those subjects on which they operate, and so making them exhibit to us new sensible ideas; therefore it is that I have reckoned these powers amongst the simple ideas which make the complex ones of the sorts of substances; though these powers, considered in themselves, are truly complex ideas. . . .

8. *And why.*—Nor are we to wonder that powers make a great part of our complex ideas of substances, since their secondary qualities are those which, in most of them, serve principally to distinguish substances one from another, and commonly make a considerable part of the complex idea of the several sorts of them. For our senses failing us in the discovery of the bulk, texture, and figure of the minute parts of bodies, on which their real constitutions and differences depend, we are fain to make use of their secondary qualities as the characteristical notes and marks whereby to frame ideas of them in our minds, and distinguish them one from another. All which secondary qualities, as has been shown, are nothing but bare powers. For the colour and taste of opium are, as well as its soporific or anodyne virtues, mere powers depending on its primary qualities, whereby it is fitted to produce different operations on different parts of our bodies.

9. *Three sorts of ideas make our complex ones of substances.*—The ideas that make our complex ones of corporeal substances are of these three sorts. First, the ideas of the primary qualities of things which are discovered by our senses, and are in them even when we perceive them not: such are the bulk, figure, number, situation, and motion of the parts of bodies, which are really in them, whether we take notice of them or no. Secondly, the sensible secondary qualities which, depending on these, are nothing but the powers those substances have to produce several ideas in us by our senses; which ideas are not in the things themselves otherwise than as anything is in its cause. Thirdly, the aptness we consider in any substance to give or receive such alterations of primary qualities as that the substance so altered should produce in us different ideas from what it did before; these are called active and passive powers: all which powers, as far as we have any notice or notion of them, terminate only in sensible simple ideas. For whatever alteration a loadstone has the power to make in the minute particles of iron, we should have no notion of any power it had at all to operate on iron, did not its sensible motion discover it; and I doubt not but there are a thousand changes

that bodies we daily handle have a power to cause in one another, which we never suspect, because they never appear in sensible effects.

10. *Powers make a great part of our complex ideas of substances.*— Powers therefore justly make a great part of our complex ideas of substances. He that will examine his complex idea of gold, will find several of its ideas that make it up to be only powers: as the power of being melted, but of not spending itself in the fire, of being dissolved in *aqua regia*, are ideas as necessary to make up our complex idea of gold, as its colour and weight: which, if duly considered, are also nothing but different powers. For to speak truly, yellowness is not actually in gold, but is a power in gold to produce that idea in us by our eyes when placed in a due light: and the heat which we cannot leave out of our idea of the sun, is no more really in the sun than the white colour it introduces into wax. . . .

11. *The now secondary qualities of bodies would disappear, if we could discover the primary ones of their minute parts.*—Had we senses acute enough to discern the minute particles of bodies, and the real constitution on which their sensible qualities depend, I doubt not but they would produce quite different ideas in us, and that which is now the yellow colour of gold would then disappear, and instead of it we should see an admirable texture of parts of a certain size and figure. This microscopes plainly discover to us; for what to our naked eyes produces a certain colour is, by thus augmenting the acuteness of our senses, discovered to be quite a different thing; and the thus altering, as it were, the proportion of the bulk of the minute parts of a coloured object to our usual sight, produces different ideas from what it did before. Thus sand, or pounded glass, which is opaque and white to the naked eye, is pellucid in a microscope: . . . blood to the naked eye appears all red; but by a good microscope, wherein its lesser parts appear, shows only some few globules of red, swimming in a pellucid liquor; and how these red globules would appear, if glasses could be found that yet could magnify them one thousand or ten thousand times more, is uncertain.

．　　　．　　　．

30. *Ideas of body and spirit compared.*—So that, in short, the idea we have of spirit, compared with the idea we have of body, stands thus: The substance of spirit is unknown to us; and so is the substance of body equally unknown to us. Two primary qualities or properties of body, viz., solid coherent parts and impulse, we have distinct clear ideas of: so likewise we know and have distinct clear ideas of two primary qualities or properties of spirit, viz., thinking, and a power of action; i.e., a power of beginning or stopping several thoughts or motions. We have also the ideas of several qualities inherent in bodies, and have the clear distinct ideas of them: which qualities are but the various modifications of the extension of cohering solid parts and their motion. We have likewise the ideas of the several modes of thinking, viz., believing, doubting, intending, fearing, hoping; all which are but the several modes of thinking. We

have also the ideas of willing, and moving the body consequent to it, and with the body itself too; for, as has been showed, spirit is capable of motion.

. . .

33. *Idea of God.*—For if we examine the idea we have of the incomprehensible Supreme Being, we shall find, that we come by it the same way; and that the complex ideas we have both of God and separate spirits are made up of the simple ideas we receive from reflection: v.g., having, from what we experiment in ourselves, got the ideas of existence and duration, of knowledge and power, of pleasure and happiness, and of several other qualities and powers which it is better to have than to be without; when we would frame an idea the most suitable we can to the Supreme Being, we enlarge every one of these with our idea of infinity; and so, putting them together, make our complex idea of God. For that the mind has such a power of enlarging some of its ideas, received from sensation and reflection, has been already showed.

. . .

35. It is infinity which, joined to our ideas of existence, power, knowledge, &c., makes that complex idea whereby we represent to ourselves, the best we can, the Supreme Being. For though in his own essence (which certainly we do not know, not knowing the real essence of a pebble, or a fly, or of our own selves) God be simple and uncompounded; yet, I think, I may say we have no other idea of him but a complex one of existence, knowledge, power, happiness, &c., infinite and eternal: which are all distinct ideas, and some of them being relative are again compounded of others; all which being, as has been shown, originally got from sensation and reflection, go to make up the idea or notion we have of God.

. . .

37. *Recapitulation.*—And thus we have seen *what kind of ideas we have of substances of all kinds,* wherein they consist, and how we come by them. From whence, I think, it is very evident,

First, That all our ideas of the several sorts of substances are nothing but collections of simple ideas, with a supposition of something to which they belong, and in which they subsist; though of this supposed something we have no clear distinct idea at all.

Secondly, That all the simple ideas that, thus united in one common substratum, make up our complex ideas of several sorts of substances, are no other but such as we have received from sensation or reflection. . . .

Thirdly, That most of the simple ideas that make up our complex ideas of substances, when truly considered, are only powers, however we are apt to take them for positive qualities: v.g., the greatest part of the ideas that make our complex idea of gold are yellowness, great weight, ductility, fusibility, and solubility in *aqua regia,* &c., all united together in an unknown substratum; all which ideas are nothing else but so many relations to other substances, and are not really in the gold considered barely in itself, though they depend on those real and primary qualities of its internal constitution, whereby it has a fitness differently to operate and be operated on by several other substances.

.   .   .

Book IV

CHAPTER I.   OF KNOWLEDGE IN GENERAL

1. *Our knowledge conversant about our ideas.*—Since the mind, in all its thoughts and reasonings, hath no other immediate object but its own ideas, which it alone does or can contemplate, it is evident that our knowledge is only conversant about them.

2. *Knowledge is the perception of the agreement or disagreement of two ideas.*—Knowledge then seems to me to be nothing but the perception of the connexion and agreement, or disagreement and repugnancy, of any of our ideas. In this alone it consists. Where this perception is, there is knowledge; and where it is not, there, though we may fancy, guess, or believe, yet we always come short of knowledge. For when we know that white is not black, what do we else but perceive that these two ideas do not agree? When we possess ourselves with the utmost security of the demonstration that the three angles of a triangle are equal to two right ones, what do we more but perceive, that equality to two right ones does necessarily agree to, and is inseparable from, the three angles of a triangle?

3. *This agreement fourfold.*—But to understand a little more distinctly wherein this agreement or disagreement consists, I think we may reduce it all to these four sorts: (1) *Identity,* or *diversity.* (2) *Relation.* (3) *Coexistence,* or *necessary connexion.* (4) *Real existence.*

4. *First, Of identity or diversity.*—As to the first sort of agreement or disagreement, viz., *identity, or diversity.* It is the first act of the mind, when it has any sentiments or ideas at all, to perceive its ideas, and, so far as it perceives them, to know each what it is, and thereby also to perceive their difference, and that one is not another. This is so absolutely necessary, that without it there could be no knowledge, no reasoning, no imagination, no distinct thoughts at all. By this the mind clearly and infallibly perceives each idea to agree with itself, and to be what it is; and all distinct ideas to disagree, i.e., the one not to be the other: and this it does without pains, labour, or deduction; but at first view, by its natural power of perception and distinction. And though men of art have reduced this into those general rules, *What is, is;* and, *It is impossible for the same thing to be and not to be,* for ready application in all cases wherein there may be occasion to reflect on it; yet it is certain that the first exercise of this

faculty is about particular ideas. A man infallibly knows, as soon as ever he has them in his mind, that the ideas he calls white and round are the very ideas they are, and that they are not other ideas which he calls red or square. Nor can any maxim or proposition in the world make him know it clearer or surer than he did before, and without any such general rule. This then is the first agreement or disagreement which the mind perceives in its ideas; which it always perceives at first sight; and if there ever happen any doubt about it, it will always be found to be about the names, and not the ideas themselves, whose identity and diversity will always be perceived as soon and as clearly as the ideas themselves are, nor can it possibly be otherwise.

5. *Secondly, Relative.*—The next sort of agreement or disagreement the mind perceives in any of its ideas may, I think, be called *relative*, and is nothing but the perception of the *relation* between any two ideas, of what kind soever, whether substances, modes, or any other. For, since all distinct ideas must eternally be known not to be the same, and so be universally and constantly denied one of another, there could be no room for any positive knowledge at all, if we could not perceive any relation between our ideas, and find out the agreement or disagreement they have one with another, in several ways the mind takes of comparing them.

6. *Thirdly, Of coexistence.*—The third sort of agreement or disagreement to be found in our ideas, which the perception of the mind is employed about, is *coexistence*, or *non-coexistence* in the same subject; and this belongs particularly to substances. Thus when we pronounce concerning gold that it is fixed, our knowledge of this truth amounts to no more but this, that fixedness, or a power to remain in the fire unconsumed, is an idea that always accompanies and is joined with that particular sort of yellowness, weight, fusibility, malleableness, and solubility in *aqua regia*, which make our complex idea, signified by the word gold.

7. *Fourthly, Of real existence.*—The fourth and last sort is that of *actual real existence* agreeing to any idea. Within these four sorts of agreement or disagreement is, I suppose, contained all the knowledge we have or are capable of; for all the enquiries that we can make concerning any of our ideas, all that we know or can affirm concerning any of them, is, that it is or is not the same with some other; that it does or does not always coexist with some other idea in the same subject; that it has this or that relation to some other idea; or that it has a real existence without the mind. Thus, 'Blue is not yellow', is of identity. 'Two triangles upon equal bases between two parallels are equal', is of relation. 'Iron is susceptible of magnetical impressions', is of coexistence. 'God is', is of real existence. Though identity and coexistence are truly nothing but relations, yet they are so peculiar ways of agreement or disagreement of our ideas, that they deserve well to be considered as distinct heads, and not under relation in general: since they are so different grounds of affirmation and negation, as will easily appear to any one who will but reflect on what is said in several places of this *Essay*. I should now proceed to examine the

several degrees of our knowledge, but that it is necessary first to consider the different acceptations of the word *knowledge*.

8. *Knowledge actual or habitual.*—There are several ways wherein the mind is possessed of truth, each of which is called knowledge.

(1) There is *actual knowledge,* which is the present view the mind has of the agreement or disagreement of any of its ideas, or of the relation they have one to another.

(2) A man is said to know any proposition which having been once laid before his thoughts, he evidently perceived the agreement or disagreement of the ideas whereof it consists; and so lodged it in his memory, that whenever that proposition comes again to be reflected on, he, without doubt or hesitation, embraces the right side, assents to and is certain of the truth of it. This, I think, one may call *habitual knowledge.* ... For our finite understandings being able to think clearly and distinctly but on one thing at once, if men had no knowledge of any more than what they actually thought on, they would all be very ignorant; and he that knew most would know but one truth, that being all he was able to think on at one time.

9. *Habitual knowledge twofold.*—Of habitual knowledge there are also, vulgarly speaking, two degrees:—

First, The one of such truths laid up in the memory as, whenever they occur to the mind, it *actually perceives the relation is between those ideas.* And this is in all those truths whereof we have an intuitive knowledge, where the ideas themselves, by an immediate view, discover their agreement or disagreement one with another.

Secondly, The other is of such truths, whereof the mind having been convinced, it *retains the memory of the conviction without the proofs.* Thus a man that remembers certainly that he once perceived the demonstration that the three angles of a triangle are equal to two right ones, is certain that he knows it, because he cannot doubt of the truth of it. In his adherence to a truth where the demonstration by which it was at first known is forgot, though a man may be thought rather to believe his memory than really to know, and this way of entertaining a truth seemed formerly to me like something between opinion and knowledge, a sort of assurance which exceeds bare belief, for that relies on the testimony of another; yet, upon a due examination, I find it comes not short of perfect certainty, and is, in effect, true knowledge. That which is apt to mislead our first thoughts into a mistake in this matter is, that the agreement or disagreement of the ideas in this case is not perceived, as it was at first, by an actual view of all the intermediate ideas whereby the agreement or disagreement of those in the proposition was at first perceived; but by other intermediate ideas, that show the agreement or disagreement of the ideas contained in the proposition whose certainty we remember. For example: in this proposition, that 'the three angles of a triangle are equal to two right ones', one who has seen and clearly perceived the demonstration of this truth knows it to be true, when that demonstration is gone out of his mind, so that at present it is not actually in view, and possibly cannot be recollected; but he knows it in a different way from what he did before. The agreement of the two ideas joined in that proposition is perceived; but it is by the intervention of other ideas than those which at first produced that perception. He remembers, i.e., he knows (for remembrance is but the reviving of some past knowledge) that he was once certain of the truth of this proposition, that 'the three angles of a triangle are equal to two right ones'. The immutability of the same relations between the same immutable things is now the idea that shows him, that if the three angles of a triangle were once equal to two right ones, they will always be equal to two right ones. And hence he comes to be certain, that what was once true in the case is always true; what ideas once agreed will always agree: and consequently, what he once knew to be true he will always know to be true, as long as he can remember that he once knew it. Upon this ground it is that particular demonstrations in mathematics afford general knowledge. If then the perception that the same ideas will eternally have the same habitudes and relations be not a sufficient ground of knowledge, there could be no knowledge of general propositions in mathematics; for no mathematical demonstration would be any other than particular: and when a man had demonstrated any proposition concerning one triangle or circle, his knowledge would not reach beyond that particular diagram. If he would extend it farther, he must renew his demonstration in another instance, before he could know it to be true in another like triangle, and so on: by which means one could never come to the knowledge of any general propositions. Nobody, I think, can deny that Mr. Newton certainly knows any proposition that he now at any time reads in his book to be true, though he has not in actual view that admirable chain of intermediate ideas whereby he at first discovered it to be true. Such a memory as that, able to retain such a train of particulars, may be well thought beyond the reach of human faculties, when the very discovery, perception, and laying together that wonderful connexion of ideas is found to surpass most readers' comprehension. But yet it is evident the author himself knows the proposition to be true, remembering he once saw the connexion of those ideas, as certainly as he knows such a man wounded another, remembering that he saw him run him through. But because the memory is not always so clear as actual perception, and does in all men more or less decay in length of time, this, amongst other differences, is one which shows that *demonstrative* knowledge is much more imperfect than *intuitive*, as we shall see in the following chapter.

CHAPTER II. OF THE DEGREES OF OUR KNOWLEDGE

1. *Intuitive.*—All our knowledge consisting, as I have said, in the view the mind has of its own ideas, which is the utmost light and greatest certainty we, with our faculties and in our way of knowledge, are capable of, it may not be amiss to consider a little the degrees of its evidence. The different clearness of our knowledge seems to me to lie in the different

way of perception the mind has of the agreement or disagreement of any of its ideas. For if we will reflect on our own ways of thinking, we shall find that sometimes the mind perceives the agreement or disagreement of two ideas immediately by themselves, without the intervention of any other: and this, I think, we may call *intuitive knowledge.* For in this the mind is at no pains of proving or examining, but perceives the truth, as the eye doth light, only by being directed towards it. Thus the mind perceives that white is not black, that a circle is not a triangle, that three are more than two, and equal to one and two. Such kind of truths the mind perceives at the first sight of the ideas together, by bare intuition, without the intervention of any other idea; and this kind of knowledge is the clearest and most certain that human frailty is capable of. This part of knowledge is irresistible, and like bright sunshine, forces itself immediately to be perceived as soon as ever the mind turns its view that way; and leaves no room for hesitation, doubt, or examination, but the mind is presently filled with the clear light of it. It is on this intuition that depends all the certainty and evidence of all our knowledge, which certainty every one finds to be so great, that he cannot imagine, and therefore not require, a greater: for a man cannot conceive himself capable of a greater certainty, than to know that any idea in his mind is such as he perceives it to be; and that two ideas wherein he perceives a difference, are different, and not precisely the same. He that demands a greater certainty than this demands he knows not what, and shows only that he has a mind to be a sceptic without being able to be so. Certainty depends so wholly on this intuition, that in the next degree of knowledge, which I call demonstrative, this intuition is necessary in all the connexions of the intermediate ideas, without which we cannot attain knowledge and certainty.

2. *Demonstrative.*—The next degree of knowledge is, where the mind perceives the agreement or disagreement of any ideas, but not immediately. . . . In this case, when the mind cannot so bring its ideas together as, by their immediate comparison and, as it were, juxtaposition or application one to another, to perceive their agreement or disagreement, it is fain, by the intervention of other ideas (one or more, as it happens), to discover the agreement or disagreement which it searches; and this is that which we call *reasoning.* Thus the mind, being willing to know the agreement or disagreement in bigness between the three angles of a triangle and two right ones, cannot, by an immediate view and comparing them, do it: because the three angles of a triangle cannot be brought at once, and be compared with any other one or two angles; and so of this the mind has no immediate, no intuitive knowledge. In this case the mind is fain to find out some other angles, to which the three angles of a triangle have an equality; and finding those equal to two right ones, comes to know their equality to two right ones.

3. *Depends on proofs.*—Those intervening ideas which serve to show the agreement of any two others, are called *proofs;* and where the agreement or disagreement is by this means plainly and clearly perceived, it is called *demonstration,* it being shown to the understanding, and the mind

made to see that it is so. A quickness in the mind to find out these inter-mediate ideas (that shall discover the agreement or disagreement of any other), and to apply them right, is, I suppose, that which is called *sagacity*.

4. *But no so easy.*—This knowledge by intervening proofs, though it be certain, yet the evidence of it is not altogether so clear and bright, nor the assent so ready, as in intuitive knowledge. For though in demonstra-tion the mind does at last perceive the agreement or disagreement of the ideas it considers, yet it is not without pains and attention: there must be more than one transient view to find it. A steady application and pur-suit is required to this discovery: and there must be a progression by steps and degrees before the mind can in this way arrive at certainty. . . .

5. *Not without precedent doubt.*—Another difference between intuitive and demonstrative knowledge is, that though in the latter all doubt be removed, when by the intervention of the intermediate ideas the agree-ment or disagreement is perceived; yet before the demonstration there was a doubt; which in intuitive knowledge cannot happen to the mind that has its faculty of perception left to a degree capable of distinct ideas, no more than it can be a doubt to the eye (that can distinctly see white and black), whether this ink and this paper be all of a colour. . . .

6. *Not so clear.*—It is true, the perception produced by demonstration is also very clear; yet it is often with a great abatement of that evident lustre and full assurance that always accompany that which I call in-tuitive; like a face reflected by several mirrors one to another, where, as long as it retains the similitude and agreement with the object, it produces a knowledge; but it is still, in every successive reflection, with a lessening of that perfect clearness and distinctness which is in the first, till at last, after many removes, it has a great mixture of dimness, and is not at first sight so knowable, especially to weak eyes. Thus it is with knowledge made out by a long train of proofs.

7. *Each step must have intuitive evidence.*—Now, in every step reason makes in demonstrative knowledge, there is an intuitive knowledge of that agreement or disagreement it seeks with the next intermediate idea, which it uses as a proof: for if it were not so, that yet would need a proof; since without the perception of such agreement or disagreement there is no knowledge produced. . . . This intuitive perception of the agreement or disagreement of the intermediate ideas, in each step and progression of the demonstration, must also be carried exactly in the mind, and a man must be sure that no part is left out: which, because in long deductions, and the use of many proofs, the memory does not always so readily and exactly retain; therefore it comes to pass, that this is more imperfect than intuitive knowledge, and men embrace often falsehood for demonstra-tions.

8. *Hence the mistake*, ex praecognitis et praeconcessis.—The necessity of this intuitive knowledge, in each step of scientifical or demonstrative reasoning, gave occasion, I imagine, to that mistaken axiom, that all reasoning was *ex praecognitus et praeconcessis;* which how far it is mis-taken, I shall have occasion to show more at large where I come to con-

sider propositions, and particularly those propositions which are called 'maxims'; and to show that it is by a mistake that they are supposed to be the foundations of all our knowledge and reasonings.

9. *Demonstration not limited to quantity.*—It has been generally taken for granted, that mathematics alone are capable of demonstrative certainty: but to have such an agreement or disagreement as may intuitively be perceived being, as I imagine, not the privilege of the ideas of number, extension, and figure alone, it may possibly be the want of due method and application in us, and not of sufficient evidence in things, that demonstration has been thought to have so little to do in other parts of knowledge, and been scarce so much as aimed at by any but mathematicians. . . .

10. *Why it has been so thought.*—The reason why it has been generally sought for and supposed to be only in those, I imagine, has been not only the general usefulness of those sciences, but because, in comparing their equality or excess, the modes of numbers have every the least difference very clear and perceivable: and though in extension every the least excess is not so perceptible, yet the mind has found out ways to examine and discover demonstratively the just equality of two angles, or extensions, or figures. . . .

11. But in other simple ideas, whose modes and differences are made and counted by degrees, and not quantity, we have not so nice and accurate a distinction of their differences as to perceive or find ways to measure their just equality or the least differences. For those other simple ideas, being appearances or sensations produced in us by the size, figure, number, and motion of minute corpuscles singly insensible, their different degrees also depend upon the variation of some or all of those causes; which since it cannot be observed by us in particles of matter whereof each is too subtile to be perceived, it is impossible for us to have any exact measures of the different degrees of these simple ideas. . . .

13. Not knowing what number of particles, nor what motion of them, is fit to produce any precise degree of whiteness, we cannot demonstrate the certain equality of any two degrees of whiteness; because we have no certain standard to measure them by, nor means to distinguish every the least real difference; the only help we have being from our senses, which in this point fail us. But where the difference is so great as to produce in the mind clearly distinct ideas, whose differences can be perfectly retained, there these ideas of colours, as we see in different kinds, as blue and red, are as capable of demonstration as ideas of number and extension. What I have here said of whiteness and colours, I think, holds true in all secondary qualities, and their modes.

14. *Sensitive knowledge of particular existence.*—These two, viz., intuition and demonstration, are the degrees of our knowledge; whatever comes short of one of these, with what assurance soever embraced, is but *faith* or *opinion*, but not knowledge, at least in all general truths. There is, indeed, another perception of the mind employed about *the particular existence of finite beings* without us; which, going beyond bare probability, and yet not reaching perfectly to either of the foregoing degrees of

certainty, passes under the name of knowledge. There can be nothing more certain, than that the idea we receive from an external object is in our minds; this is intuitive knowledge. But whether there be anything more than barely that idea in our minds, whether we can thence certainly infer the existence of anything without us which corresponds to that idea, is that whereof some men think there may be a question made; because men may have such ideas in their minds when no such thing exists, no such object affects their senses. But yet here, I think, we are provided with an evidence that puts us past doubting; for I ask any one, whether he be not invincibly conscious to himself of a different perception when he looks on the sun by day, and thinks on it by night; when he actually tastes wormwood, or smells a rose, or only thinks on that savour or odour? We as plainly find the difference there is between any idea revived in our minds by our own memory, and actually coming into our minds by our senses, as we do between any two distinct ideas. If any one say, a dream may do the same thing, and all these ideas may be produced in us without any external objects; he may please to dream that I make him this answer: (1) That it is no great matter whether I remove his scruple or no: where all is but dream, reasoning and arguments are of no use, truth and knowledge nothing. (2) That I believe he will allow a very manifest difference between dreaming of being in the fire, and being actually in it. But yet if he be resolved to appear so sceptical as to maintain, that what I call being actually in the fire is nothing but a dream; and that we cannot thereby certainly know that any such thing as fire actually exists without us; I answer, that we certainly finding that pleasure or pain follows upon the application of certain objects to us, whose existence we perceive, or dream that we perceive, by our senses; this certainly is as great as our happiness or misery, beyond which we have no concernment to know or to be. So that, I think, we may add to the two former sorts of knowledge this also, of the existence of particular external objects by that perception and consciousness we have of the actual entrance of ideas from them, and allow these three degrees of knowledge, viz., *intuitive, demonstrative,* and *sensitive:* in each of which there are different degrees and ways of evidence and certainty.

CHAPTER III. OF THE EXTENT OF HUMAN KNOWLEDGE

1. KNOWLEDGE, as has been said, lying in the perception of the agreement or disagreement of any of our ideas, it follows from hence that,

First, No farther than we have ideas.—First, We can have knowledge no farther than we have ideas.

2. *Secondly, No farther than we can perceive their agreement or disagreement.*—Secondly, That we can have no knowledge farther than we can have perception of that agreement or disagreement: which perception being, (1) Either by *intuition,* or the immediate comparing any two ideas; or, (2) By *reason,* examining the agreement or disagreement of two ideas

by the intervention of some others; or (3) By *sensation,* perceiving the existence of particular things; hence it also follows,

3.   *Thirdly, Intuitive knowledge extends itself not to all the relations of all our ideas.*—Thirdly, that we cannot have an intuitive knowledge that shall extend itself to all our ideas, and all that we would know about them; because we cannot examine and perceive all the relations they have one to another by juxtaposition, or an immediate comparison one with another. Thus having the ideas of an obtuse and an acute angled triangle, both drawn from equal bases, and between parallels, I can by intuitive knowledge perceive the one not to be the other; but cannot that way know whether they be equal or no: because their agreement or disagreement in equality can never be perceived by an immediate comparing them; the difference of figure makes their parts incapable of an exact immediate application; and therefore there is need of some intervening quantities to measure them by, which is demonstration or rational knowledge.

4.   *Fourthly, Nor demonstrative knowledge.*—Fourthly, It follows also, from what is above observed, that our rational knowledge cannot reach to the whole extent of our ideas. Because between two different ideas we would examine, we cannot always find such mediums as we can connect one to another with an intuitive knowledge, in all the parts of the deduction; and wherever that fails, we come short of knowledge and demonstration.

5.   *Fifthly, Sensitive knowledge narrower than either.*—Fifthly, Sensitive knowledge, reaching no farther than the existence of things actually present to our senses, is yet much narrower than either of the former.

NICOLAS
MALEBRANCHE   1638–1715

M alebranche has been called France's second greatest
    metaphysician, but nobody would think of ranking
him with Descartes. Of the ten men included in the present volume,
his place as a major figure is probably the least assured. Still, he is
interesting to compare with Descartes, Spinoza, Leibniz, and Berkeley.

A deformed and weak child, he was initially educated by a tutor,
but later studied theology at the Sorbonne. In 1660 he joined the
congregation of the Oratory of Jesus. He did not excel in his studies
in ecclesiastical history, and he did no better in Hebrew or Biblical
studies, which he took up next. Reading Descartes' *Traité de l'homme*
in 1664 proved the turning point of his career. His heart palpitated
so fiercely, we are told, that he had to lay aside the book again and
again. Henceforth there was no doubt about his calling: it was to be
philosophy.

In 1675 he published *De la recherche de la vérité;* in 1677, *Conver-
sations chrétiennes;* in 1680, *Traité de la nature et de la grâce;* in
1683, *Méditations chrétiennes et métaphysiques.* Other works followed. Of our two selections, the first comes from the last named
book, and the second from the first named.

To classify Malebranche, scholars have said that he fused Descartes' philosophy with the Augustinian tradition, which was cultivated by the congregation of the Oratory of Jesus. He has also been
called an occasionalist. The latter term refers to Malebranche's attempt to solve one of the difficulties of Cartesianism. According to
Descartes, there are two basically different kinds of stuff, matter and
mind, and the question arises whether the two could possibly inter-

229

act. Occasionalism is the doctrine that there is no interaction: the apparent action of material objects on each other is really due to divine action, and mental events provide the occasion for divine acts on bodies.

One of the philosophers with whose doctrines Malebranche's position invites comparison is Berkeley. It is reported that the two men met and compared their metaphysics, and that the conversation so excited Malebranche that it hastened his death, at 77.

Of the following selections, the passages on "Causation" come from the fifth and sixth *Méditations chrétiennes et métaphysiques*. Here Malebranche presents his ideas in the form of a dialogue between his own soul and the Eternal Word. The latter is also called Jesus or Universal Reason. It has been remarked that in this book the Word, instead of becoming flesh, became Cartesian.

The passages on "The Material World and the Intelligible World" fall into two parts, of which the first comes from *De la recherche de la vérité*, Book III, Part II, Chapter I, and the second from the Sixth *Eclaircissement* of the same work. All of this material was selected and translated for this volume by Professor Willis Doney at the Department of Philosophy at Dartmouth College.

CAUSATION

Listen. Listen, my son. Silence your senses; forget your prejudices and anything that is mere opinion. Empty your mind of everything introduced by your body; or at least disregard it for the time. Listen to me. Can a body—small or large, square or round, or, if you will, white or black, cold or hot—be moved by itself? Say only what you conceive. There is in the world only a foot of matter: I make this supposition in order that your mind may not be distracted. Will this body be able to move itself? In the idea that you have of matter, do you discover any power? You do not reply. But suppose that this body were in fact to have the power of moving itself. In what direction will it go? With what velocity will it move itself? You are still silent? I even suppose that this body has sufficient freedom and knowledge to determine its motion and velocity: I suppose that it is master of itself. But take care. You will again be at a loss. For suppose that this body is surrounded by an infinity of others. What will become of it when it meets another of which it knows neither the solidity nor the size? It will give to it, you will say, a part of its moving force? But who taught you this? Who told you that the other will receive it? What part of its force will the one give to the other? And how will it be able to impart or distribute it? Do you conceive all of this clearly?

My son, close the eyes of the body and open those of the mind—or at least believe only what your senses tell you. Your eyes indeed tell you that, when a body at rest is struck, it ceases to be at rest. Believe what you see. This is a fact; and concerning facts the testimony of the senses is good enough. But do not judge that bodies have in themselves a moving force or that they can distribute it in those they meet, for of this you see nothing. . . . You imagine that, because a body is never struck without being moved, bodies move one another. You go a little too fast. On the basis of what you see, you may judge that, as a consequence of the order of nature, the impact of bodies is necessary for motions to be communicated; but stop there if you do not wish to fall into error. If you wish to increase your knowledge, consult your reason and listen to me.

God is an infinitely perfect being. His volitions are efficacious in themselves, for it is a great perfection that whatever one wills be accomplished by the very efficacy of one's will. If, then, God has the volition that a body be moved, this alone will set it in motion; and the action of God's will will be the moving force of the body. God would not create beings to serve as the moving forces of bodies, for these beings would be useless. Does a wise person do in complex ways what he can execute more simply? If your volitions were efficacious, would you think of forging tools to execute your plans? Still, my son, suppose that the entity God would create as the moving force of a body were able to move itself. Would it be a body or a spirit? If a body, there would be bodies that would be able to move themselves and move others. If it were a spirit, spirits would have been created to move bodies. What order would there then be in the universe? But I shall teach you that the One who creates bodies is the only One who can move them and that the most powerful of spirits does not in fact have the force to move a so-called atom. Renew your attention.

When God has created a body, you imagine that, for it to continue to exist, it suffices for God to leave it there and, once made, it will be quite capable of subsisting by itself. When you have made something, it subsists without your doing anything more; you cannot even destroy it without some action. But, my son, do not judge of God as of yourself. Men do not bring into existence the matter with which they work: they suppose it ready made. But God makes everything and supposes nothing. A body exists because God wills that it exist; it continues to exist because God continues to will that it exist; and, if God merely ceased to will that the body exist, from that moment it would no longer exist. If the body continued to exist though God has ceased willing that it exist, it would be independent, and indeed independent in such a way that God could no longer destroy it. For God to be able to destroy such a body, He would have to be able to will that the body not exist: God would have to be capable of having a volition of which non-being would be the object. Now, in non-being there is nothing good or desirable. God cannot then desire or will it with a positive volition. God can annihilate His work because He can cease willing that His work subsist; for the volitions of God, though eternal and immutable, are not necessary and, in regard to created beings, are absolute. The world is not a necessary emanation from the Divinity. By an eternal and immutable volition God can create it for a time. But God cannot have a positive and effective volition to destroy it: He cannot act in order to do nothing; His action cannot lead to non-being. This is clear. Thus, since bodies exist because God wills that they exist and since they do not cease to exist because God does not cease willing that they exist, it is evident that in God creation and preservation are one and the same action. Let this be granted.

God must create bodies either at rest or in motion. Now, a body is at rest because God creates it or preserves it always in the same place; it is in motion because God invariably creates or preserves it successively in different places. Thus, for a spirit to move a body at rest or stop a body in motion, it would have to compel God to change His conduct or action. If God does not cease willing and consequently preserving a body in a certain place, the body will not cease being there and hence will be motionless; and, if God does not cease preserving a body successively in different places, no power will be able to stop it or fix it in one place. The moving force of bodies is the all-powerful action of God, who conserves them successively in different places. No spirit is the master of the action of God; no power can change it; and so it is God alone who can move bodies. Nor can a body in motion by itself set in motion another that it meets. For it cannot move it without imparting to it a certain moving force. Yet moving force is not in the bodies moved but in God alone, since it is nothing but the action of God who creates bodies and preserves them successively in different places. Bodies cannot then communicate a force that they do not have, nor could they communicate it even if they had it. For bodies striking one another communicate their motion with a regularity, promptitude, and proportion worthy of an infinite wisdom and power. This is only too evident.

But, my son, if God alone moves matter, He alone as true cause produces all the natural effects that certain philosophers attribute to a blind nature, to forms, faculties, and virtues of which they have no idea; for nothing takes place in the material world except through the motion of certain visible or invisible parts. If fire burns, air refreshes, and the sun gives light, it is through the motion of their parts. The earth produces flowers and fruits only because water from rain passes through the roots into the fibers of plants and, congealing, makes them grow; and, if by the motion of its parts the sun did not produce vapors above the seas condensing in rain, the earth would no longer be watered and no longer fertile. My intention here is not to teach you physics but to assure you that you will never clearly conceive principles of the changes occurring in the world other than those depending on motion, for even the shape of bodies depends on it. If there were others, it would not be difficult to show you that God alone would be their cause; but we need not attribute to God imaginary effects. Acknowledge then, my son, that God does everything. Love and fear only Him. No created being can act on you nor in what surrounds you. Disregard all those imaginary powers of a blind nature that pagan philosophers have invented to cover their ignorance, justify their idolatry, or cater to the weakness of imagination in the common run of man. . . .

You are fully convinced that God alone moves bodies by the same action by which He produces or preserves them successively in different places; and you begin to believe that no change takes place in the material world except through the motion of particles of which it is composed. Thus, you see that God does everything as true cause and as general cause. But, besides the general cause, there are an infinity of particular causes; and, besides the true cause, there are natural causes. To avoid the dangerous equivocation born of the false idea that the philosophers have of nature, you may call the latter *occasional* causes. Listen to me attentively.

To form or preserve the material world, God has established certain general laws of the communication of motion—I do not say what they are, since this is not necessary—and He invariably acts in accordance with these laws. If one body strikes another with a certain velocity, the body struck will always be moved in the same way. You may be assured of this truth by thousands of observations. You could also learn it by attentively consulting the idea that you have of a God who is infinitely wise, of a general cause and immutable nature; for the conduct of God must bear the character of His attributes. But abstract principles give you trouble, and usually it is easier to judge of the cause by the effects than of the effects by the nature of the cause. Let this be granted. When a body is in motion, it certainly has the force of moving another as a consequence of the laws of the communication of motion that God invariably follows. A body, we may say, is the physical or *natural* cause of the motion it communicates, since it acts as a result of *natural* laws. But it is by no means the true cause. In the sense of the philosophy of the pagans, it is not a natural cause; strictly, it is only an *occasional* cause determining on impact the efficacy of the general law in accordance with which a general cause—an immutable Nature and infinite Wisdom—must act. . . .

I see, however, that you are not as yet convinced that spirits have no power over bodies or over inferior spirits. You are still inclined to believe that your soul animates your body in the sense that from it the body receives all the movements produced in it, or at least those which we call voluntary and which in fact depend on your volitions. Renounce your prejudices, my son; and, regarding natural effects, never judge that one thing is the effect of another on the ground that experience teaches you that it never fails to follow the other. Of all the false principles this is the one that is most dangerous and most productive of error. Since God's volitions are immutable and His laws inviolable, His action is always uniform and constant. If you follow this false principle, though God does everything, you will conclude that He does nothing. . . . You [formerly] thought that, because bodies are never struck without being moved and are never moved without being struck, bodies striking one another are the true cause of the motion they communicate. By the same principle you also judged that fire produced heat, the sun light, and the objects surrounding you the changes you observed in them and the agreeable and disagreeable sensations you have in their presence. Today you are still inclined to believe that the soul imparts motion and life to the body, and you believe this because you suppose that the body becomes cold and motionless as a result of the absence of its soul. You also think you are the true cause of the movement of your arm and your tongue because the movement of these parts immediately follows your desires. Rid yourself entirely of this false principle. . . .

To form a judgment about the efficacy of created beings, you must enter into yourself and consult the ideas of them; and, if you can discover in their ideas some force or virtue, you must attribute it to them. For we must attribute to beings what we clearly conceive to be contained in the ideas that represent them, these being the eternal models on which they have been formed. . . . If, then, you wish to become clear whether your soul gives motion and life to your body and whether you as a true cause move your arm or your tongue, try to discover in the idea of your being whether there is a natural and necessary connection between your volitions and the movement of parts of your body; or rather, since the idea you have of yourself is not clear, as I shall some day show you, answer this question by means of the internal sensation you have of what takes place within you. This I allow. For, though the senses always deceive you, your consciousness or the internal sensation you have of what takes place within you never deceives you. Open the eyes of the mind. I am going to enlighten you and deliver you from your prejudices. . . .

Listen, my son. A man cannot move his arm unless animal spirits flow from certain muscles into their antagonists, distend and contract them, and in this way pull the bones to which they are attached by tendons; in short, the arm cannot be moved unless a certain change takes place in the parts of which it is composed. But a peasant or a juggler who does not know whether he has muscles, animal spirits, or whatever is necessary for making the arm move is able to move it as expertly as the most clever anatomist. Can we do—can we even will—what we do not know how to do? Can we will that animal spirits flow into certain muscles without knowing whether we have spirits and muscles? We can will to move our fingers because we see and know that we have them. But can we will to move spirits that we do not see and of which we are not aware? Can we transport them into muscles equally unknown through the tubes of nerves equally invisible and choose promptly and infallibly the one answering to the finger that we will to move? That we could, my son. These [animal] spirits are bodies. Remember what I have already told you: their moving force is the action of God, who creates them and preserves them successively in different places. The will of man cannot vanquish the action of God. It cannot change the position of the smallest of these spirits. It cannot place one where God does not place it, where God does not create and preserve it. Since your members are moved only by means of these spirits, your desires or your efforts are not the true causes which by their efficacy produce the movement of your members. They are only the occasional causes that God has established to determine the efficacy of the laws of the union of soul and body, by means of which you have the power of moving the members of your body. . . .

Pay attention, my son. Since you move your arm only as a consequence of the general laws of the union of soul and body, your volitions are in themselves entirely inefficacious. Your arm moves only because God has willed that it move whenever you yourself should will it and provided your body is properly disposed. Hence, when you move your arm, there are two volitions concurring in its movement, God's and yours. Now, it is a contradiction that God should will that your arm be moved and it remain motionless. You are sure that there is a necessary connection between the volitions of an all-powerful Being and their effects; whereas you see no connection between your desires and their execution. Thus, the force producing the movement of your arm comes from God as a consequence of your volition, which is in itself inefficacious. . . .

But I see what still misleads you. In order to move your arm, it is not enough that you will it: you must also make some effort. And you imagine that the effort, of which you have an internal sensation, is the true cause of the movement that follows it; you imagine this because the movement is strong and violent in proportion to the intensity of your effort. But, my son, do you clearly see some connection between what you call effort and the direction of animal spirits into the tubes of the nerves used in the movements you will to produce? Do not hold to the principle behind your errors, the falsehood of which I have already shown you in so many ways. Believe what you clearly conceive and not what you confusedly sense. You even sense, however, that your efforts are often impotent. *Effort*, then, is one thing, and *efficacy* another.

.   .   .

THE MATERIAL WORLD AND THE INTELLIGIBLE WORLD

I believe everyone agrees that we do not perceive objects which are outside of us in themselves. We see the sun, the stars, and an infinity of objects outside of us; and it is not likely that the soul leaves the body and, as it were, goes for a walk in the heavens there to contemplate these objects. It does not then see them in themselves; and when our mind sees, for instance, the sun, its immediate object is not the sun but something intimately united with our soul. It is this that I call *idea*. Thus by the word *idea* I mean here nothing other than what is the immediate or closest object of the mind when it perceives an object; i.e., what affects and modifies the mind in its perception of an object.

We must carefully note that, for the mind to perceive a certain object, it is absolutely necessary that the idea of the object be present to it. It is impossible to doubt that this is so. It is not necessary, however, that there be something external similar to the idea; for it very often happens that we perceive things that do not exist and indeed never have existed. Thus, we often have in mind real ideas of things that never were. When, for example, a man imagines a golden mountain, it is absolutely necessary that the idea of the mountain be really present to his mind. When a madman, a man with a high fever, or someone asleep sees an animal before his eyes, it is clearly the case that the idea of this animal really exists. Yet the golden mountain and the animal never did exist.

Men, however, are almost naturally led to believe that only corporeal objects exist; and they judge of the reality and existence of things quite other than they should. On sensing an object, they take it to be quite certain that the object exists, though it often happens that there is nothing external. Moreover, they would have it that the object is just as they see it, which is never the case. Yet, concerning the idea which exists necessarily and cannot be other than they see it, they usually judge unreflectingly that it is nothing. Ideas have a great number of properties, however. The idea of a square, for instance, is quite different from that of a number and represents something quite different. This cannot be the case with respect to nothing, for nothing has no property. It is indubitable, then, that ideas have a very real existence.

．　　．　　．

M. Descartes has given us the strongest arguments that reason by itself could furnish for the existence of bodies. It is evident that God is not a deceiver; and, if we were deceived in making proper use of our mind and the other faculties of which He is the author, we could say that He did in fact deceive us. Yet we may say that the existence of matter is still not perfectly demonstrated; I mean, with geometrical rigor. For in philosophic matters we should believe nothing whatever unless evidence constrains us. We should make use of our freedom so far as possible. Our judgments should extend no farther than our perceptions. Thus, when we see bodies, we are to judge only that we see them and that visible or intelligible bodies actually exist; but why are we to form the positive judgment that there is an external material world similar to the intelligible world that we see?

Perhaps you will say we see these bodies outside of us and even at a great distance from the one we animate, and so we may judge them to be outside of us without extending our judgments farther than our perceptions. But does this follow? Do we not see light outside of us and in the sun even though it is not there? None the less, I admit that the bodies we see outside of us are in fact outside of us, for indeed this is incontestable. But is it not evident that there are outsides and distances—that there are intelligible spaces—in the intelligible world that is the immediate object of our mind? The material body we animate is not, we should note, the one we see when we look at it: I mean, when we turn the eyes of our body toward it. The body we see is an intelligible body; and there are intelligible spaces between this intelligible body and the intelligible sun that we see, as there are material spaces between our body and the sun we look at. Certainly God sees that there are spaces between the bodies He has created, but He does not see these bodies or these spaces in themselves. He sees them only in the ideas He has of them—by way of intelligible bodies and intelligible spaces. God receives His light from Himself alone: He sees the material world only in the intelligible world contained in Him and in the knowledge that He has of His volitions, which confer existence and motion on all things. There are, then, intelligible spaces between the intelligible bodies we see, as there are material spaces between the material bodies we look at.

We must note that, as God alone has immediate knowledge of the volitions by which He produces all beings, we cannot know apart from Him whether there is in fact a material world outside of us similar to the one we see; for the material world is neither visible nor intelligible in itself. Hence, to be fully convinced that there are bodies, we must be shown not only that there is a God and that God is not a deceiver but also that God has assured us of having in fact created them. This I do not find proved in the works of M. Descartes.

God speaks to the mind and constrains it to believe in one of two ways: by evidence and by faith. I agree that faith constrains us to believe in the existence of bodies; but, as for evidence, it seems to me that it is incomplete and that we are not invincibly led to believe in the existence of anything other than God and our mind. It is true that we have a strong inclination to believe that there are bodies surrounding us. I concede this to M. Descartes; but this inclination, natural as it is, does not compel us through evidence but only inclines us by way of an impression. Now, in our free judgments we should follow only light and evidence; and, if we allow ourselves to be guided by sensible impressions, we shall almost always be deceived.

Why are we deceived in the judgments we make about the sensible qualities and about the size, shape, and motion of bodies if not because we follow an impression similar to the one leading us to believe that there are bodies? Do we not see that fire is hot, that snow is white, that the sun is all radiant with light? Do we not see that sensible qualities as well as bodies are outside of us? Yet it is certain that the sensible qualities we see outside of us are not in fact outside of us—or, if you wish, there is no certainty that they are. What reason have we then for judging that, besides the intelligible bodies we see, there are yet others that we look at? What evidence have we that an impression that is misleading not only in regard to the sensible qualities but also in regard to the size, shape, and motion of bodies is not misleading in regard to the actual existence of these very bodies? I ask, what evidence do we have? For, concerning probabilities, I admit we do not lack them. . . .

Indeed, faith alone can convince us that there are in fact bodies. We can have an exact demonstration of the existence of a being only if it is one that is necessary. And, if we consider the matter closely, we shall plainly see that we cannot even know with complete evidence whether God is in fact creator of a material and sensible world or not. Evidence of this sort is to be found only in the case of necessary relations, and there is no necessary relation between God and such a world. He was able not to create it; and if He created it, it is because He willed, and freely willed, to do so.

By an evident light the saints in heaven clearly perceive that the Father engenders His Son and that the Father and the Son produce the Holy Ghost; for these emanations are necessary. The world, however, is not a necessary emanation in God; and those who most clearly perceive His being do not have an evident perception of what He produces outside Himself. None the less, I believe the blessed are certain that there is a world, though only because God assures them of this by manifesting His volitions to them in a manner unknown to us; and we here below are certain there is because faith teaches us that God created the world and faith is in conformity with our natural judgments or composite sensations when they are confirmed by all our senses, corrected by our memory, and rectified by our reason.

GOTTFRIED WILHELM LEIBNIZ

1646–1716

Like many of the pre-Socratics, most of the great philosophers of the sixteenth and seventeenth centuries were prominent in public affairs and keenly interested in a vast variety of subjects besides philosophy. They published in other fields as well, and several made important contributions outside of philosophy. None can lay greater claim to having been a universal man than Leibniz.

His father was a professor of moral philosophy at the University of Leipzig, but died when Leibniz was a child. The boy was admitted to the university at 14, studied the history of philosophy, was keenly interested in Plato, Aristotle, Plotinus, scholasticism, and Descartes, and at 16 defended a thesis *De principio individui*. At 17, he went on to the University of Jena to study mathematics, and at 18 he published a treatise on law. At 20, he became a doctor of laws. He continued to write a great deal, was in close touch with many prominent men, and exerted himself toward the reunion of Protestantism and Catholicism.

He visited London, lived in Paris for several years, went to see Spinoza in Holland, and also exchanged some letters with Spinoza. His correspondence was multifarious and prolific and is a mine of philosophic ideas. He was made a member of the Royal Society in 1673, after demonstrating in London a calculating machine that he had invented. It could add, subtract, multiply, divide, and extract square roots. In 1700, he was elected a foreign member of the French Academy. He was also offered the custodianship of the Vatican Library, provided he became a Catholic; but he refused, still hoping to heal the schism of the churches.

Leibniz was a topflight mathematician; he discovered the differential and integral calculus. An unpleasant dispute concerning this discovery began in 1699 and continued after Leibniz' death, the question being whether Newton had made this discovery earlier than Leibniz. Each of the two great men was suspected of having stolen the idea from the other, and the Royal Society officially belittled Leibniz' achievement—quite unjustly according to the verdict of subsequent scholarship. It has been said that the dispute "redounded to the discredit of all concerned." Both men deserve full credit. Leibniz' notation was more convenient and is still in use.

When the *Akademie der Wissenschaften* in Berlin was founded at his instigation, in 1700, he was made the first president, for life. He was close to Sophie Charlotte, the wife of the Elector of Brandenburg who, on January 18, 1701, became the first king of Prussia. The only large systematic work in philosophy that he ever published was written at her request: *Essais de Théodicée sur la bonté de Dieu, la liberté de l'homme, et l'origine du mal* (1701). Four years later, he wrote two brief sketches of his metaphysic: *La Monadologie* and *Principes de la nature et de la grâce*. Both of these works are offered here, complete, together with Leibniz' own abridgement of the argument of his *Theodicy* and some sections from his *Discours de la métaphysique*.

His death was ignored not only by the Royal Society in London but also by the *Akademie* in Berlin and by the court at Hanover, which he had served much of his life. His secretary is said to have been his only mourner, and an eyewitness reports in his memoirs that Leibniz "was buried more like a robber than what he really was, the ornament of his country."

At his death, he left an enormous number of unpublished letters and manuscripts. One major work was first published in 1765: Leibniz' detailed critique of Locke's celebrated *Essay*, entitled *Nouveaux essais sur L'entendement humain*. Leibniz had completed the book in 1704, but had held it back when Locke died the same year. The book greatly stimulated Immanuel Kant and helped to prompt him to write his *Critique of Pure Reason*.

Around 1900, two of the outstanding philosophers of the twentieth century devoted two of their earliest works to Leibniz: Bertrand Russell in England and Ernst Cassirer in Germany. The Leibniz revered by professional philosophers in the twentieth century is not the friend of the Prussian Queen and the butt of Voltaire's *Candide*. Leibniz' dictum that this is the best of all possible worlds is gladly abondoned to Voltaire's scorn or to Bradley's briefer mockery: "and everything in it is a necessary evil." If Leibniz' *Theodicy* is still important, it is largely because it says concisely and rigorously what so many others, before and after, have said at greater length and with less care—and because, for better or for worse, Leibniz' name will always be associated with the one philosophic tome that he himself saw fit to publish. Recent philosophers, however, especially in the English-speaking world, have become far more interested in Leibniz' work in logic.

Much of Leibniz' manuscript material has not yet been published. Editions of his writings that claim to be complete are in fact quite deficient. The first really comprehensive edition has been begun, but not finished, by the *Akademie* in Berlin.

The translations that follow are those of Professor Philip P. Wiener.

THE MONADOLOGY (*complete*)

[1714]

1. The *monad* of which we shall here speak is merely a simple substance, which enters into composites; *simple,* that is to say, without parts.[1]

2. And there must be simple substances, since there are composites; for the composite is only a collection or *aggregatum* of simple substances.

3. Now where there are no parts, neither extension, nor figure, nor divisibility is possible. And these monads are the true atoms of nature, and, in a word, the elements of all things.

4. Their dissolution also is not at all to be feared, and there is no conceivable way in which a simple substance can perish naturally.[2]

5. For the same reason there is no conceivable way in which a simple substance can begin naturally, since it cannot be formed by composition.

6. Thus it may be said that the monads can only begin or end all at once, that is to say, they can only begin by creation and end by annihilation; whereas that which is composite begins or ends by parts.

7. There is also no way of explaining how a monad can be altered or changed in its inner being by any other creature, for nothing can be transposed within it, nor can there be conceived in it any internal movement which can be excited, directed, augmented or diminished within it, as can be done in composites, where there is change among the parts. The monads have no windows through which anything can enter or de-

---

[1] *Théodicée,* § 10. [All footnote references to this earlier work, *Theodicy* (1710), are Leibniz's.]

[2] § 89.

part. The accidents cannot detach themselves nor go about outside of substances, as did formerly the sensible species of the Schoolmen. Thus neither substance nor accident can enter a monad from outside.

8. Nevertheless, the monads must have some qualities, otherwise they would not even be entities. And if simple substances did not differ at all in their qualities there would be no way of perceiving any change in things, since what is in the compound can only come from the simple ingredients, and the monads, if they had no qualities, would be indistinguishable from one another, seeing also they do not differ in quantity. Consequently, a plenum being supposed, each place would always receive, in any motion, only the equivalent of what it had had before, and one state of things would be indistinguishable from another.

9. It is necessary, indeed, that each monad be different from every other. For there are never in nature two beings which are exactly alike and in which it is not possible to find an internal difference, or one founded upon an intrinsic quality (*dénomination*).

10. I take it also for granted that every created being, and consequently the created monad also, is subject to change, and even that this change is continuous in each.

11. It follows from what has just been said, that the natural changes of the monads proceed from an *internal principle,* since an external cause could not influence their inner being.[3]

12. But, besides the principle of change, there must be an individuating *detail of changes,* which forms, so to speak, the specification and variety of the simple substances.

13. This detail must involve a multitude in the unity or in that which is simple. For since every natural change takes place by degrees, something changes and something remains; and consequently, there must be in the simple substance a plurality of affections and of relations, although it has no parts.

14. The passing state, which involves and represents a multitude in unity or in the simple substance, is nothing else than what is called *perception,* which must be distinguished from apperception or consciousness, as will appear in what follows. Here it is that the Cartesians especially failed, having taken no account of the perceptions of which we are not conscious. It is this also which made them believe that spirits only are monads and that there are no souls of brutes or of other entelechies. They, with most people, have failed to distinguish between a prolonged state of unconsciousness (*étourdissement*) and death strictly speaking, and have therefore agreed with the old scholastic prejudice of entirely separate souls, and have even confirmed ill-balanced minds in the belief in the mortality of the soul.

15. The action of the internal principle which causes the change or the passage from one perception to another, may be called *appetition;* it is true that desire cannot always completely attain to the whole per-

---

[3] §§ 396 and 400.

ception to which it tends, but it always attains something of it and reaches new perceptions.

16. We experience in ourselves a multiplicity in a simple substance, when we find that the most trifling thought of which we are conscious involves a variety in the object. Thus all those who admit that the soul is a simple substance ought to admit this multiplicity in the monad, and M. Bayle ought not to have found any difficulty in it, as he has done in his Dictionary, article *Rorarius*.

17. It must be confessed, moreover, that *perception* and that which depends on it *are inexplicable by mechanical causes*, that is, by figures and motions. And, supposing that there were a machine so constructed as to think, feel and have perception, we could conceive of it as enlarged and yet preserving the same proportions, so that we might enter it as into a mill. And this granted, we should only find on visiting it, pieces which push one against another, but never anything by which to explain a perception. This must be sought for, therefore, in the simple substance and not in the composite or in the machine. Furthermore, nothing but this (namely, perceptions and their changes) can be found in the simple substance. It is also in this alone that all the *internal activities* of simple substances can consist.[4]

18. The name of *entelechies* might be given to all simple substances or created monads, for they have within themselves a certain perfection (ἔχουσι τὸ ἐντελές); there is a certain sufficiency (αὐτάρκεια) which makes them the sources of their internal activities, and so to speak, incorporeal automata.[5]

19. If we choose to give the name *soul* to everything that has *perceptions* and *desires* in the general sense which I have just explained, all simple substances or created monads may be called souls, but as feeling is something more than a simple perception, I am willing that the general name of monads or entelechies shall suffice for those simple substances which have only perception, and that those substances only shall be called *souls* whose perception is more distinct and is accompanied by memory.

20. For we experience in ourselves a state in which we remember nothing and have no distinguishable perception, as when we fall into a swoon or when we are overpowered by a profound and dreamless sleep. In this state the soul does not differ sensibly from a simple monad; but as this state is not continuous and as the soul comes out of it, the soul is something more than a mere monad.[6]

21. And it does not at all follow that in such a state the simple substance is without any perception. This is indeed impossible, for the reasons mentioned above; for it cannot perish, nor can it subsist without some affection, which is nothing else than its perception; but when there is

---

[4] Preface, p. 37 (Gerhardt edition).
[5] § 87.
[6] § 64.

a great number of minute perceptions, in which nothing is distinct, we are stunned; as when we turn continually in the same direction many times in succession, whence arises a dizziness which may make us swoon, and which does not let us distinguish anything. And death may produce for a time this condition in animals.

22. And as every present state of a simple substance is naturally the consequence of its preceding state, so its present is big with its future.[7]

23. Therefore, since on being awakened from a stupor, we are *aware* of our perceptions, we must have had them immediately before, although we were unconscious of them; for one perception can come in a natural way only from another perception, as a motion can come in a natural way only from a motion.[8]

24. From this we see that if there were nothing distinct, nothing, so to speak, in relief and of a higher flavor in our perceptions, we should always be in a dazed state. This is the condition of simply bare monads.

25. We also see that nature has given to animals heightened perceptions, by the pains she has taken to furnish them with organs which collect many rays of light or many undulations of air, in order to render these more efficacious by uniting them. There is something of the same kind in odor, in taste, in touch and perhaps in a multitude of other senses which are unknown to us. And I shall presently explain how that which takes place in the soul represents that which occurs in the organs.

26. Memory furnishes souls with a sort of *consecutiveness* [association of ideas] which imitates reason, but which ought to be distinguished from it. We observe that animals, having the perception of something which strikes them and of which they have had a similar perception before, expect, through the representation in their memory, that which was associated with it in the preceding perception, and experience feelings similar to those which they had had at that time. For instance, if we show dogs a stick, they remember the pain it has caused them and whine and run.[9]

27. And the strong imagination which impresses and moves them, arises either from the magnitude or the multitude of preceding perceptions. For often a strong impression produces all at once the effect of a long-continued *habit*, or of many oft-repeated moderate perceptions.

28. Men act like the brutes, in so far as the association of their perceptions results from the principle of memory alone, resembling the empirical physicians who practice without theory; and we are simple empirics in three-fourths of our actions. For example, when we expect that there will be daylight to-morrow, we are acting as empirics, because that has up to this time always taken place. It is only the astronomer who judges of this by reason.

29. But the knowledge of necessary and eternal truths is what distinguishes us from mere animals and furnishes us with *reason* and the

---

[7] § 360.
[8] §§ 401 to 403.
[9] Prelim., § 65.

sciences, raising us to a knowledge of ourselves and of God. This is what we call the rational soul or *spirit* in us.

30. It is also by the knowledge of necessary truths, and by their abstractions, that we rise to *acts of reflection*, which make us think of that which calls itself "*I*", and to observe that this or that is within *us:* and it is thus that, in thinking of ourselves, we think of being, of substance, simple or composite, of the immaterial and of God himself, conceiving that what is limited in us is in him without limits. And these reflective acts furnish the principal objects of our reasonings.[10]

31. Our reasonings are founded on *two great principles, that of contradiction*, in virtue of which we judge that to be *false* which involves contradiction, and that *true*, which is opposed or contradictory to the false.[11]

32. And *that of sufficient reason*, in virtue of which we hold that no fact can be real or existent, no statement true, unless there be a sufficient reason why it is so and not otherwise, although most often these reasons cannot be known to us.[12]

33. There are also two kinds of *truths*, those of *reasoning* and those of *fact*. Truths of reasoning are necessary and their opposite is impossible, and those of *fact* are contingent and their opposite is possible. When a truth is necessary its reason can be found by analysis, resolving it into more simple ideas and truths until we reach those which are primitive.[13]

34. It is thus that mathematicians by analysis reduce speculative *theorems* and practical *canons* to *definitions, axioms* and *postulates*.

35. And there are finally simple ideas, definitions of which cannot be given; there are also axioms and postulates, in a word, *primary principles*, which cannot be proved, and indeed need no proof; and these are *identical propositions*, whose opposite involves an express contradiction.

36. But there must also be a *sufficient reason* for *contingent truths* or those *of fact*,—that is, for the sequence of things diffused through the universe of created objects—where the resolution into particular reasons might run into a detail without limits, on account of the immense variety of the things in nature and the division of bodies *ad infinitum*. There is an infinity of figures and of movements, present and past, which enter into the efficient cause of my present writing, and there is an infinity of slight inclinations and dispositions, past and present, of my soul, which enter into the final cause.[14]

37. And as all this *detail* only involves other contingents, anterior or more detailed, each one of which needs a like analysis for its explanation, we make no advance: and the sufficient or final reason must be outside of the sequence or *series* of this detail of contingencies, however infinite it may be.

---

10 Pref., p. 27.
11 §§ 44, 169.
12 §§ 44, 196.
13 §§ 170, 174, 189, 280-282, 367; Abridgment, Objection 3.
14 §§ 36, 37, 44, 45, 49, 52, 121, 122, 337, 340, 344.

38. And thus it is that the final reason of things must be found in a necessary substance, in which the detail of changes exists only eminently, as in their source; and this is what we call God.[15]

39. Now this substance, being a sufficient reason of all this detail, which also is linked together thoroughout, *there is but one God, and this God is sufficient.*

40. We may also conclude that this supreme substance, which is unique, universal and necessary, having nothing outside of itself which is independent of it, and being a pure consequence of possible being, must be incapable of limitations and must contain as much of reality as is possible.

41. Whence it follows that God is absolutely perfect, *perfection* being only the magnitude of positive reality taken in its strictest meaning, setting aside the limits or bounds in things which have them. And where there are no limits, that is, in God, perfection is absolutely infinite.[16]

42. It follows also that the creatures have their perfections from the influence of God, but that their imperfections arise from their own nature, incapable of existing without limits. For it is by this that they are distinguished from God.[17]

43. It is also true that in God is the source not only of existences but also of essences, so far as they are real, or of that which is real in the possible. This is because the understanding of God is the region of eternal truths, or of the ideas on which they depend, and because, without him, there would be nothing real in the possibilities, and not only nothing existing but also nothing possible.[18]

44. For, if there is a reality in essences or possibilities or indeed in the eternal truths, this reality must be founded in something existing and actual, and consequently in the existence of the necessary being, in whom essence involves existence, or with whom it is sufficient to be possible in order to be actual.[19]

45. Hence God alone (or the necessary being) has this prerogative, that he must exist if he is possible. And since nothing can hinder the possibility of that which possesses no limitations, no negation, and, consequently, no contradiction, this alone is sufficient to establish the existence of God *a priori*. We have also proved it by the reality of the eternal truths. But we have a little while ago [§§ 36-39] proved it also *a posteriori*, since contingent beings exist, which can only have their final or sufficient reason in a necessary being who has the reason of his existence in himself.

46. Yet we must not imagine, as some do, that the eternal truths, being

---

[15] § 7.

[16] § 22; Preface, p. 27.

[17] §§ 20, 27-31, 153, 167, 377 seqq. [In the first copy, revised by Leibniz, the following is added: "This *original imperfection* of creatures is noticeable in the *natural inertia* of bodies. §§ 30, 380; Abridgment, Objection 5."]

[18] § 20.

[19] §§ 184, 189, 335.

dependent upon God, are arbitrary and depend upon his will, as Descartes seems to have held, and afterwards M. Poiret. This is true only of contingent truths, the principle of which is *fitness* or the choice of the *best*, whereas necessary truths depend solely on his understanding and are its internal object.[20]

47. Thus God alone is the primitive unity or the original simple substance; of which all created or derived monads are the products, and are generated, so to speak, by continual fulgurations of the Divinity, from moment to moment, limited by the receptivity of the creature, to whom limitation is essential.[21]

48. In God is *Power*, which is the source of all; then *Knowledge*, which contains the detail of ideas; and finally *Will*, which effects changes or products according to the principle of the best. These correspond to what in created monads form the subject or basis, the perceptive faculty, and the appetitive faculty. But in God these attributes are absolutely infinite or perfect; and in the created monads or in the *entelechies* (or *perfectihabiis*, as Harmolaus Barbarus translated the word), they are only imitations proportioned to the perfection of the monads.[22]

49. The creature is said to act extremely in so far as it has perfection, and to be *acted* on by another in so far as it is imperfect. Thus *action* is attributed to the monad in so far as it has distinct perceptions, and *passivity* in so far as it has confused perceptions.[23]

50. And one creature is more perfect than another, in this that there is found in it that which serves to account *a priori* for what takes place in the other, and it is in this way that it is said to act upon the other.

51. But in simple substances the influence of one monad upon another is purely *ideal* and it can have its effect only through the intervention of God, inasmuch as in the ideas of God a monad may demand with reason that God in regulating the others from the commencement of things, have regard to it. For since a created monad can have no physical influence upon the inner being of another, it is only in this way that one can be dependent upon another.[24]

52. And hence it is that the actions and passive reactions of creatures are mutual. For God, in comparing two simple substances, finds in each one reasons which compel him to adjust the other to it, and consequently that which in certain respects is active, is according to another point of view, passive; *active* in so far as that what is known distinctly in it, serves to account for that which takes place in another; and *passive* in so far as the reason for what takes place in it, is found in that which is distinctly known in another.[25]

53. Now, as there is an infinity of possible universes in the ideas of

[20] §§ 180, 184, 185, 335, 351, 380.
[21] §§ 382-391, 398, 395.
[22] §§ 7, 149, 150, 87.
[23] §§ 32, 66, 386.
[24] §§ 9, 54, 65, 66, 201; Abridgment, Objection 3.
[25] § 66.

God, and as only one of them can exist, there must be a sufficient reason for the choice of God, which determines him to select one rather than another.[26]

54. And this reason can only be found in the *fitness*, or in the degrees of perfection, which these worlds contain, each possible world having a right to claim existence according to the measure of perfection which it possesses.[27]

55. And this is the cause of the existence of the Best; namely, that his wisdom makes it known to God, his goodness makes him choose it, and his power makes him produce it.[28]

56. Now this *connection*, or this adaptation, of all created things to each and of each to all, brings it about that each simple substance has relations which express all the others, and that, consequently, it is a perpetual living mirror of the universe.[29]

57. And as the same city looked at from different sides appears entirely different, and is as if multiplied *perspectively;* so also it happens that, as a result of the infinite multitude of simple substances, there are as it were so many different universes, which are nevertheless only the perspectives of a single one, according to the different *points of view* of each monad.[30]

58. And this is the way to obtain as great a variety as possible, but with the greatest possible order; that is, it is the way to obtain as much perfection as possible.[31]

59. Moreover, this hypothesis (which I dare to call demonstrated) is the only one which brings into relief the grandeur of God. M. Bayle recognized this, when in his Dictionary (Art. *Rorarius*) he raised objections to it; in which indeed he was disposed to think that I attributed too much to God and more than is possible. But he can state no reason why this universal harmony, which brings it about that each substance expresses exactly all the others through the relations which it has to them, is impossible.

60. Besides, we can see, in what I have just said, the *a priori* reasons why things could not be otherwise than they are. Because God, in regulating all, has had regard to each part, and particularly to each monad, whose nature being representative, nothing can limit it to representing only a part of things; although it may be true that this representation is but confused as regards the detail of the whole universe, and can be distinct only in the case of a small part of things, that is to say, in the case of those which are nearest or greatest in relation to each of

---

[26] §§ 8, 10, 44, 173, 196 seqq., 225, 414-416.

[27] §§ 74, 167, 350, 201, 130, 352, 345 seqq., 354. [In the first copy revised by Leibniz the following is found added here: "Thus there is nothing absolutely arbitrary."]

[28] §§ 8, 78, 80, 84, 119, 204, 206, 208; Abridgment, Objections 1 and 8.

[29] §§ 130, 360.

[30] § 147.

[31] §§ 120, 124, 241 seqq., 214, 243, 275.

the monads; otherwise each monad would be a divinity. It is not as regards the object but only as regards the modification of the knowledge of the object, that monads are limited. They all tend confusedly toward the infinite, toward the whole; but they are limited and differentiated by the degrees of their distinct perceptions.

61. And composite substances are analogous in this respect with simple substances. For since the world is a *plenum*, rendering all matter connected, and since in a plenum every motion has some effect on distant bodies in proportion to their distance, so that each body is affected not only by those in contact with it, and feels in some way all that happens to them, but also by their means is affected by those which are in contact with the former, with which it itself is in immediate contact, it follows that this intercommunication extends to any distance whatever. And consequently, each body feels all that happens in the universe, so that he who sees all, might read in each that which happens everywhere, and even that which has been or shall be, discovering in the present that which is removed in time as well as in space; σύμπνοια πάντα, said Hippocrates. But a soul can read in itself only that which is distinctly represented in it. It cannot develop its laws all at once, for they reach into the infinite.

62. Thus, although each created monad represents the entire universe, it represents more distinctly the body which is particularly attached to it, and of which it forms the entelechy: and as this body expresses the whole universe through the connection of all matter in a plenum, the soul also represents the whole universe in representing this body, which belongs to it in a particular way.[32]

63. The body belonging to a monad, which is its entelechy or soul, constitutes together with the entelechy what may be called a *living being*, and together with the soul what may be called an *animal*. Now this body of a living being or of an animal is always organic, for once every monad is in its way a mirror of the universe, and since the universe is regulated in a perfect order, there must also be an order in the representative, that is, in the perceptions of the soul, and hence in the body, through which the universe is represented in the soul.[33]

64. Thus each organic body of a living being is a kind of divine machine or natural automaton, which infinitely surpasses all artificial automata. Because a machine which is made by man's art is not a machine in each one of its parts; for example, the teeth of a brass wheel have parts or fragments which to us are no longer artificial and have nothing in themselves to show the special use to which the wheel was intended in the machine. But nature's machines, that is, living bodies, are machines even in their smallest parts *ad infinitum*. Herein lies the difference between nature and art, that is, between the divine art and ours.[34]

---

[32] § 400.
[33] § 403.
[34] §§ 134, 146, 194, 403.

65. And the author of nature has been able to employ this divine and infinitely marvellous artifice, because each portion of matter is not only divisible *ad infinitum*, as the ancients recognized, but also each part is actually endlessly subdivided into parts, of which each has some motion of its own: otherwise it would be impossible for each portion of matter to express the whole universe.[35]

66. Whence we see that there is a world of creatures, of living beings, of animals, of entelechies, of souls, in the smallest particle of matter.

67. Each portion of matter may be conceived of as a garden full of plants, and as a pond full of fishes. But each branch of the plant, each member of the animal, each drop of its humors is also such a garden or such a pond.

68. And although the earth and air which lies between the plants of the garden, or the water between the fish of the pond, is neither plant nor fish, they yet contain more of them, but for the most part so tiny as to be imperceptible to us.

69. Therefore there is nothing fallow, nothing sterile, nothing dead in the universe, no chaos, no confusion except in appearance; somewhat as a pond would appear from a distance, in which we might see the confused movement and swarming, so to speak, of the fishes in the pond, without discerning the fish themselves.[36]

70. We see thus that each living body has a ruling entelechy, which in the animal is the soul; but the members of this living body are full of other living beings, plants, animals, each of which has also its entelechy or governing soul.

71. But it must not be imagined, as has been done by some people who have misunderstood my thought, that each soul has a mass or portion of matter belonging to it or attached to it forever, and that consequently it possesses other inferior living beings, destined to its service forever. For all bodies are, like rivers, in a perpetual flux, and parts are entering into them and departing from them continually.

72. Thus the soul changes its body only gradually and by degrees, so that it is never deprived of all its organs at once. There is often a metamorphosis in animals, but never metempsychosis nor transmigration of souls. There are also no entirely *separate* souls, nor *genii* without bodies. God alone is wholly without body.[37]

73. For which reason also, it happens that there is, strictly speaking, neither absolute birth nor complete death, consisting in the separation of the soul from the body. What we call *birth* is development or growth, as what we call *death* in envelopment and diminution.

74. Philosophers have been greatly puzzled over the origin of forms, entelechies, or souls; but to-day, when we know by exact investigations upon plants, insects and animals, that the organic bodies of nature are

[35] Prelim., § 70; Théod., § 195.
[36] Preface, pp. 40, 41.
[37] Théod., § 90, 124.

never products of chaos or putrefaction, but always come from seeds, in which there was undoubtedly some *pre-formation*, it has been thought that not only the organic body was already there before conception, but also a soul in this body, and, in a word, the animal itself; and that by means of conception this animal has merely been prepared for a great transformation, in order to become an animal of another kind. Something similar is seen outside of birth, as when worms become flies, and caterpillars become butterflies.[38]

75. The *animals*, some of which are raised by conception to the grade of larger animals, may be called *spermatic*; but those among them, which remain in their class, that is, the most part, are born, multiply, and are destroyed like the large animals, and it is only a small number of chosen ones which pass to a larger theatre.

76. But this is only half the truth. I have, therefore, held that if the animal never commences by natural means, neither does it end by natural means; and that not only will there be no birth, but also no utter destruction nor death, strictly speaking. And these reasonings, made *a posteriori* and drawn from experience, harmonize perfectly with my principles deduced *a priori*, as above [cf. 3, 4, 5].[39]

77. Thus it may be said that not only the soul (mirror of an indestructible universe) is indestructible, but also the animal itself, although its mechanism often perishes in part and takes on or puts off organic coatings.

78. These principles have given me the means of explaining naturally the union or rather the conformity of the soul and the organic body. The soul follows its own peculiar laws and the body also follows its own laws, and they agree in virtue of the *pre-established harmony* between all substances, since they are all representations of one and the same universe.[40]

79. Souls act according to the laws of final causes, by appetitions, ends and means. Bodies act in accordance with the laws of efficient causes or of motion. And the two realms, that of efficient causes and that of final causes, are in harmony with each other.

80. Descartes recognized that souls cannot impart any force to bodies, because there is always the same quantity of force in matter. Nevertheless he believed that the soul could change the direction of bodies. But this was because, in his day, the law of nature which affirms also the conservation of the same total direction in matter, was not known. If he had known this, he would have lighted upon my system of pre-established harmony.[41]

81. According to this system, bodies act as if (what is impossible) there were no souls, and that souls act as if there were no bodies, and that both act as if each influenced the other.

---

[38] §§ 86, 89, 90, 187, 188, 403, 397; Preface, p. 40, seq.
[39] § 90.
[40] Preface, p. 36; Théod., §§ 340, 352, 353, 358.
[41] Pref., p. 44; Théod., §§ 22, 59, 60, 63, 66, 345, 346 seqq., 354, 355.

82. As to *spirits* or rational souls, although I find that the same thing which I have stated (namely, that animals and souls begin only with the world and end only with the world) holds good at bottom with regard to all living beings and animals, yet there is this peculiarity in rational animals, that their spermatic animalcules, as long as they remain such, have only ordinary or sensitive souls; but as soon as those which are, so to speak, elected, attain by actual conception to human nature, their sensitive souls are elevated to the rank of reason and to the prerogative of spirits.[42]

83. Among other differences which exist between ordinary souls and minds (*esprits*), some of which I have already mentioned, there is also, this, that souls in general are the living mirrors or images of the universe of creatures, but minds or spirits are in addition images of the Divinity itself, or of the author of nature, able to know the system of the universe and to imitate something of it by architectonic samples, each mind being like a little divinity in its own department.[43]

84. Hence it is that spirits are capable of entering into a sort of society with God, and that he is, in relation to them, not only what an inventor is to his machine (as God is in relation to the other creatures), but also what a prince is to his subjects, and even a father to his children.

85. Whence it is easy to conclude that the assembly of all spirits (*esprits*) must compose the City of God, that is, the most perfect state which is possible, under the most perfect of monarchs.[44]

86. This City of God, this truly universal monarchy, is a moral world within the natural world, and the highest and most divine of the works of God; it is in this that the glory of God truly consists, for he would have none if his greatness and goodness were not known and admired by spirits. It is, too, in relation to this divine city that he properly has goodness; whereas his wisdom and his power are everywhere manifest.

87. As we have above established a perfect harmony between two natural kingdoms, the one of efficient, the other of final causes, we should also notice here another harmony between the physical kingdom of nature and the moral kingdom of grace; that is, between God considered as the architect of the mechanism of the universe and God considered as monarch of the divine city of spirits.[45]

88. This harmony makes things progress toward grace by natural means. This globe, for example, must be destroyed and repaired by natural means, at such times as the government of spirits may demand it, for the punishment of some and the reward of others.[46]

89. It may be said, farther, that God as architect satisfies in every respect God as legislator, and that therefore sins, by the order of nature

---

[42] §§ 91, 397.
[43] § 147.
[44] § 146; Abridgment, Objection 2.
[45] §§ 62, 72, 118, 248, 112, 130, 247.
[46] §§ 18 seqq., 110, 244, 245, 340.

and perforce even of the mechanical structure of things, must carry their punishment with them; and that in the same way, good actions will obtain their rewards by mechanical ways through their relations to bodies, although this cannot and ought not always happen immediately.

90. Finally, under this perfect government, there will be no good action unrewarded, no bad action unpunished; and everything must result in the well-being of the good, that is, of those who are not disaffected in this great State, who, after having done their duty, trust in providence, and who love and imitate, as is meet, the author of all good, finding pleasure in the contemplation of his perfections, according to the nature of truly *pure love*, which takes pleasure in the happiness of the beloved. This is what causes wise and virtuous persons to work for all which seems in harmony with the divine will, presumptive or antecedent, and nevertheless to content themselves with that which God in reality brings to pass by his secret, consequent and decisive will, recognizing that if we could sufficiently understand the order of the universe, we should find that it surpasses all the wishes of the wisest, and that it is impossible to render it better than it is, not only for all in general, but also for ourselves in particular, if we are attached, as we should be, to the author of all, not only as to the architect and efficient cause of our being, but also as to our master and final cause, who ought to be the whole aim of our will, and who, alone, can make our happiness.[47]

THE PRINCIPLES OF NATURE AND OF GRACE, BASED ON REASON (*complete*)

[1714]

1. *Substance* is a being capable of action. It is a simple or compound. *Simple substance* is that which has no parts. *Compound* substance is the collection of simple substances or *monads*. *Monas* is a Greek word which signifies unity, or that which is one.

Compounds, or bodies, are multitudes; and simple substances, lives, souls, spirits are unities. And there must be simple substances everywhere, because without simple substances there would be no compounds; and consequently all nature is full of life.

2. Monads, having no parts, cannot be formed or decomposed. They cannot begin or end naturally; and consequently last as long as the universe, which will be changed but will not be destroyed. They cannot have shapes; otherwise they would have parts. And consequently a monad, in

---

[47] §§ 134 fin., 278; Preface, pp. 27, 28.

itself and at a given moment, could not be distinguished from another except by its internal qualities and actions, which can be nothing else than its *perceptions* (that is, representations of the compound, or of what is external, in the simple), and its *appetitions* (that is, its tendencies to pass from one perception to another), which are the principles of change. For the simplicity of substance does not prevent multiplicity of modifications, which must be found together in this same simple substance, and must consist in the variety of relations to things which are external. Just as in a *centre* or point, entirely simple as it is, there is an infinity of angles formed by the lines which meet at the point.

3. All nature is a *plenum*. There are everywhere simple substances, separated in effect from one another by activities of their own which continually change their relations; and each important simple substance, or monad, which forms the centre of a composite substance (as, for example, of an animal) and the principle of its unity, is surrounded by a *mass* composed of an infinity of other monads, which constitute the body proper of this central monad; and in accordance with the affections of its body the monad represents, as in a *centre*, the things which are outside of itself. And this *body* is *organic*, though it forms a sort of automaton or natural machine, which is a machine not only in its entirety, but also in its smallest perceptible parts. And as, because the world is a *plenum*, everything is connected and each body acts upon every other body, more or less, according to the distance, and by reaction is itself affected thereby, it follows that each monad is a living mirror, or endowed with internal activity, representative according to its point of view of the universe, and as regulated as the universe itself. And the perceptions in the monad spring one from the other, by the laws of desires [*appétits*] or of the *final causes of good and evil*, which consist in observable, regulated or unregulated, perceptions; just as the changes of bodies and external phenomena spring one from another, by the laws of *efficient causes*, that is, of motions. Thus there is a perfect *harmony* between the perceptions of the monad and the motions of bodies, pre-established at the beginning between the system of efficient causes and that of final causes. And in this consists the accord and physical union of the soul and the body, although neither one can change the laws of the other.

4. Each monad, with a particular body, makes a living substance. Thus there is not only life everywhere, accompanied with members or organs, but there is also an infinity of degrees among monads, some dominating more or less over others. But when the monad has organs so adjusted that by their means prominence and distinctness appear in the impressions which they receive, and consequently in the perceptions which represent these (as, for example, when by means of the shape of the humors of the eyes, the rays of light are concentrated and act with more force), this may lead to *feeling* [*sentiment*], that is, to a perception accompanied by *memory*, namely, by a certain reverberation lasting a long time, so as to make itself heard upon occasion. And such a living being is called an *animal*, as its monad is called a soul. And when this soul is elevated to

reason, it is something more sublime and is reckoned among spirits, as will soon be explained. It is true that animals are sometimes in the condition of simple living beings, and their souls in the condition of simple monads, namely, when their perceptions are not sufficiently distinct to be remembered, as happens in a deep dreamless sleep, or in a swoon. But perceptions which have become entirely confused must be re-developed in animals, for reasons which I shall shortly (§12) enumerate. Thus it is well to make distinction between the *perception,* which is the inner state of the monad representing external things, and *apperception,* which is *consciousness* or the reflective knowledge of this inner state; the latter not being given to all souls, nor at all times to the same soul. And it is for want of this distinction that the Cartesians have failed, taking no account of the perceptions of which we are not conscious as people take no account of imperceptible bodies. It is this also which made the same Cartesians believe that only spirits are monads, that there is no soul of brutes, and still less other *principles of life.* And as they shocked too much the common opinion of men by refusing feeling to brutes, they have, on the other hand, accommodated themselves too much to the prejudices of the multitude, by confounding a *long swoon,* caused by a great confusion of perceptions, with *death strictly speaking,* where all perception would cease. This has confirmed the ill-founded belief in the destruction of some souls, and the bad opinion of some so-called strong minds, who have contended against the immortality of our soul.

5. There is a connection in the perfections of animals which bears some resemblance to reason; but it is only founded in the memory of *facts* or effects, and not at all in the knowledge of *causes.* Thus a dog shuns the stick with which it has been beaten, because memory represents to it the pain which the stick had caused it. And men, in so far as they are empirics, that is to say, in three-fourths of their actions, act simply as the brutes do. For example, we expect that there will be daylight to-morrow because we have always had the experience; only an astronomer foresees it by reason, and even this prediction will finally fail when the cause of day, which is not eternal, shall cease. But *true reasoning* depends upon necessary or eternal truths, such as those of logic, of numbers, of geometry, which establish an indubitable connection of ideas and unfailing inferences. The animals in whom these inferences are not noticed, are called *brutes;* but those which know these necessary truths are properly those which are called *rational animals,* and their souls are called *spirits.* These souls are capable of performing acts of reflection, and of considering that which is called the *ego, substance, monad, soul, spirit,* in a word, immaterial things and truths. And it is this which renders us capable of the sciences and of demonstrative knowledge.

6. Modern researches have taught us, and reason approves of it, that living beings whose organs are known to us, that is to say, plants and animals, do not come from putrefaction or from chaos, as the ancients believed, but from *pre-formed* seeds, and consequently by the transformation of pre-existing living beings. There are animalcules in the seeds of

larger animals, which by means of conception assume a new dress, which they make their own, and by means of which they can nourish themselves and increase their size, in order to pass to a larger theatre and to accomplish the propagation of the large animal. It is true that the souls of spermatic human animals are not rational, and do not become so until conception destines [*determine*] these animals to human nature. And as in general animals are not born entirely in conception or *generation*, neither do they perish entirely in what we call *death;* for it is reasonable that what does not begin naturally, should not end either in the order of nature. Therefore, quitting their mask or their rags, they merely return to a more minute theatre, where they can, nevertheless, be just as sensitive and just as well ordered as in the larger. And what we have just said of the large animals, takes place also in the generation and death of spermatic animals themselves, that is to say, they are growths of other smaller spermatic animals, in comparison with which they may pass for large; for everything extends *ad infinitum* in nature. Thus not only souls, but also animals, are ingenerable and imperishable: they are only developed, enveloped, reclothed, unclothed, transformed: souls never quit their entire body and do not pass from one body into another which is entirely new to them. There is therefore no *metempsychosis*, but there is *metamorphosis;* animals change, take and leave only parts: the same thing which happens little by little and by small invisible particles, but continually, in nutrition; and suddenly, visibly, but rarely, in conception or in death, which cause a gain or loss all at one time.

7. Thus far we have spoken as simple *physicists:* now we must advance to *metaphysics,* making use of the *great principle,* little employed in general, which teaches that *nothing happens without a sufficient reason;* that is to say, that nothing happens without its being possible for him who should sufficiently understand things, to give a reason sufficient to determine why it is so and not otherwise. This principle laid down, the first question which should rightly be asked, will be, *Why is there something rather than nothing?* For nothing is simpler and easier than something. Further, suppose that things must exist, we must be able to give a reason *why they must exist so* and not otherwise.

8. Now this sufficient reason for the existence of the universe cannot be found *in the series of contingent things,* that is, of bodies and of their representations in souls; for matter being indifferent in itself to motion and to rest, and to this or another motion, we cannot find the reason of motion in it, and still less of a certain motion. And although the present motion which is in matter, comes from the preceding motion, and that from still another preceding, yet in this way we make no progress, go as far as we may; for the same question always remains. Thus it must be that the sufficient reason, which has no need of another reason, be outside this series of contingent things and be found in a substance which is its cause, or which is a necessary being, carrying the reason of its existence within itself; otherwise we should still not have a sufficient reason in which we could rest. And this final reason of things is called *God.*

9. This primitive simple substance must contain in itself eminently the perfections contained in the derivative substances which are its effects; thus it will have perfect power, knowledge and will: that is, it will have supreme omnipotence, omniscience and goodness. And as *justice*, taken very generally, is only goodness conformed to wisdom, there must too be supreme justice in God. The reason which has caused things to exist by him, makes them still dependent upon him in existing and in working: and they continually receive from him that which gives them any perfection; but the imperfection which remains in them, comes from the essential and original limitation of the creature.

10. It follows from the supreme perfection of God, that in creating the universe he has chosen the best possible plan, in which there is the greatest variety together with the greatest order; the best arranged ground, place, time; the most results produced in the most simple ways; the most of power, knowledge, happiness and goodness in the creatures that the universe could permit. For since all the possibles in the understanding of God laid claim to existence in proportion to their perfections, the result of all these claims must be the most perfect actual world that is possible. And without this it would not be possible to give a reason why things have turned out so rather than otherwise.

11. The supreme wisdom of God led him to choose the *laws of motion* best adjusted and most suited to abstract or metaphysical reasons. There is preserved the same quantity of total and absolute force, or of action; the same quantity of respective force or of reaction; lastly the same quantity of directive force. Farther, action is always equal to reaction, and the whole effect is always equivalent to its full cause. And it is not surprising that we could not by the mere consideration of the *efficient causes* or of matter, account for those laws of motion which have been discovered in our time, and a part of which have been discovered by myself. For I have found that it was necessary to have recourse to *final causes*, and that these laws do not depend upon the *principle of necessity*, like logical, arithmetical and geometrical truths, but upon the *principle of fitness*, that is, upon the choice of wisdom. And this is one of the most effective and evident proofs of the existence of God, to those who can examine these matters thoroughly.

12. It follows, farther, from the perfection of the supreme author, that not only is the order of the entire universe the most perfect possible, but also that each living mirror representing the universe in accordance with its point of view, that is to say, that each *monad*, each substantial centre, must have its perceptions and its desires as well regulated as is compatible with all the rest. Whence it follows, still farther, that *souls*, that is, the most dominating monads, or rather, animals themselves, cannot fail to awaken from the state of stupor in which death or some other accident may put them.

13. For all is regulated in things, once for all, with as much order and harmony as is possible, supreme wisdom and goodness not being able to act except with perfect harmony. The present is big with the future, the

future might be read in the past, the distant is expressed in the near. One could become acquainted with the beauty of the universe in each soul, if one could unfold all its folds, which only develop perceptibly in time. But as each distinct perception of the soul includes innumerable confused perceptions, which embrace the whole universe, the soul itself knows the things of which it has perception only so far as it has distinct and clear perceptions of them; and it has perfection in proportion to its distinct perfections. Each soul knows the infinite, knows all, but confusedly; as in walking on the seashore and hearing the great noise which it makes, I hear the particular sounds of each wave, of which the total sound is composed, but without distinguishing them. Our confused perceptions are the result of the impressions which the whole universe makes upon us. It is the same with each monad. God alone has a distinct knowledge of all, for he is the source of all. It has been well said that he is as centre everywhere, but his circumference is nowhere, since everything is immediately present to him without any distance from this centre.

14. As regards the rational soul, or *spirit,* there is something in it more than in the monads, or even in simple souls. It is not only a mirror of the universe of creatures, but also an image of the Divinity. The *spirit* has not only a perception of the works of God, but it is even capable of producing something which resembles them, although in miniature. For, to say nothing of the marvels of dreams, in which we invent without trouble (but also involuntarily) things which, when awake, we should have to think a long time in order to hit upon, our soul is architectonic also in its voluntary actions, and, discovering the sciences according to which God has regulated things (*pondere, mensura, numero, etc.*), it imitates, in its department and in its little world, where it is permitted to exercise itself, what God does in the large world.

15. This is why all spirits, whether of men or of genii, entering by virtue of reason and of eternal truths into a sort of society with God, are members of the City of God, that is to say, of the most perfect state, formed and governed by the greatest and best of monarchs; where there is no crime without punishment, no good actions without proportionate recompense; and, finally, as much virtue and happiness as is possible; and this is not by a derangement of nature, as if what God prepares for souls disturbed the laws of bodies, but by the very order of natural things, in virtue of the harmony pre-established for all time between the *realms of nature and of grace,* between God as Architect and God as Monarch; so that *nature* itself leads to grace, and *grace,* in making use of nature, perfects it.

16. Thus although reason cannot teach us the details, reserved to Revelation, of the great future, we can be assured by this same reason that things are made in a manner surpassing our desires. God also being the most perfect and most happy, and consequently, the most lovable of substances, and *truly pure love* consisting in the state which finds pleasure in the perfections and happiness of the loved object, this love ought to

give us the greatest pleasure of which we are capable, when God is its object.

17. And it is easy to love him as we ought, if we know him as I have just described. For although God is not visible to our external senses, he does not cease to be very lovable and to give very great pleasure. We see how much pleasure honors give men, although they do not at all consist in the qualities of the external senses. Martyrs and fanatics (although the emotion of the latter is ill-regulated) show what pleasure of the spirit can accomplish; and, what is more, even sensuous pleasures are really confusedly known intellectual pleasures. Music charms us, although its beauty only consists in the harmonies of numbers and in the reckoning of the beats or vibrations of sounding bodies, which meet at certain intervals, reckonings of which we are not conscious and which the soul nevertheless does make. The pleasures which sight finds in proportions are of the same nature; and those caused by the other senses amount to almost the same thing, although we may not be able to explain it so distinctly.

18. It may even be said that from the present time on, the *love of God* makes us enjoy a foretaste of future felicity. And although it is disinterested, it itself constitutes our greatest good and interest even if we should not seek these therein and should consider only the pleasure which it gives, without regard to the utility it produces; for it gives us perfect confidence in the goodness of our author and master, producing a true tranquillity of mind; not as with the Stoics who force themselves to patience, but by a present contentment, assuring to us also a future happiness. And besides the present pleasure, nothing can be more useful for the future; for the love of God fulfills also our hopes, and leads us in the road of supreme happiness, because by virtue of the perfect order established in the universe, everything is done in the best possible way, as much for the general good as for the greatest individual good of those who are convinced of this and are content with the divine government; this conviction cannot be wanting to those who know how to love the source of all good. It is true that supreme felicity, by whatever *beatific vision* or knowledge of God it be accompanied, can never be full; because, since God is infinite, he cannot be wholly known. Therefore our happiness will never, and ought not, consist in full joy, where there would be nothing farther to desire, rendering our mind stupid; but in a perpetual progress to new pleasures and to new perfections.

THE THEODICY:

ABRIDGEMENT OF THE ARGUMENT REDUCED TO
SYLLOGISTIC FORM (*complete*)

[1710]

Some intelligent persons have desired that this supplement be made
[to the Theodicy], and I have the more readily yielded to their wishes as
in this way I have an opportunity again to remove certain difficulties and
to make some observations which were not sufficiently emphasized in the
work itself.

I. *Objection.* Whoever does not choose the best is lacking in power,
or in knowledge, or in goodness.

God did not choose the best in creating this world.

Therefore, God has been lacking in power, or in knowledge, or in
goodness.

Answer. I deny the minor, that is, the second premise of this syllogism;
and our opponent proves it by this

Prosyllogism. Whoever makes things in which there is evil, which could
have been made without any evil, or the making of which could have been
omitted, does not choose the best.

God has made a world in which there is evil; a world, I say, which
could have been made without any evil, or the making of which could
have been omitted altogether.

Therefore, God has not chosen the best.

Answer. I grant the minor of this prosyllogism; for it must be confessed that there is evil in this world which God has made, and that it
was possible to make a world without evil, or even not to create a world
at all, for its creation has depended on the free will of God; but I deny
the major, that is, the first of the two premises of the prosyllogism, and
I might content myself with simply demanding its proof; but in order to
make the matter clearer, I have wished to justify this denial by showing
that the best plan is not always that which seeks to avoid evil, since it may
happpen that *the evil is accompanied by a greater good.* For example, a
general of an army will prefer a great victory with a slight wound to a
condition without wound and without victory. We have proved this more
fully in the large work by making it clear, by instances taken from mathematics and elsewhere, that an imperfection in the part may be required
for a greater perfection in the whole. In this I have followed the opinion
of St. Augustine, who has said a hundred times, that God has permitted
evil in order to bring about good, that is, a greater good; and that of
Thomas Aquinas (in libr. II. sent. dist. 32, qu. I, art. 1), that the permitting
of evil tends to the good of the universe. I have shown that the ancients

called Adam's fall *felix culpa*, a happy sin, because it had been retrieved with immense advantage by the incarnation of the Son of God, who has given to the universe something nobler than anything that ever would have been among creatures except for it. For the sake of a clearer understanding, I have added, following many good authors, that it was in accordance with order and the general good that God allowed to certain creatures the opportunity of exercising their liberty, even when he foresaw that they would turn to evil, but which he could so well rectify; because it was not fitting that, in order to hinder sin, God should always act in an extraordinary manner. To overthrow this objection, therefore, it is sufficient to show that a world with evil might be better than a world without evil; but I have gone even farther, in the work, and have even proved that this universe must be in reality better than every other possible universe.

II. *Objection.* If there is more evil than good in intelligent creatures, then there is more evil than good in the whole work of God.

Now, there is more evil than good in intelligent creatures.

Therefore, there is more evil than good in the whole work of God.

Answer. I deny the major and the minor of this conditional syllogism. As to the major, I do not admit it at all, because this pretended deduction from a part to the whole, from intelligent creatures to all creatures, supposes tacitly and without proof that creatures destitute of reason cannot enter into comparison nor into account with those which possess it. But why may it not be that the surplus of good in the non-intelligent creatures which fill the world, compensates for, and even incomparably surpasses, the surplus of evil in the rational creatures? It is true that the value of the latter is greater; but, in compensation, the others are beyond comparison the more numerous, and it may be that the proportion of number and quantity surpasses that of value and of quality.

As to the minor, that is no more to be admitted; that is, it is not at all to be admitted that there is more evil than good in the intelligent creatures. There is no need even of granting that there is more evil than good in the human race, because it is possible, and in fact very probable, that the glory and the perfection of the blessed are incomparably greater than the misery and the imperfection of the damned, and that here the excellence of the total good in the smaller number exceeds the total evil in the greater number. The blessed approach the Divinity, by means of a Divine Mediator, as near as may suit these creatures, and make such progress in good as is impossible for the damned to make in evil, approach as nearly as they may to the nature of demons. God is infinite, and the devil is limited; the good may and does go to infinity, while evil has its bounds. It is therefore possible, and is credible, that in the comparison of the blessed and the damned, the contrary of that which I have said might happen in the comparison of intelligent and non-intelligent creatures, takes place; namely, it is possible that in the comparison of the happy and the unhappy, the proportion of degree exceeds that of number, and that in the comparison of intelligent and non-intelligent creatures, the proportion of number is greater than that of value. I have the right to suppose that a thing is possible so long as its impossibility is not proved; and indeed that which I have here advanced is more than a supposition.

But in the second place, if I should admit that there is more evil than good in the human race, I have still good grounds for not admitting that there is more evil than good in all intelligent creatures. For there is an inconceivable number of genii, and perhaps of other rational creatures. And an opponent could not prove that in all the City of God, composed as well of genii as of rational animals without number and of an infinity of kinds, evil exceeds good. And although in order to answer an objection, there is no need of proving that a thing is, when its mere possibility suffices; yet, in this work, I have not omitted to show that it is a consequence of the supreme perfection of the Sovereign of the universe, that the kingdom of God is the most perfect of all possible states or governments, and that consequently the little evil there is, is required for the consummation of the immense good which is found there.

III. *Objection.*   If it is always impossible not to sin, it is always unjust to punish.

Now, it is always impossible not to sin; or, in other words, every sin is necessary.

Therefore, it is always unjust to punish.

The minor of this is proved thus:

1. *Prosyllogism.*   All that is predetermined is necessary.

Every event is predetermined.

Therefore, every event (and consequently sin also) is necessary.

Again this second minor is proved thus:

2. *Prosyllogism.*   That which is future, that which is foreseen, that which is involved in the causes, is predetermined.

Every event is such.

Therefore, every event is predetermined.

Answer. I admit in a certain sense the conclusion of the second prosyllogism, which is the minor of the first; but I shall deny the major of the first prosyllogism, namely, that every thing predetermined is necessary; understanding by the *necessity* of sinning, for example, or by the impossibility of not sinning, or of not performing any action, the necessity with which we are here concerned, that is, that which is essential and absolute, and which destroys the morality of an action and the justice of punishments. For if anyone understood another necessity or impossibility, namely, a necessity which should be only moral, or which was only hypothetical (as will be explained shortly); it is clear that I should deny the major of the objection itself. I might content myself with this answer and demand the proof of the proposition denied; but I have again desired to explain my procedure in this work, in order to better elucidate the matter and to throw more light on the whole subject, by explaining the necessity which ought to be rejected and the determination which must take place. That *necessity* which is contrary to morality and which ought to be rejected, and which would render punishment unjust, is an insurmountable necessity which would make all opposition useless, even if we should wish with all our heart to avoid the necessary action, and should make all possible efforts to that end. Now, it is manifest that this is not applicable to voluntary actions, because we would not perform them if we did not choose to. Also their prevision and predetermination are not absolute, but presuppose the will: if it is certain that we shall perform them, it is not less certain that we shall choose to perform them. These voluntary actions and their consequences will not take place no matter what we do or whether we wish them or not; but, *through* that which we shall do and through that which we shall wish to do, which leads to them. And this is involved in prevision and in predetermination, and even constitutes their ground. And the necessity of such an event is called conditional or hypothetical, or the necessity of consequence, because it supposes the will, and the other *requisites;* whereas the necessity which destroys morality and renders punishment unjust and reward useless, exists in things which will be whatever we may do or whatever we may wish to do, and, in a word, is in that which is essential; and this is what is called an absolute necessity. Thus it is to no purpose, as regards what is absolutely necessary, to make prohibitions or commands, to propose penalties or prizes, to praise or to blame; it will be none the less. On the other hand, in voluntary actions and in that which depends upon them, precepts armed with power to punish and to recompense are very often of use and are included in the order of causes which make an action exist. And it is for this reason that not only cares and labors but also prayers are useful; God having had these prayers in view before he regulated things and having had that consideration for them which was proper. This is why the precept which says *ora et labora* (pray and work), holds altogether good; and not only those who (under the vain pretext of the necessity of events) pretend that the care which business demands may be neglected, but also those who reason against prayer, fall into what the ancients even then called the *lazy sophism.* Thus the predetermination of events by causes is just what contributes to morality instead of destroying it, and causes incline the will, without compelling it. This is why the *determination* in question is not a necessitation—it is certain (to him who knows all) that the effect will follow this inclination; but this effect does not follow by a necessary consequence, that is, one the contrary of which implies contradiction. It is also by an internal inclination such as this that the will is determined, without there being any necessity. Suppose that one has the greatest passion in the world (a great thirst, for example), you will admit to me that the soul can find some reason for resisting it, if it were only that of showing its power. Thus, although one may never be in a perfect indifference of equilibrium and there may be always a preponderance of inclination for the side taken, it, nevertheless, never renders the resolution taken absolutely necessary.

IV. *Objection.* Whoever can prevent the sin of another and does not do so, but rather contributes to it although he is well informed of it, is accessory to it.

God can prevent the sin of intelligent creatures; but he does not do so, and rather contributes to it by his concurrence and by the opportunities which he brings about, although he has a perfect knowledge of it.

Hence, etc.

Answer. I deny the major of this syllogism. For it is possible that one could prevent sin, but ought not, because he could not do it without himself committing a sin, or (when God is in question) without performing an unreasonable action. Examples have been given and the application to God himself has been made. It is possible also that we contribute to evil and that sometimes we even open the road to it, in doing things which we are obliged to do; and, when we do our duty or (in speaking of God) when, after thorough consideration, we do that which reason demands, we are not responsible for the results, even when we foresee them. We do not desire these evils; but we are willing to permit them for the sake of a greater good which we cannot reasonably help preferring to other considerations. And this is a *consequent* will, which results from *antecedent* wills by which we will the good. I know that some persons, in speaking of the antecedent and consequent will of God, have understood by the *antecedent* that which wills that all men should be saved; and by the *consequent,* that which wills, in consequence of persistent sin, that some should be damned. But these are merely illustrations of a more general idea, and it may be said for the same reason that God, by his antecedent will, wills that men should not sin; and by his consequent or final and decreeing will (that which is always followed by its effect), he wills to permit them to sin, this permission being the result of superior reasons. And we have the right to say in general that the antecedent will of God tends to the production of good and the prevention of evil, each taken in itself and as if alone (*particulariter et secundum quid,* Thom. I, qu. 19, art. 6), according to the measure of the degree of each good and of each evil; but that the divine consequent or final or total will tends toward the production of as many goods as may be put together, the combination of which becomes in this way determined, and includes also the permission of some evils and the exclusion of some goods, as the best possible plan for the universe demands. Arminius, in his *Anti-perkinsus,* has very well explained that the will of God may be called consequent, not only in relation to the action of the creature considered beforehand in the divine understanding, but also in relation to other anterior divine acts of will. But this consideration of the passage cited from Thomas Aquinas, and that from Scotus (I. dist. 46, qu. XI), is enough to show that they make this distinction as I have done here. Nevertheless, if anyone objects to this use of terms let him substitute *deliberating* will, in place of antecedent, and *final* or decreeing will, in place of consequent. For I do not wish to dispute over words.

V. *Objection.* Whoever produces all that is real in a thing, is its cause.
God produces all that is real in sin.

Hence, God is the cause of sin.

Answer. I might content myself with denying the major or the minor, since the term *real* admits of interpretations which would render these propositions false. But in order to explain more clearly, I will make a distinction. *Real* signifies either that which is positive only, or, it includes also privative beings: in the first case, I deny the major and admit the minor; in the second case, I do the contrary. I might have limited myself to this, but I have chosen to proceed still farther and give the reason for this distinction. I have been very glad therefore to draw attention to the fact that every reality purely positive or absolute is a perfection; and that imperfection comes from limitation, that is, from the privative: for to limit is to refuse progress, or the greatest possible progress. Now God is the cause of all perfections and consequently of all realities considered as purely positive. But limitations or privations result from the original imperfection of creatures, which limits their receptivity. And it is with them as with a loaded vessel, which the river causes to move more or less slowly according to the weight which it carries: thus its speed depends upon the river, but the retardation which limits this speed comes from the load. Thus in the *Theodicy*, we have shown how the creature, in causing sin, is a defective cause; how errors and evil inclinations are born of privation; and how privation is accidentally efficient; and I have justified the opinion of St. Augustine (lib. I. ad Simpl. qu. 2) who explains, for example, how God makes the soul obdurate, not by giving it something evil, but because the effect of his good impression is limited by the soul's resistance and by the circumstances which contribute to this resistance, so that he does not give it all the good which would overcome its evil. *Nec* (inquit) *ab illo erogatur aliquid quo homo fit deterior, sed tantum quo fit melior non erogatur.* But if God had wished to do more, he would have had to make either other natures for creatures or other miracles to change their natures, things which the best plan could not admit. It is as if the current of the river must be more rapid than its fall admitted or that the boats should be loaded more lightly, if it were necessary to make them move more quickly. And the original limitation or imperfection of creatures requires that even the best plan of the universe could not receive more good, and could not be exempt from certain evils, which, however, are to result in a greater good. There are certain disorders in the parts which marvellously enhance the beauty of the whole; just as certain dissonances, when properly used, render harmony more beautiful. But this depends on what has already been said in answer to the first objection.

VI. *Objection.* Whoever punishes those who have done as well as it was in their power to do, is unjust.

God does so.

Hence, etc.

Answer. I deny the minor of this argument. And I believe that God always gives sufficient aid and grace to those who have a good will, that is, to those who do not reject this grace by new sin. Thus I do not admit the damnation of infants who have died without baptism or outside of the church; nor the damnation of adults who have acted according to the light which God has given them. And I believe that if *any one has followed the light which has been given him,* he will undoubtedly receive greater light when he has need of it, as the late M. Hulseman, a profound and celebrated theologian at Leipsig, has somewhere remarked; and if such a man has failed to receive it during his lifetime he will at least receive it when at the point of death.

VII. *Objection.* Whoever gives only to some, and not to all, the means which produces in them effectively a good will and salutary final faith, has not sufficient goodness.

God does this.

Hence, etc.

Answer. I deny the major of this. It is true that God could overcome the greatest resistance of the human heart; and does it, too, sometimes, either by internal grace, or by external circumstances which have a great effect on souls; but he does not always do this. Whence comes this distinction? it may be asked, and why does his goodness seem limited? It is because, as I have already said in answering the first objection, it would not have been in order always to act in an extraordinary manner, and to reverse the connection of things. The reasons of this connection, by means of which one is placed in more favorable circumstances than another, are hidden in the depths of the wisdom of God: they depend upon the universal harmony. The best plan of the universe, which God could not fail to choose, made it so. We judge from the event itself; since God has made it, it was not possible to do better. Far from being true that this conduct is contrary to goodness, it is supreme goodness which led him to it. This objection with its solution might have been drawn from what was said in regard to the first objection; but it seemed useful to touch upon it separately.

VIII. *Objection.* Whoever cannot fail to choose the best, is not free.

God cannot fail to choose the best.

Hence, God is not free.

Answer. I deny the major of this argument; it is rather true liberty, and the most perfect, to be able to use one's free will for the best, and to always exercise this power, without ever being turned aside either by external force or by internal passions, the first of which causes slavery of the body, the second, slavery of the soul. There is nothing less servile, and nothing more in accordance with the highest degree of freedom, than to be always led toward the good, and always by one's own inclination, without any constraint and without any displeasure. And to object therefore that God had need of external things, is only a sophism. He created them freely; but having proposed to himself an end, which is to exercise his goodness, wisdom has determined him to choose the means best fitted to attain this end. To call this a *need,* is to take that term in an unusual sense which frees it from all imperfection, just as when we speak of the wrath of God.

Seneca has somewhere said that God commanded but once but that he obeys always, because he obeys laws which he willed to prescribe to himself: *semel jussit, semper paret*. But he might better have said that God always commands and that he is always obeyed; for in willing, he always follows the inclination of his own nature, and all other things always follow his will. And as this will is always the same, it cannot be said that he obeys only that will which he formerly had. Nevertheless, although his will is always infallible and always tends toward the best, the evil, or the lesser good, which he rejects, does not cease to be possible in itself; otherwise the necessity of the good would be geometrical (so to speak), or metaphysical, and altogether absolute; the contingency of things would be destroyed, and there would be no choice. But this sort of necessity, which does not destroy the possibility of the contrary, has this name only by analogy; it becomes effective, not by the pure essence of things, but by that which is outside of them, above them, namely, by the will of God. This necessity is called moral, because, to the sage, *necessity* and *what ought to be* are equivalent things; and when it always has its effect, as it really has in the perfect sage, that is, in God, it may be said that it is a happy necessity. The nearer creatures approach to it, the nearer they approach to perfect happiness. Also this kind of necessity is not that which we try to avoid and which destroys morality, rewards and praise. For that which it brings, does not happen whatever we may do or will, but because we will it so. And a will to which it is natural to choose well, merits praise so much the more; also it carries its reward with it, which is sovereign happiness. And as this constitution of the divine nature gives entire satisfaction to him who possesses it, it is also the best and the most desirable for the creatures who are all dependent on God. If the will of God did not have for a rule the principle of the best, it would either tend toward evil, which would be the worst; or it would be in some way indifferent to good and to evil, and would be guided by chance: but a will which would allow itself always to act by chance, would not be worth more for the government of the universe than the fortuitous concourse of atoms, without there being any divinity therein. And even if God should abandon himself to chance only in some cases and in a certain way (as he would do, if he did not always work entirely for the best and if he were capable of preferring a lesser work to a greater, that is, an evil to a good, since that which prevents a greater good is an evil), he would be imperfect, as well as the object of his choice; he would not merit entire confidence; he would act without reason in such a case, and the government of the universe would be like certain games, equally divided between reason and chance. All this proves that this objection which is made against the choice of the best, perverts the notions of the free and of the necessary, and represents to us the best even as evil: which is either malicious or ridiculous.

DISCOURSE ON METAPHYSICS

[1686]

. . .

XXII. Reconciliation of the two methods of explanation, the one using final causes, and the other efficient causes, thus satisfying both those who explain nature mechanically and those who have recourse to incorporeal natures.

It is worth while to make the preceding remark in order to reconcile those who hope to explain mechanically the formation of the first tissue of an animal and all the interrelation of the parts, with those who account for the same structure by referring to final causes. Both explanations are good; both are useful not only for the admiring of the work of a great artificer, but also for the discovery of useful facts in physics and medicine. And writers who take these diverse routes should not speak ill of each other. For I see that those who attempt to explain the beauty of divine anatomy ridicule those who imagine that the apparently fortuitous flow of certain liquids has been able to produce such a beautiful variety and that they regard them as overbold and irreverent. These others on the contrary treat the former as simple and superstitious, and compare them to those ancients who regarded the physicists as impious when they maintained that not Jupiter thundered but some material which is found in the clouds. The best plan would be to join the two ways of thinking. To use a practical comparison, we recognize and praise the ability of a workman not only when we show what designs he had in making the parts of his machine, but also when we explain the instruments which he employed in making each part, especially if these instruments are simple and ingeniously contrived. God is also a workman able enough to produce a machine still a thousand times more ingenious than is our body, by employing only certain quite simple liquids purposely composed in such a way that ordinary laws of nature alone are required to develop them so as to produce such a marvellous effect. But it is also true that this development would not take place if God were not the author of nature. Yet I find that the method of efficient causes, which goes much deeper and is in a measure more immediate and *a priori*, is also more difficult when we come to details, and I think that our philosophers are still very frequently far removed from making the most of this method. The method of final causes, however, is easier and can be frequently employed to find out important and useful truths which we should have to seek for a long time, if we were confined to that other more physical method of which anatomy is able to furnish many examples. It seems to me that Snellius, who was the first discoverer of the laws of refraction, would have waited a long time before finding them if he had wished to seek out first how light was formed. But he apparently followed that method which the ancients employed for Catoptrics, that is, the method of final causes. Because, while seeking for the easiest way in which to conduct a ray of light from one given point to another given point by reflection from a given plane (supposing that that was the design of nature) they discovered the equality of the angles of incidence and reflection, as can be seen from a little treatise by Heliodorus of Larissa and also elsewhere. This principle Mons. Snellius, I believe, and afterwards independently of him, M. Fermat, applied most ingeniously to refraction. For since the rays while in the same media always maintain the same proportion of sines, which in turn corresponds to the resistance of the media, it appears that they follow the easiest way, or at least that way which is the most determinate for passing from a given point in one medium to a given point in another medium. That demonstration of this same theorem which M. Descartes has given, using efficient causes, is much less satisfactory. At least we have grounds to think that he would never have found the principle by that means if he had not learned in Holland of the discovery of Snellius.

.   .   .

XXVI. Ideas are all stored up within us. Plato's doctrine of reminiscence.

In order to see clearly what an idea is, we must guard ourselves against a misunderstanding. Many regard the idea as the form or the differentiation of our thinking, and according to this opinion we have the idea in our mind, in so far as we are thinking of it, and each separate time that we think of it anew we have another idea although similar to the preceding one. Some, however, take the idea as the immediate object of thought, or as a permanent form which remains even when we are no longer contemplating it. As a matter of fact our soul has the power of representing to itself any form or nature whenever the occasion comes for thinking about it, and I think that this activity of our soul is, so far as it expresses some nature, form or essence, properly the idea of the thing. This is in us, and is always in us, whether we are thinking of it or no. (Our soul expresses God and the universe and all essences as well as all existences.) This position is in accord with my principles that naturally nothing enters into our minds from outside.

It is a bad habit we have of thinking as though our minds receive certain messengers, as it were, or as if they had doors or windows. We have in our minds all those forms for all periods of time because the mind at every moment expresses all its future thoughts and already thinks confusedly of all that of which it will ever think distinctly. Nothing can be taught us of which we have not already in our minds the idea. This idea as it were the material out of which the thought will form itself. This is what Plato has excellently brought out in his doctrine of reminiscence, a doctrine which contains a great deal of truth, provided that it is properly understood and purged of the error of pre-existence, and provided that one does not conceive of the soul as having distinctly known and thought at some other time what it learns and thinks now. Plato has also confirmed his position by a beautiful experiment. He introduces [*Meno*] a boy, whom he leads by short steps, to extremely difficult truths of geometry bearing on incommensurables, all this without teaching the boy anything, merely drawing out replies by a well arranged series of questions. This shows that the soul virtually knows those things, and needs only to be reminded (animadverted) to recognize the truths. Consequently it possesses at least the idea upon which those truths depend. We may say even that it already possesses those truths, if we consider them as the relations of the ideas.

XXVII. In what respect our souls can be compared to blank tablets and how conceptions are derived from the senses.

Aristotle preferred to compare our souls to blank tablets prepared for writing, and he maintained that nothing is in the understanding which does not come through the senses. This position is in accord with the popular conceptions, as Aristotle's approach usually is. Plato thinks more profoundly. Such tenets or practicologies are nevertheless allowable in ordinary use somewhat in the same way as those who accept the Copernican theory still continue to speak of the rising and setting of the sun. I find indeed that these usages can be given a real meaning containing no error, quite in the same way as I have already pointed out that we may truly say particular substances act upon one another. In this same sense we may say that knowledge is received from without through the medium of the senses because certain exterior things contain or express more particularly the causes which determine us to certain thoughts. Because in the ordinary uses of life we attribute to the soul only that which belongs to it most manifestly and particularly, and there is no advantage in going further. When, however, we are dealing with the exactness of metaphysical truths, it is important to recognize the powers and independence of the soul which extend infinitely further than is commonly supposed. In order, therefore, to avoid misunderstandings it would be well to choose separate terms for the two. These expressions which are in the soul whether one is conceiving of them or not may be called ideas, while those which one conceives of or constructs may be called conceptions, *conceptus.* But whatever terms are used, it is always false to say that all our conceptions come from the so-called external senses, because those conceptions which I have of myself and of my thoughts, and consequently of being, of substance, of action, of identity, and of many others come from an inner experience.

.   .   .

XXX. How God inclines our souls without necessitating them; that there are no grounds for complaint; that we must not ask why Judas sinned because this free act is contained in his concept, the only question being why Judas the sinner is admitted to existence, preferably to other possible persons; concerning the original imperfection or limitation before the fall and concerning the different degrees of grace.

Regarding the action of God upon the human will there are many quite different considerations which it would take too long to investigate here. Nevertheless the following is what can be said in general. God in co-operating with ordinary actions only follows the laws which he has established, that is to say, he continually preserves and produces our being so that the ideas come to us spontaneously or with freedom in that order which the concept of our individual substance carries with itself. In this concept they can be foreseen for all eternity. Furthermore, by virtue of the decree which God has made that the will shall always seek the apparent good in certain particular respects (in regard to which this apparent good always has in it something of reality expressing or imitating God's will), he, without at all necessitating our choice, determines it by that which appears most desirable. For absolutely speaking, our will as contrasted with necessity, is in a state of indifference, being able to act otherwise, or wholly to suspend its action, either alternative being and remaining possible. It therefore devolves upon the soul to be on guard against appearances, by means of a firm will, to reflect and to refuse to act or decide in certain circumstances, except after mature deliberation. It is, however, true and has been assured from all eternity that certain souls will not employ their power upon certain occasions.

But who could do more than God has done, and can such a soul complain of anything except itself? All these complaints after the deed are unjust, inasmuch as they would have been unjust before the deed. Would this soul shortly before committing the sin have had the right to complain of God as though he had determined the sin? Since the determination of God in these matters cannot be foreseen, how would the soul know that it was preordained to sin unless it had already committed the sin? It is merely a question of wishing to or not wishing to, and God could not have set an easier or juster condition. Therefore all judges without asking the reasons which have disposed a man to have an evil will, consider only how far this will is wrong. But, you object, perhaps it is ordained from all eternity that I will sin. Find your own answer. Perhaps it has not been. Now then, without asking for what you are unable to know and in regard to which you can have no light, act according to your duty and your knowledge. But, some one will object; whence comes it then that this man will assuredly do this sin? The reply is easy. It is that otherwise he would not be this man. God foresees from all time that there will be a certain Judas, and in the concept or idea of him which God has, is contained this future free act. The only question, therefore, which remains is why this certain Judas, the betrayer who is possible only because of the idea of God, actually exists. To this question, however, we can expect no answer here on earth excepting to say in general that it is because God has found it good that he should exist notwithstanding that sin which he foresaw. This evil will be more than overbalanced. God will derive a greater good from it, and it will finally turn out that this series of events in which is included the existence of this sinner, is the most perfect among all the possible series of events. An explanation in every case of the admirable economy of this choice cannot be given while we are sojourners on earth. It is enough to know the excellence without understanding it. It is here that we must recognize the unfathomable depth of the divine wisdom, without hesitating at a detail which involves an infinite number of considerations. It is clear, however, that God is not the cause of ill. For not only after the loss of innocence by men, has original sin possessed the soul, but even before that there was an original limitation or imperfection in the very nature of all creatures, which rendered them open to sin and able to fall. There is, therefore, no more difficulty in the supralapsarian view than there is in the other views of sin. To this also, it seems to me, can be reduced the opinion of Saint Augustine and of other authors: that the root of evil is in the privation, that is to say, in the lack or limitation of creatures which God graciously remedies by whatever degree of perfection it pleases him to give. This grace of God, whether ordinary or extraordinary, has its degrees and its measures. It is always efficacious in itself to produce a certain proportionate effect and furthermore it is always sufficient not only to keep one from sin but even to effect his salvation, provided that the man co-operates with that which is in him. It has not always, however, sufficient power to overcome the inclination, for, if it did, it would no longer be limited in any way, and this superiority to limitations is reserved to that unique grace which is absolutely efficacious. This grace is always victorious whether through its own self or through the congruity of circumstances.

.   .   .

SECOND EXPLANATION OF THE SYSTEM OF THE COMMUNICATION OF SUBSTANCES

[*Histoire des Ouvrages des Savans*, Feb. 1696]

You do not understand, you say, how I could prove what I have proposed concerning the *Communication* or *Harmony* of two *Substances* as different as the *soul* is from the *body*. It is true that I believe I have found the way, and here is how I intend to satisfy you.

Imagine two clocks or watches in perfect agreement. That can happen in three ways:

(1) The first consists in a mutual influence.

(2) The second is to have a skillful worker continually adjust them and keep them in agreement.

(3) The third is to manufacture these two time-pieces with so much art and accuracy that their agreement is guaranteed thereafter.

Now substitute the *soul* and *body* for these two time-pieces; their agreement can be obtained through one of these three ways. The *way of influence* is that of popular philosophy; but as we cannot conceive of material particles which can pass from one of these substances to another, we must abandon this idea. The way of the *continual* assistance of the Creator is that of the system of occasional causes; but I hold that this introduces *Deus ex Machinâ* in a natural and ordinary occurrence where, according to reason, it ought not intervene except as it operates in all other natural things. Thus there remains only my hypothesis, that is, the way of *Harmony*. From the beginning God has made each of these two Substances of such a nature that each by following its own laws, given to it with its being, still agrees with the other, just as though there were a mutual influence or as though God always took a hand in it beyond his general supervision of things. There is nothing further I have to prove, unless you wish to ask that I prove God is skillful enough to use this prearranged scheme, examples of which we see even among men. Now assuming that he can, you do see that this way is most admirable and most worthy of God. You suspected that my explanation would be opposed by the very different idea we have of the mind and body; but you see now that nobody has better established their independence. For while people are compelled to explain the communication of mind and body by a sort of miracle, there is cause for many people to fear that the distinction between soul and body might not be as real as they believe, since they have to go so far in order to maintain it. I shall not be vexed if learned persons sound out the thoughts I have just explained to you.

THE PERENNIAL PHILOSOPHY

[From a Letter to Remond; Vienna, August 26, 1714 *]

If I had the leisure, I should compare my doctrines with those of the ancients and of other apt men. The truth is more widespread than one thinks, but it is often covered with make-up and wrapped up, and even weakened, mutilated, and corrupted by additions that spoil it and render it less useful. If one found these traces of truth in the ancients or, to speak more generally, in one's predecessors, one would extract gold from mud,

---

* Original text in *Die philosophischen Schriften von Gottfried Wilhelm Leibniz,* ed. C. J. Gerhardt, vol. III (1887), 624f. Translation by Sylvain Bromberger and Walter Kaufmann.

the diamond from its mine, and light from darkness; and this would be, in effect, *perennis quaedam Philosophia.*

One might also say that one would find some progress in knowledge. The Orientals had beautiful and great ideas of the Deity; the Greeks added reasoning and a form of science. The Fathers of the Church rejected what was bad in the philosophy of the Greeks. But the scholastics tried to avail themselves of what was passable in pagan philosophy in a way that would be useful to Christianity. I have often said, *aurum latere in stercore illo scholastico barbariei* [that gold is hidden in this scholastic dung of barbarism]; and I wish that one could find some able man versed in this Hibernian and Spanish philosophy, who would have the inclination and the competence to extract from it what is good. I am sure that he would be rewarded for his pains with some beautiful and important truths. . . .

I do not find that the views of Father Malebranche are too far removed from mine. The transition from occasional causes to preestablished harmony does not seem difficult. A certain M. Paren, who belongs to the *Académie Royale des Sciences,* and who wants to refute me here and there, would have one believe that I have added nothing to the doctrine of occasional causes; but he does not seem to take into consideration that according to me the laws governing bodies are disturbed neither by God nor by the soul.

GEORGE
BERKELEY   1685–1753

Berkeley was born in Ireland and, though an Anglican of English descent, emphatically considered himself Irish and spent most of his life in Ireland. He studied at Kilkenny College, and in 1700 went on to Trinity College, Dublin. There he read Descartes, Newton, and Locke. In 1707 he became a Fellow, he was ordained, and he published two short mathematical tracts. In 1709, he published his *New Theory of Vision*, and the following year his most important philosophic work, *Principles of Human Knowledge*. The greater part of this is reprinted here.

In 1711, his *Discourse on Passive Obedience* appeared, and the following year he visited England and was presented at court by Swift. While in England, he published a more popular exposition of the doctrine of his *Principles* in the form of *Three Dialogues Between Hylas and Philonous* (1713). Hylas represents materialism and Philonous Berkeley's own position, that there are only spirits and ideas, but no matter in which the ideas inhere. The dialogue form serves Berkeley to expound his own philosophy with considerable literary elegance, and to show how he would meet various objections. It should be noted that his main work appeared when he was 25, and the *Dialogues* when he was 28.

In 1721, after considerable travel, he published an *Essay towards preventing the ruin of Great Britain*, then returned to Ireland as divinity lecturer and university preacher. He became Hebrew lecturer and senior proctor at the university. In 1723, Miss Vanhomrigh, Swift's Vanessa, whom he seems to have met only once, at a dinner, left him half her property. In 1724 he became Dean of Derry, but immediately exerted himself to leave for the New World.

Initially he wanted to found a college in the Bermudas; eventually, in 1728, after four years' preparation, he sailed for Rhode Island with some friends and with his newly-wed wife. The government had promised him £20,000, but when the promise was not kept, Berkeley finally had to return after three years of study.

In 1733, he published *Alciphron, or The Minute Philosopher*, and the following year he was made Bishop of Cloyne. Of his later works, *Siris* (1744), which deals with the merits of tar water, has attracted some attention. In 1751 he lost his oldest son, and the next year went to Oxford, where another son was then commencing his studies. On January 14, 1753, he died suddenly and was buried at Christ Church, Oxford.

His philosophy has struck many people as exceedingly strange, and it has been said that his arguments produce no conviction though they cannot be refuted. Dr. Johnson said, "I refute Berkeley *thus*," and kicked a stone. He only showed that he had quite failed to understand Berkeley's doctrine. For Berkeley does not claim that there are no stones, or that kicking a stone will not produce any sensation; what he does claim is that materialists and people who speak about matter give a misleading account of the nature of stones and the process of kicking a stone. Ignoring Berkeley's conception of God entails another misunderstanding of his position and also leads to irrelevant objections. This last point has received its classical formulation in two limericks:

> There was a young man who said, "God
> Must think it exceedingly odd
>   If he finds that this tree
>   Continues to be
> When there's no one about in the Quad."

> Dear Sir: Your astonishment's odd:
>   *I* am always about in the Quad.
>   And that's why the tree
>   Will continue to be,
> Since observed by, Yours faithfully, God.

OF THE PRINCIPLES OF HUMAN KNOWLEDGE

It is evident to anyone who take a survey of the objects of human knowledge, that they are either ideas (1) actually imprinted on the senses, or else such as are (2) perceived by attending to the passions and operations of the mind, or lastly (3) ideas formed by help of memory and imagination, either compounding, dividing, or barely representing those originally perceived in the aforesaid ways. By sight I have the ideas of lights and colors, with their several degrees and variations. By touch I perceive hard and soft, heat and cold, motion and resistance, and of all these more and less either as to quantity or degree. Smelling furnishes me with odors, the palate with tastes, and hearing conveys sounds to the mind in all their variety of tone and composition. And as several of these are observed to accompany each other, they come to be marked by one name, and so to be reputed as one thing. Thus, for example, a certain color, taste, smell, figure, and consistence, having been observed to go together, are accounted one distinct thing, signified by the name 'apple.' Other collections of ideas constitute a stone, a tree, a book, and the like sensible things; which, as they are pleasing or disagreeable, excite the passions of love, hatred, joy, grief, and so forth.

2. But besides all that endless variety of ideas or objects of knowledge, there is likewise something which knows or perceives them, and exercises divers operations, as willing, imagining, remembering, about them. This perceiving, active being is what I call *mind, spirit, soul,* or *myself.* By which words I do not denote any one of my ideas, but a thing entirely distinct from them wherein they exist, or, which is the same thing, whereby they are perceived; for the existence of an idea consists in being perceived.

3. That neither our thoughts, nor passions, nor ideas formed by the imagination, exist without the mind, is what everybody will allow. And it seems no less evident that the various sensations or ideas imprinted on the sense, however blended or combined together (that is, whatever objects they compose), cannot exist otherwise than in a mind perceiving them. I think an intuitive knowledge may be obtained of this by anyone that shall attend to what is meant by the term 'exist' when applied to sensible things. The table I write on I say exists—that is, I see and feel it; and if I were out of my study I should say it existed—meaning thereby that if I was in my study I might perceive it, or that some other spirit actually does perceive it. There was an odor, that is, it was smelt; there was a sound, that is, it was heard; a color or figure, and it was perceived by sight or touch. This is all that I can understand by these and the like expressions. For as to what is said of the absolute existence of unthinking things without any relation to their being perceived that seems perfectly unintelligible. Their *esse* is *percipi,* nor is it possible they should have any existence out of the minds or thinking things which perceive them.

4. It is indeed an opinion strangely prevailing amongst men, that houses, mountains, rivers, and in a word all sensible objects, have an existence, natural or real, distinct from their being perceived by the understanding. But with how great an assurance and acquiescence soever this principle may be entertained in the world, yet whoever shall find in his heart to call it in question may, if I mistake not, perceive it to

involve a manifest contradiction. For what are the forementioned objects but the things we perceive by sense? and what do we perceive *besides our own ideas or sensations?* and is it not plainly repugnant that any one of these, or any combination of them, should exist unperceived?

5. If we thoroughly examine this tenet it will perhaps be found at bottom to depend on the doctrine of *abstract ideas.* For can there be a nicer strain of abstraction than to distinguish the existence of sensible objects from their being perceived, so as to conceive them existing unperceived? Light and colors, heat and cold, extension and figures—in a word the things we see and feel—what are they but so many sensations, notions, ideas, or impressions on the sense? And is it possible to separate, even in thought, any of these from perception? For my part, I might as easily divide a thing from itself. I may, indeed, divide in my thoughts, or conceive apart from each other, those things which perhaps I never perceived by sense so divided. Thus I imagine the trunk of a human body without the limbs, or conceive the smell of a rose without thinking on the rose itself. So far, I will not deny, I can abstract, if that may properly be called abstraction which extends only to the conceiving separately such objects as it is possible may really exist or be actually perceived asunder. But my conceiving or imagining power does not extend beyond the possibility of real existence or perception. Hence, as it is impossible for me to see or feel anything without an actual sensation of that thing, so it is impossible for me to conceive in my thoughts any sensible thing or object distinct from the sensation or perception of it.

6. Some truths there are so near and obvious to the mind that a man need only open his eyes to see them. Such I take this important one to be, to wit, that all the choir of heaven and furniture of the earth, in a word all those bodies which compose the mighty frame of the world, have not any subsistence without a mind, that their *being* is to be perceived or known; that consequently so long as they are not actually perceived by me, or do not exist in my mind or that of any other created spirit, they must either have no existence at all, or else subsist in the mind of some Eternal Spirit; it being perfectly unintelligible, and involving all the absurdity of abstraction, to attribute to any single part of them an existence independent of a spirit. To be convinced of which, the reader need only reflect and try to separate in his own thoughts the *being* of a sensible thing from its *being perceived.*

7. From what has been said it follows there is not any other substance than *spirit,* or that which perceives. But for the fuller proof of this point, let it be considered the sensible qualities are color, figure, motion, smell, taste, etc.—that is, the ideas perceived by sense. Now, for an idea to exist in an unperceiving thing is a manifest contradiction, for to have an idea is all one as to perceive; that therefore wherein color, figure, and the like qualities exist must perceive them; hence it is clear there can be no unthinking substance or *substratum* of those ideas.

8. But, say you, though the ideas themselves do not exist without the mind, yet there may be things *like* them, whereof they are copies or

resemblances, which things exist without the mind in an unthinking substance. I answer, an idea can be like nothing but an idea; a color or figure can be like nothing but another color or figure. If we look but never so little into our thoughts, we shall find it impossible for us to conceive a likeness except only between our ideas. Again, I ask whether those supposed originals or external things, of which our ideas are the pictures or representations, be themselves perceivable or no? If they are, then they are ideas and we have gained our point; but if you say they are not, I appeal to anyone whether it be sense to assert a color is like something which is invisible; hard or soft, like something which is intangible; and so of the rest.

9. Some there are who make a distinction betwixt *primary* and *secondary* qualities. By the former they mean extension, figure, motion, rest, solidity or impenetrability, and number; by the latter they denote all other sensible qualities, as colors, sounds, tastes, and so forth. The ideas we have of these they acknowledge not to be the resemblances of anything existing without the mind, or unperceived, but they will have our ideas of the primary qualities to be patterns or images of things which exist without the mind, in an unthinking substance which they call *matter*. By *matter*, therefore, we are to understand an inert, senseless substance, in which extension, figure, and motion do actually subsist. But it is evident from what we have already shown, that extension, figure, and motion are only ideas existing in the mind, and that an idea can be like nothing but another idea, and that consequently neither they nor their archetypes can exist in an unperceiving substance. Hence, it is plain that the very notion of what is called *matter*, or *corporeal substance*, involves a contradiction in it.

10. They who assert that figure, motion, and the rest of the primary or original qualities do exist without the mind in unthinking substances, do at the same time acknowledge that color, sounds, heat, cold, and such-like secondary qualities, do not; which they tell us are sensations existing in the mind alone, that depend on and are occasioned by the different size, texture, and motion of the minute particles of matter. This they take for an undoubted truth, which they can demonstrate beyond all exception. Now, if it be certain that those original qualities are inseparably united with the other sensible qualities, and not, even in thought, capable of being abstracted from them, it plainly follows that they exist only in the mind. But I desire anyone to reflect and try whether he can, by any abstraction of thought, conceive the extension and motion of a body without all other sensible qualities. For my own part, I see evidently that it is not in my power to frame an idea of a body extended and moving, but I must withal give it some color or other sensible quality which is acknowledged to exist only in the mind. In short, extension, figure, and motion, abstracted from all other qualities, are inconceivable. Where therefore the other sensible qualities are, there must these be also, to wit, in the mind and nowhere else.

11. Again, *great* and *small, swift* and *slow,* are allowed to exist no-where without the mind, being entirely relative, and changing as the frame or position of the organs of sense varies. The extension therefore which exists without the mind is neither great nor small, the motion neither swift nor slow, that is, they are nothing at all. But, say you, they are extension in general, and motion in general: thus we see how much the tenet of extended movable substances existing without the mind depends on the strange doctrine of *abstract ideas.* And here I can-not but remark how nearly the vague and indeterminate description of matter or corporeal substance, which the modern philosophers are run into by their own principles, resembles that antiquated and so much rid-iculed notion of *materia prima,* to be met with in Aristotle and his fol-lowers. Without extension solidity cannot be conceived; since therefore it has been shewn that extension exists not in an unthinking substance, the same must also be true of solidity.

12. That *number* is entirely the creature of the mind, even though the other qualities be allowed to exist without, will be evident to whoever considers that the same thing bears a different denomination of number as the mind views it with different respects. Thus, the same extension is one, or three, or thirty-six, according as the mind considers it with reference to a yard, a foot, or an inch. Number is so visibly relative, and dependent on men's understanding, that it is strange to think how anyone should give it an absolute existence without the mind. We say one book, one page, one line; all these are equally units, though some contain several of the others. And in each instance, it is plain, the unit relates to some particular combination of ideas arbitrarily put together by the mind.

13. *Unity,* I know, some will have to be a simple or uncompounded idea, accompanying all other ideas into the mind. That I have any such idea answering the word 'unity' I do not find; and if I had, methinks I could not miss finding it: on the contrary, it should be the most familiar to my understanding, since it is said to accompany all other ideas, and to be perceived by all the ways of sensation and reflection. To say no more, it is an *abstract idea.*

14. I shall farther add that, after the same manner as modern philoso-phers prove certain sensible qualities to have no existence in matter, or without the mind, the same thing may be likewise proved of all other sensible qualities whatsoever. Thus, for instance, it is said that heat and cold are affections only of the mind, and not at all patterns of real be-ings, existing in the corporeal substances which excite them, for that the same body which appears cold to one hand seems warm to another. Now, why may we not as well argue that figure and extension are not patterns or resemblances of qualities existing in matter, because to the same eye at different stations, or eyes of a different texture at the same station, they appear various, and cannot therefore be the images of any-thing settled and determinate without the mind? Again, it is proved that sweetness is not really in the sapid thing, because the thing remaining unaltered the sweetness is changed into bitter, as in case of a fever or

otherwise vitiated palate. Is it not as reasonable to say that motion is not without the mind, since if the succession of ideas in the mind become swifter, the motion, it is acknowledged, shall appear slower without any alteration in any external object?

15. In short, let anyone consider those arguments which are thought manifestly to prove that colors and tastes exist only in the mind, and he shall find they may with equal force be brought to prove the same thing of extension, figure, and motion—though it must be confessed this method of arguing does not so much prove that there is no extension or color in an outward object, as that we do not know by sense which is the true extension or color of the object. But the arguments foregoing plainly show it to be impossible that any color or extension at all, or other sensible quality whatsoever, should exist in an unthinking subject without the mind, or in truth, that there should be any such thing as an outward object.

16. But let us examine a little the received opinion. It is said extension is a mode or accident of matter, and that matter is the *substratum* that supports it. Now I desire that you would explain to me what is meant by matter's *supporting* extension. Say you, I have no idea of matter and therefore cannot explain it. I answer, though you have no positive, yet, if you have any meaning at all, you must at least have a relative idea of matter; though you know not what it is, yet you must be supposed to know what relation it bears to accidents, and what is meant by its supporting them. It is evident 'support' cannot here be taken in its usual or literal sense—as when we say that pillars support a building; in what sense therefore must it be taken?

17. If we inquire into what the most accurate philosophers declare themselves to mean by *material substance*, we shall find them acknowledge they have no other meaning annexed to those sounds but the idea of *Being in general,* together with the relative notion of its supporting accidents. The general idea of Being appeareth to me the most abstract and incomprehensible of all other; and as for its supporting accidents, this, as we have just now observed, cannot be understood in the common sense of those words; it must therefore be taken in some other sense, but what that is they do not explain. So that when I consider the two parts or branches which make the signification of the words *material substance,* I am convinced there is no distinct meaning annexed to them. But why should we trouble ourselves any farther, in discussing this material *substratum* or support of figure and motion, and other sensible qualities? Does it not suppose they have an existence without the mind? And is not this a direct repugnancy, and altogether inconceivable?

18. But though it were possible that solid, figured, movable substances may exist without the mind, corresponding to the ideas we have of bodies, yet how is it possible for us to know this? Either we must know it by sense or by reason. As for our senses, by them we have the knowledge only of our sensations, ideas, or those things that are immediately perceived by sense, call them what you will; but they do not inform us

that things exist without the mind, or unperceived, like to those which are perceived. This the materialists themselves acknowledge. It remains therefore that if we have any knowledge at all of external things, it must be by reason, inferring their existence from what is immediately perceived by sense. But what reason can induce us to believe the existence of bodies without the mind, from what we perceive, since the very patrons of matter themselves do not pretend there is any necessary con nection betwixt them and our ideas? I say it is granted on all hands (and what happens in dreams, frenzies, and the like, puts it beyond dispute) that *it is possible we might be affected with all the ideas we have now, though there were no bodies existing without, resembling them.* Hence, it is evident the supposition of external bodies is not necessary for the producing our ideas; since it is granted they are produced sometimes, and might possibly be produced always in the same order we see them in at present, without their concurrence.

19. But, though we might possibly have all our sensations without them, yet perhaps it may be thought easier to conceive and explain the manner of their production by supposing external bodies in their likeness rather than otherwise; and so it might be at least probable there are such things as bodies that excite their ideas in our minds. But neither can this be said; for though we give the materialists their external bodies, they by their own confession are never the nearer knowing how our ideas are produced, since they own themselves unable to comprehend in what manner body can act upon spirit, or how it is possible it should imprint any idea in the mind. Hence it is evident the production of ideas or sensations in our minds can be no reason why we should suppose matter or corporeal substances, since that is acknowledged to remain equally inexplicable with or without this supposition. If therefore it were possible for bodies to exist without the mind, yet to hold they do so, must needs be a very precarious opinion; since it is to suppose, without any reason at all, that God has created innumerable beings that are entirely useless, and serve to no manner of purpose.

20. In short, if there were external bodies, it is impossible we should ever come to know it; and if there were not, we might have the very same reasons to think there were that we have now. Suppose (what no one can deny possible) an intelligence without the help of external bodies, to be affected with the same train of sensations or ideas that you are, imprinted in the same order and with like vividness in his mind. I ask whether that intelligence hath not all the reason to believe the existence of corporeal substances, represented by his ideas, and exciting them in his mind, that you can possibly have for believing the same thing? Of this there can be no question; which one consideration were enough to make any reasonable person suspect the strength of whatever arguments he may think himself to have for the existence of bodies without the mind.

21. Were it necessary to add any farther proof against the existence of matter after what has been said, I could instance several of those errors

and difficulties (not to mention impieties) which have sprung from that tenet. It has occasioned numberless controversies and disputes in philosophy, and not a few of far greater moment in religion. But I shall not enter into the detail of them in this place, as well because I think arguments *a posteriori* are unnecessary for confirming what has been, if I mistake not, sufficiently demonstrated *a priori*, as because I shall hereafter find occasion to speak somewhat of them.

22. I am afraid I have given cause to think I am needlessly prolix in handling this subject. For, to what purpose is it to dilate on that which may be demonstrated with the utmost evidence in a line or two, to anyone that is capable of the least reflection? It is but looking into your own thoughts, and so trying whether you can conceive it possible for a sound, or figure, or motion, or color to exist without the mind or unperceived. This easy trial may perhaps make you see that what you contend for is a downright contradiction. Insomuch that I am content to put the whole upon this issue: if you can but conceive it possible for one extended movable substance, or, in general, for any one idea, or anything like an idea, to exist otherwise than in a mind perceiving it, I shall readily give up the cause; and, as for all that compages of external bodies you contend for, I shall grant you its existence, though you cannot either give me any reason why you believe it exists, or assign any use to it when it is supposed to exist. I say, the bare possibility of your opinion's being true shall pass for an argument that it is so.

23. But, say you, surely there is nothing easier than for me to imagine trees, for instance, in a park, or books existing in a closet, and nobody by to perceive them. I answer, you may so, there is no difficulty in it; but what is all this, I beseech you, more than framing in your mind certain ideas which you call books and trees, and the same time omitting to frame the idea of anyone that may perceive them? But do not you yourself perceive or think of them all the while? This therefore is nothing to the purpose; it only shews you have the power of imagining or forming ideas in your mind: but it doth not shew that you can conceive it possible the objects of your thought may exist without the mind. To make out this, it is necessary that you conceive them existing unconceived or unthought of, which is a manifest repugnancy. When we do our utmost to conceive the existence of external bodies, we are all the while only contemplating our own ideas. But the mind taking no notice of itself, is deluded to think it can and doth conceive bodies existing unthought of or without the mind, though at the same time they are apprehended by or exist in itself. A little attention will discover to anyone the truth and evidence of what is here said, and make it unnecessary to insist on any other proofs against the existence of *material substance*.

24. It is very obvious, upon the least inquiry into our thoughts, to know whether it is possible for us to understand what is meant by the *absolute existence of sensible objects in themselves, or without the mind.* To me it is evident those words mark out either a direct contradiction, or else nothing at all. And to convince others of this, I know no readier

or fairer way than to entreat they would calmly attend to their own thoughts; and if by this attention the emptiness or repugnancy of those expressions doth appear, surely nothing more is requisite for the conviction. It is on this therefore that I insist, to wit, that the absolute existence of unthinking things are words without a meaning, or which include a contradiction. This is what I repeat and inculcate, and earnestly recommend to the attentive thoughts of the reader.

25. All our ideas, sensations, notions, or the things which we perceive, by whatsoever names they may be distinguished, are visibly inactive: there is nothing of power or agency included in them. So that one idea or object of thought cannot produce or make any alteration in another. To be satisfied of the truth of this, there is nothing else requisite but a bare observation of our ideas. For, since they and every part of them exist only in the mind, it follows that there is nothing in them but what is perceived: but whoever shall attend to his ideas, whether of sense or reflection, will not perceive in them any power or activity; there is, therefore, no such thing contained in them. A little attention will discover to us that the very being of an idea implies passiveness and inertness in it, insomuch that it is impossible for an idea to do anything, or, strictly speaking, to be the cause of anything: neither can it be the resemblance or pattern of any active being, as is evident from Sec. 8. Whence it plainly follows that extension, figure, and motion cannot be the cause of our sensations. To say, therefore, that these are the effects of powers resulting from the configuration, number, motion, and size of corpuscles, must certainly be false.

26. We perceive a continual succession of ideas, some are anew excited, others are changed or totally disappear. There is therefore some cause of these ideas, whereon they depend, and which produces and changes them. That this cause cannot be any quality or idea or combination of ideas, is clear from the preceding section. It must therefore be a substance; but it has been shewn that there is no corporeal or material substance: it remains therefore that the cause of ideas is an incorporeal active substance or Spirit.

27. A spirit is one simple, undivided, active being: as it perceives ideas it is called the *understanding*, and as it produces or otherwise operates about them it is called the *will*. Hence there can be no *idea* formed of a soul or spirit; for all ideas whatever, being passive and inert (*vide* Sec. 25), they cannot represent unto us, by way of image or likeness, that which acts. A little attention will make it plain to anyone, that to have an idea which shall be like that active principle of motion and change of ideas is absolutely impossible. Such is the nature of *spirit*, or that which acts, that it cannot be of itself perceived, but only by the effects which it produceth. If any man shall doubt of the truth of what is here delivered, let him but reflect and try if he can frame the idea of any power or active being, and whether he hath ideas of two principal powers, marked by the names *will* and *understanding*, distinct from each other as well as from a third idea of substance or being in

general, with a relative notion of its supporting or being the subject of the aforesaid powers—which is signified by the name *soul* or *spirit*. This is what some hold; but, so far as I can see, the words *will, soul, spirit,* do not stand for different ideas, or, in truth, for any idea at all, but for something which is very different from ideas, and which, being an agent, cannot be like unto, or represented by, any idea whatsoever. Though it must be owned at the same time that we have some *notion* of soul, spirit, and the operations of the mind such as willing, loving, hating; inasmuch as we know or understand the meaning of these words.

28. I find I can excite ideas in my mind at pleasure, and vary and shift the scene as oft as I think fit. It is no more than willing, and straightway this or that idea arises in my fancy; and by the same power it is obliterated and makes way for another. This making and unmaking of ideas doth very properly denominate the mind active. Thus much is certain and grounded on experience; but when we think of unthinking agents or of exciting ideas exclusive of volition, we only amuse ourselves with words.

29. But, whatever power I may have over my own thoughts, I find the ideas actually perceived by sense have not a like dependence on my will. When in broad daylight I open my eyes, it is not in my power to choose whether I shall see or no, or to determine what particular objects shall present themselves to my view; and so likewise as to the hearing and other senses, the ideas imprinted on them are not creatures of my will. There is therefore some other will or spirit that produces them.

30. The ideas of sense are more strong, lively, and distinct than those of the imagination; they have likewise a steadiness, order, and coherence, and are not excited at random, as those which are the effects of human wills often are, but in a regular train or series, the admirable connection whereof sufficiently testifies the wisdom and benevolence of its Author. Now the set rules or established methods wherein the mind we depend on excites in us the ideas of sense, are called the *laws of nature;* and these we learn by experience, which teaches us that such and such ideas are attended with such and such other ideas, in the ordinary course of things.

31. This gives us a sort of foresight which enables us to regulate our actions for the benefit of life. And without this we should be eternally at a loss: we could not know how to act anything that might procure us the least pleasure, or remove the least pain of sense. That food nourishes, sleep refreshes, and fire warms us; that to sow in the seed-time is the way to reap in the harvest; and, in general, that to obtain such or such ends, such or such means are conducive—all this we know, not by discovering any necessary connection between our ideas, but only by the observation of the settled laws of nature, without which we should be all in uncertainty and confusion, and a grown man no more know how to manage himself in the affairs of life than an infant just born.

32. And yet this insistent uniform working, which so evidently displays the goodness and wisdom of that governing Spirit whose will con-

stitutes the laws of nature, is so far from leading our thoughts to Him, that it rather sends them wandering after second causes. For, when we perceive certain ideas of sense constantly followed by other ideas and we know this is not of our own doing, we forthwith attribute power and agency to the ideas themselves, and make one the cause of another, than which nothing can be more absurd and unintelligible. Thus, for example, having observed that when we perceive by sight a certain round luminous figure we at the same time perceive by touch the idea or sensation called heat, we do from thence conclude the sun to be the cause of heat. And in like manner perceiving the motion and collision of bodies to be attended with sound, we are inclined to think the latter the effect of the former.

33. The ideas imprinted on the senses by the Author of nature are called *real things;* and those excited in the imagination, being less regular, vivid, and constant, are more properly termed *ideas,* or *images* of *things,* which they copy and represent. But then our sensations, be they never so vivid and distinct, are nevertheless ideas, that is, they exist in the mind, or are perceived by it, as truly as the ideas of its own framing. The ideas of sense are allowed to have more reality in them, that is, to be more strong, orderly, and coherent than the creatures of the mind; but this is no argument that they exist without the mind. They are also less dependent on the spirit, or thinking substance which perceives them, in that they are excited by the will of another and more powerful spirit; yet still they are *ideas,* and certainly no idea, whether faint or strong, can exist otherwise than in a mind perceiving it.

34.   Before we proceed any farther it is necessary we spend some time in answering objections which may probably be made against the principles we have hitherto laid down. In doing of which, if I seem too prolix to those of quick apprehensions, I hope it may be pardoned, since all men do not equally apprehend things of this nature, and I am willing to be understood by everyone.

First, then, it will be objected that by the foregoing principles all that is real and substantial in nature is banished out of the world, and instead thereof a chimerical scheme of *ideas* takes place. All things that exist, exist only in the mind, that is, they are purely notional. What therefore becomes of the sun, moon, and stars? What must we think of houses, rivers, mountains, trees, stones; nay, even of our own bodies? Are all these but so many chimeras and illusions on the fancy? To all which, and whatever else of the same sort may be objected, I answer that by the principles premised we are not deprived of any one thing in nature. Whatever we see, feel, hear, or anywise conceive or understand remains as secure as ever, and is as real as ever. There is a *rerum natura,* and the distinction between realities and chimeras retains its full force. This is evident from Sec. 29, 30, and 33, where we have shewn what is meant by *real things* in opposition to *chimeras* or ideas of our own framing; but then they both equally exist in the mind, and in that sense they are alike *ideas.*

35. I do not argue against the existence of any one thing that we can apprehend either by sense or reflection. That the things I see with my eyes and touch with my hands do exist, really exist, I make not the least question. The only thing whose existence we deny is that which *philosophers* call matter or corporeal substance. And in doing of this there is no damage done to the rest of mankind, who, I dare say, will never miss it. The atheist indeed will want the color of an empty name to support his impiety; and the philosophers may possibly find they have lost a great handle for trifling and disputation.

36. If any man thinks this detracts from the existence or reality of things, he is very far from understanding what hath been premised in the plainest terms I could think of. Take here an abstract of what has been said. There are spiritual substances, minds, or human souls, which will or excite ideas in themselves at pleasure; but these are faint, weak, and unsteady in respect of others they perceive by sense—which, being impressed upon them according to certain rules or laws of nature, speak themselves the effects of a mind more powerful and wise than human spirits. These latter are said to have more *reality* in them than the former; by which is meant that they are more affecting, orderly, and distinct, and that they are not fictions of the mind perceiving them. And in this sense the sun that I see by day is the real sun, and that which I imagine by night is the idea of the former. In the sense here given of 'reality' it is evident that every vegetable, star, mineral, and in general each part of the mundane system, is as much as a real being by our principles as by any other. Whether others mean anything by the term 'reality' different from what I do, I entreat them to look into their own thoughts and see.

37. It will be urged that thus much at least is true, to wit, that we take away all corporeal substances. To this my answer is that if the word 'substance' be taken in the vulgar sense—for a combination of sensible qualities, such as extension, solidity, weight, and the like—this we cannot be accused of taking away. But if it be taken in a philosophic sense—for the support of accidents or qualities without the mind—then indeed I acknowledge that we take it away, if one may be said to take away that which never had any existence, not even in the imagination.

38. But after all, say you, it sounds very harsh to say we eat and drink ideas, and are clothed with ideas. I acknowledge it does so; the word 'idea' not being used in common discourse to signify the several combinations of sensible qualities which are called 'things'; and it is certain that any expression which varies from the familiar use of language will seem harsh and ridiculous. But this doth not concern the truth of the proposition, which in other words is no more than to say, we are fed and clothed with those things which we perceive immediately by our senses. The hardness or softness, the color, taste, warmth, figure, or suchlike qualities, which combined together constitute the several sorts of victuals and apparel, have been shewn to exist only in the mind that perceives them; and this is all that is meant by calling them 'ideas';

which word if it was as ordinarily used as 'things,' would sound no harsher nor more ridiculous than it. I am not for disputing about the propriety, but the truth of the expression. If therefore you agree with me that we eat and drink and are clad with the immediate objects of sense, which cannot exist unperceived or without the mind, I shall readily grant it is more proper or conformable to custom that they should be called things rather than ideas.

39. If it be demanded why I make use of the word 'idea,' and do not rather in compliance with custom call them 'thing'; I answer, I do it for two reasons:—first, because the term 'thing' in contradistinction to 'idea,' is generally supposed to denote somewhat existing without the mind; secondly, because 'thing' hath a more comprehensive signification than 'idea,' including spirit or thinking things as well as ideas. Since therefore the objects of sense exist only in the mind, and are withal thoughtless and inactive, I chose to mark them by the word 'idea,' which implies those properties.

40. But, say what we can, someone perhaps may be apt to reply, he will still believe his senses, and never suffer any arguments, how plausible soever, to prevail over the certainty of them. Be it so; assert the evidence of sense as high as you please, we are willing to do the same. That what I see, hear, and feel doth exist, that is to say, is perceived by me, I no more doubt than I do of my own being. But I do not see how the testimony of sense can be alleged as a proof for the existence of anything which is not perceived by sense. We are not for having any man turn sceptic and disbelieve his senses; on the contrary, we give them all the stress and assurance imaginable; nor are there any principles more opposite to scepticism than those we have laid down, as shall be hereafter clearly shewn.

41. *Secondly*, it will be objected that there is a great difference betwixt real fire for instance, and the idea of fire, betwixt dreaming or imagining oneself burnt, and actually being so: if you suspect it to be only the idea of fire which you see, do but put your hand into it and you will be convinced with a witness. This and the like may be urged in opposition to our tenets. To all which the answer is evident from what hath been already said; and I shall only add in this place, that if real fire be very different from the idea of fire, so also is the real pain that it occasions very different from the idea of the same pain, and yet nobody will pretend that real pain either is, or can possibly be, in an unperceiving thing, or without the mind, any more than its idea.

42. *Thirdly*, it will be objected that we see things actually without or at distance from us, and which consequently do not exist in the mind; it being absurd that those things which are seen at the distance of several miles should be as near to us as our own thoughts. In answer to this, I desire it may be considered that in a dream we do oft perceive things as existing at a great distance off, and yet for all that, those things are acknowledged to have their existence only in the mind.

43. But, for the fuller clearing of this point, it may be worth while to

consider how it is that we perceive distance and things placed at a distance by sight. For, that we should in truth see external space, and bodies actually existing in it, some nearer, others farther off, seems to carry with it some opposition to what hath been said of their existing nowhere without the mind. The consideration of this difficulty it was that gave birth to my *Essay towards a New Theory of Vision,* which was published not long since, wherein it is shewn that distance or outness is neither immediately of itself perceived by sight, nor yet apprehended or judged of by lines and angles, or anything that hath a necessary connection with it; but that it is only suggested to our thoughts by certain visible ideas and sensations attending vision, which in their own nature have no manner of similitude or relation either with distance or things placed at a distance; but, by a connection taught us by experience, they come to signify and suggest them to us, after the same manner that words of any language suggest the ideas they are made to stand for; insomuch that a man born blind and afterwards made to see, would not, at first sight, think the things he saw to be without his mind, or at any distance from him. (See Sec. 41 of the forementioned treatise.)

44. The ideas of sight and touch make two species entirely distinct and heterogeneous. *The former are marks and prognostics of the latter.* That the proper objects of sight neither exist without mind, nor are the images of external things, was shewn even in that treatise; though throughout the same the contrary be supposed true of tangible objects— not that to suppose that vulgar error was necessary for establishing the notion therein laid down, but because it was beside my purpose to examine and refute it in a discourse concerning *vision.* So that in strict truth the ideas of sight, when we apprehend by them distance and things placed at a distance, do not suggest or mark out to us things actually existing at a distance, but only admonish us what ideas of touch will be imprinted in our minds at such and such distances of time, and in consequence of such or such actions. It is, I say, evident from what has been said in the foregoing parts of this treatise, and in Sec. 147 and elsewhere of the essay concerning vision, that visible ideas are the language whereby the governing Spirit on whom we depend informs us what tangible ideas he is about to imprint upon us, in case we excite this or that motion in our own bodies. But for a fuller information in this point I refer to the essay itself.

45. *Fourthly,* it will be objected that from the foregoing principles it follows things are every moment annihilated and created anew. The objects of sense exist only when they are perceived; the trees therefore are in the garden, or the chairs in the parlor, no longer than while there is somebody by to perceive them. Upon shutting my eyes all the furniture in the room is reduced to nothing, and barely upon opening them it is again created. In answer to all which, I refer the reader to what has been said in Sec. 3, 4, etc., and desire he will consider whether he means anything by the actual existence of an idea distinct from its being perceived. For my part, after the nicest inquiry I could make, I am not

able to discover that anything else is meant by those words; and I once more entreat the reader to sound his own thoughts, and not suffer himself to be imposed on by words. If he can conceive it possible either for his ideas or their archetypes to exist without being perceived, then I give up the cause; but if he cannot, he will acknowledge it is unreasonable for him to stand up in defense of he knows not what, and pretend to charge on me as an absurdity the not assenting to those propositions which at bottom have no meaning in them.

46. It will not be amiss to observe how far the received principles of philosophy are themselves chargeable with those pretended absurdities. It is thought strangely absurd that upon closing my eyelids all the visible objects around me should be reduced to nothing; and yet is not this what philosophers commonly acknowledge, when they agree on all hands that light and colors, which alone are the proper and immediate objects of sight, are mere sensations that exist no longer than they are perceived? Again, it may to some perhaps seem very incredible that things should be every moment creating, yet this very notion is commonly taught in the schools. For the schoolmen, though they acknowledge the existence of matter, and that the whole mundane fabric is framed out of it, are nevertheless of opinion that it cannot subsist without the divine conservation, which by them is expounded to be a continual creation.

47. Farther, a little thought will discover to us that though we allow the existence of matter or corporeal substance, yet it will unavoidably follow, from the principles which are now generally admitted, that the particular bodies, of what kind soever, do none of them exist whilst they are not perceived. For, it is evident from Sec. 11 and the following sections, that the matter philosophers contend for is an incomprehensible somewhat, which hath none of those particular qualities whereby the bodies falling under our senses are distinguished one from another. But, to make this more plain, it must be remarked that the infinite divisibility of matter is now universally allowed, at least by the most approved and considerable philosophers, who on the received principles demonstrate it beyond all exception. Hence, it follows there is an infinite number of parts in each particle of matter which are not perceived by sense. The reason therefore that any particular body seems to be of a finite magnitude, or exhibits only a finite number of parts to sense, is, not because it contains no more, since in itself it contains an infinite number of parts, but because the sense is not acute enough to discern them. In proportion therefore as the sense is rendered more acute, it perceives a greater number of parts in the object, that is, the object appears greater, and its figure varies, those parts in its extremities which were before unperceivable appearing now to bound it in very different lines and angles from those perceived by an obtuser sense. And at length, after various changes of size and shape, when the sense becomes infinitely acute the body shall seem infinite. During all which there is no alteration in the body, but only in the sense. Each body therefore, considered in itself, is infinitely extended, and consequently void of all

shape or figure. From which it follows that, though we should grant the existence of matter to be never so certain, yet it is withal as certain, the materialists themselves are by their own principles forced to acknowledge, that neither the particular bodies perceived by sense, nor anything like them, exists without the mind. Matter, I say, and each particle thereof, is according to them infinite and shapeless, and it is the mind that frames all that variety of bodies which compose the visible world, anyone whereof does not exist longer than it is perceived.

48. If we consider it, the objection proposed in Sec. 45 will not be found reasonably charged on the principles we have premised, so as in truth to make any objection at all against our notions. For, though we hold indeed the objects of sense to be nothing else but ideas which cannot exist unperceived; yet we may not hence conclude they have no existence except only while they are perceived by us, since there may be some other spirit that perceives them though we do not. Wherever bodies are said to have no existence without the mind, I would not be understood to mean this or that particular mind, but all minds whatsoever. It does not therefore follow from the foregoing principles that bodies are annihilated and created every moment, or exist not at all during the intervals between our perception of them.

49. *Fifthly*, it may perhaps be objected that if extension and figure exist only in the mind, it follows that the mind is extended and figured; since extension is a mode or attribute which (to speak with the schools) is predicted of the subject in which it exists. I answer, those qualities are in the mind only as they are perceived by it—that is, not by way of *mode* or *attribute*, but only by way of *idea;* and it no more follows the soul or mind is extended, because extension exists in it alone, than it does that it is red or blue, because those colors are on all hands acknowledged to exist in it, and nowhere else. As to what philosophers say of subject and mode, that seems very groundless and unintelligible. For instance, in this proposition, "a die is hard, extended, and square," they will have it that the word 'die' denotes a subject or substance, distinct from the hardness, extension, and figure which are predicated of it, and in which they exist. This I cannot comprehend: to me a die seems to be nothing distinct from those things which are termed its modes or accidents. And, to say a die is hard, extended, and square is not to attribute those qualities to a subject distinct from and supporting them, but only an explication of the meaning of the word 'die.'

50. *Sixthly*, you will say there have been a great many things explained by matter and motion; take away these and you destroy the whole corpuscular philosophy, and undermine those mechanical principles which have been applied with so much success to account for the phenomena. In short, whatever advances have been made, either by accident or modern philosophers, in the study of nature do all proceed on the supposition that corporeal substance or matter doth really exist. To this I answer that there is not any one phenomenon explained on that supposition which may not as well be explained without it, as might

easily be made appear by an induction of particulars. To explain the phenomena, is all one as to shew why, upon such and such occasions, we are affected with such and such ideas. But how matter should operate on a spirit, or produce any idea in it, is what no philosopher will pretend to explain; it is therefore evident there can be no use of matter in natural philosophy. Besides, they who attempt to account for things do it not by corporeal substance, but by figure, motion, and other qualities, which are in truth no more than mere ideas, and, therefore, cannot be the cause of anything, as hath been already shewn. (See Sec. 25).

51. *Seventhly,* it will upon this be demanded whether it does not seem absurd to take away natural causes, and ascribe everything to the immediate operation of spirits? We must no longer say upon these principles that fire heats, or water cools, but that a spirit heats, and so forth. Would not a man be deservedly laughed at, who should talk after this manner? I answer, he would so; in such things we ought to 'think with the learned, and speak with the vulgar.' They who to demonstration are convinced of the truth of the Copernican system do nevertheless say, "The sun rises," "The sun sets," or "comes to the meridian"; and if they affected a contrary style in common talk it would without doubt appear very ridiculous. A little reflection on what is here said will make it manifest that the common use of language would receive no manner of alteration or disturbance from the admission of our tenets.

52. In the ordinary affairs of life, any phrases may be retained, so long as they excite in us proper sentiments, or dispositions to act in such a manner as is necessary for our well-being, how false soever they may be if taken in a strict and speculative sense. Nay, this is unavoidable, since, propriety being regulated by custom, language is suited to the received opinions, which are not always the truest. Hence it is impossible, even in the most rigid, philosophic reasonings, so far to alter the bent and genius of the tongue we speak, as never to give a handle for cavilers to pretend difficulties and inconsistencies. But, a fair and ingenuous reader will collect the sense from the scope and tenor and connection of a discourse, making allowances for those inaccurate modes of speech which use has made inevitable.

53. As to the opinion that there are no corporeal causes, this has been heretofore maintained by some of the schoolmen, as it is of late by others among the modern philosophers, who though they allow matter to exist, yet will have God alone to be the immediate efficient cause of all things. These men saw that amongst all the objects of sense there was none which had any power or activity included in it; and that by consequence this was likewise true of whatever bodies they supposed to exist without the mind, like unto the immediate objects of sense. But then, that they should suppose an innumerable multitude of created beings, which they acknowledge are not capable of producing any one effect in nature, and which therefore are made to no manner of purpose, since God might have done everything as well without them: this I say,

though we should allow it possible, must yet be a very unaccountable and extravagant supposition.

54. In the *eighth* place, the universal concurrent assent of mankind may be thought by some an invincible argument in behalf of matter, or the existence of external things. Must we suppose the whole world to be mistaken? And if so, what cause can be assigned of so widespread and predominant an error? I answer, first, that, upon a narrow inquiry, it will not perhaps be found so many as is imagined do really believe the existence of matter or things without the mind. Strictly speaking, to believe that which involves a contradiction, or has no meaning in it, is impossible; and whether the foregoing expressions are not of that sort, I refer it to the impartial examination of the reader. In one sense, indeed, men may be said to believe that matter exists, that is, they *act* as if the immediate cause of their sensations, which affects them every moment, and is so nearly present to them, were some senseless unthinking being. But, that they should clearly apprehend any meaning marked by those words, and form thereof a settled speculative opinion, is what I am not able to conceive. This is not the only instance wherein men impose upon themselves, by imagining they believe those propositions which they have often heard, though at bottom they have no meaning in them.

55. But secondly, though we should grant a notion to be never so universally and steadfastly adhered to, yet this is weak argument of its truth to whoever considers what a vast number of prejudices and false opinions are everywhere embraced with the utmost tenaciousness, by the unreflecting (which are the far greater) part of mankind. There was a time when the antipodes and motion of the earth were looked upon as monstrous absurdities even by men of learning: and if it be considered what a small proportion they bear to the rest of mankind, we shall find that at this day those notions have gained but a very inconsiderable footing in the world.

56. But it is demanded that we assign a cause of this prejudice, and account for its obtaining in the world. To this I answer, that men knowing they perceived several ideas, whereof they themselves were not the authors (as not being excited from within nor depending on the operation of their wills) this made them maintain those ideas, or objects of perception had an existence independent of and without the mind, without ever dreaming that a contradiction was involved in those words. But philosophers having plainly seen that the immediate objects of perception do not exist without the mind, they in some degree corrected the mistake of the vulgar; but at the same time run into another which seems no less absurd, to wit, that there are certain objects really existing without the mind, or having a subsistence distinct from being perceived, of which our ideas are only images or resemblances, imprinted by those objects on the mind. And this notion of the philosophers owes its origin to the same cause with the former, namely, their being conscious that they were not the authors of their own sensations, which they evidently

knew were imprinted from without, and which therefore must have some cause distinct from the minds on which they are imprinted.

57. But why they should suppose the ideas of sense to be excited in us by things in their likeness, and not rather have recourse to *spirit*, which alone can act, may be accounted for, first, because they were not aware of the repugnancy there is, as well in supposing things like unto our ideas existing without, as in attributing to them power or activity. Secondly, because the Supreme Spirit, which excites those ideas in our minds, is not marked out and limited to our view by any particular finite collection of sensible ideas, as human agents are by their size, complexion, limbs, and motions. And thirdly, because His operations are regular and uniform. Whenever the course of nature is interrupted by a miracle, men are ready to own the presence of a superior agent. But, when we see things go on in the ordinary course they do not excite in us any reflection; their order and concatenation, though it be an argument of the greatest wisdom, power, and goodness in their creator, is yet so constant and familiar to us that we do not think them the immediate effects of a free spirit; especially since inconsistency and mutability in acting, though it be an imperfection, is looked on as a mark of freedom.

58. *Tenthly*, it will be objected that the notions we advance are inconsistent with several sound truths in philosophy and mathematics. For example, the motion of the earth is now universally admitted by astronomers as a truth grounded on the clearest and most convincing reasons. But, on the foregoing principles, there can be no such thing. For, motion being only an idea, it follows that if it be not perceived it exists not; but the motion of the earth is not perceived by sense. I answer, that tenet, if rightly understood, will be found to agree with the principles we have premised; for, the question whether the earth moves or no amounts in reality to no more than this, to wit, whether we have reason to conclude, from what has been observed by astronomers, that if we were placed in such and such circumstances, and such or such a position and distance both from the earth and sun, we should perceive the former to move among the choir of the planets, and appearing in all respects like one of them; and this, by the established rules of nature which we have no reason to mistrust, is reasonably collected from the phenomena.

59. We may, from the experience we have had of the train and succession of ideas in our minds, often make, I will not say uncertain conjectures, but sure and well-grounded predictions concerning the ideas we shall be affected with pursuant to a great train of actions, and be enabled to pass a right judgment of what would have appeared to us, in case we were placed in circumstances very different from those we are in at present. Herein consists the knowledge of nature, which may preserve its use and certainty very consistently with what hath been said. It will be easy to apply this to whatever objections of the like sort may be drawn from the magnitude of the stars, or any other discoveries in astronomy or nature.

60. In the *eleventh* place, it will be demanded to what purpose serves

that curious organization of plants, and the animal mechanism in the parts of animals: might not vegetables grow, and shoot forth leaves of blossoms, and animals perform all their motions as well without as with all that variety of internal parts so elegantly contrived and put together, which, being ideas, have nothing powerful or operative in them, nor have any necessary connection with the effects ascribed to them? If it be a spirit that imediately produces every effect by a *fiat* or act of His will, we must think all that is fine and artificial in the works, whether of man or nature, to be made in vain. By this doctrine, though an artist hath made the spring and wheels, and every movement of a watch, and adjusted them in such a manner as he knew would produce the motions he designed, yet he must think all this done to no purpose, and that it is an Intelligence which directs the index, and points to the hour of the day. If so, why may not the Intelligence do it, without his being at the pains of making the movements and putting them together? Why does not an empty case serve as well as another? And how comes it to pass that whenever there is any fault in the going of a watch, there is some corresponding disorder to be found in the movements, which being mended by a skillful hand all is right again? The like may be said of all the clockwork of nature, great part whereof is so wonderfully fine and subtle as scarce to be discerned by the best microscope. In short, it will be asked, how, upon our principles, any tolerable account can be given, or any final cause assigned of an innumerable multitude of bodies and machines, framed with the most exquisite art, which in the common philosophy have very apposite uses assigned them, and serve to explain abundance of phenomena?

61. To all which I answer, *first*, that though there were some difficulties relating to the administration of Providence, and the uses by it assigned to the several parts of nature, which I could not solve by the foregoing principles, yet this objection could be of small weight against the truth and certainty of those things which may be proved *a priori*, with the utmost evidence and rigor of demonstration. *Secondly*, but neither are the received principles free from the like difficulties; for, it may still be demanded to what end God should take those roundabout methods of effecting things by instruments and machines, which no one can deny might have been effected by the mere command of His will without all that apparatus; nay, if we narrowly consider it, we shall find the objection may be retorted with greater force on those who hold the existence of those machines without of mind; for it has been made evident that solidity, bulk, figure, motion, and the like have no *activity* or *efficacy* in them, so as to be capable of producing any one effect in nature. (See Sec. 25). Whoever therefore supposes them to exist (allowing the supposition possible) when they are not perceived does it manifestly to no purpose; since the only use that is assigned to them, as they exist unperceived, is that they produce those perceivable effects which in truth cannot be ascribed to anything but Spirit.

62. But, to come nigher the difficulty, it must be observed that

though the fabrication of all those parts and organs be not absolutely necessary to the producing any effect, yet it is necessary to the producing of things in a constant regular way according to the laws of nature. There are certain general laws that run through the whole chain of natural effects; these are learned by the observation and study of nature, and are by men applied as well to the framing artificial things for the use and ornament of life as to the explaining various phenomena—which explication consists only in shewing the conformity any particular phenomenon hath to the general laws of nature, or, which is the same thing, in discovering the *uniformity* there is in the production of natural effects; as will be evident to whoever shall attend to the several instances wherein philosophers pretend to account for appearances. That there is a great and conspicuous use in these regular constant methods of working observed by the Supreme Agent hath been shewn in Sec. 31. And it is no less visible that a particular size, figure, motion, and disposition of parts are necessary, though not absolutely to the producing any effect, yet to the producing it according to the standing mechanical laws of nature. Thus, for instance, it cannot be denied that God, or the Intelligence that sustains and rules the ordinary course of things, might if He were minded to produce a miracle, cause all the motions on the dial-plate of a watch, though nobody had ever made the movements and put them in it: but yet, if He will act agreeably to the rules of mechanism, by Him for wise ends established and maintained in the creation, it is necessary that those actions of the watchmaker, whereby he makes the movements and rightly adjusts them, precede the production of the aforesaid motions; as also that any disorder in them be attended with the perception of some corresponding disorder in the movements, which being once corrected all is right again.

63. It may indeed on some occasions be necessary that the Author of nature display His overruling power in producing some appearance out of the ordinary series of things. Such exceptions from the general rules of nature are proper to surprise and awe men into an acknowledgment of the Divine Being; but then they are to be used but seldom, otherwise there is a plain reason why they should fail of that effect. Besides, God seems to choose the convincing our reason of His attributes by the works of nature, which discover so much harmony and contrivance in their make, and are such plain indications of wisdom and beneficence in their Author, rather than to astonish us into a belief of His Being by anomalous and surprising events.

64. To set this matter in a yet clearer light, I shall observe that what has been objected in Sec. 60 amounts in reality to no more than this:— ideas are not anyhow and at random produced, there being a certain order and connection between them, like to that of cause and effect; there are also several combinations of them made in a very regular and artificial manner, which seem like so many instruments in the hand of nature that, being hid as it were behind the scenes, have a secret operation in producing those appearances which are seen on the theater of the world,

being themselves discernible only to the curious eye of the philosopher. But, since one idea cannot be the cause of another, to what purpose is that connection? And, since those instruments, being barely *inefficacious perceptions* in the mind, are not subservient to the production of natural effects, it is demanded why they are made; or, in other words, what reason can be assigned why God should make us, upon a close inspection into His works, behold so great variety of ideas so artfully laid together, and so much according to rule; it not being credible that He would be at the expense (if one may so speak) of all that art and regularity to no purpose.

65. To all which my answer is, first, that the connection of ideas does not imply the relation of *cause and effect,* but only of a mark or *sign* with the thing *signified.* The fire which I see is not the cause of the pain I suffer upon my approaching it, but the mark that forewarns me of it. In like manner the noise that I hear is not the effect of this or that motion or collision of the ambient bodies, but the sign thereof. Secondly, the reason why ideas are formed into machines, that is, artificial and regular combinations, is the same with that for combining letters into words. That a few original ideas may be made to signify a great number of effects and actions, it is necessary they be variously combined together. And, to the end their use be permanent and universal, these combinations must be made by *rule,* and with *wise contrivance.* By this means abundance of information is conveyed unto us, concerning what we are to expect from such and such actions, and what methods are proper to be taken for the exciting such and such ideas; which in effect is all that I conceive to be distinctly meant when it is said that, by discerning a figure, texture, and mechanism of the inward parts of bodies, whether natural or artificial, we may attain to know the several uses and properties depending thereon, or the nature of the thing.

66. Hence, it is evident that those things which, under the notion of a cause co-operating or concurring to the production of effects, are altogether inexplicable, and run us into great absurdities, may be very naturally explained, and have a proper and obvious use assigned to them, when they are considered only as marks or signs for our information. And it is the searching after and endeavoring to understand those signs instituted by the Author of Nature, that ought to be the employment of the natural philosopher; and not the pretending to explain things by corporeal causes, which doctrine seems to have too much estranged the minds of men from that active principle, that supreme and wise Spirit "in whom we live, move, and have our being."

67. In the *twelfth* place, it may perhaps be objected that—though it be clear from what has been said that there can be no such thing as an inert, senseless, extended, solid, figured, movable substance existing without the mind, such as philosophers describe matter—yet, if any man shall leave out of his idea of matter the positive ideas of extension, figure, solidity and motion, and say that he means only by that word an inert, senseless substance, that exists without the mind or unperceived,

which is the *occasion of our ideas,* or at the presence whereof God is pleased to excite ideas in us: it doth not appear but that matter taken in this sense may possibly exist. In answer to which I say, first, that it seems no less absurd to suppose a substance without accidents, than it is to suppose accidents without a substance. But secondly, though we should grant this unknown substance may possibly exist, yet where can it be supposed to be? That it exists not in the mind is agreed; and that it exists not in place is no less certain—since all place or extension exists only in the mind, as hath been already proved. It remains therefore that it exists nowhere at all.

68. Let us examine a little the description that is here given us of *matter.* It neither acts, nor perceives, nor is perceived; for this is all that is meant by saying it is an inert, senseless, unknown substance: which is a definition entirely made up of negatives, excepting only the relative notion of its standing under or supporting. But then it must be observed that it supports nothing at all, and how nearly this comes to the description of a *nonentity* I desire may be considered. But, say you, it is the *unknown occasion,* at the presence of which ideas are excited in us by the will of God. Now, I would fain know how anything can be present to us, which is neither perceivable by sense nor reflection, nor capable of producing any idea in our minds, nor is at all extended, nor hath any form, nor exists in any place. The words 'to be present,' when thus applied, must needs be taken in some abstract and strange meaning, and which I am not able to comprehend.

69. Again, let us examine what is meant by *occasion.* So far as I can gather from the common use of language, that word signifies either the agent which produces any effect, or else something that is observed to accompany or go before it in the ordinary course of things. But when it is applied to matter as above described, it can be taken in neither of those senses; for matter is said to be passive and inert, and so cannot be an agent or efficient cause. It is also unperceivable, as being devoid of all sensible qualities, and so cannot be the occasion of our perceptions in the latter sense: as when the burning my finger is said to be the occasion of the pain that attends it. What therefore can be meant by calling matter an *occasion?* The term is either used in no sense at all, or else in some very distant from its received signification.

70. You will perhaps say that matter, though it be not perceived by us, is nevertheless perceived by God, to whom it is the occasion of exciting ideas in our minds. For, say you, since we observe our sensations to be imprinted in an orderly and constant manner, it is but reasonable to suppose there are certain constant and regular occasions of their being produced. That is to say, that there are certain permanent and distinct parcels of matter, corresponding to our ideas, which, though they do not excite them in our minds, or anywise immediately affect us, as being altogether passive and unperceivable to us, they are nevertheless to God, by whom they are perceived, as it were so many occasions to remind

Him when and what ideas to imprint on our minds; that so things may go on in a constant uniform manner.

71. In answer to this, I observe that, as the notion of matter is here stated, the question is no longer concerning the existence of a thing distinct from *spirit* and *idea*, from perceiving and being perceived; but whether there are not certain ideas of I know not what sort, in the mind of God which are so many marks or notes that direct Him how to produce sensations in our minds in a constant and regular method—much after the same manner as a musician is directed by the notes of music to produce that harmonious train and composition of sound which is called a tune, though they who hear the music do not perceive the notes, and may be entirely ignorant of them. But, this notion of matter seems too extravagant to deserve a confutation. Besides, it is in effect no objection against what we have advanced, to wit, that there is no senseless unperceived substance.

72. If we follow the light of reason, we shall, from the constant uniform method of our sensations, collect the goodness and wisdom of the Spirit who excites them in our minds; but this is all that I can see reasonably concluded from thence. To me, I say, it is evident that the being of a spirit infinitely wise, good, and powerful is abundantly sufficient to explain all the appearances of nature. But as for *inert, senseless matter*, nothing that I perceive has any the least connection with it, or leads to the thoughts of it. And I would fain see anyone explain any the meanest phenomenon in nature by it, or shew any manner of reason, though in the lowest rank of probability, that he can have for its existence, or even make any tolerable sense or meaning of that supposition. For, as to its being an occasion, we have, I think, evidently shewn that with regard to us it is no occasion. It remains therefore that it must be, if at all, the occasion to God of exciting ideas in us; and what this amounts to we have just now seen.

73. It is worth while to reflect a little on the motives which inducted men to suppose the existence of *material substance;* that so having observed the gradual ceasing and expiration of those motives or reasons, we may proportionably withdraw the assent that was grounded on them. First, therefore, it was thought that color, figure, motion, and the rest of the sensible qualities or accidents, did really exist without the mind; and for this reason it seemed needful to suppose some unthinking *substratum* or substance wherein they did exist, since they could not be conceived to exist by themselves. Afterwards, in process of time, men being convinced that colors, sounds, and the rest of the sensible, secondary qualities had no existence without the mind, they stripped this *substratum* or material substance of those qualities, leaving only the primary ones, figure, motion, and suchlike, which they still conceived to exist without the mind, and consequently to stand in need of a material support. But, it having been shewn that none even of these can possibly exist otherwise than in a spirit or mind which perceives them, it follows that we have no longer any reason to suppose the being of matter; nay, that

it is utterly impossible there should be any such thing, so long as that word is taken to denote an *unthinking substratum* of qualities or accidents wherein they exist without the mind.

74. But though it be allowed by the materialists themselves that matter was thought of only for the sake of supporting accidents, and, the reason entirely ceasing, one might expect the mind should naturally, and without any reluctance at all, quit the belief of what was solely grounded thereon; yet the prejudice is riveted so deeply in our thoughts, that we can scarce tell how to part with it, and are therefore inclined, since the *thing* itself is indefensible, at least to retain the *name*, which we apply to I know not what abstracted and indefinite notions of being, or occasion, though without any show of reason, at least so far as I can see. For, what is there on our part, or what do we perceive, amongst all the ideas, sensations, notions which are imprinted on our minds, either by sense or reflection, from whence may be inferred the existence of an inert, thoughtless, unperceived occasion? And, on the other hand, on the part of an all-sufficient Spirit, what can there be that should make us believe or even suspect He is directed by an inert occasion to excite ideas in our minds?

75. It is a very extraordinary instance of the force of prejudice, and much to be lamented, that the mind of man retains so great a fondness, against all the evidence of reason, for a stupid thoughtless *somewhat*, by the interposition whereof it would as it were screen itself from the providence of God, and remove it farther off from the affairs of the world. But, though we do the utmost we can to secure the belief of *matter*, though, when reason forsakes us, we endeavor to support our opinion on the bare possibility of the thing, and though we indulge ourselves in the full scope of an imagination not regulated by reason to make out that poor possibility, yet the upshot of all is, that there are certain *unknown ideas* in the mind of God; for this, if anything, is all that I conceive to be meant by *occasion* with regard to God. And this at the bottom is no longer contending for the thing, but for the name.

76. Whether therefore there are such ideas in the mind of God, and whether they may be called by the name 'matter,' I shall not dispute. But, if you stick to the notion of an unthinking substance or support of extension, motion, and other sensible qualities, then to me it is most evidently impossible there should be any such thing; since it is a plain repugnancy that those qualities should exist in or be supported by an unperceiving substance.

77. But, say you, though it be granted that there is no thoughtless support of extension and the other qualities or accidents which we perceive, yet there may perhaps be some inert, unperceiving substance or *substratum* of some other qualities, as incomprehensible to us as colors are to a man born blind, because we have not a sense adapted to them. But, if we had a new sense, we should possibly no more doubt of their existence than a blind man made to see does of the existence of light and colors. I answer, first, if what you mean by the word 'matter' be only

the unknown support of unknown qualities, it is no matter whether there is such a thing or no, since it no way concerns us; and I do not see the advantage there is in disputing about what we know not *what*, and we know not *why*.

78. But, secondly, if we had a new sense it could only furnish us with new ideas or sensations; and then we should have the same reason against their existing in an unperceiving substance that has been already offered with relation to figure, motion, color, and the like. Qualities, as hath been shewn, are nothing else but *sensations* or *ideas*, which exist only in a *mind* perceiving them; and this is true not only of the ideas we are acquainted with at present, but likewise of all possible ideas whatsoever.

79. But, you will insist, what if I have no reason to believe the existence of matter? what if I cannot assign any use to it or explain anything by it, or even conceive what is meant by that word? yet still it is no contradiction to say that matter exists, and that this matter is in general a *substance,* or *occasion of ideas;* though indeed to go about to unfold the meaning or adhere to any particular explication of those words may be attended with great difficulties. I answer, when words are used without a meaning, you may put them together as you please without danger of running into a contradiction. You may say, for example, that twice two is equal to seven, so long as you declare you do not take the words of that proposition in their usual acceptation but for marks of you know not what. And, by the same reason, you may say there is an inert thoughtless substance without accidents which is the occasion of our ideas. And we shall understand just as much by one proposition as the other.

.　　.　　.

88. So long as we attribute a real existence to unthinking things, distinct from their being perceived, it is not only impossible for us to know with evidence the nature of any real unthinking being, but even that it exists. Hence it is that we see philosophers distrust their senses, and doubt of the existence of heaven and earth, of everything they see or feel, even of their own bodies. And, after all their labor and struggle of thought, they are forced to own we cannot attain to any self-evident or demonstrative knowledge of the existence of sensible things. But, all this doubtfulness, which so bewilders and confounds the mind and makes philosophy ridiculous in the eyes of the world, vanishes if we annex a meaning to our words, and not amuse ourselves with the terms 'absolute,' 'external,' 'exist,' and such like, signifying we know not what. I can as well doubt of my own being as of the being of those things which I actually perceive by sense; it being a manifest contradiction that any sensible object should be immediately perceived by sight or touch, and at the same time have no existence in nature, since the very *existence* of an unthinking being consists in *being perceived.*

89. Nothing seems of more importance towards erecting a firm system of sound and real knowledge, which may be proof against the assaults of scepticism, than to lay the beginning in a distinct explication of what

is meant by *thing, reality, existence;* for in vain shall we dispute concerning the real existence of things, or pretend to any knowledge thereof, so long as we have not fixed the meaning of those words. *Thing* or *Being* is the most general name of all; it comprehends under it two kinds entirely distinct and heterogeneous, and which have nothing common but the name, to wit, *spirits* and *ideas.* The former are active, indivisible substances: the latter are inert, fleeting, dependent beings, which subsist not by themselves, but are supported by, or exist in minds or spiritual substances. We comprehend our own existence by inward feeling or reflection, and that of other spirits by reason. We may be said to have some knowledge or notion of our own minds, of spirits and active beings, whereof in a strict sense we have not ideas. In like manner we know and have a notion of relations between things or ideas—which relations are distinct from the ideas or things related, inasmuch as the latter may be perceived by us without our perceiving the former. To me it seems that *ideas, spirits,* and *relations* are all in their respective kinds the object of human knowledge and subject of discourse; and that the term 'idea' would be improperly extended to signify everything we know or have any notion of.

. . .

92. For, as we have shewn the doctrine of matter or corporeal substance to have been the main pillar and support of scepticism, so likewise upon the same foundation have been raised all the impious schemes of atheism and irreligion. Nay, so great a difficulty hath it been thought to conceive matter produced out of nothing, that the most celebrated among the ancient philosophers, even of those who maintained the being of God, have thought matter to be uncreated and co-eternal with Him. How great a friend *material substance* hath been to atheists in all ages were needless to relate. All their monstrous systems have so visible and necessary a dependence on it that, when this cornerstone is once removed, the whole fabric cannot choose but fall to the ground, insomuch that it is no longer worth while to bestow a particular consideration on the absurdities of every wretched sect of atheists.

. . .

98. For my own part, whenever I attempt to frame a simple idea of *time,* abstracted from the succession of ideas in my mind, which flows uniformly and is participated by all beings, I am lost and embrangled in inextricable difficulties. I have no notion of it at all, only I hear others say it is infinitely divisible, and speak of it in such a manner as leads me to entertain odd thoughts of my existence; since that doctrine lays one under an absolute necessity of thinking, either that he passes away innumerable ages without a thought, or else that he is annihilated every moment of his life, both which seem equally absurd. Time therefore being nothing, abstracted from the succession of ideas in our minds, it follows that the duration of any finite spirit must be estimated by the

number of ideas or actions succeeding each other in that same spirit or mind. Hence, it is a plain consequence that the soul always thinks; and in truth whoever shall go about to divide in his thoughts, or abstract the *existence* of a spirit from its *cogitation,* will, I believe, find it no easy task.

.   .   .

109. As in reading other books a wise man will choose to fix his thoughts on the sense and apply it to use, rather than lay them out in grammatical remarks on the language; so, in perusing the volume of nature, it seems beneath the dignity of the mind to affect an exactness in reducing each particular phenomenon to general rules, or shewing how it follows from them. We should propose to ourselves nobler views, namely, to recreate and exalt the mind with a prospect of the beauty, order, extent, and variety of natural things: hence, by proper infer- ences, to enlarge our notions of the grandeur, wisdom, and beneficence of the Creator; and lastly, to make the several parts of the creation, so far as in us lies, subservient to the ends they were designed for, God's glory, and the sustenation and comfort of ourselves and fellow-creatures.

110. The best key or the aforesaid analogy or natural science will be easily acknowledged to be a certain celebrated treatise of *mechanics.* In the entrance of which justly admired treaties, time, space, and motion are distinguished into *absolute* and *relative, true* and *apparent, mathe- matical* and *vulgar*; which distinction, as it is at large explained by the author, does suppose these quantities to have an existence without the mind; and that they are ordinarily conceived with relation to sensible things, to which nevertheless in their own nature they bear no relation at all.

111. As for *time*, as it is there taken in an absolute or abstracted sense, for the duration or perseverance of the existence of things, I have nothing more to add concerning it after what has been already said on that subject. (Secs. 97 and 98.) For the rest, this celebrated author holds there is an *absolute space*, which, being unperceivable to sense, remains in itself similar and immovable; and relative space to be the measure thereof, which, being movable and defined by its situation in respect of sensible bodies, is vulgarly taken for immovable space. *Place* he defines to be that part of space which is occupied by any body; and according as the space is absolute or relative so also is the place. *Ab- solute motion* is said to be the translation of a body from absolute place to absolute place, as relative motion is from one relative place to an- other. And, because the parts of absolute space do not fall under our senses, instead of them we are obliged to use their sensible measures, and so define both place and motion with respect to bodies which we regard as immovable. But, it is said in philosophical matters we must abstract from our senses, since it may be that none of those bodies which seem to be quiescent are truly so, and the same thing which is moved relatively may be really at rest; as likewise one and the same body may be in relative rest and motion, or even moved with contrary

relative motions at the same time, according as its place is variously defined. All which ambiguity is to be found in the apparent motions, but not at all in the true or absolute, which should therefore be alone regarded in philosophy. And the true as we are told are distinguished from apparent or relative motions by the following properties. First, in true or absolute motion all parts which preserve the same position with respect of the whole, partake of the motions of the whole. Secondly, the place being moved, that which is placed therein is also moved; so that a body moving in a place which is in motion doth participate the motion of its place. Thirdly, true motion is never generated or changed otherwise than by force impressed on the body itself. Fourthly, true motion is always changed by force impressed on the body moved. Fifthly, in circular motion barely relative there is no centrifugal force, which, nevertheless, in that which is true or absolute, is proportional to the quantity of motion.

112. But, notwithstanding what hath been said, I must confess it doth not appear to me that there can be any motion other than *relative*; so that to conceive motion there must be at least conceived two bodies, whereof the distance or position in regard to each other is varied. Hence, if there was one only body in being it could not possibly be moved. This seems evident, in that the idea I have of motion doth necessarily include relation.

. . .

139. But it will be objected that, if there is no idea signified by the terms 'soul,' 'spirit,' and 'substance,' they are wholly insignificant, or have no meaning in them. I answer, those words do mean or signify a real thing, which is neither an idea nor like an idea, but that which perceives ideas, and wills, and reasons about them. What I am myself, that which I denote by the term 'I,' is the same with what is meant by 'soul' or 'spiritual substances.' If it be said that this is only quarreling at a word, and that, since the immediate significations of other names are by common consent called 'ideas' no reason can be assigned why that which is signified by the name 'spirit' or 'soul' may not partake in the same appellation: I answer, all the unthinking objects of the mind agree in that they are entirely passive, and their existence consists only in being perceived; whereas a soul or spirit is an active being, whose existence consists, not in being perceived, but in perceiving ideas and thinking. It is therefore necessary, in order to prevent equivocation and confounding natures perfectly disagreeing and unlike, that we distinguish between *spirit* and *idea*. (See Sec. 27.)

140. In a large sense, indeed, we may be said to have an idea or rather a notion of *spirit*, that is, we understand the meaning of the word, otherwise we could not affirm or deny anything of it. Moreover, as we conceive the ideas that are in the minds of other spirits by means of our own, which we suppose to be resemblances of them; so we know other spirits by means of our own soul; which in that sense is the im-

age or idea of them; it having a like respect to other spirits that blueness or heat by me perceived has to those ideas perceived by another.

. . .

145. From what hath been said, it is plain that we cannot know the existence of other spirits otherwise than by their operations, or the ideas by them excited in us. I perceive several motions, changes, and combinations of ideas, that inform me there are certain particular agents, like myself, which accompany them and concur in their production. Hence, the knowledge I have of other spirits is not immediate, as is the knowledge of my ideas; but depending on the intervention of ideas, by me referred to agents or spirits distinct from myself, as effects or concomitant signs.

146. But though there be some things which convince us human agents are concerned in producing them; yet it is evident to everyone that those things which are called the works of nature, that is, the far greater part of the ideas or sensations perceived by us, are not produced by, or dependent on, the wills of men. There is therefore some other Spirit that causes them; since it is repugnant that they should subsist by themselves. (See Sec. 29.) But if we attentively consider the constant regularity, order, and concatenation of natural things, the surprising magnificence, beauty, and perfection of the larger, and the exquisite contrivance of the smaller parts of creation, together with the exact harmony and correspondence of the whole, but above all the never enough admired laws of pain and pleasure, and the instincts or natural inclinations, appetites, and passions of animals; I say if we consider all these things, and at the same time attend to the meaning and import of the attributes One, Eternal, Infinitely Wise, Good, and Perfect, we shall clearly perceive that they belong to the aforesaid Spirit, "who works all in all," and "by whom all things consist."

147. Hence, it is evident that God is known as certainly and immediately as any other mind or spirit whatsoever distinct from ourselves. We may even assert that the existence of God is far more evidently perceived than the existence of men; because the effects of nature are infinitely more numerous and considerable than those ascribed to human agents. There is not any one mark that denotes a man, or effect produced by him, which does not more strongly evince the being of that Spirit who is the Author of Nature. For it is evident that in affecting other persons the will of man hath no other object than barely the motion of the limbs of his body; but that such a motion should be attended by, or excite any idea in the mind of another, depends wholly on the will of the Creator. He alone it is who, "upholding all things by the word of His power," maintains that intercourse between spirits whereby they are able to perceive the existence of each other. And yet this pure and clear light which enlightens everyone is itself invisible.

. . .

152. We should further consider that the very blemishes and defects of nature are not without their use, in that they make an agreeable sort of variety, and augment the beauty of the rest of the creation, as shades in a picture serve to set off the brighter and more enlightened parts. We would likewise do well to examine whether our taxing the waste of seeds and embryos, and accidental destruction of plants and animals, before they come to full maturity, as an imprudence in the Author of nature, be not the effect of prejudice contracted by our familiarity with impotent and saving mortals. In man indeed a thrifty management of those things which he cannot procure without much pains and industry may be esteemed wisdom. But we must not imagine that the inexplicably fine machine of an animal or vegetable costs the great Creator any more pains or trouble in its production than a pebble does; nothing being more evident than that an Omnipotent Spirit can indifferently produce everything by a mere *fiat* or act of His will. Hence, it is plain that the splendid profusion of natural things should not be interpreted weakness or prodigality in the Agent who produces them, but rather be looked on as an argument of the riches of His power.

153. As for the mixture of pain or uneasiness which is in the world, pursuant to the general laws of nature, and the actions of finite, imperfect spirits, this, in the state we are in at present, is indispensably necessary to our well-being. But our prospects are too narrow. We take, for instance, the idea of some one particular pain into our thoughts and account it *evil;* whereas, if we enlarge our view, so as to comprehend the various ends, connections, and dependencies of things, on what occasions and in what proportions we are affected with pain and pleasure, the nature of human freedom, and the design with which we are put into the world; we shall be forced to acknowledge that those particular things which, considered in themselves, appear to be evil, have the nature of good, when considered as linked with the whole system of beings.

. . .

156. For, after all, what deserves the first place in our studies is the consideration of God and our *duty;* which to promote, as it was the main drift and design of my labors, so shall I esteem them altogether useless and ineffectual if, by what I have said, I cannot inspire my readers with a pious sense of the Presence of God; and, having shewn the falseness or vanity of those barren speculations which make the chief employment of learned men, the better dispose them to reverence and embrace the salutary truths of the Gospel, which to know and to practice is the highest perfection of human nature.

DAVID
HUME   1711–1776

He was one of the greatest figures of the Enlightenment and possibly the most important of all British philosophers. A Scotsman, he was born in Edinburgh. Like Berkeley, he published his most original work before he was thirty.

A Treatise of Human Nature, Being An Attempt to introduce the experimental Method of Reasoning into Moral Subjects was written during a three-year sojourn in France and published in England, on the author's return, in three volumes (1739-40). It was a bold book that treated in three parts "Of the Understanding," "Of the Passions," and "Of Morals." It is very radical and clearly written, but, as Hume puts it in his autobiography, it "fell dead-born from the press, without reaching such distinction as even to excite a murmur among the zealots." The autobiography is reprinted below, complete.

After the success of his brilliant *Essays* in 1742, Hume decided that his earlier "want of success" must have been due to the form of presentation and he recast the material of the first part of his *Treatise* as his *Enquiry Concerning Human Understanding* (1748). Actually, the differences between the two works are not confined to the presentation, and philosophers differ in their opinions of their relative merits. Many consider the *Enquiry* far more mature and superior, while others think the *Treatise* is more brilliant. Below, the *Enquiry* is reprinted in its entirety.

Hume's *Enquiry concerning the Principles of Morals* (1751) "is another part of my Treatise that I cast anew." In 1757 he published *Four Dissertations*, the first being on "The Natural History of Religion," the second "Of the Passions," the third "Of Tragedy," and the fourth "Of the Standard of Taste."

His *Dialogues concerning natural religion* he did not choose to publish himself: they appeared posthumously in 1779. His autobiographic sketch, *My Own Life*, was published by Adam Smith in 1777. Hume's multi-volume *History of England* had appeared during his own life time.

His importance for the history of philosophy is threefold. First, his skepticism aroused Kant from his dogmatic slumber, and Kant's *Critique of Pure Reason* is partly an attempt to answer Hume. Secondly, most subsequent British philosophy is deeply indebted to Hume, both in theory of knowledge and in ethics. Finally, quite apart from any influence, it is the existence of such brilliant writers and thinkers as David Hume that makes the history of philosophy worth studying.

THE LIFE OF DAVID HUME, ESQ.

WRITTEN BY HIMSELF

MY OWN LIFE

It is difficult for a man to speak long of himself without vanity; therefore I shall be short. It may be thought an instance of vanity that I pretend at all to write my life, but this narrative shall contain little more than the history of my writings; as, indeed, almost all my life has been spent in literary pursuits and occupations. The first success of most of my writings was not such as to be an object of vanity.

I was born the twenty-sixth of April, 1711, old style, at Edinburgh. I was of a good family, both by father and mother: my father's family is a branch of the earl of Home's, or Hume's; and my ancestors had been proprietors of the estate which my brother possesses, for several generations. My mother was daughter of Sir David Falconer, president of the college of justice; the title of Lord Halkerton came by succession to her brother.

My family, however, was not rich; and being myself a younger brother, my patrimony, according to the mode of my country, was of course very slender. My father, who passed for a man of parts, died when I was an infant, leaving me, with an elder brother and a sister, under the care of our mother, a woman of singular merit, who, though young and handsome, devoted herself entirely to the rearing and educating of her children. I passed through the ordinary course of education with success, and was seized very early with a passion for literature, which has been the ruling passion of my life, and the great source of my enjoyments. My studious disposition, my sobriety, and my industry, gave my family a notion that the law was a proper profession for me; but I found an insurmountable aversion to every thing but the pursuits of philosophy and general learning; and while they fancied I was poring upon Voet and Vinnius, Cicero and Virgil were the authors which I was secretly devouring.

My very slender fortune, however, being unsuitable to this plan of life, and my health being a little broken by my ardent application, I was tempted, or rather forced, to make a very feeble trial for entering into a more active scene of life. In 1734, I went to Bristol, with some recommendations to several eminent merchants; but in a few months found that scene totally unsuitable to me. I went over to France, with a view of prosecuting my studies in a country retreat; and I there laid that plan of life which I have steadily and successfully pursued. I resolved to make a very rigid frugality supply my deficiency of fortune, to maintain unimpaired my independency, and to regard every object as contemptible, except the improvements of my talents in literature.

During my retreat in France, first at Rheims, but chiefly at La Flèche, in Anjou, I composed my Treatise of Human Nature. After passing three years very agreeably in that country, I came over to London in 1737. In the end of 1738, I published by Treatise, and immediately went down to my mother and my brother, who lived at his country house, and was employing himself very judiciously and successfully in the improvement of his fortune.

Never literary attempt was more unfortunate than my Treatise of Human Nature. It fell dead-born from the press, without reaching such distinction as even to excite a murmur among the zealots. But being naturally of a cheerful and sanguine temper, I very soon recovered the blow, and prosecuted with great ardor my studies in the country. In 1742, I printed at Edinburgh the first part of my Essays. The work was favorably received, and soon made me entirely forget my former disappointment. I continued with my mother and brother in the country, and in that time recovered the knowledge of the Greek language, which I had too much neglected in my early youth.

In 1745, I received a letter from the marquis of Annandale, inviting me to come and live with him in England; I found also that the friends and family of that young nobleman were desirous of putting him under my care and direction, for the state of his mind and health required it. I lived with him a twelve-month. My appointments during that time made a considerable accession to my small fortune. I then received in invitation from General St. Clair to attend him as a secretary to his expedition, which was at first meant against Canada, but ended in an incursion on the coast of France. Next year, to wit, 1747, I received an invitation from the general to attend him in the same station in his military embassy to the courts of Vienna and Turin. I then wore the uniform of an officer, and was introduced at these courts as aid-de-camp to the general, along with Sir Harry Erskine and Captain Grant, now General Grant. These two years were almost the only interruptions which my studies have received during the course of my life: I passed them agreeably, and in good company; and my appointments, with my frugality, had made me reach a fortune which I called independent, though most of my friends were inclined to smile when I said so: in short, I was now master of near a thousand pounds.

I had always entertained a notion, that my want of success in publishing the Treatise of Human Nature had proceeded more from the manner than the matter, and that I had been guilty of a very usual indiscretion, in going to the press too early. I, therefore, cast the first part of that work anew in the Inquiry concerning Human Understanding, which was published while I was at Turin. But this piece was at first little more successful than the Treatise on Human Nature. On my return from Italy, I had the mortification to find all England in a ferment, on account of Dr. Middleton's Free Inquiry, while my performance was entirely overlooked and neglected. A new edition, which had been published at London, of my Essays, moral and political, met not with a much better reception.

Such is the force of natural temper, that these disappointments made little or no impression on me. I went down, in 1749, and lived two years with my brother at his country house, for my mother was now dead. I there composed the second part of my Essay, which I called Political Discourses, and also my Inquiry concerning the Principles of Morals, which is another part of my Treatise that I cast anew. Meanwhile, my bookseller, A. Millar, informed me, that my former publications (all but the unfortunate Treatise) were beginning to be the subject of conversation; that the sale of them was gradually increasing, and that new editions were demanded. Answers by reverends and right reverends came out two or three in a year; and I found, by Dr. Warburton's railing, that the books were beginning to be esteemed in good company. However, I had fixed a resolution, which I inflexibly maintained, never to reply to any body; and not being very irascible in my temper, I have easily kept myself clear of all literary squabbles. These symptoms of a rising reputation gave me encouragement, as I was ever more disposed to see the favorable than unfavorable side of things; a turn of mind which it is more happy to possess, than to be born to an estate of ten thousand a year.

In 1751, I removed from the country to the town, the true scene for a man of letters. In 1752 were published at Edinburgh, where I then lived, my Political Discourses, the only work of mine that was successful on the first publication. It was well received at home and abroad. In the same year was published, at London, my Inquiry concerning the Principles of Morals; which, in my own opinion, (who ought not to judge on that subject,) is, of all my writings, historical, philosophical, or literary, incomparably the best. It came unnoticed and unobserved into the world.

In 1752, the Faculty of Advocates chose me their librarian, an office from which I received little or no emolument, but which gave me the command of a large library. I then formed the plan of writing the History of England; but being frightened with the notion of continuing a narrative through a period of seventeen hundred years, I commenced with the accession of the house of Stuart, an epoch when, I thought, the misrepresentations of faction began chiefly to take place. I was, I own, sanguine in my expectations of the success of this work. I thought that I was the only historian that had at once neglected present power, interest and authority, and the cry of popular prejudices; and as the subject was suited to every capacity, I expected proportional applause. But miserable was my disappointment; I was assailed by one cry of reproach, disapprobation, and even detestation; English, Scotch, and Irish, whig and tory, churchman and sectary, freethinker and religionist, patriot and courtier, united in their rage against the man who had presumed to shed a generous tear for the fate of Charles I. and the earl of Strafford; and after the first ebullitions of their fury were over, what was still more mortifying, the book seemed to sink into oblivion. Mr. Millar told me that in a twelvemonth he sold only forty-five copies of it. I scarcely, indeed, heard of one man in the three kingdoms, considerable for rank or letters, that could endure the book. I must only except the primate of England, Dr. Herring, and the primate of Ireland, Dr. Stone, which seem two odd exceptions. These dignified prelates separately sent me messages not to be discouraged.

I was, however, I confess, discouraged; and had not the war been at that time breaking out between France and England, I had certainly retired to some provincial town of the former kingdom, have changed my name, and never more have returned to my native country. But as this scheme was not now practicable, and the subsequent volume was considerably advanced, I resolved to pick up courage and to persevere.

In this interval, I published, at London, my Natural History of Religion, along with some other small pieces. Its public entry was rather obscure, except only that Dr. Hurd wrote a pamphlet against it, with all the illiberal petulance, arrogance, and scurrility, which distinguish the Warburtonian school. This pamphlet gave me some consolation for the otherwise indifferent reception of my performance.

In 1756, two years after the fall of the first volume, was published the second volume of my history, containing the period from the death of Charles I. till the revolution. This performance happened to give less displeasure to the whigs, and was better received. It not only rose itself, but helped to buoy up its unfortunate brother.

But though I had been taught by experience that the whig party were in possession of bestowing all places, both in the state and in literature, I was so little inclined to yield to their senseless clamor, that in above a hundred alterations, which further study, reading, or reflection engaged me to make in the reigns of the two first Stuarts, I have made all of them invariably to the tory side. It is ridiculous to consider the English constitution before that period as a regular plan of liberty.

In 1759, I published my history of the house of Tudor. The clamor against this performance was almost equal to that against the history of the two first Stuarts. The reign of Elizabeth was particularly obnoxious.

But I was now callous against the impressions of public folly, and continued very peaceably and contentedly, in my retreat at Edinburgh, to finish, in two volumes, the more early part of the English history, which I gave to the public in 1761, with tolerable, and but tolerable, success.

But, notwithstanding this variety of winds and seasons, to which my writings had been exposed, they had still been making such advances, that the copy-money given me by the booksellers much exceeded any thing formerly known in England; I was become not only independent, but opulent. I retired to my native country of Scotland, determined never more to set my foot out of it; and retaining the satisfaction of never having preferred a request to one great man, or even making advances of friendship to any of them. As I was now turned of fifty, I thought of passing all the rest of my life in this philosophical manner: when I received, in 1763, an invitation from the earl of Hertford, with whom I was not in the least acquainted, to attend him on his embassy to Paris, with a near prospect of being appointed secretary to the embassy; and, in the mean while, of performing the functions of that office. This offer, however inviting, I at first declined; both because I was reluctant to begin connections with the great, and because I was afraid that the civilities and gay company of Paris would prove disagreeable to a person of my age and humor; but on his lordship's repeating the invitation, I accepted of it. I have every reason, both of pleasure and interest, to think myself happy in my connexions with that nobleman, as well as afterwards with his brother, General Conway.

Those who have not seen the strange effects of modes, will never imagine the reception I met with at Paris, from men and women of all ranks and stations. The more I resiled from their excessive civilities, the more I was loaded with them. There is, however, a real satisfaction in living at Paris, from the great number of sensible, knowing, and polite company with which that city abounds above all places in the universe. I thought once of settling there for life.

I was appointed secretary to the embassy; and, in summer, 1765, Lord Hertford left me, being appointed lord lieutenant of Ireland. I was chargé d'affaires till the arrival of the duke of Richmond, towards the end of the year. In the beginning of 1766, I left Paris, and next summer went to Edinburgh, with the same view as formerly, of burying myself in a philosophical retreat. I returned to that place, not richer, but with much more money, and a much larger income, by means of Lord Hertford's friendship, than I left it; and I was desirous of trying what superfluity could produce, as I had formerly made an experiment of a competency But in 1767, I received from Mr. Conway an invitation to be under-secretary; and this invitation, both the character of the person, and my connexions with Lord Hertford, prevented me from declining. I returned to Edinburgh in 1769, very opulent, (for I possessed a revenue of one thousand pounds a year,) healthy, and though somewhat stricken in years, with the prospect of enjoying long my ease, and of seeing the increase of my reputation.

In spring, 1775, I was struck with a disorder in my bowels, which at first gave me no alarm, but has since, as I apprehend it, become mortal and incurable. I now reckon upon a speedy dissolution. I have suffered very little pain from my disorder; and what is more strange, have, notwithstanding the great decline of my person, never suffered a moment's abatement of my spirits; insomuch, that were I to name a period of my life which I should most choose to pass over again, I might be tempted to point to this later period. I possess the same ardor as ever in study, and the same gayety in company. I consider, besides, that a man of sixty-five, by dying, cuts off only a few years of infirmities; and though I see many symptoms of my literary reputation's breaking out at last with additional lustre, I know that I could have but few years to enjoy it. It is difficult to be more detached from life than I am at present.

To conclude historically with my own character: I am, or rather was, (for that is the style I must now use in speaking of myself, which emboldens me the more to speak my sentiments;) I was, I say, a man of mild disposition, of command of temper, of an open social, and cheerful humor, capable of attachment, but little susceptible of enmity, and of great moderation in all my passions. Even my love of literary fame, my ruling passion, never soured my temper, notwithstanding my frequent disappointments. My company was not unacceptable to the young and careless, as well as to the studious and literary; and as I took a particular pleasure in the company of modest women, I had no reason to be displeased with the reception I met with from them. In a word, though most men, anywise eminent, have found reason to complain of Calumny, I never was touched, or even attacked, by her baleful tooth; and though I wantonly exposed myself to the rage of both civil and religious factions, they seemed to be disarmed in my behalf of their wonted fury. My friends never had occasion to vindicate any one circumstance of my character and conduct; not but that the zealots, we may well suppose, would have been glad to invent and propagate any story to my disadvantage, but they could never find any which they thought would wear the face of probability. I cannot say there is no vanity in making this funeral oration of myself, but I hope it is not a misplaced one; and this is a matter of fact which is easily cleared and ascertained.

APRIL 18, 1776.

LETTER FROM ADAM SMITH LL. D.

TO WILLIAM STRAHAN, ESQ.

KIRKALDY, FIFESHIRE, Nov. 9, 1776.

DEAR SIR,

It is with a real, though a very melancholy pleasure, that I sit down to give you some account of the behaviour of our late excellent friend, Mr. Hume, during his last illness.

Though, in his own judgment, his disease was mortal and incurable, yet he allowed himself to be prevailed upon, by the entreaty of his friends, to try what might be the effects of a long journey. A few days before he set out, he wrote that account of his own life, which, together with his other papers, he has left to your care. My account, therefore, shall begin where his ends.

He set out for London towards the end of April, and at Morpeth met with Mr. John Home and myself, who had both come down from London on purpose to see him, expecting to have found him at Edinburgh. Mr. Home returned with him, and attended him during the whole of his stay in England, with that care and attention which might be expected from a temper so perfectly friendly and affectionate. As I had written to my mother that she might expect me in Scotland, I was under the necessity of continuing my journey. His disease seemed to yield to exercise and change of air; and when he arrived in London, he was apparently in much better health than when he left Edinburgh. He was advised to go to Bath to drink the waters, which appeared for some time to have so good an effect upon him, that even he himself began to entertain, what he was not apt to do, a better opinion of his own health. His symptoms, however, soon returned with their usual violence; and from that moment he gave up all thoughts of recovery, but submitted with the utmost cheerfulness, and the most perfect complacency and resignation. Upon his return to Edinburgh, though he found himself much weaker, yet his cheerfulness never abated, and he continued to divert himself, as usual, with correcting his own works for a new edition, with reading books of amusement, with the conversation of his friends; and, sometimes in the evening, with a party at his favorite game of whist. His cheerfulness was so great, and his conversation and amusements ran so much in their usual strain, that, notwithstanding all bad symptoms, many people could not believe he was dying. "I shall tell your friend, Colonel Edmonstone," said Dr. Dundas to him one day, "that I left you much better, and in a fair way of recovery." "Doctor," said he, "as I believe you would not choose to tell any thing but the truth, you had better tell him that I am dying as fast as my enemies, if I have any, could wish, and as easily and cheerfully as my best friends could desire." Colonel Edmonstone soon afterwards came to see him, and take leave of him; and on his way home he could not forbear writing him a letter, bidding him once more an eternal adieu, and applying to him, as to a dying man, the beautiful French verses in which the Abbé Chaulieu, in expectation of his own death, laments his approaching separation from his friend the Marquis de la Fare. Mr. Hume's magnanimity and firmness were such, that his most affectionate friends knew that they hazarded nothing in talking or writing to him as to a dying man, and that so far from being hurt by this frankness, he was rather pleased and flattered by it. I happened to come into his room while he was reading this letter, which he had just received, and which he immediately showed me. I told him, that though I was sensible how very much he was weakened, and that appearances were in many respects very bad, yet his cheerfulness was still so great, the spirit of life seemed still to be so very strong in him, that I could not help entertaining some faint hopes. He answered, "Your hopes are groundless. An habitual diarrhœa of more than a year's standing, would be a very bad disease at any age; at my age it is a mortal one. When I lie down in the evening, I feel myself weaker than when I rose in the morning; and when I rise in the morning, weaker than when I lay down in the evening. I am sensible, besides, that some of my vital parts are affected, so that I must soon die." "Well," said I, "if it must be so, you have at least the satisfaction of leaving all your friends, your brother's family in particular, in great prosperity." He said that he felt that satisfaction so sensibly, that when he was reading, a few days before, Lucian's *Dialogues of the Dead*, among all the excuses which are alleged to Charon for not entering readily into his boat, he could not find one that fitted him: he had no house to finish, he had no daughter to provide for, he had no enemies upon whom he wished to revenge himself. "I could not well imagine," said he, "what excuse I could make to Charon in order to obtain a little delay. I have done every thing of consequence which I ever meant to do; and I could at no time expect to leave my relations and friends in a better situation than that in which I am now likely to leave them: I, therefore, have all reason to die contented." He then diverted himself with inventing several jocular excuses, which he supposed he might make to Charon, and with imagining the very surly answers which it might suit the character of Charon to return to them. "Upon further consideration," said he, "I thought I might say to him, 'Good Charon, I have been correcting my works for a new edition. Allow me a little time, that I may see how the public receives the alterations.' But Charon would answer, 'When you have seen the effect of these, you will be for making other alterations. There will be no end of such excuses; so, honest friend, please step into the boat.' But I might still urge, 'Have a little patience, good Charon: I have been endeavouring to open the eyes of the public. If I live a few years longer, I may have the satisfaction of seeing the downfall of some of the prevailing systems of superstition.' But Charon would then lose all temper and decency. 'You loitering rogue, that will not happen these many hundred years. Do you fancy I will grant you a lease for so long a term? Get into the boat this instant, you lazy, loitering rogue.'"

But, though Mr. Hume always talked of his approaching dissolution with great cheerfulness, he never affected to make any parade of his magnanimity. He never mentioned the subject but when the conversation naturally led to it, and never dwelt longer upon it than the course of the conversation happened to require; it was a subject indeed which occurred pretty frequently, in consequence of the inquiries which his friends, who came to see him, naturally made concerning the state of his health. The conversation which I mentioned above, and which passed on Thursday the eighth of August, was the last, except one, that I ever had with him. He had now become so very weak, that the company of his most intimate friends fatigued him; for his cheerfulness was still so great, his complaisance and social disposition were still so entire, that when any friend was with him, he could not help talking more, and with greater exertion, than suited the weakness of his body. At his own desire, therefore, I agreed to leave Edinburgh, where I was staying partly upon his account and returned to my mother's house here at Kirkaldy, upon condition that he would send for me whenever he wished to see me; the physician who saw him most frequently, Dr. Black, undertaking, in the mean time, to write me occasionally an account of the state of his health.

On the twenty-second of August, the doctor wrote me the following letter:—

"Since my last, Mr. Hume has passed his time pretty easily, but is much weaker. He sits up, goes down stairs once a day, and amuses himself with reading, but seldom sees any body. He finds that even the conversation of his most intimate friends fatigues and oppresses him; and it is happy that he does not need it, for he is quite free from anxiety, impatience, or low spirits, and passes his time very well with the assistance of amusing books."

I received, the day after, a letter from Mr. Hume himself, of which the following is an extract:—

"EDINBURGH, 23d August, 1776.

"MY DEAREST FRIEND,

"I am obliged to make use of my nephew's hand in writing to you, as I do not rise to-day.

.   .   .

"I go very fast to decline, and last night had a small fever, which I hoped might put a quicker period to this tedious illness; but unluckily it has, in a great measure, gone off. I cannot submit to your coming over here on my account, as it is possilble for me to see you so small a part of the day; but Dr. Black can better inform you concerning the degree of strength which may from time to time remain with me. Adieu, etc."

Three days after, I received the following letter from Dr. Black:—

"EDINBURGH, Monday, 26th August, 1776.

"DEAR SIR,

"Yesterday, about four o'clock, afternoon, Mr. Hume expired. The near approach of his death became evident in the night between Thursday and Friday, when his disease became excessive, and soon weakened him so much, that he could no longer rise out of his bed. He continued to the last perfectly sensible, and free from much pain or feelings of distress. He never dropped the smallest expression of impatience; but when he had occasion to speak to the people about him, always did it with affection and tenderness. I thought it improper to write to bring you over, especially as I heard that he had dictated a letter to you, desiring you not to come. When he became very weak, it cost him an effort to speak; and he died in such a happy composure of mind, that nothing could exceed it."

Thus died our most excellent and never to be forgotten friend; concerning whose philosophical opinions men will, no doubt, judge variously, every one approving or condemning them, according as they happen to coincide or disagree with his own, but concerning whose character and conduct there can scarce be a difference of opinion. His temper, indeed, seemed to be more happily balanced, if I may be allowed such an expression, than that perhaps of any other man I have ever known. Even in the lowest state of his fortune, his great and necessary frugality never hindered him from exercising, upon proper occasions, acts both of charity and generosity. It was a frugality founded not upon avarice, but upon the love of independency. The extreme gentleness of his nature never weakened either the firmness of his mind or the steadiness of his resolutions. His constant pleasantry was the genuine effusion of good nature and good humour, tempered with delicacy and modesty, and without even the slightest tincture of malignity, so frequently the disagreeable source of what is called wit in other men. It never was the meaning of his raillery to mortify; and therefore, far from offending, it seldom failed to please and delight, even those who were frequently the objects of it; there was not perhaps any one of all his great and amiable qualities which contributed more to endear his conversation. And that gayety of temper, so agreeable in society, but which is so often accompanied with frivolous and superficial qualities, was in him certainly attended with the most severe application, the most extensive learning, the greatest depth of thought, and a capacity in every respect the most comprehensive. Upon the whole, I have always considered him, both in his lifetime and since his death, as approaching as nearly to the idea of a perfectly wise and virtuous man as perhaps the nature of human frailty will permit.

I ever am, dear sir,

Most affectionally yours,

ADAM SMITH.

AUTHOR'S ADVERTISEMENT

Most of the principles, and reasonings, contained in this volume, were published in a work in three volumes, called *A Treatise of Human Nature:* A work which the Author had projected before he left College, and which he wrote and published not long after. But not finding it successful, he was sensible of his error in going to the press too early, and he cast the whole anew in the following pieces, where some negligences in his former reasoning and more in the expression, are, he hopes, corrected. Yet several writers who have honoured the Author's Philosophy with answers, have taken care to direct all their batteries against that juvenile work, which the author never acknowledged, and have affected to triumph in any advantages, which, they imagined, they had obtained over it: A practice very contrary to all rules of candour and fear-dealing, and a strong instance of those polemical artifices which a bigotted zeal thinks itself authorized to employ. Henceforth, the Author desires, that the following Pieces may alone be regarded as containing his philosophical sentiments and principles.

AN ENQUIRY CONCERNING HUMAN UNDERSTANDING

(*complete*)

SECTION I.   OF THE DIFFERENT SPECIES OF PHILOSOPHY

Moral philosophy, or the science of human nature, may be treated after two different manners; each of which has its peculiar merit, and may contribute to the entertainment, instruction, and reformation of mankind. The one considers man chiefly as born for action; and as influenced in his measures by taste and sentiment; pursuing one object, and avoiding another, according to the value which these objects seem to possess, and according to the light in which they present themselves. As virtue, of all objects, is allowed to be the most valuable, this species of philosophers paint her in the most amiable colours; borrowing all helps from poetry and eloquence, and treating their subject in an easy and obvious manner, and such as is best fitted to please the imagination, and engage the affections. They select the most striking observations and instances from common life; place opposite characters in a proper contrast; and alluring us into the paths of virtue by the views of glory and happiness, direct our steps in these paths by the soundest precepts and most illustrious examples. They make us *feel* the difference between vice and virtue; they excite and regulate our sentiments; and so they can but bend our hearts to the love of probity and true honour, they think, that they have fully attained the end of all their labours.

The other species of philosophers consider man in the light of a reasonable rather than an active being, and endeavour to form his understanding more than cultivate his manners. They regard human nature as a subject of speculation; and with a narrow scrutiny examine it, in order to find those principles, which regulate our understanding, excite our sentiments, and make us to approve or blame any particular object, action, or behaviour. They think it a reproach to all literature, that philosophy should not yet have fixed, beyond controversy, the foundation of morals, reasoning, and criticism; and should for ever talk of truth and falsehood, vice and virtue, beauty and deformity, without being able to determine the source of these distinctions. While they attempt this arduous task, they are deterred by no difficulties; but proceeding from particular instances to general principles, they still push on their enquiries to principles more general, and rest not satisfied till they arrive at those original principles, by which, in every science, all human curiosity must be bounded. Though their speculations seem abstract, and even unintelligible to common readers, they aim at the approbation of the learned and the wise; and think themselves sufficiently compensated for the labour of their whole lives, if they can discover some hidden truths, which may contribute to the instruction of posterity.

It is certain that the easy and obvious philosophy will always, with the generality of mankind, have the preference above the accurate and abstruse; and by many will be recommended, not only as more agreeable, but more useful than the other. It enters more into common life; moulds the heart and affections; and, by touching those principles which actuate men, reforms their conduct, and brings them nearer to that model of perfection which it describes. On the contrary, the abstruse philosophy, being founded on a turn of mind, which cannot enter into business and action, vanishes when the philosopher leaves the shade, and comes into open day; nor can its principles easily retain any influence over our conduct and behaviour. The feelings of our heart, the agitation of our passions, the vehemence of our affections, dissipate all its conclusions, and reduce the profound philosopher to a mere plebeian.

This also must be confessed, that the most durable, as well as justest fame, has been acquired by the easy philosophy, and that abstract reasoners seem hitherto to have enjoyed only a momentary reputation, from the caprice or ignorance of their own age, but have not been able to support their renown with more equitable posterity. It is easy for a profound philosopher to commit a mistake in his subtile reasonings; and one mistake is the necessary parent of another, while he pushes on his consequences, and is not deterred from embracing any conclusion, by its unusual appearance, or its contradiction to popular opinion. But a philosopher, who purposes only to represent the common sense of mankind in more beautiful and more engaging colours, if by accident he falls into error, goes not farther; but renewing his appeal to common sense, and the natural sentiments of the mind, returns into the right path, and secures himself from any dangerous illusions. The fame of Cicero flourishes at present; but that of Aristotle is utterly decayed. La Bruyère passes the seas, and still maintains his reputation: But the glory of Malebranche is confined to his own nation, and to his own age. And Addison, perhaps, will be read with pleasure, when Locke shall be entirely forgotten.

The mere philosopher is a character, which is commonly but little acceptable in the world, as being supposed to contribute nothing either to the advantage or pleasure of society; while he lives remote from communication with mankind, and is wrapped up in principles and notions equally remote from their comprehension. On the other hand, the mere ignorant is still more despised; nor is any thing deemed a surer sign of an illiberal genius in an age and nation where the sciences flourish, than to be entirely destitute of all relish for those noble entertainments. The most perfect character is supposed to lie between those extremes; retaining an equal ability and taste for books, company, and business; preserving in conversation that discernment and delicacy which arise from polite letters; and in business, that probity and accuracy which are the natural result of a just philosophy. In order to diffuse and cultivate so accomplished a character, nothing can be more useful than compositions of the easy style and manner, which draw not too much from life, require no deep application or retreat to be comprehended, and send back the student among mankind full of noble sentiments and wise precepts, applicable to every exigence of human life. By means of such compositions, virtue becomes amiable, science agreeable, company instructive, and retirement entertaining.

Man is a reasonable being; and as such, receives from science his proper food and nourishment: But so narrow are the bounds of human understanding, that little satisfaction can be hoped for in this particular, either from the extent or security of his acquisitions. Man is a sociable, no less than a reasonable being: But neither can he always enjoy company agreeable and amusing, or preserve the proper relish for them. Man is also an active being; and from that disposition, as well as from the various necessities of human life, must submit to business and occupation: But the mind requires some relaxation, and cannot always support its bent to care and industry. It seems, then, that nature has pointed out a mixed kind of life as most suitable to the human race, and secretly admonished them to allow none of these biasses to *draw* too much, so as to incapacitate them for other occupations and entertainments. Indulge your passion for science, says she, but let your science be human, and such as may have a direct reference to action and society. Abstruse thought and profound researches I prohibit, and will severely punish, by the pensive melancholy which they introduce, by the endless uncertainty in which they involve you, and by the cold reception which your pretended discoveries shall meet with, when communicated. Be a philosopher; but, amidst all your philosophy, be still a man.

Were the generality of mankind contented to prefer the easy philosophy to the abstract and profound, without throwing any blame or contempt on the latter, it might not be improper, perhaps, to comply with this general opinion, and allow every man to enjoy, without opposition, his own taste and sentiment. But as the matter is often carried farther, even to the absolute rejecting of all profound reasonings, or what is commonly called *metaphysics*, we shall now proceed to consider what can reasonably be pleaded in their behalf.

We may begin with observing, that one considerable advantage, which results from the accurate and abstract philosophy, is, its subserviency to the easy and humane, which, without the former, can never attain a sufficient degree of exactness in its sentiments, precepts, or reasonings. All polite letters are nothing but pictures of human life in various attitudes and situations; and inspire us with different sentiments, of praise or blame, admiration or ridicule, according to the qualities of the object, which they set before us. An artist must be better qualified to succeed in this undertaking, who, besides a delicate taste and a quick apprehension, possesses an accurate knowledge of the internal fabric, the operations of the understanding, the workings of the passions, and the various species of sentiment which discriminate vice and virtue. How painful soever this inward search or enquiry may appear, it becomes, in some measure, requisite to those, who would describe with success the obvious and outward appearances of life and manners. The anatomist presents to the eye the most hideous and disagreeable objects; but his science is useful to the painter in delineating even a Venus or an Helen. While the latter employs all the richest colours of his art, and gives his figures the most graceful and engaging airs; he must still carry his attention to the inward structure of the human body, the position of the muscles, the fabric of the bones, and the use and figure of every part or organ. Accuracy is, in every case, advantageous to beauty, and just reasoning to delicate sentiment. In vain would we exalt the one by depreciating the other.

Besides, we may observe, in every art or profession, even those which most concern life or action, that a spirit of accuracy, however acquired, carries all of them nearer their perfection, and renders them more subservient to the interests of society. And though a philosopher may live remote from business, the genius of philosophy, if carefully cultivated by several, must gradually diffuse itself throughout the whole society, and bestow a similar correctness on every art and calling. The politician will acquire greater foresight and subtility, in the subdividing and balancing of power; the lawyer more method and finer principles in his reasonings; and the general more regularity in his discipline, and more caution in his plans and operations. The stability of modern governments above the ancient, and the accuracy of modern philosophy, have improved, and probably will still improve, by similar gradations.

Were there no advantage to be reaped from these studies, beyond the gratification of an innocent curiosity, yet ought not even this to be despised; as being one accession to those few safe and harmless pleasures, which are bestowed on the human race. The sweetest and most inoffensive path of life leads through the avenues of science and learning; and whoever can either remove any obstructions in this way, or open up any new prospect, ought so far to be esteemed a benefactor to mankind. And though these researches may appear painful and fatiguing, it is with some minds as with some bodies, which being endowed with vigorous and florid health, require severe exercise, and reap a pleasure from what, to the generality of mankind, may seem burdensome and laborious. Obscurity, indeed, is painful to the mind as well as to the eye; but to bring light from obscurity, by whatever labour, must needs be delightful and rejoicing.

But this obscurity in the profound and abstract philosophy, is objected to, not only as painful and fatiguing, but as the inevitable source of uncertainty and error. Here indeed lies the justest and most plausible objection against a considerable part of metaphysics, that they are not properly a science; but arise either from the fruitless efforts of human vanity, which would penetrate into subjects utterly inaccessible to the understanding, or from the craft of popular superstitions, which, being unable to defend themselves on fair ground, raise these intangling brambles to cover and protect their weakness. Chaced from the open country, these robbers fly into the forest, and lie in wait to break in upon every unguarded avenue of the mind, and overwhelm it with religious fears and prejudices. The stoutest antagonist, if he remit his watch a moment, is oppressed. And many, through cowardice and folly, open the gates to the enemies, and willingly receive them with reverence and submission, as their legal sovereigns.

But is this a sufficient reason, why philosophers should desist from such researches, and leave superstition still in possession of her retreat? Is it not proper to draw an opposite conclusion, and perceive the necessity of carrying the war into the most secret recesses of the enemy? In vain do we hope, that men, from frequent disappointment, will at last abandon such airy sciences, and discover the proper province of human reason. For, besides, that many persons find too sensible an interest in perpetually recalling such topics; besides this, I say, the motive of blind despair can never reasonably have place in the sciences; since, however unsuccessful former attempts may have proved, there is still room to hope, that the industry, good fortune, or improved sagacity of succeeding generations may reach discoveries unknown to former ages. Each adventurous genius will leap at the arduous prize, and find himself stimulated, rather than discouraged, by the failures of his predecessors; while he hopes that the glory of achieving so hard an adventure is reserved for him alone. The only method of freeing learning, at once, from these abstruse questions, is to enquire seriously into the nature of human understanding, and show, from an exact analysis of its powers and capacity, that it is by no means fitted for such remote and abstruse sub-jects. We must submit to this fatigue, in order to live at ease ever after: And must cultivate true metaphysics with some care, in order to destroy the false and adulterate. Indolence, which, to some persons, affords a safe-guard against this deceitful philosophy, is, with others, overbalanced by curiosity; and despair, which, at some moments, prevails, may give place afterwards to sanguine hopes and expectations. Accurate and just reasoning is the only catholic remedy, fitted for all persons and all dispositions; and is alone able to subvert that abstruse philosophy and metaphysical jargon, which, being mixed up with popular superstition, renders it in a manner impenetrable to careless reasoners, and gives it the air of science and wisdom.

Besides this advantage of rejecting, after deliberate enquiry, the most uncertain and disagreeable part of learning, there are many positive advantages, which result from an accurate scrutiny into the powers and faculties of human nature. It is remarkable concerning the operations of the mind, that, though most intimately present to us, yet, whenever they become the object of reflexion, they seem involved in obscurity; nor can the eye readily find those lines and boundaries, which discriminate and distinguish them. The objects are too fine to remain long in the same aspect or situation; and must be apprehended in an instant, by a superior penetration, derived from nature, and improved by habit and reflexion. It becomes, therefore, no inconsiderable part of science barely to know the different operations of the mind, to separate them from each other, to class them under their proper heads, and to correct all that seeming disorder, in which they lie involved, when made the object of reflexion and enquiry. This talk of ordering and distinguishing, which has no merit, when performed with regard to external bodies, the objects of our senses, rises in its value, when directed towards the operations of the mind, in proportion to the difficulty and labour, which we meet with in performing it. And if we can go no farther than this mental geography, or delineation of the distinct parts and powers of the mind, it is at least a satisfaction to go so far; and the more obvious this science may appear (and it is by no means obvious) the more contemptible still must the ignorance of it be esteemed, in all pretenders to learning and philosophy.

Nor can there remain any suspicion, that this science is uncertain and chimerical; unless we should entertain such a scepticism as is entirely subversive of all speculation, and even action. It cannot be doubted, that the mind is endowed with several powers and faculties, that these powers are distinct from each other, that what is really distinct to the immediate perception may be distinguished by reflexion; and consequently, that there is a truth and falsehood in all propositions on this subject, and a truth and falsehood, which lie not beyond the compass of human understanding. There are many obvious distinctions of this kind, such as those between the will and understanding, the imagination and passions, which fall within the comprehension of every human creature; and the finer and more philosophical distinctions are no less real and certain, though more difficult to be comprehended. Some instances, especially late ones, of success in these enquiries, may give us a juster notion of the certainty and solidity of this branch of learning. And shall we esteem it worthy the labour of a philosopher to give us a true system of the planets, and adjust the position and order of those remote bodies; while we affect to overlook those, who, with so much success, delineate the parts of the mind, in which we are so intimately concerned?

But may we not hope, that philosophy, if cultivated with care, and encouraged by the attention of the public, may carry its researches still farther, and discover, at least in some degree, the secret springs and principles, by which the human mind is actuated in its operations? Astronomers had long contented themselves with proving, from the phaenomena, the true motions, order, and magnitude of the heavenly bodies: Till a philosopher, at last, arose, who seems, from the happiest reasoning, to have also determined the laws and forces, by which the revolutions of the planets are governed and directed. The like has been performed with regard to other parts of nature. And there is no reason to despair of equal success in our enquiries concerning the mental powers and economy, if prosecuted with equal capacity and caution. It is probable, that one operation and principle of the mind depends on another; which, again, may be resolved into one more general and universal: And how far these researches may possibly be carried, it will be difficult for us, before, or even after, a careful trial, exactly to determine. This is certain, that attempts of this kind are very day made even by those who philosophize the most negligently: And nothing can be more requisite than to enter upon the enterprize with thorough care and attention; that, if it lie within the compass of human understanding, it may at last be happily achieved; if not, it may, however, be rejected with some confidence and security. This last conclusion, surely, is not desirable; nor ought it to be embraced too rashly. For how much must we diminish from the beauty and value of this species of philosophy, upon such a supposition? Moralists have hitherto been accustomed, when they considered the vast multitude and diversity of those actions that excite our approbation or dislike, to search for some common principle, on which this variety of sentiments might depend. And though they have sometimes carried the matter too far, by their passion for some one general principle; it must, however, be confessed, that they are excusable in expecting to find some general principles, into which all the vices and virtues were justly to be resolved. The like has been the endeavour of critics, logicians, and even politicians: Nor have their attempts been wholly unsuccessful; though perhaps longer time, greater accuracy, and more ardent application may bring these sciences still nearer their perfection. To throw up at once all pretensions of this kind may justly be deemed more rash, precipitate, and dogmatical, than even the boldest and most affirmative philosophy, that has ever attempted to impose its crude dictates and principles on mankind.

What though these reasonings concerning human nature seem abstract, and of difficult comprehension? This affords no presumption of their falsehood. On the contrary, it seems impossible, that what has hitherto escaped so many wise and profound philosophers can be very obvious and easy. And whatever pains these researches may cost us, we may think ourselves sufficiently rewarded, not only in point of profit but of pleasure, if, by that means, we can make any addition to our stock of knowledge, in subjects of such unspeakable importance.

But as, after all, the abstractedness of these speculations is no recommendation, but rather a disadvantage to them, and as this difficulty may perhaps be surmounted by care and art, and the avoiding of all unnecessary detail, we have, in the following enquiry, attempted to throw some light upon subjects, from which uncertainty has hitherto deterred the wise, and obscurity the ignorant. Happy, if we can unite the boundaries of the different species of philosophy, by reconciling profound enquiry with clearness, and truth with novelty! And still more happy, if reasoning in this easy manner, we can undermine the foundations of an abstruse philosophy, which seems to have hitherto served only as a shelter to supersition, and a cover to absurdity and error!

SECTION II. OF THE ORIGIN OF IDEAS

Every one will readily allow, that there is a considerable difference between the perceptions of the mind, when a man feels the pain of excessive heat, or the pleasure of moderate warmth, and when he afterwards recalls to his memory this sensation, or anticipates it by his imagination. These faculties may mimic or copy the perceptions of the senses; but they never can entirely reach the force and vivacity of the original sentiment. The utmost we say of them, even when they operate with greatest vigour, is, that they represent their object in so lively a manner, that we could *almost* say we feel or see it: But, except the mind be disordered by disease or madness, they never can arrive at such a pitch of vivacity, as to render these perceptions altogether undistinguishable. All the colours of poetry, however splendid, can never paint natural objects in such a manner as to make the description be taken for a real landskip. The most lively thought is still inferior to the dullest sensation.

We may observe a like distinction to run through all the other perceptions of the mind. A man in a fit of anger, is actuated in a very different manner from one who only thinks of that emotion. If you tell me, that any person is in love, I easily understand your meaning, and form a just conception of his situation; but never can mistake that conception for the real disorders and agitations of the passion. When we reflect on our past sentiments and affections, our thought is a faithful mirror, and copies its objects truly; but the colours which it employs are faint and dull, in comparison of those in which our original perceptions were clothed. It requires no nice discernment or metaphysical head to mark the distinction between them.

Here therefore we may divide all the perceptions of the mind into two classes or species, which are distinguished by their different degrees of force and vivacity. The less forcible and lively are commonly de-nominated *Thoughts* or *Ideas*. The other species want a name in our language, and in most others; I suppose, because it was not requisite for any, but philosophical purposes, to rank them under a general term or appellation. Let us, therefore, use a little freedom, and call them *Impressions*; employing that word in a sense somewhat different from the usual. By the term *impression*, then, I mean all our more lively per-ceptions, when we hear, or see, or feel, or love, or hate, or desire, or will. And impressions are distinguished from ideas which are the less lively perceptions, of which we are conscious, when we reflect on any of those sensations or movements above mentioned.

Nothing, at first view, may seem more unbounded than the thought of man, which not only escapes all human power and authority, but is not even restrained within the limits of nature and reality. To form mon-sters, and join incongruous shapes and appearances, costs the imagina-tion no more trouble than to conceive the most natural and familiar objects. And while the body is confined to one planet, along which it creeps with pain and difficulty; the thought can in an instant transport us into the most distant regions of the universe; or even beyond the universe, into the unbounded chaos, where nature is supposed to lie in total confusion. What never was seen, or heard of, may yet be con-ceived; nor is any thing beyond the power of thought, except what implies an absolute contradiction.

But though our thought seems to possess this unbounded liberty, we shall find, upon a nearer examination, that it is really confined within very narrow limits, and that all this creative power of the mind amounts to no more than the faculty of compounding, transposing, augmenting, or diminishing the materials afforded us by the senses and experience. When we think of a golden mountain, we only join two consistent ideas, *gold*, and *mountain*, with which we were formerly acquainted. A vir-tuous horse we can conceive; because, from our own feeling, we can conceive virtue; and this we may unite to the figure and shape of a horse, which is an animal familiar to us. In short, all the materials of thinking are derived either from our outward or inward sentiment: the mixture and composition of these belongs alone to the mind and will. Or, to express myself in philosophical language, all our ideas or more feeble perceptions are copies of our impressions or more lively ones.

To prove this, the two following arguments will, I hope, be sufficient. First, when we analyze our thoughts or ideas, however compounded or sublime, we always find that they resolve themselves into such simple ideas as were copied from a precedent feeling or sentiment. Even those ideas, which, at first view, seem the most wide of this origin, are found, upon a nearer scrutiny, to be derived from it. The idea of God, as meaning an infinitely intelligent, wise, and good Being, arises from re-flecting on the operations of our own mind, and augmenting, without limit, those qualities of goodness and wisdom. We may prosecute this enquiry to what length we please; where we shall always find, that every idea which we examine is copied from a similar impression. Those who would assert that this position is not universally true nor without exception, have only one, and that an easy method of refuting it; by producing that idea, which, in their opinion, is not derived from this source. It will then be incumbent on us, if we would maintain our doctrine, to produce the impression, or lively perception, which corresponds to it.

Secondly. If it happens, from a defect of the organ, that a man is not susceptible of any species of sensation, we always find that he is as little susceptible of the correspondent ideas. A blind man can form no notion of colours; a deaf man of sounds. Restore either of them that sense in which he is deficient; by opening this new inlet for his sensations, you also open an inlet for the ideas; and he finds no difficulty in conceiving these objects. The case is the same, if the object, proper for exciting any sensation, has never been applied to the organ. A Laplander or Negro has no notion of the relish of wine. And though there are few or no instances of a like deficiency in the mind, where a person has never felt or is wholly incapable of a sentiment or passion that belongs to his species; yet we find the same observation to take place in a less degree. A man of mild manners can form no idea of inveterate revenge or cruelty; nor can a selfish heart easily conceive the heights of friendship and generosity. It is readily allowed, that other beings may possess many senses of which we can have no conception, because the ideas of them have never been introduced to us in the only manner by which an idea can have access to the mind, to wit, by the actual feeling and sensation.

There is, however, one contradictory phenomenon, which may prove that it is not absolutely impossible for ideas to arise, independent of their correspondent impressions. I believe it will readily be allowed, that the several distinct ideas of colour, which enter by the eye, or those of sound, which are conveyed by the ear, are really different from each other; though, at the same time, resembling. Now if this be true of different colours, it must be no less so of the different shades of the same colour; and each shade produces a distinct idea, independent of the rest. For if this should be denied, it is possible, by the continual gradation of shades, to run a colour insensibly into what is most remote from it; and if you will not allow any of the means to be different, you cannot, without absurdity, deny the extremes to be the same. Suppose, therefore, a person to have enjoyed his sight for thirty years, and to have become perfectly acquainted with colours of all kinds except one particular shade of blue, for instance, which it never has been his fortune to meet with. Let all the different shades of that colour, except that single one, be placed before him, descending gradually from the deepest to lightest; it is plain that he will perceive a blank, where that shade is wanting, and will be sensible that there is a greater distance in that place between the contiguous colours than in any other. Now I ask, whether it be possible for him, from his own imagination, to supply this deficiency, and raise up to himself the idea of that particular shade, though it had never been conveyed to him by his senses? I believe there are few but will be of opinion that he can: and this may serve as a proof that the simple ideas are not always, in every instance, derived from the correspondent impressions; though this instance is so singular, that it is scarcely worth our observing, and does not merit that for it alone we should alter our general maxim.

Here, therefore, is a proposition, which not only seems, in itself, simple and intelligible; but, if a proper use were made of it, might render every dispute equally intelligible, and banish all that jargon, which has so long taken possession of metaphysical reasonings, and drawn disgrace upon them. All ideas, especially abstract ones, are naturally faint and obscure: the mind has but a slender hold of them: they are apt to be confounded with other resembling ideas; and when we have often employed any term, though without a distinct meaning, we are apt to imagine it has a determinate idea annexed to it. On the contrary, all impressions, that is, all sensations, either outward or inward, are strong and vivid: the limits between them are more exactly determined: nor is it easy to fall into any error or mistake with regard to them. When we entertain, therefore, any suspicion that a philosophical term is employed without any meaning or idea (as it but too frequent), we need but enquire, *from what impression is that supposed idea derived*? And if it be impossible to assign any, this will serve to confirm our suspicion.[1] By bringing ideas into so clear a light we may reasonably hope to remove all dispute, which may arise, concerning their nature and reality.

---

[1] It is probable that no more was meant by those, who denied innate ideas, than that all ideas were copies of our impressions; though it must be confessed, that the terms, which they employed, were not chosen with such caution, nor so exactly defined, as to prevent all mistakes about their doctrine. For what is meant by *innate?* If innate be equivalent to natural, then all the perceptions and ideas of the mind must be allowed to be innate or natural, in whatever sense we take the latter word, whether in opposition to what is uncommon, artificial, or miraculous. If by innate be meant, contemporary to our birth, the dispute seems to be frivolous; nor is it worth while to enquire at what time thinking begins, whether before, at, or after our birth. Again, the word *idea*, seems to be commonly taken in a very loose sense, by Locke and others; as standing for any of our perceptions, our sensations and passions, as well as thoughts. Now in this sense, I should desire to know, what can be meant by asserting, that self-love, or resentment of injuries, or the passion between the sexes is not innate?

But admitting these terms, *impressions* and *ideas*, in the sense above explained, and understanding by *innate*, what is original or copied from no precedent perception, then may we assert that all our impressions are innate and our ideas not innate.

To be ingenuous, I must own it to be my opinion, that Locke was betrayed into this question by the schoolmen, who, making use of undefined terms, draw out their disputes to a tedious length, without ever touching the point in question. A like ambiguity and circumlocution seem to run through that philosopher's reasonings on this as well as most other subjects.

SECTION III. OF THE ASSOCIATION OF IDEAS

It is evident that there is a principle of connexion between the different thoughts or ideas of the mind, and that, in their appearance to the memory or imagination, they introduce each other with a certain degree of method and regularity. In our more serious thinking or discourse this is so observable that any particular thought, which breaks in upon the regular tract or chain of ideas, is immediately remarked and rejected. And even in our wildest and most wandering reveries, nay in our very dreams, we shall find, if we reflect, that the imagination ran not altogether at adventures, but that there was still a connexion upheld among the different ideas, which succeeded each other. Were the loosest and freest conversation to be transcribed, there would immediately be observed something which connected it in all its transitions. Or where this is wanting, the person who broke the thread of discourse might still inform you, that there had secretly revolved in his mind a succession of thought, which had gradually led him from the subject of conversation. Among different languages, even where we cannot suspect the least connexion or communication, it is found, that the words, expressive of ideas, the most compounded, do yet nearly correspond to each other: a certain proof that the simple ideas, comprehended in the compound ones, were bound together by some universal principle, which had an equal influence on all mankind.

Though it be too obvious to escape observation, that different ideas are connected together; I do not find that any philosopher has attempted to enumerate or class all the principles of association; a subject, however, that seems worthy of curiosity. To me, there appear to be only three principles of connexion among ideas, namely, *Resemblance, Contiguity* in time or place, and *Cause* or *Effect.*

That these principles serve to connect ideas will not, I believe, be much doubted. A picture naturally leads our thoughts to the original: [2] the mention of one apartment in a building naturally introduces an enquiry or discourse concerning the others: [3] and if we think of a wound, we can scarcely forbear reflecting on the pain which follows it.[4] But that this enumeration is complete, and that there are no other principles of association except these, may be difficult to prove to the satisfaction of the reader, or even to a man's own satisfaction. All we can do, in such cases, is to run over several instances, and examine carefully the principle which binds the different thoughts to each other, never stopping till we render the principle as general as possible.[5] The more instances

---

[2] Resemblance.

[3] Contiguity.

[4] Cause and effect.

[5] For instance, Contrast or Contrariety is also a connexion among Ideas but it may, perhaps, be considered as a mixture of *Causation* and *Resemblance.* Where two objects are contrary, the one destroys the other; that is, the cause of its annihilation, and the idea of the annihilation of an object implies the idea of its former existence.

we examine, and the more care we employ, the more assurance shall we acquire, that the enumeration, which we form from the whole, is complete and entire.

SECTION IV.   SCEPTICAL DOUBTS CONCERNING THE OPERATIONS OF THE UNDERSTANDING

Part I

All the objects of human reason or enquiry may naturally be divided into two kinds, to wit, *Relations of Ideas*, and *Matters of Fact*. Of the first kind are the sciences of Geometry, Algebra, and Arithmetic; and in short, every affirmation which is either intuitively or demonstratively certain. *That the square of the hypothenuse is equal to the squares of the two sides*, is a proposition which expresses a relation between these figures. *That three times five is equal to the half of thirty*, expresses a relation between these numbers. Propositions of this kind are discoverable by the mere operation of thought, without dependence on what is anywhere existent in the universe. Though there never were a circle or triangle in nature, the truths demonstrated by Euclid would for ever retain their certainty and evidence.

Matters of fact, which are the second objects of human reason, are not ascertained in the same manner; nor is our evidence of their truth however great, of a like nature with the foregoing. The contrary of every matter of fact is still possible; because it can never imply a contradiction, and is conceived by the mind with the same facility and distinctness, as if ever so conformable to reality. *That the sun will not rise to-morrow* is no less intelligible a proposition, and implies no more contradiction than the affirmation, *that it will rise*. We should in vain, therefore, attempt to demonstrate its falsehood. Were it demonstratively false, it would imply a contradiction, and could never be distinctly conceived by the mind.

It may, therefore, be a subject worthy of curiosity, to enquire what is the nature of that evidence which assures us of any real existence and matter of fact, beyond the present testimony of our senses, or the records of our memory. This part of philosophy, it is observable, has been little cultivated, either by the ancients or moderns; and therefore our doubts and errors, in the prosecution of so important an enquiry, may be the more excusable; while we march through such difficult paths without any guide or direction. They may even prove useful, by exciting curiosity, and destroying that implicit faith and security, which is the bane of all reasoning and free enquiry. The discovery of defects in the common philosophy, if any such there be, will not, I presume, be a discouragement, but rather an incitement, as is usual, to attempt something more full and satisfactory than has yet been proposed to the public.

All reasonings concerning matter of fact seem to be founded on the relation of *Cause and Effect*. By means of that relation alone we can go beyond the evidence of our memory and senses. If you were to ask a man, why he believes any matter of fact, which is absent; for instance, that his friend is in the country, or in France; he would give you a reason; and this reason would be some other fact; as a letter received from him, or the knowledge of his former resolutions and promises. A man finding a watch or any other machine in a desert island, would conclude that there had once been men in that island. All our reasonings concerning fact are of the same nature. And here it is constantly supposed that there is a connexion between the present fact and that which is inferred from it. Were there nothing to bind them together, the inference would be entirely precarious. The hearing of an articulate voice and rational discourse in the dark assures us of the presence of some person: Why? because these are the effects of the human make and fabric, and closely connected with it. If we anatomize all the other reasonings of this nature, we shall find that they are founded on the relation of cause and effect, and that this relation is either near or remote, direct or collateral. Heat and light are collateral effects of fire, and the one effect may justly be inferred from the other.

If we would satisfy ourselves, therefore, concerning the nature of that evidence, which assures us of matters of fact, we must enquire how we arrive at the knowledge of cause and effect.

I shall venture to affirm, as a general proposition, which admits of no exception, that the knowledge of this relation is not, in any instance, attained by reasonings *a priori;* but arises entirely from experience, when we find that any particular objects are constantly conjoined with each other. Let an object be presented to a man of ever so strong natural reason and abilities; if that object be entirely new to him, he will not be able, by the most accurate examination of its sensible qualities, to discover any of its causes or effects. Adam, though his rational faculties be supposed, at the very first, entirely perfect, could not have inferred from the fluidity and transparency of water that it would suffocate him, or from the light and warmth of fire that it would consume him. No object ever discovers, by the qualities which appear to the senses, either the causes which produced it, or the effects which will arise from it; nor can our reason, unassisted by experience, ever draw any inference concerning real existence and matter of fact.

This proposition, *that causes and effects are discoverable, not by reason but by experience,* will readily be admitted with regard to such objects, as we remember to have once been altogether unknown to us; since we must be conscious of the utter inability, which we then lay under, of foretelling what would arise from them. Present two smooth pieces of marble to a man who has no tincture of natural philosophy; he will never discover that they will adhere together in such a manner as to require great force to separate them in a direct line, while they make so small a resistance to a lateral pressure. Such events, as bear little analogy to the common course of nature, are also readily confessed to be known only by experience; nor does any man imagine that the explosion of gunpowder, or the attraction of a loadstone, could ever be discovered by arguments *a priori*. In like manner, when an effect is supposed to depend upon an intricate machinery or secret structure of parts, we make no difficulty in attributing all our knowledge of it to experience. Who will assert that he can give the ultimate reason, why milk or bread is proper nourishment for a man, not for a lion or a tiger?

But the same truth may not appear, at first sight, to have the same evidence with regard to events, which have become familiar to us from our first appearance in the world, which bear a close analogy to the whole course of nature, and which are supposed to depend on the simple qualities of objects, without any secret structure of parts. We are apt to imagine that we could discover these effects by the mere operation of our reason, without experience. We fancy, that were we brought on a sudden into this world, we could at first have inferred that one Billiard-ball would communicate motion to another upon impulse; and that we needed not to have waited for the event, in order to pronounce with certainty concerning it. Such is the influence of custom, that, where it is strongest, it not only covers our natural ignorance, but even conceals itself, and seems not to take place, merely because it is found in the highest degree.

But to convince us that all the laws of nature, and all the operations of bodies without exception, are known only by experience, the following reflections may, perhaps, suffice. Were any object presented to us, and were we required to pronounce concerning the effect, which will result from it, without consulting past observation; after what manner, I beseech you, must the mind proceed in this operation? It must invent or imagine some event, which it ascribes to the object as its effect; and it is plain that this invention must be entirely arbitrary. The mind can never possibly find the effect in the supposed cause, by the most accurate scrutiny and examination. For the effect is totally different from the cause, and consequently can never be discovered in it. Motion in the second Billiard-ball is a quite distinct event from motion in the first: nor is there anything in the one to suggest the smallest hint of the other. A stone or piece of metal raised into the air, and left without any support, immediately falls: but to consider the matter *a priori*, is there anything we discover in this situation which can beget the idea of a downward, rather than an upward, or any other motion, in the stone or metal?

And as the first imagination or invention of a particular effect, in all natural operations, is arbitrary, where we consult not experience; so must we also esteem the supposed tie or connexion between the cause and effect, which binds them together, and renders it impossible that any other effect could result from the operation of that cause. When I see, for instance, a Billiard-ball moving in a straight line towards another; even suppose motion in the second ball should by accident be suggested to me, as the result of their contact or impulse; may I not conceive, that a hundred different events might as well follow from that cause? May not both these balls remain at absolute rest? May not the first ball return in a straight line, or leap off from the second in any line or direction? All these suppositions are consistent and conceivable. Why then should we give the preference to one, which is no more consistent or conceivable than the rest? All our reasonings *a priori* will never be able to show us any foundation for this preference.

In a word, then, every effect is a distinct event from its cause. It could not, therefore, be discovered in the cause, and the first invention or conception of it, *a priori*, must be entirely arbitrary. And even after it is suggested, the conjunction of it with the cause must appear equally arbitrary; since there are always many other effects, which, to reason, must seem fully as consistent and natural. In vain, therefore, should we pretend to determine any single event, or infer any cause or effect, without the assistance of observation and experience.

Hence we may discover the reason why no philosopher, who is rational and modest, has ever pretended to assign the ultimate cause of any natural operation, or to show distinctly the action of that power, which produces any single effect in the universe. It is confessed, that the utmost effort of human reason is to reduce the principles, productive of natural phenomena, to a greater simplicity, and to resolve the many particular effects into a few general causes, by means of reasonings from analogy, experience, and observation. But as to the causes of these general causes, we should in vain attempt their discovery; nor shall we ever be able to satisfy ourselves, by any particular explication of them. These ultimate springs and principles are totally shut up from human curiosity and enquiry. Elasticity, gravity, cohesion of parts, communication of motion by impulse; these are probably the ultimate causes and principles which we ever discover in nature; and we may esteem ourselves sufficiently happy, if, by accurate inquiry and reasoning, we can trace up the particular phenomena to, or near to, these general principles. The most perfect philosophy of the natural kind only staves off our ignorance a little longer: as perhaps the most perfect philosophy of the moral or metaphysical kind serves only to discover larger portions of it. Thus the observation of human blindness and weakness is the result of all philosophy, and meets us at every turn, in spite of our endeavours to elude or avoid it.

Nor is geometry, when taken into the assistance of natural philosophy, ever able to remedy this defect, or lead us into the knowledge of ultimate causes, by all that accuracy of reasoning for which it is so justly celebrated. Every part of mixed mathematics proceeds upon the supposition that certain laws are established by nature in her operations; and abstract reasonings are employed, either to assist experience in the discovery of these laws, or to determine their influence in particular instances, where it depends upon any precise degree of distance and quantity. Thus, it is a law of motion, discovered by experience, that the moment or force of any body in motion is in the compound ratio or proportion of its solid contents and its velocity; and consequently, that a small force may remove the greatest obstacle or raise the greatest weight, if, by any contrivance or machinery, we can increase the velocity of that force, so as to make it an overmatch for its antagonist. Geometry assists us in the application of this law, by giving us the just dimensions of all the parts and figures which can enter into any species of machines; but still the discovery of the law itself is owing merely to experience, and all the abstract reasonings in the world could never lead us one step towards the knowledge of it. When we reason *a priori,* and consider merely any object or cause, as it appears to the mind, independent of all observation, it never could suggest to us the notion of any distinct object, such as its effect; much less, show us the inseparable and inviolable connexion between them. A man must be very sagacious who could discover by reasoning that crystal is the effect of heat, and ice of cold, without being previously acquainted with the operation of these qualities.

Part II

But we have not yet attained any tolerable satisfaction with regard to the question first proposed. Each solution still gives rise to a new question as difficult as the foregoing, and leads us on to farther enquiries. When it is asked, *What is the nature of all our reasonings concerning matter of fact?* the proper answer seems to be, that they are founded on the relation of cause and effect. When again it is asked, *What is the foundation of all our reasonings and conclusions concerning that relation?* it may be replied in one word, Experience. But if we still carry on our sifting humour, and ask, *What is the foundation of all conclusions from experience?* this implies a new question, which may be of more difficult solution and explication. Philosophers, that give themselves airs of superior wisdom and sufficiency, have a hard task when they encounter persons of inquisitive dispositions, who push them from every corner to which they retreat, and who are sure at last to bring them to some dangerous dilemma. The best expedient to prevent this confusion, is to be modest in our pretensions; and even to discover the difficulty ourselves before it is objected to us. By this means, we may make a kind of merit of our very ignorance.

I shall content myself, in this section, with an easy task, and shall pretend only to give a negative answer to the question here proposed. I say then, that, even after we have experience of the operations of cause and effect, our conclusions from that experience are *not* founded on reasoning, or any process of the understanding. This answer we must endeavour both to explain and to defend.

It must certainly be allowed, that nature has kept us at a great distance from all her secrets, and has afforded us only the knowledge of a few superficial qualities of objects; while she conceals from us those powers and principles on which the influence of those objects entirely depends. Our senses inform us of the colour, weight, and consistence of bread; but neither sense nor reason can ever inform us of those qualities which fit it for the nourishment and support of a human body. Sight or feeling conveys an idea of the actual motion of bodies; but as to that wonderful force or power, which would carry on a moving body for ever in a continued change of place, and which bodies never lose but by communicating it to others; of this we cannot form the most distant conception. But notwithstanding this ignorance of natural powers [6] and principles, we always presume, when we see like sensible qualities, that they have like secret powers, and expect that effects, similar to those which we have experienced, will follow from them. If a body of like colour and consistence with that bread, which we have formerly eat, be presented to us, we make no scruple of repeating the experiment, and foresee, with certainty, like nourishment and support. Now this is a process of the mind or thought, of which I would willingly know the foundation. It is allowed on all hands that there is no known connexion between the sensible qualities and the secret powers; and consequently, that the mind is not led to form such a conclusion concerning their constant and regular conjunction, by anything which it knows of their nature. As to past *Experience*, it can be allowed to give *direct* and *certain* information of those precise objects only, and that precise period of time, which fell under its cognizance: but why this experience should be extended to future times, and to other objects, which, for aught we know, may be only in appearance similar; this is the main question on which I would insist. The bread, which I formerly eat, nourished me; that is, a body of such sensible qualities was, at that time, endued with such secret powers: but does it follow, that other bread must also nourish me at another time, and that like sensible qualities must always be attended with like secret powers? The consequence seems nowise necessary. At least, it must be acknowledged that there is here a consequence drawn by the mind; that there is a certain step taken; a process of thought, and an inference, which wants to be explained. These two propositions are far from being the same, *I have found that such an object has always been attended with such an effect,* and *I foresee, that other objects, which are, in appearance, similar, will be attended with similar effects.* I shall allow, if you please, that the one proposition may justly be inferred from the other; I know, in fact, that it always is inferred. But if you insist that the inference is made by a chain of reasoning, I desire you to produce that reasoning. The connexion between these propositions is not intuitive. There is required a medium, which may enable the mind to draw such an inference, if indeed it be drawn by reasoning and argument. What that medium is, I must confess, passes my comprehension; and it is incumbent on those to produce it, who assert that it really exists, and is the origin of all our conclusions concerning matter of fact.

This negative argument must certainly, in process of time, become altogether convincing, if many penetrating and able philosophers shall

---

[6] The word, Power, is here used in a loose and popular sense. The more accurate explication of it would give additional evidence to this argument. See Sect. 7.

turn their enquiries this way and no one be ever able to discover any connecting proposition or intermediate step, which supports the understanding in this conclusion. But as the question is yet new, every reader may not trust so far to his own penetration, as to conclude, because an argument escapes his enquiry, that therefore it does not really exist. For this reason it may be requisite to venture upon a more difficult task; and enumerating all the branches of human knowledge, endeavour to show that none of them can afford such an argument.

All reasonings may be divided into two kinds, namely, demonstrative reasoning, or that concerning relations of ideas, and moral reasoning, or that concerning matter of fact and existence. That there are no demonstrative arguments in the case seems evident; since it implies no contradiction that the course of nature may change, and that an object, seemingly like those which we have experienced, may be attended with different or contrary effects. May I not clearly and distinctly conceive that a body, falling from the clouds, and which, in all other respects, resembles snow, has yet the taste of salt or feeling of fire? Is there any more intelligible proposition than to affirm, that all the trees will flourish in December and January, and decay in May and June? Now whatever is intelligible, and can be distinctly conceived, implies no contradiction, and can never be proved false by any demonstrative argument or abstract reasoning *à priori*.

If we be, therefore, engaged by arguments to put trust in past experience, and make it the standard of our future judgement, these arguments must be probable only, or such as regard matter of fact and real existence, according to the division above mentioned. But that there is no argument of this kind, must appear, if our explication of that species of reasoning be admitted as solid and satisfactory. We have said that all arguments concerning existence are founded on the relation of cause and effect; that our knowledge of that relation is derived entirely from experience; and that all our experimental conclusions proceed upon the supposition that the future will be conformable to the past. To endeavour, therefore, the proof of this last supposition by probable arguments, or arguments regarding existence, must be evidently going in a circle, and taking that for granted, which is the very point in question.

In reality, all arguments from experience are founded on the similarity which we discover among natural objects, and by which we are induced to expect effects similar to those which we have found to follow from such objects. And though none but a fool or madman will ever pretend to dispute the authority of experience, or to reject that great guide of human life, it may surely be allowed a philosopher to have so much curiosity at least as to examine the principle of human nature, which gives this mighty authority to experience, and makes us draw advantage from that similarity which nature has placed among different objects. From causes which appear *similar* we expect similar effects. This is the sum of all our experimental conclusions. Now it seems evident that, if this conclusion were formed by reason, it would be as perfect at first, and upon one instance, as after ever so long a course of experience. But the case is far otherwise. Nothing so like as eggs; yet no one, on account of this appearing similarity, expects the same taste and relish in all of them. It is only after a long course of uniform experiments in any kind, that we attain a firm reliance and security with regard to a particular event. Now where is that process of reasoning which, from one instance, draws a conclusion, so different from that which it infers from a hundred instances that are nowise different from that single one? This question I propose as much for the sake of information, as with an intention of raising difficulties. I cannot find, I cannot imagine any such reasoning. But I keep my mind still open to instruction, if any one will vouchsafe to bestow it on me.

Should it be said that, from a number of uniform experiments, we *infer* a connexion between the sensible qualities and the secret powers; this, I must confess, seems the same difficulty, couched in different terms. The question still recurs, on what process of argument this *inference* is founded? Where is the medium, the interposing ideas, which join propositions so very wide of each other? It is confessed that the colour, consistence, and other sensible qualities of bread appear not, of themselves, to have any connexion with the secret powers of nourishment and support. For otherwise we could infer these secret powers from the first appearance of these sensible qualities, without the aid of experience; contrary to the sentiment of all philosophers, and contrary to plain matter of fact. Here, then, is our natural state of ignorance with regard to the powers and influence of all objects. How is this remedied by experience? It only shows us a number of uniform effects, resulting from certain objects, and teaches us that those particular objects, at that particular time, were endowed with such powers and forces. When a new object, endowed with similar sensible qualities, is produced, we expect similar powers and forces, and look for a like effect. From a body of like colour and consistence with bread we expect like nourishment and support. But this surely is a step or progress of the mind, which wants to be explained. When a man says, *I have found, in all past instances, such sensible qualities conjoined with such secret powers:* And when he says, *Similar sensible qualities will always be conjoined with similar secret powers,* he is not guilty of a tautology, nor are these propositions in any respect the same. You say that the one proposition is an inference from the other. But you must confess that the inference is not intuitive; neither is it demonstrative: Of what nature is it, then? To say it is experimental, is begging the question. For all inferences from experience suppose, as their foundation, that the future will resemble the past, and that similar powers will be conjoined with similar sensible qualities. If there be any suspicion that the course of nature may change, and that the past may be no rule for the future, all experience becomes useless, and can give rise to no inference or conclusion. It is impossible, therefore, that any arguments from experience can prove this resemblance of the past to the future; since all these arguments are founded on the supposition of that resemblance. Let the course of things be allowed hitherto ever so regular; that alone, without some new argument or inference, proves not that, for the future, it will continue so. In vain do you pretend to have learned the nature of bodies from your past experience. Their secret nature, and consequently all their effects and influence, may change, without any change in their sensible qualities. This happens sometimes, and with regard to some objects: Why may it happen always, and with regard to all objects? What logic, what process of argument secures you against this supposition? My practice, you say, refutes my doubts. But you mistake the purport of my question. As an agent, I am quite satisfied in the point; but as a philosopher, who has some share of curiosity, I will not say scepticism, I want to learn the foundation of this inference. No reading, no enquiry has yet been able to remove my difficulty, or give me satisfaction in a matter of such importance. Can I do better than propose the difficulty to the public, even though, perhaps, I have small hopes of obtaining a solution? We shall, at least, by this means, be sensible of our ignorance, if we do not augment our knowledge.

I must confess that a man is guilty of unpardonable arrogance who concludes, because an argument has escaped his own investigation, that therefore it does not really exist. I must also confess that, though all the learned, for several ages, should have employed themselves in fruitless search upon any subject, it may still, perhaps, be rash to conclude positively that the subject must, therefore, pass all human comprehension. Even though we examine all the sources of our knowledge, and conclude them unfit for such a subject, there may still remain a suspicion, that the enumeration is not complete, or the examination not accurate. But with regard to the present subject, there are some considerations which seem to remove all this accusation of arrogance or suspicion of mistake.

It is certain that the most ignorant and stupid peasants—nay infants, nay even brute beasts—improve by experience, and learn the qualities of natural objects, by observing the effects which result from them. When a child has felt the sensation of pain from touching the flame of a candle, he will be careful not to put his hand near any candle; but will expect a similar effect from a cause which is similar in its sensible qualities and appearance. If you assert, therefore, that the understanding of the child is led into this conclusion by any process of argument or ratiocination, I may justly require you to produce that argument; nor have you any pretense to refuse so equitable a demand. You cannot say that the argument is abtruse, and may possibly escape your enquiry; since you confess that it is obvious to the capacity of a mere infant. If you hesitate, therefore, a moment, or if, after reflection, you produce any intricate or profound argument, you, in a manner, give up the question, and confess that it is not reasoning which engages us to suppose the past resembling the future, and to expect similar effects from causes which are, to appearance, similar. This is the proposition which I intended to enforce in the present section. If I be right, I pretend not to have made any mighty discovery. And if I be wrong, I must acknowledge myself to be indeed a very backward scholar; since I cannot now discover an argument which, it seems, was perfectly familiar to me long before I was out of my cradle.

SECTION V. SCEPTICAL SOLUTION OF THESE DOUBTS

Part I

The passion for philosophy, like that for religion, seems liable to this inconvenience, that, though it aims at the correction of our manners, and extirpation of our vices, it may only serve, by imprudent management, to foster a predominant inclination, and push the mind, with more determined resolution, towards that side which already *draws* too much, by the bias and propensity of the natural temper. It is certain that, while we aspire to the magnanimous firmness of the philosophic sage, and endeavour to confine our pleasures altogether within our own minds, we may, at last, render our philosophy like that of Epictetus, and other *Stoics*, only a more refined system of selfishness, and reason ourselves out of all virtue as well as social enjoyment. While we study with attention the vanity of human life, and turn all our thoughts towards the empty and transitory nature of riches and honours, we are, perhaps, all the while flattering our natural indolence, which, hating the bustle of the world, and drudgery of business, seeks a pretence of reason to give itself a full and uncontrolled indulgence. There is, however, one species of philosophy which seems little liable to this inconvenience, and that because it strikes in with no disorderly passion of the human mind, nor can mingle itself with any natural affection or propensity; and that is the Academic or Sceptical philosophy. The academics always talk of doubt and suspense of judgement, of danger in hasty determinations, of confining to very narrow bounds the enquiries of the understanding, and of renouncing all speculations which lie not within the limits of common life and practice. Nothing, therefore, can be more contrary than such a philosophy to the supine indolence of the mind, its rash arrogance, its lofty pretensions, and its superstitious credulity. Every passion is mortified by it, except the love of truth; and that passion never is, nor can be, carried to too high a degree. It is surprising, therefore, that this philosophy, which, in almost every instance, must be harmless and innocent, should be the subject of so much groundless reproach and obloquy. But, perhaps, the very circumstance which renders it so innocent is what chiefly exposes it to the public hatred and resentment. By flattering no irregular passion, it gains few partizans: By opposing so many vices and follies, it raises to itself abundance of enemies, who stigmatize it as libertine, profane, and irreligious.

Nor need we fear that this philosophy, while it endeavours to limit our enquiries to common life, should ever undermine the reasonings of common life, and carry its doubts so far as to destroy all action, as well as speculation. Nature will always maintain her rights, and prevail in the end over any abstract reasoning whatsoever. Though we should conclude, for instance, as in the foregoing section, that, in all reasonings from experience, there is a step taken by the mind which is not supported by any argument or process of the understanding; there is no danger that these reasonings, on which almost all knowledge depends, will ever be affected by such a discovery. If the mind be not engaged by argument to make this step, it must be induced by some other principle of equal weight and authority; and that principle will preserve its influence as long as human nature remains the same. What that principle is may well be worth the pains of enquiry.

Suppose a person, though endowed with the strongest faculties of reason and reflection, to be brought on a sudden into this world; he would, indeed, immediately observe a continual succession of objects, and one event following another; but he would not be able to discover anything farther. He would not, at first, by any reasoning, be able to reach the idea of cause and effect; since the particular powers, by which all natural operations are performed, never appear to the senses; nor is it reasonable to conclude, merely because one event, in one instance, precedes another, that therefore the one is the cause, the other the effect. Their conjunction may be arbitrary and casual. There may be no reason to infer the existence of one from the appearance of the other. And in a word, such a person, without more experience, could never employ his conjecture or reasoning concerning any matter of fact, or be assured of anything beyond what was immediately present to his memory and senses.

Suppose, again, that he has acquired more experience, and has lived so long in the world as to have observed familiar objects or events to be constantly conjoined together; what is the consequence of this experience? He immediately infers the existence of one object from the appearance of the other. Yet he has not, by all his experience, acquired any idea or knowledge of the secret power by which the one object produces the other; nor is it, by any process of reasoning, he is engaged to draw this inference. But still he finds himself determined to draw it: And though he should be convinced that his understanding has no part in the operation, he would nevertheless continue in the same course of thinking. There is some other principle which determines him to form such a conclusion.

This principle is Custom or Habit. For wherever the repetition of any particular act or operation produces a propensity to renew the same act or operation, without being impelled by any reasoning or process of the understanding, we always say, that this propensity is the effect of *Custom*. By employing that word, we pretend not to have given the ultimate reason of such a propensity. We only point out a principle of human nature, which is universally acknowledged, and which is well known by its effects. Perhaps we can push our enquiries no farther, or pretend to give the cause of this cause; but must rest contented with it as the ultimate principle, which we can assign, of all our conclusions from experience. It is sufficient satisfaction, that we can go so far, without repining at the narrowness of our faculties because they will carry us no farther. And it is certain we here advance a very intelligible proposition at least, if not a true one, when we assert that, after the constant conjunction of two objects—heat and flame, for instance, weight and solidity—we are determined by custom alone to expect the one from the appearance of the other. This hypothesis seems even the only one which explains the difficulty, why we draw, from a thousand instances, an inference which we are not able to draw from one instance, that is, in no respect, different from them. Reason is incapable of any such variation. The conclusions which it draws from considering one circle are the same which it would form upon surveying all the circles in the universe. But no man, having seen only one body move after being impelled by another, could infer that every other body will move after a like impulse. All inferences from experience, therefore, are effects of custom, not of reasoning.[7]

---

[7] Nothing is more useful than for writers, even, on *moral, political,* or *physical* subjects, to distinguish between *reason* and *experience,* and to suppose, that these species of argumentation are entirely different from each other. The former are taken for the mere result of our intellectual faculties, which, by considering *à priori* the nature of things, and examining the effects, that must follow from their operation, establish particular principles of science and philosophy. The latter are supposed to be derived entirely from sense and observation, by which we learn what has actually resulted from the operation of particular objects, and are thence able to infer, what will, for the future, result from them. Thus, for instance, the limitations and restraints of civil government, and a legal constitution, may be defended, either from *reason,* which reflecting on the great frailty and corruption of human nature, teaches, that no man can safely be trusted with unlimited authority; or from *experience* and history, which inform us of the enormous abuses, that ambition, in every age and country, has been found to make of so imprudent a confidence.

The same distinction between reason and experience is maintained in all our deliberations concerning the conduct of life; while the experienced statesman, general, physician, or merchant is trusted and followed; and the unpractised novice, with whatever natural talents endowed, neglected and despised. Though it be allowed, that reason may form very plausible conjectures with regard to the consequences of such a particular conduct in such particular circumstances; it is still supposed imperfect, without the assistance of experience, which is alone able to give stability and certainty to the maxims, derived from study and reflection.

But notwithstanding that this distinction be thus universally received, both in the active speculative scenes of life, I shall not scruple to pronounce, that it is, at bottom, erroneous, at least, superficial.

If we examine those arguments, which, in any of the sciences above mentioned, are supposed to be the mere effects of reasoning and reflection, they will be found to terminate, at last, in some general principle or conclusion, for which we can assign no reason but observation and experience. The only difference between them and those maxims, which are vulgarly esteemed the result of pure experience, is, that the former cannot be established without

Custom, then, is the great guide of human life. It is that principle alone which renders our experience useful to us, and makes us expect, for the future, a similar train of events with those which have appeared in the past. Without the influence of custom, we should be entirely ignorant of every matter of fact beyond what is immediately present to the memory and senses. We should never know how to adjust means to ends, or to employ our natural powers in the production of any effect. There would be an end at once of all action, as well as of the chief part of speculation.

But here it may be proper to remark, that though our conclusions from experience carry us beyond our memory and senses, and assure us of matters of fact which happened in the most distant places and most remote ages, yet some fact must always be present to the senses or memory, from which we may first proceed in drawing these conclusions. A man, who should find in a desert country the remains of pompous buildings, would conclude that the country had, in ancient times, been cultivated by civilized inhabitants; but did nothing of this nature occur to him, he could never form such an inference. We learn the events of former ages from history; but then we must peruse the volumes in which this instruction is contained, and thence carry up our inferences from one testimony to another, till we arrive at the eyewitnesses and spectators of these distant events. In a word, if we proceed not upon some fact, present to the memory or senses, our reasonings would be merely hypothetical; and however the particular links might be connected with

---

some process of thought, and some reflection on what we have observed, in order to distinguish its circumstances, and trace its consequences: Whereas in the latter, the experienced event is exactly and fully familiar to that which we infer as the result of any particular situation. The history of a Tiberius or a Nero makes us dread a like tyranny, were our monarchs freed from the restraints of laws and senates. But the observation of any fraud or cruelty in private life is sufficient, with the aid of a little thought, to give us the same apprehension; while it serves as an instance of the general corruption of human nature, and shows us the danger which we must incur by reposing an entire confidence in mankind. In both cases, it is experience which is ultimately the foundation of our inference and conclusion.

There is no man so young and unexperienced, as not to have formed, from observation, many general and just maxims concerning human affairs and the conduct of life; but it must be confessed, that, when a man comes to put these in practice, he will be extremely liable to error, till time and farther experience both enlarge these maxims, and teach him their proper use and application. In every situation or incident, there are many particular and seemingly minute circumstances, which the man of greatest talent is, at first, apt to overlook, though on them the justness of his conclusions, and consequently the prudence of his conduct, entirely depend. Not to mention, that, to a young beginner, the general observations and maxims occur not always on the proper occasions, nor can be immediately applied with due calmness and distinction. The truth is, an unexperienced reasoner could be no reasoner at all, were he absolutely unexperienced; and when we assign that character to any one, we mean it only in a comparative sense, and suppose him possessed of experience, in a smaller and more imperfect degree.

each other, the whole chain of inferences would have nothing to support it, nor could we ever, by its means, arrive at the knowledge of any real existence. If I ask why you believe any particular matter of fact, which you relate, you must tell me some reason; and this reason will be some other fact, connected with it. But as you cannot proceed after this manner, *in infinitum*, you must at last terminate in some fact, which is present to your memory or senses; or must allow that your belief is entirely without foundation.

What, then, is the conclusion of the whole matter? A simple one; though, it must be confessed, pretty remote from the common theories of philosophy. All belief of matter of fact or real existence is derived merely from some object, present to the memory or senses, and a customary conjunction between that and some other object. Or in other words; having found in many instances, that any two kinds of objects—flame and heat, snow and cold—have always been conjoined together; if flame or snow be presented anew to the senses, the mind is carried by custom to expect heat or cold, and to *believe* that such a quality does exist, and will discover itself upon a nearer approach. This belief is the necessary result of placing the mind in such circumstances. It is an operation of the soul, when we are so situated, as unavoidable as to feel the passion of love, when we receive benefits; or hatred, when we meet with injuries. All these operations are a species of natural instincts, which no reasoning or process of the thought and understanding is able either to produce or to prevent.

At this point, it would be very allowable for us to stop our philosophical researches. In most questions we can never make a single step farther; and in all questions we must terminate here at last, after our most restless and curious enquiries. But still our curiosity will be pardonable, perhaps commendable, if it carry us on to still farther researches, and make us examine more accurately the nature of this *belief*, and of the *customary conjunction*, whence it is derived. By this means we may meet with some explications and analogies that will give satisfaction; at least to such as love the abstract sciences, and can be entertained with speculations, which, however accurate, may still retain a degree of doubt and uncertainty. As to readers of a different taste; the remaining part of this section is not calculated for them, and the following enquiries may well be understood, though it be neglected.

Part II

Nothing is more free than the imagination of man; and though it cannot exceed that original stock of ideas furnished by the internal and external senses, it has unlimited power of mixing, compounding, separating, and dividing these ideas, in all the varieties of fiction and vision. It can feign a train of events, with all the appearance of reality, ascribe to them a particular time and place, conceive them as existent, and paint them out to itself with every circumstance, that belongs to any historical fact, which it believes with the greatest certainty. Wherein, therefore, consists the difference between such a fiction and belief? It lies not merely in any peculiar idea, which is annexed to such a conception as commands our assent, and which is wanting to every known fiction. For as the mind has authority over all its ideas, it could voluntarily annex this particular idea to any fiction, and consequently be able to believe whatever it pleases; contrary to what we find by daily experience. We can, in our conception, join the head of a man to the body of a horse; but it is not in our power to believe that such an animal has ever really existed.

It follows, therefore, that the difference between *fiction* and *belief* lies in some sentiment or feeling, which is annexed to the latter, not to the former, and which depends not on the will, nor can be commanded at pleasure. It must be excited by nature, like all other sentiments; and must arise from the particular situation, in which the mind is placed at any particular juncture. Whenever any object is presented to the memory or senses, it immediately, by the force of custom, carries the imagination to conceive that object, which is usually conjoined to it; and this conception is attended with a feeling or sentiment, different from the loose reveries of the fancy. In this consists the whole nature of belief. For as there is no matter of fact which we believe so firmly that we cannot conceive the contrary, there would be no difference between the conception assented to and that which is rejected, were it not for some sentiment which distinguishes the one from the other. If I see a billiard-ball moving towards another, on a smooth table, I can easily conceive it to stop upon contact. This conception implies no contradiction; but still it feels very differently from that conception by which I represent to myself the impulse and the communication of motion from one ball to another.

Were we to attempt a *definition* of this sentiment, we should, perhaps, find it a very difficult, if not an impossible task; in the same manner as if we should endeavour to define the feeling of cold or passion of anger, to a creature who never had any experience of these sentiments. Belief is the true and proper name of this feeling; and no one is ever at a loss to know the meaning of that term; because every man is every moment conscious of the sentiment represented by it. It may not, however, be improper to attempt a *description* of this sentiment; in hopes we may, by that means, arrive at some analogies, which may afford a more perfect explication of it. I say, then, that belief is nothing but a more vivid, lively, forcible, firm, steady conception of an object, than what the imagination alone is ever able to attain. This variety of terms, which may seem so unphilosophical, is intended only to express that act of the mind, which renders realities, or what is taken for such, more present to us than fictions, causes them to weigh more in the thought, and gives them a superior influence on the passions and imagination. Provided we agree about the thing, it is needless to dispute about the terms. The imagination has the command over all its ideas, and can join and mix and vary them, in all the ways possible. It may conceive fictitious objects with all the circumstances of place and time. It may set them, in a manner, before our eyes, in their true colours, just as they might have existed. But as it is impossible that this faculty of imagination can ever, of itself, reach belief, it is evident that belief consists not in the peculiar nature or order of ideas, but in the *manner* of their conception, and in their *feeling* to the mind. I confess, that it is impossible perfectly to explain this feeling or manner of conception. We may make use of words which express something near it. But its true and proper name, as we observed before, is *belief;* which is a term that every one sufficiently understands in common life. And in philosophy, we can go no farther than assert, that *belief* is something felt by the mind, which distinguishes the ideas of the judgement from the fictions of the imagination. It gives them more weight and influence; makes them appear of greater importance; enforces them in the mind; and renders them the governing principle of our actions. I hear at present, for instance, a person's voice, with whom I am acquainted; and the sound comes as from the next room. This impression of my senses immediately conveys my thought to the person, together with all the surrounding objects. I paint them out to myself as existing at present, with the same qualities and relations, of which I formerly knew them possessed. These ideas take faster hold of my mind than ideas of an enchanted castle. They are very different to the feeling, and have a much greater influence of every kind, either to give pleasure or pain, joy or sorrow.

Let us, then, take in the whole compass of this doctrine, and allow, that the sentiment of belief is nothing but a conception more intense and steady than what attends the mere fictions of the imagination, and that this *manner* of conception arises from a customary conjunction of the object with something present to the memory or senses: I believe that it will not be difficult, upon these suppositions, to find other operations of the mind analogous to it, and to trace up these phenomena to principles still more general.

We have already observed that nature has established connexions among particular ideas, and that no sooner one idea occurs to our thoughts than it introduces its correlative, and carries our attention towards it, by a gentle and insensible movement. These principles of connexion or association we have reduced to three, namely, *Resemblance, Contiguity* and *Causation;* which are the only bonds that unite our thoughts together, and beget that regular train of reflection or discourse, which, in a greater or less degree, takes place among mankind. Now here arises a question, on which the solution of the present difficulty will depend. Does it happen, in all these relations, that, when one of the objects is presented to the senses or memory, the mind is not only carried to the conception of the correlative, but reaches a steadier and stronger conception of it than what otherwise it would have been able to attain? This seems to be the case with that belief which arises from the relation of cause and effect. And if the case be the same with the other relations or principles of associations, this may be established as a general law, which takes place in all the operations of the mind.

We may, therefore, observe, as the first experiment to our present purpose, that, upon the appearance of the picture of an absent friend, our idea of him is evidently enlivened by the *resemblance*, and that every passion, which that idea occasions, whether of joy or sorrow, acquires new force and vigour. In producing this effect, there concur both a relation and a present impression. Where the picture bears him no resemblance, at least was not intended for him, it never so much as conveys our thought to him: And where it is absent, as well as the person, though the mind may pass from the thought of the one to that of the other, it feels its idea to be rather weakened than enlivened by that transition. We take a pleasure in viewing the picture of a friend, when it is set before us; but when it is removed, rather choose to consider him directly than by reflection in an image, which is equally distant and obscure.

The ceremonies of the Roman Catholic religion may be considered as instances of the same nature. The devotees of that superstition usually plead in excuse for the mummeries, with which they were upbraided, that they feel the good effect of those external motions, and postures, and actions, in enlivening their devotion and quickening their fervour, which otherwise would decay, if directed entirely to distant and immaterial objects. We shadow out the objects of our faith, say they, in sensible types and images, and render them more present to us by the immediate presence of these types, than it is possible for us to do merely by an intellectual view and contemplation. Sensible objects have always a greater influence on the fancy than any other; and this influence they readily convey to those ideas to which they are related, and which they resemble. I shall only infer from these practices, and this reasoning, that the effect of resemblance in enlivening the ideas is very common; and as in every case a resemblance and a present impression must concur, we are abundantly supplied with experiments to prove the reality of the foregoing principle.

We may add force to these experiments by others of a different kind, in considering the effects of *contiguity* as well as of *resemblance*. It is certain that distance diminishes the force of every idea, and that, upon our approach to any object; though it does not discover itself to our senses; it operates upon the mind with an influence, which imitates an immediate impression. The thinking on any object readily transports the mind to what is contiguous; but it is only the actual presence of an object, that transports it with a superior vivacity. When I am a few miles from home, whatever relates to it touches me more nearly than when I am two hundred leagues distant; though even at that distance the re-flecting on any thing in the neighbourhood of my friends or family naturally produces an idea of them. But as in this latter case, both the objects of the mind are ideas; notwithstanding there is an easy transition between them; that transition alone is not able to give a superior vivacity to any of the ideas, for want of some immediate impression.[8]

No one can doubt but causation has the same influence as the other two relations of resemblance and contiguity. Superstitious people are fond of the reliques of saints and holy men, for the same reason, that they seek after types or images, in order to enliven their devotion, and give them a more intimate and strong conception of those exemplary lives, which they desire to imitate. Now it is evident, that one of the best reliques, which a devotee could procure, would be the handywork of a saint; and if his cloaths and furniture are ever to be considered in this light, it is because they were once at his disposal, and were moved and affected by him; in which respect they are to be considered as imperfect effects, and as connected with him by a shorter chain of consequences than any of those, by which we learn the reality of his existence.

Suppose, that the son of a friend, who had been long dead or absent, were presented to us; it is evident, that this object would instantly revive its correlative idea, and recall to our thoughts all past intimacies and familiarities, in more lively colours than they would otherwise have appeared to us. This is another phaenomenon, which seems to prove the principle above mentioned.

We may observe, that, in these phaenomena, the belief of the correlative object is always presupposed; without which the relation could have no effect. The influence of the picture supposes, that we *believe* our friend to have once existed. Contiguity to home can never excite our ideas of home, unless we *believe* that it really exists. Now I assert, that this belief, where it reaches beyond the memory or senses, is of a similar nature, and arises from similar causes, with the transition of thought and vivacity of conception here explained. When I throw a piece of dry wood into a fire, my mind is immediately carried to conceive, that it augments, not extinguishes the flame. This transition of thought from the cause to the effect proceeds not from reason. It derives its origin altogether from custom and experience. And as it first begins from an object, present to the senses, it renders the idea or conception of flame more strong and lively than any loose, floating reverie of the imagination. That idea arises immediately. The thought moves instantly towards it, and conveys to it

---

[8] 'Naturane nobis, inquit, datum dicam, an errore quodam, ut, cum ea loca videamus, in quibus memoria dignos viros acceperimus multum esse versatos, magis moveamur, quam siquando eorum ipsorum aut facta audiamus aut scriptum aliquod legamus? Velut ego nunc moveor. Venit enim mihi Plato in mentem, quem accepimus primum hic disputare solitum: cuius etiam illi hortuli propinqui non memoriam solum mihi afferunt, sed ipsum videntur in conspectu meo hic ponere. Hic Speusippus, hic Xenocrates, hic eius auditor Polemo; cuius ipsa illa sessio fuit, quam videmus. Equidem etiam curiam nostram, Hostiliam dico, non hanc novam, quae mihi minor esse videtur postquam est maior, solebam intuens, Scipionem, Catonem, Laelium; nostrum vero in primis avum cogitare. Tanta vis admonitionis est in locis; ut non sine causa ex his memoriae deducta sit disciplina.'

Cicero de Finibus. Lib. v.

all that force of conception, which is derived from the impression present to the senses. When a sword is levelled at my breast, does not the idea of wound and pain strike me more strongly, than when a glass of wine is presented to me, even though by accident this idea should occur after the appearance of the latter object? But what is there in this whole matter to cause such a strong conception, except only a present object and a customary transition to the idea of another object, which we have been accustomed to conjoin with the former? This is the whole operation of the mind, in all our conclusions concerning matter of fact and existence; and it is a satisfaction to find some analogies, by which it may be explained. The transition from a present object does in all cases give strength and solidity to the related idea.

Here, then, is a kind of pre-established harmony between the course of nature and the succession of our ideas; and though the powers and forces, by which the former is governed, be wholly unknown to us; yet our thoughts and conceptions have still, we find, gone on in the same train with the other work of nature. Custom is that principle, by which this correspondence has been effected; so necessary to the subsistence of our species, and the regulation of our conduct, in every circumstance and occurrence of human life. Had not the presence of an object, instantly excited the idea of those objects, commonly conjoined with it, all our knowledge must have been limited to the narrow sphere of our memory and senses; and we should never have been able to adjust means to ends, or employ our natural powers, either to the producing of good, or avoiding of evil. Those, who delight in the discovery and contemplation of *final causes,* have here ample subject to employ their wonder and admiration.

I shall add, for a further confirmation of the foregoing theory, that, as this operation of the mind, by which we infer like effects from like causes, and *vice versa,* is so essential to the subsistence of all human creatures, it is not probable, that it could be trusted to the fallacious deductions of our reason, which is slow in its operations; appears not, in any degree, during the first years of infancy; and at best is, in every age and period of human life, extremely liable to error and mistake. It is more conformable to the ordinary wisdom of nature to secure so necessary an act of the mind, by some instinct or mechanical tendency, which may be infallible in its operations, may discover itself at the first appearance of life and thought, and may be independent of all the laboured deductions of the understanding. As nature has taught us the use of our limbs, without giving us the knowledge of the muscles and nerves, by which they are actuated; so has she implanted in us an instinct, which carries forward the thought in a correspondent course to that which she has established among external objects; though we are ignorant of those powers and forces, on which this regular course and succession of objects totally depends.

SECTION VI. OF PROBABILITY [9]

Though there be no such thing as *Chance* in the world; our ignorance of the real cause of any event has the same influence on the understanding, and begets a like species of belief or opinion.

There is certainly a probability, which arises from a superiority of chances on any side; and according as this superiority encreases, and surpasses the opposite chances, the probability receives a proportionable encrease, and begets still a higher degree of belief or assent to that side, in which we discover the superiority. If a dye were marked with one figure or number of spots on four sides, and with another figure or number of spots on the two remaining sides, it would be more probable, that the former would turn up than the latter; though, if it had a thousand sides marked in the same manner, and only one side different, the probability would be much higher, and our belief or expectation of the event more steady and secure. This process of the thought or reasoning may seem trivial and obvious; but to those who consider it more narrowly, it may, perhaps, afford matter for curious speculation.

It seems evident, that, when the mind looks forward to discover the event, which may result from the throw of such a dye, it considers the turning up of each particular side as alike probable; and this is the very nature of chance, to render all the particular events, comprehended in it, entirely equal. But finding a greater number of sides concur in the one event than in the other, the mind is carried more frequently to that event, and meets it oftener, in revolving the various possibilities or chances, on which the ultimate result depends. This concurrence of several views in one particular event begets immediately, by an inexplicable contrivance of nature, the sentiment of belief, and gives that event the advantage over its antagonist, which is supported by a smaller number of views, and recurs less frequently to the mind. If we allow, that belief is nothing but a firmer and stronger conception of an object than what attends the mere fictions of the imagination, this operation may, perhaps, in some measure, be accounted for. The concurrence of these several views or glimpses imprints the idea more strongly on the imagination; gives it superior force and vigour; renders its influence on the passions and affections more sensible; and in a word, begets that reliance or security, which constitutes the nature of belief and opinion.

The case is the same with the probability of causes, as with that of chance. There are some causes, which are entirely uniform and constant in producing a particular effect; and no instance has ever yet been found

---

[9] Mr. Locke divides all arguments into demonstrative and probable. In this view, we must say, that it is only probable all men must die, or that the sun will rise to-morrow. But to conform our language more to common use, we ought to divide arguments into *demonstrations, proofs,* and *probabilities.* By proofs meaning such arguments from experience as leave no room for doubt or opposition.

of any failure or irregularity in their operation. Fire has always burned, and water suffocated every human creature: The production of motion by impulse and gravity is an universal law, which has hitherto admitted of no exception. But there are other causes which have been found more irregular and uncertain; nor has rhubarb always proved a purge, or opium a soporific to every one, who has taken these medicines. It is true, when any cause fails of producing its usual effect, philosophers ascribe not this to any irregularity in nature; but suppose, that some secret causes, in the particular structure of parts, have prevented the operation. Our reasonings, however, and conclusions concerning the event are the same as if this principle had no place. Being determined by custom to transfer the past to the future, in all our inferences; where the past has been entirely regular and uniform, we expect the event with the greatest assurance, and leave no room for any contrary supposition. But where different effects have been found to follow from causes, which are to *appearance* exactly similar, all these various effects must occur to the mind in transferring the past to the future, and enter into our consideration, when we determine the probability of the event. Though we give the preference to that which has been found most usual, and believe that this effect will exist, we must not overlook the other effects, but must assign to each of them a particular weight and authority, in proportion as we have found it to be more or less frequent. It is more probable, in almost every country of Europe, that there will be frost sometime in January, than that the weather will continue open throughout the whole month; though this probability varies according to the different climates, and approaches to a certainty in the more northern kingdoms. Here then it seems evident, that, when we transfer the past to the future, in order to determine the effect, which will result from any cause, we transfer all the different events, in the same proportion as they have appeared in the past, and conceive one to have existed a hundred times, for instance, another ten times, and another once. As a great number of views do here concur in one event, they fortify and confirm it to the imagination, beget that sentiment which we call *belief*, and give its object the preference above the contrary event, which is not supported by an equal number of experiments, and recurs not so frequently to the thought in transferring the past to the future. Let any one try to account for this operation of the mind upon any of the received systems of philosophy, and he will be sensible of the difficulty. For my part, I shall think it sufficient, if the present hints excite the curiosity of philosophers, and make them sensible how defective all common theories are in treating of such curious and such sublime subjects

SECTION VII.   OF THE IDEA OF NECESSARY CONNEXION

Part I

The great advantage of the mathematical sciences above the moral consists in this, that the ideas of the former, being sensible, are always clear and determinate, the smallest distinction between them is immediately perceptible, and the same terms are still expressive of the same ideas, without ambiguity or variation. An oval is never mistaken for a circle, nor an hyperbola for an ellipsis. The isosceles and scalenum are distinguished by boundaries more exact than vice and virtue, right and wrong. If any term be defined in geometry, the mind readily, of itself, substitutes, on all occasions, the definition for the term defined: Or even when no definition is employed, the object itself may be presented to the senses, and by that means be steadily and clearly apprehended. But the finer sentiments of the mind, the operations of the understanding, the various agitations of the passions, though really in themselves distinct, easily escape us, when surveyed by reflection; nor is it in our power to recall the original object, as often as we have occasion to contemplate it. Ambiguity, by this means, is gradually introduced into our reasonings: Similar objects are readily taken to be the same: And the conclusion becomes at last very wide of the premises.

One may safely, however, affirm, that, if we consider these sciences in a proper light, their advantages and disadvantages nearly compensate each other, and reduce both of them to a state of equality. If the mind, with greater facility, retains the ideas of geometry clear and determinate, it must carry on a much longer and more intricate chain of reasoning, and compare ideas much wider of each other, in order to reach the abstruser truths of that science. And if moral ideas are apt, without extreme care, to fall into obscurity and confusion, the inferences are always much shorter in these disquisitions, and the intermediate steps, which lead to the conclusion, much fewer than in the sciences which treat of quantity and number. In reality, there is scarcely a proposition in Euclid so simple, as not to consist of more parts, than are to be found in any moral reasoning which runs not into chimera and conceit. Where we trace the principles of the human mind through a few steps, we may be very well satisfied with our progress; considering how soon nature throws a bar to all our enquiries concerning causes, and reduces us to an acknowledgment of our ignorance. The chief obstacle, therefore, to our improvement in the moral or metaphysical sciences is the obscurity of the ideas, and ambiguity of the terms. The principal difficulty in the mathematics is the length of inferences and compass of thought, requisite to the forming of any conclusion. And, perhaps, our progress in natural philosophy is chiefly retarded by the want of proper experiments and phaenomena, which are often discovered by chance, and cannot always be found, when requisite, even by the most diligent and prudent enquiry. As moral philosophy seems hitherto to have received less improvement than either geometry or physics, we may conclude, that, if there be any difference in this respect among these sciences, the difficulties, which obstruct the progress of the former, require superior care and capacity to be surmounted.

There are no ideas, which occur in metaphysics, more obscure and uncertain, than those of *power, force, energy* or *necessary connexion*, of which it is every moment necessary for us to treat in all our disquisitions. We shall, therefore, endeavour, in this section, to fix, if possible, the precise meaning of these terms, and thereby remove some part of that obscurity, which is so much complained of in this species of philosophy.

It seems a proposition, which will not admit of much dispute, that all our ideas are nothing but copies of our impressions, or, in other words, that it is impossible for us to *think* of any thing, which we have not antecedently *felt*, either by our external or internal senses. I have endeavoured [10] to explain and prove this proposition, and have expressed my hopes, that, by a proper application of it, men may reach a greater clearness and precision in philosophical reasonings, than what they have hitherto been able to attain. Complex ideas may, perhaps, be well known by definition, which is nothing but an enumeration of those parts or simple ideas, that compose them. But when we have pushed up definitions to the most simple ideas, and find still some ambiguity and obscurity; what resource are we then possessed of? By what invention can we throw light upon these ideas, and render them altogether precise and determinate to our intellectual view? Produce the impressions or original sentiments, from which the ideas are copied. These impressions are all strong and sensible. They admit not of ambiguity. They are not only placed in a full light themselves, but may throw light on their correspondent ideas, which lie in obscurity. And by this means, we may, perhaps, attain a new microscope or species of optics, by which, in the moral sciences, the most minute, and most simple ideas may be so enlarged as to fall readily under our apprehension, and be equally known with the grossest and most sensible ideas, that can be the object of our enquiry.

To be fully acquainted, therefore, with the idea of power or necessary connexion, let us examine its impression; and in order to find the impression with greater certainty, let us search for it in all the sources, from which it may possibly be derived.

When we look about us towards external objects, and consider the operation of causes, we are never able, in a single instance, to discover any power or necessary connexion; any quality, which binds the effect to the cause, and renders the one an infallible consequence of the other. We only find, that the one does actually, in fact, follow the other. The impulse of one billiard-ball is attended with motion in the second. This is the whole that appears to the *outward* senses. The mind feels no senti-

---

[10] Section II.

ment or *inward* impression from this succession of objects: Consequently there is not, in any single, particular instance of cause and effect, any thing which can suggest the idea of power or necessary connexion.

From the first appearance of an object, we never can conjecture what effect will result from it. But were the power or energy of any cause discoverable by the mind, we could foresee the effect, even without experience; and might, at first, pronounce with certainty concerning it, by mere dint of thought and reasoning.

In reality, there is no part of matter, that does ever, by its sensible qualities, discover any power or energy, or give us ground to imagine, that it could produce any thing, or be followed by any other object, which we could denominate its effect. Solidity, extension, motion; these qualities are all complete in themselves, and never point out any other event which may result from them. The scenes of the universe are continually shifting, and one object follows another in an uninterrupted succession; but the power of force, which actuates the whole machine, is entirely concealed from us, and never discovers itself in any of the sensible qualities of body. We know, that, in fact, heat is a constant attendant of flame; but what is the connexion between them, we have no room so much as to conjecture or imagine. It is impossible, therefore, that the idea of power can be derived from the contemplation of bodies, in single instances of their operation; because no bodies ever discover any power, which can be the original of this idea.[11]

Since, therefore, external objects as they appear to the senses, give us no idea of power or necessary connexion, by their operation in particular instances, let us see, whether this idea be derived from reflexion on the operations of our own minds, and be copied from any internal impression. It may be said, that we are every moment conscious of internal power; while we feel, that, by the simple command of our will, we can move the organs of our body, or direct the faculties of our mind. An act of volition produces motion in our limbs, or raises a new idea in our imagination. This influence of the will we know by consciousness. Hence we acquire the idea of power or energy; and are certain, that we ourselves and all other intelligent beings are possessed of power. This idea, then, is an idea of reflection, since it arises from reflecting on the operations of our own mind, and on the command which is exercised by will, both over the organs of the body and faculties of the soul.

We shall proceed to examine this pretension; and first with regard to the influence of volition over the organs of the body. This influence, we may observe, is a fact, which, like all other natural events, can be known only by experience, and can never be foreseen from any apparent energy

---

[11] Mr. Locke, in his chapter of power, says, that, finding from experience, that there are several new productions in matter, and concluding that there must somewhere be a power capable of producing them, we arrive at last by this reasoning at the idea of power. But no reasoning can ever give us a new, original, simple idea; as this philosopher himself confesses. This, therefore, can never be the origin of that idea.

or power in the cause, which connects it with the effect, and renders the one an infallible consequence of the other. The motion of our body follows upon the command of our will. Of this we are every moment conscious. But the means, by which this is effected; the energy, by which the will performs so extraordinary an operation; of this we are so far from being immediately conscious, that it must for ever escape our most diligent enquiry.

For *first;* is there any principle in all nature more mysterious than the union of soul with body; by which a supposed spiritual substance acquires such an influence over a material one, that the most refined thought is able to actuate the grossest matter? Were we empowered, by a secret wish, to remove mountains, or control the planets in their orbit; this extensive authority would not be more extraordinary, nor more beyond our comprehension. But if by consciousness we perceived any power or energy in the will, we must know this power; we must know its connexion with the effect; we must know the secret union of soul and body, and the nature of both these substances; by which the one is able to operate, in so many instances, upon the other.

Secondly, We are not able to move all the organs of the body with a like authority; though we cannot assign any reason besides experience, for so remarkable a difference between one and the other. Why has the will an influence over the tongue and fingers, not over the heart and liver? This question would never embarrass us, were we conscious of a power in the former case, not in the latter. We should then perceive, independent of experience, why the authority of will over the organs of the body is circumscribed within such particular limits. Being in that case fully acquainted with the power or force, by which it operates, we should also know, why its influence reaches precisely to such boundaries, and no farther.

A man, suddenly struck with palsy in the leg or arm, or who had newly lost those members, frequently endeavours, at first to move them, and employ them in their usual offices. Here he is as much conscious of power to command such limbs, as a man in perfect health is conscious of power to actuate any member which remains in its natural state and condition. But consciousness never deceives. Consequently, neither in the one case nor in the other, are we ever conscious of any power. We learn the influence of our will from experience alone. And experience only teaches us, how one event constantly follows another; without instructing us in the secret connexion, which binds them together, and renders them inseparable.

Thirdly, We learn from anatomy, that the immediate object of power in voluntary motion, is not the member itself which is moved, but certain muscles, and nerves, and animal spirits, and, perhaps, something still more minute and more unknown, through which the motion is successfully propagated, ere it reach the member itself whose motion is the immediate object of volition. Can there be a more certain proof that the power, by which this whole operation is performed, so far from being directly and fully known by an inward sentiment or consciousness, is, to the last degree, mysterious and unintelligible? Here the mind wills a certain event: Immediately another event, unknown to ourselves, and totally different from the one intended, is produced: This event produces another, equally unknown: Till at last, through a long succession, the desired event is produced. But if the original power were felt, it must be known: Were it known, its effect also must be known; since all power is relative to its effect. And *vice versa*, if the effect be not known, the power cannot be known nor felt. How indeed can we be conscious of a power to move our limbs, when we have no such power; but only that to move certain animal spirits, which, though they produce at last the motion of our limbs, yet operate in such a manner as is wholly beyond our comprehension?

We may, therefore, conclude from the whole, I hope, without any temerity, though with assurance; that our idea of power is not copied from any sentiment or consciousness of power within ourselves, when we give rise to animal motion, or apply our limbs, to their proper use and office. That their motion follows the command of the will is a matter of common experience, like other natural events: But the power or energy by which this is effected, like that in other natural events, is unknown and inconceivable.[12]

Shall we then assert, that we are conscious of a power or energy in our own minds, when, by an act or command of our will, we raise up a new idea, fix the mind to the contemplation of it, turn it on all sides, and at last dismiss it for some other idea, when we think that we have surveyed it with sufficient accuracy? I believe the same arguments will prove, that even this command of the will gives us no real idea of force or energy.

First, It must be allowed, that, when we know a power, we know that very circumstance in the cause, by which it is enabled to produce the effect: For these are supposed to be synonimous. We must, therefore, know both the cause and effect, and the relation between them. But do we pretend to be acquainted with the nature of the human soul and the nature of an idea, or the aptitude of the one to produce the other? This

---

[12] It may be pretended, that the resistance which we meet with in bodies, obliging us frequently to exert our force, and call up all our power, this gives us the idea of force and power. It is this *nisus*, or strong endeavour, of which we are conscious, that is the original impression from which this idea is copied. But, first, we attribute power to a vast number of objects, where we never can suppose this resistance or exertion of force to take place; to the Supreme Being, who never meets with any resistance; to the mind in its command over its ideas and limbs, in common thinking and motion, where the effect follows immediately upon the will, without any exertion or summoning up of force; to inanimate matter, which is not capable of this sentiment. *Secondly,* This sentiment of an endeavour to overcome resistance has no known connexion with any event: What follows it, we know by experience; but could not know it *à priori*. It must, however, be confessed, that the animal *nisus,* which we experience, though it can afford no accurate precise idea of power, enters very much into that vulgar, inaccurate idea, which is formed of it.

is a real creation; a production of something out of nothing: Which implies a power so great, that it may seem, at first sight, beyond the reach of any being, less than infinite. At least it must be owned, that such a power is not felt, nor known, nor even conceivable by the mind. We only feel the event, namely, the existence of an idea, consequent to a command of the will: But the manner, in which this operation is performed, the power by which it is produced, is entirely beyond our comprehension.

Secondly, The command of the mind over itself is limited, as well as its command over the body; and these limits are not known by reason, or any acquaintance with the nature of cause and effect, but only by experience and observation, as in all other natural events and in the operation of external objects. Our authority over our sentiments and passions is much weaker than that over our ideas; and even the latter authority is circumscribed within very narrow boundaries. Will any one pretend to assign the ultimate reason of these boundaries, or show why the power is deficient in one case, not in another.

Thirdly, This self-command is very different at different times. A man in health possesses more of it than one languishing with sickness. We are more master of our thoughts in the morning than in the evening: Fasting, than after a full meal. Can we give any reason for these variations, except experience? Where then is the power, of which we pretend to be conscious? Is there not here, either in a spiritual or material substance, or both, some secret mechanism or structure of parts, upon which the effect depends, and which, being entirely unknown to us, renders the power or energy of the will equally unknown and incomprehensible?

Volition is surely an act of the mind, with which we are sufficiently acquainted. Reflect upon it. Consider it on all sides. Do you find anything in it like this creative power, by which it raises from nothing a new idea, and with a knd of *Fiat,* imitates the omnipotence of its Maker, if I may be allowed so to speak, who called forth into existence all the various scenes of nature? So far from being conscious of this energy in the will, it requires as certain experience as that of which we are possessed, to convince us that such extraordinary effects do ever result from a simple act of volition.

The generality of mankind never find any difficulty in accounting for the more common and familiar operations of nature—such as the descent of heavy bodies, the growth of plants, the generation of animals, or the nourishment of bodies by food: But suppose that, in all these cases, they perceive the very force or energy of the cause, by which it is connected with its effect, and is for ever infallible in its operation. They acquire, by long habit, such a turn of mind, that, upon the appearance of the cause, they immediately expect with assurance its usual attendant, and hardly conceive it possible that any other event could result from it. It is only on the discovery of extraordinary phaenomena, such as earthquakes, pestilence, and prodigies of any kind, that they find themselves at a loss to assign a proper cause, and to explain the manner in which the effect is produced by it. It is usual for men, in such difficulties, to have recourse to some invisible intelligent principle as the immediate cause of that event which surprises them, and which, they think, cannot be accounted for from the common powers of nature. But philosophers, who carry their scrutiny a little farther, immediately perceive that, even in the most familiar events, the energy of the cause is as unintelligible as in the most unusual, and that we only learn by experience the frequent *Conjunction* of objects, without being ever able to comprehend anything like *Connexion* between them. Here, then, many philosophers think themselves obliged by reason to have recourse, on all occasions, to the same principle, which the vulgar never appeal to but in cases that appear miraculous and supernatural. They acknowledge mind and intelligence to be, not only the ultimate and original cause of all things, but the immediate and sole cause of every event which appears in nature. They pretend that those objects which are commonly denominated *causes,* are in reality nothing but *occasions;* and that the true and direct principle of every effect is not any power or force in nature, but a volition of the Supreme Being, who wills that such particular objects should for ever be conjoined with each other. Instead of saying that one billiard-ball moves another by a force which it has derived from the author of nature, it is the Deity himself, they say, who, by a particular volition, moves the second ball, being determined to this operation by the impulse of the first ball, in consequence of those general laws which he has laid down to himself in the government of the universe. But philosophers advancing still in their inquiries, discover that, as we are totally ignorant of the power on which depends the mutual operation of bodies, we are no less ignorant of that power on which depends the operation of mind on body, or of body on mind; nor are we able, either from our sense or consciousness, to assign the ultimate principle in one case more than in the other. The same ignorance, therefore, reduces them to the same conclusion. They assert that the Deity is the immediate cause of the union between soul and body; and that they are not the organs of sense, which, being agitated by external objects, produce sensations in the mind; but that it is a particular volition of our omnipotent Maker, which excites such a sensation, in consequence of such a motion in the organ. In like manner, it is not any energy in the will that produces local motion in our members: It is God himself, who is pleased to second our will, in itself impotent, and to command that motion which we erroneously attribute to our own power and efficacy. Nor do philosophers stop at this conclusion. They sometimes extend the same inference to the mind itself, in its internal operations. Our mental vision or conception of ideas is nothing but a revelation made to us by our Maker. When we voluntarily turn our thoughts to any object, and raise up its image in the fancy, it is not the will which creates that idea: It is the universal Creator, who discovers it to the mind, and renders it present to us.

Thus, according to these philosophers, every thing is full of God. Not content with the principle, that nothing exists but by his will, that nothing possesses any power but by his concession: They rob nature, and all created beings, of every power, in order to render their dependence on the Deity still more sensible and immediate. They consider not that, by this theory, they diminish, instead of magnifying, the grandeur of those attributes, which they affect so much to celebrate. It argues surely more power in the Deity to delegate a certain degree of power to inferior creatures, than to produce every thing by his own immediate volition. It argues more wisdom to contrive at first the fabric of the world with such perfect foresight that, of itself, and by its proper operation, it may serve all the purposes of providence, than if the great Creator were obliged every moment to adjust its parts, and animate by his breath all the wheels of that stupendous machine.

But if we would have a more philosophical confutation of this theory, perhaps the two following reflections may suffice.

First, it seems to me that this theory of the universal energy and operation of the Supreme Being is too bold ever to carry conviction with it to a man, sufficiently apprized of the weakness of human reason, and the narrow limits to which it is confined in all its operations. Though the chain of arguments which conduct to it were ever so logical, there must arise a strong suspicion, if not an absolute assurance, that it has carried us quite beyond the reach of our faculties, when it leads to conclusions so extraordinary, and so remote from common life and experience. We are got into fairy land, long ere we have reached the last steps of our theory; and *there* we have no reason to trust our common methods of argument, or to think that our usual analogies and probabilities have any authority. Our line is too short to fathom such immense abysses. And however we may flatter ourselves that we are guided, in every step which we take, by a kind of verisimilitude and experience, we may be assured that this fancied experience has no authority when we thus apply it to subjects that lie entirely out of the sphere of experience. But on this we shall have occasion to touch afterwards.[13]

Secondly, I cannot perceive any force in the arguments on which this theory is founded. We are ignorant, it is true, of the manner in which bodies operate on each other: Their force or energy is entirely incomprehensible: But are we not equally ignorant of the manner or force by which a mind, even the supreme mind, operates either on itself or on body? Whence, I beseech you, do we acquire any idea of it? We have no sentiment or consciousness of this power in ourselves. We have no idea of the Supreme Being but what we learn from reflection on our own faculties. Were our ignorance, therefore, a good reason for rejecting any thing, we should be led into that principle of denying all energy in the Supreme Being as much as in the grossest matter. We surely comprehend as little the operations of one as of the other. Is it more difficult

---

[13] Section XII.

to conceive that motion may arise from impulse than that it may arise from volition? All we know is our profound ignorance in both cases.[14]

Part II

But to hasten to a conclusion of this argument, which is already drawn out to too great a length: We have sought in vain for an idea of power or necessary connexion in all the sources from which we could suppose it to be derived. It appears that, in single instances of the operation of bodies, we never can, by our utmost scrutiny, discover any thing but one event following another, without being able to comprehend any force or power by which the cause operates, or any connexion between it and its supposed effect. The same difficulty occurs in contemplating the operations of mind on body—where we observe the motion of the latter to follow upon the volition of the former, but are not able to observe or conceive the tie which binds together the motion and volition, or the energy by which the mind produces this effect. The authority of the will over its own faculties and ideas is not a whit more comprehensible: So that, upon the whole, there appears not, throughout all nature, any one instance of connexion which is conceivable by us. All events seem entirely loose and separate. One event follows another; but we never can observe any tie between them. They seem *conjoined*, but never *connected*. And as we can have no idea of any thing which never appeared to our outward sense or inward sentiment, the necessary conclusion *seems* to be that we have no idea of connexion or power at all, and that these words are absolutely without any meaning, when employed either in philosophical reasonings or common life.

But there still remains one method of avoiding this conclusion, and one source which we have not yet examined. When any natural object

---

14 I need not examine at length the *vis inertiae* which is so much talked of in the new philosophy, and which is ascribed to matter. We find by experience, that a body at rest or in motion continues for ever in its present state, till put from it by some new cause; and that a body impelled takes as much motion from the impelling body as it acquires itself. These are facts. When we call this a *vis inertiae*, we only mark these facts, without pretending to have any idea of the inert power; in the same manner as, when we talk of gravity, we mean certain effects, without comprehending that active power. It was never the meaning of Sir Isaac Newton to rob second causes of all force or energy; though some of his followers have endeavoured to establish that theory upon his authority. On the contrary, that great philosopher had recourse to an etherial active fluid to explain his universal attraction; though he was so cautious and modest as to allow, that it was a mere hypothesis, not to be insisted on, without more experiments. I must confess, that there is something in the fate of opinions a little extraordinary. Des Cartes insinuated that doctrine of the universal and sole efficacy of the Deity, without insisting on it. Malebranche and other Cartesians made it the foundation of all their philosophy. It had, however, no authority in England. Locke, Clarke, and Cudworth, never so much as take notice of it, but suppose all along, that matter has a real, though subordinate and derived power. By what means has it become so prevalent among our modern metaphysicians?

or event is presented, it is impossible for us, by any sagacity or penetration, to discover, or even conjecture, without experience, what event will result from it, or to carry our foresight beyond that object which is immediately present to the memory and senses. Even after one instance or experiment where we have observed a particular event to follow upon another, we are not entitled to form a general rule, or foretell what will happen in like cases; it being justly esteemed an unpardonable temerity to judge of the whole course of nature from one single experiment, however accurate or certain. But when one particular species of event has always, in all instances, been conjoined with another, we make no longer any scruple of foretelling one upon the appearance of the other, and of employing that reasoning which can alone assure us of any matter of fact or existence. We then call the one object, *Cause;* the other, *Effect.* We suppose that there is some connexion between them; some power in the one, by which it infallibly produces the other, and operates with the greatest certainty and strongest necessity.

It appears, then, that this idea of a necessary connexion among events arises from a number of similar instances which occur of the constant conjunction of these events; nor can that idea ever be suggested by any one of these instances, surveyed in all possible lights and positions. But there is nothing in a number of instances, different from every single instance, which is supposed to be exactly similar; except only, that after a repetition of similar instances, the mind is carried by habit, upon the appearance of one event, to expect its usual attendant, and to believe that it will exist. This connexion, therefore, which we *feel* in the mind, this customary transition of the imagination from one object to its usual attendant, is the sentiment or impression from which we form the idea of power or necessary connexion. Nothing farther is in the case. Contemplate the subject on all sides; you will never find any other origin of that idea. This is the sole difference between one instance, from which we can never receive the idea of connexion, and a number of similar instances, by which it is suggested. The first time a man saw the communication of motion by impulse, as by the shock of two billiard balls, he could not pronounce that the one event was *connected:* but only that it was *conjoined* with the other. After he has observed several instances of this nature, he then pronounces them to be *connected.* What alteration has happened to give rise to this new idea of *connexion?* Nothing but that he now *feels* these events to be *connected* in his imagination, and can readily foretell the existence of one from the appearance of the other. When we say, therefore, that one object is connected with another, we mean only that they have acquired a connexion in our thought, and give rise to this inference, by which they become proofs of each other's existence: A conclusion which is somewhat extraordinary, but which seems founded on sufficient evidence. Nor will its evidence be weakened by any general diffidence of the understanding, or sceptical suspicion concerning every conclusion which is new and extraordinary. No conclusions can be more agreeable to scepticism than such as make discoveries concerning the weakness and narrow limits of human reason and capacity.

And what stronger instance can be produced of the surprising ignorance and weakness of the understanding than the present? For surely, if there be any relation among objects which it imports to us to know perfectly, it is that of cause and effect. On this are founded all our reasonings concerning matter of fact or existence. By means of it alone we attain any assurance concerning objects which are removed from the present testimony of our memory and senses. The only immediate utility of all sciences, is to teach us, how to control and regulate future events by their causes. Our thoughts and enquiries are, therefore, every moment, employed about this relation: Yet so imperfect are the ideas which we form concerning it, that it is impossible to give any just definition of cause, except what is drawn from something extraneous and foreign to it. Similar objects are always conjoined with similar. Of this we have experience. Suitably to this experience, therefore, we may define a cause to be *an object, followed by another, and where all the objects similar to the first are followed by objects similar to the second.* Or in other words *where, if the first object had not been, the second never had existed.* The appearance of a cause always conveys the mind, by a customary transition, to the idea of the effect. Of this also we have experience. We may, therefore, suitably to this experience, form another definition of cause, and call it, *an object followed by another and whose appearance always conveys the thought to that other.* But though both these definitions be drawn from circumstances foreign to the cause, we cannot remedy this inconvenience, or attain any more perfect definition, which may point out that circumstance in the cause, which gives it a connexion with its effect. We have no idea of this connexion, nor even any distinct notion what it is we desire to know, when we endeavour at a conception of it. We say, for instance, that the vibration of this string is the cause of this particular sound. But what do we mean by that affirmation? We either mean *that this vibration is followed by this sound, and that all similar vibrations have been followed by similar sounds:* Or, *that this vibration is followed by this sound, and that upon the appearance of one the mind anticipates the senses, and forms immediately an idea of the other.* We may consider the relation of cause and effect in either of these two lights; but beyond these, we have no idea of it.[15]

---

[15] According to these explications and definitions, the idea of *power* is relative as much as that of *cause;* and both have a reference to an effect, or some other event constantly conjoined with the former. When we consider the *unknown* circumstance of an object, by which the degree or quantity of its effect is fixed and determined, we call that its power: And accordingly, it is allowed by all philosophers, that the effect is the measure of the power. But if they had any idea of power, as it is in itself, why could not they measure it in itself? The dispute whether the force of a body in motion be as its velocity, or the square of its velocity; this dispute, I say, needed not be de-

To recapitulate, therefore, the reasonings of this section: Every idea is copied from some preceding impression or sentiment; and where we cannot find any impression, we may be certain that there is no idea. In all single instances of the operation of bodies or minds, there is nothing that produces any impression, nor consequently can suggest any idea of power or necessary connexion. But when many uniform instances appear, and the same object is always followed by the same event; we then begin to entertain the notion of cause and connexion. We then *feel* a new sentiment or impression, to wit, a customary connexion in the thought or imagination between one object and its usual attendant; and this sentiment is the original of that idea which we seek for. For as this idea arises from a number of similar instances, and not from any single instance, it must arise from that circumstance, in which the number of instances differ from every individual instance. But this customary connexion or transition of the imagination is the only circumstance in which they differ. In every other particular they are alike. The first instance which we saw of motion communicated by the shock of two billiard balls (to return to this obvious illustration) is exactly similar to any instance that may, at present, occur to us; except only, that we could not, at first, *infer* one event from the other; which we are enabled to do at present, after so long a course of uniform experience. I know not whether the reader will readily apprehend this reasoning. I am afraid that, should I multiply words about it, or throw it into a greater variety of lights, it would only become more obscure and intricate. In all abstract reasonings there is one point of view which, if we can happily hit, we shall go farther towards illustrating the subject than by all the eloquence in the world. This point of view we should endeavour to reach, and reserve the flowers of rhetoric for subjects which are more adapted to them.

----

cided by comparing its effects in equal or unequal times; but by a direct mensuration and comparison.

As to the frequent use of the words, Force, Power, Energy, &c., which every where occur in common conversation, as well as in philosophy; that is no proof, that we are acquainted, in any instance, with the connecting principle between cause and effect, or can account ultimately for the production of one thing to another. These words, as commonly used, have very loose meanings annexed to them; and their ideas are very uncertain and confused. No animal can put external bodies in motion without the sentiment of a *nisus* or endeavour; and every animal has a sentiment or feeling from the stroke or blow of an external object, that is in motion. These sensations, which are merely animal, and from which we can *à priori* draw no inference, we are apt to transfer to inanimate objects, and to suppose, that they have some such feelings, whenever they transfer or receive motion. With regard to energies, which are exerted, without our annexing to them any idea of communicated motion, we consider only the constant experienced conjunction of the events; and as we *feel* a customary connexion between the ideas, we transfer that feeling to the objects; as nothing is more usual than to apply to external bodies every internal sensation which they occasion.

SECTION VIII. OF LIBERTY AND NECESSITY

Part I

It might reasonably be expected in questions which have been canvassed and disputed with great eagerness, since the first origin of science and philosophy, that the meaning of all the terms, at least, should have been agreed upon among the disputants; and our enquiries, in the course of two thousand years, been able to pass from words to the true and real subject of the controversy. For how easy may it seem to give exact definitions of the terms employed in reasoning, and make these definitions, not the mere sound of words, the object of future scrutiny and examination? But if we consider the matter more narrowly, we shall be apt to draw a quite opposite conclusion. From this circumstance alone, that a controversy has been long kept on foot, and remains still undecided, we may presume that there is some ambiguity in the expression, and that the disputants affix different ideas to the terms employed in the controversy. For as the faculties of the mind are supposed to be naturally alike in every individual; otherwise nothing could be more fruitless than to reason or dispute together; it were impossible, if men affix the same ideas to their terms, that they could so long form different opinions of the same subject; especially when they communicate their views, and each party turn themselves on all sides, in search of arguments which may give them the victory over their antagonists. It is true, if men attempt the discussion of questions which lie entirely beyond the reach of human capacity, such as those concerning the origin of worlds, or the economy of the intellectual system or region of spirits, they may long beat the air in their fruitless contests, and never arrive at any determinate conclusion. But if the question regard any subject of common life and experience, nothing, one would think, could preserve the dispute so long undecided but some ambiguous expressions, which keep the antagonists still at a distance, and hinder them from grappling with each other.

This has been the case in the long disputed question concerning liberty and necessity; and to so remarkable a degree that, if I be not much mistaken, we shall find, that all mankind, both learned and ignorant, have always been of the same opinion with regard to this subject, and that a few intelligible definitions would immediately have put an end to the whole controversy. I own that this dispute has been so much canvassed on all hands, and has led philosophers into such a labyrinth of obscure sophistry, that it is no wonder, if a sensible reader indulge his ease so far as to turn a deaf ear to the proposal of such a question, from which he can expect neither instruction nor entertainment. But the state of the argument here proposed may, perhaps, serve to renew his attention; as it has more novelty, promises at least some decision of the controversy, and will not much disturb his ease by any intricate or obscure reasoning.

I hope, therefore, to make it appear that all men have ever agreed in the doctrine both of necessity and of liberty, according to any reasonable sense, which can be put on these terms; and that the whole controversy has hitherto turned merely upon words. We shall begin with examining the doctrine of necessity.

It is universally allowed that matter, in all its operations, is actuated by a necessary force, and that every natural effect is so precisely determined by the energy of its cause that no other effect, in such particular circumstances, could possibly have resulted from it. The degree and direction of every motion is, by the laws of nature, prescribed with such exactness that a living creature may as soon arise from the shock of two bodies as motion in any other degree or direction than what is actually produced by it. Would we, therefore, form a just and precise idea of *necessity*, we must consider whence that idea arises when we apply it to the operation of bodies.

It seems evident that, if all the scenes of nature were continually shifted in such a manner that no two events bore any resemblance to each other, but every object was entirely new, without any similitude to whatever had been seen before, we should never, in that case, have attained the least idea of necessity, or of a connexion among these objects. We might say, upon such a supposition, that one object or event has followed another; not that one was produced by the other. The relation of cause and effect must be utterly unknown to mankind. Inference and reasoning concerning the operations of nature would, from that moment, be at an end; and the memory and senses remain the only canals, by which the knowledge of any real existence could possibly have access to the mind. Our idea, therefore, of necessity and causation arises entirely from the uniformity observable in the operations of nature, where similar objects are constantly conjoined together, and the mind is determined by custom to infer the one from the appearance of the other. These two circumstances form the whole of that necessity, which we ascribe to matter. Beyond the constant *conjunction* of similar objects, and the consequent *inference* from one to the other, we have no notion of any necessity or connexion.

If it appear, therefore, that all mankind have ever allowed, without any doubt or hesitation, that these two circumstances take place in the voluntary actions of men, and in the operations of mind; it must follow, that all mankind have ever agreed in the doctrine of necessity, and that they have hitherto disputed, merely for not understanding each other.

As to the first circumstance, the constant and regular conjunction of similar events, we may possibly satisfy ourselves by the following considerations. It is universally acknowledged that there is a great uniformity among the actions of men, in all nations and ages, and that human nature remains still the same, in its principles and operations. The same motives always produce the same actions: The same events follow from the same causes. Ambition, avarice, self-love, vanity, friendship, generosity, public spirit: these passions, mixed in various degrees, and distributed through society, have been, from the beginning of the world, and still are, the source of all the actions and enterprises, which have ever been observed among mankind. Would you know the sentiments, inclinations, and course of life of the Greeks and Romans? Study well the temper and actions of the French and English: You cannot be much mistaken in transferring to the former *most* of the observations which you have made with regard to the latter. Mankind are so much the same, in all times and places, that history informs us of nothing new or strange in this particular. Its chief use is only to discover the constant and universal principles of human nature, by showing men in all varieties of circumstances and situations, and furnishing us with materials from which we may form our observations and become acquainted with the regular springs of human action and behaviour. These records of wars, intrigues, factions, and revolutions, are so many collections of experiments, by which the politician or moral philosopher fixes the principles of his science, in the same manner as the physician or natural philosopher becomes acquainted with the nature of plants, minerals, and other external objects, by the experiments which he forms concerning them. Nor are the earth, water, and other elements, examined by Aristotle, and Hippocrates, more like to those which at present lie under our observation than the men described by Polybius and Tacitus are to those who now govern the world.

Should a traveller, returning from a far country, bring us an account of men, wholly different from any with whom we were ever acquainted; men, who were entirely divested of avarice, ambition, or revenge; who knew no pleasure but friendship, generosity, and public spirit; we should immediately, from these circumstances, detect the falsehood, and prove him a liar, with the same certainty as if he had stuffed his narration with stories of centaurs and dragons, miracles and prodigies. And if we would explode any forgery in history, we cannot make use of a more convincing argument, than to prove, that the actions ascribed to any person are directly contrary to the course of nature, and that no human motives, in such circumstances, could ever induce him to such a conduct. The veracity of Quintus Curtius is as much to be suspected, when he describes the supernatural courage of Alexander, by which he was hurried on singly to attack multitudes, as when he describes his supernatural force and activity, by which he was able to resist them. So readily and universally do we acknowledge a uniformity in human motives and actions as well as in the operations of body.

Hence likewise the benefit of that experience, acquired by long life and a variety of business and company, in order to instruct us in the principles of human nature, and regulate our future conduct, as well as speculation. By means of this guide, we mount up to the knowledge of men's inclinations and motives, from their actions, expressions, and even gestures; and again descend to the interpretation of their actions from our knowledge of their motives and inclinations. The general observations treasured up by a course of experience, give us the clue of human nature, and teach us to unravel all its intricacies. Pretexts and appearances no longer deceive us. Public declarations pass for the specious colouring of a cause. And though virtue and honour be allowed their proper weight and authority, that perfect disinterestedness, so often pretended to, is never expected in multitudes and parties; seldom in their leaders; and scarcely even in individuals of any rank or station. But were there no uniformity in human actions, and were every experiment which we could form of this kind irregular and anomalous, it were impossible to collect any general observations concerning mankind; and no experience, however accurately digested by reflection, would ever serve to any purpose. Why is the aged husbandman more skilful in his calling than the young beginner but because there is a certain uniformity in the operation of the sun, rain, and earth towards the production of vegetables; and experience teaches the old practitioner the rules by which this operation is governed and directed.

We must not, however, expect that this uniformity of human actions should be carried to such a length as that all men, in the same circumstances, will always act precisely in the same manner, without making any allowance for the diversity of characters, prejudices, and opinions. Such a uniformity in every particular, is found in no part of nature. On the contrary, from observing the variety of conduct in different men, we are enabled to form a greater variety of maxims, which still suppose a degree of uniformity and regularity.

Are the manners of men different in different ages and countries? We learn thence the great force of custom and education, which mould the human mind from its infancy and form it into a fixed and established character. Is the behaviour and conduct of the one sex very unlike that of the other? Is it thence we become acquainted with the different characters which nature has impressed upon the sexes, and which she preserves with constancy and regularity? Are the actions of the same person much diversified in the different periods of his life, from infancy to old age? This affords room for many general observations concerning the gradual change of our sentiments and inclinations, and the different maxims which prevail in the different ages of human creatures. Even the characters, which are peculiar to each individual, have a uniformity in their influence; otherwise our acquaintance with the persons and our observation of their conduct could never teach us their dispositions, or serve to direct our behaviour with regard to them.

I grant it possible to find some actions, which seem to have no regular connexion with any known motives, and are exceptions to all the measures of conduct which have ever been established for the government of men. But if we would willingly know what judgement should be formed of such irregular and extraordinary actions, we may consider the sentiments commonly entertained with regard to those irregular events which appear in the course of nature, and the operations of external objects. All causes are not conjoined to their usual effects with like uniformity. An artificer, who handles only dead matter, may be disappointed of his aim, as well as the politician, who directs the conduct of sensible and intelligent agents.

The vulgar, who take things according to their first appearance, attribute the uncertainty of events to such an uncertainty in the causes as makes the latter often fail of their usual influence; though they meet with no impediment in their operation. But philosophers, observing that, almost in every part of nature, there is contained a vast variety of springs and principles, which are hid, by reason of their minuteness or remoteness, find, that it is at least possible the contrariety of events may not proceed from any contingency in the cause, but from the secret operation of contrary causes. This possibility is converted into certainty by farther observation, when they remark that, upon an exact scrutiny, a contrariety of effects always betrays a contrariety of causes, and proceeds from their mutual opposition. A peasant can give no better reason for the stopping of any clock or watch than to say that it does not commonly go right: But an artist easily perceives that the same force in the spring or pendulum has always the same influence on the wheels; but fails of its usual effect, perhaps by reason of a grain of dust, which puts a stop to the whole movement. From the observation of several parallel instances, philosophers form a maxim that the connexion between all causes and effects is equally necessary, and that its seeming uncertainty in some instances proceeds from the secret opposition of contrary causes.

Thus, for instance, in the human body, when the usual symptoms of health or sickness disappoint our expectation; when medicines operate not with their wonted powers; when irregular events follow from any particular cause; the philosopher and physician are not surprised at the matter, nor are ever tempted to deny, in general, the necessity and uniformity of those principles by which the animal economy is conducted. They know that a human body is a mighty complicated machine: That many secret powers lurk in it, which are altogether beyond our comprehension: That to us it must often appear very uncertain in its operations: And that therefore the irregular events, which outwardly discover themselves, can be no proof that the laws of nature are not observed with the greatest regularity in its internal operations and government.

The philosopher, if he be consistent, must apply the same reasoning to the actions and volitions of intelligent agents. The most irregular and unexpected resolutions of men may frequently be accounted for by those who know every particular circumstance of their character and situation. A person of an obliging disposition gives a peevish answer: But he has the toothache, or has not dined. A stupid fellow discovers an uncommon alacrity in his carriage: But he has met with a sudden piece of good fortune. Or even when an action, as sometimes happens, cannot be particularly accounted for, either by the person himself or by others; we know, in general, that the characters of men are, to a certain degree, inconstant and irregular. This is, in a manner, the constant character of human nature; though it be applicable, in a more particular manner, to some persons who have no fixed rule for their conduct, but proceed in a continued course of caprice and inconstancy. The internal principles and motives may operate in a uniform manner, notwithstanding these seeming irregularities; in the same manner as the winds, rain, clouds, and other variations of the weather are supposed to be governed by steady principles; though not easily discoverable by human sagacity and enquiry.

Thus it appears, not only that the conjunction between motives and voluntary actions is as regular and uniform as that between the cause and effect in any part of nature; but also that this regular conjunction has been universally acknowledged among mankind, and has never been the subject of dispute, either in philosophy or common life. Now, as it is from past experience that we draw all inferences concerning the future, and as we conclude that objects will always be conjoined together which we find to have always been conjoined; it may seem superfluous to prove that this experienced uniformity in human actions is a source whence we draw *inferences* concerning them. But in order to throw the argument into a greater variety of lights we shall also insist, though briefly, on this latter topic.

The mutual dependence of men is so great in all societies that scarce any human action is entirely complete in itself, or is performed without some reference to the actions of others, which are requisite to make it answer fully the intention of the agent. The poorest artificer, who labours alone, expects at least the protection of the magistrate, to ensure him the enjoyment of the fruits of his labour. He also expects that, when he carries his goods to market, and offers them at a reasonable price, he shall find purchasers, and shall be able, by the money he acquires, to engage others to supply him with those commodities which are requisite for his subsistence. In proportion as men extend their dealings, and render their intercourse with others more complicated, they always comprehend, in their schemes of life, a greater variety of voluntary actions, which they expect, from the proper motives, to co-operate with their own. In all these conclusions they take their measures from past experience, in the same manner as in their reasonings concerning external objects; and firmly believe that men, as well as all the elements, are to continue, in their operations, the same that they have ever found them. A manufacturer reckons upon the labour of his servants for the execution of any work as much as upon the tools which he employs, and would be equally surprised were his expectations disappointed. In short, this experimental inference and reasoning concerning the actions of others enters so much into human life, that no man, while awake, is ever a moment without employing it. Have we not reason, therefore, to affirm that all mankind have always agreed in the doctrine of necessity according to the foregoing definition and explication of it?

Nor have philosophers ever entertained a different opinion from the people in this particular. For, not to mention that almost every action of their life supposes that opinion, there are even few of the speculative parts of learning to which it is not essential. What would become of *history,* had we not a dependence on the veracity of the historian accord-ing to the experience which we have had of mankind? How could *politics* be a science, if laws and forms of government had not a uniform influence upon society? Where would be the foundation of *morals,* if particular characters had no certain or determinate power to produce particular sentiments, and if these sentiments had no constant operation on actions? And with what pretence could we employ our *criticism* upon any poet or polite author, if we could not pronounce the conduct and sentiments of his actors either natural or unnatural to such characters, and in such circumstances? It seems almost impossible, therefore, to engage either in science or action of any kind without acknowledging the doctrine of necessity, and this *inference* from motive to voluntary actions, from characters to conduct.

And indeed, when we consider how aptly *natural* and *moral* evidence link together, and form only one chain of argument, we shall make no scruple to allow that they are of the same nature, and derived from the same principles. A prisoner who has neither money nor interest, discovers the impossibility of his escape, as well when he considers the obstinacy of the gaoler, as the walls and bars with which he is surrounded; and, in all attempts for his freedom, chooses rather to work upon the stone and iron of the one, than upon the inflexible nature of the other. The same prisoner, when conducted to the scaffold, foresees his death as certainly from the constancy and fidelity of his guards, as from the opera-tion of the axe or wheel. His mind runs along a certain train of ideas: The refusal of the soldiers to consent to his escape; the action of the executioner; the separation of the head and body; bleeding, convulsive motions, and death. Here is a connected chain of natural causes and voluntary actions; but the mind feels no difference between them in passing from one link to another: Nor is less certain of the future event than if it were connected with the objects present to the memory or senses, by a train of causes, cemented together by what we are pleased to call a *physical* necessity. The same experienced union has the same effect on the mind, whether the united objects be motives, volition, and actions; or figure and motion. We may change the name of things; but their nature and their operation on the understanding never change.

Were a man, whom I know to be honest and opulent, and with whom I live in intimate friendship, to come into my house, where I am sur-rounded with my servants, I rest assured that he is not to stab me before he leaves it in order to rob me of my silver standish; and I no more sus-pect this event than the falling of the house itself, which is new, and solidly built and founded.—*But he may have been seized with a sudden and unknown frenzy.*—So may a sudden earthquake arise, and shake and tumble my house about my ears. I shall therefore change the suppo-sitions. I shall say that I know with certainty that he is not to put his hand into the fire and hold it there till it be consumed: And this event, I think I can foretell with the same assurance, as that, if he throw himself out at the window, and meet with no obstruction, he will not remain a moment suspended in the air. No suspicion of an unknown frenzy can give the least possibility to the former event, which is so contrary to all the known principles of human nature. A man who at noon leaves his purse full of gold on the pavement at Charing-Cross, may as well expect that it will fly away like a feather, as that he will find it untouched an hour after. Above one half of human reasonings contain inferences of a similar nature, attended with more or less degrees of certainty proportioned to our experience of the usual conduct of mankind in such particular situations.

I have frequently considered, what could possibly be the reason why all mankind, though they have ever, without hesitation, acknowledged the doctrine of necessity in their whole practice and reasoning, have yet not discovered such a reluctance to acknowledge it in words, and have rather shown a propensity, in all ages, to profess the contrary opinion. The matter, I think, may be accounted for after the following manner. If we examine the operations of body, and the production of effects from their causes, we shall find that all our faculties can never carry us farther in our knowledge of this relation than barely to observe that particular objects are *constantly conjoined* together, and that the mind is carried, by a *customary transition,* from the appearance of one to the belief of the other. But though this conclusion concerning human ignorance be the result of the strictest scrutiny of this subject, men still entertain a strong propensity to believe that they penetrate farther into the powers of nature, and perceive something like a necessary connexion between the cause and the effect. When again they turn their reflections towards the operations of their own minds, and *feel* no such connexion of the motive and the action; they are thence apt to suppose, that there is a difference between the effects which result from material force, and those which arise from thought and intelligence. But being once convinced that we know nothing farther of causation of any kind than merely the *constant conjunction* of objects, and the consequent *inference* of the mind from one to another, and finding that these two circumstances are universally allowed to have place in voluntary actions; we may be more easily led to own the same necessity common to all causes. And though this reasoning may contradict the systems of many philosophers, in ascribing necessity to the determinations of the will, we shall find, upon reflection, that they dissent from it in words only, not in their real sentiment. Necessity, according to the sense in which it is here taken, has never yet been rejected, nor can ever, I think, be rejected by any philosopher. It may only, perhaps, be pretended that the mind can perceive, in the operations of matter, some farther connexion between the cause and effect; and connexion that has not place in voluntary actions of intelligent beings. Now whether it be so or not, can only appear upon examination; and it is incumbent on these philosophers to make good their assertion, by defining or describing that necessity, and pointing it out to us in the operations of material causes.

It would seem, indeed, that men begin at the wrong end of this question concerning liberty and necessity, when they enter upon it by examining the faculties of the soul, the influence of the understanding, and the operations of the will. Let them first discuss a more simple question, namely, the operations of body and of brute unintelligent matter; and try whether they can there form any idea of causation and necessity, except that of a constant conjunction of objects, and subsequent inference of the mind from one to another. If these circumstances form, in reality, the whole of that necessity, which we conceive in matter, and if these circumstances be also universally acknowledged to take place in the operations of the mind, the dispute is at an end; at least, must be owned to be thenceforth merely verbal. But as long as we will rashly suppose, that we have some farther idea of necessity and causation in the operations of external objects; at the same time, that we can find nothing farther in the voluntary actions of the mind; there is no possibility of bringing the question to any determinate issue, while we proceed upon so erroneous a supposition. The only method of undeceiving us is to mount up higher; to examine the narrow extent of science when applied to material causes; and to convince ourselves that all we know of them is the constant conjunction and inference above mentioned. We may, perhaps, find that it is with difficulty we are induced to fix such narrow limits to human understanding: But we can afterwards find no difficulty when we come to apply this doctrine to the actions of the will. For as it is evident that these have a regular conjunction with motives and circumstances and characters, and as we always draw inferences from one to the other, we must be obliged to acknowledge in words that necessity, which we have already avowed, in every deliberation of our lives, and in every step of our conduct and behaviour.[16]

---

[16] The prevalence of the doctrine of liberty may be accounted for, from another cause, viz. a false sensation or seeming experience which we have, or may have, of liberty or indifference, in many of our actions. The necessity of any action, whether of matter or of mind, is not, properly speaking, a quality in the agent, but in any thinking or intelligent being, who may consider the action; and it consists chiefly in the determination of his thoughts to infer the existence of that action from some preceding objects; as liberty, when opposed to necessity, is nothing but the want of that determination, and a certain looseness or indifference, which we feel, in passing, or not passing, from the idea of one object to that of any succeeding one. Now we may observe, that, though, in *reflecting* on human actions, we seldom feel such a looseness, or indifference, but are commonly able to infer them with considerable certainty from their motives, and from the dispositions of the agent; yet it frequently happens, that, in *performing* the actions themselves, we are sensible of something like it: And as all resembling objects are readily taken for each other, this has been employed as a demonstrative and even intuitive proof of human liberty. We feel, that our actions are subject to our will, on most occasions; and imagine we feel, that the will itself is subject to nothing, because, when by a denial of it we are provoked to try, we feel, that it moves easily every way, and produces an image of itself (or a *Velleity*,

But to proceed in this reconciling project with regard to the question of liberty and necessity; the most contentious question of metaphysics, the most contentious science; it will not require many words to prove, that all mankind have ever agreed in the doctrine of liberty as well as in that of necessity, and that the whole dispute, in this respect also, has been hitherto merely verbal. For what is meant by liberty, when applied to voluntary actions? We cannot surely mean that actions have so little connexion with motives, inclinations, and circumstances, that one does not follow with a certain degree of uniformity from the other, and that one affords no inference by which we can conclude the existence of the other. For these are plain and acknowledged matters of fact. By liberty, then, we can only mean *a power of acting or not acting, according to the determinations of the will;* that is, if we choose to remain at rest, we may; if we choose to move, we also may. Now this hypothetical liberty is universally allowed to belong to every one who is not a prisoner and in chains. Here, then, is no subject of dispute.

Whatever definition we may give of liberty, we should be careful to observe two requisite circumstances; *first,* that it be consistent with plain matter of fact; *secondly,* that it be consistent with itself. If we observe these circumstances, and render our definition intelligible, I am persuaded that all mankind will be found of one opinion with regard to it.

It is universally allowed that nothing exists without a cause of its existence, and that chance, when strictly examined, is a mere negative word, and means not any real power which has anywhere a being in nature. But it is pretended that some causes are necessary, some not necessary. Here then is the advantage of definitions. Let any one *define* a cause, without comprehending, as a part of the definition, a *necessary connexion* with its effect; and let him show distinctly the origin of the idea, expressed by the definition; and I shall readily give up the whole controversy. But if the foregoing explication of the matter be received, this must be absolutely impracticable. Had not objects a regular conjunction with each other, we should never have entertained any notion of cause and effect; and this regular conjunction produces that inference of the understanding, which is the only connexion, that we can have any comprehension of. Whoever attempts a definition of cause, exclusive of these circumstances, will be obliged either to employ unintelligible terms or such as are synonymous to the term which he endeavours to

---

as it is called in the schools) even on that side, on which it did not settle. This image, or faint motion, we persuade ourselves, could, at that time, have been compleated into the thing itself; because, should that be denied, we find, upon a second trial, that, at present, it can. We consider not, that the fantastical desire of shewing liberty, is here the motive of our actions. And it seems certain, that, however we may imagine we feel a liberty within ourselves, a spectator can commonly infer our actions from our motives and character; and even where he cannot, he concludes in general, that he might, were he perfectly acquainted with every circumstance of our situation and temper, and the most secret springs of our complexion and disposition. Now this is the very essence of necessity, according to the foregoing doctrine.

define.[17] And if the definition above mentioned be admitted; liberty, when opposed to necessity, not to constraint, is the same thing with chance; which is universally allowed to have no existence.

Part II

There is no method of reasoning more common, and yet none more blameable, than, in philosophical disputes, to endeavour the refutation of any hypothesis, by a pretence of its dangerous consequences to religion and morality. When any opinion leads to absurdities, it is certainly false; but it is not certain that an opinion is false, because it is of dangerous consequence. Such topics, therefore, ought entirely to be forborne; as serving nothing to the discovery of truth, but only to make the person of an antagonist odious. This I observe in general, without pretending to draw any advantage from it. I frankly submit to an examination of this kind, and shall venture to affirm that the doctrines, both of necessity and of liberty, as above explained, are not only consistent with morality, but are absolutely essential to its support.

Necessity may be defined two ways, conformably to the two definitions of *cause*, of which it makes an essential part. It consists either in the constant conjunction of like objects, or in the inference of the understanding from one object to another. Now necessity, in both these senses, (which, indeed, are at bottom the same) has universally, though tacitly, in the schools, in the pulpit, and in common life, been allowed to belong to the will of man; and no one has ever pretended to deny that we can draw inferences concerning human actions, and that those inferences are founded on the experienced union of like actions, with like motives, inclinations, and circumstances. The only particular in which any one can differ, is, that either, perhaps, he will refuse to give the name of necessity to this property of human actions: But as long as the meaning is understood, I hope the word can do no harm: Or that he will maintain it possible to discover something farther in the operations of matter. But this, it must be acknowledged, can be of no consequence to morality or religion, whatever it may be to natural philosophy or metaphysics. We may here be mistaken in asserting that there is no idea of any other necessity or connexion in the actions of body: But surely we ascribe nothing to the actions of the mind, but what everyone does, and must readily allow of. We change no circumstance in the received orthodox system with regard to the will, but only in that with regard to material

---

[17] Thus, if a cause be defined, *that which produces any thing;* it is easy to observe, that *producing* is synonimous to *causing*. In like manner, if a cause be defined, *that by which any thing exists;* this is liable to the same objection. For what is meant by these words, *by which?* Had it been said, that a cause is *that* after which *any thing constantly exists;* we should have understood the terms. For this is, indeed, all we know of the matter. And this constancy forms the very essence of necessity, nor have we any other idea of it.

objects and causes. Nothing, therefore, can be more innocent, at least, than this doctrine.

All laws being founded on rewards and punishments, it is supposed as a fundamental principle, that these motives have a regular and uniform influence on the mind, and both produce the good and prevent the evil actions. We may give to this influence what name we please; but, as it is usually conjoined with the action, it must be esteemed a *cause*, and be looked upon as an instance of that necessity, which we would here establish.

The only proper object of hatred or vengeance is a person or creature, endowed with thought and consciousness; and when any criminal or injurious actions excite that passion, it is only by their relation to the person, or connexion with him. Actions are, by their very nature, temporary and perishing; and where they proceed not from some *cause* in the character and disposition of the person who performed them, they can neither redound to his honour, if good; not infamy, if evil. The actions themselves may be blameable; they may be contrary to all the rules of morality and religion: But the person is not answerable for them; and as they proceeded from nothing in him that is durable and constant, and leave nothing of that nature behind them, it is impossible he can, upon their account, become the object of punishment or vengeance. According to the principle, therefore, which denies necessity, and consequently causes, a man is as pure and untainted, after having committed the most horrid crime, as at the first moment of his birth, nor is his character anywise concerned in his actions, since they are not derived from it, and the wickedness of the one can never be used as a proof of the depravity of the other.

Men are not blamed for such actions as they perform ignorantly and casually, whatever may be the consequences. Why? but because the principles of these actions are only momentary, and terminate in them alone. Men are less blamed for such actions as they perform hastily and unpremeditately than for such as proceed from deliberation. For what reason? but because a hasty temper, though a constant cause or principle in the mind, operates only by intervals, and infects not the whole character. Again, repentance wipes off every crime, if attended with a reformation of life and manners. How is this to be accounted for? but by asserting that actions render a person criminal merely as they are proofs of criminal principles in the mind; and when, by an alteration of these principles, they cease to be just proofs, they likewise cease to be criminal. But, except upon the doctrine of necessity, they never were just proofs, and consequently never were criminal.

It will be equally easy to prove, and from the same arguments, that *liberty*, according to that definition above mentioned, in which all men agree, is also essential to morality, and that no human actions, where it is wanting, are susceptible of any moral qualities, or can be the objects either of approbation or dislike. For as actions are objects of our moral sentiment, so far only as they are indications of the internal character, passions, and affections; it is impossible that they can give rise either to praise or blame, where they proceed not from these principles, but are derived altogether from external violence.

I pretend not to have obviated or removed all objections to this theory, with regard to necessity and liberty. I can foresee other objections, de- rived from topics which have not here been treated of. It may be said, for instance, that, if voluntary actions be subjected to the same laws of necessity with the operations of matter, there is a continued chain of necessary causes, pre-ordained and pre-determined, reaching from the original cause of all to every single volition of every human creature. No contingency anywhere in the universe; no indifference; no liberty. While we act, we are, at the same time, acted upon. The ultimate Author of all our volitions is the Creator of the world, who first bestowed motion on this immense machine, and placed all beings in that particular position, whence every subsequent event, by an inevitable necessity, must result. Human actions, therefore, either can have no moral turpitude at all, as proceeding from so good a cause; or if they have any turpitude, they must involve our Creator in the same guilt, while he is acknowledged to be their ultimate cause and author. For as a man, who fired a mine, is answerable for all the consequences whether the train he employed be long or short; so wherever a continued chain of necessary causes is fixed, that Being, either finite or infinite, who produces the first, is likewise the author of all the rest, and must both bear the blame and acquire the praise which belong to them. Our clear and unalterable ideas of morality establish this rule, upon unquestionable reasons, when we examine the conse- quences of any human action; and these reasons must still have greater force when applied to the volitions and intentions of a Being infinitely wise and powerful. Ignorance or impotence may be pleaded for so limited a creature as man; but those imperfections have no place in our Creator. He foresaw, he ordained, he intended all those actions of men, which we so rashly pronounce criminal. And we must therefore conclude, either that they are not criminal, or that the Deity, not man, is accountable for them. But as either of these positions is absurd and impious, it follows, that the doctrine from which they are deduced cannot possibly be true, as being liable to all the same objections. An absurd consequence, if necessary, proves the original doctrine to be absurd in the same manner as criminal actions render criminal the original cause, if the connexion between them be necessary and evitable.

This objection consists of two parts, which we shall examine separately; *First*, that, if human actions can be traced up, by a necessary chain, to the Deity, they can never be criminal; on account of the infinite perfection of that Being from whom they are derived, and who can intend nothing but what is altogether good and laudable. Or, *Secondly*, if they be crim- inal, we must retract the attribute of perfection, which we ascribe to the Deity, and must acknowledge him to be the ultimate author of guilt and moral turpitude in all his creatures.

The answer to the first objection seems obvious and convincing. There are many philosophers who, after an exact scrutiny of all the phenomena

of nature, conclude, that the WHOLE, considered as one system is, in every
period of its existence, ordered with perfect benevolence; and that the utmost possible happiness will, in the end, result to all created beings,
without any mixture of positive or absolute ill or misery. Every physical
ill, say they, makes an essential part of this benevolent system, and could
not possibly be removed, even by the Deity himself, considered as a
wise agent, without giving entrance to greater ill, or excluding greater
good, which will result from it. From this theory, some philosophers, and
the ancient *Stoics* among the rest, derived a topic of consolation under
all afflictions, while they taught their pupils that those ills under which
they laboured were, in reality, goods to the universe; and that to an
enlarged view, which could comprehend the whole system of nature,
every event became an object of joy and exultation. But though this topic
be specious and sublime, it was soon found in practice weak and ineffectual. You would surely more irritate than appease a man lying under
the racking pains of the gout by preaching up to him the rectitude of
those general laws, which produced the malignant humours in his body,
and led them through the proper canals, to the sinews and nerves, where
they now excite such acute torments. These enlarged views may, for a
moment, please the imagination of a speculative man, who is placed in
ease and security; but neither can they dwell with constancy on his mind,
even though undisturbed by the emotions of pain or passion; much less
can they maintain their ground when attacked by such powerful antagonists. The affections take a narrower and more natural survey of their
object; and by an economy, more suitable to the infirmity of human minds,
regard alone the beings around us, and are actuated by such events as
appear good or ill to the private system.

The case is the same with *moral* as with *physical* ill. It cannot reasonably be supposed, that those remote considerations, which are found of so
little efficacy with regard to one, will have a more powerful influence with
regard to the other. The mind of man is so formed by nature that, upon
the appearance of certain characters, dispositions, and actions, it immediately feels the sentiment of approbation or blame; nor are there any
emotions more essential to its frame and constitution. The characters
which engage our approbation are chiefly such as contribute to the peace
and security of human society; as the characters which excite blame are
chiefly such as tend to public detriment and disturbance: Whence it may
reasonably be presumed, that the moral sentiments arise, either mediately
or immediately, from a reflection of these opposite interests. What though
philosophical meditations establish a different opinion or conjecture; that
everything is right with regard to the WHOLE, and that the qualities, which
disturb society, are, in the main, as beneficial, and are as suitable to the
primary intention of nature as those which more directly promote its
happiness and welfare? Are such remote and uncertain speculations able
to counterbalance the sentiments which arise from the natural and immediate view of the objects? A man who is robbed of a considerable
sum; does he find his vexation for the loss anywise diminished by these

sublime reflections? Why then should his moral resentment against the crime be supposed incompatible with them? Or why should not the acknowledgment of a real distinction between vice and virtue be reconcileable to all speculative systems of philosophy, as well as that of a real distinction between personal beauty and deformity? Both these distinctions are founded in the natural sentiments of the human mind: And these sentiments are not to be controuled or altered by any philosophical theory or speculation whatsoever.

The *second* objection admits not of so easy and satisfactory an answer; nor it is possible to explain distinctly, how the Deity can be the mediate cause of all the actions of men, without being the author of sin and moral turpitude. These are mysteries, which mere natural and unassisted reason is very unfit to handle; and whatever system she embraces, she must find herself involved in inextricable difficulties, and even contradictions, at every step which she takes with regard to such subjects. To reconcile the indifference and contingency of human actions with prescience; or to defend absolute decrees, and yet free the Deity from being the author of sin, has been found hitherto to exceed all the power of philosophy. Happy, if she be thence sensible of her temerity, when she pries into these sublime mysteries; and leaving a scene so full of obscurities and perplexities, return, with suitable modesty, to her true and proper province, the examination of common life; where she will find difficulties enough to employ her enquiries, without launching into so boundless an ocean of doubt, uncertainty, and contradiction!

SECTION IX. OF THE REASON OF ANIMALS

All our reasonings concerning matter of fact are founded on a species of Analogy, which leads us to expect from any cause the same events, which we have observed to result from similar causes. Where the causes are entirely similar, the analogy is perfect, and the inference, drawn from it, is regarded as certain and conclusive: nor does any man ever entertain a doubt, when he sees a piece of iron, that it will have weight and cohesion of parts; as in all other instances, which have ever fallen under his observation. But where the objects have not so exact a similarity, the analogy is less perfect, and the inference is less conclusive; though still it has some force, in proportion to the degree of similarity and resemblance. The anatomical observations, formed upon one animal, are, by this species of reasoning, extended to all animals; and it is certain, that when the circulation of the blood, for instance, is clearly proved to have place in one creature, as a frog, or fish, it forms a strong presumption, that the same principle has place in all. These analogical observations may be carried farther, even to this science, of which we are now treating; and any theory, by which we explain the operations of the understanding, or the origin and connexion of the passions in man, will acquire additional authority, if we find, that the same theory is requisite to explain the same phenomena in all other animals. We shall make trial of this, with regard to the hypothesis, by which we have, in the foregoing discourse, endeavoured to account for all experimental reasonings; and it is hoped, that this new point of view will serve to confirm all our former observations.

First, It seems evident, that animals as well as men learn many things from experience, and infer, that the same events will always follow from the same causes. By this principle they become acquainted with the more obvious properties of external objects, and gradually, from their birth, treasure up a knowledge of the nature of fire, water, earth, stones, heights, depths, &c., and of the effects which result from their operation. The ignorance and inexperience of the young are here plainly distinguishable from the cunning and sagacity of the old, who have learned, by long observation, to avoid what hurt them, and to pursue what gave ease or pleasure. A horse, that has been accustomed to the field, becomes acquainted with the proper height which he can leap, and will never attempt what exceeds his force and ability. An old greyhound will trust the more fatiguing part of the chace to the younger, and will place himself so as to meet the hare in her doubles; nor are the conjectures, which he forms on this occasion, founded in any thing but his observation and experience.

This is still more evident from the effects of discipline and education on animals, who, by the proper application of rewards and punishments, may be taught any course of action, and most contrary to their natural instincts and propensities. Is it not experience, which renders a dog apprehensive of pain, when you menace him, or lift up the whip to beat him? Is it not even experience, which makes him answer to his name, and infer, from such an arbitrary sound, that you mean him rather than any of his fellows, and intend to call him, when you pronounce it in a certain manner, and with a certain tone and accent?

In all these cases, we may observe, that the animal infers some fact beyond what immediately strikes his senses; and that this inference is altogether founded on past experience, while the creature expects from the present object the same consequences, which it has always found in its observation to result from similar objects.

Secondly, It is impossible, that this inference of the animal can be founded on any process of argument or reasoning, by which he concludes, that like events must follow like objects, and that the course of nature will always be regular in its operations. For it there be in reality any arguments of this nature, they surely lie too abstruse for the observation of such imperfect understandings; since it may well employ the utmost care and attention of a philosophic genius to discover and observe them. Animals, therefore, are not guided in these inferences by reasoning: Neither are children: Neither are the generality of mankind, in their ordinary actions and conclusions: Neither are philosophers themselves, who, in all the active parts of life, are, in the main, the same with the vulgar, and are governed by the same maxims. Nature must have provided some other principle, of more ready, and more general use and application; nor can an operation of such immense consequence in life, as that of inferring effects from causes, be trusted to the uncertain process of reasoning and argumentation. Were this doubtful with regard to men, it seems to admit of no question with regard to the brute creation; and the conclusion being once firmly established in the one, we have a strong presumption, from all the rules of analogy, that it ought to be universally admitted, without any exception or reserve. It is custom alone, which engages animals, from every object, that strikes their senses, to infer its usual attendant, and carries their imagination, from the appearance of the one, to conceive the other, in that particular manner, which we denominate *belief*. No other explication can be given of this operation, in all the higher, as well as lower classes of sensitive beings, which fall under our notice and observation.[18]

------

[18] Since all reasonings concerning facts or causes is derived merely from custom, it may be asked how it happens, that men so much surpass animals in reasoning, and one man so much surpasses another? Has not the same custom the same influence on all?

We shall here endeavour briefly to explain the great difference in human understandings: After which the reason of the difference between men and animals will easily be comprehended.

1. When we have lived any time, and have been accustomed to the uniformity of nature, we acquire a general habit, by which we always transfer the known to the unknown, and conceive the latter to resemble the former. By means of this general habitual principle, we regard even one experiment as the foundation of reasoning, and expect a similar event with some degree of certainty, where the experiment has been made accurately, and free from all foreign circumstances. It is therefore considered as a matter of great importance to observe the consequences of things; and as one man may very much surpass another in attention and memory and observation, this will make a very great difference in their reasoning.

2. Where there is a complication of causes to produce any effect, one mind may be much larger than another, and better able to comprehend the whole system of objects, and to infer justly their consequences.

3. One man is able to carry on a chain of consequences to a greater length than another.

4. Few men can think long without running into a confusion of ideas, and mistaking one for another; and there are various degrees of this infirmity.

5. The circumstance, on which the effect depends, is frequently involved in other circumstances, which are foreign and extrinsic. The separation of it often requires great attention, accuracy, and subtilty.

6. The forming of general maxims from particular observation is a very nice operation; and nothing is more usual, from haste or narrowness of mind which sees not on all sides, than to commit mistakes in this particular.

7. When we reason from analogies, the man, who has the greater experience or the greater promptitude of suggesting analogies, will be the better reasoner.

8. Byasses from prejudice, education, passion, party, &c., hang more upon one mind than another.

9. After we have acquired a confidence in human testimony, books and conversation enlarge much more the sphere of one man's experience and thought than those of another.

It would be easy to discover many other circumstances that make a difference in the understandings of men.

But though animals learn many parts of their knowledge from observation, there are also many parts of it, which they derive from the original hand of nature; which much exceed the share of capacity they possess on ordinary occasions; and in which they improve, little or nothing, by the longest practice and experience. These we denominate Instincts, and are so apt to admire as something very extraordinary, and inexplicable by all the disquisitions of human understanding. But our wonder will, perhaps, cease or diminish, when we consider, that the experimental reasoning itself, which we possess in common with beasts, and on which the whole conduct of life depends, is nothing but a species of instinct or mechanical power, that acts in us unknown to ourselves; and in its chief operations, is not directed by any such relations or comparisons of ideas, as are the proper objects of our intellectual faculties. Though the instinct be different, yet still it is an instinct, which teaches a man to avoid the fire; as much as that, which teaches a bird, with such exactness, the art of incubation, and the whole economy and order of its nursery.

SECTION X.　OF MIRACLES

Part I

There is, in Dr. Tillotson's writings, an argument against the *real presence*, which is as concise, and elegant, and strong as any argument can possibly be supposed against a doctrine, so little worthy of a serious refutation. It is acknowledged on all hands, says that learned prelate, that the authority, either of the scripture or of tradition, is founded merely in the testimony of the apostles, who were eye-witnesses to those miracles of our Saviour, by which he proved his divine mission. Our evidence, then, for the truth of the *Christian* religion is less than the evidence for the truth of our senses; because, even in the first authors of our religion, it was no greater; and it is evident it must diminish in passing from them to their disciples; nor can any one rest such confidence in their testimony, as in the immediate object of his senses. But a weaker evidence can never destroy a stronger; and therefore, were the doctrine of the real presence ever so clearly revealed in scripture, it were directly contrary to the rules of just reasoning to give our assent to it. It contradicts sense, though both the scripture and tradition, on which it is supposed to be built, carry not such evidence with them as sense, when they are considered merely as external evidences, and are not brought home to every one's breast, by the immediate operation of the Holy Spirit.

Nothing is so convenient as a decisive argument of this kind, which must at least *silence* the most arrogant bigotry and superstition, and free us from their impertinent solicitations. I flatter myself, that I have discovered an argument of a like nature, which, if just, will, with the wise and learned, be an everlasting check to all kinds of superstitious delusion, and consequently, will be useful as long as the world endures, For so long, I presume, will the accounts of miracles and prodigies be found in all history, sacred and profane.

Though experience be our only guide in reasoning concerning matters of fact; it must be acknowledged, that this guide is not altogether infallible, but in some cases is apt to lead us into errors. One, who in our climate, should expect better weather in any week of June than in one of December, would reason justly, and conformably to experience; but it is certain, that he may happen, in the event, to find himself mistaken. However, we may observe, that, in such a case, he would have no cause to complain of experience; because it commonly informs us beforehand of the uncertainty, by that contrariety of events, which we may learn from a diligent observation. All effects follow not with like certainty from their supposed causes. Some events are found, in all countries and all ages, to have been constantly conjoined together: Others are found to have been more variable, and sometimes to disappoint our expectations; so that, in our reasonings concerning matter of fact, there are all imaginable degrees of assurance, from the highest certainty to the lowest species of moral evidence.

A wise man, therefore, proportions his belief to the evidence. In such conclusions as are founded on an infallible experience, he expects the event with the last degree of assurance, and regards his past experience as a full *proof* of the future existence of that event. In other cases, he proceeds with more caution: He weighs the opposite experiments: He considers which side is supported by the greater number of experiments: to that side he inclines, with doubt and hesitation; and when at last he fixes his judgement, the evidence exceeds not what we properly call *probability*. All probability, then, supposes an opposition of experiments and observations, where the one side is found to overbalance the other, and to produce a degree of evidence, proportioned to the superiority. A hundred instances or experiments on one side, and fifty on another, afford a doubtful expectation of any event; though a hundred uniform experiments, with only one that is contradictory, reasonably begets a pretty strong degree of assurance. In all cases, we must balance the opposite experiments, where they are opposite, and deduct the smaller number from the greater, in order to know the exact force of the superior evidence.

To apply these principles to a particular instance; we may observe, that there is no species of reasoning more common, more useful, and even necessary to human life, than that which is derived from the testimony of men, and the reports of eye-witnesses and spectators. This species of reasoning, perhaps, one may deny to be founded on the relation of cause and effect. I shall not dispute about a word. It will be sufficient to observe that our assurance in any argument of this kind is derived from no other principle than our observation of the veracity of human testimony, and of the usual conformity of facts to the reports of witnesses. It being a general maxim, that no objects have any discoverable connexion together, and that all the inferences, which we can draw from one to another, are founded merely on our experience of their constant and regular conjunction; it is evident, that we ought not to make an exception to this maxim in favour of human testimony, whose connexion with any event seems, in itself, as little necessary as any other. Were not the memory tenacious to a certain degree; had not men commonly an inclination to truth and a principle of probity, were they not sensible to shame, when detected in a falsehood: Were not these, I say, discovered by *experience* to be qualities, inherent in human nature, we should never repose the least confidence in human testimony. A man delirious, or noted for falsehood and villany, has no manner of authority with us.

And as the evidence, derived from witnesses and human testimony, is founded on past experience, so it varies with the experience, and is regarded either as *proof* or a *probability*, according as the conjunction between any particular kind of report and any kind of object has been found to be constant or variable. There are a number of circumstances to be taken into consideration in all judgements of this kind; and the ultimate standard, by which we determine all disputes, that may arise concerning them, is always derived from experience and observation. Where this experience is not entirely uniform on any side, it is attended with an unavoidable contrariety in our judgements, and with the same opposition and mutual destruction of argument as in every other kind of evidence. We frequently hesitate concerning the reports of others. We balance the opposite circumstances, which cause any doubt or uncertainty; and when we discover a superiority on one side, we incline to it; but still with a diminution of assurance, in proportion to the force of its antagonist.

This contrariety of evidence, in the present case, may be derived from several different causes; from the opposition of contrary testimony; from the character or number of the witnesses; from the manner of their delivering their testimony; or from the union of all these circumstances. We entertain a suspicion concerning any matter of fact, when the witnesses contradict each other; when they are but few, or of a doubtful character; when they have an interest in what they affirm; when they deliver their testimony with hesitation, or on the contrary, with too violent asseverations. There are many other particulars of the same kind, which may diminish or destroy the force of any argument, derived from human testimony.

Suppose, for instance, that the fact, which the testimony endeavours to establish, partakes of the extraordinary and the marvellous; in that case, the evidence, resulting from the testimony, admits of a diminution, greater or less, in proportion as the fact is more or less unusual. The reason why we place any credit in witnesses and historians, is not derived from any *connexion*, which we perceive *a priori*, between testimony and reality, but because we are accustomed to find a conformity between them. But when the fact attested is such a one as has seldom fallen under our observation, here is a contest of two opposite experiences; of which the one destroys the other, as far as its force goes, and the superior can only operate on the mind by the force, which remains. The very same principle of experience, which gives us a certain degree of assurance in the testimony of witnesses, gives us also, in this case, another degree of assurance against the fact, which they endeavour to establish; from which contradiction there necessarily arises a counterpoize, and mutual destruction of belief and authority.

I should not believe such a story were it told me by Cato, was a proverbial saying in Rome, even during the lifetime of that philosophical patriot.[19] The incredibility of a fact, it was allowed, might invalidate so great an authority.

The Indian prince, who refused to believe the first relations concerning the effects of frost, reasoned justly; and it naturally required very strong testimony to engage his assent to facts, that arose from a state of nature, with which he was unacquainted, and which bore so little analogy to those events, of which he had had constant and uniform experience. Though they were not contrary to his experience, they were not conformable to it.[20]

But in order to encrease the probability against the testimony of witnesses, let us suppose, that the fact, which they affirm, instead of being only marvellous, is really miraculous; and suppose also, that the testimony considered apart and in itself, amounts to an entire proof; in that case, there is proof against proof, of which the strongest must prevail, but still with a diminution of its force, in proportion to that of its antagonist.

A miracle is a violation of the laws of nature; and as a firm and unalterable experience has established these laws, the proof against a miracle, from the very nature of the fact, is as entire as any argument from experience can possibly be imagined. Why is it more than probable, that all men must die; that lead cannot, of itself, remain suspended in the air; that fire consumes wood, and is extinguished by water; unless it be, that these events are found agreeable to the laws of nature, and

---

[19] Plutarch, in vita Catonis.

[20] No Indian, it is evident, could have experience that water did not freeze in cold climates. This is placing nature in a situation quite unknown to him; and it is impossible for him to tell *a priori* what will result from it. It is making a new experiment, the consequence of which is always uncertain. One may sometimes conjecture from analogy what will follow; but still this is but conjecture. And it must be confessed, that, in the present case of freezing, the event follows contrary to the rules of analogy, and is such as a rational Indian would not look for. The operations of cold upon water are not gradual, according to the degrees of cold; but whenever it comes to the freezing point, the water passes in a moment, from the utmost liquidity to perfect hardness. Such an event, therefore, may be denominated *extraordinary,* and requires a pretty strong testimony, to render it credible to people in a warm climate: But still it is not *miraculous,* nor contrary to uniform experience of the course of nature in cases where all the circumstances are the same. The inhabitants of Sumatra have always seen water fluid in their own climate, and the freezing of their rivers ought to be deemed a prodigy: But they never saw water in Muscovy during the winter; and therefore they cannot reasonably be positive what would there be the consequence.

there is required a violation of these laws, or in other words, a miracle to prevent them? Nothing is esteemed a miracle, if it ever happen in the common course of nature. It is no miracle that a man, seemingly in good health, should die on a sudden: because such a kind of death, though more unusual than any other, has yet been frequently observed to happen. But it is a miracle, that a dead man should come to life; because that has never been observed in any age or country. There must, therefore, be a uniform experience against every miraculous event, otherwise the event would not merit that appellation. And as a uniform experience amounts to a proof, there is here a direct and full *proof*, from the nature of the fact, against the existence of any miracle; nor can such a proof be destroyed, or the miracle rendered credible, but by an opposite proof, which is superior.[21]

The plain consequence is (and it is a general maxim worthy of our attention), 'That no testimony is sufficient to establish a miracle, unless the testimony be of such a kind, that its falsehood would be more miraculous, than the fact, which it endeavours to establish; and even in that case there is a mutual destruction of arguments, and the superior only gives us an assurance suitable to that degree of force, which remains, after deducting the inferior.' When anyone tells me, that he saw a dead man restored to life, I immediately consider with myself, whether it be more probable, that this person should either deceive or be deceived, or that the fact, which he relates, should really have happened. I weigh the one miracle against the other; and according to the superiority, which I discover, I pronounce my decision, and always reject the greater miracle. If the falsehood of his testimony would be more miraculous, than the event which he relates; then, and not till then, can he pretend to command my belief or opinion.

---

[21] Sometimes an event may not, *in itself, seem* to be contrary to the laws of nature, and yet, if it were real, it might, by reason of some circumstances, be denominated a miracle; because, *in fact*, it is contrary to these laws. Thus if a person, claiming a divine authority, should command a sick person to be well, a healthful man to fall down dead, the clouds to pour rain, the winds to blow, in short, should order many natural events, which immediately follow upon his command; these might justly be esteemed miracles, because they are really, in this case, contrary to the laws of nature. For if any suspicion remain, that the event and command concurred by accident, there is no miracle and no transgression of the laws of nature. If this suspicion be removed, there is evidently a miracle, and a transgression of these laws; because nothing can be more contrary to nature than that the voice or command of a man should have such an influence. A miracle may be accurately defined, *a transgression of a law of nature by a particular volition of the Deity, or by the interposition of some invisible agent.* A miracle may either be discoverable by men or not. This alters not its nature and essence. The raising of a house or ship into the air is a visible miracle. The raising of a feather, when the wind wants ever so little of a force requisite for that purpose, is as real a miracle, though not so sensible with regard to us.

Part II

In the foregoing reasoning we have supposed, that the testimony, upon which a miracle is founded, may possibly amount to an entire proof, and that the falsehood of that testimony would be a real prodigy: But it is easy to shew, that we have been a great deal too liberal in our concession, and that there never was a miraculous event established on so full an evidence.

For *first*, there is not to be found, in all history, any miracle attested by a sufficient number of men, of such unquestioned good-sense, education, and learning, as to secure us against all delusion in themselves; of such undoubted integrity, as to place them beyond all suspicion of any design to deceive others; of such credit and reputation in the eyes of mankind, as to have a great deal to lose in case of their being detected in any falsehood; and at the same time, attesting facts performed in such a public manner and in so celebrated a part of the world, as to render the detection unavoidable: All which circumstances are requisite to give us a full assurance in the testimony of men.

Secondly. We may observe in human nature a principle which, if strictly examined, will be found to diminish extremely the assurance, which we might, from human testimony, have, in any kind of prodigy. The maxim, by which we commonly conduct ourselves in our reasonings, is, that the objects, of which we have no experience, resemble those, of which we have; that what we have found to be most usual is always most probable; and that where there is an opposition of arguments, we ought to give the preference to such as are founded on the greatest number of past observations. But though, in proceeding by this rule, we readily reject any fact which is unusual and incredible in an ordinary degree; yet in advancing farther, the mind observes not always the same rule; but when anything is affirmed utterly absurd and miraculous, it rather the more readily admits of such a fact, upon account of that very circumstance, which ought to destroy all its authority. The passion of *surprise* and *wonder*, arising from miracles, being an agreeable emotion, gives a sensible tendency towards the belief of those events, from which it is derived. And this goes so far, that even those who cannot enjoy this pleasure immediately, nor can believe those miraculous events, of which they are informed, yet love to partake of the satisfaction at second-hand or by rebound, and place a pride and delight in exciting the admiration of others.

With what greediness are the miraculous accounts of travellers received, their descriptions of sea and land monsters, their relations of wonderful adventures, strange men, and uncouth manners? But if the spirit of religion join itself to the love of wonder, there is an end of common sense; and human testimony, in these circumstances, loses all pretensions to authority. A religionist may be an enthusiast, and imagine he sees what has no reality: he may know his narrative to be false, and yet persevere in it, with the best intentions in the world, for the sake of promoting so holy a cause: or even where this delusion has not place, vanity, excited by so strong a temptation, operates on him more powerfully than on the rest of mankind in any other circumstances; and self-interest with equal force. His auditors may not have, and commonly have not, sufficient judgement to canvass his evidence: what judgement they have, they renounce by principle, in these sublime and mysterious subjects: or if they were ever so willing to employ it, passion and a heated imagination disturb the regularity of its operations. Their credulity increases his impudence: and his impudence overpowers their credulity.

Eloquence, when at its highest pitch, leaves little room for reason or reflection; but addressing itself entirely to the fancy or the affections, captivates the willing hearers, and subdues their understanding. Happily, this pitch it seldom attains. But what a Tully or a Demosthenes could scarcely effect over a Roman or Athenian audience, every *Capuchin*, every itinerant or stationary teacher can perform over the generality of mankind, and in a higher degree, by touching such gross and vulgar passions.

The many instances of forged miracles, and prophecies, and supernatural events, which, in all ages, have either been detected by contrary evidence, or which detect themselves by their absurdity, prove sufficiently the strong propensity of mankind to the extraordinary and the marvellous, and ought reasonably to beget a suspicion against all relations of this kind. This is our natural way of thinking, even with regard to the most common and most credible events. For instance: There is no kind of report which rises so easily, and spreads so quickly, especially in country places and provincial towns, as those concerning marriages; insomuch that two young persons of equal condition never see each other twice, but the whole neighbourhood immediately join them together. The pleasure of telling a piece of news so interesting, of propagating it, and of being the first reporters of it, spreads the intelligence. And this is so well known, that no man of sense gives attention to these reports, till he find them confirmed by some greater evidence. Do not the same passions, and others still stronger, incline the generality of mankind to believe and report, with the greatest vehemence and assurance, all religious miracles?

Thirdly. It forms a strong presumption against all supernatural and miraculous relations, that they are observed chiefly to abound among ignorant and barbarous nations; or if a civilized people has ever given admission to any of them, that people will be found to have received them from ignorant and barbarous ancestors, who transmitted them with that inviolable sanction and authority, which always attend received opinions. When we peruse the first histories of all nations, we are apt to imagine ourselves transported into some new world; where the whole frame of nature is disjointed, and every element performs its operations in a different manner, from what it does at present. Battles, revolutions, pestilence, famine and death, are never the effect of those natural causes, which we experience. Prodigies, omens, oracles, judgements, quite obscure the few natural events, that are intermingled with them. But as the former grow thinner every page, in proportion as we advance nearer the enlightened ages, we soon learn, that there is nothing mysterious or supernatural in the case, but that all proceeds from the usual propensity of mankind towards the marvellous, and that, though this inclination may at intervals receive a check from sense and learning, it can never be thoroughly extirpated from human nature.

It is strange, a judicious reader is apt to say, upon the perusal of these wonderful historians, *that such prodigious events never happen in our days*. But it is nothing strange, I hope, that men should lie in all ages. You must surely have seen instances enough of that frailty. You have yourself heard many such marvellous relations started, which, being treated with scorn by all the wise and judicious, have at last been abandoned even by the vulgar. Be assured, that those renowned lies, which have spread and flourished to such a monstrous height, arose from like beginnings; but being sown in a more proper soil, shot up at last into prodigies almost equal to those which they relate.

It was a wise policy in that false prophet, Alexander, who though now forgotten, was once so famous, to lay the first scene of his impostures in Paphlagonia, where, as Lucian tells us, the people were extremely ignorant and stupid, and ready to swallow even the grossest delusion. People at a distance, who are weak enough to think the matter at all worth enquiry, have no opportunity of receiving better information. The stories come magnified to them by a hundred circumstances. Fools are industrious in propagating the imposture; while the wise and learned are contented, in general, to deride its absurdity, without informing themselves of the particular facts, by which it may be distinctly refuted. And thus the impostor above mentioned was enabled to proceed, from his ignorant Paphlagonians, to the enlisting of votaries, even among the Grecian philosophers, and men of the most eminent rank and distinction in Rome: nay, could engage the attention of that sage emperor Marcus Aurelius; so far as to make him trust the success of a military expedition to his delusive prophecies.

The advantages are so great, of starting an imposture among an ignorant people, that, even though the delusion should be too gross to impose on the generality of them (*which, though seldom, is sometimes the case*) it has a much better chance for succeeding in remote countries, than if the first scene had been laid in a city renowned for arts and knowledge. The most ignorant and barbarous of these barbarians carry the report abroad. None of their countrymen have a large correspondence, or sufficient credit and authority to contradict and beat down the delusion. Men's inclination to the marvellous has full opportunity to display itself. And thus a story, which is universally exploded in the place where it was first started, shall pass for certain at a thousand miles distance. But had Alexander fixed his residence at Athens, the philosophers of that renowned mart of learning had immediately spread, throughout the whole Roman empire, their sense of the matter; which, being supported by so great authority, and displayed by all the force of reason and eloquence, had entirely opened the eyes of mankind. It is true; Lucian, passing by chance through Paphlagonia, had an opportunity of performing this good office. But, though much to be wished, it does not always happen, that every Alexander meets with a Lucian, ready to expose and detect his impostures.

I may add as a *fourth* reason, which diminishes the authority of prodigies, that there is no testimony for any, even those which have not been expressly detected, that is not opposed by an infinite number of witnesses; so that not only the miracle destroys the credit of testimony, but the testimony destroys itself. To make this the better undersood, let us consider, that, in matters of religion, whatever is different is contrary; and that it is impossible the religions of ancient Rome, of Turkey, of Siam, and of China should, all of them, be established on any solid foundation. Every miracle, therefore, pretended to have been wrought in any of these religions (and all of them abound in miracles), as its direct scope is to establish the particular system to which it is attributed; so has it the same force, though more indirectly, to overthrow every other system. In destroying a rival system, it likewise destroys the credit of those miracles, on which that system was established; so that all the prodigies of different religions are to be regarded as contrary facts, and the evidences of these prodigies, whether weak or strong, as opposite to each other. According to this method of reasoning, when we believe any miracle of Mahomet or his successors, we have for our warrant the testimony of a few barbarous Arabians: And on the other hand, we are to regard the authority of Titus Livius, Plutarch, Tacitus, and, in short, of all the authors and witnesses, Grecian, Chinese, and Roman Catholic, who have related any miracle in their particular religion; I say, we are to regard their testimony in the same light as if they had mentioned that Mahometan miracle, and had in express terms contradicted it, with the same certainty as they have for the miracle they relate. This argument may appear over subtile and refined; but is not in reality different from the reasoning of a judge, who supposes, that the credit of two witnesses, maintaining a crime against any one, is destroyed by the testimony of two others, who affirm him to have been two hundred leagues distant, at the same instant when the crime is said to have been committed.

One of the best attested miracles in all profane history, is that which Tacitus reports of Vespasian, who cured a blind man in Alexandria, by means of his spittle, and a lame man by the mere touch of his foot; in obedience to a vision of the god Serapis, who had enjoined them to have recourse to the Emperor, for these miraculous cures. The story may be seen in that fine historian; [22] where every circumstance seems to add weight to the testimony, and might be displayed at large with all the force of argument and eloquence, if any one were now concerned to enforce the evidence of that exploded and idolatrous superstition. The gravity, solidity, age, and probity of so great an emperor, who, through

---

22 Hist. lib. v. cap. 8. Suetonius gives nearly the same account *in vita* Vesp.

the whole course of his life, conversed in a familiar manner with his friends and courtiers, and never affected those extraordinary airs of divinity assumed by Alexander and Demetrius. The historian, a contemporary writer, noted for candour and veracity, and withal, the greatest and most penetrating genius, perhaps, of all antiquity; and so free from any tendency to credulity, that he even lies under the contrary imputation, of atheism and profaneness: The persons, from whose authority he related the miracle, of established character for judgement and veracity, as we may well presume; eye-witnesses of the fact, and confirming their testimony, after the Flavian family was despoiled of the empire, and could no longer give any reward, as the price of a lie. *Utrumque, qui interfuere, nunc quoque memorant, postquam nullum mendacio pretium.* To which if we add the public nature of the facts, as related, it will appear, that no evidence can well be supposed stronger for so gross and so palpable a falsehood.

There is also a memorable story related by Cardinal de Retz, which may well deserve our consideration. When that intriguing politician fled into Spain, to avoid the persecution of his enemies, he passed through Saragossa, the capital of Arragon, where he was shewn, in the cathedral, a man, who had served seven years as a doorkeeper, and was well known to every body in town, that had ever paid his devotions at that church. He had been seen, for so long a time, wanting a leg; but recovered that limb by the rubbing of holy oil upon the stump; and the cardinal assures us that he saw him with two legs. This miracle was vouched by all the canons of the church; and the whole company in town were appealed to for a confirmation of the fact; whom the cardinal found, by their zealous devotion, to be thorough believers of the miracle. Here the relater was also cotemporary to the supposed prodigy, of an incredulous and libertine character, as well as of great genius; the miracle of so *singular* a nature as could scarcely admit of a counterfeit, and the witnesses very numerous, and all of them, in a manner, spectators of the fact, to which they gave their testimony. And what adds mightily to the force of the evidence, and may double our surprise on this occasion, is, that the cardinal himself, who relates the story, seems not to give any credit to it, and consequently cannot be suspected of any concurrence in the holy fraud. He considered justly, that it was not requisite, in order to reject a fact of this nature, to be able accurately to disprove the testimony, and to trace its falsehood, through all the circumstances of knavery and credulity which produced it. He knew, that, as this was commonly altogether impossible at any small distance of time and place; so was it extremely difficult, even where one was immediately present, by reason of the bigotry, ignorance, cunning, and roguery of a great part of mankind. He therefore concluded, like a just reasoner, that such an evidence carried falsehood upon the very face of it, and that a miracle, supported by any human testimony, was more properly a subject of derision than of argument.

There surely never was a greater number of miracles ascribed to one person, than those, which were lately said to have been wrought in

France upon the tomb of Abbé Paris, the famous Jansenist, with whose sanctity the people were so long deluded. The curing of the sick, giving hearing to the deaf, and sight to the blind, were every where talked of as the usual effects of that holy sepulchre. But what is more extraordinary; many of the miracles were immediately proved upon the spot, before judges of unquestioned integrity, attested by witnesses of credit and distinction, in a learned age, and on the most eminent theatre that is now in the world. Nor is this all: a relation of them was published and dispersed everywhere; nor were the *Jesuits,* though a learned body, supported by the civil magistrate, and determined enemies to those opinions, in whose favour the miracles were said to have been wrought, ever able distinctly to refute or detect them. Where shall we find such a number of circumstances, agreeing to the corroboration of one fact? And what have we to oppose to such a cloud of witnesses, but the absolute impossibility or miraculous nature of the events, which they relate? And this surely, in the eyes of all reasonable people, will alone be regarded as a sufficient refutation.

Is the consequence just, because some human testimony has the utmost force and authority in some cases, when it relates the battle of Philippi or Pharsalia for instance; that therefore all kinds of testimony must, in all cases, have equal force and authority? Suppose that the Cæsarean and Pompeian factions had, each of them, claimed the victory in these battles, and that the historians of each party had uniformly ascribed the advantage to their own side; how could mankind, at this distance, have been able to determine between them? The contrariety is equally strong between the miracles related by Herodotus or Plutarch, and those delivered by Mariana, Bede, or any monkish historian.

The wise lend a very academic faith to every report which favours the passion of the reporter; whether it magnifies his country, his family, or himself, or in any other way strikes in with his natural inclinations and propensities. But what greater temptation than to appear a missionary, a prophet, an ambassador from heaven? Who would not encounter many dangers and difficulties, in order to attain so sublime a character? Or if, by the help of vanity and a heated imagination, a man has first made a convert of himself, and entered seriously into the delusion; who ever scruples to make use of pious frauds, in support of so holy and meritorious a cause?

The smallest spark may here kindle into the greatest flame; because the materials are always prepared for it. The *avidum genus auricularum,*[23] the gazing populace, receive greedily, without examination, whatever soothes superstition, and promotes wonder.

How many stories of this nature have, in all ages, been detected and exploded in their infancy? How many more have been celebrated for a time, and have afterwards sunk into neglect and oblivion? Where such reports, therefore, fly about, the solution of the phenomenon is obvious;

---

[23] Lucret.

and we judge in conformity to regular experience and observation, when we account for it by the known and natural principles of credulity and delusion. And shall we, rather than have a recourse to so natural a solution, allow of a miraculous violation of the most established laws of nature?

I need not mention the difficulty of detecting a falsehood in any private or even public history, at the place, where it is said to happen; much more when the scene is removed to ever so small a distance. Even a court of judicature, with all the authority, accuracy, and judgement, which they can employ, find themselves often at a loss to distinguish between truth and falsehood in the most recent actions. But the matter never comes to any issue, if trusted to the common method of altercations and debate and flying rumours; especially when men's passions have taken part on either side.

In the infancy of new religions, the wise and learned commonly esteem the matter too inconsiderable to deserve their attention or regard. And when afterwards they would willingly detect the cheat, in order to undeceive the deluded multitude, the season is now past, and the records and witnesses, which might clear up the matter, have perished beyond recovery.

No means of detection remain, but those which must be drawn from the very testimony itself of the reporters: and these, though always sufficient with the judicious and knowing, are commonly too fine to fall under the comprehension of the vulgar.

Upon the whole, then, it appears, that no testimony for any kind of miracle has ever amounted to a probability, much less to a proof; and that, even supposing it amounted to a proof, it would be opposed by another proof; derived from the very nature of the fact, which it would endeavour to establish. It is experience only, which gives authority to human testimony; and it is the same experience, which assures us of the laws of nature. When, therefore, these two kinds of experience are contrary, we have nothing to do but substract the one from the other, and embrace an opinion, either on one side or the other, with that assurance which arises from the remainder. But according to the principle here explained, this substraction, with regard to all popular religions, amounts to an entire annihilation; and therefore we may establish it as a maxim, that no human testimony can have such force as to prove a miracle, and make it a just foundation for any such system of religion.

I beg the limitations here made may be remarked, when I say, that a miracle can never be proved, so as to be the foundation of a system of religion. For I own, that otherwise, there may possibly be miracles, or violations of the usual course of nature, of such a kind as to admit of proof from human testimony; though, perhaps, it will be impossible to find any such in all the records of history. Thus, suppose, all authors, in all languages, agree, that, from the first of January 1600, there was a total darkness over the whole earth for eight days: suppose that the tradition of this extraordinary event is still strong and lively among the people:

that all travellers, who return from foreign countries, bring us accounts of the same tradition, without the least variation or contradiction: it is evident, that our present philosophers, instead of doubting the fact, ought to receive it as certain, and ought to search for the causes whence it might be derived. The decay, corruption, and dissolution of nature, is an event rendered probable by so many analogies, that any phenomenon, which seems to have a tendency towards that catastrophe, comes within the reach of human testimony, if that testimony be very extensive and uniform.

But suppose, that all the historians who treat of England, should agree, that, on the first of January 1600, Queen Elizabeth died; that both before and after her death she was seen by her physicians and the whole court, as is usual with persons of her rank; that her successor was acknowledged and proclaimed by the parliament; and that, after being interred a month, she again appeared, resumed the throne, and governed England for three years: I must confess that I should be surprised at the concurrence of so many odd circumstances, but should not have the least inclination to believe so miraculous an event. I should not doubt of her pretended death, and of those other public circumstances that followed it: I should only assert it to have been pretended, and that it neither was, nor possibly could be real. You would in vain object to me the difficulty, and almost impossibility of deceiving the world in an affair of such consequence; the wisdom and solid judgement of that renowned queen; with the little or no advantage which she could reap from so poor an artifice: All this might astonish me; but I would still reply, that the knavery and folly of men are such common phenomena, that I should rather believe the most extraordinary events to arise from their concurrence, then admit of so signal a violation of the laws of nature.

But should this miracle be ascribed to any new system of religion; men, in all ages, have been so much imposed on by ridiculous stories of that kind, that this very circumstance would be a full proof of a cheat, and sufficient, with all men of sense, not only to make them reject the fact, but even reject it without farther examination. Though the Being to whom the miracle is ascribed, be, in this case, Almighty, it does not, upon that account, become a whit more probable; since it is impossible for us to know the attributes or actions of such a Being, otherwise than from the experience which we have of his productions, in the usual course of nature. This still reduces us to past observation, and obliges us to compare the instances of the violation of truth in the testimony of men, with those of the violation of the laws of nature by miracles, in order to judge which of them is most likely and probable. As the violations of truth are more common in the testimony concerning religious miracles, than in that concerning any other matter of fact; this must diminish very much the authority of the former testimony, and make us form a general resolution, never to lend any attention to it, with whatever specious pretence it may be covered.

Lord Bacon seems to have embraced the same principles of reasoning.

'We ought,' says he, 'to make a collection or particular history of all monsters and prodigious births or productions, and in a word of every thing new, rare, and extraordinary in nature. But this must be done with the most severe scrutiny, lest we depart from truth. Above all, every relation must be considered as suspicious, which depends in any degree upon religion, as the prodigies of Livy: And no less so, every thing that is to be found in the writers of natural magic or alchimy, or such authors, who seem, all of them, to have an unconquerable appetite for falsehood and fable.' [24]

I am the better pleased with the method of reasoning here delivered, as I think it may serve to confound those dangerous friends or disguised enemies to the *Christian Religion*, who have undertaken to defend it by the principles of human reason. Our most holy religion is founded on *Faith*, not on reason; and it is a sure method of exposing it to put it to such a trial as it is, by no means, fitted to endure. To make this more evident, let us examine those miracles, related in scripture; and not to lose ourselves in too wide a field, let us confine ourselves to such as we find in the *Pentateuch*, which we shall examine, according to the principles of these pretended Christians, not as the word or testimony of God himself, but as the production of a mere human writer and historian. Here then we are first to consider a book, presented to us by a barbarous and ignorant people, written in a age when they were still more barbarous, and in all probability long after the facts which it relates, corroborated by no concurring testimony, and resembling those fabulous accounts, which every nation gives of its origin. Upon reading this book, we find it full of prodigies and miracles. It gives an account of a state of the world and of human nature entirely different from the present: Of our fall from that state: Of the age of man, extended to near a thousand years: Of the destruction of the world by a deluge: Of the arbitrary choice of one people, as the favourites of heaven; and that people the countrymen of the author: Of their deliverance from bondage by prodigies the most astonishing imaginable: I desire any one to lay his hand upon his heart, and after a serious consideration declare, whether he thinks that the falsehood of such a book, supported by such a testimony, would be more extraordinary and miraculous than all the miracles it relates; which is, however, necessary to make it be received, according to the measures of probability above established.

What we have said of miracles may be applied, without any variation, to prophecies; and indeed, all prophecies are real miracles, and as such only, can be admitted as proofs of any revelation. If it did not exceed the capacity of human nature to foretell future events, it would be absurd to employ any prophecy as an argument for a divine mission or authority from heaven. So that, upon the whole, we may conclude, that the *Christian Religion* not only was at first attended with miracles, but even at this day cannot be believed by any reasonable person without one. Mere reason

---

[24] Nov. Org. lib. ii aph. 29.

is insufficient to convince us of its veracity: And whoever is moved by
Faith to assent to it, is conscious of a continued miracle in his own person,
which subverts all the principles of his understanding, and gives him a
determination to believe what is most contrary to custom and experience.

SECTION XI.   OF A PARTICULAR PROVIDENCE AND OF A FUTURE STATE

I was lately engaged in conversation with a friend who loves sceptical
paradoxes; where, though he advanced many principles, of which I can by
no means approve, yet as they seem to be curious, and to bear some relation to the chain of reasoning carried on throughout this enquiry, I shall
here copy them from my memory as accurately as I can, in order to submit
them to the judgement of the reader.

Our conversation began with my admiring the singular good fortune
of philosophy, which, as it requires entire liberty above all other privi-
leges, and chiefly flourishes from the free opposition of sentiments and
argumentation, received its first birth in an age and country of freedom
and toleration, and was never cramped, even in its most extravagant principles, by any creeds, concessions, or penal statutes. For, except the
banishment of Protagoras, and the death of Socrates, which last event
proceeded partly from other motives, there are scarcely any instances to
be met with, in ancient history, of this bigotted jealousy, with which the
present age is so much infested. Epicurus lived at Athens to an advanced age, in peace and tranquillity: Epicureans were even admitted
to receive the sacerdotal character, and to officiate at the altar, in the
most sacred rites of the established religion: And the public encouragement of pensions and salaries was afforded equally, by the wisest of all
the Roman emperors, to the professors of every sect of philosophy. How
requisite such kind of treatment was to philosophy, in her early youth,
will easily be conceived, if we reflect, that, even at present, when she
may be supposed more hardy and robust, she bears with much difficulty
the inclemency of the seasons, and those harsh winds of calumny and
persecution, which blow upon her.

You admire, says my friend, as the singular good fortune of philosophy,
what seems to result from the natural course of things, and to be unavoidable in every age and nation. This pertinacious bigotry, of which you
complain, as so fatal to philosophy, is really her offspring, who, after
allying with superstition, separates himself entirely from the interest of
his parent, and becomes her most inveterate enemy and persecutor. Speculative dogmas of religion, the present occasions of such furious dispute,
could not possibly be conceived or admitted in the early ages of the
world; when mankind, being wholly illiterate, formed an idea of religion
more suitable to their weak apprehension, and composed their sacred tenets
of such tales chiefly as were the objects of traditional belief, more than of
argument or disputation. After the first alarm, therefore, was over, which
arose from the new paradoxes and principles of the philosophers; these

teachers seem ever after, during the ages of antiquity, to have lived in great harmony with the established superstition, and to have made a fair partition of mankind between them; the former claiming all the learned and wise, the latter possessing all the vulgar and illiterate.

It seems then, say I, that you leave politics entirely out of the question, and never suppose, that a wise magistrate can justly be jealous of certain tenets of philosophy, such as those of Epicurus, which, denying a divine existence, and consequently a providence and a future state, seem to loosen, in a great measure, the ties of morality, and may be supposed, for that reason, pernicious to the peace of civil society.

I know, replied he, that in fact these persecutions never, in any age, proceeded from calm reason, or from experience of the pernicious consequences of philosophy; but arose entirely from passion and prejudice. But what if I should advance farther, and assert, that if Epicurus had been accused before the people, by any of the *sycophants* or informers of those days, he could easily have defended his cause, and proved his principles of philosophy to be as salutary as those of his adversaries, who endeavoured, with such zeal, to expose him to the public hatred and jealousy?

I wish, said I, you would try your eloquence upon so extraordinary a topic, and make a speech for Epicurus, which might satisfy, not the mob of Athens, if you will allow that ancient and polite city to have contained any mob, but the more philosophical part of his audience, such as might be supposed capable of comprehending his arguments.

The matter would not be difficult, upon such conditions, replied he: And if you please, I shall suppose myself Epicurus for a moment, and make you stand for the Athenian people, and shall deliver you such an harangue as will fill all the urn with white beans, and leave not a black one to gratify the malice of my adversaries.

Very well: Pray proceed upon these suppositions.

I come hither, O ye Athenians, to justify in your assembly what I maintained in my school, and I find myself impeached by furious antagonists, instead of reasoning with calm and dispassionate enquirers. Your deliberations, which of right should be directed to questions of public good, and the interest of the commonwealth, are diverted to the disquisitions of speculative philosophy; and these magnificent, but perhaps fruitless enquiries, take place of your more familiar but more useful occupations. But so far as in me lies, I will prevent this abuse. We shall not here dispute concerning the origin and government of worlds. We shall only enquire how far such questions concern the public interest. And if I can persuade you, that they are entirely indifferent to the peace of society and security of government, I hope that you will presently send us back to our schools, there to examine, at leisure, the question the most sublime, but at the same time, the most speculative of all philosophy.

The religious philosophers, not satisfied with the tradition of your forefathers, and doctrine of your priests (in which I willingly acquiesce), indulge a rash curiosity, in trying how far they can establish religion upon the principles of reason; and they thereby excite, instead of satisfying, the doubts, which naturally arise from a diligent and scrutinous enquiry. They paint, in the most magnificent colours, the order, beauty, and wise arrangement of the universe; and then ask, if such a glorious display of intelligence could proceed from the fortuitous concourse of atoms, or if chance could produce what the greatest genius can never sufficiently admire. I shall not examine the justness of this argument. I shall allow it to be as solid as my antagonists and accusers can desire. It is sufficient, if I can prove, from this very reasoning, that the question is entirely speculative, and that, when, in my philosophical disquisitions, I deny a providence and a future state, I undermine not the foundations of society, but advance principles, which they themselves, upon their own topics, if they argue consistently, must allow to be solid and satisfactory.

You then, who are my accusers, have acknowledged, that the chief or sole argument for a divine existence (which I never questioned) is derived from the order of nature; where there appear such marks of intelligence and design, that you think it extravagant to assign for its cause, either chance, or the blind and unguided force of matter. You allow, that this is an argument drawn from effects to causes. From the order of the work, you infer, that there must have been project and forethought in the workman. If you cannot make out this point, you allow, that your conclusion fails; and you pretend not to establish the conclusion in a greater latitude than the phenomena of nature will justify. These are your concessions. I desire you to mark the consequences.

When we infer any particular cause from an effect, we must proportion the one to the other, and can never be allowed to ascribe to the cause any qualities, but what are exactly sufficient to produce the effect. A body of ten ounces raised in any scale may serve as a proof, that the counterbalancing weight exceeds ten ounces; but can never afford a reason that it exceeds a hundred. If the cause, assigned for any effect, be not sufficient to produce it, we must either reject that cause, or add to it such qualities as will give it a just proportion to the effect. But if we ascribe to it further qualities, or affirm it capable or producing other effects, we can only indulge the licence of conjecture, and arbitrarily suppose the existence of qualities and energies, without reason or authority.

The same rule holds, whether the cause assigned be brute unconscious matter, or a rational intelligent being. If the cause be known only by the effect, we never ought to ascribe to it any qualities, beyond what are precisely requisite to produce the effect: Nor can we, by any rules of just reasoning, return back from the cause, and infer other effects from it, beyond those by which alone it is known to us. No one, merely from the sight of one of Zeuxis's pictures, could know, that he was also a statuary or architect, and was an artist no less skilful in stone and marble than in colours. The talents and taste, displayed in the particular work before us; these we may safely conclude the workmen to be possessed of. The cause must be proportioned to the effect; and if we exactly and precisely proportion it, we shall never find in it any qualities, that point farther, or afford an inference concerning any other design or performance. Such qualities must be somewhat beyond what is merely requisite for producing the effect, which we examine.

Allowing, therefore, the gods to be the authors of the existence or order of the universe; it follows, that they possess that precise degree of power, intelligence, and benevolence, which appears in their workmanship; but nothing farther can ever be proved, except we call in the assistance of exaggeration and flattery to supply the defects of argument and reasoning. So far as the traces of any attributes, at present, appear, so far may we conclude these attributes to exist. The supposition of farther attributes is mere hypothesis; much more the supposition, that, in distant regions of space or periods of time, there has been, or will be, a more magnificent display of these attributes, and a scheme of administration more suitable to such imaginary virtues. We can never be allowed to mount up from the universe, the effect, to Jupiter, the cause; and then descend downwards, to infer any new effect from that cause; as if the present effects alone were not entirely worthy of the glorious attributes, which we ascribe to that deity. The knowledge of the cause being derived solely from the effect, they must be exactly adjusted to each other; and the one can never refer to anything farther, or be the foundation of any new inference and conclusion.

You find certain phenomena in nature. You seek a cause or author. You imagine that you have found him. You afterwards become so enamoured of this offspring of your brain, that you imagine it impossible, but he must produce something greater and more perfect than the present scene of things, which is so full of ill and disorder. You forget, that this superlative intelligence and benevolence are entirely imaginary, or, at least, without any foundation in reason; and that you have no ground to ascribe to him any qualities, but what you see he has actually exerted and displayed in his productions. Let your gods, therefore, O philosophers, be suited to the present appearances of nature: and presume not to alter these appearances by arbitrary suppositions, in order to suit them to the attributes, which you so fondly ascribe to your deities.

When priests and poets, supported by your authority, O Athenians, talk of a golden or silver age, which preceded the present state of vice and misery, I hear them with attention and with reverence. But when philosophers, who pretend to neglect authority, and to cultivate reason, hold the same discourse, I pay them not, I own, the same obsequious submission and pious deference. I ask, who carried them into the celestial regions, who admitted them into the councils of the gods, who opened to them the book of fate, that they thus rashly affirm, that their deities have executed, or will execute, any purpose beyond what has actually appeared? If they tell me, that they have mounted on the steps or by the gradual ascent of reason, and by drawing inferences from effects to causes, I still insist, that they have aided the ascent of reason by the wings of imagination; otherwise they could not thus change their manner of inference, and argue from causes to effects; presuming, that a more perfect production than the present world would be more suitable to such perfect beings as the gods, and forgetting that they have no reason to ascribe to these celestial beings any perfection or any attribute, but what can be found in the present world.

Hence all the fruitless industry to account for the ill appearance of nature, and save the honour of the gods; while we must acknowledge the reality of that evil and disorder, with which the world so much abounds. The obstinate and intractable qualities of matter, we are told, or the observance of general laws, or some such reason, is the sole cause, which controlled the power and benevolence of Jupiter, and obliged him to create mankind and every sensible creature so imperfect and so unhappy. These attributes then, are, it seems, beforehand, taken for granted, in their greatest latitude. And upon that supposition, I own that such conjectures may, perhaps, be admitted as plausible solutions of the ill phenomena. But still I ask, Why take these attributes for granted, or why ascribe to the cause any qualities but what actually appear in the effect? Why torture your brain to justify the course of nature upon suppositions, which, for aught you know, may be entirely imaginary, and of which there are to be found no traces in the course of nature?

The religious hypothesis, therefore, must be considered only as a particular method of accounting for the visible phenomena of the universe: but no just reasoner will ever presume to infer from it any single fact, and alter or add to the phenomena, in any single particular. If you think, that the appearances of things prove such causes, it is allowable for you to draw an inference concerning the existence of these causes. In such complicated and sublime subjects, every one should be indulged in the liberty of conjecture and argument. But here you ought to rest. If you come backward, and arguing from your inferred causes, conclude, that any other fact has existed, or will exist, in the course of nature, which may serve as a fuller display of particular attributes; I must admonish you, that you have departed from the method of reasoning, attached to the present subject, and have certainly added something to the attributes of the cause, beyond what appears in the effect; otherwise you could never, with tolerable sense or propriety, add anything to the effect, in order to render it more worthy of the cause.

Where, then, is the odiousness of that doctrine, which I teach in my school, or rather, which I examine in my gardens? Or what do you find in this whole question, wherein the security of good morals, or the peace and order of society, is in the least concerned?

I deny a providence, you say, and supreme governor of the world, who guides the course of events, and punishes the vicious with infamy and disappointment, and rewards the virtuous with honour and success, in all their undertakings. But surely, I deny not the course itself of events, which lies open to every one's inquiry and examination. I acknowledge, that, in the present order of things, virtue is attended with more peace of mind than vice, and meets with a more favourable reception from the world. I am sensible, that, according to the past experience of mankind, friendship is the chief joy of human life, and moderation the only source of tranquillity and happiness. I never balance between the virtuous and the vicious course of life; but am sensible, that, to a well-disposed mind, every advantage is on the side of the former. And what can you say more, allowing all your suppositions and reasonings? You tell me, indeed, that this disposition of things proceeds from intelligence and design. But whatever it proceeds from, the disposition itself, on which depends our happiness or misery, and consequently our conduct and deportment in life is still the same. It is still open for me, as well as you, to regulate my behaviour, by my experience of past events. And if you affirm, that, while a divine providence is allowed, and a supreme distributive justice in the universe, I ought to expect some more particular reward of the good, and punishment of the bad, beyond the ordinary course of events; I here find the same fallacy, which I have before endeavoured to detect. You persist in imagining, that, if we grant that divine existence, for which you so earnestly contend, you may safely infer consequences from it, and add something to the experienced order of nature, by arguing from the attributes which you ascribe to your gods. You seem not to remember, that all your reasonings on this subject can only be drawn from effects to causes; and that every argument, deducted from causes to effects, must of necessity be a gross sophism; since it is impossible for you to know anything of the cause, but what you have antecedently, not inferred, but discovered to the full, in the effect.

But what must a philosopher think of those vain reasoners, who, instead of regarding the present scene of things as the sole object of their contemplation, so far reverse the whole course of nature, as to render this life merely a passage to something farther; a porch, which leads to a greater, and vastly different building; a prologue, which serves only to introduce the piece, and give it more grace and propriety? Whence, do you think, can such philosophers derive their idea of the gods? From their own conceit and imagination surely. For if they derived it from the present phenomena, it would never point to anything farther, but must be exactly adjusted to them. That the divinity may *possibly* be endowed with attributes, which we have never seen exerted, may be governed by principles of action, which we cannot discover to be satisfied: all this will freely be allowed. But still this is mere *possibility* and hypothesis. We never can have reason to *infer* any attributes, or any principles of action in him, but so far as we know them to have been exerted and satisfied.

Are there any marks of a distributive justice in the world? If you answer in the affirmative, I conclude, that, since justice here exerts itself, it is satisfied. If you reply in the negative, I conclude, that you have then no reason to ascribe justice, in our sense of it, to the gods. If you hold a medium between affirmation and negation, by saying, that the justice of the gods, at present, exerts itself in part, but not in its full extent; I answer, that you have no reason to give it any particular extent, but only so far as you see it, *at present,* exert itself.

Thus I bring the dispute, O Athenians, to a short issue with my antagonists. The course of nature lies open to my contemplation as well as to theirs. The experienced train of events is the great standard, by which we all regulate our conduct. Nothing else can be appealed to in the field, or in the senate. Nothing else ought ever to be heard of in the schools, or in the closet. In vain would our limited understanding break through those boundaries, which are too narrow for our fond imagination. While we argue from the course of nature, and infer a particular intelligent cause, which first bestowed, and still preserves order in the universe, we embrace a principle, which is both uncertain and useless. It is uncertain; because the subject lies entirely beyond the reach of human experience. It is useless; because our knowledge of this cause being derived entirely from the course of nature, we can never, according to the rules of just reasoning, return back from the cause with any new inference, or making additions to the common and experienced course of nature, establish any new principles of conduct and behaviour.

I observe (said I, finding he had finished his harangue) that you neglect not the artifice of the demagogues of old; and as you were pleased to make me stand for the people, you insinuate yourself into my favour by embracing those principles, to which, you know, I have always expressed a particular attachment. But allowing you to make experience (as indeed I think you ought) the only standard of our judgement concerning this, and all other questions of fact; I doubt not but, from the very same experience, to which you appeal, it may be possible to refute this reasoning, which you have put into the mouth of Epicurus. If you saw, for instance, a half-finished building, surrounded with heaps of brick and stone and mortar, and all the instruments of masonry; could you not *infer* from the effect, that it was a work of design and contrivance? And could you not return again, from this inferred cause, to infer new additions to the effect, and conclude, that the building would soon be finished, and receive all the further improvements, which art could bestow upon it? If you saw upon the sea-shore the print of one human foot, you would conclude, that a man had passed that way, and that he had also left the traces of the other foot, though effaced by the rolling of the sands or inundation of the waters. Why then do you refuse to admit the same method of reasoning with regard to the order of nature? Consider the world and the present life only as an imperfect building, from which you can infer a superior intelligence; and arguing from that superior intelligence, which can leave nothing imperfect; why may you not infer a more finished scheme or plan, which will receive its completion in some distant point of space or time? Are not these methods of reasoning exactly similar? And under what pretence can you embrace the one, while you reject the other?

The infinite difference of the subjects, replied he, is a sufficient foundation for this difference in my conclusions. In works of *human* art and contrivance, it is allowable to advance from the effect to the cause, and returning back from the cause, to form new inferences concerning the effect, and examine the alterations, which it has probably undergone, or may still undergo. But what is the foundation of this method of reasoning? Plainly this: that man is a being, whom we know by experience, whose motives and designs we are acquainted with, and whose projects and inclinations have a certain connexion and coherence, according to the laws which nature has established for the government of such a creature. When, therefore, we find, that any work has proceeded from the skill and industry of man; as we are otherwise acquainted with the nature of the animal, we can draw a hundred inferences concerning what may be expected from him; and these inferences will all be founded in experience and observation. But did we know man only from the single work or production which we examine, it were impossible for us to argue in this manner; because our knowledge of all the qualities, which we ascribe to him, being in that case derived from the production, it is impossible they could point to anything further, or be the foundation of any new inference. The print of a foot in the sand can only prove, when considered alone, that there was some figure adapted to it, by which it was produced: but the print of a human foot proves likewise, from our other experience, that there was probably another foot, which also left its impression, though effaced by time or other accidents. Here we mount from the effect to the cause; and descending again from the cause, infer alterations in the effect; but this is not a continuation of the same simple chain of reasoning. We comprehend in this case a hundred other experiences and observations, concerning the *usual* figure and members of that species of animal, without which this method of argument must be considered as fallacious and sophistical.

The case is not the same with our reasonings from the works of nature. The Deity is known to us only by his productions, and is a single being in the universe, not comprehended under any species or genus, from whose experienced attributes or qualities, we can, by analogy, infer may attribute or quality in him. As the universe shews wisdom and goodness, we infer wisdom and goodness. As it shews a particular degree of these perfections, we infer a particular degree of them, precisely adapted to the effect which we examine. But further attributes or further degrees of the same attributes, we can never be authorised to infer or suppose, by any rules of just reasoning. Now, without some such license of supposition, it is impossible for us to argue from the cause, or infer any alteration in the effect, beyond what as immediately fallen under our observation. Greater good produced by this Being must still prove a greater degree of goodness: a more impartial distribution of rewards and punishments must proceed from a greater regard to justice and equity. Every supposed addition to the works of nature makes an addition to the attributes of the Author of nature; and consequently, being entirely unsupported by any reason or argument, can never be admitted but as mere conjecture and hypothesis.[25]

The great source of our mistake in this subject, and of the unbounded licence of conjecture, which we indulge, is, that we tacitly consider ourselves, as in the place of the Supreme Being, and conclude, that he will, on every occasion, observe the same conduct, which we ourselves, in his situation, would have embraced as reasonable and eligible. But, besides that the ordinary course of nature may convince us, that almost everything is regulated by principles and maxims very different from ours; besides, this, I say, it must evidently appear contrary to all rules of analogy to reason, from the intentions and project of men, to those of a Being so different, and so much superior. In human nature, there is a certain experienced coherence of designs and inclinations; so that when, from any fact, we have discovered one intention of any man, it may often be reasonable, from experience, to infer another, and draw a long chain of conclusions concerning his past or future conduct. But this method of reasoning can never have place with regard to a Being, so remote and incomprehensible, who bears much less analogy to any other being in the universe than the sun to a waxen taper, and who discovers himself only by some faint traces or outlines, beyond which we have no authority to ascribe to him any attribute or perfection. What we imagine to be a superior perfection, may really be a defect. Or were it ever so much a perfection, the ascribing of it to the Supreme Being, where it appears not to have been really exerted, to the full, in his works, savours more of flattery and panegyric, than of just reasoning and sound philosophy. All the philosophy, therefore, in the world, and all the religion, which is nothing but a species of philosophy, will never be able to carry us beyond the usual course of experience, or give us measures of conduct and behaviour different from those which are furnished by reflections on common life. No new fact can ever be inferred from the religious hypothesis; no event foreseen or foretold: no reward or punishment expected or

---

[25] In general, it may, I think, be established as a maxim, that where any cause is known only by its particular effects, it must be impossible to infer any new effects from that cause; since the qualities, which are requisite to produce these new effects along with the former, must either be different, or superior, or of more extensive operation, than those which simply produced the effect, whence alone the cause is supposed to be known to us. We can never, therefore, have any reason to suppose the existence of these qualities. To say, that the new effects proceed only from a continuation of the same energy, which is already known from the first effects, will not remove the difficulty. For even granting this to be the case (which can seldom be supposed), the very continuation and exertion of a like energy (for it is impossible it can be absolutely the same), I say, this exertion of a like energy, in a different period of space and time, is a very arbitrary supposition, and what there cannot possibly be any traces of in the effects, from which all our knowledge of the cause is originally derived. Let the *inferred* cause be exactly proportioned (as it should be) to the known effect; and it is impossible that it can possess any qualities, from which new or different effects can be *inferred*.

dreaded, beyond what is already known by practice and observation. So that my apology for Epicurus will still appear solid and satisfactory; nor have the political interests of society any connexion with the philosophical disputes concerning metaphysics and religion.

There is still one circumstance, replied I, which you seem to have overlooked. Though I should allow your premises, I must deny your conclusion. You conclude, that religious doctrines and reasonings *can* have no influence on life, because they *ought* to have no influence; never considering, that men reason not in the same manner you do, but draw many consequences from the belief of a divine Existence, and suppose that the Deity will inflict punishments on vice, and bestow rewards on virtue, beyond what appear in the ordinary course of nature. Whether this reasonings of theirs be just or not, is no matter. Its influence on their life and conduct must still be the same. And, those, who attempt to disabuse them of such prejudices, may, for aught I know, be good reasoners, but I cannot allow them to be good citizens and politicians; since they free men from one restraint upon their passions, and make the infringement of the laws of society, in one respect, more easy and secure.

After all, I may, perhaps, agree to your general conclusion in favour of liberty, though upon different premises from those, on which you endeavour to found it. I think, that the state ought to tolerate every principle of philosophy; nor is there an instance, that any government has suffered in its political interests by such indulgence. There is no enthusiasm among philosophers; their doctrines are not very alluring to the people; and no restraint can be put upon their reasonings, but what must be of dangerous consequences to the sciences, and even to the state, by paving the way for persecution and oppression in points, where the generality of mankind are more deeply interested and concerned.

But there occurs to me (continued I) with regard to your main topic, a difficulty, which I shall just propose to you without insisting on it; lest it lead into reasonings of too nice and delicate a nature. In a word, I much doubt whether it be possible for a cause to be known only by its effect (as you have all along supposed) or to be of so singular and particular a nature as to have no parallel and no similarity with any other cause or object, that has ever fallen under our observation. It is only when two *species* of objects are found to be constantly conjoined, that we can infer the one from the other; and were an effect presented, which was entirely singular, and could not be comprehended under any known *species*, I do not see, that we could form any conjecture or inference at all concerning its cause. If experience and observation and analogy be, indeed, the only guides which we can reasonably follow in inferences of this nature; both the effect and cause must bear a similarity and resemblance to other effects and causes, which we know, and which we have found, in many instances, to be conjoined with each other. I leave it to your own reflection to pursue the consequences of this principle. I shall just observe, that, as the antagonists of Epicurus always suppose the universe, an effect quite singular and unparalleled, to be the proof of a Deity, a cause no less singular and unparalleled; your reasonings, upon that supposition, seem, at least, to merit our attention. There is, I own, some difficulty, how we can ever return from the cause to the effect, and, reasoning from our ideas of the former, infer any alteration on the latter, or any addition to it.

SECTION XII.   OF THE ACADEMICAL OR SCEPTICAL PHILOSOPHY

Part I

There is not a greater number of philosophical reasonings, displayed upon any subject, than those, which prove the existence of a Deity, and refute the fallacies of *Atheists;* and yet the most religious philosophers still dispute whether any man can be so blinded as to be a speculative atheist. How shall we reconcile these contradictions? The knights-errant, who wandered about to clear the world of dragons and giants, never entertained the least doubt with regard to the existence of these monsters.

The *Sceptic* is another enemy of religion, who naturally provokes the indignation of all divines and graver philosophers; though it is certain, that no man ever met with any such absurd creature, or conversed with a man, who had no opinion or principle concerning any subject, either of action or speculation. This begets a very natural question; What is meant by a sceptic? And how far is it possible to push these philosophical principles of doubt and uncertainty?

There is a species of scepticism, *antecedent* to all study and philosophy, which is much inculcated by Des Cartes and others, as a sovereign preservative against error and precipitate judgement. It recommends an universal doubt, not only of all our former opinions and principles, but also of our very faculties; of whose veracity, say they, we must assure ourselves, by a chain of reasoning, deduced from some original principle, which cannot possibly be fallacious or deceitful. But neither is there any such original principle, which has a prerogative above others, that are self-evident and convincing: or if there were, could we advance a step beyond it, but by the use of those very faculties, of which we are supposed to be already diffident. The Cartesian doubt, therefore, were it ever possible to be attained by any human creature (as it plainly is not) would be entirely incurable; and no reasoning could ever bring us to a state of assurance and conviction upon any subject.

It must, however, be confessed, that this species of scepticism, when more moderate, may be understood in a very reasonable sense, and is a necessary preparative to the study of philosophy, by preserving a proper impartiality in our judgements, and weaning our mind from all those prejudices, which we may have imbibed from education or rash opinion. To begin with clear and self-evident principles, to advance by timorous and sure steps, to review frequently our conclusions, and examine accurately all their consequences; though by these means we shall make both a slow and a short progress in our systems; are the only methods, by which we can ever hope to reach truth, and attain a proper stability and certainty in our determinations.

There is another species of scepticism, *consequent* to science and enquiry, when men are supposed to have discovered either the absolute fallaciousness of their mental faculties, or their unfitness to reach any fixed determination in all those curious subjects of speculation, about which they are commonly employed. Even our very senses are brought into dispute, by a certain species of philosophers; and the maxims of common life are subjected to the same doubt as the most profound principles or conclusions of metaphysics and theology. As these paradoxical tenets (if they may be called tenets) are to be met with in some philosophers, and the refutation of them in several, they naturally excite our curiosity, and make us enquire into the arguments, on which they may be founded.

I need not insist upon the more trite topics, employed by the sceptics in all ages, against the evidence of *sense;* such as those which are derived from the imperfection and fallaciousness of our organs, on numberless occasions; the crooked appearance of an oar in water; the various aspects of objects, according to their different distances; the double images which arise from the pressing one eye; with many other appearances of a like nature. These sceptical topics, indeed, are only sufficient to prove, that the senses alone are not implicitly to be depended on; but that we must correct their evidence by reason, and by considerations, derived from the nature of the medium, the distance of the object, and the disposition of the organ, in order to render them, without their sphere, the proper *criteria* of truth and falsehood. There are other more profound arguments against the senses, which admit not of so easy a solution.

It seems evident, that men are carried, by a natural instinct or prepossession, to repose faith in their senses; and that, without any reasoning, or even almost before the use of reason, we always suppose an external universe, which depends not on our perception, but would exist, though we and every sensible creature were absent or annihilated. Even the animal creation are governed by a like opinion, and preserve this belief of external objects, in all their thoughts, designs, and actions.

It seems also evident, that, when men follow this blind and powerful instinct of nature, they always suppose the very images, presented by the senses, to be the external objects, and never entertain any suspicion, that the one are nothing but representations of the other. This very table, which we see white, and which we feel hard, is believed to exist, independent of our perception, and to be something external to our mind, which perceives it. Our presence bestows not being on it: our absence does not annihilate it. It preserves its existence uniform and entire, independent of the situation of intelligent beings, who perceive or contemplate it.

But this universal and primary opinion of all men is soon destroyed by the slightest philosophy, which teaches us, that nothing can ever be present to the mind but an image or perception, and that the senses are only the inlets, through which these images are conveyed, without being able to produce any immediate intercourse between the mind and the object. The table, which we see, seems to diminish, as we remove farther from it: but the real table, which exists independent of us, suffers no alteration: it was, therefore, nothing but its image, which was present to the mind. These are the obvious dictates of reason; and no man, who reflects, ever doubted, that the existences, which we consider, when we say, *this house* and *that tree*, are nothing but perceptions in the mind, and fleeting copies or representations of other existences, which remain uniform and independent.

So far, then, are we necessitated by reasoning to contradict or depart from the primary instincts of nature, and to embrace a new system with regard to the evidence of our senses. But here philosophy finds herself extremely embarrassed, when she would justify this new system, and obviate the cavils and objections of the sceptics. She can no longer plead the infallible and irresistible instinct of nature: for that led us to a quite different system, which is acknowledged fallible and even erroneous. And to justify this pretended philosophical system, by a chain of clear and convincing argument, or even any appearance of argument, exceeds the power of all human capacity.

By what argument can it be proved, that the perceptions of the mind must be caused by external objects, entirely different from them, though resembling them (if that be possible) and could not arise either from the energy of the mind itself, or from the suggestion of some invisible and unknown spirit, or from some other cause still more unknown to us? It is acknowledged, that, in fact, many of these perceptions arise not from anything external, as in dreams, madness, and other diseases. And nothing can be more explicable than the manner, in which body should so operate upon mind as ever to convey an image of itself to a substance, supposed of so different, and even contrary a nature.

It is a question of fact, whether the perceptions of the senses be produced by external objects, resembling them: how shall this question be determined? By experience surely; as all other questions of a like nature. But here experience is, and must be entirely silent. The mind has never anything present to it but the perceptions, and cannot possibly reach any experience of their connexion with objects. The supposition of such a connexion is, therefore, without any foundation in reasoning.

To have recourse to the veracity of the supreme Being, in order to prove the veracity of our senses, is surely making a very unexpected circuit. If his veracity were at all concerned in this matter, our senses would be entirely infallible; because it is not possible that he can ever deceive. Not to mention, that, if the external world be once called in question, we shall be at a loss to find arguments, by which we may prove the existence of that Being or any of his attributes.

This is a topic, therefore, in which the profounder and more philosophical sceptics will always triumph, when they endeavour to introduce an universal doubt into all subjects of human knowledge and enquiry. Do you follow the instincts and propensities of nature, may they say, in assenting to the veracity of sense? But these lead you to believe that the very perception or sensible image is the external object. Do you disclaim this principle, in order to embrace a more rational opinion, that the perceptions are only representations of something external? You here depart from your natural propensities and more obvious sentiments; and yet are not able to satisfy your reason, which can never find any convincing argumen from experience to prove, that the perceptions are connected with any external objects.

There is another sceptical topic of a like nature, derived from the most profound philosophy, which might merit our attention, were it requisite to dive so deep, in order to discover arguments and reasonings, which can so little serve to any serious purpose. It is universally allowed by modern enquirers, that all the sensible qualities of objects, such as hard, soft, hot, cold, white, black, &c. are merely secondary, and exist not in the objects themselves, but are perceptions of the mind, without any external archetype or model, which they represent. If this be allowed, with regard to secondary qualities, it must also follow, with regard to the supposed primary qualities of extension and solidity; nor can the latter be any more entitled to that denomination than the former. The idea of extension is entirely acquired from the senses of sight and feeling; and if all the qualities, perceived by the senses, be in the mind, not in the object, the same conclusion must reach the idea of extension, which is wholly dependent on the sensible ideas or the ideas of secondary qualities. Nothing can save us from this conclusion, but the asserting, that the ideas of those primary qualities are attained by *Abstraction*, an opinion, which, if we examine it accurately, we shall find to be unintelligible, and even absurd. An extension, that is neither tangible nor visible, cannot possibly be conceived: and a tangible or visible extension, which is neither hard nor soft, black or white, is equally beyond the reach of human conception. Let any man try to conceive a triangle in general, which is neither *Isosceles* nor *Scalenum*, nor has any particular length or proportion of sides; and he will soon perceive the absurdity of all the scholastic notions with regard to abstraction and general ideas.[26]

Thus the first philosophical objection to the evidence of sense or to the opinion of external existence consists in this, that such an opinion, if

---

[26] This argument is drawn from Dr. Berkeley; and indeed most of the writings of that very ingenious author form the best lessons of scepticism, which are to be found either among the ancient or modern philosophers. Bayle not excepted. He professes, however, in his title-page (and undoubtedly with great truth) to have composed his book against the sceptics as well as against the atheists and free-thinkers. But that all his arguments, though otherwise intended, are, in reality, merely sceptical, appears from this, *that they admit of no answer and produce no conviction.* Their only effect is to cause that momentary amazement and irresolution and confusion, which is the result of scepticism.

rested on natural instinct, is contrary to reason, and if referred to reason, is contrary to natural instinct, and at the same time carries no rational evidence with it, to convince an impartial enquirer. The second objection goes farther, and represents this opinion as contrary to reason: at least, if it be a principle of reason, that all sensible qualities are in the mind, not in the object. Bereave matter of all its intelligible qualities, both primary and secondary, you in a manner annihilate it, and leave only a certain unknown, inexplicable *something*, as the cause of our perceptions; a notion so imperfect, that no sceptic will think it worth while to contend against it.

Part II

It may seem a very extravagant attempt of the sceptics to destroy *reason* by argument and ratiocination; yet is this the grand scope of all their enquiries and disputes. They endeavour to find objections, both to our abstract reasonings, and to those which regard matter of fact and existence.

The chief objection against all *abstract* reasonings is derived from the ideas of space and time; ideas, which, in common life and to a careless view, are very clear and intelligible, but when they pass through the scrutiny of the profound sciences (and they are the chief object of these sciences) afford principles, which seem full of absurdity and contradiction. No priestly *dogmas*, invented on purpose to tame and subdue the rebellious reason of mankind, ever shocked common sense more than the doctrine of the infinite divisibility of extension, with its consequences; as they are pompously displayed by all geometricians and metaphysicians, with a kind of triumph and exultation. A real quantity, infinitely less than any finite quantity, containing quantities infinitely less than itself, and so on *in infinitum;* this is an edifice so bold and prodigious, that it is too weighty for any pretended demonstration to support, because it shocks the clearest and most natural principles of human reason.[27] But what renders the matter more extraordinary, is, that these seemingly absurd opinions are supported by a chain of reasoning, the clearest and most natural; nor is it possible for us to allow the premises without admitting the consequences. Nothing can be more convincing and satisfactory than all the conclusions concerning the properties of circles and triangles; and yet, when these are once received, how can we deny, that the angle of

---

[27] Whatever disputes there may be about mathematical points, we must allow that there are physical points; that is, parts of extension, which cannot be divided or lessened, either by the eye or imagination. These images, then, which are present to the fancy or senses, are absolutely indivisible, and consequently must be allowed by mathematicians to be infinitely less than any real part of extension; and yet nothing appears more certain to reason, than that an infinite number of them composes an infinite extension. How much more an infinite number of those infinitely small parts of extension, which are still supposed infinitely divisible.

contact between a circle and its tangent is infinitely less than any recti-lineal angle, that as you may increase the diameter of the circle *in infini-tum*, this angle of contact becomes still less, even *in infinitum*, and that the angle of contact between other curves and their tangents may be infinitely less than those between any circle and its tangent, and so on, *in infinitum?* The demonstration of these principles seems as unexceptionable as that which proves the three angles of a triangle to be equal to two right ones, though the latter opinion be natural and easy, and the former big with contradiction and absurdity. Reason here seems to be thrown into a kind of amazement and suspence, which, without the suggestions of any sceptic, gives her a diffidence of herself, and of the ground on which she treads. She sees a full light, which illuminates certain places; but that light borders upon the most profound darkness. And between these she is so dazzled and confounded, that she scarcely can pronounce with certainty and assurance concerning any one object.

The absurdity of these bold determinations of the abstract sciences seems to become, if possible, still more palpable with regard to time than extension. An infinite number of real parts of time, passing in succession, and exhausted one after another, appears so evident a contradiction, that no man, one should think, whose judgment is not corrupted, instead of being improved, by the sciences, would ever be able to admit of it.

Yet still reason must remain restless, and unquiet, even with regard to that scepticism, to which she is driven by these seeming absurdities and contradictions. How any clear, distinct idea can contain circumstances, contradictory to itself, or to any other clear, distinct idea, is absolutely incomprehensible; and is, perhaps, as absurd as any proposition, which can be formed. So that nothing can be more sceptical, or more full of doubt and hesitation, than this scepticism itself, which arises from some of the paradoxical conclusions of geometry or the science of quantity.[28]

The sceptical objections to *moral* evidence, or to the reasonings concerning matter of fact, are either *popular* or *philosophical.* The popular

---

[28] It seems to me not impossible to avoid these absurdities and contradictions, if it be admitted, that there is no such thing as abstract or general ideas, properly speaking; but that all general ideas are, in reality, particular-ones, attached to a general term, which recalls, upon occasion, other particular ones, that resemble, in certain circumstances, the idea, present to the mind. Thus when the term Horse is pronounced, we immediately figure to ourselves the idea of a black or a white animal, of a particular size or figure: But as that term is also usually applied to animals of other colours, figures and sizes, these ideas, though not actually present to the imagination, are easily recalled; and our reasoning and conclusion proceed in the same way, as if they were actually present. If this be admitted (as seems reasonable) it follows that all the ideas of quantity, upon which mathematicians reason, are nothing but particular, and such as are suggested by the senses and imagination, and consequently, cannot be infinitely divisible. It is sufficient to have dropped this hint at present, without prosecuting it any farther. It certainly concerns all lovers of science not to expose themselves to the ridicule and contempt of the ignorant by their conclusions; and this seems the readiest solution of these difficulties.

objections are derived from the natural weakness of human understanding; the contradictory opinions, which have been entertained in different ages and nations; the variations of our judgement in sickness and health, youth and old age, prosperity and adversity; the perpetual contradiction of each particular man's opinions and sentiments; with many other topics of that kind. It is needless to insist farther on this head. These objections are but weak. For as, in common life, we reason every moment concerning fact and existence, and cannot possibly subsist, without continually employing this species of argument, any popular objections, derived from thence, must be insufficient to destroy that evidence. The great subverter of *Pyrrhonism* or the excessive principles of scepticism is action, and employment, and the occupations of common life. These principles may flourish and triumph in the schools; where it is, indeed, difficult, if not impossible, to refute them. But as soon as they leave the shade, and by the presence of the real objects, which actuate our passions and sentiments, are put in opposition to the more powerful principles of our nature, they vanish like smoke, and leave the most determined sceptic in the same condition as other mortals.

The sceptic, therefore, had better keep within his proper sphere, and display those *philosophical* objections, which arise from more profound researches. Here he seems to have ample matter of triumph; while he justly insists, that all our evidence for any matter of fact, which lies beyond the testimony of sense or memory, is derived entirely from the relation of cause and effect; that we have no other idea of this relation than that of two objects, which have been frequently *conjoined* together; that we have no argument to convince us, that objects, which have, in our experience, been frequently conjoined, will likewise, in other instances, be conjoined in the same manner; and that nothing leads us to this inference but custom or a certain instinct of our nature; which it is indeed difficult to resist, but which, like other instincts, may be fallacious and deceitful. While the sceptic insists upon these topics, he shows his force, or rather, indeed, his own and our weakness; and seems, for the time at least, to destroy all assurance and conviction. These arguments might be displayed at greater length, if any durable good or benefit to society could ever be expected to result from them.

For here is the chief and most confounding objection to *excessive* scepticism, that no durable good can ever result from it; while it remains in its full force and vigour. We need only ask a sceptic, *What his meaning is? And what he proposes by all these curious researches?* He is immediately at a loss, and knows not what to answer. A Copernican or Ptolemaic, who supports each his different system of astronomy, may hope to produce a conviction, which will remain constant and durable, with his audience. A Stoic or Epicurean displays principles, which may not be durable, but which have an effect on conduct and behaviour. But a Pyrrhonian cannot expect, that his philosophy will have any constant influence on the mind: or if it had, that its influence would be beneficial to society. On the contrary, he must acknowledge, if he will acknowledge anything, that all human life must perish, were his principles universally and steadily to prevail. All discourse, all action would immediately cease; and men remain in a total lethargy, till the necessities of nature, unsatisfied, put an end to their miserable existence. It is true; so fatal an event is very little to be dreaded. Nature is always too strong for principle. And though a Pyrrhonian may throw himself or others into a momentary amazement and confusion by his profound reasonings; the first and most trivial event in life will put to flight all his doubts and scruples, and leave him the same, in every point of action and speculation, with the philosophers of every other sect, or with those who never concerned themselves in any philosophical researches. When he awakes from his dream, he will be the first to join in the laugh against himself, and to confess, that all his objections are mere amusement, and can have no other tendency than to show the whimsical condition of mankind, who must act and reason and believe; though they are not able, by their most diligent enquiry, to satisfy themselves concerning the foundation of these operations, or to remove the objections, which may be raised against them.

Part III

There is, indeed, a more *mitigated* scepticism or *academical* philosophy, which may be both durable and useful, and which may, in part, be the result of this Pyrrhonism, or *excessive* scepticism, when its undistinguished doubts are, in some measure, corrected by common sense and reflection. The greater part of mankind are naturally apt to be affirmative and dogmatical in their opinions; and while they see objects only on one side, and have no idea of any counterpoising argument, they throw themselves precipitately into the principles, to which they are inclined; nor have they any indulgence for those who entertain opposite sentiments. To hesitate or balance perplexes their understanding, checks their passion, and suspends their action. They are, therefore, impatient till they escape from a state, which to them is so uneasy: and they think, that they could never remove themselves far enough from it, by the violence of their affirmations and obstinacy of their belief. But could such dogmatical reasoners become sensible of the strange infirmities of human understanding, even in its most perfect state, and when most accurate and cautious in its determinations; such a reflection would naturally inspire them with more modesty and reserve, and diminish their fond opinion of themselves, and their prejudice against antagonists. The illiterate may reflect on the disposition of the learned, who, amidst all the advantages of study and reflection, are commonly still diffident in their determinations: and if any of the learned be inclined, from their natural temper, to haughtiness and obstinacy, a small tincture of Pyrrhonism might abate their pride, by showing them, that the few advantages, which they may have attained over their fellows, are but inconsiderable, if compared with the universal perplexity and confusion, which is inherent in human nature. In general, there is a degree of doubt, and caution, and modesty, which, in all kinds of scrutiny and decision, ought for ever to accompany a just reasoner.

Another species of *mitigated* scepticism which may be of advantage to mankind, and which may be the natural result of the Pyrrhonian doubts and scruples, is the limitation of our enquiries to such subjects as are best adapted to the narrow capacity of human understanding. The *imagination* of man is naturally sublime, delighted with whatever is remote and extraordinary, and running, without control, into the most distant parts of space and time in order to avoid the objects, which custom has rendered too familiar to it. A correct *judgement* observes a contrary method, and avoiding all distant and high enquiries, confines itself to common life, and to such subjects as fall under daily practice and experience; leaving the more sublime topics to the embellishment of poets and orators, or to the arts of priests and politicians. To bring us to so salutary a determination, nothing can be more serviceable, than to be once thoroughly convinced of the force of the Pyrrhonian doubt, and of the impossibility, that anything, but the strong power of natural instinct, could free us from it. Those who have a propensity to philosophy, will still continue their researches; because they reflect, that, besides the immediate pleasure, attending such an occupation, philosophical decisions are nothing but the reflections of common life, methodized and corrected. But they will never be tempted to go beyond common life, so long as they consider the imperfection of those faculties which they employ, their narrow reach, and their inaccurate operations. While we cannot give a satisfactory reason, why we believe, after a thousand experiments, that a stone will fall, or fire burn; can we ever satisfy ourselves concerning any determination, which we may form, with regard to the origin of worlds, and the situation of nature, from, and to eternity?

This narrow limitation, indeed, of our enquiries, is, in every respect, so reasonable, that it suffices to make the slightest examination into the natural powers of the human mind and to compare them with their objects, in order to recommend it to us. We shall then find what are the proper subjects of science and enquiry.

It seems to me, that the only objects of the abstract science or of demonstration are quantity and number, and that all attempts to extend this more perfect species of knowledge beyond these bounds are mere sophistry and illusion. As the component parts of quantity and number are entirely similar, their relations become intricate and involved; and nothing can be more curious, as well as useful, than to trace, by a variety of mediums their equality or inequality, through their different appearances. But as all other ideas are clearly distinct and different from each other, we can never advance farther, by our utmost scrutiny, than to observe this diversity, and, by an obvious reflection, pronounce one thing not to be another. Or if there be any difficulty in these decisions, it proceeds entirely from the undeterminate meaning of words, which is corrected by juster definitions. That *the square of the hypothenuse is equal to the squares of the other two sides*, cannot be known, let the terms be ever so exactly defined, without a train of reasoning and enquiry. But to convince us of this proposition, *that where there is no property, there can be no injustice,* it is only necessary to define the terms, and explain injustice to be a violation of property. This proposition is, indeed, nothing but a more imperfect definition. It is the same case with all those pretended syllogistical reasonings, which may be found in every other branch of learning, except the sciences of quantity and number; and these may safely, I think, be pronounced the only proper objects of knowledge and demonstration.

All other enquiries of men regard only matter of fact and existence; and these are evidently incapable of demonstration. Whatever *is* may *not be.* No negation of a fact can involve a contradiction. The non-existence of any being, without exception, is as clear and distinct an idea as its existence. The proposition, which affirms it not to be, however false, is no less conceivable and intelligible, than that which affirms it to be. The case is different with the sciences, properly so called. Every proposition, which is not true, is there confused and unintelligible. That the cube root of 64 is equal to the half of 10, is a false proposition, and can never be distinctly conceived. But that Cæsar, or the angel Gabriel, or any being never existed, may be a false proposition, but still is perfectly conceivable, and implies no contradiction.

The existence, therefore, of any being can only be proved by arguments from its cause or its effect; and these arguments are founded entirely on experience. If we reason *a priori,* anything may appear able to produce anything. The falling of a pebble may, for aught we know, extinguish the sun; or the wish of a man control the planets in their orbits. It is only experience, which teaches us the nature and bounds of cause and effect, and enables us to infer the existence of one object from that of another.[29] Such is the foundation of moral reasoning, which forms the greater part of human knowledge, and is the source of all human action and behaviour.

Moral reasonings are either concerning particular or general facts. All deliberations in life regard the former; as also all disquisitions in history, chronology, geography, and astronomy.

The sciences, which treat of general facts, are politics, natural philosophy, physic, chemistry, &c. where the qualities, causes and effects of a whole species of objects are enquired into.

Divinity or Theology, as it proves the existence of a Deity, and the immortality of souls, is composed partly of reasonings concerning particular, partly concerning general facts. It has a foundation in *reason,* so far as it is supported by experience. But its best and most solid foundation is *faith* and divine revelation.

---

[29] That impious maxim of the ancient philosophy, *Ex nihilo, nihil fit,* by which the creation of matter was excluded, ceases to be a maxim according to this philosophy. Not only the will of the supreme Being may create matter; but, for aught we know *a priori,* the will of any other being might create it, or any other cause, that the most whimsical imagination can assign.

Morals and criticism are not so properly objects of the understanding as of taste and sentiment. Beauty, whether moral or natural, is felt, more properly than perceived. Or if we reason concerning it, and endeavour to fix its standard, we regard a new fact, to wit, the general tastes of mankind, or some such fact, which may be the object of reasoning and enquiry.

When we run over libraries, persuaded of these principles, what havoc must we make? If we take in our hand any volume; of divinity or school metaphysics, for instance; let us ask, *Does it contain any abstract reasoning concerning quantity or number?* No. *Does it contain any experimental reasoning concerning matter of fact and existence?* No. Commit it then to the flames: for it can contain nothing but sophistry and illusion.

IMMANUEL KANT 1724–1804

Kant is widely considered the greatest modern philosopher; his influence has been enormous. He was born in, and died in, Königsberg, in East Prussia—annexed by the Soviet Union after World War II and rechristened Kaliningrad. Kant never left the environs of his home town, but students came from far away to study with him.

As a young man, he was under the spell of the comprehensive scholasticism of Christian Wolff (1679-1754), who had developed Leibniz' philosophy into a dogmatic rationalistic system. But Kant read widely and also studied theology, physics, and mathematics. For roughly ten years, he served as a private tutor in several families before he became a lecturer at the university, in 1755. For fifteen years, he was unable to obtain a professorship, but in 1766 "Magister Kant, apt and made famous by his scholarly writings," was appointed assistant librarian at the royal Schlossbibliothek, to supplement his salary. In 1770 he was finally made a professor—and thus became the first important modern philosopher who made his living as a professor of philosophy. Like most of the great philosophers up to his time, he did not marry. His way of life was simple and rather pedantic: what saved it from monotony and boredom was the richness of his mind and his stunning capacity for conceiving and developing exciting ideas.

Among his early works, his *Allgemeine Naturgeschichte und Theorie des Himmels* (General Natural History and Theory of the Heavens), subtitled "An Essay treating the Constitution and Mechanical Origin of the Whole Cosmos according to Newtonian Principles," deserves special note. The work was printed in 1755, but the publisher failed, and so publication was delayed. The work was dedicated to Frederick the Great, then King of Prussia, but appeared anonymously. Its agreement with Laplace's *Exposition du système du monde* (1796) is sufficient for scholars to speak generally of the Kant-Laplace theory of the origin of the solar system.

Philosophically, Kant received decisive stimulation from reading Hume and from Leibniz' *Nouveaux Essais* (1765). But he took his time about publishing his radically new ideas. In a letter of August 18, 1783, he told Moses Mendelssohn how he finally composed his masterpiece: confronted with the results of at least twelve years of reflection, he wrote his main work "within four or five months, with the utmost attention to the contents, but with less concern for the presentation or for making things easy for the reader." The book thus described was Kant's *Critique of Pure Reason*, which appeared in 1781. Moses Mendelssohn, a celebrated and influential writer and popular philosopher of the Enlightenment, the grandfather of the composer, called Kant, on the basis of this work, "the all-smasher." For to him, and by no means only to him, it seemed that Kant had smashed traditional metaphysics and theology—the whole of so-called rational psychology, rational cosmology, and natural theology.

Although 1781 has become a crucial date in the history of ideas, since it is firmly associated with Kant's *Kritik der reinen Vernunft,* some translations are based on the second edition of 1787, which differs in content as well as in the mode of presentation. Schopenhauer, and not only he, argued that the earlier edition was bolder, more radical, and altogether preferable.

It happens that there is an excellent English version of the first edition, made by an ideally suitable translator: Max Müller. Born in Germany of a culturally distinguished family, he spent most of his adult life as a teacher at Oxford, lecturing and writing in English, and he established a reputation as an absolutely first-rate translator. An outstanding linguist, he conceived and edited one of the greatest scholarly projects of the nineteenth century, the multi-volume *Sacred Books of the East;* and he himself translated the Upanishads and the Dhammapada. His English versions of these classics of Oriental thought are unsurpassed. Since he was completely bilingual as far as English and German were concerned, he was perfectly equipped to translate Kant's *Kritik.* Indeed, only one later translation of that work is in the same class with his: that of Norman Kemp-Smith, which is based on Kant's second edition. Each of the two translators supplies the variant readings in notes and appendices. Kemp-Smith's is often smoother reading; but when it is, it is smoother not only than Müller's version, but also than Kant's original. Where Kant is less than clear, Kemp-Smith considered it his duty to make up Kant's mind for him, resolving difficulties in favor of some univocal solution. Müller stays closer to the original. The copious selections from Kant's *Critique* that follow are all offered in Müller's translation, and almost all of them come from Kant's first edition. In the end, however, a few of the variants from Kant's second edition have been added.

The page numbers in brackets are those of the first edition. In scholarly citations they are preceded by an *A*, to distinguish them from references to the second edition, which are preceded by a *B*. Parts of the text that appear in brackets are peculiar to the first edition and were changed in the second edition. The footnotes are Kant's, except for clearly editorial notes, which are Müller's. I have deleted Müller's occasional references to the "Supplements" in his edition, in which the second edition variants are offered; and this has involved some very slight rewording in some of his footnotes. I have also changed his translation of the section title on A 820, supplied a title for A 856, and added the words "Chapter I" and "Chapter II" on A 67 and A 84, where Kant had them and Müller inadvertently omitted them. That I have made no revisions is a sign of my respect for Müller's version, which is a classic. Those who wonder whether Kemp-Smith's translation might not be better after all may perhaps be reassured by the experience of C. I. Lewis, to whom this volume of *Philosophic Classics* is dedicated. For a generation, he taught a celebrated course on Kant's *Critique of Pure Reason* at Harvard. At first, he used Müller. Later he switched to Kemp-Smith. In the end he went back to Müller, finding that "with it in hand, the class meetings seemed to go a little better." (The year I assisted him, both of these translations were out of print, and the students had to make do with another version that clearly did not belong in the same league.)

In 1783, Kant published a popular condensation of his argument, the *Prolegomena zu einer jeden künftigen Metaphysik* (Prolegomena to Any Future Metaphysics). Although, like most of Kant's prolific writings, it bears the stamp of his genius, it is no substitute for his *Critique,* and was not meant to be. Many of the best things in the *Critique* were completely omitted.

In 1785, Kant's first major work on ethics appeared under the title *Grundlegung zur Metaphysik der Sitten* (Foundation for the Metaphysics of Morals). Though short, it is one of the most important works on ethics ever written. The selections from this book that follow are offered in the translation of Thomas Kingsmill Abbott. Kant's *Critique of Practical Reason* appeared in 1788, a year after the second edition of his first *Critique.* In spite of the titles,

Kant did not intend any contrast between "Pure Reason" and "Practical Reason." The contrast he did intend was between "Pure Theoretical Reason" and "Pure Practical Reason," the point being that the first *Critique* sought to determine the limits of speculative, theorizing reason—of what we generally call "reason"—while the second *Critique* suggests that there is something rational about man's moral sense, and that this rationality is rooted in our "practical reason." The whole conception of man's practical reason is controversial; many who profoundly admire Kant's *Critique of Pure Reason* and his earlier work on ethics, the so-called *Grundlegung*, reject the notion of practical reason; and hardly any professional philosopher accepts Kant's claim that the practical reason "postulates" the freedom of the will, the immortality of the soul, and the existence of God. Kant, himself, insists that we cannot know whether any of these postulates are true, that the *Critique of Pure Reason* only shows that they *might* be true; but he argues that reason—meaning our rational moral sense—demands that they should be true.

In 1790, Kant published his third and last *Critique, the Critique of Judgment (Kritik der Urteilskraft)*. It is concerned mainly with aesthetic judgments, and the question of whether there is any purpose in nature.

His many other important works include: *Die Religion innerhalb der Grenzen der blossen Vernunft* (Religion Within the Bounds of Mere Reason, 1793); *Zum ewigen Frieden* (Toward Eternal Peace, 1795); *Metaphysik der Sitten* (Metaphysics of Morals, 2 volumes, 1797); and *Anthropologie* (1798). An earlier essay, *Idee zu einer allgemeinen Geschichte in weltbürgerlicher Absicht*, which was initially published in a journal in 1784, deserves special mention. This "Idea for a Universal History with Cosmopolitan Intent" is a fine example of Kant at his non-technical best. Here he shows himself as a brilliant citizen of the world who could write with incisive clarity on subjects of general import, and he introduces the conception of a League of Nations (*Völkerbund*):

"Nature has again made use of conflict among men, even between large societies and states, to create a situation of rest and security out of this inevitable antagonism. By means of wars and the high tension of never relaxed armaments for these wars, and by means of the distress which every nation must thus suffer even during times of peace, she drives man at first to imperfect attempts, but finally, after many devastations and disturbances and even exhaustion of all powers, she drives toward a situation which reason might have anticipated without so many sad experiences: Men leave the lawless state of savages and enter a League of Nations. Thus every state, including the smallest, can find a guarantee for its security and its rights, not in its own power or in its own views of what is just, but in this great League of Nations..."

CRITIQUE OF PURE REASON

CONTENTS

The first edition had a fifteen-line table of contents; the second had none at all; the third featured the first-edition table as an appendix. In the fourth edition (1794), and in most editions ever since, the table of contents continued for pages and pages and comprised well over one hundred items. The table offered here was constructed especially for the present edition, merely to help a little to clarify the structure of the book. Brackets indicate parts omitted in the following pages. The page numbers are those of the first edition.

Preface [1]

Our reason has this peculiar fate that, with reference to one class of its knowledge, it is always troubled with questions which cannot be ignored, because they spring from the very nature of reason, and which cannot be answered, because they transcend the powers of human reason.

Nor is human reason to be blamed for this. It begins with principles which, in the course of experience, it *must* follow, and which are sufficiently confirmed by experience. With these again, according to the necessities of its nature, it rises higher and higher to more remote conditions. But when it pereceives that in this way its work remains for ever incomplete, because the questions never cease, it finds itself constrained to take refuge in principles which exceed every possible experimental application, and nevertheless seem so unobjectionable that even ordinary common sense agrees with them. Thus, however, reason becomes involved in darkness and contradictions, from which, no doubt, it may conclude that errors must be lurking somewhere, but without being able to discover them, because the principles which it follows transcend all the limits of experience and therefore withdraw themselves from all experimental tests. It is the battle-field of these endless controversies which is called *Metaphysic*.

There was a time when Metaphysic held a royal place among all the sciences, and, if the will were taken for the deed, the exceeding importance of her subject might well have secured to her that place of honour. At present it is the fashion to despise Metaphysic, and the poor matron, forlorn and forsaken, complains like Hecuba, *Modo maxima rerum, tot generis natisque potens—nunc trahor exul, inops* (Ovid, Metam. xiii. 508).

At first the rule of Metaphysic, under the dominion of the dogmatists, was despotic. But as the laws still bore the traces of an old barbarism, intestine wars and complete anarchy broke out, and the sceptics, a kind of nomads, despising all settled culture of the land, broke up from time to time all civil society. Fortunately their number was small, and they could not prevent the old settlers from returning to cultivate the ground afresh, though without any fixed plan or agreement. Not long ago one might have thought, indeed, that all these quarrels were to have been settled and the legitimacy of her claims decided once for all through a certain physiology of the human understanding, the work of the celebrated *Locke*. But, though the descent of that royal pretender, traced

---

[1] This preface was left out in later editions, and replaced by a new preface.

back as it had been to the lowest mob of common experience, ought to have rendered her claims very suspicious, yet, as that genealogy turned out to be in reality a false invention, the old queen (Metaphysic) continued to maintain her claims, everything fell back into the old rotten dogmatism, and the contempt from which metaphysical science was to have rescued, remained the same as ever. At present, after everything has been tried, so they say, and tried in vain, there reign in philosophy weariness and complete indifferentism, the mother of chaos and night in all sciences but, at the same time, the spring or, at least, the prelude of their near reform and of a new light, after an ill-applied study has rendered them dark, confused, and useless.

It is in vain to assume a kind of artificial indifferentism in respect to enquiries the object of which cannot be indifferent to human nature. Nay, those pretended indifferentists (however they may try to disguise themselves by changing scholastic terminology into popular language), if they think at all, fall back inevitably into those very metaphysical dogmas which they profess to despise. Nevertheless this indifferentism, showing itself in the very midst of the most flourishing state of all sciences, and affecting those very sciences the teachings of which, if they could be had, would be the last to be surrendered, is a phenomenon well worthy of our attention and consideration. It is clearly the result, not of the carelessness, but of the matured judgment [2] of our age, which will no longer rest satisfied with the mere appearance of knowledge. It is, at the same time, a powerful appeal to reason to undertake anew the most difficult of its duties, namely, self-knowledge, and to institute a court of appeal which should protect the just rights of reason, but dismiss all groundless claims, and should do this not by means of irresponsible decrees, but according to the eternal and unalterable laws of reason. This court of appeal is no other than the *Critique of Pure Reason*.

I do not mean by this a criticism of books and systems, but of the faculty of reason in general, touching that whole class of knowledge which it may strive after, unassisted by experience. This must decide the question of the possibility or impossibility of metaphysic in general, and the determination of its sources, its extent, and its limits—and all this according to fixed principles.

---

[2] We often hear complaints against the shallowness of thought in our own time, and the decay of sound knowledge. But I do not see that sciences which rest on a solid foundation, such as mathematics, physics, etc., deserve this reproach in the least. On the contrary, they maintain their old reputation of solidity, and with regard to physics, even surpass it. The same spirit would manifest itself in other branches of knowledge, if only their principles had first been properly determined. Till that is done, indifferentism and doubt, and ultimately severe criticism, are rather signs of honest thought. Our age is, in every sense of the word, the age of criticism, and everything must submit to it. Religion, on the strength of its sanctity, and law, on the strength of its majesty, try to withdraw themselves from it; but by so doing they arouse just suspicions, and cannot claim that sincere respect which reason pays to those only who have been able to stand its free and open examination.

This, the only way that was left, I have followed, and I flatter myself that I have thus removed all those errors which have hitherto brought reason, whenever it was unassisted by experience, into conflict with itself. I have not evaded its questions by pleading the insufficiency of human reason, but I have classified them according to principles, and, after showing the point where reason begins to misunderstand itself, solved them satisfactorily. It is true that the answer of those questions is not such as a dogma-enamoured curiosity might wish for, for such curiosity could not have been satisfied except by juggling tricks in which I am no adept. But this was not the intention of the natural destiny of our reason, and it became the duty of philosophy to remove the deception which arose from a false interpretation, even though many a vaunted and cherished dream should vanish at the same time. In this work I have chiefly aimed at completeness, and I venture to maintain that there ought not to be one single metaphysical problem that has not been solved here, or to the solution of which the key at least has not been supplied. In fact Pure Reason is so perfect a unity that, if its principle should prove insufficient to answer any one of the many questions started by its very nature, one might throw it away altogether, as insufficient to answer the other questions with perfect certainty.

While I am saying this I fancy I observe in the face of my readers an expression of indignation, mixed with contempt, at pretensions apparently so self-glorious and extravagant; and yet they are in reality far more moderate than those made by the writer of the commonest essay professing to prove the simple nature of the soul or the necessity of a first beginning of the world. For, while he pretends to extend human knowledge beyond the limits of all possible experience, I confess most humbly that this is entirely beyond my power. I mean only to treat of reason and its pure thinking, a knowledge of which is not very far to seek, considering that it is to be found within myself. Common logic gives an instance how all the simple acts of reason can be enumerated completely and systematically. Only between the common logic and my work there is this difference, that my question is,—what can we hope to achieve with reason, when all the material and assistance of experience is taken away?

So much with regard to the completeness in our laying hold of every single object, and the thoroughness in our laying hold of all objects, as the material of our critical enquiries—a completeness and thoroughness determined, not by a casual idea, but by the nature of our knowledge itself.

Besides this, certainty and clearness with regard to form are two essential demands that may very properly be addressed to an author who ventures on so slippery an undertaking.

First, with regard to certainty, I have pronounced judgment against myself by saying that in this kind of enquiries it is in no way permissible to propound mere opinions, and that everything looking like a hypothesis is counterband, that must not be offered for sale at however low a price, but must, as soon as it has been discovered, be confiscated. For every kind of knowledge which professes to be certain *a priori*, proclaims itself that it means to be taken for absolutely necessary. And this applies, therefore, still more to a definition of all pure knowledge *a priori*, which is to be the measure, and therefore also an example, of all apodictic philosophical certainty. Whether I have fulfilled what I have here undertaken to do, must be left to the judgment of the reader; for it only behoves the author to propound his arguments, and not to determine beforehand the effect which they ought to produce on his judges. But, in order to prevent any unnecessary weakening of those arguments, he may be allowed to point out himself certain passages which, though they refer to collateral objects only, might occasion some mistrust, and thus to counteract in time the influence which the least hesitation of the reader in respect to these minor points might exercise with regard to the principal object.

I know of no enquiries which are more important for determining that faculty which we call understanding (Verstand), and for fixing its rules and its limits, than those in the Second Chapter of my Transcendental Analytic, under the title of 'Deduction of the Pure Concepts of the Understanding.' They have given me the greatest but, I hope, not altogether useless trouble. The enquiry, which rests on a deep foundation, has two sides. The one refers to the objects of the pure understanding, and is intended to show and explain the objective value of its concepts *a priori*. It is, therefore, of essential importance for my purposes. The other is intended to enquire into the pure understanding itself, its possibility, and the powers of knowledge on which it rests, therefore its subjective character; a subject which, though important for my principal object, yet forms no essential part of it, because my principal problem is and remains, What and how much may understanding (Verstand) and reason (Vernunft) know without all experience? and not, How is the faculty of thought possible? The latter would be an enquiry into a cause of a given effect; it would, therefore, be of the nature of an hypothesis (though, as I shall show elsewhere, this is not quite so); and it might seem as if I had here allowed myself to propound a mere opinion, leaving the reader free to hold another opinion also. I therefore warn the reader, in case my subjective deduction should not produce that complete conviction which I expect, that the objective deduction, in which I am here chiefly concerned, must still retain its full strength. For this, what has been said on pp. 92,93 [3] may possibly by itself be sufficient.

Secondly, as to clearness, the reader has a right to demand not only what may be called logical or discursive clearness, which is based on concepts, but also what may be called æsthetic or intiutive clearness produced by intuitions, i.e. by examples and concrete illustrations. With regard to the former I have made ample provision. That arose from the very nature of my purpose, but it became at the same time the reason why

---

[3] Omitted in the present volume.

I could not fully satisfy the latter, if not absolute, yet very just claim. Nearly through the whole of my work I have felt doubtful what to do. Examples and illustrations seemed always to be necessary, and therefore found their way into the first sketch of my work. But I soon perceived the magnitude of my task and the number of objects I should have to treat; and, when I saw that even in their driest scholastic form they would considerably swell my book, I did not consider it expedient to extend it still further through examples and illustrations required for popular purposes only. This work can never satisfy the popular taste, and the few who know, do not require that help which, though it is always welcome, yet might here have defeated its very purpose. The Abbé Terrasson writes indeed that, if we measured the greatness of a book, not by the number of its pages, but by the time we require for mastering it, many a book might be said to be much shorter, if it were not so short. But, on the other hand, if we ask how a complicated, yet in principle coherent whole of speculative thought can best be rendered intelligible, we might be equally justified in saying that many a book would have been more intelligible, if it had not tried to be so very intelligible. For the helps to clearness, though they may help with regard to details, often distract with regard to the whole. The reader does not arrive quickly enough at a survey of the whole, because the bright colours of illustrations hide and distort the articulation and concatenation of the whole system, which, after all, if we want to judge of its unity and sufficiency, are more important than anything else.

Surely it should be an attraction to the reader if he is asked to join his own efforts with those of the author in order to carry out a great and important work, according to the plan here proposed, in a complete and lasting manner. Metaphysic, according to the definitions here given, is the only one of all sciences which, through a small but united effort, may count on such completeness in a short time, so that nothing will remain for posterity but to arrange everything according to its own views for didactic purposes, without being able to add anything to the subject itself. For it is in reality nothing but an inventory of all our possessions acquired through Pure Reason, systematically arranged. Nothing can escape us, because whatever reason produces entirely out of itself, cannot hide itself, but is brought to light by reason itself, so soon as the common principle has been discovered. This absolute completeness is rendered not only possible, but necessary, through the perfect unity of this kind of knowledge, all derived from pure concepts, without any influence from experience, or from special intuitions leading to a definite kind of experience, that might serve to enlarge and increase it. *Tecum habita et noris quam sit tibi curta supellex* (Persius, Sat. iv. 52).

Such a system of pure (speculative) reason I hope myself to produce under the title of 'Metaphysic of Nature.' It will not be half so large, yet infinitely richer than this Critique of Pure Reason, which has, first of all, to discover its source, nay, the conditions of its possibility, in fact, to clear and level a soil quite overgrown with weeds. Here I expect from my readers the patience and impartiality of a judge, there the goodwill and aid of a fellow-worker. For however completely all the principles of the system have been propounded in my Critique, the completeness of the whole system requires also that no derivative concepts should be omitted, such as cannot be found out by an estimate *a priori*, but have to be discovered step by step. There the synthesis of concepts has been exhausted, here it will be requisite to do the same for their analysis, a task which is easy and an amusement rather than a labour.

I have only a few words to add with respect to the printing of my book. As the beginning had been delayed, I was not able to see the clean sheets of more than about half of it. I now find some misprints...

Introduction [1]

I. THE IDEA OF TRANSCENDENTAL PHILOSOPHY

[Experience [4] is no doubt the first product of our understanding, while employed in fashioning the raw material of our sensations. It is therefore our first instruction, and in its progress so rich in new lessons that the chain of all future generations will never be in want of new information that may be gathered on that field. Nevertheless, experience is by no means the only field to which our understanding can be confined. Experience tells us what is, but not that it must be necessarily as it is, and not otherwise. It therefore never gives us any really general truths, and our reason, which is particularly anxious for that class of knowledge, is roused by it rather than satisfied. General truths, which at the [2] same time bear the character of an inward necessity, must be independent of experience,—clear and certain by themselves. They are therefore called knowledge *a priori*, while what is simply taken from experience is said to be, in ordinary parlance, known *a posteriori* or empirically only.

Now it appears, and this is extremely curious, that even with our experiences different kinds of knowledge are mixed up, which must have their origin *a priori*, and which perhaps serve only to produce a certain connection between our sensuous representations. For even if we remove from experience everything that belongs to the senses, there remain nevertheless certain original concepts, and certain judgments derived from them, which must have had their origin entirely *a priori*, and independent of all experience, because it is owing to them that we are able, or imagine we are able, to predicate more of the objects of our senses than can be learnt from mere experience, and that our propositions contain real generality and strict necessity, such as mere empirical knowledge can never supply.]

---

[4] The beginning of this Introduction down to 'But what is still more extraordinary,' differs in the Second Edition.

But [5] what is still more extraordinary is this, that certain kinds of knowledge leave the field of all possible experience, and seem to [3] enlarge the sphere of our judgments beyond the limits of experience by means of concepts to which experience can never supply any corresponding objects.

And it is in this very kind of knowledge which transcends the world of the senses, and where experience can neither guide nor correct us, that reason prosecutes its investigations, which by their importance we consider far more excellent and by their tendency far more elevated than anything the understanding can find in the sphere of phenomena. Nay, we risk rather anything, even at the peril of error, than that we should surrender such investigations, either on the ground of their uncertainty, or from any feeling of indifference or contempt.[6]

Now it might seem natural that, after we have left the solid ground of experience, we should not at once proceed to erect an edifice with knowledge which we possess without knowing whence it came, and trust to principles the origin of which is unknown, without having made sure of the safety of the foundations by means of careful examination. It would seem natural, I say, that philosophers should first of all have asked the question how the mere understanding could arrive at all this knowledge *a priori,* and what extent, what truth, and what value it could possess. If we take natural to mean what is just and reasonable, [4] then indeed nothing could be more natural. But if we understand by natural what takes place ordinarily, then, on the contrary, nothing is more natural and more intelligible than that this examination should have been neglected for so long a time. For one part of this knowledge, namely, the mathematical, has always been in possession of perfect trustworthiness; and thus produces a favourable presumption with regard to other parts also, although these may be of a totally different nature. Besides, once beyond the precincts of experience, and we are certain that experience can never contradict us, while the charm of enlarging our knowledge is so great that nothing will stop our progress until we encounter a clear contradiction. This can be avoided if only we are cautious in our imaginations, which nevertheless remain what they are, imaginations only. How far we can advance independent of all experience in *a priori* knowledge is shown by the brilliant example of mathematics. It is true they deal with objects and knowledge so far only as they can be represented in intuition. But this is easily overlooked, because that intuition itself may be given *a priori,* and be difficult to distinguish from a pure concept.

_____

5 The Second Edition gives here a new heading:—III, Philosophy requires a science to determine the possibility, the principles, and the extent of all cognitions *a priori.*

6 The Second Edition adds here: 'These inevitable problems of pure reason itself are, *God, Freedom,* and *Immortality.* The science which with all its apparatus is really intended for the solution of these problems, is called *Metaphysic.* Its procedure is at first *dogmatic,* i.e. unchecked by a previous examination of what reason can and cannot do, before it engages confidently in so arduous an undertaking.'

Thus inspirited by a splendid proof of the power of reason, the [5] desire of enlarging our knowledge sees no limits. The light dove, piercing in her easy flight the air and perceiving its resistance, imagines that flight would be easier still in empty space. It was thus that Plato left the world of sense, as opposing so many hindrances to our understanding, and ventured beyond on the wings of his ideas into the empty space of pure understanding. He did not perceive that he was making no progress by these endeavours, because he had no resistance as a fulcrum on which to rest or to apply his powers, in order to cause the understanding to advance. It is indeed a very common fate of human reason first of all to finish its speculative edifice as soon as possible, and then only to enquire whether the foundation be sure. Then all sorts of excuses are made in order to assure us as to its solidity, or to decline altogether such a late and dangerous enquiry. The reason why during the time of building we feel free from all anxiety and suspicion and believe in the apparent solidity of our foundation, is this:—A great, perhaps the greatest portion of what our reason finds to do consists in the analysis of our concepts of objects. This gives us a great deal of knowledge which, though it consists in no more than in simplifications and explanations of what [6] is comprehended in our concepts (though in a confused manner), is yet considered as equal, at least in form, to new knowledge. It only separates and arranges our concepts, it does not enlarge them in matter or contents. As by this process we gain a kind of real knowledge *a priori*, which progresses safely and usefully, it happens that our reason, without being aware of it, appropriates under that pretence propositions of a totally different character, adding to given concepts new and strange ones *a priori*, without knowing whence they come, nay without even thinking of such a question. I shall therefore at the very outset treat of the distinction between these two kinds of knowledge.

Of the Distinction between Analytical and Synthetical Judgments

In all judgments in which there is a relation between subject and predicate (I speak of affirmative judgments only, the application to negative ones being easy), that relation can be of two kinds. Either the predicate B belongs to the subject A as something contained (though covertly) in the concept A; or B lies outside the sphere of the concept A, though somehow connected with it. In the former case I call the judgment analytical, in the latter synthetical. Analytical judgments (affirmative) are therefore those in which the connection of the predicate with the [7] subject is conceived through identity, while others in which that connection is conceived without identity, may be called synthetical. The former might be called illustrating, the latter expanding judgments, because in the former nothing is added by the predicate to the concept of the subject, but the concept is only divided into its constituent concepts which were always conceived as existing within it, though confusedly;

while the latter add to the concept of the subject a predicate not conceived as existing within it, and not to be extracted from it by any process of mere analysis. If I say, for instance, All bodies are extended, this is an analytical judgment. I need not go beyond the concept connected with the name of body, in order to find that extension is connected with it. I have only to analyse that concept and become conscious of the manifold elements always contained in it, in order to find that predicate. This is therefore an analytical judgment. But if I say, All bodies are heavy, the predicate is something quite different from what I think as the mere concept of body. The addition of such a predicate gives us a synthetical judgment.

[It becomes clear from this,⁷

[1. That our knowledge is in no way extended by analytical judgments, but that all they effect is to put the concepts which we   [8] possess into better order and render them more intelligible.

2. That in synthetical judgments I must have besides the concept of the subject something else (*x*) on which the understanding relies in order to know that a predicate, not contained in the concept, nevertheless belongs to it.

In empirical judgments this causes no difficulty, because this *x* is here simply the complete experience of an object which I conceive by the concept A, that concept forming one part only of my experience. For though I do not include the predicate of gravity in the general concept of body, that concept nevertheless indicates the complete experience through one of its parts, so that I may add other parts also of the same experience, all belonging to that concept. I may first, by an analytical process, realise the concept of body through the predicates of extension, impermeability, form, etc., all of which are contained in it. Afterwards I expand my knowledge, and looking back to the experience from which my concept of body was abstracted, I find gravity always connected with the before-mentioned predicates. Experience therefore is the *x* which lies beyond the concept A, and on which rests the possibility of a synthesis of the predicate of gravity B with the concept A.]

In synthetical judgments *a priori*, however, that help is entirely   [9] wanting. If I want to go beyond the concept A in order to find another concept B connected with it, where is there anything on which I may rest and through which a synthesis might become possible, considering that I cannot have the advantage of looking about in the field of experience? Take the proposition that all which happens has its cause. In the concept of something that happens I no doubt conceive of something existing preceded by time, and from this certain analytical judgments may be deduced. But the concept of cause is entirely outside that concept, and indicates something different from that which happens, and is by no means contained in that representation. How can I venture then to

⁷ The next two paragraphs to 'In synthetical judgments *a priori*, however,' differ in the Second Edition.

predicate of that which happens something totally different from it, and to represent the concept of cause, though not contained in it, as belonging to it, and belonging to it by necessity? What is here the unknown *x,* on which the understanding may rest in order to find beyond the concept A a foreign predicate B, which nevertheless is believed to be connected with it? It cannot be experience, because the proposition that all which happens has its cause represents this second predicate as added to the subject not only with greater generality than experience can ever supply, but also with a character of necessity, and therefore purely *a priori,* and based on concepts. All our speculative knowledge *a priori* aims at and rests on such synthetical, i.e. expanding propositions, [10] for the analytical are no doubt very important and necessary, yet only in order to arrive at that clearness of concepts which is requisite for a safe and wide synthesis, serving as a really new addition to what we possess already.

[We [8] have here a certain mystery [9] before us, which must be cleared up before any advance into the unlimited field of a pure knowledge of the understanding can become safe and trustworthy. We must discover on the largest scale the ground of the possibility of synthetical judgments *a priori;* we must understand the conditions which render every class of them possible, and endeavour not only to indicate in a sketchy outline, but to define in its fulness and practical completeness, the whole of that knowledge, which forms a class by itself, systematically arranged according to its original sources, its divisions, its extent and its limits. So much for the present with regard to the peculiar character of synthetical judgments.]

It will now be seen how there can be a special science serving [11] as a critique of pure reason. [Every kind of knowledge is called pure, if not mixed with anything heterogeneous. But more particularly is that knowledge called absolutely pure, which is not mixed up with any experience or sensation, and is therefore possible entirely *a priori.*] Reason is the faculty which supplies the principles of knowledge *a priori.* Pure reason therefore is that faculty which supplies the principles of knowing anything entirely *a priori.* An Organum of pure reason ought to comprehend all the principles by which pure knowledge *a priori* can be acquired and fully established. A complete application of such an Organum would give us a System of Pure Reason. But as that would be a difficult task, and as at present it is still doubtful whether and when such an expansion of our knowledge is here possible, we may look on a mere criticism of pure reason, its sources and limits, as a kind of preparation for a complete system of pure reason. It should be called a critique,

---

[8] This paragraph differs in the Second Edition.
[9] If any of the ancients had ever thought of asking this question, this alone would have formed a powerful barrier against all systems of pure reason to the present day, and would have saved many vain attempts undertaken blindly and without a true knowledge of the subject in hand.

not a doctrine, of pure reason. Its usefulness would be negative only, serving for a purging rather than for an expansion of our reason, and, what after all is a considerable gain, guarding reason against errors.

I call all knowledge *transcendental* which is occupied not so much with objects, as with our *a priori* concepts of objects.[10] A system of such concepts might be called Transcendental Philosophy. But for the [12] present this is again too great an undertaking. We should have to treat therein completely both of analytical knowledge, and of synthetical knowledge *a priori*, which is more than we intend to do, being satisfied to carry on the analysis so far only as is indispensably necessary in order to recognise in their whole extent the principles of synthesis *a priori*, which alone concern us. This investigation which should be called a transcendental critique, but not a systematic doctrine, is all we are occupied with at present. It is not meant to extend our knowledge, but only to rectify it, and to become the test of the value of all *a priori* knowledge. Such a critique therefore is a preparation for a New Organum, or, if that should not be possible, for a Canon at least, according to which hereafter a complete system of a philosophy of pure reason, whether it serve for an expansion or merely for a limitation of it, may be carried out, both analytically and synthetically. That such a system is possible, nay that it need not be so comprehensive as to prevent the hope of its completion, may be gathered from the fact that it would have to deal, not with the nature of things, which is endless, but with the understanding which judges of the nature of things, and this again so far [13] only as its knowledge *a priori* is concerned. Whatever the understanding possesses *a priori*, as it has not to be looked for without, can hardly escape our notice, nor is there any reason to suppose that it will prove too extensive for a complete inventory, and for such a valuation as shall assign to it its true merits or demerits.[11]

II. DIVISION OF TRANSCENDENTAL PHILOSOPHY

Transcendental Philosophy is with us an idea (of a science) only, for which the critique of pure reason should trace, according to fixed principles, an architectonic plan, guaranteeing the completeness and certainty of all parts of which the building consists. (It is a system of all principles of pure reason.)[12] The reason why we do not call such a critique a transcendental philosophy in itself is simply this, that in order to be a complete system, it ought to contain likewise a complete analysis of the whole of human knowledge *a priori*. It is true that our critique must produce a complete list of all the fundamental concepts which constitute pure knowledge. But it need not give a detailed analysis of these concepts, nor a complete list of all derivative concepts. Such an

---

10 'As with our manner of knowing objects, so far as this is meant to be possible *a priori*.' Second Edition.
11 Here a paragraph was added in the Second Edition.
12 Addition in the Second Edition.

analysis would be out of place, because it is not beset with the   [14] doubts and difficulties which are inherent in synthesis, and which alone necessitate a critique of pure reason. Nor would it answer our purpose to take the responsibility of the completeness of such an analysis and derivation. This completeness of analysis, however, and of derivation from such *a priori* concepts as we shall have to deal with presently, may easily be supplied, if only they have first been laid down as perfect principles of synthesis, and nothing is wanting to them in that respect.

All that constitutes transcendental philosophy belongs to the critique of pure reason, nay it is the complete idea of transcendental philosophy, but not yet the whole of that philosophy itself, because it carries the analysis so far only as is requisite for a complete examination of synthetical knowledge *a priori*.

The most important consideration in the arrangement of such a science is that no concepts should be admitted which contain anything empirical, and that the *a priori* knowledge shall be perfectly pure. Therefore, although the highest principles of morality and their fundamental concepts are *a priori* knowledge, they do not belong to transcendental   [15] philosophy, because the concepts of pleasure and pain, desire, inclination, free-will, etc., which are all of empirical origin, must here be presupposed. Transcendental philosophy is the wisdom of pure speculative reason. Everything practical, so far as it contains motives, has reference to sentiments, and these belong to empirical sources of knowledge.

If we wish to carry out a proper division of our science systematically, it must contain first *a doctrine of the elements,* secondly, *a doctrine of the method* of pure reason. Each of these principal divisions will have its subdivisions, the grounds of which cannot however be explained here. So much only seems necessary for previous information, that there are two stems of human knowledge, which perhaps may spring from a common root, unknown to us, viz. *sensibility* and the *understanding*, objects being given by the former and thought by the latter. If our sensibility should contain *a priori* representations, constituting conditions under which alone objects can be given, it would belong to transcendental philosophy, and the doctrine of this transcendental sense-perception would necessarily form the first part of the doctrine of elements, because   [16] the conditions under which alone objects of human knowledge can be given must precede those under which they are thought.

The Elements of Transcendentalism   [19]

FIRST PART.   TRANSCENDENTAL ÆSTHETIC

Whatever the process and the means may be by which knowledge reaches its objects, there is one that reaches them directly, and forms the ultimate material of all thought, viz. intuition (Anschauung). This is possible only when the object is given, and the object can be given only (to human beings at least) through a certain affection of the mind (Gemüth).

This faculty (receptivity) of receiving representations (Vorstellungen), according to the manner in which we are affected by objects, is called sensibility (Sinnlichkeit).

Objects therefore are given to us through our sensibility. Sensibility alone supplies us with intuitions (Anschauungen). These intuitions become thought through the understanding (Verstand), and hence arise conceptions (Begriffe). All thought therefore must, directly or indirectly, go back to intuitions (Anschauungen), i.e. to our sensibility, because in no other way can objects be given to us.

The effect produced by an object upon the faculty of representation (Vorstellungsfähigkeit), so far as we are affected by it, is called   [20] sensation (Empfindung). An intuition (Anschauung) of an object, by means of sensation, is called empirical. The undefined object of such an empirical intuition is called phenomenon (Erscheinung).

In a phenomenon I call that which corresponds to the sensation its *matter;* but that which causes the manifold matter of the phenomenon to to be perceived as arranged in a certain order, I call its form.

Now it is clear that it cannot be sensation again through which sensations are arranged and placed in certain forms. The matter only of all phenomena is given us *a posteriori;* but their form must be ready for them in the mind (Gemüth) *a priori*, and must therefore be capable of being considered as separate from all sensations.

I call all representations in which there is nothing that belongs to sensation, *pure* (in a transcendental sense). The pure form therefore of all sensuous intuitions, that form in which the manifold elements of the phenomena are seen in a certain order, must be found in the mind *a priori*. And this pure form of sensibility may be called the pure intuition (Anschauung).

Thus, if we deduct from the representation (Vorstellung) of a body what belongs to the thinking of the understanding, viz. substance, force, divisibility, etc., and likewise what belongs to sensation, viz. impermeability, hardness, colour, etc., there still remains something of that   [21] empirical intuition (Anschauung), viz. extension and form. These belong to pure intuition, which *a priori*, and even without a real object of the senses or of sensation, exists in the mind as a mere form of sensibility.

The science of all the principles of sensibility *a priori* I call *Transcendental Æsthetic*.[13] There must be such a science, forming the first

---

13 The Germans are the only people who at present (1781) use the word *æsthetic* for what others call criticism of taste. There is implied in that name a false hope, first conceived by the excellent analytical philosopher, Baumgarten, of bringing the critical judgment of the beautiful under rational principles, and to raise its rules to the rank of a science. But such endeavours are vain. For such rules or criteria are, according to their principal sources, empirical only, and can never serve as definite *a priori* rules for our judgment in matters of taste; on the contrary, our judgment is the real test of the truth

part of the Elements of Transcendentalism, as opposed to that which treats of the principles of pure thought, and which should be called *Transcendental Logic.*

In Transcendental Æsthetic therefore we shall first isolate sen- [22] sibility, by separating everything which the understanding adds by means of its concepts, so that nothing remains but empirical intuition (Anschauung).

Secondly, we shall separate from this all that belongs to sensation (Enfindung), so that nothing remains but pure intuition (reine Anschauung) or the mere form of the phenomena, which is the only thing which sensibility *a priori* can supply. In the course of this investigation it will appear that there are, as principles of *a priori* knowledge, two pure forms of sensuous intuition (Anschauung), namely, *Space* and *Time*. We now proceed to consider these more in detail.

FIRST SECTION OF THE TRANSCENDENTAL ÆSTHETIC

Of Space

By means of our external sense, a property of our mind (Gemüth), we represent to ourselves objects as external or outside ourselves, and all of these in space. It is within space that their form, size, and relative position are fixed or can be fixed. The internal sense by means of which the mind perceives itself or its internal state, does not give an intuition (Anschauung) of the soul (Seele) itself, as an object, but it is nevertheless a fixed form under which alone an intuition of its internal state is [23] possible, so that whatever belongs to its internal determinations (Bestimmungen) must be represented in relations of time. Time cannot be perceived (angeschaut) externally, as little as space can be perceived as something within us. What then are space and time? Are they real beings? Or, if not that, are they determinations or relations of things, but such as would belong to them even if they were not perceived? Or lastly, are they determinations and relations which are inherent in the form of intuition only, and therefore in the subjective nature of our mind, without which such predicates as space and time would never be ascribed to anything?

In order to understand this more clearly, let us first consider space.

1. Space is not an empirical concept which has been derived from external experience. For in order that certain sensations should be referred to something outside myself, i.e. to something in a different part

---

of such rules. It would be advisable therefore to drop the name in that sense, and to apply it to a doctrine which is a real science, thus approaching more nearly to the language and meaning of the ancients with whom the division into αἰσθητὰ καὶ νοητά was very famous (or to share that name in common with speculative philosophy, and thus to use æsthetic sometimes in a transcendental, sometimes in a psychological sense).

of space from that where I am; again, in order that I may be able to represent them (vorstellen) as side by side, that is, not only as different, but as in different places, the representation (Vorstellung) of space must already be there. Therefore the representation of space cannot be borrowed through experience from relations of external phenomena, but, on the contrary, this external experience becomes possible only by means of the representation of space.

2. Space is a necessary representation *a priori*, forming the very foundation of all external intuitions. It is impossible to imagine that [24] there should be no space, though one might very well imagine that there should be space without objects to fill it. Space is therefore regarded as a condition of the possibility of phenomena, not as a determination produced by them; it is a representation *a priori* which necessarily precedes all external phenomena.

[3. On this necessity of an *a priori* representation of space rests the apodictic certainty of all geometrical principles, and the possibility of their construction *a priori*. For if the intuition of space were a concept gained *a posteriori*, borrowed from general external experience, the first principles of mathematical definition would be nothing but perceptions. They would be exposed to all the accidents of perception, and there being but one straight line between two points would not be a necessity, but only something taught in each case by experience. Whatever is derived from experience possesses a relative generality only, based on induction. We should therefore not be able to say more than that, so far as hitherto observed, no space has yet been found having more than three dimensions.]

4. Space is not a discursive or so-called general concept of the [25] relations of things in general, but a pure intuition. For, first of all, we can imagine one space only and if we speak of many spaces, we mean parts only of one and the same space. Nor can these parts be considered as antecedent to the one and all-embracing space and, as it were, its component parts out of which an aggregate is formed, but they can be thought of as existing within it only. Space is essentially one; its multiplicity, and therefore the general concept of spaces in general, arises entirely from limitations. Hence it follows that, with respect to space, an intuition *a priori*, which is not empirical, must form the foundation of all conceptions of space. In the same manner all geometrical principles, e.g. 'that in every triangle two sides together are greater than the third,' are never to be derived from the general concepts of side and triangle, but from an intuition, and that *a priori*, with apodictic certainty.

[5. Space is represented as an infinite quantity. Now a general concept of space, which is found in a foot as well as in an ell, could tell us nothing in respect to the quantity of the space. If there were not infinity in the progression of intuition, no concept of relations of space could ever contain a principle of infinity.[14]]

---

[14] This paragraph is differently worded in the Second Edition.

Conclusions from the Foregoing Concepts [26]

a. Space does not represent any quality of objects by themselves, or objects in their relation to one another; i.e. space does not represent any determination which is inherent in the objects themselves, and would remain, even if all subjective conditions of intuition were removed. For no determinations of objects, whether belonging to them absolutely or in relation to others, can enter into our intuition before the actual existence of the objects themselves, that is to say, they can never be intuitions *a priori.*

b. Space is nothing but the form of all phenomena of the external senses; it is the subjective condition of our sensibility, without which no external intuition is possible for us. If then we consider that the receptivity of the subject, its capacity of being affected by objects, must necessarily precede all intuition of objects, we shall understand how the form of all phenomena may be given before all real perceptions, may be, in fact, *a priori* in the soul, and may, as a pure intuition, by which all objects must be determined, contain, prior to all experience, principles regulating their relations.

It is therefore from the human standpoint only that we can speak of space, extended objects, etc. If we drop the subjective condition under which alone we can gain external intuition, that is, so far as we ourselves may be affected by objects, the representation of space means nothing. For this predicate is applied to objects only in so far as they appear to us, and are objects of our senses. The constant form of this receptivity,   [27] which we call sensibility, is a necessary condition of all relations in which objects, as without us, can be perceived; and, when abstraction is made of these objects, what remains is that pure intuition which we call space. As the peculiar conditions of our sensibility cannot be looked upon as conditions of the possibility of the objects themselves, but only of their appearance as phenomena to us, we may say indeed that space comprehends all things which may appear to us externally, but not all things by themselves, whether perceived by us or not, or by any subject whatsoever. We cannot judge whether the intuitions of other thinking beings are subject to the same conditions which determine our intuition, and which for us are generally binding. If we add the limitation of a judgment to a subjective concept, the judgment gains absolute validity. The proposition 'all things are beside each other in space,' is valid only under the limitation that things are taken as objects of our sensuous intuition (Anschauung). If I add that limitation to the concept and say 'all things, as external phenomena, are beside each other in space,' the rule obtains universal and unlimited validity. Our discussions teach therefore the reality, i.e. the objective validity, of space with regard to all that can come to us externally as an object, but likewise the *ideality* of space   [28] with regard to things, when they are considered in themselves by our reason, and independent of the nature of our senses. We maintain the empirical reality of space, so far as every possible external experience is concerned, but at the same time its transcendental ideality; that is to say, we maintain that space is nothing, if we leave out of consideration the condition of a possible experience, and accept it as something on which things by themselves are in any way dependent.

With the exception of space there is no other subjective representation (Vorstellung) referring to something external, that would be called *a priori* objective. [This [15] subjective condition of all external phenomena cannot therefore be compared to any other. The taste of wine does not belong to the objective determinations of wine, considered as an object, even as a phenomenal object, but to the peculiar nature of the sense belonging to the subject that tastes the wine. Colours are not qualities of a body, though inherent in its intuition, but they are likewise modifications only of the sense of sight, as it is affected in different ways by light. Space, on the contrary, as the very condition of external objects, is essential to their appearance or intuition. Taste and colour are by no means necessary conditions under which alone things can become   [29] to us objects of sensuous perception. They are connected with their appearance, as accidentally added effects only of our peculiar organisation. They are not therefore representations *a priori*, but are dependent on sensation (Empfindung), nay taste even on an affection (Gefühl) of pleasure and pain, which is the result of a sensation. No one can have *a priori*, an idea (Vorstellung) either of colour or of taste, but space refers to the pure form of intuition only, and involves no kind of sensation, nothing empirical; nay all kinds and determinations of space can and must be represented *a priori*, if concepts of forms and their relations are to arise. Through it alone is it possible that things should become external objects to us.]

My object in what I have said just now is only to prevent people from imagining that they can elucidate the ideality of space by illustrations which are altogether insufficient, such as colour, taste, etc., which should never be considered as qualities of things, but as modifications of the subject, and which therefore may be different with different people. For in this case that which originally is itself a phenomenon only, as for instance, a rose, is taken by the empirical understanding for a thing by itself, which nevertheless, with regard to colour, may appear dif-   [30] ferent to every eye. The transcendental conception, on the contrary, of all phenomena in space, is a critical warning that nothing which is seen in space is a thing by itself, nor space a form of things supposed to belong to them by themselves, but that objects by themselves are not known to us at all, and that what we call external objects are nothing but representations of our senses, the form of which is space, and the true correlative of which, that is the thing by itself, is not known, nor can be known by these representations, nor do we care to know anything about it in our daily experience.

---

15 This passage to 'my object in what I have said' is differently worded in the Second Edition.

SECOND SECTION OF THE TRANSCENDENTAL ÆSTHETIC [16]

Of Time

I. Time is not an empirical concept deduced from any experience, for neither coexistence nor succession would enter into our perception, if the representation of time were not given *a priori*. Only when this representation *a priori* is given, can we imagine that certain things happen at the same time (simultaneously) or at different times (successively).   [31]

II. Time is a necessary representation on which all intuitions depend. We cannot take away time from phenomena in general, though we can well take away phenomena out of time. Time therefore is given *a priori*. In time alone is reality of phenomena possible. All phenomena may vanish, but time itself (as the general condition of their possibility) cannot be done away with.

III. On this *a priori* necessity depends also the possibility of apodictic principles of the relations of time, or of axioms of time in general. Time has one dimension only; different times are not simultaneous, but successive, while different spaces are never successive, but simultaneous. Such principles cannot be derived from experience, because experience could not impart to them absolute universality nor apodictic certainty. We should only be able to say that common experience teaches us that it is so, but not that it must be so. These principles are valid as rules under which alone experience is possible; they teach us before experience, not by means of experience.[17]

IV. Time is not a discursive, or what is called a general concept, but a pure form of sensuous intuition. Different times are parts only of one and the same time. Representation, which can be produced by a [32] single object only, is called an intuition. The proposition that different times cannot exist at the same time cannot be deduced from any general concept. Such a proposition is synthetical, and cannot be deduced from concepts only. It is contained immediately in the intuition and representation of time.

V. To say that time is infinite means no more than that every definite quantity of time is possible only by limitations of one time which forms the foundation of all times. The original representation of time must therefore be given as unlimited. But when the parts themselves and every quantity of an object can be represented as determined by limitation only, the whole representation cannot be given by concepts (for in that case

---

[16] In the Second Edition the title is, Metaphysical exposition of the concept of time, with reference to par. 5, Transcendental exposition of the concept of time.

[17] I retain the reading of the First Edition, *vor derselben, nicht durch dieselbe. Von denselben,* the reading of later editions, is wrong; the emendation of Rosenkranz, *vor derselben, nicht durch dieselben,* unnecessary. The Second Edition has likewise *vor derselben.* M.M.

the partial representations come first), but it must be founded on immediate intuition.[18]

Conclusions from the foregoing concepts

a. Time is not something existing by itself, or inherent in things as an objective determination of them, something therefore that might remain when abstraction is made of all subjective conditions of intuition. For in the former case it would be something real, without being a real object. In the latter it could not, as a determination or order inherent in   [33] things themselves, be antecedent to things as their condition, and be known and perceived by means of synthetical propositions *a priori*. All this is perfectly possible if time is nothing but a subjective condition under which alone [19] intuitions take place within us. For in that case this form of internal intuition can be represented prior to the objects themselves, that is, *a priori*.

b. Time is nothing but the form of the internal sense, that is, of our intuition of ourselves, and of our internal state. Time cannot be a determination peculiar to external phenomena. It refers neither to their shape, nor their position, etc., it only determines the relation of representations in our internal state. And exactly because this internal intuition supplies no shape, we try to make good this deficiency by means of analogies, and represent to ourselves the succession of time by a line progressing to infinity, in which the manifold constitutes a series of one dimension only; and we conclude from the properties of this line as to all the properties of time, with one exception, i.e. that the parts of the former are simultaneous, those of the latter successive. From this it becomes clear also, that the representation of time is itself an intuition, because all its relations can be expressed by means of an external intuition.

c. Time is the formal condition, *a priori*, of all phenomena whatsoever. Space, as the pure form of all external intuition, is a condition,   [34] *a priori*, of external phenomena only. But, as all representations, whether they have for their objects external things or not, belong by themselves, as determinations of the mind, to our inner state, and as this inner state falls under the formal conditions of internal intuition, and therefore of time, time is a condition, *a priori*, of all phenomena whatsoever, and is so directly as a condition of internal phenomena (of our mind) and thereby indirectly of external phenomena also. If I am able to say, *a priori*, that all external phenomena are in space, and are determined, *a priori*, according to the relations of space, I can, according to the principle of the internal sense, make the general assertion that all phenomena, that is, all objects of the senses, are in time, and stand necessarily in relations of time.

If we drop our manner of looking at ourselves internally, and of comprehending by means of that intuition all external intuitions also within

---

[18] Here follows in the Second Edition, another paragraph.
[19] Read *allein* instead of *alle*.

our power of representation, and thus take objects as they may be by themselves, then time is nothing. Time has objective validity with reference to phenomena only, because these are themselves things which we accept as objects of our senses; but time is no longer objective, if we [35] remove the sensuous character of our intuitions, that is to say, that mode of representation which is peculiar to ourselves, and speak of things in general. Time is therefore simply a subjective condition of our (human) intuition (which is always sensuous, that is so far as we are affected by objects), but by itself, apart from the subject, nothing. Nevertheless, with respect to all phenomena, that is, all things which can come within our experience, time is necessarily objective. We cannot say that all things are in time, because, if we speak of things in general, nothing is said about the manner of intuition, which is the real condition under which time enters into our representation of things. If therefore this condition is added to the concept, and if we say that all things as phenomena (as objects of sensuous intuition) are in time, then such a proposition has its full objective validity and *a priori* universality.

What we insist on therefore is the empirical reality of time, that is, its objective validity, with reference to all objects which can ever come before our senses. And as our intuition must at all times be sensuous, no object can ever fall under our experience that does not come under the conditions of time. What we deny is, that time has any claim on absolute reality, so that, without taking into account the form of our sensuous [36] condition, it should by itself be a condition or quality inherent in things; for such qualities which belong to things by themselves can never be given to us through the senses. This is what constitutes the transcendental ideality of time, so that, if we take no account of the subjective conditions of our sensuous intuitions, time is nothing, and cannot be added to the objects by themselves (without their relation to our intuition) whether as subsisting or inherent. This ideality of time, however, as well as that of space, should not be confounded with the deceptions of our sensations, because in their case we always suppose that the phenomenon to which such predicates belong has objective reality, which is not at all the case here, except so far as this objective reality is purely empirical, that is, so far as the object itself is looked upon as a mere phenomenon. On this subject see a previous note, in section i, on Space.

Explanation

Against this theory which claims empirical, but denies absolute and transcendental reality to time, even intelligent men have protested so unanimously, that I suppose that every reader who is unaccustomed to these considerations may naturally be of the same opinion. What they object to is this: Changes, they say, are real (this is proved by the change of our own representations, even if all external phenomena and [37] their changes be denied). Changes, however, are possible in time only, and therefore time must be something real. The answer is easy enough. I grant the whole argument. Time certainly is something real, namely, the real form of our internal intuition. Time therefore has subjective reality with regard to internal experience: that is, I really have the representation of time and of my determinations in it. Time therefore is to be considered as real, not so far as it is an object, but so far as it is the representation of myself as an object. If either I myself or any other being could see me without this condition of sensibility, then these self-same determinations which we now represent to ourselves as changes, would give us a kind of knowledge in which the representation of time, and therefore of change also, would have no place. There remains therefore the empirical reality of time only, as the condition of all our experience, while absolute reality cannot, according to what has just been shown, be conceded to it. Time is nothing but the form of our own internal intuition.[20] Take away the peculiar condition of our sensibility, and the idea of time vanishes, because it is not inherent in the objects, but in the subject only that perceives them.   [38]

The reason why this objection is raised so unanimously, and even by those who have nothing very tangible to say against the doctrine of the ideality of space, is this. They could never hope to prove apodictically the absolute reality of space, because they are confronted by idealism, which has shown that the reality of external objects does not admit to strict proof, while the reality of the object of our internal perceptions (the perception of my own self and of my own status) is clear immediately through our consciousness. The former might be merely phenomenal, but the latter, according to their opinion, is undeniably something real. They did not see that both, without denying to them their reality as representations, belong nevertheless to the phenomenon only, which must always have two sides, the one when the object is considered by itself (without regard to the manner in which it is perceived, its quality therefore remaining always problematical), the other, when the form of the perception of the object is taken into consideration; this form belonging not to the object itself, but to the subject which perceives it, though nevertheless belonging really and necessarily to the object as a phenomenon.

Time and space are therefore two sources of knowledge from which various *a priori* synthetical cognitions can be derived. Of this pure   [39] mathematics give a splendid example in the case of our cognitions of space and its various relations. As they are both pure forms of sensuous intuition, they render synthetical propositions *a priori* possible. But these sources of knowledge *a priori* (being conditions of our sensibility only) fix their own limits, in that they can refer to objects only in so far as they are considered as phenomena, but cannot represent things as they are by themselves. That is the only field in which they are valid; beyond it they

---

[20] I can say indeed that my representations follow one another, but this means no more than that we are conscious of them as in a temporal succession, that is, according to the form of our own internal sense. Time, therefore, is nothing by itself, nor is it a determination inherent objectively in things.

admit of no objective application. This ideality of space and time, however, leaves the truthfulness of our existence quite untouched, because we are equally sure of it, whether these forms are inherent in things by themselves, or by necessity in our intuition of them only. Those, on the contrary, who maintain the absolute reality of space and time, whether as subsisting or only as inherent, must come into conflict with the principles of experience itself. For if they admit space and time as subsisting (which is generally the view of mathematical students of nature) they have to admit two eternal infinite and self-subsisting nonentities (space and time), which exist without their being anything real, only in order to comprehend all that is real. If they take the second view (held by some metaphysical students of nature), and look upon space and time   [40] as relations of phenomena, simultaneous or successive, abstracted from experience, though represented confusedly in their abstracted form, they are obliged to deny to mathematical propositions *a priori* their validity with regard to real things (for instance in space), or at all events their apodictic certainty, which cannot take place *a posteriori*, while the *a priori* conceptions of space and time are, according to their opinion, creations of our imagination only. Their source, they hold, must really be looked for in experience, imagination framing out of the relations abstracted from experience something which contains the general character of these relations, but which cannot exist without the restrictions which nature has imposed on them. The former gain so much that they keep at least the sphere of phenomenon free for mathematical propositions; but, as soon as the understanding endeavours to transcend that sphere, they become bewildered by these very conditions. The latter have this advantage that they are not bewildered by the representations of space and time when they wish to form judgments of objects, not as phenomena, but only as considered by the understanding; but they can neither account for the possibility of mathematical knowledge *a priori* (there being, according to them, no true and objectively valid intuition *a priori*), nor can they bring the laws of experience into true harmony with the *a priori* doctrines of mathematics. According to our theory of the true character of these original forms of sensibility, both difficulties vanish.   [41]

Lastly, that transcendental æsthetic cannot contain more than these two elements, namely, space and time, becomes clear from the fact that all other concepts belonging to the senses, even that of motion, which combines both, presuppose something empirical. Motion presupposes the perception of something moving. In space, however, considered by itself, there is nothing that moves. Hence that which moves must be something which, as in space, can be given by experience only, therefore an empirical datum. On the same ground, transcendental æsthetic cannot count the concept of change among its *a priori* data, because time itself does not change, but only something which is in time. For this, the perception of something existing and of the succession of its determinations, in other words, experience, is required.

.   .   .

SECOND PART.   TRANSCENDENTAL LOGIC

Introduction: The Idea of a Transcendental Logic

I

Of Logic in General

Our knowledge springs from two fundamental sources of our soul; the first receives representations (receptivity of impressions), the second is the power of knowing an object by these representations (spontaneity of concepts). By the first an object is *given* us, by the second the object is *thought,* in relation to that representation which is a mere determination of the soul. Intuition therefore and concepts constitute the elements of all our knowledge, so that neither concepts without an intuition corresponding to them, nor intuition without concepts can yield any real knowledge.

Both are either pure or empirical. They are empirical when sensation, presupposing the actual presence of the object, is contained in it. They are pure when no sensation is mixed up with the representation. The latter may be called the material of sensuous knowledge. Pure intuition therefore contains the form only by which something is seen, and   [51] pure conception the form only by which an object is thought. Pure intuitions and pure concepts only are possible *a priori,* empirical intuitions and empirical concepts *a posteriori.*

We call *sensibility* the *receptivity* of our soul, or its power of receiving representations whenever it is in any wise affected, while the *understanding,* on the contrary, is with us the power of producing representations, or the *spontaneity* of knowledge. We are so constituted that our intuition must always be sensuous, and consists of the mode in which we are affected by objects. What enables us to think the objects of our sensuous intuition is the understanding. Neither of these qualities or faculties is preferable to the other. Without sensibility objects would not be given to us, without understanding they would not be thought by us. *Thoughts without contents are empty, intuitions without concepts are blind.* Therefore it is equally necessary to make our concepts sensuous, i.e. to add to them their object in intuition, as to make our intuitions intelligible, i.e. to bring them under concepts. These two powers or faculties cannot exchange their functions. The understanding cannot see, the senses cannot think. By their union only can knowledge be produced. But this is no reason for confounding the share which belongs to each in the production of knowledge. On the contrary, they should always be carefully   [52] separated and distinguished, and we have therefore divided the science of the rules of sensibility in general, i.e. æsthetic, from the science of the rules of the understanding in general, i.e. logic.

.   .   .

IV

Of the Division of Transcendental Logic into Transcendental Analytic and Dialectic

In transcendental logic we isolate the understanding, as before in transcendental æsthetic the sensibility, and fix our attention on that part of thought only which has its origin entirely in the understanding. The application of this pure knowledge has for its condition that objects are given in intuition, to which it can be applied, for without intuition all our knowledge would be without objects, and it would therefore remain entirely empty. That part of transcendental logic therefore which teaches the elements of the pure knowledge of the understanding, and the principles without which no object can be thought, is transcendental Analytic, and at the same time a logic of truth. No knowledge can contradict it without losing at the same time all contents, that is, all relation to   [63] any object, and therefore all truth. But as it is very tempting to use this pure knowledge of the understanding and its principles by themselves, and even beyond the limits of all experience, which alone can supply the material or the objects to which those pure concepts of the understanding can be applied, the understanding runs the risk of making, through mere sophisms, a material use of the purely formal principles of the pure understanding, and thus of judging indiscriminately of objects which are not given to us, nay, perhaps can never be given. As it is properly meant to be a mere canon for criticising the empirical use of the understanding, it is a real abuse if it is allowed as an organum of its general and unlimited application, by our venturing, with the pure understanding alone, to judge synthetically of objects in general, or to affirm and decide anything about them. In this case the employment of the pure understanding would become dialectical.

The second part of transcendental logic must therefore form a critique of that dialectical semblance, and is called transcendental Dialectic, not as an art of producing dogmatically such semblance (an art but too popular with many metaphysical jugglers), but as a critique of the understanding and reason with regard to their hyperphysical employment, in order thus to lay bare the false semblance of its groundless pretensions, and to reduce its claims to discovery and expansion, which   [64] was to be achieved by means of transcendental principles only, to a mere critique, serving as a protection of the pure understanding against all sophistical illusions.

TRANSCENDENTAL LOGIC—FIRST DIVISION:

Transcendental Analytic

Transcendental Analytic consists in the dissection of all our knowledge *a priori* into the elements which constitute the knowledge of the pure understanding. Four points are here essential: first, that the concepts should be pure and not empirical; secondly, that they should not belong to intuition and sensibility, but to thought and understanding; thirdly, that the concepts should be elementary and carefully distinguished from derivative or composite concepts; fourthly, that our tables should be complete and that they should cover the whole field of the pure understanding.

This completeness of a science cannot be confidently accepted on the strength of a mere estimate, or by means of repeated experiments only; what is required for it is an idea of the totality of the *a priori* knowledge of the understanding, and a classification of the concepts based [65] upon it; in fact, a systematic treatment. Pure understanding must be distinguished, not merely from all that is empirical, but even from all sensibility. It constitutes therefore a unity independent in itself, self-sufficient, and not to be increased by any additions from without. The sum of its knowledge must constitute a system, comprehended and determined by one idea, and its completeness and articulation must form the test of the correctness and genuineness of its component parts.

This part of transcendental logic consists of two books, the one containing the *concepts*, the other the *principles* of pure understanding.

Book I: Analytic of Concepts

. . .

CHAPTER I. TRANSCENDENTAL METHOD OF THE DISCOVERY OF
ALL PURE CONCEPTS OF THE UNDERSTANDING

Section I

Of the Logical Use of the Understanding in General

We have before defined the understanding negatively only, as a non-sensuous faculty of knowledge. As without sensibility we cannot have any intuition, it is clear that the understanding is not a faculty of intui- [68] tion. Besides inuition, however, there is no other kind of knowledge except by means of concepts. The knowledge therefore of every understanding, or at least of the human understanding, must be by means of concepts, not intuitive, but discursive. All intuitions, being sensuous, depend on affections, concepts on functions. By this function I mean the unity of the act of arranging different representations under one common representation. Concepts are based therefore on the spontaneity of thought, sensuous intuitions on the receptivity of impressions. The only use which the understanding can make of these concepts is to form judgments by them. As no representation, except the intuitional, refers immediately to an object, no concept is ever referred to an object immediately, but to some other representation of it, whether it be an intuition, or itself a concept. A judgment is therefore a mediate knowledge of an object, or a representation of a representation of it. In every judgment we find a concept applying to many, and comprehending among the many one single representation, which is referred immediately to the object. Thus in the judgment that all bodies are divisible,[21] the concept of divisible applies to various other concepts, but is here applied in particular to the concept of body, and this concept of body to certain phenomena of our experience. These objects therefore are represented   [69] mediately by the concept of divisibility. All judgements therefore are functions of unity among our representations, the knowledge of an object being brought about, not by an immediate representation, but by a higher one, comprehending this and several others, so that many possible cognitions are collected into one. As all acts of the understanding can be reduced to judgments, the understanding may be defined as *the faculty of judging.* For we saw before that the understanding is the faculty of thinking, and thinking is knowledge by means of concepts, while concepts, as predicates of possible judgments, refer to some representation of an object yet undetermined. Thus the concept of body means something, for instance, metal, which can be known by that concept. It is only a concept, because it comprehends other representations, by means of which it can be referred to objects. It is therefore the predicate of a possible judgment, such as, that every metal is a body. Thus the functions of the understanding can be discovered in their completeness, if it is possible to represent the functions of unity in *judgments.* That this is possible will be seen in the following section.

Section II   [70]

Of the Logical Function of the Understanding in Judgments

If we leave out of consideration the contents of any judgment and fix our attention on the mere form of the understanding, we find that the function of thought in a judgment can be brought under four heads, each

---

[21] *Veränderlich* in the First Edition is rightly corrected into *theilbar* in later editions, though in the Second it is still *veränderlich.*

of them with three subdivisions. They may be represented in the following table:—

I

Quantity of Judgments
Universal.
Particular.
Singular.

II

Quality
Affirmative.
Negative.
Infinite.

III

Relation
Categorical.
Hypothetical.
Disjunctive.

IV

Modality
Problematical.
Assertory.
Apodictic.

.   .   .

Section III

Of the Pure Concepts of the Understanding, or of the Categories

General logic, as we have often said, takes no account of the contents of our knowledge, but expects that representations will come from elsewhere in order to be turned into concepts by an analytical process. Transcendental logic, on the contrary, has before it the manifold contents of sensibility a priori, supplied by transcendental æsthetic as the [77] material for the concepts of the pure understanding, without which those concepts would be without any contents, therefore entirely empty. It is true that space and time contain what is manifold in the pure intuition *a priori,* but they belong also to the conditions of the receptivity of our mind under which alone it can receive representations of objects, and which therefore must affect the concepts of them also. The spontaneity of our thought requires that which is manifold in the pure intuition should first be in a certain way examined, received, and connected, in order to produce a knowledge of it. This act I call *synthesis.*

In its most general sense, I understand by synthesis the act of arranging different representations together, and of comprehending what is manifold in them under one form of knowledge. Such a synthesis is pure, if the manifold is not given empirically, but *a priori* (as in time and space). Before we can proceed to an analysis of our representations, these must first be given, and, as far as their contents are concerned, no concepts can arise analytically. Knowledge is first produced by the synthesis of what is manifold (whether given empirically or *a priori*). That knowledge may at first be crude and confused and in need of analysis, but it is synthesis which really collects the elements of knowledge, and unites them to a certain extent. It is therefore the first thing which we have to con- [78] sider, if we want to form an opinion on the first origin of our knowledge.

We shall see hereafter that synthesis in general is the mere result of what I call the faculty of imagination, a blind but indispensable function of the soul, without which we should have no knowledge whatsoever, but of the existence of which we are scarcely conscious. But to reduce this synthesis to concepts is a function that belongs to the understanding, and by which the understanding supplies us for the first time with knowledge properly so called.

Pure synthesis in its most general meaning gives us the pure concept of the understanding. By this pure synthesis I mean that which rests on the foundation of what I call synthetical unity *a priori*. Thus our counting (as we best perceive when dealing with higher numbers) is a synthesis according to concepts, because resting on a ground of unity, as for instance, the decade. The unity of the synthesis of the manifold becomes necessary under this concept.

By means of analysis different representations are brought under one concept, a task treated of in general logic; but how to bring, not the representations, but the pure synthesis of representations, under concepts, that is what transcendental logic means to teach. The first that must be given us *a priori* for the sake of knowledge of all objects, is the manifold in pure intuition. The second is, the synthesis of the manifold by [79] means of imagination. But this does not yet produce true knewledge. The concepts which impart unity to this pure synthesis and consist entirely in the representation of this necessary synthetical unity, add the third contribution towards the knowledge of an object, and rest on the understanding.

The same function which imparts unity to various representations in one judgment imparts unity likewise to the mere synthesis of various representations in one intuition, which in a general way may be called the pure concept of the understanding. The same understanding, and by the same operations by which in concepts it achieves through analytical unity the logical form of a judgment, introduces also, through the synthetical unity of the manifold in intuition, a transcendental element into its representations. They are therefore called pure concepts of the understanding, and they refer *a priori* to objects, which would be quite impossible in general logic.

In this manner there arise exactly so many pure concepts of the understanding which refer *a priori* to objects of intuition in general, as there were in our table logical functions in all possible judgments, because those functions completely exhaust the understanding, and comprehend every one of its faculties. Borrowing a term of Aristotle, we shall call these concepts *categories,* our intention being originally the same as his, [80] though widely diverging from it in its practical application.

TABLE of CATEGORIES

I

Of Quantity
Unity.
Plurality
Totality.

II

Of Quality
Reality.
Negation.
Limitation.

III

Of Relation
Of Inherence and Subsistence (*substantia et accidens*).
Of Causality and Dependence (cause and effect).
Of Community (reciprocity between the active and the passive).

IV

Of Modality
Possibility. Impossibility.
Existence. Non-existence.
Necessity. Contingency.

This then is a list of all original pure concepts of synthesis, which belong to the understanding *a priori*, and for which alone it is called pure understanding; for it is by them alone that it can understand something in the manifold of intuition, that is, think an object in it. The classification is systematical, and founded on a common principle, namely, the faculty of judging (which is the same as the faculty of thinking). It is not the result of a search after pure concepts undertaken at hap- [81] hazard, the completeness of which, as based on induction only, could never be guaranteed. Nor could we otherwise understand why these concepts only, and no others, abide in the pure understanding. It was an enterprise worthy of an acute thinker like Aristotle to try to discover these fundamental concepts; but as he had no guiding principle he merely picked them up as they occurred to him, and at first gathered up ten of them, which he called *categories* or *predicaments*. Afterwards he thought he had discovered five more of them, which he added under the name of *post-predicaments*. But his table remained imperfect for all that, not to mention that we find in it some modes of pure sensibility (*quando, ubi, situs,* also *prius, simul*), also an empirical concept (*motus*), none of which can belong to this genealogical register of the understanding. Besides, there are some derivative concepts, counted among the fundamental concepts (*actio, passio*), while some of the latter are entirely wanting.

.   .   .

CHAPTER II. DEDUCTION OF THE PURE CONCEPTS OF THE   [84]
UNDERSTANDING *

.   .   .

Section II

Of the a priori Grounds for the Possibility of Experience

[That a concept should be produced entirely *a priori* and yet refer to an object, though itself neither belonging to the sphere of possible experience, nor consisting of the elements of such an experience, is self-contradictory and impossible. It would have no contents, because no intuition corresponds to it, and intuitions by which objects are given to us constitute the whole field or the complete object of possible experience. An *a priori* concept therefore not referring to experience would be the logical form only of a concept, but not the concept itself by which something is thought.

If therefore there exist any pure concepts *a priori*, though they cannot contain anything empirical, they must nevertheless all be conditions *a priori* of a possible experience, on which alone their objective reality depends.

If therefore we wish to know how pure concepts of the understanding are possible, we must try to find out what are the conditions *a priori* on which the possibility of experience depends, nay, on which it is   [96] founded, apart from all that is empirical in phenomena. A concept expressing this formal and objective condition of experience with sufficient generality might properly be called a pure concept of the understanding. If we once have these pure concepts of the understanding, we may also imagine objects which are either impossible, or, if not impossible in themselves, yet can never be given in any experience. We have only in the connection of those concepts to leave out something which necessarily belongs to the conditions of a possible experience (concept of a spirit), or to extend pure concepts of the understanding beyond what can be reached by experience (concept of God). But the elements of all knowledge *a priori*, even of gratuitous and preposterous fancies, though not borrowed from experience (for in that case they would not be knowledge *a priori*) must nevertheless contain the pure conditions *a priori* of a possible experience and its object, otherwise not only would nothing be thought by them, but they themselves, being without data, could never arise in our mind.

Such concepts, then, which comprehend the pure thinking *a priori*

---

* The "deduction," down through page A 130, was substantially changed in the Second Edition. Parts of the revised version are offered below on pp. 564-567. W.K.

involved in every experience, are discovered in the categories, and it is really a sufficient deduction of them and a justification of their objective validity, if we succeed in proving that by them alone an object can   [97] be thought. But as in such a process of thinking more is at work than the faculty of thinking only, namely, the understanding, and as the understanding, as a faculty of knowledge which is meant to refer to objects, requires quite as much an explanation as to the possibility of such a reference, it is necessary for us to consider the subjective sources which form the foundation *a priori* for the possibility of experience, not according to their empirical, but according to their transcendental character.

If every single representation stood by itself, as if isolated and separated from the others, nothing like what we call knowledge could ever arise, because knowledge forms a whole of representations connected and compared with each other. If therefore I ascribe to the senses a synopsis, because in their intuition they contain something manifold, there corresponds to it always a synthesis, and receptivity can make knowledge possible only when joined with spontaneity. This spontaneity, now, appears as a threefold synthesis which must necessarily take place in every kind of knowledge, namely, first, that of the *apprehension* of representations as modifications of the soul in intuition, secondly, of the *reproduction* of them in the imagination, and, thirdly, that of their *recognition* in concepts. This leads us to three subjective sources of knowledge which render possible the understanding, and through it all experience as an empirical product of the understanding.   [98]

Preliminary Remark

The deduction of the categories is beset with so many difficulties and obliges us to enter so deeply into the first grounds of the possibility of our knowledge in general, that I thought it more expedient, in order to avoid the lengthiness of a complete theory, and yet to omit nothing in so essential an investigation, to add the following four paragraphs with a view of preparing rather than instructing the reader. After that only I shall in the third section proceed to a systematical discussion of these elements of the understanding. Till then the reader must not allow himself to be frightened by a certain amount of obscurity which at first is inevitable on a road never trodden before, but which, when we come to that section, will give way, I hope, to a complete comprehension.

I

Of the Synthesis of Apprehension in Intuition

Whatever the origin of our representations may be, whether they be due to the influence of external things or to internal causes, whether they have arisen *a priori* or empirically as phenomena, as modifications of the mind they must always belong to the internal sense, and all our   [99] knowledge must therefore finally be subject to the formal condition of that internal sense, namely, time, in which they are all arranged, joined, and brought into certain relations to each other. This is a general remark which must never be forgotten in all that follows.

Every representation contains something manifold, which could not be represented as such, unless the mind distinguished the time in the succession of one impression after another; for as contained in one moment, each representation can never be anything but absolute unity. In order to change this manifold into a unity of intuition (as, for instance, in the representation of space), it is necessary first to run through the manifold and then to hold it together. It is this act which I call the synthesis of apprehension, because it refers directly to intuition which no doubt offers something mainfold, but which, without a synthesis, can never make it such, as it is contained in *one* representation.

This synthesis of apprehension must itself be carried out *a priori* also, that is, with reference to representations which are not empirical. For without it we should never be able to have the representations either of space or time *a priori*, because these cannot be produced except [100] by a synthesis of the manifold which the senses offer in their original receptivity. It follows therefore that we have a pure synthesis of apprehension.

II

Of the Synthesis of Reproduction in Imagination

It is no doubt nothing but an empirical law according to which representations which have often followed or accompanied one another, become associated in the end and so closely united that, even without the presence of the object, one of these representations will, according to an invariable law, produce a transition of the mind to the other. This law of reproduction, however, presupposes that the phenomena themselves are really subject to such a rule, and that there is in the variety of these representations a sequence and concomitancy subject to certain rules; for without this the faculty of empirical imagination would never find anything to do that it is able to do, and remain therefore buried within our mind as a dead faculty, unknown to ourselves. If cinnabar were sometimes red and sometimes black, sometimes light and sometimes heavy, if a man could be changed now into this, now into another animal shape, if on the longest day the fields were sometimes covered with fruit, sometimes with ice and snow, the faculty of my em- [101] pirical imagination would never be in a position, when representing red colour, to think of heavy cinnabar. Nor, if a certain name could be given sometimes to this, sometimes to that object, or if that the same object could sometimes be called by one, and sometimes by another name, without any rule to which representations are subject by themselves, would it be possible that any empirical synthesis of reproduction should ever take place.

There must therefore be something to make this reproduction of phenomena possible by being itself the foundation *a priori* of a necessary synthetical unity of them. This becomes clear if we only remember that all phenomena are not things by themselves, but only the play of our representations, all of which are in the end determinations only of the internal sense. If therefore we could prove that even our purest intuitions *a priori* give us no knowledge, unless they contain such a combination of the manifold as to render a constant synthesis of reproduction possible, it would follow that this synthesis of the imagination is, before all experience, founded on principles *a priori*, and that we must admit a pure transcendental synthesis of imagination which forms even the foundation of the possibility of all experience, such experience being impossible without the reproductibility of phenomena. Now,   [102] when I draw a line in thought, or if I think the time from one noon to another, or if I only represent to myself a certain number, it is clear that I must first necessarily apprehend one of these manifold representations after another. If I were to lose from my thoughts what precedes, whether the first parts of a line or the antecedent portions of time, or the numerical unities representing one after the other, and if, while I proceed to what follows, I were unable to reproduce what came before, there would never be a complete representation, and none of the before-mentioned thoughts, not even the first and purest representations of space and time, could ever arise within us.

The synthesis of apprehension is therefore inseparably connected with the synthesis of reproduction, and as the former constitutes the transcendental ground of the possibility of all knowledge in general (not only of empirical, but also of pure *a priori* knowledge), it follows that a reproductive synthesis of imagination belongs to the transcendental acts of the soul. We may therefore call this faculty the transcendental faculty of imagination.

III   [103]

Of the Synthesis of Recognition in Concepts

Without our being conscious that what we are thinking now is the same as what we thought a moment before, all reproduction in the series of representations would be vain. Each representation would, in its present state, be a new one, and in no wise belonging to the act by which it was to be produced by degrees, and the manifold in it would never form a whole, because deprived of that unity which consciousness alone can impart to it. If in counting I forget that the unities which now present themselves to my mind have been added gradually one to the other, I should not know the production of the quantity by the successive addition of one to one, nor should I know consequently the number, produced by the counting, this number being a concept consisting entirely in the consciousness of that unity of synthesis.

The very word of concept (Begriff) could have suggested this remark, for it is the *one* consciousness which unites the manifold that has been perceived successively, and afterwards reproduced into one representation. This consciousness may often be very faint, and we may connect it with the effect only, and not with the act itself, i.e. with the production of a representation. But in spite of this, that conscious- [104] ness, though deficient in pointed clearness, must always be there, and without it, concepts, and with them, knowledge of objects are perfectly impossible.

And here we must needs arrive at a clear understanding of what we mean by an object of representations. We said before that phenomena are nothing but sensuous representations, which therefore by themselves must not be taken for objects outside our faculty of representation. What then do we mean if we speak of an object corresponding to, and therefore also different from our knowledge? It is easy to see that such an object can only be conceived as something in general $= x$: because, beside our knowledge, we have absolutely nothing which we could put down as corresponding to that knowledge.

Now we find that our conception of the relation of all knowledge to its object contains something of necessity, the object being looked upon as that which prevents our knowledge from being determined at haphazard, and causes it to be determined *a priori* in a certain way, because, as they are all to refer to an object, they must necessarily, with regard to that object, agree with each other, that is to say, possess that [105] unity which constitutes the concept of an object.

It is clear also that, as we can only deal with the manifold in our representations, and as the x corresponding to them (the object), since it is to be something different from all our representations, is really nothing to us, it is clear, I say, that the unity, necessitated by the object, cannot be anything but the formal unity of our consciousness in the synthesis of the manifold in our representations. Then and then only do we say that we know an object, if we have produced synthetical unity in the manifold of intuition. Such unity is impossible, if the intuition could not to be produced, according to a rule, by such a function of synthesis as makes the reproduction of the manifold *a priori* necessary, and a concept in which that manifold is united, possible. Thus we conceive a triangle as an object, if we are conscious of the combination of three straight lines, according to a rule, which renders such an intuition possible at all times. This *unity of rule* determines the manifold and limits it to conditions which render the unity of apperception possible, and the concept of that unity is really the representation of the object $= x$, which I think, by means of the predicates of a triangle.

No knowledge is possible without a concept, however obscure [106] or imperfect it may be, and a concept is always, with regard to its form, something general, something that can serve as a rule. Thus the concept of body serves as a rule to our knowledge of external phenomena, according to the unity of the manifold which is thought by it. It can only be such a rule of intuitions because representing, in any given phenomena, the necessary reproduction of their manifold elements, or the synthetical unity in our consciousness of them. Thus the concept of body, whenever we perceive something outside us, necessitates the representation of extension, and, with it, those of impermeability, shape, etc.

Necessity is always founded on transcendental conditions. There must be therefore a transcendental ground of the unity of our consciousness in the synthesis of the manifold of all our intuitions, and therefore also a transcendental ground of all concepts of objects in general, and therefore again of all objects of experience, without which it would be impossible to add to our intuitions the thought of an object, for the object is no more than that something of which the concept predicates such a necessity of synthesis.

That original and transcendental condition is nothing else but what I call *transcendental apperception.* The consciousness of oneself, [107] according to the determinations of our state, is, with all our internal perceptions, empirical only, and always transient. There can be no fixed or permanent self in that stream of internal phenomena. It is generally called the *internal sense*, or the empirical apperception. What is necessarily to be represented as numerically identical with itself, cannot be thought as such by means of empirical data only. It must be a condition which precedes all experience, and in fact renders it possible, for thus only could such a transcendental supposition acquire validity.

No knowledge can take place in us, no conjunction or unity of one kind of knowledge with another, without that unity of consciousness which precedes all data of intuition, and without reference to which no representation of objects is possible. This pure, original, and unchangeable consciousness I shall call *transcendental apperception.* That it deserves such a name may be seen from the fact that even the purest objective unity, namely, that of the concepts a priori (space and time), is possible only by a reference of all intuitions to it. The numerical unity of that apperception therefore forms the *a priori* condition of all concepts, as does the manifoldness of space and time of the intuitions of the senses.

The same transcendental unity of apperception constitutes, in [108] all possible phenomena which may come together in our experience, a connection of all these representations according to laws. For that unity of consciousness would be impossible, if the mind, in the knowledge of the manifold, could not become conscious of the identity of function, by which it unites the manifold synthetically in one knowledge. Therefore the original and necessary consciousness of the identity of oneself is at the same time a consciousness of an equally necessary unity of the synthesis of all phenomena according to concepts, that is, according to rules, which render them not only necessarily reproducible, but assign also to their intuition an object, that is, a concept of something in which they are necessarily united. The mind could never conceive the identity of itself in the manifoldness of its representations (and this *a priori*) if it did not clearly perceive the identity of its action, by which it subjects all synthesis of apprehension (which is empirical) to a transcendental unity, and thus renders its regular coherence *a priori* possible. When we have clearly perceived this, we shall be able to determine more accurately our concept of an object in general. All representations have, as representations, their object, and can themselves in turn become objects of other representations. The only objects which can be given to us immediately are phenomena, and whatever in them refers immediately to the object is called intuition. These phenom- [109] ena, however, are not things in themselves, but representations only which have their object, but an object that can no longer be seen by us, and may therefore be called the not-empirical, that is, the transcendental object, = *x*.

The pure concept of such a transcendental object (which in reality in all our knowledge is always the same = *x*) is that which alone can give to all our empirical concepts a relation to an object or objective reality. That concept cannot contain any definite intuition, and can therefore refer to that unity only, which must be found in the manifold of our knowledge, so far as it stands in relation to an object. That relation is nothing else but a necessary unity of consciousness, and therefore also of the synthesis of the manifold, by a common function of the mind, which unites it in one representation. As that unity must be considered as *a priori* necessary (because, without it, our knowledge would be without an object), we may conclude that the relation to a transcendental object, that is, the objective reality of our empirical knowledge, rests on a transcendental law, that all phenomena, if they are to give us objects, must be subject to rules *a priori* of a syn- [110] thetical unity of these objects, by which rules alone their mutual relation in an empirical intuition becomes possible: that is, they must be subject, in experience, to the conditions of the necessary unity of apperception quite as much as, in mere intuition, to the formal conditions of space and time. Without this no knowledge is possible.

IV

Preliminary Explanation of the Possibility of the Categories as Knowledge a priori

There is but one experience in which all perceptions are represented as in permanent and regular connection, as there is but one space and one time in which all forms of phenomena and all relations of being or not being take place. If we speak of different experiences, we only mean different perceptions so far as they belong to one and the same general experience. It is the permanent and synthetical unity of perceptions that constitutes the form of experience, and experience is nothing but the synthetical unity of phenomena according to concepts.

Unity of synthesis, according to empirical concepts, would be purely

accidental, nay, unless these were founded on a transcendental   [111]
ground of unity, a whole crowd of phenomena might rush into our soul,
without ever forming real experience. All relation between our knowledge and its objects would be lost at the same time, because that knowledge would no longer be held together by general and necessary laws;
it would therefore become thoughtless intuition, never knowledge, and
would be to us the same as nothing.

The conditions *a priori* of any possible experience in general are
at the same time conditions of the possibility of any objects of our experience. Now I maintain that the categories of which we are speaking
are nothing but the conditions of thought which make experience possible, as much as space and time contain the conditions of that intuition
which forms experience. These categories therefore are also fundamental
concepts by which we think objects in general for the phenomena, and
have therefore *a priori* objective validity. This is exactly what we wish
to prove.

The possibility, nay the necessity of these categories rests on the relation between our whole sensibility, and therefore all possible phenomena, and that original apperception in which everything must be necessarily subject to the conditions of the permanent unity of self-consciousness, that is, must submit to the general functions of that synthesis   [112]
which we call synthesis according to concepts, by which alone our appre-
ciation can prove its permanent and necessary identity *a priori*. Thus the
concept of cause is nothing but a synthesis of that which follows in
temporal succession, with other phenomena, but a synthesis according
to concepts: and without such a unity which rests on a rule *a priori*,
and subjects all phenomena to itself, no permanent and general, and
therefore necessary unity of consciousness would be formed in the
manifold of our perceptions. Such perceptions would then belong to no
experience at all, they would be without an object, a blind play of representation,—less even than a dream.

All attempts therefore at deriving those pure concepts of the understanding from experience, and ascribing to them a purely empirical
origin, are perfectly vain and useless. I shall not dwell here on the fact
that a concept of cause, for instance, contains an element of necessity,
which no experience can ever supply, because experience, though it
teaches us that after one phenomenon something else follows habitually,
can never teach us that it follows necessarily, nor that we could *a priori*,
and without any limitation, derive from it, as a condition, any conclusion
as to what must follow. And thus I ask with reference to that empirical
rule of association, which must always be admitted if we say that everything in the succession of events is so entirely subject to rules that
nothing ever happens without something preceding it on which it   [113]
always follows,—What does it rest on, if it is a law of nature, nay, how
is that very association possible? You call the ground for the possibility
of the association of the manifold, so far as it is contained in the objects
themselves, the *affinity* of the manifold. I ask, therefore, how do you

make that permanent affinity by which phenomena stand, nay, must stand, under permanent laws, conceivable to yourselves?

According to my principles it is easily conceivable. All possible phenomena belong, as representations, to the whole of our possible self-consciousness. From this, as a transcendental representation, numerical identity is inseparable and *a priori* certain, because nothing can become knowledge except by means of that original apperception. As this identity must necessarily enter into the synthesis of the whole of the manifold of phenomena, if that synthesis is to become empirical knowledge, it follows that the phenomena are subject to conditions *a priori* to which their synthesis (in apprehension) must always conform. The representation of a general condition according to which something manifold *can* be arranged (with uniformity) is called *a rule,* if it *must* be so arranged, *a law.* All phenomena therefore stand in a permanent connection according to necessary laws, and thus possess that transcendental [114] affinity of which the empirical is a mere consequence.

It sounds no doubt very strange and absurd that nature should have to conform to our subjective ground of apperception, nay, be dependent on it, with respect to her laws. But if we consider that what we call nature is nothing but a whole of phenomena, not a thing by itself, but a number of representations in our soul, we shall no longer be surprised that we only see her through the fundamental faculty of all our knowledge, namely, the transcendental apperception, and in that unity without which it could not be called the object (or the whole) of all possible experience, that is, nature. We shall thus also understand why we can recognise this unity *a priori,* and therefore as necessary, which would be perfectly impossible if it were given by itself and independent of the first sources of our own thinking. In that case I could not tell whence we should take the synthetical propositions of such general unity of nature. They would have to be taken from the objects of nature themselves, and as this could be done empirically only, we could derive from it none but an accidental unity, which is very different from that necessary connection which we mean when speaking of nature.

Section III [115]

Of the Relation of the Understanding to Objects in General, and the Possibility of Knowing Them a priori

What in the preceding section we have discussed singly and separately we shall now try to treat in connection with each other and as a whole. We saw that there are three subjective sources of knowledge on which the possibility of all experience and of the knowledge of its objects depends, namely, *sense, imagination, and apperception.* Each of them may be considered as empirical in its application to given phenomena; all, however, are also elements or grounds *a priori* which render their empirical application possible. *Sense* represents phenomena empirically in *perception, imagination* in *association* (and reproduction), *apperception* in the *empirical consciousness* of the identity of these reproductive representations with the phenomena by which they were given; therefore in *recognition.*

The whole of our perception rests *a priori* on pure intuition (if the perception is regarded as representation, then on time, as the form of our internal intuition), the association of it (the whole) on the pure   [116] synthesis of imagination, and our empirical consciousness of it on pure apperception, that is, on the permanent identity of oneself in the midst of all possible representations.

If we wish to follow up the internal ground of this connection of representations to that point towards which they must all converge, and where they receive for the first time that unity of knowledge which is requisite for every possible experience, we must begin with pure apperception. Intuitions are nothing to us, and do not concern us in the least, if they cannot be received into our consciousness, into which they may enter either directly or indirectly. Knowledge is impossible in any other way. We are conscious *a priori* of our own permanent identity with regard to all representations that can ever belong to our knowledge, as forming a necessary condition of the possibility of all representations (because these could not represent anything in me, unless they belonged with everything else to one consciousness and could at least be connected within it). This principle stands stands firm *a priori,* and may be called the *transcendental principle of the unity* of all the manifold of our representations (therefore also of intuition). This unity of the manifold in one subject is synthetical; the pure apperception therefore supplies us with a principle of the synthetical unity of the manifold in all   [117] possible intuitions.[22]

---

22 This point is of great importance and should be carefully considered. All representations have a necessary relation to some possible empirical consciousness, for if they did not possess that relation, and if it were entirely impossible to become conscious of them, this would be the same as if they did not exist. All empirical consciousness has a necessary relation to a transcendental consciousness, which precedes all single experiences, namely, the consciousness of my own self as the original apperception. It is absolutely necessary therefore that in my knowledge all consciousness should belong to one consciousness of my own self. Here we have a synthetical unity of the manifold (consciousness) which can be known *a priori,* and which may thus supply a foundation for synthetical propositions *a priori* concerning pure thinking in the same way as space and time supply a foundation for synthetical propositions which concern the form of mere intuition.

The synthetical proposition that the different kinds of empirical consciousness must be connected in one self-consciousness, is the very first and synthetical foundation of all our thinking. It should be remembered that the mere representation of the Ego in reference to all other representations (the collective unity of which would be impossible without it) constitutes our transcendental consciousness. It does not matter whether that representation is clear (empirical consciousness) or confused, not even whether it is real; but the possibility of the logical form of all knowledge rests necessarily on the relation to this apperception *as a faculty.*

This synthetical unity, however, presupposes or involves a [118] synthesis, and if that unity is necessary *a priori*, the synthesis also must be *a priori*. The transcendental unity of apperception therefore refers to the pure synthesis of imagination as a condition *a priori* of the possibility of the manifold being united in one knowledge. Now there can take place *a priori* the productive synthesis of imagination only, because the reproductive rests on conditions of experience. The principle therefore of the necessary unity of the pure (productive) synthesis of imagination, before all apperception, constitutes the ground of the possibility of all knowledge, nay, of all experience.

The synthesis of the manifold in imagination is called transcendental, if, without reference to the difference of intuitions, it affects only the *a priori* conjunction of the manifold; and the unity of that synthesis is called transcendental, if, with reference to the original unity of apperception, it is represented as *a priori* necessary. As the possibility of all knowledge depends on the unity of that apperception, it follows that the transcendental unity of the synthesis of imagination is the pure form of all possible knowledge through which therefore all objects of possible experience must be represented *a priori*.

This unity of apperception with reference to the synthesis of [119] imagination is the *understanding*, and the same unity with reference to the transcendental synthesis of the imagination, the *pure understanding*. It must be admitted therefore that there exist in the understanding pure forms of knowledge *a priori*, which contain the necessary unity of the pure synthesis of the imagination in reference to all possible phenomena. These are the categories, that is, the pure concepts of the understanding. The empirical faculty of knowledge of man contains therefore by necessity an understanding which refers to all objects of the senses, though by intuition only, and by its synthesis through imagination, and all phenomena, as data of a possible experience, must conform to that understanding. As this relation of phenomena to a possible experience is likewise necessary, (because, without it, we should receive no knowledge through them, and they would not in the least concern us), it follows that the pure understanding constitutes by the means of the categories a formal and synthetical principle of all experience, and that phenomena have thus a necessary relation to the understanding.

We shall now try to place the necessary connection of the understanding with the phenomena by means of the categories more clearly before the reader, by beginning with the beginning, namely, with the empirical.

The first that is given us is the *phenomenon*, which, if connected [120] with consciousness, is called *perception*. (Without its relation to an at least possible consciousness, the phenomenon could never become to us an object of knowledge. It would therefore be nothing to us; and because it has no objective reality in itself, but exists only in being known, it would be nothing altogether.) As every phenomenon contains a manifold, and different perceptions are found in the mind singly and scattered, a connection of them is necessary, such as they cannot have in the senses by themselves. There exists therefore in us an active power for the synthesis of the manifold which we call imagination, and the function of which, as applied to perceptions, I call *apprehension*.[23] This imagination is meant to change the manifold of intuition into an image, it must therefore first receive the impressions into its activity, which I call *to apprehend*.

It must be clear, however, that even this apprehension of the　[121] manifold could not alone produce a coherence of impressions or an image, without some subjective power of calling one perception from which the mind has gone over to another back to that which follows, and thus forming whole series of perceptions. This is the reproductive faculty of imagination which is and can be empirical only.

If representations, as they happen to meet with one another, could reproduce each other at haphazard, they would have no definite coherence, but would form irregular agglomerations only, and never produce knowledge. It is necessary therefore that their reproduction should be subject to a rule by which one representation connects itself in imagination with a second and not with a third. It is this subjective and empirical ground of reproduction according to rules, which is called the *association* of representations.

If this unity of association did not possess an objective foundation also, which makes it impossible that phenomena should be apprehended by imagination in any other way but under the condition of a possible synthetical unity of that apprehension, it would be a mere accident that phenomena lend themselves to a certain connection in human knowledge. Though we might have the power of associating perceptions, it would still be a matter of uncertainty and chance whether they them-　[122] selves are associable; and, in case they should not be so, a number of perceptions, nay, the whole of our sensibility, might possibly contain a great deal of empirical consciousness, but in a separate state, nay, without belonging to the *one* consciousness of myself, which, however, is impossible. Only by ascribing all perceptions to one consciousness (the original apperception) can I say of all of them that I am conscious of them. It must be therefore an objective ground, that is, one that can be understood as existing *a priori*, and before all empirical laws of imagination, on which alone the possibility, nay, even the necessity of a law can rest, which pervades all phenomena, and which makes us look upon them all, without exception, as data of the senses, associable by themselves, and subject to general rules of a permanent connection in their reproduction. This objective ground of all association of phenomena I call their affinity, and this can nowhere be found except in the principle

---

23 It has hardly struck any psychologist that this imagination is a necessary ingredient of perception. This was partly owing to their confining this faculty to reproduction, partly to our belief that the senses do not only give us impressions, but compound them also for us, thus producing pictures of objects. This, however, beyond our receptivity of impressions, requires something more, namely, a function for their synthesis.

of the unity of apperception applied to all knowledge which is to belong to me. According to it all phenomena, without exception, must so enter into the mind or be apprehended as to agree with the unity of apperception. This, without a synthetical unity in their connection, which is therefore necessary objectively also, would be impossible.

We have thus seen that the objective unity of all (empirical)   [123] consciousness in one consciousness (that of the original apperception) is the necessary condition even of all possible perception, while the affinity of all phenomena (near or remote) is a necessary consequence of a synthesis in imagination which is *a priori* founded on rules.

Imagination is therefore likewise the power of a synthesis *a priori* which is the reason why we called it productive imagination, and so far as this aims at nothing but the necessary unity in the synthesis of all the manifold in phenomena, it may be called the transcendental function of imagination. However strange therefore it may appear at first, it must nevertheless have become clear by this time that the affinity of phenomena and with it their association, and through that, lastly, their reproduction also according to laws, that is, the whole of our experience, becomes possible only by means of that transcendental function of imagination, without which no concepts of objects could ever come together in one experience.

It is the permanent and unchanging Ego (or pure apperception) which forms the correlative of all our representations, if we are to become conscious of them, and all consciousness belongs quite as much to such an all-embracing pure apperception as all sensuous intuitions belongs, as a representation, to a pure internal intuition, namely,   [124] time. This apperception it is which must be added to pure imagination, in order to render its function intellectual. For by itself, the synthesis of imagination, though carried out *a priori*, is always sensuous, and only connects the manifold as it appears in intuition, for instance, the shape of a triangle. But when the manifold is brought into relation with the unity of apperception, concepts which belong to the understanding become possible, but only as related to sensuous intuition through imagination.

We have therefore a pure imagination as one of the fundamental faculties of the human soul, on which all knowledge *a priori* depends. Through it we bring the manifold of intuition on one side in connection with the condition of the necessary unity of pure apperception on the other. These two extreme ends, sense and understanding, must be brought into contact with each other by means of the transcendental function of imagination, because, without it, the senses might give us phenomena, but no objects of empirical knowledge, therefore no experience. Real experience, which is made up of apprehension, association (reproduction), and lastly recognition of phenomena, contains in this last and highest (among the purely empirical elements of expe-   [125] rience) concepts, which render possible the formal unity of experience, and with it, all objective validity (truth) of empirical knowledge. These grounds for the recognition of the manifold, so far as they concern the form only of experience in general, are our categories. On them is founded the whole formal unity in the synthesis of imagination and, through it, of [24] the whole empirical use of them (in recognition, reproduction, association, and apprehension) down to the very phenomena, because it is only by means of those elements of knowledge that the phenomena can belong to our consciousness and therefore to ourselves.

It is we therefore who carry into the phenomena which we call nature, order and regularity, nay, we should never find them in nature, if we ourselves, or the nature of our mind, had not originally placed them there. For the unity of nature is meant to be a necessary and *a priori* certain unity in the connection of all phenomena. And how should we *a priori* have arrived at such a synthetical unity, if the subjective grounds of such unity were not contained *a priori* in the original sources of our knowledge, and if those subjective conditions did not at the same time possess objective validity, as being the grounds on which alone an object becomes possible in our experience? [126]

We have before given various definitions of the understanding, by calling it the spontaneity of knowledge (as opposed to the receptivity of the senses), or the faculty of thinking, or the faculty of concepts or of judgments; all of these explanations, if more closely examined, coming to the same. We may now characterise it as *the faculty of rules*. This characteristic is more significant, and approaches nearer to the essence of the understanding. The senses give us forms (of intuition), the understanding rules, being always busy to examine phenomena, in order to discover in them some kind of rule. Rules, so far as they are objective (therefore necessarily inherent in our knowledge of an object), are called laws. Although experience teaches us many laws, yet these are only particular determinations of higher laws, the highest of them, to which all others are subject, springing *a priori* from the understanding; not being derived from experience, but, on the contrary, imparting to the phenomena their regularity, and thus making experience possible. The understanding therefore is not only a power of making rules by a comparison of phenomena, it is itself the lawgiver of nature, and without the understanding nature, that is, a synthetical unity of the manifold of phenomena, according to rules, would be nowhere to be found, [127] because phenomena, as such, cannot exist without us, but exist in our sensibility only. This sensibility, as an object of our knowledge in any experience, with everything it may contain, is possible only in the unity of apperception, which unity of apperception is transcendental ground of the necessary order of all phenomena in an experience. The same unity of apperception with reference to the manifold of representations (so as to determine it out of one) [25] forms what we call the rule, and the faculty of these rules I call the understanding. As possible experience

---

[24] *Of* may be omitted, if we read *aller empirischer Gebrauch.*
[25] That is, out of one, or out of the unity of apperception.

therefore, all phenomena depend in the same way *a priori* on the understanding, and receive their formal possibility from it as, when looked upon as mere intuitions, they depend on sensibility, and become possible through it, so far as their form is concerned.

However exaggerated therefore, and absurd it may sound, that the understanding is itself the source of the laws of nature, and of its formal unity, such a statement is nevertheless correct and in accordance with experience. It is quite true, no doubt, that empirical laws, as such, cannot derive their origin from the pure understanding, as little as the infinite manifoldness of phenomena could be sufficiently comprehended through the pure form of sensuous intuition. But all empirical laws are only particular determinations of the pure laws of the under- [128] standing, under which and according to which the former become possible, and phenomena assume a regular form, quite as much as all phenomena, in spite of the variety of their empirical form, must always submit to the conditions of the pure form of sensibility.

The pure understanding is therefore in the categories the law of the synthetical unity of all phenomena, and thus makes experience, so far as its form is concerned, for the first time possible. This, and no more than this, we were called upon to prove in the transcendental deduction of the categories, namely, to make the relation of the understanding to our sensibility, and through it to all objects of experience, that is the objective validity of the pure concepts *a priori* of the understanding, conceivable, and thus to establish their origin and their truth.

SUMMARY REPRESENTATION

OF THE CORRECTNESS AND OF THE ONLY POSSIBILITY OF THIS DEDUCTION OF THE PURE CONCEPTS OF THE UNDERSTANDING

If the objects with which our knowledge has to deal were things by themselves, we could have no concepts *a priori* of them. For where should we take them? If we took them from the object (without asking even the question, how that object could be known to us) our [129] concepts would be empirical only, not concepts *a priori*. If we took them from within ourselves, then that which is within us only, could not determine the nature of an object different from our representations, that is, supply a ground why there should be a thing to which something like what we have in our thoughts really belongs, and why all this representation should not rather be altogether empty. But if, on the contrary, we have to deal with phenomena only, then it becomes not only possible, but necessary, that certain concepts *a priori* should precede our empirical knowledge of objects. For being phenomena, they form an object that is within us only, because a mere modification of our sensibility can never exist outside us. The very idea that all these phenomena, and therefore all objects with which we have to deal, are altogether within me, or determinations of my own identical self, implies by itself the necessity of a permanent unity of them in one and the same apperception. In that unity of a possible consciousness consists also the form of all knowledge of objects, by which the manifold is thought as belonging to *one* object. The manner therefore in which the manifold of sensuous representation (intuition) belongs to our consciousness, precedes all knowledge of an object, as its intellectual form, and constitutes a kind of formal *a priori* knowledge of all objects in general, if they are to be thought (categories). Their synthesis by means of pure imagination, [130] and the unity of all representations with reference to the original apperception, precede all empirical knowledge. Pure concepts of the understanding are therefore *a priori* possible, nay, with regard to experience, necessary, for this simple reason, because our knowledge has to deal with nothing but phenomena, the possibility of which depends on ourselves, and the connection and unity of which (in the representation of an object) can be found in ourselves only, as antecedent to all experience, nay, as first rendering all experience possible, so far as its form is concerned. On this ground, as the only possible one, our deduction of the categories has been carried out.]

· · ·

Book II: Analytic of Principles (The Transcendental Doctrine of the Faculty of Judgment)

CHAPTER I. OF THE SCHEMATISM OF THE PURE CONCEPTS OF THE UNDERSTANDING

In comprehending any object under a concept, the representation of the former must be homogeneous with the latter,[26] that is, the concept must contain that which is represented in the object to be comprehended under it, for this is the only meaning of the expression that an object is comprehended under a concept. Thus, for instance, the empirical concept of a plate is homogeneous with the pure geometrical concept of a circle, the roundness which is conceived in the first forming an object of intuition in the latter.

Now it is clear that pure concepts of the understanding, as compared with empirical or sensuous impressions in general, are entirely heterogeneous, and can never be met with in any intuition. How then can the latter be comprehended under the former, or how can the categories be applied to phenomena, as no one is likely to say that causality, for instance, could be seen through the senses, and was contained in the phenomenon? It is really this very natural and important question [138] which renders a transcendental doctrine of the faculty of judgment necessary, in order to show how it is possible that any of the pure con-

---

26 Read *dem letzteren*, as corrected by Rosenkranz, for *der letzteren*.

cepts of the understanding can be applied to phenomena. In all other sciences in which the concepts by which the object is thought in general are not so heterogeneous or different from those which represent it *in concreto,* and as it is given, there is no necessity to enter into any discussions as to the applicability of the former to the latter.

In our case there must be some third thing homogeneous on the one side with the category, and on the other with the phenomenon, to render the application of the former to the latter possible. This intermediate representation must be pure (free from all that is empirical) and yet intelligible on the one side, and sensuous on the other. Such a representation is the *transcendental schema.*

The concept of the understanding contains pure synthetical unity of the manifold in general. Time, as the formal condition of the manifold in the internal sense, consequently of the conjunction of all representations, contains a manifold *a priori* in pure intuition. A transcendental determination of time is so far homogeneous with the category (which constitutes its unity) that it is general and founded on a rule *a priori;* and it is on the other hand so far homogeneous with the phenom-   [139] enon, that time must be contained in every empirical representation of the manifold. The application of the category to phenomena becomes possible therefore by means of the transcendental determination of time, which, as a *schema* of the concepts of the understanding, allows the phenomena to be comprehended under the category.

After what has been said in the deduction of the categories, we hope that nobody will hesitate in answering the question whether these pure concepts of the understanding allow only of an empirical or also of a transcendental application, that is, whether, as conditions of a possible experience, they refer *a priori* to phenomena only, or whether, as conditions of the possibility of things in general, they may be extended to objects by themselves (without restriction to our sensibility). For there we saw that concepts are quite impossible, and cannot have any meaning unless there be an object given either to them or, at least, to some of the elements of which they consist, and that they can never refer to things by themselves (without regard as to whether and how things may be given to us). We likewise saw that the only way in which objects can be given to us, consists in a modification of our sensibility, and lastly, that pure concepts *a priori* must contain, besides the function of the understanding in the category itself, formal conditions *a priori* of sensibility (par-   [140] ticularly of the internal sense) which form the general condition under which alone the category may be applied to any object. We shall call this formal and pure condition of sensibility, to which the concept of the understanding is restricted in its application, its *schema;* and the function of the understanding in these schemata, the *schematism of the pure understanding.*

The schema by itself is no doubt a product of the imagination only, but as the synthesis of the imagination does not aim at a single intuition, but at some kind of unity alone in the determination of sensibility, the schema ought to be distinguished from the image. Thus, if I place five points, one after the other . . . . . , this is an image of the number five. If, on the contrary, I think of a number in general, whether it be five or a hundred, this thinking is rather the representation of a method of representing in one image a certain quantity (for instance a thousand) according to a certain concept, than the image itself, which in the case of a thousand, I could hardly take in and compare with the concept. This representation of a general procedure of the imagination by which a concept receives its image, I call the schema of such concept.

The fact is that our pure sensuous concepts do not depend on images of objects, but on schemata. No image of a triangle in general [141] could ever be adequate to its concept. It would never attain to that generality of the concept, which makes it applicable to all triangles, whether right-angled, or acute-angled, or anything else, but would always be restricted to one portion only of the sphere of the concept. The schema of the triangle can exist nowhere but in thought, and is in fact a rule for the synthesis of imagination with respect to pure forms in space. Still less does an object of experience or its image ever cover the empirical concept, which always refers directly to the schema of imagination as a rule for the determination of our intuitions, according to a certain general concept. The concept of dog means a rule according to which my imagination can always draw a general outline of the figure of a four-footed animal, without being restricted to any particular figure supplied by experience or to any possible image which I may draw in the concrete. This schematism of our understanding applied to phenomena and their mere form is an art hidden in the depth of the human soul, the true secrets of which we shall hardly ever be able to guess and reveal. So much only we can say, that the *image* is a product of the empirical faculty of the productive imagination, while the *schema* of sensuous concepts (such as of figures in space) is a product and so to say a monogram of the pure imagination *a priori,* through which and [142] according to which images themselves become possible, though they are never fully adequate to the concept, and can be connected with it by means of their schema only. The schema of a pure concept of the understanding, on the contrary, is something which can never be made into an image; for it is nothing but the pure synthesis determined by a rule of unity, according to concepts, a synthesis as expressed by the category, and represents a transcendental product of the imagination, a product which concerns the determination of the internal sense in general, under the conditions of its form (time), with reference to all representations, so far as these are meant to be joined *a priori* in one concept, according to the unity of apperception.

Without dwelling any longer on a dry and tedious determination of all that is required for the transcendental schemata of the pure concepts of the understanding in general, we shall proceed at once to represent them according to the order of the categories, and in connection with them.

The pure image of all quantities (*quanta*) before the external sense, is space; that of all objects of the senses in general, time. The pure schema of quantity (*quantitas*), however, as a concept of the understanding, is *number,* a representation which comprehends the successive addition of one to one (homogeneous). Number therefore is nothing but the [143] unity of the synthesis of the manifold (repetition) of a homogeneous intuition in general, I myself producing the time in the apprehension of the intuition.

Reality is, in the pure concept of the understanding, that which corresponds to a sensation in general: that, therefore, the concept of which indicates by itself being (in time), while negation is that the concept of which represents not-being (in time). The opposition of the two takes place therefore by a distinction of one and the same time, as either filled or empty. As time is only the form of intuition, that is, of objects as phenomena, that which in the phenomena corresponds to sensation, constitutes the transcendental matter of all objects, as things by themselves (reality, Sachheit). Every sensation, however, has a degree of quantity by which it can fill the same time (that is, the internal sense, with reference to the same representation of an object), more or less, till it vanishes into nothing (equal to nought or negation). There exists, therefore, a relation and connection, or rather a transition from reality to negation, which makes every reality representable as a quantum; and the schema of a reality, as the quantity of something which fills time, is this very continuous and uniform production of reality in time; while we either descend from the sensation which has a certain degree, to its vanishing in time, or ascend from the negation of sensation to some quantity of it.

The schema of substance is the permanence of the real in time, [144] that is, the representation of it as a substratum for the empirical determination of time in general, which therefore remains while everything else changes. (It is not time that passes, but the existence of the changeable passes in time. What corresponds therefore in the phenomena to time, which in itself is unchangeable and permanent, is the unchangeable in existence, that is, substance; and it is only in it that the succession and the coexistence of phenomena can be determined according to time.)

The schema of cause and of the causality of a thing in general is the real which, when once supposed to exist, is always followed by something else. It consists therefore in the succession of the manifold, in so far as that succession is subject to a rule.

The schema of community (reciprocal action) or of the reciprocal causality of substances, in respect to their accidents, is the coexistence, according to a general rule, of the determinations of the one with those of the other.

The schema of possibility is the agreement of the synthesis of different representations with the conditions of time in general, as, for instance, when opposites cannot exist at the same time in the same thing, but only one after the other. It is therefore the determination of the representation of a thing at any time whatsoever.

The schema of reality is existence at a given time.   [145]

The schema of necessity is the existence of an object at all times.

It is clear, therefore, if we examine all the categories, that the schema of quantity contains and represents the production (synthesis) of time itself in the successive apprehension of an object; the schema of quality, the synthesis of sensation (perception) with the representation of time or the filling-up of time; the schema of relation, the relation of perceptions to each other at all times (that is, according to a rule which determines time); lastly, the schema of modality and its categories, time itself as the correlative of the determination of an object as to whether and how it belongs to time. The schemata therefore are nothing but determinations of time *a priori* according to rules, and these, as applied to all possible objects, refer in the order of the categories to the *series of time*, the *contents of time*, the *order of time*, and lastly, the *comprehension of time*.

We have thus seen that the schematism of the understanding, by means of a transcendental synthesis of imagination, amounts to nothing else but to the unity of the manifold in the intuition of the internal sense, and therefore indirectly to the unity of apperception, as an active function corresponding to the internal sense (as receptive). These schemata therefore of the pure concepts of the understanding are the true   [146] and only conditions by which these concepts can gain a relation to objects, that is, a *significance*, and the categories are thus in the end of no other but a possible empirical use, serving only, on account of an *a priori* necessary unity (the necessary connection of all consciousness in one original apperception) to subject all phenomena to general rules of synthesis, and thus to render them capable of a general connection in experience.

All our knowledge is contained within this whole of possible experience, and transcendental truth, which precedes all empirical truth and renders it possible, consists in general relation of it to that experience.

But although the schemata of sensibility serve thus to realize the categories, it must strike everybody that they at the same time restrict them, that is, limit them by conditions foreign to the understanding and belonging to sensibility. Hence the schema is really the phenomenon, or the sensuous concept of an object in agreement with the category (nu-merus *est quantitas phaenomenon*, sensatio *realitas phaenomenon*, con-stans et perdurabile rerum *substantia phaenomenon*—aeternitas *necessitas phaenomenon*, etc.). If we omit a restrictive condition, it would seem that we amplify a formerly limited concept, and that therefore the   [147] categories in their pure meaning, free from all conditions of sensibility, should be valid of things in general, *as they are*, while their schemata represent them only *as they appear*, so that these categories might claim a far more extended power, independent of all schemata. And in truth we must allow to these pure concepts of the understanding, apart from all sensuous conditions, a certain significance, though a logical one only, with regard to the mere unity of representations produced by them, although these representations have no object and therefore no meaning that could give us a concept of an object. Thus substance, if we leave out the sensuous condition of permanence, would mean nothing but a something that may be conceived as a subject, without being the predicate of anything else. Of such a representation we can make nothing, because it does not teach us how that thing is determined which is thus to be considered as the first subject. Categories, therefore, without schemata are functions only of the understanding necessary for concepts, but do not themselves represent any object. This character is given to them by sensibility only, which realises the understanding by, at the time time, restricting it.

. . .

CHAPTER III. ON THE GROUND OF DISTINCTION OF ALL SUBJECTS INTO PHENOMENA AND NOUMENA

We have now not only traversed the whole domain of the pure understanding, and carefully examined each part of it, but we have also measured its extent, and assigned to everything in it its proper place. This domain, however, is an island and enclosed by nature itself within limits that can never be changed. It is the country of truth (a very attractive name), but surrounded by a wide and stormy ocean, the true home of illusion, where many a fog bank and ice that soon melts away tempt us to believe in new lands, while constantly deceiving the adventurous mariner with vain hopes, and involving him in adventures which [236] he can never leave, and yet can never bring to an end. Before we venture ourselves on this sea, in order to explore it on every side, and to find out whether anything is to be hoped for there, it will be useful to glance once more at the map of that country which we are about to leave, and to ask ourselves, first, whether we might not be content with what it contains, nay, whether we must not be content with it, supposing that there is no solid ground anywhere else on which we could settle; secondly, by what title we possess even that domain, and may consider ourselves safe against all hostile claims. Although we have sufficiently answered these questions in the course of the analytic, a summary recapitulation of their solutions may help to strength our conviction, by uniting all arguments in one point.

We have seen that the understanding possesses everything which it draws from itself, without borrowing from experience, for no other purpose but for experience. The principles of the pure understanding, whether constitutive *a priori* (as the mathematical) or simply relative (as the dynamical), contain nothing but, as it were, the pure schema of possible experience; for that experience derives its unity from that [237] synthetical unity alone which the understanding originally and spontaneously imparts to the synthesis of imagination, with reference to apperception, and to which all phenomena, as data of a possible knowledge, must conform *a priori*. But although these rules of the understanding are not only true *a priori*, but the very source of all truth, that is, of the agreement of our knowledge with objects, because containing the conditions of the possibility of experience, as the complete sphere of all knowledge in which objects can be given to us, nevertheless we do not seem to be content with hearing only what is true, but want to know a great deal more. If therefore this critical investigation does not teach us any more than what, even without such subtle researches, we should have practised ourselves in the purely empirical use of the understanding, it would seem as if the advantages derived from it were hardly worth the labour. One might reply that nothing would be more prejudicial to the enlargement of our knowledge than that curiosity which, before entering upon any researches, wishes to know beforehand the advantages likely to accrue from them, though quite unable as yet to form the least conception of such advantages, even though they were placed before our eyes. There is, however, one advantage in this transcendental investigation [238] which can be rendered intelligible, nay, even attractive to the most troublesome and reluctant apprentice, namely this, that the understanding confined to its empirical use only and unconcerned with regard to the sources of its own knowledge, may no doubt fare very well in other respects, but can never determine for itself the limits of its own use and know what is inside or outside its own sphere. It is for that purpose that such profound investigations are required as we have just instituted. If the understanding cannot decide whether certain questions lie within its own horizon or not, it can never feel certain with regard to its claims and possessions, but must be prepared for many humiliating corrections, when constantly transgressing, as it certainly will, the limits of its own domain, and losing itself in follies and fancies.

That the understanding cannot make any but an empirical, and never a transcendental, use of all its principles *a priori*, nay, of all its concepts, is a proposition which, if thoroughly understood, leads indeed to most important consequences. What we call the transcendental use of a concept in any proposition is its being referred to things in general and to things by themselves, while its empirical use refers to phenomena only, that is, to objects of a possible experience. That the latter use alone is admissible will be clear from the following considerations. What is required [239] for every concept is, first, the logical form of a concept (of thought) in general; and, secondly, the possibility of an object to which it refers. Without the latter, it has no sense, and is entirely empty, though it may still contain the logical function by which a concept can be formed out of any data. The only way in which an object can be given to a concept is in intuition, and though a pure intuition is possible *a priori* and before the object, yet even that pure intuition can receive its object, and with it its objective validity, by an empirical intuition only, of which it is itself nothing but the form. All concepts, therefore, and with them all principles, though they may be possible *a priori,* refer nevertheless to empirical intuitions, that is, to data of a possible experience. Without this, they can claim no objective validity, but are a mere play, whether of the imagination or of the understanding with their respective representations. Let us take the concepts of mathematics as an example, and, first, with regard to pure intuitions. Although such principles as 'space has three dimensions,' 'between two points there can be only one straight line,' as well as the representation of the object with which that science is occupied, may be produced in the mind *a priori,* they would have no meaning, if we were not able at all times to show their meaning as ap- [240] plied to phenomena (empirical objects). It is for this reason that an abstract concept is required to be made *sensuous,* that is, that its corresponding object is required to be shown in intuition, because, without this, the concept (as people say) is without *sense,* that is, without meaning. Mathematics fulfil this requirement by the construction of the figure, which is a phenomenon present to the senses (although constructed *a priori*). In the same science the concept of quantity finds its support and sense in number; and this in turn in the fingers, the beads of the abacus, or in strokes and points which can be presented to the eyes. The concept itself was produced *a priori,* together with all the synthetical principles or formulas which can be derived from such concepts; but their use and their relation to objects can nowhere be found except in experience, of which those concepts contain *a priori* the (formal) possibility only.

That this is the case with all categories and with all the principles drawn from them, becomes evident from the fact that we could not define any one of them (really, that is, make conceivable the possibility of their object),[27] without at once having recourse to the conditions of sensibility or the form of phenomena, to which, as their only possible objects, these categories must necessarily be restricted, it being impossible, if we take away these conditions, to assign to them any [241] meaning, that is, any relation to an object, or to make it intelligible to ourselves by an example what kind of thing could be intended by such concepts.

[When representing the table of the categories, we dispensed with the definition of every one of them, because at that time it seemed unnecessary for our purpose, which concerned their synthetical use only, and because entailing responsibilities which we were not bound to incur. This was not a mere excuse, but a very important prudential rule, viz. not to rush into definitions, and to attempt or pretend completeness or precision in the definition of a concept, when one or other of its characteristic marks is sufficient without a complete enumeration of all that constitute the whole concept. Now, however, we can perceive that this caution had even a deeper ground, namely, that we could not have defined them, even if we

---

[27] Additions of the Second Edition.

had wished; [28] for, if we remove all conditions of sensibility, [242] which distinguish them as the concepts of a possible empirical use, and treat them as concepts of things in general (therefore as of transcendental use), nothing remains but to regard the logical function in judgments as the condition of the possibility of the things themselves, without the slightest indication as to where they could have their application and their object, or how they could have any meaning or objective validity in the pure understanding, apart from sensibility.] [29]

No one can explain the concept of quantity in general, except, it may be, by saying that it is the determination of an object, by which we may know how many times the one is supposed to exist in it. But this 'how many times' is based on successive repetition, that is on time, and on the synthesis in it of the homogeneous.

Reality, again, can only be explained in opposition to a negation, if we think of time (as containing all being) being either filled or empty.

Were I to leave out permanence (which means existence at all times), nothing would remain of my concept of substance but the logical representation of a subject which I think I can realise by imagining [243] something which is a subject only, without being a predicate of anything. But in this case we should not only be ignorant of all conditions under which this logical distinction could belong to anything, but we should be unable to make any use of it or draw any conclusions from it, because no object is thus determined for the use of this concept, and no one can tell whether such a concept has any meaning at all.

Of the concept of cause also (if I leave out time, in which something follows on something else by rule) I should find no more in the pure category than that it is something which enables us to conclude the existence of something else, so that it would not only be impossible to distinguish cause and effect from each other, but the concept of cause would possess no indication as to how it can be applied to any object, because, in order to form any such conclusion, certain conditions require to be known of which the concept itself tells us nothing. The so-called principle that everything contingent has a cause, comes no doubt before us with great solemnity and self-assumed dignity. But, if I ask what you understand by contingent and you answer, something of which the non-existence is possible, I should be glad to know how you can recognise this possibility of non-existence, if you do not represent to yourselves, in the series of phenomena, some kind of succession, and in it an existence that follows upon non-existence (or *vice versa*), and consequently a

---

[28] I am treating here of the real definition, which not only puts in place of the name of a thing other and more intelligible words, but that which contains a clear mark by which the object (*definitum*) can at all times be safely recognised, and by which the defined concept becomes fit for practical use. A real definition (*Realarklärung*) must therefore render clear the concept itself, and its objective reality also. Of this kind are the mathematical explanations which represent an object in intuition, according to its concept.

[29] Read *nimmt* instead of *nehmen,* and *können* instead of *könne.*

change? To say that the non-existence of a thing is not self-   [244] contradictory is but a lame appeal to a logical condition which, though it is necessary for the concept, yet is by no means sufficient for its real possibility. I can perfectly well remove in thought every existing substance, without contradicting myself, but I can by no means conclude from this as to its objective contingency in its existence, that is, the possibility of its non-existence in itself.

As regards the concept of community, it is easy to see that, as the pure categories of substance and causality admit of no explanation that would determine their object, neither could such an explanation apply to the reciprocal causality in the relation of substances to each other (*commercium*).

As to possibility, existence, and necessity, no one has yet been able to explain them, except by a manifest tautology, so long as their definition is to be exclusively drawn from the pure understanding. To substitute the transcendental possibility of things (when an object corresponds to a concept) for the logical possibility of the concept (when the concept does not contradict itself) is a quibble such as could deceive and satisfy the inexperienced only.

[It seems to be something strange and even illogical [30] that there should be a concept which must have a meaning, and yet is incapable of any explanation. But the case of these categories is peculiar, because it is only by means of the general sensuous condition that they can acquire a definite meaning, and a reference to any objects. That condition being left out in the pure category, it follows that it can contain   [245] nothing but the logical function by which the manifold is brought into a concept. By means of this function, that is, the pure form of the concept, nothing can be known nor distinguished as to the object belonging to it, because the sensuous condition, under which alone objects can belong to it, has been removed. Thus we see that the categories require, besides the pure concept of the understanding, certain determinations of their application to sensibility in general (schemata). Without them, they would not be concepts by which an object can be known and distinguished from other objects, but only so many ways of thinking an object for possible intuitions, and giving to it, according to one of the functions of the understanding, its meaning (certain requisite conditions being given). They are needed to define an object, and cannot therefore be defined themselves. The logical functions of judgments in general, namely, unity and plurality, assertion and negation, subject and predicate, cannot be defined without arguing in a circle, because the definition would itself be a judgment and contain these very functions. The pure categories are nothing but representations of things in general, so far as the manifold in intuition must be thought by one or the other of these functions. Thus, magnitude is the determination which can [only be thought by a judg-

---

[30] The passage from 'It seems to be' to 'objective concepts' is left out in the Second Edition, and replaced by a short note.

ment possessing quantity (*judicium commune*); reality, the de-   [246] termination which can only be thought by an affirmative judgment; while substance is that which, in regard to intuition, must be the last subject of all other determinations. With all this it remains perfectly undetermined, what kind of things they may be with regard to which we have to use one rather than another of these functions, so that, without the condition of sensuous intuition, for which they supply the synthesis, the categories have no relation to any definite object, cannot define any object, and consequently have not in themselves the validity of objective concepts.]

From this it follows incontestably, that the pure concepts of the understanding never admit of a transcendental, but only of an empirical use, and that the principles of the pure understanding can only be referred, as general conditions of a possible experience, to objects of the senses, never to things by themselves (without regard to the manner in which we have to look at them).

Transcendental Analytic has therefore yielded us this important result, that the understanding *a priori* can never do more than anticipate the form of a possible experience; and as nothing can be an object of experience except the phenomenon, it follows that the understanding can never go beyond the limits of sensibility, within which alone objects are given to us. Its principles are principles for the exhibition of phe-   [247] nomena only; and the proud name of Ontology, which presumes to supply in a systematic form different kinds of synthetical knowledge *a priori* of things by themselves (for instance the principle of causality), must be replaced by the more modest name of a mere Analytic of the pure understanding.

Thought is the act of referring a given intuition to an object. If the mode of such intuition is not given, the object is called transcendental, and the concept of the understanding admits then of a transcendental use only, in producing a unity in the thought of the manifold in general. A pure category therefore, in which every condition of sensuous intuition, the only one that is possible for us, is left out, cannot determine an object, but only the thought of an object in general, according to different modes. Now, if we want to use a concept, we require in addition some function of the faculty of judgment, by which an object is subsumed under a concept, consequently the at least formal condition under which something can be given in intuition. If this condition of the faculty of judgment (schema) is wanting, all subsumption is impossible, because nothing is given that could be subsumed under the concept. The purely transcendental use of categories therefore is in reality of no use at all, and has no definite or even, with regard to its form only, definable object. Hence it follows that a pure category is not fit for any synthetical *a*   [248] *priori* principle, and that the principles of the pure understanding admit of empirical only, never of transcendental application, nay, that no synthetical principles *a priori* are possible beyond the field of possible experience.

It might therefore be advisable to express ourselves in the following way: the pure categories, without the formal conditions of sensibility, have a transcendental character only, but do not admit of any transcendental use, because such use in itself is impossible, as the categories are deprived of all the conditions of being used in judgments, that is, of the formal conditions of the subsumption of any possible object under these concepts. As therefore (as pure categories) they are not meant to be used empirically, and cannot be used transcendentally, they admit, if separated from sensibility, of no use at all; that is, they cannot be applied to any possible object, and are nothing but the pure form of the use of the understanding with reference to objects in general, and of thought, without ever enabling us to think or determine any object by their means alone.

[Appearances,[31] so far as they are thought as objects under the unity of the categories, are called *phenomena*. But if I admit things which are objects of the understanding only, and nevertheless can be given   [249] as objects of an intuition, though not of sensuous intuition (as *coram intuitu intellectuali*), such things would be called *noumena* (*intelligibilia*).

One might feel inclined to think that the concept of *Phenomena*, as limited by the transcendental æsthetic, suggested by itself the objective reality of the *Noumena*, and justified a division of objects into phenomena and noumena, and consequently of the world into a *sensible* and *intelligible* world (*mundus sensibilis et intelligibilis*); and this in such a way that the distinction between the two should not refer to the logical form only of a more or less clear knowledge of one and the same object, but to a difference in their original presentation to our knowledge, which makes them to differ in themselves from each other in kind. For if the senses only represent to us something as it appears, that something must by itself also be a thing, and an object of a non-sensuous intuition, i.e. of the understanding. That is, there must be a kind of knowledge in which there is no sensibility, and which alone possesses absolute objective reality, representing objects as they are, while through the empirical use of our understanding we know things only as they appear. Hence it would seem to follow that, beside the empirical use   [250] of the categories (limited by sensuous conditions), there was another one, pure and yet objectively valid, and that we could not say, as we have hitherto done, that our knowledge of the pure understanding contained nothing but principles for the exhibition of phenomena, which, even *a priori*, could not apply to anything but the formal possibility of experience. Here, in fact, quite a new field would seem to be open, a world, as it were, realised in thought (nay, according to some, even in intuition), which would be a more, and not a less, worthy object for the pure understanding.

---

[31] The passage from 'Appearances' to 'given to me in intuition' differs in the Second Edition.

All our representations are no doubt referred by the understanding to some sort of object, and as phenomena are nothing but representations, the understanding refers them to a *something*, as the object of our sensuous intuition, this something being however the transcendental object only. This means a something equal to *x*, of which we do not, nay, with the present constitution of our understanding, cannot know anything, but which [32] can only serve, as a correlatum of the unity of apperception, for the unity of the manifold in sensuous intuition, by means of which the understanding unites the manifold into the concept of an object. This transcendental object cannot be separated from the sensuous data, because in that case nothing would remain by which it could be   [251] thought. It is not therefore an object of knowledge in itself, but only the representation of phenomena, under the concept of an object in general, which can be defined by the manifold of sensuous intuition.

For this very reason the categories do not represent a peculiar object, given to the understanding only, but serve only to define the transcendental object (the concept of something in general) by that which is given us through the senses, in order thus to know empirically phenomena under the concepts of objects.

What then is the cause why people, not satisfied with the substratum of sensibility, have added to the phenomena the noumena, which the understanding only is supposed to be able to realise? It is this, that sensibility and its sphere, that is the sphere of phenomena, is so limited by the understanding itself that it should not refer to things by themselves, but only to the mode in which things appear to us, in accordance with our own subjective qualification. This was the result of the whole transcendental æsthetic, and it really follows quite naturally from the concept of a phenomenon in general, that something must correspond to it, which in itself is not a phenomenon, because a phenomenon cannot be anything by itself, apart from our mode of representation. Unless therefore   [252] we are to move in a constant circle, we must admit that the very word *phenomenon* indicates a relation to something the immediate representation of which is no doubt sensuous, but which nevertheless, even without this qualification of our sensibility (on which the form of our intuition is founded) must be something by itself, that is an object independent of our sensibility.

Hence arises the concept of a noumenon, which however is not positive, nor a definite knowledge of anything, but which implies only the thinking of something, without taking any account of the form of sensuous intuition. But in order that a noumenon may signify a real object that can be distinguished from all phenomena, it is not enough that I should free my thought of all conditions of sensuous intuition, but I must besides have some reason for admitting another kind of intuition besides the sensuous, in which such an object can be given; otherwise my thought would be empty, however free it may be from contradictions. It is true

---

[32] Read *welches* instead of *welcher*.

that we were not able to prove that the sensuous is the only possible intuition, though it is so for us: but neither could we prove that another kind of intuition was possible; and although our thought may take no account of any sensibility, the question always remains whether, after that, it is not a mere form of a concept, and whether any real [253] object would thus be left.

The object to which I refer the phenomenon in general is the transcendental object, that is, the entirely indefinite thought of something in general. This cannot be called the noumenon, for I know nothing of what it is by itself, and have no conception of it, except as the object of sensuous intuition in general, which is therefore the same for all phenomena. I cannot lay hold of it by any of the categories, for these are valid for empirical intuitions only, in order to bring them under the concept of an object in general. A pure use of the categories is no doubt possible, that is, not self-contradictory, but it has no kind of objective validity, because it refers to no intuition to which it is meant to impart the unity of an object. The categories remain for ever mere functions of thought by which no object can be given to me, but by which I can only think whatever may be given to me in intuition.]

If all thought (by means of categories) is taken away from empirical knowledge, no knowledge of any object remains, because nothing can be thought by mere intuition, and the mere fact that there is within me an affection of my sensibility, establishes in no way any relation of such a representation to any object. If, on the contrary, all intuition is taken away, there always remains the form of thought, that is, the [254] mode of determining an object for the manifold of a possible intuition. In this sense the categories may be said to extend further than sensuous intuition, because they can think objects in general without any regard to the special mode of sensibility in which they may be given; but they do not thus prove a larger sphere of objects, because we cannot admit that such objects can be given, without admitting the possibility of some other but sensuous intuition, for which we have no right whatever.

I call a concept problematic, if it is not self-contradictory, and if, as limiting other concepts, it is connected with other kinds of knowledge, while its objective reality cannot be known in any way. Now the concept of a noumenon, that is of a thing which can never be thought as an object of the senses, but only as a thing by itself (by the pure understanding), is not self-contradictory, because we cannot maintain that sensibility is the only form of intuition. That concept is also necessary, to prevent sensuous intuition from extending to things by themselves; that is, in order to limit the objective validity of sensuous knowledge (for all the rest to which sensuous intuition does not extend is called nou- [255] menon, for the very purpose of showing that sensuous knowledge cannot extend its domain over everything that can be thought by the understanding). But, after all, we cannot understand the possibility of such noumena, and whatever lies beyond the sphere of phenomena is (to us) empty; that is, we have an understanding which *problematically* extends beyond that sphere, but no intuition, nay not even the conception of a possible intuition, by which, outside the field of sensibility, objects could be given to us, and our understanding could extend beyond that sensibility in its assertory use. The concept of a noumenon is therefore merely limitative, and intended to keep the claims of sensibility within proper bounds, therefore of negative use only. But it is not a mere arbitrary fiction, but closely connected with the limitation of sensibility, though incapable of adding anything positive to the sphere of the senses.

A real division of objects into phenomena and noumena, and of the world into a sensible and intelligible world (in a positive sense),[33] is therefore quite inadmissible, although concepts may very well be divided into sensuous and intellectual. For no objects can be assigned to these intellectual concepts, nor can they be represented as objectively valid. If we drop the senses, how are we to make it conceivable that   [256] our categories (which would be the only remaining concepts for noumena) have any meaning at all, considering that, in order to refer them to any object, something more must be given than the mere unity of thought, namely, a possible intuition, to which the categories could be applied? With all this the concept of a noumenon, if taken as problematical only, remains not only admissible, but, as a concept to limit the sphere of sensibility, indispensable. In this case, however, it is not a particular *intelligible object* for *our* understanding, but an understanding to which it could belong is itself a problem, if we ask how it could know an object, not discursively by means of categories, but intuitively, and yet in a nonsensuous intuition,—a process of which we could not understand even the bare possibility. Our understanding thus acquires a kind of negative extension, that is, it does not become itself limited by sensibility, but, on the contrary, limits it, by calling things by themselves (not considered as phenomena) noumena. In doing this, it immediately proceeds to prescribe limits to itself, by admitting that it cannot know these noumena by means of the categories, but can only think of them under the name of something unknown.

In the writings of modern philosophers, however, I meet with a totally different use of the terms of *mundus sensibilis* and *intelligibilis*,[34] totally different from the meaning assigned to these terms by the ancients.   [257] Here all difficulty seems to disappear. But the fact is, that there remains nothing but mere word-mongery. In accordance with this, some people have been pleased to call the whole of phenomena, so far as they are seen, the world of sense; but so far as their connection, according to general laws of the understanding, is taken into account, the world of the understanding. Theoretical astronomy, which only teaches the actual observation of the starry heavens, would represent the former; contemplative astronomy, on the contrary (taught according to the Copernican system, or, it may be, according to Newton's laws of gravitation), the latter, namely,

---

[33] Addition of the Second Edition.
[34] An additional note is found in the Second Edition.

a purely intelligible world. But this twisting of words is a mere sophistical excuse, in order to avoid a troublesome question, by changing its meaning according to one's own convenience. Understanding and reason may be applied to phenomena, but it is very questionable whether they can be applied at all to an object which is not a phenomenon, but a noumenon; and it is this, when the object is represented as purely intelligible, that is, as given to the understanding only, and not to the senses. The question therefore is whether, besides the empirical use of the understanding (even in the Newtonian view of the world), a transcendental use is possible, referring to the noumenon, as its object; and that question we have answered decidedly in the negative.

When *we* therefore say that the senses represent objects to us [258] as they *appear*, and the understanding as they *are*, the latter is not to be taken in a transcendental, but in a purely empirical meaning, namely, as to how they, as objects of experience, must be represented, according to the regular connection of phenomena, and not according to what they may be, as objects of the pure understanding, apart from their relation to possible experience, and therefore to our senses. This will always remain unknown to us; nay, we shall never know whether such a transcendental and exceptional knowledge is possible at all, at least as comprehended under our ordinary categories. With us understanding and sensibility cannot determine objects, unless they are joined together. If we separate them, we have intuitions without concepts, or concepts without intuitions, in both cases representations which we cannot refer to any definite object.

If, after all these arguments, anybody should still hesitate to abandon the purely transcendental use of the categories, let him try an experiment with them for framing any synthetical proposition. An analytical proposition does not in the least advance the understanding, which, as in such a proposition it is only concerned with what is already thought in the concept, does not ask whether the concept in itself has any reference to objects, or expresses only the unity of thought in general (this [259] completely ignoring the manner in which an object may be given). The understanding in fact is satisfied if it knows what it contained in the concept of an object; it is indifferent as to the object to which the concept may refer. But let him try the experiment with any synthetical and so-called transcendental proposition, as for instance, 'Everything that exists, exists as a substance, or as a determination inherent in it,' or 'Everything contingent exists as an effect of some other thing, namely, its cause,' etc. Now I ask, whence can the understanding take these synthetical propositions, as the concepts are to apply, not to some possible experience, but to things by themselves (noumena)? Where is that third term to be found which is always required for a synthetical proposition, in order thus to join concepts which have no logical (analytical) relation with each other? It will be impossible to prove such a proposition, nay even to justify the possibility of any such pure assertion, without appealing to the empirical use of the understanding, and thus renouncing entirely the so-called pure and nonsensuous judgment. There are no principles therefore according to which the concepts of pure and merely intelligible objects could ever be applied, because we cannot imagine any way in which they could be given, and the problematic thought, which leaves a place open to them, serves only, like empty space, to limit the sphere of empirical principles, without containing or indicating any other object of knowledge,   [260] lying beyond that sphere.

.   .   .

TRANSCENDENTAL LOGIC—SECOND DIVISION:

Transcendental Dialectic

.   .   .

A. *Of Reason in General*

All our knowledge begins with the senses, proceeds thence to the understanding, and ends with reason. There is nothing higher than reason, for working up the material of intuition, and comprehending it under the highest unity of thought. As it here becomes necessary   [299] to give a definition of that highest faculty of knowledge, I begin to feel considerable misgivings. There is of reason, as there is of the understanding, a purely formal, that is logical use, in which no account is taken of the contents of knowledge; but there is also a real use, in so far as reason itself contains the origin of certain concepts and principles, which it has not borrowed either from the senses or from the understanding. The former faculty has been long defined by logicians as the faculty of mediate conclusions, in contradistinction to immediate ones (*consequentiae immediatae*); but this does not help us to understand the latter, which itself produces concepts. As this brings us face to face with the division of reason into a logical and a transcendental faculty, we must look for a higher concept for this source of knowledge, to comprehend both concepts: though, according to the analogy of the concepts of the understanding, we may expect that the logical concept will give us the key to the transcendental, and that the table of the functions of the former will give us the genealogical outline of the concepts of reason.

In the first part of our transcendental logic we defined the understanding as the *faculty of rules*, and we now distinguish reason from it, by calling it the *faculty of principles*.   [300]

The term *principle* is ambiguous, and signifies commonly some kind of knowledge only that may be used as a principle, though in itself, and according to its origin, it is no principle at all. Every general proposition, even though it may have been derived from experience (by induction), may serve as a major in a syllogism of reason; but it is not on that account a principle. Mathematical axioms, as, for instance, that between two points there can be only one straight line, constitute even general knowledge *a priori*, and may therefore, with reference to the cases which can be brought under them, rightly be called principles. Nevertheless it would be wrong to say, that this property of a straight line, in general and by itself, is known to us from principles, for it is known from pure intuition only.

I shall therefore call it knowledge from principles, whenever we know the particular in the general, by means of concepts. Thus every syllogism of reason is a form of deducing some kind of knowledge from a principle, because the major always contains a concept which enables us to know, according to a principle, everything that can be comprehended under the conditions of that concept. As every general knowledge may serve as a major in such a syllogism, and as the understanding supplies such general propositions *a priori*, these no doubt may, with reference to their possible use, be called principles. [301]

But, if we consider these principles of the pure understanding in themselves, and according to their origin, we find that they are anything rather than knowledge from concepts. They would not even be possible *a priori*, unless we relied on pure intuition (in mathematics) or on conditions of a possible experience in general. That everything which happens has a cause, can by no means be concluded from the concept of that which happens; on the contrary, that very principle shows in what manner alone we can form a definite empirical concept of that which happens.

It is impossible therefore for the understanding to supply us with synthetical knowledge from concepts, and it is really that kind of knowledge which I call principles absolutely; while all general propositions may be called principles relatively.

It is an old desideratum, which at some time, however distant, may be realised, that, instead of the endless variety of civil laws, their principles might be discovered, for thus alone the secret might be found of what is called simplifying legislation. Such laws, however, are only limitations of our freedom under conditions by which it always agrees with itself; they refer to something which is entirely our own work, and of which we ourselves can be the cause, by means of these concepts. But that objects in themselves, as for instance material nature, should be subject to principles, and be determined according to mere concepts, [302] is something, if not impossible, at all events extremely contradictory. But be that as it may (for on this point we have still all investigations before us), so much at least is clear, that knowledge from principles (by itself) is something totally different from mere knowledge of the understanding, which, in the form of a principle, may no doubt precede other knowledge, but which by itself (in so far as it is synthetical) is not based on mere thought, nor contains anything general, according to concepts.

If the understanding is a faculty for producing unity among phenomena, according to rules, reason is the faculty for producing unity among the rules of the understanding, according to principles. Reason therefore never looks directly to experience, or to any object, but to the understanding, in order to impart *a priori* through concepts to its manifold kinds of knowledge a unity that may be called the unity of reason, and is very different from the unity which can be produced by the understanding.

This is a general definition of the faculty of reason, so far as it was possible to make it intelligible without the help of illustrations, which are to be given hereafter.

.   .   .

Book II: Of the Dialectical Conclusions of Pure Reason

CHAPTER I.   OF THE PARALOGISMS OF PURE REASON

The logical paralogism consists in the formal faultiness of a conclusion, without any reference to its contents. But a transcendental paralogism arises from a transcendental cause, which drives us to a formally false conclusion. Such a paralogism, therefore, depends most likely on the very nature of human reason, and produces an illusion which is inevitable, though not insoluble.

We now come to a concept which was not inserted in our general list of transcendental concepts, and yet must be reckoned with them, without however changing that table in the least, or proving it to be deficient. This is the concept, or, if the term is preferred, the judgment, *I think*. It is easily seen, however, that this concept is the vehicle of all concepts in general, therefore of transcendental concepts also, being always comprehended among them, and being itself transcendental also, though without any claim to a special title, inasmuch as it serves only to introduce all thought, as belonging to consciousness. However free that concept may be from all that is empirical (impressions of the senses), it serves nevertheless to distinguish two objects within the nature of our   [342] faculty of representation. *I*, as thinking, am an object of the internal sense, and am called soul. That which is an object of the external senses is called body. The term *I*, as a thinking being, signifies the object of psychology, which may be called the rational science of the soul, supposing that we want to know nothing about the soul except what, independent of all experience (which determines that I more especially and *in concreto*), can be deduced from the concept of I, so far as it is present in every act of thought.

Now the rational science of the soul is really such an undertaking; for if the smallest empirical element of my thought or any particular perception of my internal state were mixed up with the sources from which that science derives its materials, it would be an empirical, and no longer a purely rational science of the soul. There is therefore a pretended science, founded on the single proposition of *I think*, and the soundness or unsoundness of which may well be examined in this place, according to the principles of transcendental philosophy. It should not be objected that even in that proposition, which expresses the perception of oneself, I have an internal experience, and that therefore the rational science of the soul, which is founded on it, can never be quite pure, but rests,   [343] to a certain extent, on an empirical principle. For this inner perception is nothing more than the mere apperception, *I think*, without which even all transcendental concepts would be impossible, in which we really say, I think the substance, I think the cause, etc. This internal experience in general and its possibility, or perception in general and its relation to other perceptions, there being no special distinction or empirical determination of it, cannot be regarded as empirical knowledge, but must be regarded as knowledge of the empirical in general, and falls therefore under the investigation of the possibility of all experience, which investigation is certainly transcendental. The smallest object of perception (even pleasure and pain), if added to the general representation of self-consciousness, would at once change rational into empirical psychology.

I think is, therefore, the only text of rational psychology, out of which it must evolve all its wisdom. It is easily seen that this thought, if it is to be applied to any object (my self), cannot contain any but transcendental predicates, because the smallest empirical predicate would spoil the rational purity of the science, and its independence of all experience.

We shall therefore follow the thread of the categories, with this   [344] difference, however, that as here the first thing which is given is a thing, the I, a thinking being, we must begin with the category of substance, by which a thing in itself is represented, and then proceed backwards, though without changing the respective order of the categories, as given before in our table. The topic of the rational science of the soul, from which has to be derived whatever else that science may contain, is therefore the following.

I

The Soul is *substance*.

II

As regards its quality, *simple*.

III

As regards the different times in which it exists, numerically identical, that is *unity* (not plurality).

IV

It is in relation to *possible* objects in space.[35]

---

[35] The reader, who may not guess at once the psychological purport of these transcendental and abstract terms, or understand why the latter attribute of the soul belongs to the category of existence, will find their full explanation and justification in the sequel. Moreover, I have to apologise for the many

All concepts of pure psychology arise from these elements, [345] simply by way of combination, and without the admixture of any other principle. This substance, taken simply as the object of the internal sense, gives us the concept of *immateriality;* and as simple substance, that of *incorruptibility;* its identity, as that of an intellectual substance, gives us *personality;* and all these three together, *spirituality;* its relation to objects in space give us the concept of *commercium* (intercourse) with *bodies;* the pure psychology thus representing the thinking substance as the principle of life in matter, that is, as soul (*anima*), and as the ground of *animality;* which again, as restricted by spirituality, gives us the concept of *immortality.*

To these concepts refer four paralogisms of a transcendental psychology, which is falsely supposed to be a science of pure reason, concerning the nature of our thinking being. We can, however, use as the foundation of such a science nothing but the single, and in itself perfectly empty, representation of the *I*, of which we cannot even say [346] that it is a concept, but merely a consciousness that accompanies all concepts. By this *I*, or *he*, or *it* (the thing), which thinks, nothing is represented beyond a transcendental subject of thoughts $= x$, which is known only through the thoughts that are its predicates, and of which, apart from them, we can never have the slightest concept, so that we are really turning round it in a perpetual circle, having already to use its representation, before we can form any judgment about it. And this inconvenience is really inveitable, because consciousness in itself is not so much a representation, distinguishing a particular object, but really a form of representation in general, in so far as it is to be called knowledge, of which alone I can say that I think something by it.

It must seem strange, however, from the very beginning, that the condition under which I think, and which therefore is a property of my own subject only, should be valid at the same time for everything which thinks, and that, depending on a proposition which seems to be empirical, we should venture to found the apodictical and general judgment, namely, that everything which thinks is such as the voice of my own consciousness declares it to be within me. The reason of it is, that we are constrained to attribute *a priori* to things all the qualities which form the conditions, under which alone we are able to think them. [347] Now it is impossible for me to form the smallest representation of a thinking being by any external experience, but I can do it through self-consciousness only. Such objects therefore are nothing but a transference of my own consciousness to other things, which thus, and thus only, can be represented as thinking beings. The proposition *I think* is

---

Latin expressions which, contrary to good taste, have crept in instead of their native equivalents, not only here, but throughout the whole of the work. My only excuse is, that I thought it better to sacrifice something of the elegance of language, rather than to throw any impediments in the way of real students, by the use of inaccurate and obscure expressions.

used in this case, however, as problematical only; not so far as it may contain the perception of an existence (the Cartesian, *cogito, ergo sum*), but with regard to its mere possibility, in order to see what properties may be deduced from such a simple proposition with regard to its subject, whether such subject exists or not.

If our knowledge of thinking beings in general, so far as it is derived from pure reason, were founded on more than the *cogito*, and if we made use at the same time of observations on the play of our thoughts and the natural laws of the thinking self, derived from them, we should have before us an empirical psychology, which would form a kind of physiology of the internal sense, and perhaps explain its manifestations, but would never help us to understand such properties as do not fall under any possible experience (as, for instance, simplicity), or to teach apodictically anything touching the nature of thinking beings in general. It would not therefore be a rational psychology.

As the proposition *I think* (taken problematically) contains [348] the form of every possible judgment of the understanding, and accompanies all categories as their vehicle, it must be clear that the conclusions to be drawn from it can only contain a transcendental use of the understanding, which declines all admixture of experience, and of the achievements of which, after what has been said before, we cannot form any very favourable anticipations. We shall therefore follow it, with a critical eye, through all the predicaments of pure psychology.[36]

[*The First Paralogism of Substantiality*

That the representation of which is the absolute subject of our judgments, and cannot be used therefore as the determination of any other thing, is the *substance*.

I, as a thinking being, am the absolute subject of all my possible judgments, and this representation of myself can never be used as the predicate of any other thing.

Therefore I, as a thinking being (Soul), am *Substance*.

Criticism of the First Paralogism of Pure [37] *Psychology*

We showed in the analytical portion of transcendental logic, that pure categories, and among them that of substance, have in themselves no objective meaning, unless they rest on some intuition, and are applied

---

[36] All that follows from here to the beginning of the second chapter, differs in the Second Edition.
[37] Afterwards *transcendental* instead of *pure*.

to the manifold of such intuitions as functions of synthetical [349]
unity. Without this they are merely functions of a judgment without contents. I may say of everything, that it is a substance, so far as I distinguish it from what are mere predicates and determinations. Now in
all our thinking the I is the subject, in which thoughts are inherent as
determinations only; nor can that I ever be used as a determination of
any other thing. Thus everybody is constrained to look upon himself
as the substance, and on thinking as the accidents only of his being, and
determinations of his state.

But what use are we to make of such a concept of a substance? That
I, as a thinking being, *continue* for myself, and naturally neither *arise*
nor *perish*, is no legitimate deduction from it; and yet this conclusion
would be the only advantage that could be gained from the concept of
the substantiality of my own thinking subject, and, but for that, I could
do very well without it.

So far from being able to deduce these properties from the pure
category of substance, we have on the contrary to observe the permanency of an object in our experience and then lay hold of this permanency, if we wish to apply to it the empirically useful concept of substance. In this case, however, we had no experience to lay hold of, but
have only formed a deduction from the concept of the relation [350]
which all thinking has to the I, as the common subject to which it belongs. Nor should we, whatever we did, succeed by any certain observation in proving such permanency. For though the I exists in all thoughts,
not the slightest intuition is connected with that representation, by
which it might be distinguished from other objects of intuition. We may
very well perceive therefore that this representation appears again and
again in every act of thought, but not that it is a constant and permanent
intuition, in which thoughts, as being changeable, come and go.

Hence it follows that in the first syllogism of transcendental psychology
reason imposes upon us an apparent knowledge only, by representing
the constant logical subject of thought as the knowledge of the real
subject in which that knowledge inheres. Of that subject, however, we
have not and cannot have the slightest knowledge, because consciousness is that which alone changes representations into thoughts, and in
which therefore, as the transcendental subject, all our perceptions must
be found. Beside this logical meaning of the I, we have no knowledge
of the subject in itself, which forms the substratum and foundation of
it and of all our thoughts. In spite of this, the proposition that the soul is a
substance may well be allowed to stand, if only we see that this concept
cannot help us on in the least or teach us any of the ordinary conclusions
of rationalising psychology, as, for instance, the everlasting con- [351]
tinuance of the soul amid all changes and even in death, and that it therefore signifies a substance in idea only, and not in reality.

.   .   .

CONSIDERATION ON THE WHOLE OF PURE PSYCHOLOGY, AS [381]
AFFECTED BY THESE PARALOGISMS

If we compare the science of the soul, as the physiology of the internal sense, with the science of the body, as a physiology of the objects of external senses, we find, besides many things which in both must be known empirically, this important difference, that in the latter many things can be known *a priori* from the mere concept of an extended and impermeable being, while in the former nothing can be known *a priori* and synthetically from the concept of a thinking being. The cause is this. Though both are phenomena, yet the phenomena of the external sense have something permanent, which suggests a substratum of varying determinations, and consequently a synthetical concept, namely, that of space, and of a phenomenon in space; while time, the only form of our internal intuition, has nothing permanent, and makes us to know the change of determinations only, but not the determinable object. For in what we call soul there is a continuous flux, and nothing permanent, except it may be (if people will so have it) the simple *I*, so simple because this representation has no contents, consequently nothing manifold, so that it seems to represent, or more accurately to indicate, a simple object. This I or Ego would have to be an intuition, which, being [382] presupposed in all thought (before all experience), might as an intuition *a priori* supply synthetical propositions, if it should be possible to get any knowledge by pure reason of the nature of a thinking being in general. But this I is neither an intuition nor a concept of any object, but the mere form of consciousness which can accompany both classes of representations, and impart to them the character of knowledge, provided something else be given in intuition which supplies matter for a representation of an object. Thus we see that the whole of rational psychology is impossible as transcending the powers of human reason, and nothing remains to us but to study our soul under the guidance of experience, and to keep ourselves within the limits of questions which do not go beyond the line where the material can be supplied by possible internal experience.

But although rational psychology is of no use in extending our knowledge, but as such is made up of paralogisms only, we cannot deny to it an important negative utility, if it does not pretend to be more than a critical investigation of our dialectical syllogisms, as framed by our common and natural reason.

What purpose can be served by psychology founded on pure [383] principles of reason? Its chief purpose is meant to be to guard our thinking self against the danger of materialism. This purpose however is answered, as we have shown, by the concept which reason gives of our thinking self. For, so far from there being any fear lest, if matter be taken away, all thought, and even the existence of thinking beings might vanish, it has been on the contrary clearly shown that, if we take away the thinking subject, the whole material world would vanish, because it is nothing but a phenomenon in the sensibility of our own subject, and a certain class of its representations.

It is true that I do not know thus this thinking self any better according to its qualities, nor can I perceive its permanence, or even the independence of its existence from the problematical transcendental substratum of external phenomena, both being necessarily unknown to us. But as it is nevertheless possible that I may find reason, from other than purely speculative causes, to hope for an independent, and, during every possible change of my states, permanently abiding existence of my thinking nature, much is gained if, though I freely confess my own ignorance, I can nevertheless repel the dogmatical attacks of a speculative opponent, showing to him that he can never know more of the [384] nature of the subject, in order to deny the possibility of my expectations, than I can know, in order to cling to them.

Three dialectical questions, which form the real object of all rational psychology, are founded on this transcendental illusion of our psychological concepts, and cannot be answered except by means of the considerations in which we have just been engaged, namely, (1) the question of the possibility of the association of the soul with an organic body, that is, of animality and the state of the soul in the life of man; (2) the question of the beginning of that association of the soul at the time and before the time of our birth; (3) the question of the end of that association of the soul at and after the time of death (immortality).

What I maintain is, that all the difficulties which we imagine to exist in these questions, and with which, as dogmatical objections, people wish to give themselves an air of deeper insight into the nature of things than the common understanding can ever claim, rest on a mere illusion, which leads us to hypostasise what exists in thought only, and to accept it in the same quality in which it is thought as a real object, outside the thinking subject, taking in fact extension, which is phenomenal only, for a quality of external things, existing without our sensibility also, [385] and movement as their effect, taking place by itself also, and independently of our senses. For matter, the association of which with the soul causes so much misgiving, is nothing but a mere form, or a certain mode of representing an unknown object by that intuition which we call the external sense. There may, therefore, well be something outside us to which the phenomenon which we call matter corresponds; though in its quality of phenomenon it cannot be outside us, but merely as a thought within us, although that thought represents it through the external sense as existing outside us. Matter, therefore, does not signify a class of substances totally heterogeneous and different from the object of the internal sense (the soul), but only the different nature of the phenomenal appearance of objects (in themselves unknown to us), the representations of which we call external, as compared with those which we assign to the internal sense, although, like other thoughts, those external representations also belong to the thinking subject only. They possess however this illusion that, as they represent objects in space, they seem to separate themselves from the soul and to move outside it, although even the space, in which they are seen, is nothing but a representation of which no homogeneous original can ever be found outside the soul. The question therefore is no longer as to the possibility of an association of the soul with other known and foreign substances outside us, but only as [386] to the connection of the representations of the internal sense with the modifications of our external sensibility, and how these can be connected with each other according to constant laws, and acquire cohesion in experience.

So long as we connect internal and external phenomena with each other as mere representations in our experience, there is nothing irrational, nor anything to make the association of both senses to appear strange. As soon however as we hypostatise the external phenomena, looking upon them no longer as representations, but *as things existing by themselves and outside us, with the same quality in which they exist inside us*, and referring to our own thinking subject their acts which they, as phenomena, show in their mutual relation, the effective causes outside us assume a character which will not harmonise with their effects within us, because that character refers to the external senses only, but the effects to the internal sense, both being entirely unhomogeneous, though united in the same subject. We then have no other external effects but changes of place, and no forces but tendencies, which have for their effects relations in space only. Within us, on the contrary, those effects are mere thoughts, without any relations of space, movement, shape, or local determination between them; and we entirely lose the thread [387] of the causes in the effects which ought to show themselves in the internal sense. We ought to consider therefore that bodies are not objects by themselves which are present to us, but a mere appearance of we do not know what unknown object, and that movement likewise is not the effect of that unknown cause, but only the appearance of its influence on our senses. Both are not something outside us, but only representation within us, and consequently it is not the movement of matter which produces representations within us, but that motion itself (and matter also, which makes itself known through it) is representation only. Our whole self-created difficulty turns on this, how and why the representations of our sensibility are so connected with each other that those which we call external intuitions can, according to empirical laws, be represented as objects outside us; a question which is entirely free from the imagined difficulty of explaining the origin of our representations from totally heterogeneous efficient causes, existing outside us, the confusion arising from our mistaking the phenomenal appearance of an unknown cause for the very cause outside us. In judgments in which there is a misapprehension confirmed by long habit, it is impossible to bring its correction at

once to that clearness which can be produced in other cases, where   [388]
no inevitable illusion confuses our concept. Out attempt therefore at freeing reason from these sophistical theories can hardly claim as yet that per-
spicuity which would render it perfectly satisfactory. I hope however to
arrive at greater lucidity in the following manner.

All *objections* may be divided into *dogmatical, critical* and *sceptical*.
The dogmatical attacks the *proposition*, the critical the *proof* of a proposition. The former presupposes an insight into the peculiar nature of the
object in order to be able to assert the contrary of what the proposition
asserts. It is therefore itself dogmatical, and pretends to know the peculiar
nature of the object in question better than the opponent. The critical
objection, as it says nothing about the worth or worthlessness of the
proposition, and attacks the proof only, need not know the object itself
better, or claim a better knowledge of it. All it wants to show is, that a
proposition is not well grounded, not that it is false. The sceptical objection, lastly, places assertion and denial side by side, as of equal value,
taking one or the other now as dogma, and now as denial; and being thus
in appearance dogmatical on both sides, it renders every judgment   [389]
on the object impossible. Both the dogmatical and sceptical objections
must pretend to so much knowledge of their object as is necessary in
order to assert or deny anything about it. The critical objection, on the
contrary, wishes only to show that something purely futile and fanciful
has been used in support of a proposition, and thus upsets a theory
by depriving it of its pretended foundation, without wishing to establish
itself anything else about the nature of the object.

According to the ordinary concepts of our reason with regard to the
association between our thinking subject and the things outside us, we
are dogmatical, and look upon them as real objects, existing independently of ourselves, in accordance with a certain transcendental dualism
which does not reckon external phenomena as representations belonging
to the subject, but places them, as they are given us in sensuous intuition,
as objects outside us and entirely separated from the thinking subject.
This mere assumption is the foundation of all theories on the association
between soul and body. It is never asked whether this objective reality of
phenomena is absolutely true, but it is taken for granted, and the only
question seems to be, how it is to be explained and understood. The
three systems which are commonly suggested, and which in   [390]
fact are alone possible, are those, 1st, of *physical influence,* 2nd, of
pre-established harmony and 3rd, of *supernatural assistance*.

The second and third explanations of the association between soul and
matter arise from objections to the first, which is that of the ordinary understanding, the objection being, that what appears as matter cannot by
its immediate influence be the cause of representations, these being a
totally heterogeneous class of effects. Those who start this objection cannot understand by the objects of the external senses matter, conceived
as phenomenon only, and therefore itself a mere representation produced
by whatever external objects. For in that case they would really say that

the representations of external objects (phenomena) cannot be the external causes of the representations in our mind, which would be a meaningless objection, because nobody would think of taking for an external cause what he knows to be a mere representation. According to our principles the object of their theory can only be, that that which is the true (transcendental) object of our external senses cannot be the cause of those representations (phenomena) which we mean by the name of matter. As no one has any right to say that he knows [391] anything of the transcendental cause of the representations of our external senses, their assertion is entirely groundless. And if the pretended reformers of the doctrine of physical influence represent, according to the ordinary views of transcendental dualism, matter, as such, as a thing by itself (not simply as a mere phenomenal appearance of an unknown thing), and then proceed in their objections to show that such an external object, which shows no causality but that of movements, can never be the efficient cause of representations, but that a third being must intervene in order to produce, if not reciprocal action, at least correspondence and harmony between the two, they would really begin their refutation by admitting in their dualism the πρῶτον ψεῦδος of a physical influence, and thus refute by their objection, not so much the physical influence as their own dualistic premisses. For all the difficulties with regard to a possible connection between a thinking nature and matter arise, without exception, from that too readily admitted dualistic representation, namely, that matter, as such, is not phenomenal, that is, a mere representation of the mind to which an unknown object corresponds, but the object itself, such as it exists outside us, and independent of all sensibility. [392]

It is impossible, therefore, to start a dogmatical objection against the commonly received theory of a physical influence. For if the opponent were to say that matter and its movements are purely phenomenal and therefore mere representations, the only difficulty remaining to him would be that the unknown object of our senses could not be the cause of our representations, and this he has no right to say, because no one is able to determine what an unknown object may or may not be able to effect; and, according to our former arguments, he must necessarily admit this transcendental idealism, unless he wishes to hypostasise mere representations and place them outside himself as real things.

What is quite possible, however, is to raise a well-founded *critical objection* to the commonly received opinion of a physical influence. For the pretended association between two kinds of substances, the one thinking, the other extended, rests on a coarse dualism, and changes the latter, though they are nothing but representations of the thinking subject, into things existing by themselves. Thus the misunderstood physical influence may be entirely upset by showing that the proof which was to establish it, was surreptitiously obtained, and therefore, valueless.

The notorious problem, therefore, as to a possible association between the thinking and the extended, would, when all that is purely imaginative

is deducted, come to this, *how external intuition,* namely, that   [393]
of space (or what fills space, namely, form and movement), *is possible
in any thinking subject?* To this question, however, no human being
can return an answer, and instead of attempting to fill this gap in our
knowledge, all we can do is to indicate it by ascribing external phenomena to a transcendental object as the cause of this class of representations, but which we shall never know, nor be able to form any
concept of. In all practical questions we treat phenomena as objects by
themselves, without troubling ourselves about the first cause of their
possibility (as phenomena). But as soon as we go beyond, the concept
of a transcendental object becomes inevitable.

The decision of all the discussions on the state of a thinking being,
before this association with matter (life) or after the ceasing of such
association (death), depends on the remarks which we have just made
on the association between the thinking and the extended. The opinion
that the thinking subject was able to think before any association with
bodies, would assume the following form, that before the beginning of
that kind of sensibility through which something appears to us   [394]
in space, the same transcendental objects, which in our present state
appear as bodies, could have been seen in a totally different way. The
other opinion that, after the cessation of its association with the material
world, the soul could continue to think, would be expressed as follows:
that, if that kind of sensibility through which transcendental and, for
the present, entirely unknown objects appear to us as a material world,
should cease, it would not follow that thereby all intuition of them would
be removed: it being quite possible that the same unknown objects
should continue to be known by the thinking subject, although no longer
in the quality of bodies.

Now it is quite true that no one can produce from speculative principles the smallest ground for such an assertion, or do more than presuppose its possibility, but neither can any valid dogmatical objection
be raised against it. For whoever would attempt to do so, would know
neither more nor less than I myself, or anybody else, about the absolute
and internal cause of external and material phenomena. As he cannot
pretend to know on what the reality of external phenomena in our present
state (in life) really rests, neither can he know that the condition of all
external intuition, or the thinking subject itself, will cease afer this state
(in death).   [395]

We thus see that all the wrangling about the nature of a thinking
being, and its association with the material world, arises simply from our
filling the gap, due to our ignorance, with paralogisms of reason, and by
changing thoughts into things and hypostasising them. On this an imaginary science is built up, both by those who assert and by those who deny,
some pretending to know about objects of which no human being has any
conception, while others make their own representations to be objects,
all turning round in a constant circle of ambiguities and contradictions.
Nothing but a sober, strict, and just criticism can free us of this dogmat-

ical illusion, which, through theories and systems, deceives so many by an imaginary happiness. It alone can limit our speculative pretensions to the sphere of possible experience, and this not by a shallow scoffing at repeated failures or by pious sighs over the limits of our reason, but by a demarcation made according to well-established principles, writing the *nihil ulterious* with perfect assurance on those Herculean columns which Nature herself has erected, in order that the voyage of our reason should be continued so far only as the continuous shores of experience extend— shores which we can never forsake without being driven upon a [396] boundless ocean, which, after deceiving us again and again, makes us in the end cease all our laborious and tedious endeavours as perfectly hopeless.]

.   .   .

CHAPTER II. THE ANTIMONY OF PURE REASON

In the Introduction to this part of our work we showed that all the transcendental illusion of pure reason depended on three dialectical syllogisms, the outline of which is supplied to us by logic in the three formal kinds of the ordinary syllogism, in about the same way in which the logical outline of the categories was derived from the four [406] functions of all judgments. *The first class* of these rationalising syllogisms aimed at the unconditioned unity of the subjective conditions of all representations (of the subject or the soul) as corresponding to the *categorical* syllogisms of reason, the major of which, as the principle, asserts the relation of a predicate to a subject. *The second class* of the dialectical arguments will, therefore, in analogy with the *hypothetical* syllogisms, take for its object the unconditioned unity of the objective conditions in phenomenal appearance, while the *third class,* which has to be treated in the following chapter, will be concerned with the unconditioned unity of the objective conditions of the possibility of objects in general.

It is strange, however, that a transcendental paralogism caused a one-sided illusion only, with regard to our idea of the subject of our thought; and that it is impossible to find in mere concepts of reason the slightest excuse for maintaining the contrary. All the advantage is on the side of pneumatism, although it cannot hide the hereditary taint by which it evaporates into nought, when subjected to the ordeal of our critique.

The case is totally different when we apply reason to the *objective synthesis* of phenomena; here reason tries at first, with great plausibility, to establish its principle of unconditioned unity, but becomes soon [407] entangled in so many contradictions, that it must give up its pretensions with regard to cosmology also.

For here we are met by a new phenomenon in human reason, namely, a perfectly natural Antithetic, which is not produced by any artificial efforts, but into which reason falls by itself, and inevitably. Reason is no doubt preserved thereby from the slumber of an imaginary conviction, which is often produced by a purely one-sided illusion; but it is tempted at the same time, either to abandon itself to sceptical despair, or to assume a dogmatical obstinacy, taking its stand on certain assertions, without granting a hearing and doing justice to the arguments of the opponent. In both cases, a death-blow is dealt to sound philosophy, although in the former we might speak of the *Euthanasia* of pure reason.

Before showing the scenes of discord and confusion produced by the conflict of the laws (antinomy) of pure reason, we shall have to make a few remarks in order to explain and justify the method which we mean to follow in the treatment of this subject. I shall call all transcendental ideas, so far as they relate to the absolute totality in the synthesis of phenomena, *cosmical concepts,* partly, because of even this uncon- [408] ditioned totality on which the concept of the cosmical universe also rests (which is itself an idea only), partly, because they refer to the synthesis of phenomena only, which is empirical, while the absolute totality in the synthesis of the conditions of all possible things must produce an ideal of pure reason, totally different from the cosmical concept, although in a certain sense related to it. As therefore the paralogisms of pure reason formed the foundation for a dialectical psychology, the antinomy of pure reason will place before our eyes the transcendental principles of a pretended pure (rational) cosmology, not in order to show that it is valid and can be accepted, but, as may be guessed from the very name of the antinomy of reason, in order to expose it as an idea surrounded by deceptive and false appearances, and utterly irreconcileable with phenomena.

Section I

System of Cosmological Ideas

Before we are able to enumerate these ideas according to a principle and with systematic precision, we must bear in mind,

1st, That pure and transcendental concepts arise from the understanding only, and that reason does not in reality produce any [409] concept, but only *frees,* it may be, the *concept of the understanding* of the inevitable limitation of a possible experience, and thus tries to enlarge it, beyond the limits of experience, yet in connection with it. Reason does this by demanding for something that is given as conditioned, absolute totality on the side of the conditions (under which the understanding subjects all phenomena to the synthetical unity). It thus changes the category into a transcendental idea, in order to give absolute completeness to the empirical synthesis, by continuing it up to the unconditioned (which can never be met with in experience, but in the idea only). In doing this, reason follows the principle that, *if the conditioned is given, the whole sum of conditions, and therefore the absolutely unconditioned must be given likewise,* the former being impossible without the latter. Hence the transcendental ideas are in reality nothing but categories, enlarged till they reach the unconditioned, and those ideas must admit of being arranged in a table, according to the titles of the categories.

2ndly, Not all categories will lend themselves to this, but those only in which the synthesis constitutes a *series*, and a series of subordinated (not of co-ordinated) conditions. Absolute totality is demanded by reason, with regard to an ascending series of conditions only, not there- [410] fore when we have to deal with a descending line of consequences, or with an aggregate of co-ordinated conditions. For, with reference to something given as conditioned, conditions are presupposed and considered as given with it, while, on the other hand, as consequences do not render their conditions possible, but rather presuppose them, we need not, in proceeding to the consequences (or in descending from any given condition to the conditioned), trouble ourselves whether the series comes to an end or not, the question as to their totality being in fact no presupposition of reason whatever.

Thus we necessarily conceive time past up to a given moment, as given, even if not determinable by us. But with regard to time future, which is not a condition of arriving at time present, it is entirely indifferent, if we want to conceive the latter, what we may think about the former, whether we take it, as coming to an end somewhere, or as going on to infinity. Let us take the series, *m, n, o*, where *n* is given as conditioned by *m*, and at the same time as a condition of *o*. Let that series ascend from the conditioned *n* to its condition *m* (*l, k, i*, etc.), and descend from the condition *n* to the conditioned *o* (*p, q, r*, etc.). I must then presuppose the former series, in order to take *n* as given, and according to reason (the totality of conditions) *n* is possible only by means of that series, while its possibility depends in no way on the subse- [411] quent series, *o, p, q, r*, which therefore cannot be considered as given, but only as *dabilis*, capable of being given.

I shall call the synthesis of a series on the side of the conditions, beginning with the one nearest to a given phenomenon, and advancing to the more remote conditions, *regressive*; the other, which on the side of the conditioned advances from the nearest effect to the more remote ones, *progressive*. The former proceeds in *antecedentia*, the second in *consequentia*. Cosmological ideas therefore, being occupied with the totality of regressive synthesis, proceed in *antecedentia*, not in *consequentia*. If the latter should take place, it would be a gratuitous, not a necessary problem of pure reason, because for a complete comprehension of what is given us in experience we want to know the causes, but not the effects.

In order to arrange a table of ideas in accordance with the table of the categories, we must take, *first*, the two original *quanta* of all our intuition, time and space. Time is in itself a series (and the formal condition of all series), and in it, therefore, with reference to any given present, we have to distinguish *a priori* the *antecedentia* as conditions (the past) from the *consequentia* (the future). Hence the transcendental idea of the absolute totality of the series of conditions of anything [412] conditioned refers to time past only. The whole of time past is looked upon, according to the idea of reason, as a necessary condition of the given moment. With regard to space there is in it no difference between *progressus* and *regressus*, because all its parts exist together and form an aggregate, but *no series*. We can look upon the present moment, with reference to time past, as conditioned only, but never as condition, because this moment arises only through time past (or rather through the passing of antecedent time). But as the parts of space are not subordinate to one another, but co-ordinate, no part of it is in the condition of the possibility of another, nor does it, like time, constitute a series in itself. Nevertheless the synthesis by which we apprehend the many parts of space is successive, takes place in time, and contains a series. And as in that series of aggregated spaces (as, for instance, of feet in a rood) the spaces added to a given space a are always the *condition of the limit* of the preceding spaces, we ought to consider the *measuring* of a space also a synthesis of a series of conditions of something given as conditioned, with this difference only, that the side of the conditions is by   [413] itself not different from the other side which comprehends the conditioned, so that *regressus* and *progressus* seem to be the same in space. As however every part of space is limited only, and not given by another, we must look upon every limited space as conditioned also, so far as it presupposes another space as the condition of its limit, and so on. With reference to limitation therefore *progressus* in space is also *regressus*, and the transcendental idea of the absolute totality of the synthesis in the series of conditions applies to space also. I may ask then for the absolute totality of phenomena in space, quite as well as in time past, though we must wait to see whether an answer is ever possible.

Secondly, reality in space, that is, matter, is something conditioned, the parts of which are its internal conditions, and the parts of its parts, its remoter conditions. We have therefore here a regressive synthesis the absolute totality of which is demanded by reason, but which cannot take place except by a complete division, whereby the reality of matter dwindles away into nothing, or into that at least which is no longer matter, namely, the simple; consequently we have here also a series of conditions, and a progress to the unconditioned.

Thirdly, when we come to the categories of the real relation between phenomena, we find that the category of substance with its acci-   [414] dents does not lend itself to a transcendental idea; that is, reason has here no inducement to proceed regressively to conditions. We know that accidents, so far as they inhere in one and the same substance, are co-ordinated with each other, and do not constitute a series; and with reference to the substance, they are not properly subordinate to it, but are the mode of existence of the substance itself. The concept of the *substantial* might seem to be here an idea of transcendental reason. This, however, signifies nothing but the concept of the object in general, which *subsists*, so far as we think in it the transcendental subject only, without any predicates; and, as we are here speaking only of the unconditioned in the series of phenomena, it is clear that the substantial cannot be a part of it. The same applies to substances in community, which are aggregates only, without having an exponent of a series, since they are not subordinate to each other, as conditions of their possibility, in the same way as spaces were, the limits of which can never be determined by itself, but always through another space. There remains therefore only the category of *causality*, which offers a series of causes to a given effect, enabling us to ascend from the latter, as the conditioned, to the former as the conditions, and thus to answer the question of reason. [415]

Fourthly, the concepts of the possible, the real, and the necessary do not lead to any series, except so far as the *accidental* in existence must always be considered as conditioned, and point, according to a rule of the understanding, to a condition which makes it necessary to ascend to a higher condition, till reason finds at last, only, in the totality of that series, the unconditioned *necessity* which it requires.

If therefore we select those categories which necessarily imply a series in the synthesis of the manifold, we shall have no more than four cosmological ideas, according to the four titles of the categories.

I

Absolute completeness
of the composition
of the given whole of all phenomena.

II	III
Absolute completeness of the division of a given whole in phenomenal appearance.	Absolute completeness of the origination of a phenomenon in general.

IV

Absolute completeness
of the dependence of the existence
of the changeable in phenomenal appearance.

[416]

It should be remarked, *first*, that the idea of absolute totality refers to nothing else but the exhibition of phenomena, and not therefore to the pure concept, formed by the understanding, of a totality of things in general. Phenomena, therefore, are considered here as given, and reason postulates the absolute completeness of the conditions of their possibility, so far as these conditions constitute a series, that is, an absolutely (in every respect) complete synthesis, whereby phenomena could be exhibited according to the laws of the understanding.

Secondly, it is in reality the unconditioned alone which reason is looking for in the synthesis of conditions, continued regressively and serially, as it were a completeness in the series of premisses, which taken together require no further premisses. This *unconditioned* is always contained in *the absolute totality of a series,* as represented in imagination. But this absolutely complete synthesis is again an idea only, for it is impossible to know beforehand, whether such a synthesis be possible in phenomena. If we represent everything by means of pure concepts of the understanding only, and without the conditions of sensuous intuition, we might really say that of everything given as conditioned the whole series also of conditions, subordinated to each other, is given, for the conditioned is given through the conditions only. When we come to phenomena, however, we find a particular limitation of the mode in which conditions are given, namely, through the successive synthesis of the manifold [417] of intuition which should become complete by the *regressus.* Whether this completeness, however, is possible, with regard to sensuous phenomena, is still a question. But the idea of that completeness is no doubt contained in reason, without reference to the possibility or impossibility of connecting with it adequate empirical concepts. As therefore in the absolute totality of the regressive synthesis of the manifold in intuition (according to the categories which represent that totality as a series of conditions of something given as conditioned) the unconditioned is necessarily contained without attempting to determine whether and how such a totality be possible, reason here takes the road to start from the idea of totality, though her final aim is the *unconditioned,* whether of the whole series or of a part thereof.

This unconditioned may be either conceived as existing in the whole series only, in which all members without exception are conditioned and the whole of them only absolutely unconditioned—and in this case the *regressus* is called infinite—or the absolutely unconditioned is only a part of the series, the other members being subordinate to it, while it is itself conditioned by nothing else.[38] In the former case the series is without limits *a parte priori* (without a beginning), that is infinite; given [418] however as a whole in which the *regressus* is never complete, and can therefore be called infinite potentially only. In the latter case there is something that stands first in the series, which, with reference to time past, is called the *beginning of the world;* with reference to space, the *limit of the world;* with reference to the parts of a limited given whole, the *simple;* with reference to causes, absolute *spontaneity* (liberty); with reference to the existence of changeable things, the absolute *necessity of nature.*

We have two expressions, *world* and *nature,* which frequently run into each other. The first denotes the mathematical total of all phenomena and the totality of their synthesis of large and small in its progress whether by

---

[38] The absolute total of a series of conditions of anything given as conditioned, is itself always unconditioned; because there are no conditions beyond on which it could depend. Such an absolute total of a series is, however, an idea only, or rather a problematical concept, the possibility of which has to be investigated with reference to the mode in which the unconditioned, that is, in reality, the transcendental idea with which we are concerned, may be contained in it.

composition or division. That world, however, is called nature [39] if we look upon it as a dynamical whole, and consider not the aggrega- [419] tion in space and time, in order to produce a quantity, but the unity in the *existence* of phenomena. In this case the condition of that which happens is called *cause*, the unconditioned causality of the cause as phenomenal, *liberty*, while the conditioned causality, in its narrower meaning, is called *natural cause*. That of which the existence is conditioned is called *contingent*, that of which it is unconditioned, *necessary*. The unconditioned necessity of phenomena may be called *natural necessity*.

I have called the ideas, which we are at present discussing, cosmological, partly because we understand by *world* the totality of all phenomena, our ideas being directed to that only which is unconditioned among the phenomena; partly, because world, in its transcendental meaning, denotes the totality of all existing things, and we are concerned only with the completeness of the synthesis (although properly only in the *regressus* to the conditions). Considering, therefore, that all these [420] ideas are transcendent because, though not transcending in kind their object, namely, phenomena, but restricted to the world of sense (and excluded from all noumena) they nevertheless carry synthesis to a *degree* which transcends all possible experience, they may, according to my opinion, very properly be called *cosmical concepts*. With reference to the distinction, however, between the mathematically or the dynamically unconditioned at which the *regressus* aims, I might call the two former, in a narrower sense, *cosmical concepts* (macrocosmically or microcosmically) and the remaining two *transcendent concepts of nature*. This distinction, though for the present of no great consequence, may become important hereafter.

Section II

Antithetic of Pure Reason

If every collection of dogmatical doctrines is called *Thetic*, I may denote by *Antithetic*, not indeed dogmatical assertions of the opposite, but the conflict between different kinds of apparently dogmatical knowledge (*thesis cum antithesi*), to none of which we can ascribe a su- [421] perior claim to our assent. This antithetic, therefore, has nothing to do with one-sided assertions, but considers general knowledge of reason with reference to the conflict only that goes on in it, and its causes. The

---

[39] Nature, if taken *adjective* (*formaliter*), is meant to express the whole complex of the determinations of a thing, according to an inner principle of causality; while, if taken *substantive* (*materialiter*), it denotes the totality of phenomena, so far as they are all held together by an internal principle of causality. In the former meaning we speak of the nature of liquid matter, of fire, etc., using the word *adjective;* while, if we speak of the objects of nature, or of natural objects, we have in our mind the idea of a subsisting whole.

transcendental antithetic is in fact an investigation of the antinomy of pure reason, its causes and its results. If we apply our reason, not only to objects of experience, in order to make use of the principles of the understanding, but venture to extend it beyond the limit of experience, there arise rationalising or sophistical propositions, which can neither hope for confirmation nor need fear refutation from experience. Every one of them is not only in itself free from contradiction, but can point to conditions of its necessity in the nature of reason itself, only that, unfortunately, its opposite can produce equally valid and necessary grounds for its support.

The questions which naturally arise in such a Dialectic of pure reason are the following. 1. In what propositions is pure reason inevitably subject to an antinomy? 2. On what causes does this antinomy depend? 3. Whether, and in what way, reason may, in spite of this contradiction, find a way to certainty?

A dialectical proposition of pure reason must have this characteristic to distinguish it from all purely sophistical propositions, *first,* that it does not refer to a gratuitous question, but to one which human reason   [422] in its natural progress must necessarily encounter, and, *secondly,* that it, as well as its opposite, carries with itself not a merely artificial illusion, which when once seen through disappears, but a natural and inevitable illusion, which, even when it deceives us no longer, always remains, and though rendered harmless, cannot be annihilated.

This dialectical doctrine will not refer to the unity of the understanding in concepts of experience, but to the unity of reason in mere ideas, the condition of which, as it is meant to agree, as a synthesis according to rules, with the understanding, and yet at the same time, as the absolute unity of that synthesis, with reason, must either, if it is adequate to the unity of reason, be too great for the understanding, or, if adequate to the understanding, too small for reason. Hence a conflict must arise, which cannot be avoided, do what we will.

These apparently rational, but really sophistical assertions open a dialectical battle-field, where that side always obtains the victory which is allowed to make the attack, and where those must certainly   [423] succumb who are obliged to keep on the defensive. Hence doughty knights, whether fighting for the good or the bad cause, are sure to win their laurels, if only they take care that they have the right to make the last attack, and are not obliged to stand a new onslaught of the enemy. We can easily imagine that this arena has often been entered, and many victories have been won on both sides, the last decisive victory being always guarded by the defender of the good cause maintaining his place, his opponent being forbidden ever to carry arms again. As impartial judges we must take no account of whether it be the good or the bad cause which the two champions defend. It is best to let them fight it out between themselves in the hope that, after they have rather tired out than injured each other, they may themselves perceive the uselessness of their quarrel, and part as good friends.

This method of watching or even provoking such a conflict of assertions, not in order to decide in favour of one or the other side, but in order to find out whether the object of the struggle be not a mere illusion, which everybody tries to grasp in vain, and which never can be of any use to any one, even if no resistance were made to him, this method, I [424] say, may be called the *sceptical method*. It is totally different from *scepticism*, or that artificial and scientific agnosticism which undermines the foundations of all knowledge, in order if possible to leave nothing trustworthy and certain anywhere. The sceptical method, on the contrary, aims at certainty, because, while watching a contest which on both sides is carried on honestly and intelligently, it tries to discover the point where the misunderstanding arises, in order to do what is done by wise legislators, namely, to derive from the embarrassments of judges in law-suits information as to what is imperfectly, or not quite accurately, determined in their laws. The antinomy which shows itself in the application of laws, is, considering our limited wisdom, the best criterion of the original legislation (nomothetic), and helps to attract the attention of reason, which in abstract speculations does not easily become aware of its errors, to the important points in the determination of its principles.

This sceptical method is essential in transcendental philosophy only, while it may be dispensed with in other fields of investigation. It would be absurd in mathematics, for no false assertions can there be hidden or rendered invisible, because the demonstrations must always be [425] guided by pure intuition, and proceed by evident synthesis. In experimental philosophy a doubt, which causes delay, may be useful, but at least no misunderstanding is possible that could not be easily removed, and the final means for deciding a question, whether found sooner or later, must always be supplied by experience. Moral philosophy too can always produce its principles and their practical consequences in the concrete also, or at least in possible experience, and thus avoid the misunderstandings inherent in abstraction. Transcendental assertions, on the contrary, pretending to knowledge far beyond the field of possible experience, can never produce their abstract synthesis in any intuition *a priori*, nor can their flaws be discovered by means of any experience. Transcendental reason, therefore, admits of no other criterion but an attempt to combine its conflicting assertions, and therefore, previous to this, unrestrained conflict between them. This is what we shall now attempt to do.[40]

---

[40] The antinomies follow each other, according to the order of the transcendental ideas mentioned before.

Thesis   [426]

The world has a beginning in time, and is limited also with regard to space.

Proof

For if we assumed that the world had no beginning in time, then an eternity must have elapsed up to every given point of time, and therefore an infinite series of successive states of things must have passed in the world. The infinity of a series, however, consists in this, that it never can be completed by means of a successive synthesis. Hence an infinite past series of worlds is impossible, and the beginning of the world a necessary condition of its existence. This was what had to be proved first.

With regard to the second, let us assume again the opposite. In that case the world would be given as an infinite whole of co-existing things. Now we cannot conceive in any way the extension of a quantum, which is not given within certain limits to every intuition,[41] except through the synthesis of its parts, nor the totality of such a quantum in any   [428] way, except through a completed synthesis, or by the repeated addition of unity to itself.[42] In order therefore to conceive the world, which fills all space, as a whole, the successive synthesis of the parts of an infinite world would have to be looked upon as completed; that is, an infinite time would have to be looked upon as elapsed, during the enumeration of all co-existing things. This is impossible. Hence an infinite aggregate of real things cannot be regarded as a given whole, nor, therefore, as given at the same time. Hence it follows that the world is not infinite, as regards extension in space, but enclosed in limits. This was the second that had to be proved.

---

41 We may perceive an indefinite quantum as a whole, if it is included in limits, without having to build up its totality by means of measuring, that is, by the successive synthesis of its parts. The limits themselves determine its completeness, by cutting off everything beyond.

42 The concept of totality is in this case nothing but the representation of the completed synthesis of its parts, because, as we cannot deduce the concept from the intuition of the whole (this being in this case impossible), we can conceive it only through the synthesis of its parts, up to the completion of the infinite, at least in the idea.

TRANSCENDENTAL IDEAS

Antithesis [427]

The world has no beginning and no limits in space, but is infinite, in respect both to time and space.

Proof

For let us assume that it has a beginning. Then, as beginning is an existence which is preceded by a time in which the thing is not, it would follow that antecedently there was a time in which the world was not, that is, an empty time. In an empty time, however, it is impossible that anything should take its beginning, because of such a time no part possesses any condition as to existence rather than non-existence, which condition could distinguish that part from any other (whether produced by itself or through another cause). Hence, though many a series of things may take its beginning in the world, the world itself can have no beginning, and in reference to time past is infinite.

With regard to the second, let us assume again the opposite, namely, that the world is finite and limited in space. In that case the world would exist in an empty space without limits. We should therefore have not only a relation of things *in space,* but also of things *to space.* As however the world is an absolute whole, outside of which no object of in- [429] tuition, and therefore no correlate of the world can be found, the relation of the world to empty space would be a relation to *no object.* Such a relation, and with it the limitation of the world by empty space, is nothing, and therefore the world is not limited with regard to space, that is, it is infinite in extension.[43]

---

43 Space is merely the form of external intuition (formal intuition) and not a real object that can be perceived by external intuition. Space, as prior to all things which determine it (fill or limit it), or rather which give an empirical intuition determined by its form, is, under the name of absolute space, nothing but a mere possibility of external phenomena, so far as they either exist already, or can be added to given phenomena. Empirical intuition, therefore, is not a compound of phenomena and of space (perception and empty intuition). The one is not a correlate of the other in a synthesis, but the two are only connected as matter and form in one and the same empirical intuition. If we try to separate one from the other, and to place space outside all phenomena, we arrive at a number of empty determinations of external intuition, which, however, can never be possible perceptions; for instance, motion or rest of the world in an infinite empty space, i.e. a determination of the mutual relation of the two, which can never be perceived, and is therefore nothing but the predicate of a mere idea.

I

On the Thesis

In exhibiting these conflicting arguments I have not tried to avail myself of mere sophisms for the sake of what is called special pleading, which takes advantage of the want of caution of the opponent, and gladly allows his appeal to a misunderstood law, in order to establish his own illegitimate claims on its refutation. Every one of our proofs has been deduced from the nature of the case, and no advantage has been taken of the wrong conclusions of dogmatists on either side.

I might have apparently proved my thesis too by putting forward, as is the habit of dogmatists, a wrong definition of the infinity of a given quantity. I might have said that the quantity is *infinite,* if no greater quantity (that is, greater than the number of given units contained in it) is possible. As no number is the greatest, because one or more units can always be added to it, I might have argued that an infinite given quantity, and therefore also an infinite world (infinite as regards both the past series of time and extension in space) is impossible, and therefore the world limited in space and time. I might have done this, but, in that case, my definition would not have agreed with the true concept of an infinite whole. We do not represent by it how large it is, and the concept of it is not therefore the concept of a *maximum,* but we conceive by it its relation only to any possible unit, in regard to which it is greater than any   [432] number. According as this unit is either greater or smaller, the infinite would be greater or smaller, while infinity, consisting in the relation only to this given unit, would always remain the same, although the absolute quantity of the whole would not be known by it. This, however, does not concern us at present.

The true transcendental concept of infinity is, that the successive synthesis of units in measuring a quantum, can never be completed.[44] Hence it follows with perfect certainty, that an eternity of real and successive states cannot have elapsed up to any given (the present) moment, and that the world therefore must have a beginning.

With regard to the second part of the thesis, the difficulty of an endless and yet past series does not exist; for the manifold of a world, infinite in extension, is given at *one and the same time.* But, in order to conceive the totality of such a multitude of things, as we cannot appeal to those limits which in intuition produce that totality by themselves, we must render an account of our concept, which in our case cannot proceed from the whole to the determined multitude of the parts, but has to demonstrate

---

[44] This quantum contains therefore a multitude (of given units) which is greater than any number; this is the mathematical concept of the infinite.

II

On the Antithesis [431]

The proof of the infinity of the given series of world, and of the totality of the world, rests on this, that in the opposite case an empty time, and likewise an empty space, would form the limits of the world. Now I am quite aware that people have tried to escape from this conclusion by saying that a limit of the world, both in time and space, is quite possible, without our having to admit an absolute time before the beginning of the world or an absolute space outside the real world, which is impossible. I have nothing to say against the latter part of this opinion, held by the philosophers of the school of Leibniz. Space is only the form of external intuition, and not a real object that could be perceived externally, nor is it a correlate of phenomena, but the form of phenomena themselves. Space, therefore, cannot exist absolutely (by itself) as something determining the existence of things, because it is no object, but only the form of possible objects. Things, therefore, as phenomenal, may indeed determine space, that is, impart reality to one or other of its predicates (quantity and relation); but space, on the other side, as something existing by itself, cannot determine the reality of things in regard to quantity or form, because it is nothing real in itself. Space therefore (whether full or empty [45]) may be limited by phenomena, but phenomena cannot be limited *by empty space* outside them. The [433] same applies to time. But, granting all this, it cannot be denied that we should be driven to admit these two monsters, empty space outside, and empty time before the world, if we assumed the limit of the world, whether in space or time.

For as to the plea by which people try to escape from the conclusion, that if the world has limits in time or space, the infinite void would determine the existence of real things, so far as their dimensions are concerned, it is really no more than a covered attempt at putting some unknown *intelligible* world in the place of our *sensuous* world, and an existence in general, which *presupposes no other condition* in the world, in the place of a first beginning (an existence preceded by a time of non-existence), and *boundaries* of the universe in place of the limits of extension,—thus getting rid of time and space. But we have to deal here with the *mundus phaenomenon* and its quantity, and we could not ignore the conditions of sensibility, without destroying its very essence. The world of sense, if it is limited, lies necessarily within the infinite void.

---

[45] It is easily seen that what we wish to say is that empty space, so far as limited *by phenomena,* that is, space *within* the world, does not at least contradict transcendental principles, and may be admitted, therefore, so far as they are concerned, though by this its possibility is not asserted.

the possibility of a whole by the successive synthesis of the parts. As such a synthesis would constitute a series that would never be completed, it is impossible to conceive a totality either before it, or through it. For the concept of totality itself is in this case the representation of a completed synthesis of parts, and such a completion, and therefore its concept also, is impossible.

SECOND CONFLICT OF THE

Thesis   [434]

Every compound substance in the world consists of simple parts, and nothing exists anywhere but the simple, or what is composed of it.

Proof

For let us assume that compound substances did not consist of simple parts, then, if all composition is removed in thought, there would be no compound part, and (as no simple parts are admitted) no simple part either, that is, there would remain nothing, and there would therefore be no substance at all. Either, therefore, it is impossible to remove all composition in thought, or, after its removal, there must remain something that exists without composition, that is the simple. In the former case the compound could not itself consist of substances (because with them composition is only an accidental relation of substances, which substances, as permanent beings, must subsist without it). As this contradicts [436] the supposition, there remains only the second view, namely, that the substantial compounds in the world consist of simple parts.

It follows as an immediate consequence that all the things in the world are simple beings, that their composition is only an external condition, and that, though we are unable to remove these elementary substances from their state of composition and isolate them, reason must conceive them as the first subjects of all composition, and therefore, antecedently to it, as simple beings.

If we ignore this, and with it, space in general, as an *a priori* condition of the possibility of phenomena, the whole world of sense vanishes, which alone forms the object of our enquiry. The *mundus intelligibilis* is nothing but the general concept of any world, which takes no account of any of the conditions of intuition, and which therefore admits of no synthetical proposition, whether affirmative or negative.

TRANSCENDENTAL IDEAS

Antithesis [435]

No compound thing in the world consists of simple parts, and there exists nowhere in the world anything simple.

Proof

Assume that a compound thing, a substance, consists of simple parts. Then as all external relation, and therefore all composition of substances also, is possible in space only, it follows that space must consist of as many parts as the parts of the compound that occupies the space. Space, however, does not consist of simple parts, but of spaces. Every part of a compound, therefore, must occupy a space. Now the absolutely primary parts of every compound are simple. It follows therefore that the simple occupies a space. But as everything real, which occupies a space, contains a manifold, the parts of which are by the side of each other, and which therefore is compounded, and, as a real compound, compounded not of accidents (for these could not exist by the side of each other, without a substance), but of substances, it would follow that the simple is a substantial compound, which is self-contradictory.

The second proposition of the antithesis, that there exists nowhere in the world anything simple, is not intended to mean more than that the existence of the absolutely simple cannot be proved from any ex- [437] perience or perception, whether external or internal, and that the absolutely simple is a mere idea, the objective reality of which can never be shown in any possible experience, so that in the explanation of phenomena it is without any application or object. For, if we assumed that an object of this transcendental idea might be found in experience, the empirical intuition of some one object would have to be such as to contain absolutely nothing manifold by the side of each other, and combined to a unity. But as, from our not being conscious of such a manifold, we cannot form any valid conclusion as to the entire impossibility of it in any objective intuition, and as without this no absolute simplicity can be established, it follows that such simplicity cannot be inferred from any perception whatsoever. As, therefore, an absolutely simple object can never be given in any possible experience, while the

Observations on the Second Antinomy [438]

I

On the Thesis

If I speak of a whole as necessarily consisting of separate parts, I understand by it a substantial whole only, as a real compound, that is, that contingent unity of the manifold, which, given as *separate* (at least in thought), is brought into a mutual connection, and thus constitutes one whole. We ought not to call space a compositum, but a totum, because in it its parts are possible only in the whole, and not the whole by its parts. It might therefore be called a *compositum ideale,* but not *reale.* But this is an unnecessary distinction. As space is no compound of substances, not even of real accidents, nothing remains of it, if I remove all composition in it, not even the point, for a point is possible only as the limit of a space, and therefore of a compound. Space and time do [440] not therefore consist of simple parts. What belongs only to the condition of a substance, even though it possesses quantity (as, for instance, change), does not consist of the simple; that is to say, a certain degree of change does not arise through the accumulation of many simple changes. We can infer the simple from the compound in self-subsisting objects only. Accidents of a state, however, are not self-subsisting. The proof of the necessity of the simple, as the component parts of all that is substantially composite, can therefore easily be injured, if it is extended too far, and applied to all compounds without distinction, as has often been the case.

I am, however, speaking here of the simple only so far as it is necessarily given in the composite, which can be dissolved into the former, as its component parts. The true meaning of the word *Monas* (as used [442] by Leibniz) should refer to that simple only, which is given *immediately* as simple substance (for example in self-consciousness), and not as an element of the composite, in which case it is better called an *Atomus.*[46]

---

[46] Rosenkranz thinks that *atomus* is here used intentionally by Kant as a *masculine,* to distinguish it from the *atomon,* translated by scholastic philosophers, as *inseparable, indiscernible, simplex,* etc., while with the Greek philosophers *atomus* is feminine. Erdman, however, has shown that Kant has used *atomus* elsewhere also as masculine.

world of sense must be looked upon as the sum total of all possible experience, it follows that nothing simple exists in it.

This second part of the antithesis goes far beyond the first, which only banished the simple from the intuition of the composite, while the second drives it out of the whole of nature. Hence we could not attempt to prove it out of the concept of any given object of external intuition (of the compound), but from its relation to a possible experience in general.

II [439]

On the Antithesis

Against the theory of the infinite divisibility of matter, the proof of which is mathematical only, objections have been raised by the *Monadists*, which become suspicious by their declining to admit the clearest mathematical proofs as founded on a true insight into the quality of space, so far as space is indeed the formal condition of the possibility of all matter, but treating them only as conclusions derived from abstract but arbitrary concepts, which ought not to be applied to real things. But how is it possible to conceive a different kind of intuition from that given in the original intuition of space, and how can its determinations *a priori* not apply to everything, since it becomes possible only by its filling that space? If we were to listen to them, we should have to admit, beside the mathematical point, which is simple, but no part, but only the limit of a space, other physical points, simple likewise, but possessing this privilege that, as parts of space, they are able, by mere aggregation, to fill space. Without repeating here the many clear refutations of this absurdity, it being quite futile to attempt to reason away by purely discursive concepts the evidence of mathematics, I only remark, that if philosophy in this case seems to play tricks with mathematics, it does so because it forgets that in this discussion we are concerned with [441] *phenomena* only, and their conditions. Here, however, it is not enough to find for the pure *concept*, produced by the understanding, of the composite the concept of the simple, but we must find for the *intuition* of the composite (matter) the intuition of the simple; and this, according to the laws of sensibility, and therefore with reference to the objects of the senses, is totally impossible. Though it may be true, therefore, with regard to a whole, consisting of substances, which is conceived by the pure understanding only, that before its composition there must be the simple, this does not apply to the *totum substantiale phaenomenon* which, as an empirical intuition in space, carries with it the necessary condition that no part of it is simple, because no part of space is simple. The monadists, however, have been clever enough to try to escape from this difficulty, by not admitting space as a condition of the possibility of

As I wish to prove the existence of simple substances, as the elements of the composite only, I might call the thesis [47] of the second antinomy transcendental *Atomistic*. But as this word has long been used as the name of a particular explanation of material phenomena (*moleculae*) and presupposes, therefore, empirical concepts, it will be better to call it the dialectic principle of *monadology*.

THIRD CONFLICT OF THE

Thesis   [444]

Causality, according to the laws of nature, is not the only causality from which all the phenomena of the world can be deduced. In order to account for these phenomena it is necessary also to admit another causality, that of freedom.

Proof

Let us assume that there is no other causality but that according to the laws of nature. In that case everything that *takes place*, presupposes

---

[47] *Antithesis* is a misprint.

the objects of external intuition (bodies), but by presupposing these and the dynamical relation of substances in general as the condition of the possibility of space. But we have no concept of bodies, except as phenomena, and, as such, they presuppose space as the necessary condition of the possibility of all external phenomena. The argument of the monadists, therefore, is futile, and has been sufficiently answered in the transcendental Æsthetic. If the bodies were things by themselves, then, and then only, the argument of the monadists would be valid.

The second dialectical assertion possesses this peculiarity, that [443] it is opposed by dogmatical assertion which, among all sophistical assertions, is the only one which undertakes to prove palpably in an object of experience the reality of that which we counted before as belonging only to transcendental ideas, namely, the absolute simplicity of a substance,—I mean the assertion that the object of the internal sense, or the thinking I, is an absolutely simple substance. Without entering upon this question (as it has been fully discussed before), I only remark, that if something is conceived as an object only, without adding any synthetical determination of its intuition (and this is the case in the bare representation of the I), it would no doubt be impossible that anything manifold or composite could be perceived in such a representation. Besides, as the predicates through which I conceive this object are only intuitions of the internal sense, nothing can occur in them to prove a manifold (one by the side of another), and therefore a real composition. It follows, therefore, from the nature of self-consciousness that, as the thinking subject is at the same time its own object, it cannot divide itself (though it might divide its inherent determinations); for in regard to itself every object is absolute unity. Nevertheless, when this subject is looked upon externally, as an object of intuition, it would most likely exhibit some kind of composition as a phenomenon, and it must always be looked upon in this light, if we wish to know whether its manifold constituent elements are *by the side* of each other or not.

TRANSCENDENTAL IDEAS

Antithesis [445]

There is no freedom, but everything in the world takes place entirely according to the laws of nature.

Proof

If we admit that there is *freedom*, in the transcendental sense, as a particular kind of causality, according to which the events in the world could take place, that is a faculty of absolutely originating a state, and with it a series of consequences, it would follow that not only a series would have its absolute beginning through this spontaneity, but the determination of that spontaneity itself to produce the series, that is, the

an anterior state, on which it follows inevitably according to a rule. But that anterior state must itself be something which has taken place (which has come to be in time, and did not exist before), because, if it had always existed, its effect too would not have only just arisen, but have existed always. The causality, therefore, of a cause, through which something takes place, is itself an *event,* which again, according to the law of nature, presupposes an anterior state and its causality, and this again an anterior state, and so on. If, therefore, everything takes place according to mere laws of nature, there will always be a secondary   [446] only, but never a primary beginning, and therefore no completeness of the series, on the side of successive causes. But the law of nature consists in this, that nothing takes place without a cause sufficiently determined *a priori.* Therefore the proposition, that all causality is possible according to the laws of nature only, contradicts itself, if taken in unlimited generality, and it is impossible, therefore, to admit that causality as the only one.

We must therefore admit another causality, through which something takes place, without its cause being further determined according to necessary laws by a preceding cause, that is, an *absolute spontaneity* of causes, by which a series of phenomena, proceeding according to natural laws, begins by itself; we must consequently admit transcendental freedom, without which, even in the course of nature, the series of phenomena on the side of causes, can never be perfect.

Observations on the Third Antinomy   [448]

I

On the Thesis

The transcendental idea of freedom is far from forming the whole content of the psychological concept of that name, which is chiefly empirical, but only that of the absolute spontaneity of action, as the real ground of imputability; it is, however, the real stone of offence in the eyes of philosophy, which finds its unsurmountable difficulties in admitting this kind of unconditioned causality. That element in the question of the freedom of the will, which has always so much embarrassed speculative reason, is therefore in reality *transcendental* only, and refers merely to the question whether we must admit a faculty of *spontaneously* originating a series of successive things or states. How such a faculty is possible need not be answered, because, with regard to the causality, according to the laws of nature also, we must be satisfied to know *a priori* that such a causality has to be admitted, though we can in no wise understand causality, would have an absolute beginning, nothing preceding it by which this act is determined according to permanent laws. Every beginning of an act, however, presupposes a state in which the cause is not yet active, and a dynamically primary beginning of an act presupposes a state which has no causal connection with the preceding state of that cause, that is, in no wise follows from it. Transcendental freedom is therefore opposed to the law of causality, and represents such a con- [447] nection of successive states of effective causes, that no unity of experience is possible with it. It is therefore an empty fiction of the mind, and not to be met with in any experience.

We have, therefore, nothing but *nature*, in which we must try to find the connection and order of cosmical events. Freedom (independence) from the laws of nature is no doubt a *deliverance* from restraint, but also from the *guidance* of all rules. For we cannot say that, instead of the laws of nature, laws of freedom may enter into the causality of the course of the world, because, if determined by laws, it would not be freedom, but nothing else but nature. Nature, therefore, and transcendental freedom differ from each other like legality and lawlessness. The former, no doubt, imposes upon the understanding the difficult task of looking higher and higher for the origin of events in the series of causes, because their causality is always conditioned. In return for this, however, it promises a complete and well-ordered unity of experience; while, on the other side, the fiction of freedom promises, no doubt, to the enquiring mind, rest in the chain of causes, leading him up to an unconditioned causality, which begins to act by itself, but which, as it is blind itself, tears the thread of rules by which alone a complete and coherent experience is possible.

II [449]

On the Antithesis

He who stands up for the omnipotence of nature (transcendental *physiocracy*), in opposition to the doctrine of freedom, would defend his position against the sophistical conclusions of that doctrine in the following manner. *If you do not admit something mathematically the first in the world with reference to time, there is no necessity why you should look for something dynamically the first with reference to causality.* Who has told you to invent an absolutely first state of the world, and with it an absolute beginning of the gradually progressing series of phenomena, and to set limits to unlimited nature in order to give to your imagination something to rest on? As substances have always existed in the world, or as the unity of experience renders at least such a supposition necessary, there is no difficulty in assuming that a change of their states, that is, a series of their changes, has always existed also, so that there is no neces-

the possibility how, through one existence, the existence of another is given, but must for that purpose appeal to experience alone. The necessity of a first beginning of a series of phenomena from freedom has been proved so far only as it is necessary in order to comprehend an origin of the world, while all successive states may be regarded as a result in succession according to mere laws of nature. But as thus the [450] faculty of originating a series in time by itself has been proved, though by no means understood, it is now permitted also to admit, within the course of the world, different series, beginning by themselves, with regard to their causality, and to attribute to their substances a faculty of acting with freedom. But we must not allow ourselves to be troubled by a misapprehension, namely that, as every successive series in the world can have only a relatively primary beginning, some other state of things always preceding in the world, therefore no absolutely primary beginning of different series is possible in the course of the world. For we are speaking here of the absolutely first beginning, not according to time, but according to causality. If, for instance, at this moment I rise from my chair with perfect freedom, without the necessary determining influence of natural causes, a new series has its absolute beginning in this event, with all its natural consequences *ad infinitum,* although, with regard to time, this event is only the continuation of a preceding series. For this determination and this act do not belong to the succession of merely natural effects, nor are they a mere continuation of them, but the determining natural causes completely stop before it, so far as this event is concerned, which no doubt follows them, and does not *result* from them, and may therefore be called an absolutely first beginning in a series of phenomena, not with reference to time, but with reference to causality.

This requirement of reason to appeal in the series of natural causes to a first and free beginning is fully confirmed if we see that, with the exception of the Epicurean school, all philosophers of antiquity have felt themselves obliged to admit, for the sake of explaining all cosmical movements, a *prime mover,* that is, a freely acting cause which, first and by itself, started this series of states. They did not attempt to make a first beginning comprehensible by an appeal to nature only.

FOURTH CONFLICT OF THE

Thesis [452]

There exists an absolutely necessary Being belonging to the world, either as a part or as a cause of it.

Proof

The world of sense, as the sum total of all phenomena, contains a series of changes without which even the representation of a series of time,

sity for looking for a first beginning either mathematically or dynamically. It is true we cannot render the possibility of such an infinite descent comprehensible without the first member to which everything else is subsequent. But, if for this reason you reject this riddle of nature, you will feel yourselves constrained to reject many synthetical fundamental properties (natural forces), which you cannot comprehend any more, nay, the very possibility of change in general would be full of difficulties. [451] For if you did not know from experience that change exists, you would never be able to conceive *a priori* how such a constant succession of being and not being is possible.

And, even if the transcendental faculty of freedom might somehow be conceded to start the changes of the world, such faculty would at all events have to be outside the world (though it would always remain a bold assumption to admit, outside the sum total of all possible intuitions, an object that cannot be given in any possible experience). But to attribute in the world itself a faculty to substances can never be allowed, because in that case the connection of phenomena determining each other by necessity and according to general laws, which we call nature, and with it the test of empirical truth, which distinguishes experience from dreams, would almost entirely disappear. For by the side of such a lawless faculty of freedom, nature could hardly be conceived any longer, because the laws of the latter would be constantly changed through the influence of the former, and the play of phenomena which, according to nature, is regular and uniform, would become confused and incoherent.

TRANSCENDENTAL IDEAS

Antithesis [453]

There nowhere exists an absolutely necessary Being, either within or without the world, as the cause of it.

Proof

If we supposed that the world itself is a necessary being, or that a necessary being exists in it, there would then be in the series of changes

which forms the condition of the possibility of the world of sense, would not be given us.[48] But every change has its condition which precedes it in time, and renders it necessary. Now, everything that is given as conditional presupposes, with regard to its existence, a complete series of conditions, leading up to that which is entirely unconditioned, and alone absolutely necessary. Something absolutely necessary therefore must exist, if there exists a change as its consequence. And this absolutely necessary belongs itself to the world of sense. For if we supposed that it existed outside that world, then the series of changes in the world would derive its origin from it, while the necessary cause itself would not belong   [454] to the world of sense. But this is impossible. For as the beginning of a temporal series can be determined only by that which precedes it in time, it follows that the highest condition of the beginning of a series of changes must exist in the time when that series was not yet (because the beginning is an existence, preceded by a time in which the thing which begins was not yet). Hence the causality of the necessary cause of changes and that cause itself belong to time and therefore to phenomena (in which alone time, as their form, is possible), and it cannot therefore be conceived as separated from the world of sense, as the sum total of all phenomena. It follows, therefore, that something absolutely necessary is contained in the world, whether it be the whole cosmical series itself, or only a part of it.

Observations on the Fourth Antinomy   [456]

I

On the Thesis

In order to prove the existence of a necessary Being, I ought not, in this place, to use any but the *cosmological* argument, which ascends from what is conditioned in the phenomena to what is unconditioned in concept, that being considered as the necessary condition of the absolute totality of the series. To undertake that proof from the mere idea of a Supreme Being belongs to another principle of reason, and will have to be treated separately.

The pure cosmological proof cannot establish the existence of a necessary Being, without leaving it open, whether that Being be the world itself, or a Being distinct from it. In order to settle this question, principles are required which are no longer cosmological, and do not proceed in the series of phenomena. We should have to introduce concepts of contingent beings in general (so far as they are considered as objects of

---

[48] As formal condition of the possibility of changes, time is no doubt objectively prior to them (read *diesen* instead of *dieser*); subjectively, however, and in the reality of our consciousness the representation of time, like every other, is occasioned solely by perceptions.

either a beginning, unconditionally necessary, and therefore without a cause, which contradicts the dynamical law of the determination of all phenomena in time; or the series itself would be without any beginning, and though contingent and conditioned in all its parts, yet entirely necessary and unconditioned as a whole. This would be self-contradictory, because the existence of a multitude cannot be necessary, if no single part of it possesses necessary existence.

If we supposed, on the contrary, that there exists an absolutely necessary cause of the world, outside the world, then that cause, as the highest member in *the series of causes* of cosmical changes, would begin [455] the existence of the latter and their series.[49] In that case, however, that cause would have to begin to act, and its causality would belong to time, and therefore to the sum total of phenomena. It would belong to the world, and would therefore not be outside the world, which is contrary to our supposition. Therefore, neither in the world, nor outside the world (yet in causal connection with it), does there exist anywhere an absolutely necessary Being.

II [457]

On the Antithesis

If, in ascending the series of phenomena, we imagine we meet with difficulties militating against the existence of an absolutely necessary supreme cause, such difficulties ought not to be derived from mere concepts of the necessary existence of a thing in general. They ought not to be ontological, but ought to arise from the causal connection with a series of phenomena for which a condition is required which is itself unconditioned, that is, they ought to be cosmological, and dependent on empirical laws. It must be shown that our ascending in the series of causes (in the world of sense) can never end with a condition empirically unconditioned, and that the cosmological argument, based on the contingency of cosmical states, as proved by their changes, ends in a verdict against the admission of a first cause, absolutely originating the whole series.

---

[49] The word *to begin* is used in two senses. The first is active when the cause begins, or starts (*infit*), a series of states as its effect. The second is passive (or neuter) when the causality begins in the cause itself (*fit*). I reason here from the former to the latter meaning.

the understanding only), and also a principle according to which we might connect them, by means of concepts only, with a necessary Being. All this belongs to a *transcendent* philosophy, for which this is not [458] yet the place.

If, however, we once begin our proof cosmologically, taking for our foundation the series of phenomena, and the regressus in it, according to the empirical laws of causality, we cannot afterwards suddenly leave this line of argument and pass over to something which does not belong as a member to this series. For the condition must be taken in the same meaning in which the relation of the condition to that condition was taken in the series which, by continuous progress, was to lead to that highest condition. If therefore that relation is sensuous and intended for a possible empirical use of the understanding, the highest condition or cause can close the regressus according to the laws of sensibility only, and therefore as belonging to that temporal series itself. The necessary Being must therefore be regarded as the highest member of the cosmical series.

Nevertheless, certain philosophers have taken the liberty of making such a salto (μετάβασις εἰς ἄλλο γένος). From the changes in the world they concluded their empirical contingency, that is, their dependence on empirically determining causes, and they thus arrived at an ascending series of empirical conditions. This was quite right. As, however, in this way they could not find a first beginning, or any highest member, they suddenly left the empirical concept of contingency, and took to the pure category. This led to a purely intelligible series, the completeness of which depended on the existence of an absolutely necessary cause, which cause, as no longer subject to any sensuous conditions, was freed also from the temporal condition of itself beginning its causality. Such a proceeding is entirely illegitimate, as may be seen from what follows.

In the pure sense of the category we call contingent that the contradictory opposite of which is possible. Now we cannot conclude that intelligible contingency from empirical contingency. Of what is [460] being changed we may say that the opposite (of its state) is real, and therefore possible also at another time. But this is not the contradictory opposite of the preceding state. In order to establish that, it is necessary that, at the same time, when the previous state existed, its opposite could have existed in its place, and this can never be concluded from change. A body, for instance, which, when in motion, was A, comes to be, when at rest, = non A. From the fact that the state opposite to the state A follows upon it, we can in no wise conclude that the contradictory opposite of A is possible, and therefore A contingent only. In order to establish this, it would be necessary to prove that, at the same time when there was motion, there might have been, instead of it, rest. But we know no more than that, at a subsequent time, such rest was real and therefore possible also. Motion at one time, and rest at another, are not contradictory opposites. Therefore the succession of opposite determinations, that is, change, in no way proves contingency, according to the concepts of

A curious contrast however meets us in this antinomy. From [459] the same ground on which, in the thesis, the existence of an original Being was proved, its non-existence is proved in the antithesis with equal stringency. We were first told, that *a necessary Being exists*, because the whole of time past comprehends the series of all conditions, and with it also the unconditioned (the necessary). We are now told *there is no necessary Being*, for the very reason that the whole of past time comprehends the series of all conditions (which therefore altogether are themselves conditioned). The explanation is this. The first argument regards only the *absolute totality* of the series of conditions determining each other in time, and thus arrives at something unconditioned and necessary. The second, on the contrary, regards the *contingency* of all that is determined *in the temporal series* (everything being preceded by a time in which the condition itself must again be determined as conditioned), in which case everything unconditioned, and every absolute necessity, must absolutely vanish. In both, the manner [461] of concluding is quite in conformity with ordinary human reason, which frequently comes into conflict with itself, from considering its object from two different points of view. Herr von Mairan considered the controversy between two famous astronomers, which arose from a similar difficulty, as the choice of the true standpoint, as something sufficiently important to write a separate treatise on it. The one reasoned thus, the *moon revolves on its own axis*, because it always turns the same side towards the earth. The other concluded, the *moon does not revolve on its own axis*, because it always turns the same side towards the earth. Both conclusions were correct, according to the point of view from which one chose to consider the motion of the moon.

.　　.　　.

the pure understanding, and can therefore never lead us on to the existence of a necessary Being, according to the pure concepts of the understanding. Change proves empirical contingency only; it proves that the new state could not have taken place according to the law of causality by itself, and without a cause belonging to a previous time. This cause, even if it is considered as absolutely necessary, must, as we see, exist in time, and belong to the series of phenomena.

.   .   .

Section VI

Transcendental Idealism as the Key to the Solution of Cosmological Dialectic

It has been sufficiently proved in the transcendental Æsthetic that everything which is perceived in space and time, therefore all objects of an experience possible to us, are nothing but phenomena, that is, mere representations which, such as they are represented, namely, as   [491] extended beings, or series of changes, have no independent existence outside our thoughts. This system I call *Transcendental Idealism*.[50] Transcendental realism changes these modifications of our sensibility into self-subsistent things, that is, it changes *mere representations* into things by themselves.

It would be unfair to ask us to adopt that long-decried empirical idealism which, while it admits the independent reality of space, denies the existence of extended beings in it, or at all events considers it as doubtful and does not admit that there is in this respect a sufficiently established difference between dream and reality. It sees no difficulty with regard to the phenomena of the internal sense in time, being real things; nay, it even maintains that this internal experience alone sufficiently proves the real existence of its object (by itself), with all the determinations in time.

Our own transcendental idealism, on the contrary, allows that the objects of external intuition may be real, as they are perceived in space, and likewise all changes in time, as they are represented by the internal sense. For as space itself is a form of that intuition which we call external, and as there would be no emipirical representation at all, unless   [492] there were objects in space, we can and must admit the extended beings in it as real; and the same applies to time. Space itself, however, as well

---

50 In a footnote added in the Second Edition, Kant says: "I have sometimes called it *formal* idealism also, in order to distinguish it from the *material* or common idealism, which doubts or denies the very existence of external things. . . ." W.K.

as time, and with them all phenomena, are not *things* by themselves, but representations, and cannot exist outside our mind; and even the internal sensuous intuition of our mind (as an object of consciousness) which is represented as determined by the succession of different states in time, is not a real self, as it exists by itself, or what is called the transcendental subject, but a phenomenon only, given to the sensibility of this to us unknown being. It cannot be admitted that this internal phenomenon exists as a thing by itself, because it is under the condition of time, which can never be the determination of anything by itself. In space and time, however, the empirical truth of phenomena is sufficiently established, and kept quite distinct from a dream, if both are properly and completely connected together in experience, according to empirical laws.

The objects of experience are therefore *never given by themselves*, but in our experience only, and do not exist outside it. That there may be inhabitants in the moon, though no man has ever seen them, must [493] be admitted; but it means no more than that, in the possible progress of our experience, we may meet with them; for everything is real that hangs together with a perception, according to the laws of empirical progress. They are therefore real, if they are empirically connected with any real consciousness, although they are not therefore real by themselves, that is, apart from that progress of experience.

Nothing is really given to us but perception, and the empirical progress from this to other possible perceptions. For by themselves phenomena, as mere representations, are real in perception only, which itself is nothing but the reality of an empirical representation, that is, phenomenal appearance. To call a phenomenon a real thing, before it is perceived, means either, that in the progress of experience we must meet with such a perception, or it means nothing. For that it existed by itself, without any reference to our senses and possible experience, might no doubt be said when we speak of a thing by itself. We here are speaking, however, of a phenomenon only in space and time, which are not determinations of things by themselves, but only of our sensibility. Hence that which exists in them (phenomena) is not something by itself, but consists in representations only, which, unless they are given in us [494] (in perception), exist nowhere.

The faculty of sensuous intuition is really some kind of receptivity only, according to which we are affected in a certain way by representations the mutual relation of which is a pure intuition of space and time (mere forms of our sensibility), and which, if they are connected and determined in that relation of space and time, according to the laws of the unity of experience, are called objects. The non-sensuous cause of these representations is entirely unknown to us, and we can never perceive it as an object, for such a cause would have to be represented neither in space nor in time, which are conditions of sensuous representations only, and without which we cannot conceive any intuition. We may, however, call that purely intelligible cause of phenomena in general, the transcendental object, in order that we may have something which corresponds to sensibility as a kind of receptivity. We may ascribe to that transcendental object the whole extent and connection of all our possible perceptions, and we may say that it is given by itself antecedently to all experience. Phenomena, however, are given accordingly, not by themselves, but in experience only, because they are mere representations which as perceptions only, signify a real object, provided that [495] the perception is connected with all others, according to the rules of unity in experience. Thus we may say that the real things of time past are given in the transcendental object of experience, but they only are objects to me, and real in time past, on the supposition that I conceive that a regressive series of possible perceptions (whether by the light of history, or by the vestiges of causes and effects), in one word, the course of the world, leads, according to empirical laws, to a past series of time, as a condition of the present time. It is therefore represented as real, not by itself, but in connection with a possible experience, so that all past events from time immemorial and before my own existence mean after all nothing but the possibility of an extension of the chain of experience, beginning with present perception and leading upwards to the conditions which determine it in time.

If, therefore, I represent to myself all existing objects of the senses, at all times and in all spaces, I do not place them before experience into space and time, but the whole representation is nothing but the idea of a possible experience, in its absolute completeness. In that alone those objects (which are nothing but mere representations) are given; and if we say that they exist before my whole experience, this only means [496] that they exist in that part of experience to which, starting from perception, I have first to advance. The cause of empirical conditions of that progress, and consequently with what members, or how far I may meet with certain members in that regressus, is transcendental, and therefore entirely unknown to me. But that cause does not concern us, but only the rule of the progress of experience, in which objects, namely phenomena, are given to me. In the end it is just the same whether I say, that in the empirical progress in space I may meet with stars a hundred times more distant than the most distant which I see, or whether I say that such stars are perhaps to be met with in space, though no human being did ever or will ever see them. For though, as things by themselves, they might be given without any relation to possible experience, they are nothing to me, and therefore no objects, unless they can be comprehended in the series of the empirical regressus. Only in another relation, when namely these phenomena are meant to be used for the cosmological idea of an absolute whole, and when we have to deal with a question that goes beyond the limits of possible experience, the distinction of the mode in which the reality of those objects of the senses is taken becomes of importance, in order to guard against a de- [497] ceptive error that would inevitably arise from a misinterpretation of our own empirical concepts.

Section VII

Critical Decision of the Cosmological Conflict of Reason with itself

The whole antinomy of pure reason rests on the dialectical argument that, if the conditioned is given, the whole series of conditions also is given. As therefore the objects of the senses are given us as conditioned, it follows, etc. Through this argument, the major of which seems so natural and self-evident, cosmological ideas have been introduced corresponding in number to the difference of conditions (in the synthesis of phenomena) which constitute a series. These cosmological ideas postulate the absolute totality of those series, and thus place reason in inevitable contradiction with itself. Before, however, we show what is deceptive in this sophistical argument, we must prepare ourselves for it by correcting and defining certain concepts occurring in it.

First, the following proposition is clear and admits of no doubt, that if the conditioned is given, it imposes on us the regressus in the series of all conditions of it; for it follows from the very concept of the [498] conditioned that through it something is referred to a condition, and, if that condition is again conditioned, to a more distant condition, and so on through all the members of the series. This proposition is really analytical, and need not fear any transcendental criticism. It is a logical postulate of reason to follow up through the understanding, as far as possible, that connection of a concept with its conditions, which is inherent in the concept itself.

Further, if the conditioned as well as its conditions are things by themselves, then, if the former be given, the regressus to the latter is not only *required,* but is really *given*; and as this applies to all the members of the series, the complete series of conditions and with it the unconditioned also is given, or rather it is presupposed that the conditioned, which was possible through that series only, is given. Here the synthesis of the conditioned with its condition is a synthesis of the understanding only, which represents things *as they are,* without asking whether and how we can arrive at the knowledge of them. But if I have to deal with phenomena, which, as mere representations, are not given at all, unless I attain to a knowledge of them (that is, to the phe- [499] nomena themselves, for they are nothing but empirical knowledge), then I cannot say in the same sense that, if the conditioned is given, all its conditions (as phenomena) are also given, and can therefore by no means conclude the absolute totality of the series. For *phenomena* in their apprehension are themselves nothing but an empirical synthesis (in space and time), and are given therefore in *that synthesis* only. Now it follows by no means that, if the conditioned (as phenomenal) is given, the synthesis also that constitutes its empirical condition should thereby be given at the same time and presupposed; for this takes place in the regressus only, and never without it. What we may say in such a case is this, that a regressus to the conditions, that is, a continued empirical synthesis in that direction is required, and that conditions cannot be wanting that are given through that regressus.

Hence we see that the major of the cosmological argument takes the conditioned in the transcendental sense of a pure category, while the minor takes it in the empirical sense of a concept of the understanding, referring to mere phenomena, so that it contains that dialectical deceit which is called *Sophisma figurae dictionis*. That deceit, however, [500] is not artificial, but a perfectly natural illusion of our common reason. It is owing to it that, in the major, we presuppose the conditions and their series as it were *on trust*, if anything is given as conditioned, because this is no more than the logical postulate to assume complete premisses for any given conclusion. Nor does there exist in the connection of the conditioned with its condition any order of time, but they are presupposed in themselves as given *together*. It is equally natural also in the minor to look on phenomena as things by themselves, and as objects given to the understanding only in the same manner as in the major, as no account was taken of all the conditions of intuition under which alone objects can be given. But there is an important distinction between these concepts, which has been overlooked. The synthesis of the conditioned with its condition, and the whole series of conditions in the major, was in no way limited by time, and was free from any concept of succession. The empirical synthesis, on the contrary, and the series of conditions in phenomena, which was subsumed in the minor, is necessarily successive and given as such in time only. Therefore I had no right to assume the absolute *totality* of the synthesis and of the series represented by it in this case as well as in the former. For in the former all the members of the series are given by themselves (without determination in time), while here they are possible through the successive regressus only, [501] which cannot exist unless it is actually carried out.

After convicting them of such a mistake in the argument adopted by both parties as the foundation of their cosmological assertions, both might justly be dismissed as not being able to produce any good title in support of their claims. But even thus their quarrel is not yet ended, as if it had been proved that both parties, or one of them, were wrong in the matter contended for (in the conclusion), though they had failed to support it by valid proof. Nothing seems clearer than that, if one maintains that the world has a beginning, and the other that it has no beginning, but exists from all eternity, one or the other must be right. But if this were so, as the arguments on both sides are equally clear, it would still remain impossible ever to find out on which side the truth lies, and the suit continues, although both parties have been ordered to keep the peace before the tribunal of reason. Nothing remains therefore in order to settle the quarrel once for all, and to the satisfaction of both parties, but to convince them that, though they can refute each other so eloquently, they are really quarrelling about nothing, and that a certain transcendental illusion has mocked them with a reality where no reality exists. We shall [502] enter upon this way of adjusting a dispute, which cannot be adjudicated.

The Eleatic philosopher Zeno, a subtle dialectician, was severely reprimanded by Plato as a heedless Sophist who, in order to display his skill, would prove a proposition by plausible arguments and subvert the same immediately afterwards by arguments equally strong. He maintained, for instance, that God (which to him was probably nothing more than the universe) is neither finite nor infinite, neither in motion nor at rest, neither similar nor dissimilar to any other thing. It seemed to his critics as if he had intended to deny completely both of the two self-contradictory propositions which would be absurd. But I do not think that he can be rightly charged with this. We shall presently consider the first of these propositions more carefully. With regard to the others, if by the word *God* he meant the universe, he could not but say that it is neither permanently present in its place (at rest) nor that it changes it (in motion), because all places exist in the universe only, while the universe exists in no place. If the universe comprehends in itself everything that exists, it follows that it cannot be similar or dissimilar to any other thing, because there is no other thing besides it with which it could be compared. If two opposite judgments presuppose an inadmissible [503] condition, they both, in spite of their contradiction (which, however, is no real contradiction), fall to the ground, because the condition fails under which alone either of the propositions was meant to be valid.

If somebody were to say that everybody has either a good or a bad smell, a third case is possible, namely, that it has no smell at all, in which case both contradictory propositions would be false. If I say that it is either good smelling or not good smelling (*vel suaveolens vel non suaveolens*), in that case the two judgments are contradictory, and the former only is wrong, while its contradictory opposite, namely, that some bodies are not good smelling, comprehends those bodies also which have no smell at all. In the former opposition (*per disparata*) the contingent condition of the concept of a body (smell) still remained in the contradictory judgment and was not eliminated by it, so that the latter could not be called the contradictory opposite of the former.

If I say therefore that the world is either infinite in space or is not infinite (*non est infinitus*), then, if the former proposition is wrong, its contradictory opposite, that the world is not infinite, must be true. I should thus only eliminate an infinite world without affirming another, namely, the finite. But if I had said the world is either infinite or [504] finite (not-infinite), both statements may be false. For I then look upon the world, as by itself, determined in regard to its extent, and I do not only eliminate in the opposite statement the infinity, and with it, it may be, its whole independent existence, but I add a determination to the world as a thing existing by itself, which may be false, because the world may not be a thing by itself, and therefore, with regard to extension, neither

infinite nor finite. This kind of opposition I may be allowed to call
dialectical, that the real contradiction, the *analytical opposition.* Thus
then of two judgments opposed to each other dialectically both may be
false, because the one does not only contradict the other, but says something more than is requisite for a contradiction.

If we regard the two statements that the world is infinite in extension,
and that the world is finite in extension, as contradictory opposites, we
assume that the world (the whole series of phenomena) is a thing by
itself; for it remains, whether I remove the infinite or the finite regressus
in the series of its phenomena. But if we remove this suppositon, or this
transcendental illusion, and deny that it is a thing by itself, then the
contradictory opposition of the two statements becomes purely   [505]
dialectical, and as the world does not exist by itself (independently of
the regressive series of my representations), it exists neither as a whole
by itself infinite, nor as a whole *by itself finite.* It exists only in the empirical regressus in the series of phenomena, and nowhere by itself.
Hence, if that series is always conditioned, it can never exist as complete, and the world is therefore not an inconditioned whole, and does
not exist as such, either with infinite or finite extension.

What has here been said of the first cosmological idea, namely, that of
the absolute totality of extension in phenomena, applies to the others also.
The series of conditions is to be found only in the regressive synthesis,
never by itself, as complete, in phenomenon as an independent thing,
existing prior to every regressus. Hence I shall have to say that the
number of parts in any given phenomenon is by itself neither finite nor
infinite, because a phenomenon does not exist by itself, and its parts are
only found through the regressus of the decomposing synthesis through
and in the regressus, and that regressus can never be given as absolutely
complete, whether as finite or as infinite. The same applies to the series of
causes, one being prior to the other, and to the series leading from conditioned to unconditioned necessary existence, which can never be regarded either by itself finite in its totality or infinite, because, as   [506]
a series of subordinated representations, it forms a dynamical regressus
only, and cannot exist prior to it, by itself, as a self-subsistent series of
things.

The antinomy of pure reason with regard to its cosmological ideas is
therefore removed by showing that it is dialectical only, and a conflict
of an illusion produced by our applying the idea of absolute totality,
which exists only as a condition of things by themselves, to phenomena,
which exist in our representation only, and if they form a series, in the
successive regressus, but nowhere else. We may, however, on the other
side, derive from that antinomy a true, if not dogmatical, at least critical
and doctrinal advantage, namely, by proving through it indirectly the
transcendental ideality of phenomena, in case anybody should not have
been satisfied by the direct proof given in the transcendental Æsthetic.
The proof would consist in the following dilemma. If the world is a whole
existing by itself, it is either finite or infinite. Now the former as well as

the latter proposition is false, as has been shown by the proofs given in the antithesis on one and in the thesis on the other side. It is false, therefore, that the world (the sum total of all phenomena) is a whole [507] existing by itself. Hence it follows that phenomena in general are nothing outside our representations, which was what we meant by their transcendental ideality.

This remark is of some importance, because it shows that our proofs of the fourfold antinomy were not mere sophistry, but honest and correct, always under the (wrong) supposition that phenomena, or a world of sense which comprehends them all, are things by themselves. The conflict of the conclusions drawn from this shows, however, that there is a flaw in the supposition, and thus leads us to the discovery of the true nature of things, as objects of the senses. This transcendental Dialectic therefore does not favour scepticism, but only the sceptical method, which can point to it as an example of its great utility, if we allow the arguments of reason to fight against each other with perfect freedom, from which something useful and serviceable for the correction of our judgments will always result, though it may not be always that which we were looking for.

Section VIII [508]

The Regulative Principle of Pure Reason with Regard to the Cosmological Ideas

As through the cosmological principle of totality no real maximum is *given* of the series of conditions in the world of sense, as a thing by itself, but can only be *required* in the regressus of that series, that principle of pure reason, if thus amended, still retains its validity, not indeed as an *axiom*, requiring us to think the totality in the object as real, but as a *problem* for the understanding, and therefore for the subject, encouraging us to undertake and to continue, according to the completeness in the idea, the regressus in the series of conditions of anything given as conditioned. In our sensibility, that is, in space and time, every condition which we can reach in examining given phenomena is again conditioned, because these phenomena are not objects by themselves, in which something absolutely unconditioned might possibly exist, but empirical representations only, which always must have their condition in intuition, whereby they are determined in space and time. The principle of reason is therefore properly a rule only, which in the series of conditions of given phenomena postulates a regressus which is [509] never allowed to stop at anything absolutely unconditioned. It is therefore no principle of the possibility of experience and of the empirical knowledge of the objects of the senses, and not therefore a principle of the understanding, because every experience is (according to a given intuition) within its limits; nor is it a *constitutive principle* of reason, enabling us to extend the concept of the world of sense beyond all possible experience, but it is merely a principle of the greatest possible continuation and extension of our experience, allowing no empirical limit to be taken as an absolute limit. It is therefore a principle of reason, which, as a *rule*, postulates what we ought to do in the regressus, but does *not anticipate* what may be given in the *object*, before such regressus. I therefore call it a *regulative* principle of reason, while, on the contrary, the principle of the absolute totality of the series of conditions, as given in the object (the phenomena) by itself, would be a constitutive cosmological principle, the hollowness of which I have tried to indicate by this very distinction, thus preventing what otherwise would have inevitably happened (through a transcendental surreptitious proceeding), namely, an idea, which is to serve as a rule only, being invested with objective reality.

In order properly to determine the meaning of this rule of pure reason it should be remarked, first of all, that it cannot tell us what *the object is*, but only *how the empirical regressus is to be carried* [510] *out*, in order to arrive at the complete concept of the object. If we attempted the first, it would become a constitutive principle, such as pure reason can never supply. It cannot therefore be our intention to say through this principle, that a series of conditions of something, given as conditioned, is by itself either finite or infinite; for in that case a mere idea of absolute totality, produced in itself only, would represent in thought an object such as can never be given in experience, and an objective reality, independent of empirical synthesis, would have been attributed to a series of phenomena. This idea of reason can therefore do no more than prescribe a rule to the regressive synthesis in the series of conditions, according to which that synthesis is to advance from the conditioned, through all subordinate conditions, towards the unconditioned, though it can never reach it, for the absolutely unconditioned can never be met with in experience.

To this end it is necessary, first of all, to define accurately the synthesis of a series, so far as it never is complete. People are in the habit of using for this purpose two expressions which are meant to establish a difference, though they are unable clearly to define the ground of the distinction. Mathematicians speak only of a *progressus in infinitum*. Those who enquire into concepts (philosophers) will admit instead the expression of a *progressus in indefinitum* only. Without losing any time in the [511] examination of the reasons which may have suggested such a distinction, and of its useful or useless application, I shall at once endeavour to define these concepts accurately for my own purpose.

Of a straight line it can be said correctly that it may be produced to infinity; and here the distinction between an infinite and an indefinite progress (*progressus in indefinitum*) would be mere subtilty. No doubt, if we are told to carry on a line, it would be more correct to add *in indefinitum,* than *in infinitum,* because the former means no more than, produce it as far as *you wish,* but the second, *you shall* never cease producing it (which can never be intended). Nevertheless, if we speak only of what is possible, the former expression is quite correct, because we can always make it longer, if we like, without end. The same applies in all cases where we speak only of the progressus, that is, of our proceeding from the condition to the conditioned, for such progress proceeds in the series of phenomena without end. From a given pair of parents we may, in the descending line of generation, proceed without end, and conceive quite well that that line should so continue in the world. For here reason never requires an absolute totality of the series, because [512] it is not presupposed as a condition, and as it were given (*datum*), but only as something conditioned, that is, capable only of being given (*dabile*), and can be added to without end.

The case is totally different with the problem, how far the regressus from something given as conditioned may ascend in a series to its conditions; whether I may call it *a regressus into the infinite*, or only into the indefinite (*in indefinitum*); and whether I may ascend, for instance, from the men now living, through the series of their ancestors, *in infinitum*; or whether I may only say that, so far as I have gone back, I have never met with an empirical ground for considering the series limited anywhere, so that I feel justified, and at the same time obliged to search for an ancestor of every one of these ancestors, though not to presuppose them.

I say, therefore, that where the whole is given in empirical intuition, the regressus in the series of its internal conditions proceeds *in infinitum*, while if a member only of a series is given, from which the regressus to the absolute totality has first to be carried out, the regressus is only *in indefinitum*. Thus we must say that the division of matter, as given [513] between its limits (a body), goes on *in infinitum*, because that matter is complete and therefore, with all its possible parts, given in empirical intuition. As the condition of that whole consists in its part, and the condition of that part in the part of that part, and so on, and as in this regressus of decomposition we never meet with an unconditioned (indivisible) member of that series of conditions, there is nowhere an empirical ground for stopping the division; nay, the further members of that continued division are themselves empirically given before the continuation of the division, and therefore the division goes on *in infinitum*. The series of ancestors, on the contrary, of any given man, exists nowhere in its absolute totality, in any possible experience, while the regressus goes on from every link in the generation to a higher one, so that no empirical limit can be found which should represent a link as absolutely unconditioned. As, however, the links too, which might supply the condition, do not exist in the empirical intuition of the whole, prior to the regressus, that regressus does not proceed *in infinitum* (by a division of what is given), but to an indefinite distance, in its search for more links in addition to those which are given, and which themselves are again always conditioned only.

In neither case—the *regressus in infinitum* nor the *regressus in* [514] *indefinitum*—is the series of conditions to be considered as given as infinite in the object. They are not things by themselves, but phenomena only, which, as conditions of each other, are given only in the regressus itself. Therefore the question is no longer how great this series of conditions may be by itself, whether finite or infinite, for it is nothing by itself, but only how we are to carry out the empirical regressus, and how far we may continue it. And here we see a very important difference with regard to the rule of that progress. If the whole is given empirically, it is possible to go back in the series of its conditions *in infinitum*. But if the whole is not given, but has first to be given through an empirical regressus, I can only say that it is possible to proceed to still higher conditions of the series. In the former case I could say that more members exist and are empirically given than I can reach through the regressus (of decomposition); in the latter I can only say that I may advance still further in the regressus, because no member is empirically given as absolutely unconditioned, and a higher member therefore always possible, and therefore the enquiry for it necessary. In the former case it was necessary to *find* more members of the series, in the latter it is necessary to *enquire* for more, because no experience is absolutely limiting.   [515] For either you have no perception which absolutely limits your empirical regressus, and in that case you cannot consider that regressus as complete, or you have a perception which limits your series, and in that case it cannot be a part of your finished series (because what *limits* must be different from that which is *limited by it*), and you must therefore continue your regressus to that condition also, and so on for ever.

.   .   .

Possibility of a Causality through Freedom, in   [538]
Harmony with the Universal Law of Natural Necessity

Whatever in an object of the senses is not itself phenomenal, I call *intelligible*. If, therefore, what in the world of sense must be considered as phenomenal, possesses in itself a faculty which is not the object of sensuous intuition, but through which it can become the cause of phenomena, the *causality* of that being may be considered from *two sides*, as *intelligible* in its *action*, as the causality of a thing by itself, and as *sensible* in the *effects* of the action, as the causality of a phenomenon in the world of sense. Of the faculty of such a being we should have to form both an *empirical* and an *intellectual concept* of its causality, both of which consist together in one and the same effect. This twofold way of conceiving the faculty of an object of the senses does not contradict any of the concepts which we have to form of phenomena and of a possible experience. For as all phenomena, not being things by themselves, must have for their foundation a transcendental object, determining them as mere representations, there is nothing to prevent us from attributing to that transcendental object, besides the quality through which   [539] it becomes phenomenal, a *causality* also which is not phenomenal, although its *effect* appears in the phenomenon. Every efficient cause, however, must have a *character*, that is, a rule according to which it manifests its causality, and without which it would not be a cause. According to this we should have in every subject of the world of sense, first, an *empirical character*, through which its acts, as phenomena, stand with other phenomena in an unbroken connection, according to permanent laws of nature, and could be derived from them as their conditions, and in connection with them form the links of one and the same series in the order of nature. Secondly, we should have to allow to it an *intelligible character* also, by which, it is true, it becomes the cause of the same acts as phenomena, but which itself is not subject to any conditions of sensibility, and never phenomenal. We might call the former the character of such a thing as a phenomenon, in the latter the character of the thing by itself.

According to its intelligible character, this active subject would not depend on conditions of time, for time is only the condition of phenomena, and not of things by themselves. In it no *act* would *arise* or *perish*, neither would it be subject therefore to the law of determination   [540] in time and of all that is changeable, namely, that everything *which happens* must have its cause in *the phenomena* (of the previous state). In one word its causality, so far as it is intelligible, would not have a place in the series of empirical conditions by which the event is rendered necessary in the world of sense. It is true that that intelligible character could never be known immediately, because we cannot perceive anything, except so far as it appears, but it would nevertheless have to be conceived, according to the empirical character, as we must always admit in thought a transcendental object, as the foundation of phenomena, though we know nothing of what it is by itself.

In its empirical character, therefore, that subject, as a phenomenon, would submit, according to all determining laws, to a causal nexus, and in that respect it would be nothing but a part of the world of sense, the effects of which, like every other phenomenon, would arise from nature without fail. As soon as external phenomena began to influence it, and as soon as its empirical character, that is the law of its causality, had been known through experience, all its actions ought to admit of explanation, according to the laws of nature, and all that is requisite for its complete and necessary determination would be found in a possible experience.

In its intelligible character, however (though we could only   [541] have a general concept of it), the same subject would have to be considered free from all influence of sensibility, and from all determination through phenomena: and as in it, so far as it is a *noumenon*, nothing *happens,* and no change which requires dynamical determination of time, and therefore no connection with phenomena as causes, can exist, that active being would so far be quite independent and free in its acts from all natural necessity, which can exist in the world of sense only. One might say of it with perfect truth that it originates its effects in the world of sense *by itself,* though the act does not begin *in itself.* And this would be perfectly true, though the effects in the world of sense need not therefore originate by themselves, because in it they are always determined previously through empirical conditions in the previous time, though only by means of the empirical character (which is the phenomenal appearance of the intelligible character), and therefore impossible, except as a continuation of the series of natural causes. In this way freedom and nature, each in its complete signification, might exist together and without any conflict in the same action, according as we refer it to its intelligible or to its sensible cause.

Explanation of the Cosmological Idea of Freedom   [542]
in Connection with the General Necessity of Nature

I thought it best to give first this sketch of the solution of our transcendental problem, so that the course which reason has to adopt in its solution might be more clearly surveyed. We shall now proceed to explain more fully the points on which the decision properly rests, and examine each by itself.

The law of nature, that everything which happens has a cause,—that the causality of that cause, that is, its *activity* (as it is anterior in time, and with regard to an effect which has *arisen*, cannot itself have always existed, but must have *happened* at some time), must have its cause among the phenomena by which it is determined, and that therefore all events in the order of nature are empirically determined, this law, I say, through which alone phenomena become *nature* and objects of experience, is a law of the understanding, which can on no account be surrendered, and from which no single phenomenon can be exempted; because in doing this we should place it outside all possible experience, separate from all objects of possible experience, and   [543] change it into a mere fiction of the mind or a cobweb of the brain.

But although this looks merely like a chain of causes, which in the regressus to its conditions admits of no *absolute totality*, this difficulty does not detain us in the least, because it has already been removed in the general criticism of the antinomy of reason when, starting from the series of phenomena, it aims at the unconditioned. Were we to yield to the illusion of transcendental realism, we should have neither nature nor freedom. The question therefore is, whether, if we recognise in the whole series of events nothing but natural necessity, we may yet regard the same event which on one side is an effect of nature only, on the other side, as an effect of freedom; or whether there is a direct contradiction between these two kinds of causality?

There can certainly be nothing among phenomenal causes that could originate a series absolutely and by itself. Every action, as a phenomenon, so far as it produces an event, is itself an event, presupposing another state, in which its cause can be discovered; and thus everything that happens is only a continuation of the series, and no beginning, happening by itself, is possible in it. Actions of natural causes in the succession of time are therefore themselves effects, which likewise presuppose [544] causes in the series of time. A *spontaneous* and original action by which something takes place, which did not exist before, cannot be expected from the causal nexus of phenomena.

But is it really necessary that, if effects are phenomena, the causality of their cause, which cause itself is phenomenal, could be nothing but empirical; or is it not possible, although for every phenomenal effect a connection with its cause, according to the laws of empirical causality, is certainly required, that empirical causality itself could nevertheless, without breaking in the least its connection with the natural causes, represent an effect of a non-empirical and intelligible causality, that is, of a caused action, original in respect to phenomena, and in so far not phenomenal; but, with respect to this faculty, intelligible, although, as a link in the chain of nature, to be regarded as entirely belonging to the world of sense?

We require the principle of the causality of phenomena among themselves, in order to be able to look for and to produce natural conditions, that is, phenomenal causes of natural events. If this is admitted and not weakened by any exceptions, the understanding, which in its empirical employment recognises in all events nothing but nature, and is quite justified in doing so, has really all that it can demand, and the [545] explanations of physical phenomena may proceed without let or hindrance. The understanding would not be wronged in the least, if we assumed, though it be a mere fiction, that some among the natural causes have a faculty which is intelligible only, and whose determination to activity does not rest on empirical conditions, but on mere grounds of the intellect, if only the *phenomenal activity* of that cause is in accordance with all the laws of empirical causality. For in this way the active subject, as *causa phaenomenon*, would be joined with nature through the indissoluble dependence of all its actions, and the noumenon [51] only of that subject (with all its phenomenal causality) would contain certain conditions which, if we want to ascend from the empirical to the transcendental object, would have to be considered as intelligible only. For, if only we follow the rule of nature in that which may be the cause among phenomena, it is indifferent to us what kind of ground of those phenomena, and of their connection, may be conceived to exist in the transcendental subject, which is empirically unknown to us. This intelligible ground does not touch the empirical questions, but concerns only, as it would seem, the thought in the pure understanding; and although the effects of that thought and action of the pure understanding may [546] be discovered in the phenomena, these have nevertheless to be completely explained from their phenomenal cause, according to the laws of nature, by taking their empirical character as the highest ground of explanation, and passing by the intelligible character, which is the

---

[51] It seems better to read *noumenon* instead of *phenomenon*.

transcendental cause of the other, as entirely unknown, except so far as it is indicated by the empirical, as its sensuous sign. Let us apply this to experience. Man is one among the phenomena of the world of sense, and in so far one of the natural causes the causality of which must be subject to empirical laws. As such he must therefore have an empirical character, like all other objects of nature. We perceive it through the forces and faculties which he shows in his actions and effects. In the lifeless or merely animal nature we see no ground for admitting any faculty, except as sensuously conditioned. Man, however, who knows all the rest of nature through his senses only, knows himself through mere apperception also, and this in actions and internal determinations, which he cannot ascribe to the impressions of the senses. Man is thus to himself partly a phenomenon, partly, however, namely with reference to certain faculties, a purely intelligible object, because the actions of these faculties cannot be ascribed to the receptivity of sensibility. We [547] call these faculties understanding and reason. It is the latter, in particular, which is entirely distinguished from all empirically conditioned forces or faculties, because it weighs its objects according to ideas, and determines the understanding accordingly, which then makes an empirical use of its (by themselves, however pure) concepts.

That our reason possesses causality, or that we at least represent to ourselves such a causality in it, is clear from the *imperatives* which, in all practical matters, we impose as rules on our executive powers. The *ought* expresses a kind of necessity and connection with causes, which we do not find elsewhere in the whole of nature. The understanding can know in nature only what is present, past, or future. It is impossible that anything in it *ought to be* different from what it is in reality, in all these relations of time. Nay, if we only look at the course of nature, the ought has no meaning whatever. We cannot ask, what ought to be in nature, as little as we can ask, what qualities a circle ought to possess. We can only ask what happens in it, and what qualities that which happens has.

This ought expresses a possible action, the ground of which cannot be anything but a mere concept; while in every merely natural action the ground must always be a phenomenon. Now it is quite true that [548] the action to which the ought applies must be possible under natural conditions, but these natural conditions do not affect the determination of the will itself, but only its effects and results among phenomena. There may be ever so many natural grounds which impel me to *will* and ever so many sensuous temptations, but they can never produce the *ought*, but only a willing which is always conditioned, but by no means necessary, and to which the ought, pronounced by reason, opposes measure, ay, prohibition and authority. Whether it be an object of the senses merely (pleasure), or of pure reason (the good), reason does not yield to the impulse that is given empirically, and does not follow the order of things, as they present themselves as phenomena, but frames for itself, with perfect spontaneity, a new order according to ideas to which it adapts the empirical conditions, and according to which it declares actions to be necessary, even though they *have not taken place,* and, maybe, never will take place. Yet it is presupposed that reason may have causality with respect to them, for otherwise no effects in experience could be expected to result from these ideas.

Now let us take our stand here and admit it at least as possible, that reason really possesses causality with reference to phenomena. [549] In that case, reason though it be, it must show nevertheless an empirical character, because every cause presupposes a rule according to which certain phenomena follow as effects, and every rule requires in the effects a homogeneousness, on which the concept of cause (as a faculty) is founded. This, so far as it is derived from mere phenomena, may be called the empirical character, which is *permanent,* while the effects, according to a diversity of concomitant, and in part, restraining conditions, appear in *changeable* forms.

Every man therefore has an empirical character of his (arbitrary) will, which is nothing but a certain causality of his reason, exhibiting in its phenomenal actions and effects a rule, according to which one may infer the motives of reason and its actions, both in kind and in degree, and judge of the subjective principles of his will. As that empirical character itself must be derived from phenomena, as an effect, and from their rule which is supplied by experience, all the acts of a man, so far as they are phenomena, are determined from his empirical character and from the other concomitant causes, according to the order of nature; and if we could investigate all the manifestations of his will to the very bottom, there would be not a single human action which we could not [550] predict with certainty and recognise from its preceding conditions as necessary. There is no freedom therefore with reference to this empirical character, and yet it is only with reference to it that we can consider man, when we are merely *observing,* and, as is the case in anthropology, trying to investigate the motive causes of his actions physiologically.

If, however, we consider the same actions with reference to reason, not with reference to speculative reason, in order to *explain* their origin, but solely so far as reason is the cause which *produces* them; in one word, if we compare actions with reason, with reference to *practical* purposes, we find a rule and order, totally different from the order of nature. For, from this point of view, everything, it may be, *ought not to have happened,* which according to the course of nature *has happened,* and according to its empirical grounds, was inevitable. And sometimes we find, or believe at least that we find, that the ideas of reason have really proved their causality with reference to human actions as phenomena, and that these actions have taken place, not because they were determined by empirical causes, but by the causes of reason.

Now supposing one could say that reason possesses causality [551] in reference to phenomena, could the action of reason be called free in that case, as it is accurately determined by the empirical character (the disposition) and rendered necessary by it? That character again is deter-

mined in the intelligible character (way of thinking). The latter, however, we do not know, but signify only through phenomena, which in
reality give us immediately a knowledge of the disposition (empirical
character) only.[52] An action, so far as it is to be attributed to the way of
thinking as its cause, does nevertheless not result from it according to empirical laws, that is, it is not *preceded* by the conditions of pure reason,
but only by its effects in the phenomenal form of the internal sense. Pure
reason, as a simple intelligible faculty, is not subject to the form of time,
or to the conditions of the succession of time. The causality of reason in
its intelligible character does *not arise* or begin at a certain time in order
to produce an effect; for in that case it would be subject to the natural
law of phenomena, which determines all causal series in time, and [552]
its causality would then be nature and not freedom. What, therefore, we
can say is, that if reason can possess causality with reference to phenomena, it is a faculty *through which* the sensuous condition of an empirical series of effects first begins. For the condition that lies in reason
is not sensuous, and therefore does itself not begin. Thus we get what
we missed in all empirical series, namely, that the *condition* of a successive series of events should itself be empirically unconditioned. For
here the condition is really *outside* the series of phenomena (in the intelligible), and therefore not subject to any sensuous condition, nor to
any temporal determination through preceding causes.

Nevertheless the same cause belongs also, in another respect, to the
series of phenomena. Man himself is a phenomenon. His will has an
empirical character, which is the (empirical) cause of all his actions.
There is no condition, determining man according to this character, that
is not contained in the series of natural effects and subject to their law,
according to which there can be no empirically unconditioned causality
of anything that happens in time. No given action therefore (as it can
be perceived as a phenomenon only) can begin absolutely by itself. Of
pure reason, however, we cannot say that the state in which it [553]
determines the will is preceded by another in which that state itself is
determined. For as reason itself is not a phenomenon, and not subject
to any of the conditions of sensibility, there exists in it, even in reference
to its causality, no succession of time, and the dynamical law of nature,
which determines the succession of time according to rules, cannot be
applied to it.

Reason is therefore the constant condition of all free actions by which
man takes his place in the phenomenal world. Every one of them is determined beforehand in his empirical character, before it becomes actual.
With regard to the intelligible character, however, of which the empirical

---

52 The true morality of actions (merit or guilt), even that of our own conduct,
remains therefore entirely hidden. Our imputations can refer to the empirical
character only. How much of that may be the pure effect of freedom, how
much should be ascribed to nature only, and to the faults of temperament,
for which man is not responsible, or its happy constitution (*merito fortunae*),
no one can discover, and no one can judge with perfect justice.

is only the sensuous schema, there is neither *before* nor *after;* and every action, without regard to the temporal relation which connects it with other phenomena, is the immediate effect of the intelligible character of pure reason. That reason therefore acts freely, without being determined dynamically, in the chain of natural causes, by external or internal conditions, anterior in time. That freedom must then not only be regarded negatively, as independence of empirical conditions (for in that case the faculty of reason would cease to be a cause of phenomena), but should be determined positively also, as the faculty of beginning spontaneously a series of events. Hence nothing begins in reason itself, and [554] being itself the unconditioned condition of every free action, reason admits of no condition antecedent in time above itself, while nevertheless its effect takes its beginning in the series of phenomena, though it can never constitute in that series an *absolutely* first beginning.

In order to illustrate the regulative principle of reason by an example of its empirical application, not in order to confirm it (for such arguments are useless for transcendental propositions), let us take a voluntary action, for example, a malicious lie, by which a man has produced a certain confusion in society, and of which we first try to find out the motives, and afterwards try to determine how far it and its consequences may be imputed to the offender. With regard to the first point, one has first to follow up his empirical character to its very sources, which are to be found in wrong education, bad society, in part also in the viciousness of a natural disposition, and a nature insensible to shame, or ascribed to frivolity and heedlessness, not omitting the occasioning causes at the time. In all this the procedure is exactly the same as in the investigation of a series of determining causes of a given natural effect. But although one believes that the act was thus determined, one nevertheless [555] blames the offender, and not on account of his unhappy natural disposition, not on account of influencing circumstances, not even on account of his former course of life, because one supposes one might leave entirely out of account what that course of life may have been, and consider the past series of conditions as having never existed, and the act itself as totally unconditioned by previous states, as if the offender had begun with it a new series of effects, quite by himself. This blame is founded on a law of reason, reason being considered as a cause which, independent of all the before-mentioned empirical conditions, would and should have determined the behaviour of the man otherwise. Nay, we do not regard the causality of reason as a concurrent agency only, but as complete in itself, even though the sensuous motives did not favour, but even oppose it. The action is imputed to a man's intelligible character. At the moment when he tells the lie, the guilt is entirely his; that is, we regard reason, in spite of all empirical conditions of the act, as completely free, and the act has to be imputed entirely to a fault of reason.

Such an imputation clearly shows that we imagine that reason is not affected at all by the influences of the senses, and that it does not change (although its manifestations, that is the mode in which it shows itself by its effects, do change): that in it no state precedes as deter-   [556] mining a following state, in fact, that reason does not belong to the series of sensuous conditions which render phenomena necessary, according to laws of nature. Reason, it is supposed, is present in all the actions of man, in all circumstances of time, and always the same; but it is itself never in time, never in a new state in which it was not before; it is *determining,* never *determined.* We cannot ask, therefore, why reason has not determined itself differently, but only why it has not differently determined the *phenomena* by its causality. And here no answer is really possible. For a different intelligible character would have given a different empirical character, and if we say that, in spite of the whole of his previous course of life, the offender could have avoided the lie, this only means that it was in the power of reason, and that reason, in its causality, is subject to no phenomenal and temporal conditions, and lastly, that the difference of time, though it makes a great difference in phenomena and their relation to each other, can, as these are neither things nor causes by themselves, produce no difference of action in reference to reason.

We thus see that, in judging of voluntary actions, we can, so   [557] far as their causality is concerned, get only so far as the intelligible cause, but not beyond. We can see that that cause is free, that it determines as independent of sensibility, and therefore is capable of being the sensuously unconditioned condition of phenomena. To explain why that intelligible character should, under present circumstances, give these phenomena and this empirical character, and no other, transcends all the powers of our reason, nay, all its rights of questioning, as if we were to ask why the transcendental object of our external sensuous intuition gives us intuition in *space* only and no other. But the problem which we have to solve does not require us to ask or to answer such questions. Our problem was, whether freedom is contradictory to natural necessity in one and the same action: and this we have sufficiently answered by showing that freedom may have relation to a very different kind of conditions from those of nature, so that the law of the latter does not affect the former, and both may exist independent of, and undisturbed by, each other.

It should be clearly understood that, in what we have said, we had no intention of establishing the *reality* of freedom, as one of the faculties which contain the cause of the phenomenal appearances in our   [558] world of sense. For not only would this have been no transcendental consideration at all, which is concerned with concepts only, but it could never have succeeded, because from experience we can never infer anything but what must be represented in thought according to the laws of experience. It was not even our intention to prove the *possibility* of freedom, for in this also we should not have succeeded, because from mere concepts *a priori* we can never know the possibility of any real ground or any causality. We have here treated freedom as a transcendental idea only, which makes reason imagine that it can absolutely begin the series of phenomenal conditions through what is sensuously unconditioned, but by which reason becomes involved in an antinomy with its own laws, which it had prescribed to the empirical use of the understanding. That this antinomy rests on a mere illusion, and that nature does *not contradict* the causality of freedom, that was the only thing which we could prove, and cared to prove.

. . .

CHAPTER III.   THE IDEAL OF PURE REASON   [567]

. . .

There are only three kinds of proofs of the existence of God from speculative reason.

All the paths that can be followed to this end begin either from definite experience and the peculiar nature of the world of sense, known to us through experience, and ascend from it, according to the laws of causality, to the highest cause, existing outside the world; or they rest on indefinite experience only, that is, on any existence which is empirically given; or lastly, they leave all experience out of account, and conclude, entirely *a priori* from mere concepts, the existence of a supreme cause.   [591] The first proof is the *physico-theological,* the second the *cosmological,* the third the *ontological* proof. There are no more, and there can be no more.

I shall show that neither on the one path, the empirical, nor on the other, the transcendental, can reason achieve anything, and that it stretches its wings in vain, if it tries to soar beyond the world of sense by the mere power of speculation. With regard to the order in which these three arguments should be examined, it will be the opposite of that, followed by reason in its gradual development, in which we placed them also at first ourselves. For we shall be able to show that, although experience gives the first impulse, it is the transcendental concept only which guides reason in its endeavours, and fixes the last goal which reason wishes to retain. I shall therefore begin with the examination of the transcendental proof, and see afterwards how far it may be strengthened by the addition of empirical elements.

Section IV   [592]

*Of the Impossibility of an Ontological Proof of the
Existence of God*

It is easily perceived, from what has been said before, that the concept of an absolutely necessary Being is a concept of pure reason, that is, a mere idea, the objective reality of which is by no means proved by the fact that reason requires it. That idea does no more than point to a certain but unattainable completeness, and serves rather to limit the understanding, than to extend its sphere. It seems strange and absurd, however, that a conclusion of an absolutely necessary existence from a given existence in general should seem urgent and correct, and that yet all the conditions under which the understanding can form a concept of such a necessity should be entirely against us.

People have at all times been talking of an *absolutely necessary* Being, but they have tried, not so much to understand whether and how a thing of that kind could even be conceived, as rather to prove its existence. No doubt a verbal definition of that concept is quite easy, if we say that it is something the non-existence of which is impossible. This, however, does not make us much wiser with reference to the conditions that [593] make it necessary [53] to consider the non-existence of a thing as absolutely inconceivable. It is these conditions which we want to know, and whether by that concept we are thinking anything or not. For to use the word *unconditioned,* in order to get rid of all the conditions which the understanding always requires, when wishing to conceive something as necessary, does not render it clear to us in the least whether, after that, we are still thinking anything or perhaps nothing, by the concept of the unconditionally necessary.

Nay, more than this, people have imagined that by a number of examples they had explained this concept, at first risked at haphazard, and afterwards become quite familiar, and that therefore all further inquiry regarding its intelligibility were unnecessary. It was said that every proposition of geometry, such as, for instance, that a triangle has three angles, is absolutely necessary, and people began to talk of an object entirely outside the sphere of our understanding, as if they understood perfectly well what, by that concept, they wished to predicate of it.

But all these pretended examples are taken without exception from *judgments* only, not from *things,* and their existence. Now the unconditioned necessity of judgments is not the same thing as an absolute necessity of things. The absolute necessity of a judgment is only a conditioned necessity of the thing, or of the predicate in the judg- [594] ment. The above proposition did not say that three angles were absolutely necessary, but that under the condition of the existence of a triangle, three angles are given (in it) by necessity. Nevertheless, this pure logical necessity has exerted so powerful an illusion, that, after having formed of a thing a concept *a priori* so constituted that it seemed to include existence in its sphere, people thought they could conclude with certainty that, because existence necessarily belongs to the object of that concept, provided always that I accept the thing as given (existing), its existence also must necessarily be accepted (according to the rule of identity), and that the Being therefore must itself be absolutely necessary, because its existence is implied in a concept, which is accepted voluntarily only, and always under the condition that I accept the object of it as given.

---

[53] Read *nothwendig* instead of *unmöglich.* Noiré

If in an identical judgment I reject the predicate and retain the subject, there arises a contradiction, and hence, I say, that the former belongs to the latter necessarily. But if I reject the subject as well as the predicate, there is no contradiction, because there is nothing left that can be contradicted. To accept a triangle and yet to reject its three angles is contradictory, but there is no contradiction at all in admitting the non-existence of the triangle and of its three angles. The same applies to the concept of an absolutely necessary Being. Remove its existence, [595] and you remove the thing itself, with all its predicates, so that a contradiction becomes impossible. There is nothing external to which the contradiction could apply, because the thing is not meant to be externally necessary; nor is there anything internal that could be contradicted, for in removing the thing out of existence, you have removed at the same time all its internal qualities. If you say, God is almighty, that is a necessary judgment, because almightiness cannot be removed, if you accept a deity, that is, an infinite Being, with the concept of which that other concept is identical. But if you say, God is not, then neither his almightiness, nor any other of his predicates is given; they are all, together with the subject, removed out of existence, and therefore there is not the slightest contradiction in that sentence.

We have seen therefore that, if I remove the predicate of a judgment together with its subject, there can never be an internal contradiction, whatever the predicate may be. The only way of evading this conclusion would be to say that there are subjects which cannot be removed out of existence, but must always remain. But this would be the same as to say that there exist absolutely necessary subjects, an assumption the correctness of which I have called in question, and the possibility of which you had undertaken to prove. For I cannot form to myself the smallest concept of a thing which, if it had been removed together with all its predicates, should leave behind a contradiction; and except con- [596] tradiction, I have no other test of impossibility by pure concepts *a priori*. Against all these general arguments (which no one can object to) you challenge me with a case, which you represent as a proof by a fact, namely, that there is one, and this one concept only, in which the non-existence or the removal of its object would be self-contradictory, namely, the concept of the most real Being (*ens realissimum*). You say that it possesses all reality, and you are no doubt justified in accepting such a Being as possible. This for the present I may admit, though the absence of self-contradictoriness in a concept is far from proving the possibility of its object.[54] Now reality comprehends existence, and therefore exist-

---

[54] A concept is always possible, if it is not self-contradictory. This is the logical characteristic of possibility, and by it the object of the concept is distinguished from the *nihil negativum*. But it may nevertheless be an empty concept, unless the objective reality of the synthesis, by which the concept is generated, has been distinctly shown. This, however, as shown above, must always rest on principles of possible experience, and not on the principle of analysis (the principle of contradiction). This is a warning against inferring at once from the possibility of concepts (logical) the possibility of things (real).

ence is contained in the concept of a thing possible. If that thing is removed, the internal possibility of the thing would be removed, [597] and this is self-contradictory.

I answer:—Even in introducing into the concept of a thing, which you wish to think in its possibility only, the concept of its existence, under whatever disguise it may be, you have been guilty of a contradiction. If you were allowed to do this, you would apparently have carried your point; but in reality you have achieved nothing, but have only committed a tautology. I simply ask you, whether the proposition, that *this or that thing* (which, whatever it may be, I grant you as possible) *exists,* is an analytical or a synthetical proposition? If the former, then by its existence you add nothing to your thought of the thing; but in that case, either the thought within you would be the thing itself, or you have presupposed existence, as belonging to possibility, and have according to your own showing deduced existence from internal possibility, which is nothing but a miserable tautology. The mere word *reality,* which in the concept of a thing sounds different from existence in the concept of the predicate, can make no difference. For if you call all accepting or positing (without determining what it is) reality, you have placed a thing, with all its predicates, within the concept of the subject, and accepted it as real, and you do nothing but repeat it in the predicate. If, on the contrary, you [598] admit, as every sensible man must do, that every proposition involving existence is synthetical, how can you say that the predicate of existence does not admit of removal without contradiction, a distinguishing property which is peculiar to analytical propositions only, the very character of which depends on it?

I might have hoped to put an end to this subtle argumentation, without many words, and simply by an accurate definition of the concept of existence, if I had not seen that the illusion, in mistaking a logical predicate for a real one (that is the predicate which determines a thing), resists all correction. Everything can become a *logical predicate,* even the subject itself may be predicated of itself, because logic takes no account of any contents of concepts. *Determination,* however, is a predicate, added to the concept of the subject, and enlarging it, and it must not therefore be contained in it.

Being is evidently not a real predicate, or a concept of something that can be added to the concept of a thing. It is merely the admission of a thing, and of certain determinations in it. Logically, it is merely the copula of a judgment. The proposition, *God is almighty,* contains two concepts, each having its object, namely, God and almightiness. [599] The small word *is,* is not an additional predicate, but only serves to put the predicate *in relation* to the subject. If, then, I take the subject (God) with all its predicates (including that of almightiness), and say, *God is,* or there is a God, I do not put a new predicate to the concept of God, but I only put the subject by itself, with all its predicates, in relation to my concept, as its object. Both must contain exactly the same kind of thing, and nothing can have been added to the concept, which expresses possibility only, by my thinking its object as simply given and saying, it is. And thus the real does not contain more than the possible. A hundred real dollars do not contain a penny more than a hundred possible dollars. For as the latter signify the concept, the former the object and its position by itself, it is clear that, in case the former contained more than the latter, my concept would not express the whole object, and would not therefore be its adequate concept. In my financial position no doubt there exists more by one hundred real dollars, than by their concept only (that is their possibility), because in reality the object is not only contained analytically in my concept, but is added to my concept (which is a determination of my state), synthetically; but the conceived hundred dollars are not in the least increased through the existence which is outside my concept.

By whatever and by however many predicates I may think [600] a thing (even in completely determining it) nothing is really added to it, if I add that the thing exists. Otherwise, it would not be the same that exists, but something more than was contained in the concept, and I could not say that the exact object of my concept existed. Nay, even if I were to think in a thing all reality, except one, that one missing reality would not be supplied by my saying that so defective a thing exists, but it would exist with the same defect with which I thought it; or what exists would be different from what I thought. If, then, I try to conceive a being, as the highest reality (without any defect), the question still remains, whether it exists or not. For though in my concept there may be wanting nothing of the possible real content of a thing in general, something is wanting in its relation to my whole state of thinking, namely, that the knowledge of that object should be possible *a posteriori* also. And here we perceive the cause of our difficulty. If we were concerned with an object of our senses, I could not mistake the existence of a thing for the mere concept of it; for by the concept the object is thought as only in harmony with the general conditions of a possible empirical knowledge, while by its existence it is thought as contained in the whole content of experience. Through this connection with the content of the whole experience, the concept [601] of an object is not in the least increased; our thought has only received through it one more possible perception. If, however, we are thinking existence through the pure category alone, we need not wonder that we cannot find any characteristic to distinguish it from mere possibility.

Whatever, therefore, our concept of an object may contain, we must always step outside it, in order to attribute to it existence. With objects of the senses, this takes place through their connection with any one of my perceptions, according to empirical laws; with objects of pure thought, however, there is no means of knowing their existence, because it would have to be known entirely *a priori*, while our consciousness of every kind of existence, whether immediately by perception, or by conclusions which connect something with perception, belongs entirely to the unity of experience, and any existence outside that field, though it cannot be declared to be absolutely impossible, is a presupposition that cannot be justified by anything.

The concept of a Supreme Being is, in many respects, a very useful idea, but, being an idea only, it is quite incapable of increasing, by itself alone, our knowledge with regard to what exists. It cannot even   [602] do so much as to inform us any further as to its possibility. The analytical characteristic of possibility, which consists in the absence of contradiction in mere positions (realities), cannot be denied to it; but the connection of all real properties in one and the same thing is a synthesis the possibility of which we cannot judge *a priori* because these realities are not given to us as such, and because, even if this were so, no judgment whatever takes place, it being necessary to look for the characteristic of the possibility of synthetical knowledge in experience only, to which the object of an idea can never belong. Thus we see that the celebrated Leibniz is far from having achieved what he thought he had, namely, to understand *a priori* the possibility of so sublime an ideal Being.

Time and labour therefore are lost on the famous ontological (Cartesian) proof of the existence of a Supreme Being from mere concepts; and a man might as well imagine that he could become richer in knowledge by mere ideas, as a merchant in capital, if, in order to improve his position, he were to add a few noughts to his cash account.

Section V   [603]

Of the Impossibility of a Cosmological Proof of the Existence of God

It was something quite unnatural, and a mere innovation of scholastic wisdom, to attempt to pick out of an entirely arbitrary idea the existence of the object corresponding to it. Such an attempt would never have been made, if there had not existed beforehand a need of our reason of admitting for existence in general something necessary, to which we may ascend and in which we may rest; and if, as that necessity must be unconditioned and *a priori* certain, reason had not been forced to seek a concept which, if possible, should satisfy such a demand and give us a knowledge of an existence entirely *a priori*. Such a concept was supposed to exist in the idea of an *ens realissimum,* and that idea was therefore used for a more definite knowledge of that, the existence of which one had admitted or been persuaded of independently, namely, of the necessary Being. This very natural procedure of reason was carefully concealed, and instead of ending with that concept, an attempt was made to begin with it, and thus to derive from it the necessity of existence, which it was only meant to supplement. Hence arose that un-   [604] fortunate ontological proof, which satisfies neither the demands of our natural and healthy understanding, nor the requirements of the schools.

The *cosmological proof,* which we have now to examine, retains the connection of absolute necessity with the highest reality, but instead of concluding, like the former, from the highest reality necessity in existence, it concludes from the given unconditioned necessity of any being, its unlimited reality. It thus brings everything at least into the groove of a natural, though I know not whether of a really or only apparently rational syllogism, which carries the greatest conviction, not only for the common, but also for the speculative understanding, and has evidently drawn the first outline of all proofs of natural theology, which have been followed at all times, and will be followed in future also, however much they may be hidden and disguised. We shall now proceed to exhibit and to examine this cosmological proof which Leibniz calls also the proof *a contingentia mundi.*

It runs as follows: If there exists anything, there must exist an absolutely necessary Being also. Now I, at least, exist; therefore there exists an absolutely necessary Being. The minor contains an experience, the major the conclusion from experience in general to the existence of [605] the necessary.[55] This proof therefore begins with experience, and is not entirely *a priori*, or ontological; and, as the object of all possible experience is called the world, this proof is called the *cosmological proof.* As it takes no account of any peculiar property of the objects of experience, by which this world of ours may differ from any other possible world, it is distinguished, in its name also, from the physico-theological proof, which employs as arguments, observations of the peculiar property of this our world of sense.

The proof then proceeds as follows: The necessary Being can be determined in one way only, that is, by one only of all possible opposite predicates; it must therefore be determined completely by its own concept. Now, there is only one concept of a thing possible, which *a priori* completely determines it, namely, that of the *ens realissimum*. It follows, therefore, that the concept of the *ens realissimum* is the only one by which a necessary Being can be thought, and therefore it is concluded [606] that a highest Being exists by necessity.

There are so many sophistical propositions in this cosmological argument, that it really seems as if speculative reason had spent all her dialectical skill in order to produce the greatest possible transcendental illusion. Before examining it, we shall draw up a list of them, by which reason has put forward an old argument disguised as a new one, in order to appeal to the agreement of two witnesses, one supplied by pure reason, the other by experience, while in reality there is only one, namely, the first, who changes his dress and voice in order to be taken for a second. In order to have a secure foundation, this proof takes its stand on experience, and pretends to be different from the ontological proof, which

---

[55] This conclusion is too well known to require detailed exposition. It rests on the apparently transcendental law of causality in nature, that everything *contingent* has its cause, which, if contingent again, must likewise have a cause, till the series of subordinate causes ends in an absolutely necessary cause, without which it could not be complete.

places its whole confidence in pure concepts *a priori* only. The cosmological proof, however, uses that experience only in order to make one
step, namely, to the existence of a necessary Being in general. What
properties that Being may have, can never be learnt from the empirical
argument, and for that purpose reason takes leave of it altogether, and
tries to find out, from among concepts only, what properties an absolutely
necessary Being ought to possess, i.e. which among all possible things
contains in itself the requisite conditions (*requisita*) of absolute [607]
necessity. This requisite is believed by reason to exist in the concept of
an *ens realissimum* only, and reason concludes at once that this must be
the absolutely necessary Being. In this conclusion it is simply assumed
that the concept of a being of the highest reality is perfectly adequate to
the concept of absolute necessity in existence; so that the latter might
be concluded from the former. This is the same proposition as that maintained in the ontological argument, and is simply taken over into the
cosmological proof, nay, made its foundation, although the intention was
to avoid it. For it is clear that absolute necessity is an existence from
mere concepts. If, then, I say that the concept of the *ens realissimum*
is such a concept, and is the only concept adequate to necessary existence,
I am bound to admit that the latter may be deduced from the former.
The whole conclusive strength of the so-called cosmological proof rests
therefore in reality on the ontological proof from mere concepts, while
the appeal to experience is quite superfluous, and, though it may lead us
on to the concept of absolute necessity, it cannot demonstrate it with any
definite object. For as soon as we intend to do this, we must at once
abandon all experience, and try to find out which among the pure concepts
may contain the conditions of the possibility of an absolutely [608]
necessary Being. But if in this way the possibility of such a Being has
been perceived, its existence also has been proved: for what we are really
saying is this, that under all possible things there is one which carries
with it absolute necessity, or that this Being exists with absolute necessity.

Sophisms in arguments are most easily discovered, if they are put
forward in a correct scholastic form. This we shall now proceed to do.

If the proposition is right, that every absolutely necessary Being is, at
the same time, the most real Being (and this is the *nervus probandi* of the
cosmological proof), it must, like all affirmative judgments, be capable of
conversion, at least *per accidens*. This would give us the proposition that
some *entia realissima* are at the same time absolutely necessary beings.
One *ens realissimum*, however, does not differ from any other on any
point, and what applies to one, applies also to all. In this case, therefore,
I may employ absolute conversion, and say, that every *ens realissimum* is
a necessary Being. As this proposition is determined by its concepts *a
priori* only, it follows that the mere concept of the *ens realissimum* must
carry with it its absolute necessity; and this, which was maintained by
the ontological proof, and not recognised by the cosmological, forms really
the foundation of the conclusions of the latter, though in a disguised
form.   [609]

We thus see that the second road taken by speculative reason, in order to prove the existence of the highest Being, is not only as illusory as the first, but commits in addition an *ignoratio elenchi,* promising to lead us by a new path, but after a short circuit bringing us back to the old one, which we had abandoned for its sake.

I said before that a whole nest of dialectical assumptions was hidden in that cosmological proof, and that transcendental criticism might easily detect and destroy it. I shall here enumerate them only, leaving it to the experience of the reader to follow up the fallacies and remove them.

We find, first, the transcendental principle of inferring a cause from the accidental. This principle, that everything contingent must have a cause, is valid in the world of sense only, and has not even a meaning outside it. For the purely intellectual concept of the contingent cannot produce a synthetical proposition like that of causality, and the principle of causality has no meaning and no criterion of its use, except in the world of sense, while here it is meant to help us beyond the world of sense.

Secondly. The inference of a first cause, based on the im- [610] possibility of an infinite ascending series of given causes in this world of sense,—an inference which the principles of the use of reason do not allow us to draw even in experience, while here we extend that principle beyond experience, whither that series can never be prolonged.

Thirdly. The false self-satisfaction of reason with regard to the completion of that series, brought about by removing in the end every kind of condition, without which, nevertheless, no concept of necessity is possible, and by then, when any definite concepts have become impossible, accepting this as a completion of our concept.

Fourthly. The mistaking the logical possibility of a concept of all united reality (without any internal contradiction) for the transcendental, which requires a principle for the practicability of such a synthesis, such principle however being applicable to the field of possible experience only, etc.

The trick of the cosmological proof consists only in trying to avoid the proof of the existence of a necessary Being *a priori* by mere concepts. Such a proof would have to be ontological, and of this we feel ourselves quite incapable. For this reason we take a real existence (of any experience whatever), and conclude from it, as well as may be, some absolutely necessary condition of it. In that case there is no necessity for explaining its possibility, because, if it has been proved that it exists, the [611] question as to its possibility is unnecessary. If then we want to determine that necessary Being more accurately, according to its nature, we do not seek what is sufficient to make us understand from its concept the necessity of its existence. If we could do this, no empirical presupposition would be necessary. No, we only seek the negative condition (*conditio sine qua non*), without which a Being would not be absolutely necessary. Now, in every other kind of syllogisms leading from a given effect to its cause, this might well be feasible. In our case, however, it happens unfortunately that the condition which is required for absolute necessity exists in one single Being only, which, therefore, would have to contain in its concept all that is required for absolute necessity, and that renders a conclusion *a priori*, with regard to such necessity, possible. I ought therefore to be able to reason conversely, namely, that everything is absolutely necessary, if that concept (of the highest reality) belongs to it. If I cannot do this (and I must confess that I cannot, if I wish to avoid the ontological proof), I have suffered shipwreck on my new course, and have come back again from where I started. The concept of the highest Being may satisfy all questions *a priori* which can be asked regarding the internal determinations of a thing, and it is therefore an ideal, without an equal, because the general concept distinguishes it at the same time as an individual being among all possible things. But it does   [612] not satisfy the really important question regarding its own existence; and if some one who admitted the existence of a necessary Being were to ask us which of all things in the world could be regarded as such, we could not answer: This here is the necessary Being.

It may be allowable to *admit* the existence of a Being entirely sufficient to serve as the cause of all possible effects, simply in order to assist reason in her search for unity of causes. But to go so far as to say that *such a Being exists necessarily,* is no longer the modest language of an admissible hypothesis, but the bold assurance of apodictic certainty; for the knowledge of that which is absolutely necessary must itself possess absolute necessity.

The whole problem of the transcendental Ideal is this, either to find a concept compatible with absolute necessity, or to find the absolute necessity compatible with the concept of anything. If the one is possible, the other must be so also, for reason recognises that only as absolutely necessary which is necessary according to its concept. Both these tasks baffle our attempts at *satisfying* our understanding on this point, and likewise our endeavours to comfort it with regard to its impotence.   [613]

That unconditioned necessity, which we require as the last support of all things, is the true abyss of human reason. Eternity itself, however terrible and sublime it may have been depicted by Haller, is far from producing the same giddy impression, for it only *measures* the duration of things, but does not *support* them. We cannot put off the thought, nor can we support it, that a Being, which we represent to ourselves as the highest among all possible beings, should say to himself, I am from eternity to eternity, there is nothing beside me, except that which is something through my will,—*but whence am I?* Here all sinks away from under us, and the highest perfection, like the smallest, passes without support before the eyes of speculative reason, which finds no difficulty in making the one as well as the other to disappear without the slightest impediment.

Many powers of nature, which manifest their existence by certain effects, remain perfectly inscrutable to us, because we cannot follow them up far enough by observation. The transcendental object, which forms the foundation of all phenomena, and with it the ground of our sensibility having this rather than any other supreme conditions, is and always will be inscrutable. The thing no doubt is given, but it is incomprehensible. An ideal of pure reason, however, cannot be called [614] inscrutable, because it cannot produce any credentials of its reality beyond the requirement of reason to perfect all synthetical unity by means of it. As, therefore, it is not even given as an object that can be thought, it cannot be said to be, as such, inscrutable; but, being a mere idea, it must find in the nature of reason its place and its solution, and in that sense be capable of scrutiny. For it is the very essence of reason that we are able to give an account of all our concepts, opinions, and assertions either on objective or, if they are a mere illusion, on subjective grounds.

Discovery and Explanation of the Dialectical Illusion in all Transcendental Proofs of the Existence of a Necessary Being

Both proofs, hitherto attempted, were transcendental, that is, independent of empirical principles. For although the cosmological proof assumes for its foundation an experience in general, it does not rest on any particular quality of it, but on pure principles of reason, with reference to an existence given by the empirical consciousness in general, and abandons even that guidance in order to derive its support from pure concepts only. What then in these transcendental proofs is the [615] cause of the dialectical, but natural, illusion which connects the concepts of necessity and of the highest reality, and realises and hypostasises that which can only be an idea? What is the cause that renders it inevitable to admit something as necessary in itself among existing things, and yet makes us shrink back from the existence of such a Being as from an abyss? What is to be done that reason should understand itself on this point, and, escaping from the wavering state of hesitatingly approving or disapproving, acquire a calm insight into the matter?

It is surely extremely strange that, as soon as we suppose that something exists, we cannot avoid the conclusion that something exists necessarily. On this quite natural, though by no means, therefore, certain conclusion, rests the whole cosmological argument. On the other side, I may take any concept of anything, and I find that its existence has never to be represented by me as absolutely necessary, nay, that nothing prevents me, whatever may exist, from thinking its non-existence. I may, therefore, have to admit something necessary as the condition of existing things in general, but I need not think any single thing as necessary in itself. In other words I can never *complete* the regressus to the [616] conditions of existence without admitting a necessary Being, but I can never *begin* with such a Being.

If, therefore, I am obliged to think something necessary for all existing things, and at the same time am not justified in thinking of anything as in itself necessary, the conclusion is inevitable: that necessity and contingency do not concern things themselves, for otherwise there would be a contradiction, and that therefore neither of the two principles can be objective; but that they may possibly be subjective principles of reason only, according to which, on one side, we have to find for all that is given as existing, something that is necessary, and thus never to stop except when we have reached an *a priori* complete explanation; while on the other we must never hope for that completion, that is, never admit anything empirical as unconditioned, and thus dispense with its further derivation. In that sense both principles as purely heuristic and *regulative,* and affecting the formal interests of reason only, may well stand side by side. For the one tells us that we ought to philosophise on nature as if there was a necessary first cause for everything that exists, if only in order to introduce systematical unity into our knowledge, by always looking for such an idea as an imagined highest cause. The other   [617] warns us against mistaking any single determination concerning the existence of things for such a highest cause, i.e. for something absolutely necessary, and bids us to keep the way always open for further derivation, and to treat it always as conditioned. If, then, everything that is perceived in things has to be considered by us as only conditionally necessary, nothing that is empirically given can ever be considered as absolutely necessary.

It follows from this that the absolutely necessary must be accepted as *outside the world,* because it is only meant to serve as a principle of the greatest possible unity of phenomena, of which it is the highest cause, and that it can never be reached *in the world,* because the second rule bids you always to consider all empirical causes of that unity as derived.

The philosophers of antiquity considered all form in nature as contingent, but matter, according to the judgment of common reason, as primitive and necessary. If, however, they had considered matter, not relatively as the substratum of phenomena, but as existing *by itself,* the idea of absolute necessity would have vanished at once, for there is nothing that binds reason absolutely to that existence, but reason can at any time and without contradiction remove it in thought, and it   [618] was in thought only that it could claim absolute necessity. The ground of this persuasion must therefore have been a certain regulative principle. And so it is; for extension and impermeability (which together constitute the concept of matter) furnish the highest empirical principle of the unity of phenomena, and possess, so far as this principle is empirically unconditioned, the character of a regulative principle. Nevertheless, as every determination of matter, which constitutes its reality, and hence the impermeability of matter also, is an effect (action) which must have a cause, and therefore be itself derived, matter is not adequate to the idea of a necessary Being, as a principle of all derived unity, because every one of its real qualities is derived and, therefore, conditionally necessary only, so that it could be removed, and with it would be removed the whole existence of matter. If this were not so, we should have reached the highest cause of unity, empirically, which is forbidden by the second regulative principle. It follows from all this that matter and everything in general that belongs to the world are not fit for the idea of a necessary original Being, as a mere principle of the greatest empirical unity, but that we must place it outside the world. In that case there is no reason why we should not simply derive the phenomena of the world and their existence from other phenomena, as if there were no necessary Being at all, while at the same time we might always strive towards the completeness of that derivation, just as if such a Being, as the high- [619] est cause, were presupposed.

The ideal of the Supreme Being is therefore, according to these remarks, nothing but a *regulative principle* of reason, which obliges us to consider all connection in the world as if it arose from an all-sufficient necessary cause, in order to found on it the rule of a systematical unity necessary according to general laws for the explanation of the world; it does not involve the assertion of an existence necessary by itself. It is impossible, however, at the same time, to escape from a transcendental *subreptio,* which leads us to represent that formal principle as constitutive, and to think that unity as hypostasised. It is the same with space. (Space, though it is only a principle of sensibility, yet serves originally to make all forms possible, these being only limitations of it. For that very reason, however, it is mistaken for something absolutely necessary and independent, nay, for an object *a priori* existing in itself.) It is the same here, and as this systematical unity of nature can in no wise become the principle of the empirical use of our reason, unless we base it on the idea of an *ens realissimum* as the highest cause, it happens quite naturally that we thus represent that idea as a real object, and that object again, as it is the highest condition, as necessary. Thus a *regulative* principle has been changed into a constitutive principle, which substitution becomes evident [620] at once because, as soon as I consider that highest Being, which with regard to the world was absolutely (unconditionally) necessary, as a thing by itself, that necessity cannot be conceived, and can therefore have existed in my reason as a formal condition of thought only, and not as a material and substantial condition of existence.

Section VI

Of the Impossibility of the Physico-theological Proof

If, then, neither the concept of things in general, nor the experience of any *existence in general,* can satisfy our demands, there still remains one way open, namely, to try whether any *definite experience,* and consequently that of things in the world as it is, their constitution and disposition, may not supply a proof which could give us the certain conviction of the existence of a Supreme Being. Such a proof we should call *physico-theological.* If that, however, should prove impossible too, then it is clear that no satisfactory proof whatever, from merely speculative reason, is possible, in support of the existence of a Being, corresponding to our transcendental idea.

After what has been said already, it will be easily understood [621] that we may expect an easy and complete answer to this question. For how could there ever be an experience that should be adequate to an idea? It is the very nature of an idea that no experience can ever be adequate to it. The transcendental idea of a necessary and all-sufficient original Being is so overwhelming, so high above everything empirical, which is always conditioned, that we can never find in experience enough material to fill such a concept, and can only grope about among things conditioned, looking in vain for the unconditioned, of which no rule of any empirical synthesis can ever give us an example, or even show the way towards it.

If the highest Being should stand itself in that chain of conditions, it would be a link in the series, and would, exactly like the lower links, above which it is placed, require further investigation with regard to its own still higher cause. If, on the contrary, we mean to separate it from that chain, and, as a purely intelligible Being, not comprehend it in the series of natural causes, what bridge is then open for reason to reach it, considering that all rules determining the transition from effect to cause, nay, all synthesis and extension of our knowledge in general, refer to nothing but possible experience, and therefore to the objects of the world of sense only, and are valid nowhere else? [622]

This present world presents to us so immeasurable a stage of variety, order, fitness, and beauty, whether we follow it up in the infinity of space or in its unlimited division, that even with the little knowledge which our poor understanding has been able to gather, all language, with regard to so many and inconceivable wonders, loses its vigour, all numbers their power of measuring, and all our thoughts their necessary determination; so that our judgment of the whole is lost in a speechless, but all the more eloquent astonishment. Everywhere we see a chain of causes and effects, of means and ends, of order in birth and death, and as nothing has entered by itself into the state in which we find it, all points to another thing as its cause. As that cause necessitates the same further enquiry, the whole universe would thus be lost in the abyss of nothing, unless we admitted something which, existing by itself, original and independent, outside the chain of infinite contingencies, should support it, and, as the cause of its origin, secure to it at the same time its permanence. Looking at all the things in the world, what greatness shall we attribute to that highest cause? We do not know the whole contents of the world, still less can we measure its magnitude by a comparison with all that is possible. But, as with regard to [623] causality, we cannot do without a last and highest Being, why should we not fix the degree of its perfection *beyond everything else that is possible?* This we can easily do, though only in the faint outline of an abstract concept, if we represent to ourselves all possible perfections united in it as in one substance. Such a concept would agree with the demand of our reason, which requires parsimony in the number of principles; it would have no contradictions in itself, would be favourable to the extension of the employment of reason in the midst of experience, by guiding it towards order and system, and lastly, would never be decidedly opposed to any experience.

This proof will always deserve to be treated with respect. It is the oldest, the clearest, and most in conformity with human reason. It gives life to the study of nature, deriving its own existence from it, and thus constantly acquiring new vigour.

It reveals aims and intention, where our own observation would not by itself have discovered them, and enlarges our knowledge of nature by leading us towards that peculiar unity the principle of which exists outside nature. This knowledge reacts again on its cause, namely, the transcendental idea, and thus increases the belief in a supreme [624] Author to an irresistible conviction.

It would therefore be not only extremely sad, but utterly vain to attempt to diminish the authority of that proof. Reason, constantly strengthened by the powerful arguments that come to hand by themselves, though they are no doubt empirical only, cannot be discouraged by any doubts of subtle and abstract speculation. Roused from every inquisitive indecision, as from a dream, by one glance at the wonders of nature and the majesty of the cosmos, reason soars from height to height till it reaches the highest, from the conditioned to conditions, till it reaches the supreme and unconditioned Author of all.

But although we have nothing to say against the reasonableness and utility of this line of argument, but wish, on the contrary, to commend and encourage it, we cannot approve of the claims which this proof advances to apodictic certainty, and to an approval on its own merits, requiring no favour, and no help from any other quarter. It cannot injure the good cause, if the dogmatical language of the overweening sophist is toned down to the moderate and modest statements of a faith which does not require unconditioned submission, yet is sufficient to give rest and comfort. I therefore maintain that the physico-theological proof can never establish by itself alone the existence of a Supreme Being, but must always [625] leave it to the ontological proof (to which it serves only as an introduction), to supply its deficiency; so that, after all, it is the ontological proof which contains the *only possible argument* (supposing always that any speculative proof is possible), and human reason can never do without it.

The principal points of the physico-theological proof are the following. 1st. There are everywhere in the world clear indications of an intentional arrangement carried out with great wisdom, and forming a whole indescribably varied in its contents and infinite in extent.

2ndly. The fitness of this arrangement is entirely foreign to the things existing in the world, and belongs to them contingently only; that is, the nature of different things could never spontaneously, by the combination of so many means, co-operate towards definite aims, if these means had not been selected and arranged on purpose by a rational disposing principle, according to certain fundamental ideas.

3rdly. There exists, therefore, a sublime and wise cause (or many), which must be the cause of the world, not only as a blind and all-powerful nature, by means of unconscious *fecundity*, but as an intelligence, by *freedom*.

4thly. The unity of that cause may be inferred with certainty from the unity of the reciprocal relation of the parts of the world, as [626] portions of a skilful edifice, so far as our experience reaches, and beyond it, with plausibility, according to the principles of analogy.

Without wishing to argue, for the sake of argument only, with natural reason, as to its conclusion in inferring from the analogy of certain products of nature with the works of human art, in which man does violence to nature, and forces it not to follow its own aims, but to adapt itself to ours (that is, from the similarity of certain products of nature with houses, ships, and watches), in inferring from this, I say, that a similar causality, namely, understanding and will, must be at the bottom of nature, and in deriving the internal possibility of a freely acting nature (which, it may be, renders all human art and even human reason possible) from another though superhuman art—a kind of reasoning, which probably could not stand the severest test of transcendental criticism; we are willing to admit, nevertheless, that if we have to name such a cause, we cannot do better than to follow the analogy of such products of human design, which are the only ones of which we know completely both cause and effect. There would be no excuse, if reason were to surrender a causality which it knows, and have recourse to obscure and indemonstrable principles of explanation, which it does not know.

According to this argument, the fitness and harmony existing in so many works of nature might prove the contingency of the form, [627] but not of the matter, that is, the substance in the world, because, for the latter purpose, it would be necessary to prove in addition, that the things of the world were in themselves incapable of such order and harmony, according to general laws, unless there existed, even in their *substance*, the product of a supreme wisdom. For this purpose, very different arguments would be required from those derived from the analogy of human art. The utmost, therefore, that could be established by such a proof would be an *architect of the world*, always very much hampered by the quality of the material with which he has to work, not a *creator*, to whose idea everything is subject. This would by no means suffice for the purposed aim of proving an all-sufficient original Being. If we wished to prove the contingency of matter itself, we must have recourse to a transcendental argument, and this is the very thing which was to be avoided.

The inference, therefore, really proceeds from the order and design that can everywhere be observed in the world, as an entirely contingent arrangement, to the existence of a cause, *proportionate to it*. The concept of that cause must therefore teach us something quite *definite* about it, and can therefore be no other concept but that of a Being which possesses all might, wisdom, etc., in one word, all perfection of an all-sufficient Being. The predicates of a *very great*, of an astounding, [628] of an immeasurable might and virtue give us no definite concept, and never tell us really what the thing is by itself. They are only relative representations of the magnitude of an object, which the observer (of the world) compares with himself and his own power of comprehension, and which would be equally grand, whether we magnify the object, or reduce the observing subject to smaller proportions in reference to it. Where we are concerned with the magnitude (of the perfection) of a thing in general, there exists no definite concept, except that which comprehends all possible perfection, and only the all (*omnitudo*) of reality is thoroughly determined in the concept.

Now I hope that no one would dare to comprehend the relation of that part of the world which he has observed (in its extent as well as in its contents) to omnipotence, the relation of the order of the world to the highest wisdom, and the relation of the unity of the world to the absolute unity of its author, etc. Physico-theology, therefore, can never give a definite concept of the highest cause of the world, and is insufficient, therefore, as a principle of theology, which is itself to form the basis of religion.

The step leading to absolute totality is entirely impossible on the empirical road. Nevertheless, that step is taken in the physico-theological proof. How then has this broad abyss been bridged over?   [629]

The fact is that, after having reached the stage of admiration of the greatness, the wisdom, the power, etc. of the Author of the world, and seeing no further advance possible, one suddenly leaves the argument carried on by empirical proofs, and lays hold of that contingency which, from the very first, was inferred from the order and design of the world. The next step from that contingency leads, by means of transcendental concepts only, to the existence of something absolutely necessary, and another step from the absolute necessity of the first cause to its completely determined or determining concept, namely, that of an all-embracing reality. Thus we see that the physico-theological proof, baffled in its own undertaking, takes suddenly refuge in the cosmological proof, and as this is only the ontological proof in disguise, it really carries out its original intention by means of pure reason only; though it so strongly disclaimed in the beginning all connection with it, and professed to base everything on clear proofs from experience.

Those who adopt the physico-theological argument have no reason to be so very coy towards the transcendental mode of argument, and with the conceit of enlightened observers of nature to look down upon them as the cobwebs of dark speculators. If they would only examine themselves, they would find that, after they had advanced a good way on the soil of nature and experience, and found themselves nevertheless as much removed as ever from the object revealed to their reason,   [630] they suddenly leave that soil, to enter the realm of pure possibilities, where on the wings of ideas they hope to reach that which had withdrawn itself from all their empirical investigations. Imagining themselves to be on firm ground after that desperate leap, they now proceed to expand the definite concept which they have acquired, they do not know how, over the whole field of creation; and they explain the ideal, which was merely a product of pure reason, by experience, though in a very poor way, and totally beneath the dignity of the object, refusing all the while to admit that they have arrived at that knowledge or supposition by a very different road from that of experience.

Thus we have seen that the physico-theological proof rests on the cosmological, and the cosmological on the ontological proof of the existence of one original Being as the Supreme Being; and, as besides these three, there is no other path open to speculative reason, the ontological proof, based exclusively on pure concepts of reason, is the only possible one, always supposing that any proof of a proposition, so far transcending the empirical use of the understanding, is possible at all.

Section VII   [631]

*Criticism of all Theology based on Speculative Principles
of Reason*

If by *Theology* we understand the knowledge of the original Being, it is derived either from reason only (*theologia rationalis*), or from revelation (*revelata*). The former thinks its object either by pure reason and through transcendental concepts only (*ens originarium, realissimum, ens entium*), and is then called *transcendental* theology, or by a concept, borrowed from the nature (of our soul), as the highest intelligence, and ought then to be called *natural* theology. Those who admit a transcendental theology only are called *Deists*, those who admit also a *natural* theology Theists. The former admit that we may know the existence of an original Being by mere reason, but that our concept of it is transcendental only, as of a Being which possesses all reality, but a reality that cannot be further determined. The latter maintain that reason is capable of determining that object more accurately in analogy with nature, namely, as a Being which, through understanding and freedom, contains within itself the original ground of all other things. The former admits *a cause of the world* only (whether through the necessity   [632] of its nature or through freedom, remains undecided), the latter an *author of the world.*

Transcendental theology, again, either derives the existence of the original Being from an experience in general (without saying anything about the world, to which it belongs), and is then called *Cosmotheology;* or it believes that it can know its existence, without the help of any experience whatsoever, and by mere concepts, and is then called *Ontotheology.*

Natural theology infers the qualities and the existence of an author of the world from the constitution, the order, and the unity, which are seen in this world, in which two kinds of causality with their rules must be admitted, namely, nature and freedom. It ascends from this world to the highest intelligence as the principle either of all natural or of all moral order and perfection. In the former case it is called *Physico-theology*, in the other *Ethico-theology*.[56]

As we are accustomed to understand by the concept of God, not only a blindly working eternal nature, as the root of all things, but a Supreme Being, which, through understanding and freedom, is supposed to be the author of all things, and it is this concept alone in which we [633] really take an interest, one might strictly deny to the *Deist* all belief in God, and allow him only the maintaining of an original Being, or a supreme cause. But as no one, simply because he does not dare to assert, ought to be accused of denying a thing, it is kinder and juster to say, that the *Deist* believes in a God, but the *Theist* in a *living* God (*summa intelligentia*). We shall now try to discover the possible sources of all these attempts of reason.

I shall not do more, at present, than define theoretical knowledge as one by which I know what *there is*, practical knowledge as one by which I represent to myself what *ought to be*. Hence the theoretical use of reason is that by which I know *a priori* (as necessary) that something is, while the practical use of reason is that by which I know *a priori* what ought to be. If then it is certain, beyond the possibility of doubt, that something is, or that something ought to be, though both are conditioned, then a certain definite condition of it may be either absolutely necessary or presupposed only as possible and contingent. In the former case, the condition is postulated (*per thesin*), in the latter supposed (*per hypothesin*). As there are practical laws, which are absolutely necessary (the moral laws), it follows, if they necessarily presuppose any ex- [634] istence as the condition of the possibility of their *obligatory* power, that the existence of that condition must be *postulated*, because the conditioned, from which we infer that condition, has been recognised *a priori* as absolutely necessary. On a future occasion we shall show that the moral laws not only presuppose the existence of a Supreme Being, but that, as they are in other respects absolutely necessary, they postulate it by right, though of course practically only. For the present we leave this mode of argument untouched.

If we only speak of that which is, not of that which ought to be, the conditioned given to us in experience is always conceived as contingent, and the condition belonging to it can therefore not be known as absolutely necessary, but serves only as a relatively necessary, or rather *needful*, though in itself an *a priori* arbitrary supposition for a rational understanding of the conditioned. If, therefore, we wish to know in our theoretical knowledge the absolute necessity of a thing, this could only

---

[56] Not theological Ethics; for these contain moral laws, which *presuppose* the existence of a supreme ruler of the world, while Ethico-theology is the conviction of the existence of a Supreme Being, founded on moral laws.

be done from concepts *a priori,* and never as of a cause in reference to an existence which is given in experience.

I call a theoretical knowledge *speculative,* if it relates to an object, or such concepts of an object, which we can never reach in any experience. It is opposed to our *knowledge of nature,* which relates to no other objects or predicates of them except those that can be given in   [635] a possible experience.

From something that happens (the empirically contingent) as an effect, to infer a cause, is a principle of natural, though not of speculative knowledge. For if we no longer use it as a principle involving the condition of possible experience, and, leaving out everything that is empirical, try to apply it to the contingent in general, there does not remain the smallest justification of such a synthetical proposition, showing how from something which is, there can be a transition to something totally different, which we call cause; nay, in such purely speculative application, the concepts both of cause and of the contingent lose all meaning, the objective reality of which would be made intelligible in the concrete.

If from the existence of *things* in the world we infer their cause, we are using reason not *naturally,* but *speculatively.* Naturally, reason refers not the things themselves (substances), but only that which *happens,* their *states,* as empirically contingent, to some cause; but it could know speculatively only that a substance itself (matter) is contingent in its existence. And even if we were thinking only of the form of the   [636] world, the manner of its composition and the change of this composition, and tried to infer from this a cause totally different from the world, this would be again a judgment of speculative reason only; because the object here is not an object of any possible experience. In this case the principle of causality, which is valid within the field of experience only, and utterly useless, nay, even meaningless, outside it, would be totally diverted from its proper destination.

What I maintain then is, that all attempts at a purely speculative use of reason, with reference to theology, are entirely useless and intrinsically null and void, while the principles of their natural use can never lead to any theology, so that unless we depend on moral laws, or are guided by them, there cannot be any theology of reason. For all synthetical principles of the understanding are applicable immanently only, i.e. within its own sphere, while, in order to arrive at the knowledge of a Supreme Being, we must use them transcendentally, and for this our understanding is not prepared. If the empirically valid law of causality is to conduct us to the original Being, that Being must belong to the chain of objects of experience, and in that case it would, like all phenomena, be itself conditioned. And even if that sudden jump beyond the limits of experience, according to the dynamical law of the   [637] relation of effects to their causes, could be allowed, what concept could we gain by this proceeding? Certainly no concept of a Supreme Being, because experience never presents to us the greatest of all possible effects, to bear witness of its cause. If we claim to be allowed, only in order to leave no void in our reason, to supply this defect in the complete determination of that cause by the mere idea of the highest perfection and of original necessity, this may possibly be granted as a favour, but can never be demanded on the strength of an irresistible proof. The physico-theological proof, as connecting speculation with intuition, might possibly therefore be used in support of other proofs (if they existed); it cannot, however, finish the task for itself, but can only prepare the understanding for theological knowledge, and impart to it the right and natural direction.

It must have been seen from this that transcendental questions admit of transcendental answers only, that is, of such which consist of mere concepts *a priori* without any empirical admixture. Our question, however, is clearly synthetical, and requires an extension of our knowledge beyond all limits of experience, till it reaches the existence of a Being which is to correspond to our pure idea, though no experience can ever be adequate to it. According to our former proofs, all synthetical [638] knowledge *a priori* is possible only, if it conforms to the formal conditions of a possible experience. All these principles therefore are of immanent validity only, that is, they must remain within the sphere of objects of empirical knowledge, or of phenomena. Nothing, therefore, can be achieved by a transcendental procedure with reference to the theology of a purely speculative reason.

If people, however, should prefer to call in question all the former proofs of the Analytic, rather than allow themselves to be robbed of their persuasion of the value of the proofs on which they have rested so long, they surely cannot decline my request, when I ask them to justify themselves, at least on this point, in what manner, and by what kind of illumination they trust themselves to soar above all possible experience, on the wings of pure ideas. I must ask to be excused from listening to new proofs, or to the tinkered workmanship of the old. No doubt the choice is not great, for all speculative proofs end in the one, namely, the ontological; nor need I fear to be much troubled by the inventive fertility of the dogmatical defenders of that reason which they have delivered from the bondage of the senses; nor should I even, without considering myself a very formidable antagonist, decline the challenge to detect the fallacy in every one of their attempts, and thus to dispose of their pretensions. But I know too well that the hope of better success will never be sur- [639] rendered by those who have once accustomed themselves to dogmatical persuasion, and I therefore restrict myself to the one just demand, that my opponents should explain in general, from the nature of the human understanding, or from any other sources of knowledge, what we are to do in order to extend our knowledge entirely *a priori*, and to carry it to a point where no possible experience, and therefore no means whatever, is able to secure to a concept invented by ourselves its objective reality. In whatever way the understanding may have reached that concept, it is clearly impossible that the *existence* of its object could be found in it through analysis, because the very knowledge of the existence of the object implies that it exists *outside our thoughts*. We cannot in fact go beyond concepts, nor, unless we follow the empirical connection by which nothing but phenomena can be given, hope to discover new objects and imaginary beings.

Although then reason, in its purely speculative application, is utterly insufficient for this great undertaking, namely, to prove the existence of a Supreme Being, it has nevertheless this great advantage of being able to *correct* our knowledge of it, if it can be acquired from else-   [640] where, to make it consistent with itself and every intelligible view, and to purify it from everything incompatible with the concept of an original Being, and from all admixture of empirical limitations.

In spite of its insufficiency, therefore, transcendental theology has a very important negative use, as a constant test of our reason, when occupied with pure ideas only, which, as such, admit of a transcendental standard only. For suppose that on practical grounds the *admission* of a highest and all-sufficient Being, as the highest intelligence, were to maintain its validity without contradiction, it would be of the greatest importance that we should be able to determine that concept accurately on its transcendental side, as the concept of a necessary and most real Being, to remove from it what is contradictory to that highest reality and purely phenomenal (anthropomorphic in the widest sense), and at the same time to put an end to all opposite assertions, whether *atheistic*, *deistic*, or *anthropomorphistic*. Such a critical treatment would not be difficult, because the same arguments by which the insufficiency of human reason in asserting the existence of such a Being has been proved, must be sufficient also to prove the invalidity of opposite as-   [641] sertions. For whence can anybody, through pure speculation of reason, derive his knowledge that there is no Supreme Being, as the cause of all that exists, or that it can claim none of those qualities which we, to judge from their effects, represent to ourselves as compatible with the dynamical realities of a thinking Being, or that, in the latter case, they would be subject to all those limitations which sensibility imposes inevitably on all the intelligences known to us by experience?

For the purely speculative use of reason, therefore, the Supreme Being remains, no doubt, an ideal only, but an ideal *without a flaw*, a concept which finishes and crowns the whole of human knowledge, and the objective reality of which, though it cannot be proved, can neither be disproved in that way. If then there should be an Ethico-theology to supply that deficiency, transcendental theology, which before was problematical only, would prove itself indispensable in determining its concept, and in constantly testing reason, which is so often deceived by sensibility, and not even always in harmony with its own ideas. Necessity, infinity, unity, extra-mundane existence (not as a world-soul), eternity, free from conditions of time, omnipresence, free from conditions of space, omnipotence, etc., all these are transcendental predicates, and their purified concepts, which are so much required for every   [642] theology, can therefore be derived from transcendental theology only.

.   .   .

Of Opinion, Knowledge, and Belief [820]

. . .

Now we must admit that the doctrine of the existence of God [826] belongs to doctrinal belief. For although, with reference to my theoretical knowledge of the world, I can *produce* nothing which would make this thought a necessary supposition as a condition of my being able to explain the phenomena of the world, but on the contrary am bound to use my reason as if everything were mere nature, nevertheless, the unity of design is so important a condition of the application of reason to nature that I cannot ignore it, especially as experience supplies so many examples of it. Of that unity of design, however, I know no other condition, which would make it a guidance in my study of nature, but the supposition that a supreme intelligence has ordered all things according to the wisest ends. As a condition, therefore, of, it may be, a contingent, but not unimportant end, namely, in order to have a guidance in the investigation of nature, it is necessary to admit a wise author of the world. The result of my experiment confirms the usefulness of this supposition so many times, while nothing decisive can be adduced against it, that I am really saying far too little, if I call my acceptation of it a mere opinion, and it may be said, even with regard to these theoretical matters, that I firmly believe in God. Still, if we use our words strictly, this belief must always be called doctrinal, and not practical, such as the *theology* of nature (physical theology) must always and necessarily produce. In [827] the same wisdom, and in the prominent endowments of human nature, combined with the inadequate shortness of life, another sufficient ground may be found for the doctrinal belief in the future life of the human soul.

The expression of belief is in such cases an expression of modesty from the *objective* point of view, and yet, at the same time, a firm confidence from a *subjective*. If even I were to call this purely theoretical acceptance an hypothesis only, which I am entitled to assume, I should profess to be in possession of a more complete concept of the nature of a cause of the world, and of another world, than I really can produce. If I accept anything, even as an hypothesis only, I must know it at least so much according to its properties, that I need *not* imagine *its concepts*, but *its existence* only. But the word *belief* refers only to the guidance which an idea gives me, and to its subjective influence on the conduct of my reason, which makes me hold it fast, though I may not be able to give an account of it from a speculative point of view.

Purely doctrinal belief, however, has always a somewhat unstable character. Speculative difficulties often make us lose hold of it, though in the end we always return to it. [828]

It is quite different with *moral belief*. For here action is absolutely necessary, that is, I must obey the moral law on all points. The end is here firmly established, and, according to all we know, one only condition is possible under which that end could agree with all other ends, and thus acquire practical validity, namely, the existence of a God and of a future world. I also know it for certain that no one is cognisant of other conditions which could lead to the same unity of ends under the moral law. As, then, the moral precept is at the same time my maxim, reason commanding that it should be so, I shall inevitably believe in the existence of God, and in a future life, and I feel certain that nothing can shake this belief, because all my moral principles would be overthrown at the same time, and I cannot surrender them without becoming hateful in my own eyes.

We see, therefore, that, even after the failure of all the ambitious schemes of reason to pass beyond the limits of all experience, enough remains to make us satisfied for practical purposes. No one, no doubt, will be able to boast again that he *knows* that there is a God and a future life. For a man who knows that, is the very man whom I   [829] have been so long in search of. As all knowledge, if it refers to an object of pure reason, can be communicated, I might hope that, through his teaching, my own knowledge would be increased in the most wonderful way. No, that conviction is not a *logical,* but a *moral* certainty; and, as it rests on subjective grounds (of the moral sentiment), I must not even say that *it is* morally certain that there is a God, etc., but that *I* am morally certain, etc. What I really mean is, that the belief in a God and in another world is so interwoven with my moral sentiment, that as there is little danger of my losing the latter, there is quite as little fear lest I should ever be deprived of the former.

The only point that may arouse misgivings is that this rational belief is based on the supposition of moral sentiments. If we surrender this, and take a man who is entirely indifferent with regard to moral laws, the question proposed by reason becomes merely a problem for speculation, and may in that case be still supported with strong grounds from analogy, but not such to which the most obstinate scepticism has to submit.[57]

No man, however, is with regard to these questions free from all   [830] interest. For although in the absence of good sentiments he may be rid of all moral interest, enough remains even thus to make him *fear* the existence of God and a future life. For nothing is required for this but his inability to plead *certainty* with regard to the *non-existence* of such a being and of a future life. As this would have to be proved by mere reason, and therefore apodictically, he would have to establish the im-

---

[57] The interest which the human mind takes in morality (an interest which, as I believe, is necessary to every rational being) is natural, though it is not undivided, and always practically preponderant. If you strengthen and increase that interest, you will find reason very docile, and even more enlightened, so as to be able to join the speculative with the practical interests. If you do not take care that you first make men at least moderately good, you will never make them honest believers.

possibility of both, which I feel certain no rational being would venture to do. This would be a *negative* belief which, though it could not produce morality and good sentiments, would still produce something analogous, namely, a check on the outbreak of evil.

But, it will be said, is this really all that pure reason can achieve in opening prospects beyond the limits of experience? Nothing more than two articles of faith? Surely even the ordinary understanding could have achieved as much without taking counsel of philosophers!   [831]

I shall not here dwell on the benefits which, by the laborious efforts of its criticism, philosophy has conferred on human reason, granting even that in the end they should turn out to be merely negative. On this point something will have to be said in the next section. But I ask, do you really require that knowledge, which concerns all men, should go beyond the common understanding, and should be revealed to you by philosophers only? The very thing which you find fault with, is the best confirmation of the correctness of our previous assertions, since it reveals to us what we could not have grasped before, namely, that in matters which concern all men without distinction, nature cannot be accused of any partial distribution of her gifts; and that with regard to the essential interests of human nature, the highest philosophy can achieve no more than that guidance which nature has vouchsafed even to the meanest understanding.

.   .   .

(*The Conclusion of the Book*)   [856]

As regards those who follow a *scientific* method, they have the choice to proceed either *dogmatically* or *sceptically*, but at all events, *systematically*. When I have mentioned in relation to the former the celebrated *Wolf*, and in relation to the other *David Hume*, I may for my present purpose leave all the rest unnamed.

The only path that is still open is the *critical*. If the reader has been kind and patient enough to follow me to the end along this path, he may judge for himself whether, if he will help, as far as in him lies, towards making this footpath a highroad, it may not be possible to achieve, even before the close of the present century, what so many centuries have not been able to achieve, namely, to give complete satisfaction to human reason with regard to those questions which have in all ages exercised its desire for knowledge, though hitherto in vain.

THREE ADDITIONS TO THE SECOND EDITION

The Deduction of the Categories (A 95-130) was substantially changed in the Second Edition. Two sections (§§ 16-17) from the revised version (B 131-39) are reprinted here, followed by Kant's "Refutation of Idealism" (B 274-79), inserted in the Second Edition in the argument on A 226. In Max Müller's translation, these additions are found in Supplements XIV and XXI.

The Original Synthetical Unity of Apperception

It must be *possible* that the *I think* should accompany all my representations: for otherwise something would be represented within me that could not be thought, in other words, the representation would either be impossible or nothing, at least so far as I am concerned. That representation which can be given before all thought, is called *intuition*, and all the manifold of intuition has therefore a necessary relation to the *I think* in the same subject in which that manifold of intuition is found. That representation, however (that *I think*), is an act of *spontaneity*, that is, it cannot be considered as belonging to sensibility. I call it *pure apperception*, in order to distinguish it from empirical apperception, or *original apperception* also, because it is that self-consciousness which by producing the representation, *I think* (which must accompany all others, and is one and the same in every act of consciousness), cannot itself be accompanied by any other. I also call the unity of it the transcendental unity of self-consciousness, in order to indicate that it contains the possibility of knowledge *a priori*.

For the manifold representations given in any intuition would not all be *my* representations, if they did not all belong to one self-consciousness. What I mean is that, as my representations (even though I am not conscious of them as such), they must be in accordance with that condition, under which alone they can stand together in one common self-consciousness, because otherwise they would not all belong to me. From this original connection the following important conclusions can be deduced.

The unbroken identity of apperception of the manifold that is given in intuition contains a synthesis of representations, and is possible only through the consciousness of that synthesis. The empirical consciousness, which accompanies various representations, is itself various and disunited, and without reference to the identity of the subject. Such a relation takes place, not by my simply accompanying every relation with consciousness, but by my *adding* one to the other and being conscious of that act of adding, that is, of that synthesis. Only because I am able to connect the manifold of given representations in *one consciousness*, is it possible for me to represent to myself the *identity* of the *consciousness* in these *representations*, that is, only under the supposition of some synthetical unity of apperception does the analytical unity of apperception become possible.[58]

The thought that the representations given in intuition belong all of them to me, is therefore the same as that I connect them in one self-consciousness, or am able at least to do so; and though this is not yet the *consciousness* of the *synthesis* of representations, it nevertheless presupposes the possibility of this synthesis. In other words, it is only because I am able to comprehend the manifold of representations in one consciousness, that I call them altogether my representations, for otherwise, I should have as manifold and various a self as I have representations of which I am conscious. The synthetical unity of the manifold of intuitions as given *a priori* is therefore the ground also of the identity of that apperception itself which precedes *a priori* all definite thought. Connection, however, does never lie in the objects, and cannot be borrowed from them by perception, and thus be taken into the understanding, but it is always an act of the understanding, which itself is nothing but a faculty of connecting *a priori*, and of bringing the manifold of given representations under the unity of apperception, which is, in fact, the highest principle of all human knowledge.

It is true, no doubt, that this principle of the necessary unity of apperception is itself identical, and therefore an analytical proposition; but it shows, nevertheless, the necessity of a synthesis of the manifold which is given in intuition, without which synthesis it would be impossible to think the unbroken identity of self-consciousness. For through the *Ego*, as a simple representation, nothing manifold is given; in the intuition, which is different from that, it can be given only, and then, by *connection*, be thought in one consciousness. An understanding in which, by self-consciousness, all the manifold would be given at the same time, would possess *intuition*; our understanding can do nothing but think, and must seek for its intuition in the senses. I am conscious, therefore, of the identical self with respect to the manifold of the representations, which are given to me in an intuition, because I call them, altogether, my representations, as constituting *one*. This means, that I am conscious of a

---

[58] This analytical unity of consciousness belongs to all general concepts, as such. If, for instance, I think *red* in general, I represent to myself a property, which (as a characteristic mark) may be found in something, or can be connected with other representations; that is to say, only under a presupposed possible synthetical unity can I represent to myself the analytical. A representation which is to be thought as common to *different* representations, is looked upon as belonging to such as possess, besides it, something *different*. It must therefore have been thought in synthetical unity with other (though only possible) representations, before I can think in it that analytical unity of consciousness which makes it a *conceptus communis*. The synthetical unity of apperception is, therefore, the highest point with which all employment of the understanding, and even the whole of logic, and afterwards the whole of transcendental philosophy, must be connected; ay, that faculty is the understanding itself.

necessary synthesis of them *a priori*, which is called the original synthetical unity of apperception under which all representations given to me must stand, but have to be brought there, first, by means of a synthesis.

The Principle of the Synthetical Unity of Apperception is the Highest Principle of all Employment of the Understanding

The highest principle of the possibility of all intuition, in relation to sensibility, was, according to the transcendental Æsthetic, that all the manifold in it should be subject to the formal conditions of space and time. The highest principle of the same possibility in relation to the understanding is, that all the manifold in intuition must be subject to the conditions of the original synthetical unity of apperception.[59]

All the manifold representations of intuition, so far as they are *given* us, are subject to the former, so far as they must admit of being connected in one consciousness, to the latter; and without that nothing can be thought or known by them, because the given representations would not share the act of apperception (I think) in common, and could not be comprehended in one self-consciousness.

The *understanding* in its most general sense is the faculty of *cognitions*. These consist in a definite relation of given representations to an object; and an *object* is that in the concept of which the manifold of a given intuition is *connected*. All such connection of representations requires of course the unity of the consciousness in their synthesis: consequently, the unity of consciousness is that which alone constitutes the relation of representations to an object, that is, their objective validity, and consequently their becoming cognitions, so that the very possibility of the understanding depends on it.

The first pure cognition of the understanding, therefore, on which all the rest of its employment is founded, and which at the same time is entirely independent of all conditions of sensuous intuition, is this very principle of the original synthetical unity of apperception. Space, the mere form of external sensuous intuition, is not yet cognition: it only supplies the manifold of intuition *a priori* for a possible cognition. In order to know anything in space, for instance, a line, I must *draw* it, and produce synthetically a certain connection of the manifold that is given, so that the unity of that act is at the same time the unity of the consciousness (in the concept of a line), and (so that) an object (a deter-

---

[59] Space and time, and all portions thereof, are *intuitions,* and consequently single representations with the manifold of their content. (See the transcendental Æsthetic.) They are not, therefore, mere concepts, through which the same consciousness, as existing in many representations, but intuitions through which many representations are brought to us, as contained in one and in its consciousness; this latter, therefore, is compounded, and these intuitions represent the unity of consciousness as *synthetical,* but yet as primitive. This character of *singleness* in them is practically of great importance (see § 25).

minate space) is then only known for the first time. The synthetical unity of consciousness is, therefore, an objective condition of all knowledge; a condition, not necessary for myself only, in order to know an object, but one to which each intuition must be subject, in order to become an *object* for me, because the manifold could not become connected in one consciousness in any other way, and without such a synthesis.

No doubt, that proposition, as I said before, is itself analytical, though it makes synthetical unity a condition of all thought, for it really says no more than that all my representations in any given intuition must be subject to the condition under which alone I can ascribe them, as my representations, to the identical self, and therefore comprehend them, as synthetically connected, in one apperception through the general expression, *I think.*

And yet this need not be a principle for every possible understanding, but only for that which gives nothing manifold through its pure apperception in the representation, *I am.* An understanding which through its self-consciousness could give the manifold of intuition, and by whose representation the objects of that representation should at the same time exist, would not require a special act of the synthesis of the manifold for the unity of its consciousness, while the human understanding, which possesses the power of thought only, but not of intuition, requires such an act. To the human understanding that first principle is so indispensable that it really cannot form the least concept of any other possible understanding, whether it be intuitive by itself, or possessed of a sensuous intuition, different from that in space and time.

Refutation of Idealism

IDEALISM (I mean *material* idealism) is the theory which declares the existence of objects in space, without us, as either doubtful only and not demonstrable, or as false and impossible. The *former* is the *problematical* idealism of Descartes, who declares one empirical assertion only to be undoubted, namely, that of *I am*; the latter is the *dogmatical* idealism of Berkeley, who declares space and all things to which it belongs as an inseparable condition, as something impossible in itself, and, therefore, the things in space as mere imaginations. Dogmatic idealism is inevitable, if we look upon space as a property belonging to things by themselves, for in that case space and all of which it is a condition, would be a non-entity. The ground on which that idealism rests has been removed by us in the transcendental Æsthetic. Problematical idealism, which asserts nothing, but only pleads our inability of proving any existence except our own by means of immediate experience, is reasonable and in accordance with a sound philosophical mode of thought, which allows of no decisive judgment, before a sufficient proof has been found. The required proof will have to demonstrate that we may have not only an *imagination*, but also an *experience* of external things, and this it seems can hardly be effected in any other way except by proving that even our internal experience, which Descartes considers as undoubted, is possible only under the supposition of external experience.

Theorem

The simple, but empirically determined Consciousness of my own existence, proves the Existence of objects in space outside myself.

Proof

I am conscious of my own existence as determined in time, and all determination in time presupposes something *permanent* in the perception.[60] That *permanent*, however, cannot be an intuition within me, because all the causes which determine my existence, so far as they can be found within me, are representations, and as such require themselves something permanent, different from them, in reference to which their change, and therefore my existence in time in which they change, may be determined. The perception of this permanent, therefore, is possible only through a thing *outside* me, and not through the mere *representation* of a thing outside me, and the determination of my existence in time is, consequently, possible only by the existence of real things, which I perceive outside me. Now, as the consciousness in time is necessarily connected with the consciousness of the possibility of that determination of time, it is also necessarily connected with the existence of things outside me, as the condition of the determination of time. In other words, the consciousness of my own existence is, at the same time, an immediate consciousness of the existence of other things.

NOTE 1.—It will have been perceived that in the foregoing proof the trick played by idealism has been turned against it, and with greater justice. Idealism assumed that the only immediate experience is the internal, and that from it we can no more than *infer* external things, though in an untrustworthy manner only, as always happens if from given effects we infer *definite* causes: it being quite possible that the cause of the representations, which are ascribed by us, it may be wrongly, to external things, may lie within ourselves. We, however, have proved that external experience is really immediate,[61] and that only by means of it, though

---

60 This passage has been translated as amended by Kant himself in the Preface to the Second Edition (p. 386).

61 The *immediate* consciousness of the existence of external things is not simply assumed in the preceding theorem, but proved, whether we can understand the possibility of this consciousness or not. The question with regard to that possibility would come to this, whether we have an internal sense only, and no external sense, but merely an external imagination. It is clear, however, that, even in order to imagine only something as external, that is, to represent it to the senses in intuition, we must have an external sense, and thus distinguish immediately the mere receptivity of an external intuition from that spontaneity which characterizes every act of imagination. For merely to imagine an external *sense* would really be to destroy the faculty of intuition, which is to be determined by the faculty of imagination.

not the consciousness of our own existence, yet its determination in time, that is, internal experience, becomes possible. No doubt the representation of *I am*, which expresses the consciousness that can accompany all thought, is that which immediately includes the existence of a subject: but it does not yet include a *knowledge* of it, and therefore no empirical knowledge, that, is experience. For that we require, besides the thought of something existing, intuition also, and in this case internal intuition in respect to which, that is, to time, the subject must be determined. For that purpose external objects are absolutely necessary, so that internal experience itself is possible, mediately only, and through external experience.

NOTE 2. — This view is fully confirmed by the empirical use of our faculty of knowledge, as applied to the determination of time. Not only are we unable to perceive any determination of time, except through a change in external relations (motion) with reference to what is permanent in space (for instance, the movement of the sun with respect to terrestrial objects), but we really have nothing permanent to which we could refer the concept of a substance, as an intuition, except *matter* only: and even its permanence is not derived from external experience, but presupposed *a priori* as a necessary condition of all determination of time, and therefore also of [62] the determination of the internal sense with respect to our own existence through the existence of external things. The consciousness of myself, in the representation of the *ego*, is not an intuition, but a merely *intellectual* representation of the spontaneity of a thinking subject. Hence that *ego* has not the slightest predicate derived from intuition, which predicate, as *permanent*, might serve as the correlate of the determination of time in the internal sense: such as is, for instance, *impermeability* in matter, as an *empirical* intuition.

NOTE 3. — Because the existence of external objects is required for the possibility of a definite consciousness of ourselves, it does not follow that every intuitional representation of external things involves, at the same time, their existence; for such a representation may well be the mere effect of the faculty of imagination (in dreams as well as in madness); but it can be such an effect only through the reproduction of former external perceptions, which, as we have shown, is impossible without the reality of *external* objects. What we wanted to prove here was only that internal experience in general is possible only through external experience in general. Whether this or that supposed experience be purely imaginary, must be settled according to its own particular determinations, and through a comparison with the criteria of all real experience.

---

[62] Read *der* instead of *als*.

PROLEGOMENA TO ANY FUTURE METAPHYSICS

§ 27. Now we are prepared to remove Hume's doubt. He justly maintains, that we cannot comprehend by reason the possibility of Causality, that is, of the reference of the existence of one thing to the existence of another, which is necessitated by the former. I add, that we comprehend just as little the concept of Subsistence, that is, the necessity that at the foundation of the existence of things here lies a subject which cannot itself be a predicate of any other thing; nay, we cannot even form a notion of the possibility of such a thing (though we can point out examples of its use in experience). The very same incomprehensibility affects the Community of things, as we cannot comprehend how from the state of one thing an inference to the state of quite another thing beyond it, and *vice versa*, can be drawn, and how substances which have each their own separate existence should depend upon one another necessarily. But I am very far from holding these concepts to be derived merely from experience, and the necessity represented in them, to be imaginary and a mere illusion produced in us by long habit. On the contrary, I have amply shown, that they and the theorems derived from them are firmly established *a priori*, or before all experience, and have their undoubted objective value, though only with regard to experience.

§ 28. Though I have no notion of such a connexion of things in themselves, that they can either exist as substances, or act as causes, or stand in community with others (as part of a real whole), and I can just as little conceive such properties in appearances as such (because those concepts contain nothing that lies in the appearances, but only what the understanding alone must think): we have yet a notion of such a connexion of representations in our understanding, and in judgments generally; consisting in this, that representations appear in one sort of judgments as subject in relation to predicates, in another as reason in relation to consequences, and in a third as parts, which constitute together a total possible cognition. Besides we cognise *a priori* that without considering the representation of an object as determined in some of these respects, we can have no valid cognition of the object, and, if we should occupy ourselves about the object in itself, there is no possible attribute, by which I could know that it is determined under any of these aspects, that is, under the concept either of substance, or of cause, or (in relation to other substances) of community, for I have no notion of the possibility of such a connexion of existence. But the question is not how things in themselves, but how the empirical cognition of things is determined, as regards the above aspects of judgments in general, that is, how things, as objects of experience, can and shall be subsumed under these concepts of the understanding. And then it is clear, that I completely comprehend not only the possibility, but also the necessity of subsuming all phenomena under these concepts, that is, of using them for principles of the possibility of experience.

§ 29. When making an experiment with Hume's problematical concept (his *crux metaphysicorum*), the concept of cause, we have, in the first place, given *a priori*, by means of logic, the form of a conditional judgment in general, i.e., we have one given cognition as antecedent and another as consequence. But it is possible, that in perception we may meet with a rule of relation, which runs thus: that a certain phenomenon is constantly followed by another (though not conversely), and this is a case for me to use the hypothetical judgment, and, for instance, to say, if the sun shines long enough upon a body, it grows warm. Here there is indeed as yet no necessity of connexion, or concept of cause. But I proceed and say, that if this proposition, which is merely a subjective connexion of perceptions, is to be a judgment of experience, it must be considered as necessary and universally valid. Such a proposition would be, "the sun is by its light the cause of heat." The empirical rule is now considered as a law, and as valid not merely of appearances but valid of them for the purposes of a possible experience which requires universal and therefore necessarily valid rules. I therefore easily comprehend the concept of cause, as a concept necessarily belonging to the mere form of experience, and its possibility as a synthetical union of perceptions in consciousness generally; but I do not at all comprehend the possibility of a thing generally as a cause, because the concept of cause denotes a condition not at all belonging to things, but to experience. It is nothing in fact but an objectively valid cognition of appearances and of their succession, so far as the antecedent can be conjoined with the consequent according to the rule of hypothetical judgments.

§ 30. Hence if the pure concepts of the understanding do not refer to objects of experience but to things in themselves (*noumena*), they have no signification whatever. They serve, as it were, only to decipher appearances, that we may be able to read them as experience. The principles which arise from their reference to the sensible world, only serve our understanding for empirical use. Beyond this they are arbitrary combinations, without objective reality, and we can neither cognise their possibility *a priori*, nor verify their reference to objects, let alone make it intelligible by any example; because examples can only be borrowed from some possible experience, consequently the objects of these concepts can be found nowhere but in a possible experience.

This complete (though to its originator unexpected) solution of Hume's problem rescues for the pure concepts of the understanding their *a priori* origin, and for the universal laws of nature their validity, as laws of the understanding, yet in such a way as to limit their use to experience, because their possibility depends solely on the reference of the understanding to experience, but with a completely reversed mode of connexion which never occurred to Hume, not by deriving them from experience, but by deriving experience from them.

This is therefore the result of all our foregoing inquiries: "All synthetical principles *a priori* are nothing more than principles of possible experience, and can never be referred to things in themselves, but to appearances as objects of experience. And hence pure mathematics as well as a pure science of nature can never be referred to anything more than mere appearances, and can only represent either that which makes experience generally possible, or else that which, as it is derived from these principles, must always be capable of being represented in some possible experience."

°   ·   ·

§ 36 . . . HOW IS NATURE ITSELF POSSIBLE?

This question—the highest point that transcendental philosophy can ever reach, and to which, as its boundary and completion, it must proceed—properly contains two questions.

FIRST: How is nature at all possible in the material sense, by intuition, considered as the totality of appearances; how are space, time, and that which fills both—the object of sensation, in general possible? The answer is: By means of the constitution of our Sensibility, according to which it is specifically affected by objects, which are in themselves unknown to it, and totally distinct from those phenomena. This answer is given in the *Critique* itself in the transcendental Aesthetic, and in these *Prolegomena* by the solution of the first general problem.

SECOND: How is nature possible in the formal sense, as the totality of the rules, under which all phenomena must come, in order to be thought as connected in experience? The answer must be this: It is only possible by means of the constitution of our Understanding, according to which all the above representations of the sensibility are necessarily referred to a consciousness, and by which the peculiar way in which we think (viz., by rules), and hence experience also, are possible, but must be clearly distinguished from an insight into the objects in themselves. This answer is given in the *Critique* itself in the transcendental Logic, and in these *Prolegomena,* in the course of the solution of the second main problem.

But how this peculiar property of our sensibility itself is possible, or that of our understanding and of the apperception which is necessarily its basis and that of all thinking, cannot be further analysed or answered, because it is of them that we are in need for all our answers and for all our thinking about objects.

There are many laws of nature, which we can only know by means of experience; but conformity to law in the connexion of appearances, i.e., in nature in general, we cannot discover by any experience, because experience itself requires laws which are *a priori* at the basis of its possibility.

The possibility of experience in general is therefore at the same time the universal law of nature, and the principles of the experience are the very laws of nature. For we do not know nature but as the totality of appearances, i.e., of representations in us, and hence we can only derive the laws of its connexion from the principles of their connexion in us, that is, from the conditions of their necessary union in consciousness, which constitutes the possibility of experience.

Even the main proposition expounded throughout this section—that universal laws of nature can be distinctly cognised *a priori*—leads naturally to the proposition: that the highest legislation of nature must lie in ourselves, i.e., in our understanding, and that we must not seek the universal laws of nature in nature by means of experience, but conversely must seek nature, as to its universal conformity to law, in the conditions of the possibility of experience, which lie in our sensibility and in our understanding. For how were it otherwise possible to know *a priori* these laws, as they are not rules of analytical cognition, but truly synthetical extensions of it?

Such a necessary agreement of the principles of possible experience with the laws of the possibility of nature, can only proceed from one of two reasons: either these laws are drawn from nature by means of experience, or conversely nature is derived from the laws of the possibility of experience in general, and is quite the same as the mere universal conformity to law of the latter. The former is self-contradictory, for the universal laws of nature can and must be cognised *a priori* (that is, independent of all experience), and be the foundation of all empirical use of the understanding; the latter alternative therefore alone remains.[1]

But we must distinguish the empirical laws of nature, which always presuppose particular perceptions, from the pure or universal laws of nature, which, without being based on particular perceptions, contain merely the conditions of their necessary union in experience. In relation to the latter, nature and possible experience are quite the same, and as the conformity to law here depends upon the necessary connexion of appearances in experience (without which we cannot cognise any object whatever in the sensible world), consequently upon the original laws of the understanding, it seems at first strange, but is not the less certain, to say:

The understanding does not derive its laws (a priori) from, but prescribes them to, nature.

.   .   .

[1] Crusius alone thought of a compromise: that a Spirit, who can neither err nor deceive, implanted these laws in us originally. But since false principles often intrude themselves, as indeed the very system of this man shows in not a few examples, we are involved in difficulties as to the use of such a principle in the absence of sure criteria to distinguish the genuine origin from the spurious, as we never can know certainly what the Spirit of truth or the father of lies may have instilled into us.

GENERAL REMARK ON THE TRANSCENDENTAL IDEAS

§ 56. The objects, which are given us by experience, are in many respects incomprehensible, and many questions, to which the law of nature leads us, when carried beyond a certain point (though quite conformably to the laws of nature), admit of no answer; as for example the question: why substances attract one another? But if we entirely quit nature, or in pursuing its combinations, exceed all possible experience, and so enter the realm of mere ideas, we cannot then say that the object is incomprehensible, and that the nature of things proposes to us insoluble problems. For we are not then concerned with nature or in general with given objects, but with concepts, which have their origin merely in our reason, and with mere creations of thought; and all the problems that arise from our notions of them must be solved, because of course reason can and must give a full account of its own procedure.[2] As the psychological, cosmological, and theological Ideas are nothing but pure concepts of reason, which cannot be given in any experience, the questions which reason asks us about them are put to us not by the objects, but by mere maxims of our reason for the sake of its own satisfaction. They must all be capable of satisfactory answers, which is done by showing that they are principles which bring our use of the understanding into thorough agreement, completeness, and synthetical unity, and that they so far hold good of experience only, but of experience as a whole.

Although an absolute whole of experience is impossible, the idea of a whole of cognition according to principles must impart to our knowledge a peculiar kind of unity, that of a system, without which it is nothing but piecework, and cannot be used for proving the existence of a highest purpose (which can only be the general system of all purposes), I do not here refer only to the practical, but also to the highest purpose of the speculative use of reason.

The transcendental Ideas therefore express the peculiar application of reason as a principle of systematic unity in the use of the understanding. Yet if we assume this unity of the mode of cognition to be attached to the object of cognition, if we regard that which is merely regulative to be constitutive, and if we persuade ourselves that we can by means of these

---

[2] Herr Platner in his Aphorisms acutely says (§§ 728, 729), "If reason be a criterion, no concept, which is incomprehensible to human reason, can be possible. Incomprehensibility has place in what is actual only. Here incomprehensibility arises from the insufficiency of the acquired ideas." It sounds paradoxical, but is otherwise not strange to say, that in nature there is much incomprehensible (e.g., the faculty of generation) but if we mount still higher, and even go beyond nature, everything again becomes comprehensible; for we then quit entirely the objects, which can be given us, and occupy ourselves merely about ideas, in which occupation we can easily comprehend the law that reason prescribes by them to the understanding for its use in experience, because the law is the reason's own production.

Ideas enlarge our cognition transcendently, or far beyond all possible experience, while it only serves to render experience within itself as nearly complete as possible, i.e., to limit its progress by nothing that cannot belong to experience: we suffer from a mere misunderstanding in our estimate of the proper application of our reason and of its principles, and from a Dialectic, which both confuses the empirical use of reason, and also sets reason at variance with itself.

FOUNDATION FOR THE METAPHYSIC OF MORALS

.   .   .

Nothing can possibly be conceived in the world, or even out of it, which can be called good without qualification, except a Good Will. Intelligence, wit, judgment, and the other *talents* of the mind, however they may be named, or courage, resolution, perseverance, as qualities of temperament, are undoubtedly good and desirable in many respects; but these gifts of nature may also become extremely bad and mischievous if the will which is to make use of them, and which, therefore, constitutes what is called *character,* is not good. It is the same with the *gifts of fortune.* Power, riches, honour, even health, and the general well-being and contentment with one's condition which is called *happiness,* inspire pride, and often presumption, if there is not a good will to correct the influence of these on the mind, and with this also to rectify the whole principle of acting, and adapt it to its end. The sight of a being who is not adorned with a single feature of a pure and good will, enjoying unbroken prosperity, can never give pleasure to an impartial rational spectator. Thus a good will   [12] *
appears to constitute the indispensable condition even of being worthy of happiness.

There are even some qualities which are of service to this good will itself, and may facilitate its action, yet which have no intrinsic unconditional value, but always presuppose a good will, and this qualifies the esteem that we justly have for them, and does not permit us to regard them as absolutely good. Moderation in the affections and passions, self-control and calm deliberation are not only good in many respects, but even seem to constitute part of the intrinsic worth of the person; but they are far from deserving to be called good without qualification, although they have been so unconditionally praised by the ancients. For without the principles of a good will, they may become extremely bad, and the coolness of a villain not only makes him far more dangerous, but also directly makes him more abominable in our eyes than he would have been without it.

---

* In this selection, page numbers in brackets refer to Kant's *Sämmtliche Werke,* ed. Karl Rosenkranz and F. W. Schubert, vol. VIII (1838). W. K.

A good will is good not because of what it performs or effects, not by its aptness for the attainment of some proposed end, but simply by virtue of the volition, that is, it is good in itself, and considered by itself is to be esteemed much higher than all that can be brought about by it in favour of any inclination, nay, even of the sum total of all inclinations. Even if it should happen that, owing to special disfavour of fortune, or the niggardly provision of a step-motherly nature, this will should wholly lack power to accomplish its purpose, if with its greatest efforts it should yet achieve nothing, and there should remain only the good will (not, to be sure, a mere wish, but the summoning of all means in our power), then, like a jewel, it would still shine by its own light, as a thing which has its whole value in itself. Its usefulness or fruitlessness can neither add [13] to nor take away anything from this value. It would be, as it were, only the setting to enable us to handle it the more conveniently in common commerce, or to attract to it the attention of those who are not yet connoisseurs, but not to recommend it to true connoisseurs, or to determine its value.

There is, however, something so strange in this idea of the absolute value of the mere will, in which no account is taken of its utility, that notwithstanding the thorough assent of even common reason to the idea, yet a suspicion must arise that it may perhaps really be the product of mere high-flown fancy, and that we may have misunderstood the purpose of nature in assigning reason as the governor of our will. Therefore we will examine this idea from this point of view.

In the physical constitution of an organized being, that is, a being adapted suitably to the purposes of life, we assume it as a fundamental principle that no organ for any purpose will be found but what is also the fittest and best adapted for that purpose. Now in a being which has reason and a will, if the proper object of nature were its *conservation,* its *welfare,* in a word, its *happiness,* then nature would have hit upon a very bad arrangement in selecting the reason of the creature to carry out this purpose. For all the actions which the creature has to perform with a view to this purpose, and the whole rule of its conduct, would be far more surely prescribed to it by instinct, and that end would have been attained thereby much more certainly than it ever can be by reason. Should reason have been communicated to this favoured creature over and above, it must only have served it to contemplate the happy constitution of its nature, to admire it, to congratulate itself thereon, and to feel thank- [14] ful for it to the beneficent cause, but not that it should subject its desires to that weak and delusive guidance, and meddle bunglingly with the purpose of nature. In a word, nature would have taken care that reason should not break forth into *practical exercise,* nor have the presumption, with its weak insight, to think out for itself the plan of happiness, and of the means of attaining it. Nature would not only have taken on herself the choice of the ends, but also of the means, and with wise foresight would have entrusted both to instinct.

.   .   .

We have then to develop the notion of a will which deserves to be highly esteemed for itself, and is good without a view to anything further, a notion which exists already in the sound natural understanding, requiring rather to be cleared up than to be taught, and which in estimating the value of our actions always takes the first place, and constitutes the condition of all the rest. In order to do this we will take the notion of duty, which includes that of a good will, although implying certain subjective restrictions and hindrances. These, however, far from concealing it, or rendering it unrecognizable, rather bring it out by contrast, and make it shine forth so much the brighter.

I omit here all actions which are already recognised as inconsistent with duty, although they may be useful for this or that purpose, for with these the question whether they are done *from duty* cannot arise at all, since they even conflict with it. I also set aside those actions which really conform to duty, but to which men have *no* direct *inclination*, performing them because they are impelled thereto by some other inclination. For in this case we can readily distinguish whether the action which agrees with duty is done *from duty*, or from a selfish view. It is much harder to make this distinction when the action accords with duty, and the subject has besides a *direct* inclination to it. For example, it is always a matter of duty that a dealer should not overcharge an inexperienced purchaser, and wherever there is much commerce the prudent tradesman does not overcharge, but keeps a fixed price for everyone, so that a child buys of him as well as any other. Men are thus *honestly* served; but this is not enough to make us believe that the tradesman has so acted from duty and from principles of honesty: his own advantage required it; it is out of the question in this case to suppose that he might besides have a direct inclination in favour of the buyers, so that, as it were, from love he should give   [17] no advantage to one over another. Accordingly the action was done neither from duty nor from direct inclination, but merely with a selfish view.

On the other hand, it is a duty to maintain one's life; and, in addition, every one has also a direct inclination to do so. But on this account the often anxious care which most men take for it has no intrinsic worth, and their maxim has no moral import. They preserve their life *as duty requires*, no doubt, but not *because duty requires.* On the other hand, if adversity and hopeless sorrow have completely taken away the relish for life; if the unfortunate one, strong in mind, indignant at his fate rather than desponding or dejected, wishes for death, and yet preserves his life without loving it—not from inclination or fear, but from duty—then his maxim has a moral worth.

To be beneficent when we can is a duty; and besides this, there are many minds so sympathetically constituted that, without any other motive of vanity or self-interest, they find a pleasure in spreading joy around them, and can take delight in the satisfaction of others so far as it is their own work. But I maintain that in such a case an action of this kind, however proper, however amiable it may be, has nevertheless no true moral worth, but is on a level with other inclinations, *e. g.* the inclination to honour, which, if it is happily directed to that which is in fact of public utility and accordant with duty, and consequently honourable, deserves praise and encouragement, but not esteem. For the maxim lacks the moral import, namely, that such actions be done *from duty*, not from inclination. Put the case that the mind of that philanthropist were clouded by sorrow of his own, extinguishing all sympathy with the lot of others, and   [18] that while he still has the power to benefit others in distress, he is not touched by their trouble because he is absorbed with his own; and now suppose that he tears himself out of this dead insensibility, and performs the action without any inclination to it, but simply from duty, then first has his action its genuine moral worth. Further still; if nature has put little sympathy in the heart of this or that man; if he, supposed to be an upright man, is by temperament cold and indifferent to the sufferings of others, perhaps because in respect of his own he is provided with the special gift of patience and fortitude, and supposes, or even requires, that others should have the same—and such a man would certainly not be the meanest product of nature—but if nature had not specially framed him for a philanthropist, would he not still find in himself a source from whence to give himself a far higher worth than that of a good-natured temperament could be? Unquestionably. It is just in this that the moral worth of the character is brought out which is incomparably the highest of all, namely, that he is beneficent, not from inclination, but from duty.

. . .

The second [1] proposition is: That an action done from duty derives its moral worth, *not from the purpose* which is to be attained by it, but from the maxim by which it is determined, and therefore does not depend on the realization of the object of the action, but merely on the *principle of volition* by which the action has taken place, without regard to any object of desire. It is clear from what precedes that the purposes which   [20] we may have in view in our actions, or their effects regarded as ends and springs of the will, cannot give to actions any unconditional or moral worth. In what, then, can their worth lie, if it is not to consist in the will and in reference to its expected effect? It cannot lie anywhere but in the *principle of the will* without regard to the ends which can be attained by the action. For the will stands between its *à priori* principle, which is formal, and its *à posteriori* spring, which is material, as between two roads, and as it must be determined by something, it follows that it must be determined by the formal principle of volition when an action is done from duty, in which case every material principle has been withdrawn from it.

The third proposition, which is a consequence of the two preceding, I would express thus: *Duty is the necessity of acting from respect for the law.* I may have *inclination* for an object as the effect of my proposed action, but I cannot have *respect* for it, just for this reason, that it is an

---

[1] [The first proposition was that to have moral worth an action must be done from duty.]

effect and not an energy of will. Similarly, I cannot have respect for inclination, whether my own or another's; I can at most, if my own, approve
it; if another's, sometimes even love it; *i. e.* look on it as favourable to my
own interest. It is only what is connected with my will as a principle, by
no means as an effect—what does not subserve my inclination, but overpowers it, or at least in case of choice excludes it from its calculation—in
other words, simply the law of itself, which can be an object of respect,
and hence a command. Now an action done from duty must wholly exclude the influence of inclination, and with it every object of the will, so
that nothing remains which can determine the will except objectively the
law, and subjectively *pure respect* for this practical law, and conse-   [21]
sequently the maxim ² that I should follow this law even to the thwarting
of all my inclinations.

Thus the moral worth of an action does not lie in the effect expected
from it, nor in any principle of action which requires to borrow its motive from this expected effect. For all these effects—agreeableness of one's
condition, and even the promotion of the happiness of others—could have
been also brought about by other causes, so that for this there would have
been no need of the will of a rational being; whereas it is in this alone that
the supreme and unconditional good can be found. The pre-eminent good
which we call moral can therefore consist in nothing else than *the conception of law* in itself, *which certainly is only possible in a rational being,*
in so far as this conception, and not the expected effect, determines the
will. This is a good which is already present in the person who acts accordingly, and we have not to wait for it to appear in the result.³   [22]

---

² A *maxim* is the subjective principle of volition. The objective principle (*i.e.*
that which would also serve subjectively as a practical principle to all rational
beings if reason had full power over the faculty of desire) is the practical *law.*

³ It might be here objected to me that I take refuge behind the word *respect* in
an obscure feeling, instead of giving a distinct solution of the question by a
concept of the reason. But although respect is a feeling, it is not a feeling
received through influence, but is *self-wrought* by a rational concept, and,
therefore, is specifically distinct from all feelings of the former kind, which may
be referred either to inclination or fear. What I recognise immediately as a
law for me, I recognise with respect. This merely signifies the consciousness
that my will is *subordinate* to a law, without the intervention of other influences on my sense. The immediate determination of the will by the law, and
the consciousness of this is called *respect,* so that this is regarded as an *effect* of
the law on the subject, and not as the *cause* of it. Respect is properly the   [22]
conception of a worth which thwarts my self-love. Accordingly it is something
which is considered neither as an object of inclination nor of fear, although it
has something analogous to both. The *object* of respect is the *law* only, and
that, the law which we impose on *ourselves,* and yet recognise as necessary in
itself. As a law, we are subjected to it without consulting self-love; as imposed
by us on ourselves, it is a result of our will. In the former aspect it has an
analogy to fear, in the latter to inclination. Respect for a person is properly
only respect for the law (of honesty, &c.), of which he gives us an example.
Since we also look on the improvement of our talents as a duty, we consider
that we see in a person of talents, as it were, the *example of a law* (viz., to become like him in this by exercise), and this constitutes our respect. All so-called
moral *interest* consists simply in *respect* for the law.

But what sort of law can that be, the conception of which must determine the will, even without paying any regard to the effect expected from it, in order that this will may be called good absolutely and without qualification? As I have deprived the will of every impulse which could arise to it from obedience to any law, there remains nothing but the universal conformity of its actions to law in general, which alone is to serve the will as a principle, *i. e.* I am never to act otherwise than so *that I could also will that my maxim should become a universal law.* Here now, it is the simple conformity to law in general, without assuming any particular law applicable to certain actions, that serves the will as its principle, and must so serve it, if duty is not to be a vain delusion and a chimerical notion. The common reason of men in its practical judgments perfectly coincides with this, and always has in view the principle here suggested. Let the question be, for example: May I when in distress make a promise with the intention not to keep it? I readily distinguish here between the two significations which the question may have: Whether it is prudent, or   [23] whether it is right, to make a false promise. The former may undoubtedly often be the case. I see clearly indeed that it is not enough to extricate myself from a present difficulty by means of this subterfuge, but it must be well considered whether there may not hereafter spring from this lie much greater inconvenience than that from which I now free myself, and as, with all my supposed *cunning*, the consequences cannot be so easily foreseen but that credit once lost may be much more injurious to me than any mischief which I seek to avoid at present, it should be considered whether it would not be more *prudent* to act herein according to a universal maxim, and to make it a habit to promise nothing except with the intention of keeping it. But it is soon clear to me that such a maxim will still only be based on the fear of consequences. Now it is a wholly different thing to be truthful from duty, and to be so from apprehension of injurious consequences. In the first case, the very notion of the action already implies a law for me; in the second case, I must first look about elsewhere to see what results may be combined with it which would affect myself. For to deviate from the principle of duty is beyond all doubt wicked; but to be unfaithful to my maxim of prudence may often be very advantageous to me, although to abide by it is certainly safer. The shortest way, however, and an unerring one, to discover the answer to this question whether a lying promise is consistent with duty, is to ask myself, Should I be content that my maxim (to extricate myself from difficulty by a false promise) should hold good as a universal law, for myself as well as for others? and should I be able to say to myself, "Every one may make a deceitful promise when he finds himself in a difficulty from which he cannot otherwise extricate himself?" Then I presently become aware   [24] that while I can will the lie, I can by no means will that lying should be a universal law. For with such a law there would be no promises at all, since it would be in vain to allege my intention in regard to my future actions to those who would not believe this allegation, or if they overhastily did so would pay me back in my own coin. Hence my maxim, as soon as it should be made a universal law, would necessarily destroy itself.

I do not, therefore, need any far-reaching penetration to discern what I have to do in order that my will may be morally good. Inexperienced in the course of the world, incapable of being prepared for all its contingencies, I only ask myself: Canst thou also will that thy maxim should be a universal law? If not, then it must be rejected, and that not because of a disadvantage accruing from it to myself or even to others, but because it cannot enter as a principle into a possible universal legislation, and reason extorts from me immediate respect for such legislation. I do not indeed as yet *discern* on what this respect is based (this the philosopher may inquire), but at least I understand this, that it is an estimation of the worth which far outweighed all worth of what is recommended by inclination, and that the necessity of acting from *pure* respect for the practical law is what constitutes duty, to which every other motive must give place, because it is the condition of a will being good *in itself,* and the worth of such a will is above everything.

. . .

Now all *imperatives* command either *hypothetically* or *categorically.* The former represent the practical necessity of a possible action as means to something else that is willed (or at least which one might possibly will). The categorical imperative would be that which represented an action as necessary of itself without reference to another end, *i. e.* as objectively necessary.

. . .

Finally, there is an imperative which commands a certain conduct immediately, without having as its condition any other purpose to be attained by it. This imperative is Categorical. It concerns not the matter of the action, or its intended result, but its form and the principle of which it is itself a result; and what is essentially good in it consists in the   [41] mental disposition, let the consequence be what it may. This imperative may be called that of Morality.

. . .

When I conceive a hypothetical imperative in general I do not know beforehand what it will contain until I am given the condition. But when I conceive a categorical imperative I know at once what it contains. For as the imperative contains besides the law only the necessity that the maxims [4] shall conform to this law, while the law contains no conditions

---

[4] A MAXIM is a subjective principle of action, and must be distinguished from the *objective principle,* namely, practical law. The former contains the practical rule set by reason according to the conditions of the subject (often its ignorance or its inclinations), so that it is the principle on which the subject *acts;* but the law is the objective principle valid for every rational being, and is the principle on which it *ought to act* that is an imperative.

restricting it, there remains nothing but the general statement that the maxim of the action should conform to a universal law, and it is this [47] conformity alone that the imperative properly represents as necessary.[5]

There is therefore but one categorical imperative, namely this: *Act only on that maxim whereby you can at the same time will that it should become a universal law.*

Now if all imperatives of duty can be deduced from this one imperative as from their principle, then, although it should remain undecided whether what is called duty is not merely a vain notion, yet at least we shall be able to show what we understand by it and what this notion means.

Since the universality of the law according to which effects are produced constitutes what is properly called *nature* in the most general sense (as to form), that is the existence of things so far as it is determined by general laws, the imperative of duty may be expressed thus: *Act as if the maxim of your action were to become by your will a universal law of nature.*

We will now enumerate a few duties, adopting the usual division of them into duties to ourselves and to others, and into perfect and imperfect duties.[6]

1. A man reduced to despair by a series of misfortunes feels wearied of life, but is still so far in possession of his reason that he can ask himself whether it would not be contrary to his duty to himself to take his own life. Now he inquires whether the maxim of his action could become a universal law of nature. His maxim is: From self-love I adopt it as a principle to shorten my life when its longer duration is likely to bring more evil than satisfaction. It is asked then simply whether this principle founded on self-love can become a universal law of nature. Now we see at once that a system of nature of which it should be a law to destroy life by means of the very feeling whose special nature it is to impel to the improvement of life would contradict itself, and therefore could not exist as a system of nature; hence that maxim cannot possibly exist as a universal law of nature, and consequently would be wholly inconsistent with the supreme principle of all duty.

---

[5] [I have no doubt that "den" in the original before "Imperativ" is a misprint for "der," and have translated accordingly. Mr. Semple has done the same. The editions that I have seen agree in reading "den," and M. Barni so translates. With this reading, it is the conformity that presents the imperative as necessary.]

[6] It must be noted here that I reserve the division of duties for a future *metaphysic of morals;* so that I give it here only as an arbitrary one (in order to arrange my examples). For the rest, I understand by a perfect duty one that admits no exception in favour of inclination, and then I have not merely external, but also internal perfect duties. This is contrary to the use of the word adopted in the schools; but I do not intend to justify it here, as it is all one for my purpose whether it is admitted or not. [*Perfect* duties are usually understood to be those which can be enforced by external law; *imperfect,* those which cannot be enforced. They are also called respectively *determinate* and *indeterminate, officia juris* and *officia virtutis.*]

2. Another finds himself forced by necessity to borrow money. He knows that he will not be able to repay it, but sees also that nothing will be lent to him, unless he promises stoutly to repay it in a definite time. He desires to make this promise, but he has still so much conscience as to ask himself: Is it not unlawful and inconsistent with duty to get out of a difficulty in this way? Suppose however that he resolves to do so, then the maxim of his action would be expressed thus: When I think myself in want of money, I will borrow money and promise to repay it, although I know that I never can do so. Now this principle of self-love or of one's own advantage may perhaps be consistent with my whole future welfare; but the question now is, Is it right? I change then the suggestion of self-love into a universal law, and state the question thus: How would   [49] it be if my maxim were a universal law? Then I see at once that it could never hold as a universal law of nature, but would necessarily contradict itself. For supposing it to be a universal law that everyone when he thinks himself in a difficulty should be able to promise whatever he pleases, with the purpose of not keeping his promise, the promise itself would become impossible, as well as the end that one might have in view in it, since no one would consider that anything was promised to him, but would ridicule all such statements as vain pretences.

3. A third finds in himself a talent which with the help of some culture might make him a useful man in many respects. But he finds himself in comfortable circumstances, and prefers to indulge in pleasure rather than to take pains in enlarging and improving his happy natural capacities. He asks, however, whether his maxim of neglect of his natural gifts, besides agreeing with his inclination to indulgence, agrees also with what is called duty. He sees then that a system of nature could indeed subsist with such a universal law although men (like the South Sea islanders) should let their talents rest, and resolve to devote their lives merely to idleness, amusement, and propagation of their species—in a word, to enjoyment; but he cannot possibly *will* that this should be a universal law of nature, or be implanted in us as such by a natural instinct. For, as a rational being, he necessarily wills that his faculties be developed, since they serve him, and have been given him, for all sorts of possible purposes.

4.   A fourth, who is in prosperity, while he sees that others have to contend with great wretchedness and that he could help them, thinks: What concern is it of mine? Let everyone be as happy as heaven   [50] pleases, or as he can make himself; I will take nothing from him nor even envy him, only I do not wish to contribute anything to his welfare or to his assistance in distress! Now no doubt if such a mode of thinking were a universal law, the human race might very well subsist, and doubtless even better than in a state in which everyone talks of sympathy and goodwill, or even takes care occasionally to put it into practice, but on the other side, also cheats when he can, betrays the rights of men, or otherwise violates them. But although it is possible that a universal law of nature might exist in accordance with that maxim, it is impossible to *will* that such a principle should have the universal validity of a law of nature.

For a will which resolved this would contradict itself, inasmuch as many cases might occur in which one would have need of the love and sympathy of others, and in which, by such a law of nature, sprung from his own will, he would deprive himself of all hope of the aid he desires.

[56]

·   ·   ·

Now I say: man and generally any rational being *exists* as an end in himself, *not merely as a means* to be arbitrarily used by this or that will, but in all his actions, whether they concern himself or other rational beings, must be always regarded at the same time as an end. All objects of the inclinations have only a conditional worth, for if the inclinations and the wants founded on them did not exist, then their object would be without value. But the inclinations themselves being sources of want, are so far from having an absolute worth for which they should be desired, that on the contrary it must be the universal wish of every rational being to be wholly free from them. Thus the worth of any object which is *to be acquired* by our action is always conditional. Beings whose existence depends not on our will but on nature's, have nevertheless, if they are irrational beings, only a relative value as means, and are therefore called *things;* rational beings, on the contrary, are called *persons,* because their very nature points them out as ends in themselves, that is as something which must not be used merely as means, and so far therefore restricts freedom of action (and is an object of respect). These, therefore, are not merely subjective ends whose existence has a worth *for us* as an effect of our action, but *objective ends,* that is things whose existence is an end in itself: an end moreover for which no other can be substituted, which they should subserve *merely* as means, for otherwise nothing whatever would possess *absolute worth;* but if all worth were conditioned and therefore contingent, then there would be no supreme practical principle of reason whatever.

If then there is a supreme practical principle or, in respect of the human will, a categorical imperative, it must be one which, being drawn   [57] from the conception of that which is necessarily an end for every one because it is *an end in itself,* constitutes an *objective* principle of will, and can therefore serve as a universal practical law. The foundation of this principle is: *rational nature exists as an end in itself.* Man necessarily conceives his own existence as being so: so far then this is a *subjective* principle of human actions. But every other rational being regards its existence similarly, just on the same rational principle that holds for me: so that it is at the same time an objective principle, from which as a supreme practical law all laws of the will must be capable of being deduced. Accordingly the practical imperative will be as follows: So *act as to treat humanity, both in your own person and in that of any other person, always as an end also, never as a means only.*

·   ·   ·